A SOCIAL AND RELIGIOUS
HISTORY OF THE JEWS

Late Middle Ages and Era of European Expansion
1200–1650

VOLUME XI
CITIZEN OR ALIEN CONJURER

About the Author

After 35 years as a member of the Columbia University Faculty of Political Science, Salo Wittmayer Baron became Professor Emeritus of Jewish History, Literature, and Institutions on the Miller Foundation in 1963. At present he is Director of the Center of Israel and Jewish Studies at Columbia; Visiting Professor in the Department of Religious Studies at Brown University; Philip J. Levin Visiting Professor at Rutgers University; and Alexander Marx Visiting Professor at the Jewish Theological Seminary of America. He is a Fellow of the American Academy of Arts and Sciences; a corresponding member of the International Commission for a Scientific and Cultural History of Mankind; and has been editor of the quarterly *Jewish Social Studies* since its founding in 1939.

Other books by Professor Baron include *The Jewish Community, Modern Nationalism and Religion, The Russian Jew Under Tsars and Soviets,* and *History and Jewish Historians: Essays and Addresses.* He is co-editor, with Joseph L. Blau, of *The Jews of the United States, 1790-1840: A Documentary History* (3 vols.).

A SOCIAL
AND RELIGIOUS
HISTORY OF
THE JEWS

By SALO WITTMAYER BARON

Second Edition, Revised and Enlarged

Late Middle Ages and Era of European Expansion
1200–1650

VOLUME XI

CITIZEN OR ALIEN CONJURER

Columbia University Press
New York and London 1967

The Jewish Publication Society of America
Philadelphia 5727

PREFACE

THE CONTENTS and chapter arrangement of Volumes XI and XII have been explained in the Preface to Volume IX. As in the preceding two volumes, the present treatment covers in the main the last three centuries of the Middle Ages. It tries to probe in depth some major Jewish facets of late-medieval political and economic history, thus elaborating the more chronological and topographical description of the earlier volumes. Once again "the reader is urgently advised to view the picture presented in Volumes IX-XII as integral parts of the same treatment."

Similarly, the expression of indebtedness to the institutions and persons enumerated in that Preface applies with equal force to the two volumes here submitted. Without their help, the completion of these volumes would have been greatly delayed, and whatever merit they possess would have been seriously impaired. But I wish to take this occasion to add to that large list the authorities of the British Museum in London and of the Zentralbibliothek in Zurich, whose unfailing courtesy helped me clarify many details still left open after the research done in the other libraries and archives. Finally, it gives me great pleasure to add to the names of my wife and secretary that of Miss Elisabeth L. Shoemaker of Columbia University Press, to all of whom I am deeply indebted for their valuable assistance in the preparation and editing of the manuscript and in seeing the two volumes through the press.

SALO W. BARON

New York, N.Y.
February 24, 1967

CONTENTS

A SOCIAL AND RELIGIOUS HISTORY
OF THE JEWS

PUBLISHED VOLUMES

Ancient Times

I. TO THE BEGINNING OF THE CHRISTIAN ERA

II. CHRISTIAN ERA: THE FIRST FIVE CENTURIES

High Middle Ages

III. HEIRS OF ROME AND PERSIA

IV. MEETING OF EAST AND WEST

V. RELIGIOUS CONTROLS AND DISSENSIONS

VI. LAWS, HOMILIES, AND THE BIBLE

VII. HEBREW LANGUAGE AND LETTERS

VIII. PHILOSOPHY AND SCIENCE

INDEX TO VOLUMES I–VIII

Late Middle Ages and Era of European Expansion

IX. UNDER CHURCH AND EMPIRE

X. ON THE EMPIRE'S PERIPHERY

XI. CITIZEN OR ALIEN CONJURER

XII. ECONOMIC CATALYST

CITIZEN OR ALIEN CONJURER

XLVII

CITIZEN OR BONDSMAN

SUCH kaleidoscopic variety of legislation, state-wide, provincial or local, as was reflected in our geographic-chronological review of the last two volumes seems to defy generalization. Not only did laws differ from one country to another, even from one locality to another, but they were also subject to rapid changes within each community. The medieval preference for local custom over any established general laws, so well epitomized in the Teuton principle of *Landrecht bricht Reichsrecht,* assured a modicum of continuity within each locality and region, but it also makes any general analysis doubly precarious.

Yet, particularly in the Jewish sphere, the overwhelming impact of tradition, both ecclesiastical and sociopolitical, was so great that the basic similarity of institutions governing Jewish life throughout medieval Europe becomes manifest to any observer. Apart from the fundamentally consistent practice and theory of canon law, the heritage of the Carolingian legislation concerning Jews came to the fore in almost all aspects of law and judicial practice under Latin Christendom. The principles adopted by Charlemagne and Louis the Pious may, indeed, be pursued, with but relatively few modifications, in all successor states of the Carolingian Empire. Through the ordinances of the two contemporary Frederick IIs of 1238–44, they also deeply influenced the legislative approaches to the Jewish question by the newly rising kingdoms of east-central Europe. They were supplemented, rather than controverted, by the surviving vestiges of Roman law, particularly in the Mediterranean lands.

It may be possible, therefore, to subject this entire vast and multifarious body of decrees, ordinances, parliamentary resolutions, and judicial decisions to systematic analysis. By paying primary attention, to be sure, to subject matter, rather than chronology or geography, such an analysis is often apt to obscure the dynamism of the changes which occurred in different periods and regions. This shortcoming of any systematic review, however, is not only compensated by the inherent clarification of major issues but it also is minimized here by reference to the geographic and chronological diversities analyzed in the last two volumes.

SIGNIFICANCE OF JEWISH SERFDOM

Crucial for the understanding of the entire Jewish position in the medieval world is the institution of "Jewish serfdom." Although that phrase did not appear in any formal decree until the 1230s when, curiously, the general system of medieval servitude was declining, the term seemed most descriptive of the Jews' dependence on individual rulers. It is small wonder, then, that the terms *servitus Judaeorum* and *servi camerae,* or the related expressions of Jews being chests (*cofres*) or treasures of kings, frequently encountered in the sources, readily conjured up in the minds of modern historians the specter of medieval villeinage. Some extreme theological formulations, such as St. Bernard of Clairvaux' emotional assertion that "no serfdom is more shameful and harsh than the serfdom of the Jews which they carry with them wherever they go and everywhere they offend their masters," were sometimes taken as mirroral of existing legal relationships. Such phrases were grist for the mill of the adherents of the prevailing "lachrymose conception of Jewish history," especially since this conception seemed borne out by many arbitrary acts of the Jews' royal or ecclesiastical masters. Certainly, the ruthless exploitation of Jewish subjects by many French and English kings, the occasional transfers of Jewish groups from one lord to another, the oft-debated treaties of extradition between the thirteenth-century French kings and their powerful vassals—all seemed to lend credence to the equation of Jewish serfdom with villeinage.[1]

Nor were the complexities of the German evolution likely to alter that image. The simultaneous claims upon Jewish services by the conflicting sovereignties in the Empire, combined with the retention by the emperor of his own overriding title, contributed to the Jews' general insecurity and to the chaotic picture of their legal status. The resulting instability was compounded by the impermanence of any privilege granted to Jews since, according to the then regnant legal theory, no ruler could formally bind his successor and hence every privilege had to be renewed by the latter in order to retain its validity. Emperor Charles IV, for example, handed over on February 6, 1350, to three German lords "all Jews, collectively and individually," residing in their territories, as well as in three named cities, together with all the services and contributions "which they [the Jews] owe Us and the Holy Roman Empire as confirmed from ancient times by the law and custom of Roman rule." Yet almost immediately he claimed imperial overlordship over these very Jews. Margrave Albert III Achilles of Brandenburg went further and, in 1462, formulated the theory of Jewish serfdom in its extreme fashion:

Upon his coronation each Roman king or emperor may take away from the Jews throughout the Empire all their goods, even their lives, and kill them all, except for the few who ought to be preserved for remembrance. Hence all the Jews in the lands of the German Empire had been granted the opportunity to avoid such an eventuality by giving each new emperor a third part of their possessions, in order thus to redeem their bodies, lives and property.

The margrave repeated that statement somewhat more concisely in 1463. His views are doubly significant as he was not merely an imperial official, but also an important German prince who, like his confreres, wished to arrogate to himself as many of the empire's *regalia* as possible. However, primarily intended to justify his raid upon the Jewish communal treasuries in the emperor's behalf, Albert's sharp definitions actually contrasted with his own rather humane and moderate treatment of Brandenburg Jewry.[2]

Easy generalizations of this kind were facilitated by their very terminological vagueness. Neither medieval legislators nor jurists writing judicial decisions and law books sought to give clear-cut definitions of what they meant by Jewish "serfdom." Many doubtless realized that clarity would merely tie the hands of rulers and administrators, whereas obscurity in legal terminology would leave the gate wide open for any use, or abuse, which officials might wish to make of the existing regulations. Most modern students of medieval Jewish status have dealt with this complex subject from too narrowly conceived juridical criteria. Even historians of law have increasingly come to the realization that legal institutions cannot be fully comprehended through exclusively juristic categories of thinking. For the general historian this entire realm of the juridical norms, the *Sollen,* is only a small segment of the world of actual living, the *Sein,* with all its logical inconsistencies. Comparing these difficulties of contemporary legal historians with the relative ease of the strictly legalistic analysis of two generations ago, Heinrich Mitteis has rightly observed, "We no longer believe that we can *explain* everything rationally; we rather endeavor to *understand* the historic dynamism [of the juridical institutions]. And understanding, as Dilthey and Max Weber have taught us, is, in contrast to mere explanation, the superior form of historic cognition." In the case of medieval Jewish serfdom, too, we must try to penetrate behind the façade of the legalistic verbiage to its true juridical meaning within the total context of the existing legislation and, as a second even more important step, seek to detect behind it the multihued richness of historic reality.[3]

Of course, such a task is much more difficult. Legal enactments are more likely to be deposited and preserved in archives than other records, except for literary works of high quality or great popularity. Beneficiaries of decrees frequently found it to their advantage to secure several copies for use in various localities or courts and in subsequent requests for renewal. Documents of this type are also, for the most part, well dated and of known authorship. The peril of mistaking the numerous forgeries for genuine enactments can, with a modicum of effort, be minimized by the use of accepted critical techniques. Laws are further elucidated by court decisions and illustrated by commercial and other deeds, whether these were written in full conformity with, or in deviation from, the existing regulations. In contrast, the extralegal world of historical reality can be but partially reconstructed from very subjective chronicles, letters and other biographical records, or a multitude of informal sources preserved by mere chance. The sporadic rays of light shed by them on certain phases of life merely underscore the obscurity in which other, equally or more important, aspects remain enveloped. For one example, the extant rich documentation on Jewish moneylenders in medieval England has almost completely diverted the attention of scholars from the pulsating life of what probably was the non-moneylending majority of English Jews, just as the one-sidedness of sources relating to kings, nobles, clerics, and patrician burghers made many historians oblivious of the life of the overwhelming inarticulate majority of villeins and urban proletarians. Only the patient toil of generations of students, braving these difficulties, may ultimately help lift the veil from these fundamental realities.

In the first place, it ought to give us pause that almost all early decrees mentioning the Jews' specific allegiance to the royal power were intended for the former's *protection*. For the most part Jewish "serfdom" was cited as a reason why kings felt obliged to safeguard the rights of their Jewish wards. The Majorcan decree of 1387 was granted "to those who, as the said Jews, are obliged to sustain Our needs from their possessions. We must promote their liberties and favors in their capacity of Our property and treasure [*nostrum peculium et thesaurum*]." Similarly, in his extensive privilege of April 2, 1451, for Sicilian Jewry, Alphonso V explained why he had withdrawn from the papal commissioner, Jacob Xarch, an earlier authorization to intervene in Jewish affairs. The king argued that "the Jews are in their persons and possessions the serfs and the domain of the royal Chamber and the jurisdiction over their matters pertains exclusively to the Royal Majesty." To bring this point home with renewed emphasis he concluded, "We are thus [concerned] about the preservation of the said Jews and Jewesses who are Our royal domain [*herarium*]." Such examples can easily be multiplied. At times the Jews themselves invoked that legal attachment to the Crown as a means of staving off some unwelcome outside interference. Although long accustomed to paying allegiance, as well as a variety of taxes, to the local abbot, the Jews of Leonese Sahagún joined forces with the burghers then embroiled in a protracted controversy with the monastery and "claimed that they in no manner were subject to the jurisdiction of the abbot, for they were the serfs of the Lord King and were obliged in all matters to be of service to the royal power." Ultimately, the king resolved the controversy in the abbot's favor without in any way relinquishing his overlordship over his Jewish subjects. Exclusive allegiance to the Crown was also invoked by Ratisbon Jewry in its protracted struggle against the burghers. On occasion the kings felt obliged to intervene even in the inner affairs of Jewish communities if internal conflicts threatened to undermine the latter's strength. In agreeing, for example, to the enlargement of the Jewish communal council of Perpignan to twenty-three members, the Aragonese Infante John emphasized that, because the Jews were the king's and his "treasure," he had to take action "for the public good of that community and its preservation" (1380, 1384).[4]

Moreover, the term *servitus* had many shades of meaning in medieval juristic and theological terminology. Certainly, being subject to a king in a period when jurists often quoted the old Roman adage, "What pleases the prince has the power of law," was an entirely different matter from villeinage under private masters. While the distinction between public and private law was not yet sharply drawn, everyone realized that a Jew belonged to the ruler *qua* representative of government, rather than as private owner of an estate. Certainly, upon an emperor's demise it was his elected successor on the German throne, not the immediate heir of his hereditary possessions, who assumed the tutelage over the "serfs" of the imperial Chamber. In general, under a monarchy bestowed by grace divine, few persons could claim to be entirely free in the sense suggested in Albertus Magnus' definition, "We consider a man free when he is the cause of his own behavior and whom an outside power cannot force to do anything." Even technically the term *servus,* as Otto Stobbe pointed out, was still applied in Germany to the *ministeriales* at the time when they had status wholly equal to that of free vassals and above that of free peasants or burghers. At the other extreme the term *servitus* was frequently used as the equivalent of the English word "service." For example, in his letter of June 1075 to Henry IV, Bishop Hexilo of Hildesheim constantly reassured the emperor of his faithful allegiance (*fidelis* or *fidelissima servitus*).[5]

We also must bear in mind the specific implications of the medieval concept of liberty which always presupposed a certain measure of dependence. Adolf Waas may have gone too far in contending that in the Middle Ages liberty existed "only under dominion, whereas the nineteenth century saw liberty only in the absence of dominion." Nevertheless the political outlook on liberty, like all of medieval life, was too deeply colored by ecclesiastical conceptions not to diverge greatly from our modern ideas of freedom. No church even today is able to grant to its individual adherents full freedom of deciding about the truths of their religious tradition. Explaining the views held by Pope Gregory VII, A. Nitschke declared that "under liberty Gregory understands not the freedom of human decision, but on the contrary man's freedom from purely human decisions by his full submission to the will divine." These theological presuppositions necessarily carried over into the sociopolitical sphere. According to Eberhard Otto, the medieval jurists saw in the free man "a protected individual . . . originally anyone who was not unprotected or rightless was called free. . . . The very idea of freedom necessarily presupposed a master who protects and safeguards." In this sense the Jewish "serfs" were indeed free men living under royal protection but enjoying a considerable measure of self-determination and individual mobility.[6]

Numerous medieval documents attest this clear-cut distinction between Jewish serfdom and real slavery or villeinage. Time and again the kings of England, Castile, or Aragon threatened Jews with the loss of freedom in case of disobedience. Even at the height of legal discrimination against Iberian Jewry during the quarter century of 1391–1415, the anti-Jewish decree of January 2, 1412, tried to stem Jewish emigration by warning the would-be culprits that they would lose all their property and become "My captives forever." This decree was repeated, as we recall, by Ferdinand I of Aragon in the following year. Similar sanctions had been placed in 1380 upon the illicit circumcision of Moorish or Tartar slaves by Jewish masters. Obviously, not until a court found a Jew guilty of these "crimes" was he to lose that personal liberty which he had theretofore fully enjoyed. Equally revealing were the phrases used by the German king William in his privilege for the city of Goslar of 1252. Here the king promised that "the city's Jews shall suffer no undue molestation or *captivity* from Us, and We shall protect them amicably and benevolently as *special serfs* of Our Chamber; but as it is proper, they shall *serve* Us as their lord and Roman king." [7]

Viewing the conditions in the Spanish realms which, with modifications, largely applied also to other Western countries, the keen jurist, Martin Didaci d'Aux, commented:

A Saracen or a Jew cannot oblige himself by contract or loan to become anybody's slave. They must not do it even on account of hunger, for their persons belong to the king. Not even the king can sell them except in retribution for a crime. Neither do they really deserve to be called captives or serfs in the sense that they may be sold, because according to law they have the liberty of moving about [*liberum habent volatum juxta forum*], but they may be given away.

We have seen that this right to give them away, or for that matter to mortgage them as security for a loan, but superficially resembled a private transaction. Even in France the extradition treaties between princes and the transfers, by gift or sale, of individual Jews or groups of Jews from one lord to another still bore the unmistakable earmarks of transfers of rights, particularly of fiscal rights, under public law. In Germany, where the rivaling authorities often made the Jews' dependence on particular masters quite ambiguous, Archbishop Baldwin of Mayence exacted in 1334 from Rose Welen of Kaiserlauten the remarkable pledge that he would not leave the archbishop's domain and that if he did the archbishop could insist upon his return. More significantly, Welen promised that, after his demise, his estate would not fall to his usual heirs, but be turned over *in toto* to the archbishop—a singular exception to the general rule of the undisturbed inheritance rights of the Jewish families and communities, subject only to some compromises concerning the estate taxes. To reassure the Jews returning to France that they would not be exposed to similar pressures, Philip V provided in his ordinance of 1317 that "they could not be subjected to, nor held in *mortmain* [that is, be made serfs] in a manner that the property which anyone of them holds should not devolve to his nearest relative." [8]

Long before Welen's promise some rabbis tried to forestall such involuntary commitments, often reinforced by guarantors personally responsible for their fulfillment. R. Jacob Tam is reputed to have "forbidden under oath, to any Jew, man or woman, living under Christian domination to serve as guarantor [of this kind] for the lord. To forestall violations of this prohibition we have forbidden the pledgee to pay any compensation to him [the guarantor] and ordered all coreligionists not to appoint judges to adjudicate such claims." Tam's nephew, Isaac b. Samuel of Dampierre, went further and, contrary to general rabbinic practice, counseled the Jew forced to take such an anti-emigration oath to nullify it by some mental reservation. "He may swear in general terms that he would not leave and add in his heart [the qualification,] 'today,' or if he must spell out that he would not leave for the rest of his life, add [silently], 'if he will see no need to do so.' If he is able to whisper that he annuls the oath, so much the better." [9]

Despite the sharp verbiage of even the most outspoken French extradition treaties their main purpose was less to impede voluntary migrations of Jews than to prevent the respective rulers from raiding one another's Jewish subjects. This objective is, indeed, clearly spelled out in the treaties between the kings of France and the counts of Champagne of 1210, 1228, and 1246, as well as in the convention of Melun of 1230. Even the occasionally recorded transfers of particular Jews and the acquisition, by one lord from another, of a single Jew or of three Jews really meant that the new masters had the right to tax these individuals, not that the latter were forcibly removed from one locality to another. In substance, therefore, these agreements amounted to little more than a change of address to which the Jew had to deliver his taxes. In contrast, it was common practice in Norman England, according to Reginald Lennard, "to combine a donation of the tithe with the assignment to the recipient monastery of a peasant's services," the lord often feeling free even to detach his villein from the cultivation of the land. Ironically, such detachment gave the serf a sense of elevation in rank. Nor, for that matter, was the kings' authority to regulate the movements of their subjects limited to unfree populations. In his decree of 1302 referring to the seditions of various barons, Philip the Fair wrote, "By virtue of Our royal authority We strictly forbid, under the sanction of corporal punishment and [the loss of] all temporal possessions, any of Our faithful subjects or natives of the said kingdom, of whatever dignity, status, nation, or condition he may be, to leave the boundaries of Our kingdom without special license by Our letters patent. Only merchants, foreigners, and the merchants' employees are excepted." But such regulations concerning nobles, burghers, or Jews were much less frequently enforced in the weak medieval states than in modern times, when more powerful regimes, both totalitarian and democratic, have often instituted effective controls over exit permits for travel abroad.[10]

Because of the overwhelming power of custom, practice often greatly diverged from theory. Even today, as Cyril M. Picciotto has pointed out, "the King is the ultimate overlord of every yard of land in England. . . . [He] can in law do innumerable things which he never does, such as attending Parliament, refusing his assent to a Bill, or sitting in the Court of King's bench. King Charles I lost his head for much less." The mere fact that both the state and the Church had to engage in protracted, often futile, struggles against the Jews' employment of Christian servants, even ownership of Christian slaves, demonstrated the inefficacy of royal controls, further weakened by the jurisdictional conflicts among the various claimants to such mastery over Jews which were particularly frequent in thirteenth-century France. We recall the controversy between the king and the duke of Burgundy in 1270 concerning the authority over a single Jew, Abraham. The Parlement decided, according to Abraham's wishes, that he was to remain with the king. In 1281 an agreement was reached that the older Jews of the County of Alençon should belong to the count, whereas new Jewish settlers hailing from the royal domain should remain under the king's authority. When, in 1295, the bishop of Nîmes complained to Philip the Fair about the seizure of some of his Jews, the king ordered their release, but stressed that these Jews belonged to him, too, and that only in so far as they contributed to the royal Treasury were they to be allowed to engage in moneylending. At one point the Paris Parlement decided that even after being banished Jewish émigrés had to pay allegiance to the king. On the other hand, it made clear that Jews could stay in baronial lands possessing superior jurisdiction (*altam justiciam*) only with the barons' permission. In the same year (1288) the Parlement also declared that prelates could exact no fines from Jews, but could only forbid the faithful to maintain contacts with them. There was little exaggeration, therefore, in Isidore Loeb's contention that the French kings used their Jewish controls as a weapon in their struggle for the unification of France.[11]

At times such conflicts arose among the royal vassals themselves. In the community of Narbonne a protracted controversy between viscount and bishop was finally settled by arbitration. In his remarkable decision of May 13, 1276, the arbiter, after listening to the arguments from both sides and "carefully considering that the Jews are subject to the laws and ought to live in accordance with Roman law," decided to establish as the main criteria the origin of each Jewish family from the bishop's or the viscount's quarter back to the fifth generation; in the case of newcomers, to follow the location of the Jew's property. Only in the absence of such objective criteria was a new settler to be free to choose his residence, as also could a native propertyless woman who had followed her husband to another quarter. However, the Jewish *nasi* himself, often styled the Jewish king, possessed allodial lands outside the Jewish quarter. These feudal possessions remained substantially unchanged, according to two records dating from 1217 and 1307. Even at a later date the burghers of Narbonne took advantage of the ancient authority of the Jewish leader. They argued in 1364 that the royal provost should reside in their city because "at the time of Charlemagne of blessed memory, it had been a royal city; it had had two kings, a Jew and a Saracen." [12]

In essence, these numerous conflicts, as well as the voluntary transfers of Jews from one sovereignty or semisovereignty to another, merely reflected the general diffusion of power under the feudal order. As duke of Normandy, the king of England was a vassal of the French king. Charles of Anjou, Louis IX's brother, was simultaneously his brother's vassal as ruler of Anjou, that of the emperor through his wife's hereditary rights in the Provence, and that of the pope from whom he held Sicily and Naples. Just as in antiquity many individuals, including Jews, held more than one "citizenship," so did many medieval Jews share with their non-Jewish compatriots an often confusing array of political loyalties to emperor or king, to bishop, prince, or municipality. Rather than lowering the status of medieval Jewry, this confusion often served as a safety valve, preventing the recurrent outbreaks of local intolerance from engulfing many communities at once.

MEANING OF CITIZENSHIP

Not surprisingly, this state of dependence, varying in both degree and clarity, was wholly reconcilable with that of free citizenship (*civitas*), recorded in the case of many medieval Jewish communities. We recall the agreement of 1283 between the city of Worms and the bishop, in which the latter promised to observe all the privileges and good customs "enjoyed by his dear citizens of Worms, both Christian and Jewish." A Jew was actually received into the burghers' association by a procedure resembling the admission of Christians, the major difference being that the Jewish newcomer had first to secure acceptance from the elders of the Jewish community. Worms Jews also automatically secured citizens' rights through birth from citizen parents or through marriage to daughters of Jewish burghers. Minor children born before their parents' naturalization were treated as burghers until reaching maturity when they had the option of either retaining these rights or renouncing them. The Worms situation may have been somewhat exceptional, but in many other German cities, too, the status of Jews was generally comparable to that of their Christian neighbors. In the privilege issued for the Jews of Stendal in 1297, the Margraves Otto and Konrad of Brandenburg emphasized that the Jews should enjoy the benefits of all existing laws and be held in the city as its burghers. Similarly, when in 1320 the sovereignty over the cities of Prenzlau, Pasewalk, and Templin was transferred to the king of Denmark, clear reservations were inserted into each treaty concerning the burghers' rights of the local Jews. King Henry VII likewise used the term "burghers' rights" quite advisedly when in 1313 he ordered the admission to them of new Jewish settlers in Nuremberg. Thirty-four years later (November 30, 1347) Charles IV provided "that a Jew whom the Jewish community of Nuremberg accepts as its burgher shall have the same rights as the others. He who leaves the city in order to establish a residence elsewhere shall not therefore suffer any damage to his property." In Ratisbon the municipality issued the usual letters of accreditation as burghers to individual Jews; for instance, to one Nachman in 1338. As late as 1389, we recall, King Wenceslaus considered the Jews of Eger as forming one community (*ein Ding*) with the burghers.[13]

Remarkably, the sources fail to mention certain technical difficulties which must have arisen from the religious disparity. We may perhaps assume that Jews, newly admitted to burghers' rights, either through special "naturalization" or through reaching the required age of fifteen or sixteen, were allowed to take their burghers' oath according to their own rites, possibly without the humiliating features of the oath *more judaico*. But it is somewhat difficult to envisage all Jews sharing with the rest of the burghers the repeated, sometimes annual, ceremony of retaking the oath of fealty to the city, wherever such reiteration was required by law, without leaving any traces in the contemporary records. The ever present social differences between the Christian and Jewish burghers must also have in many ways impinged on the latter's legal status. Although the class structure in medieval towns was relatively fluid and low-born persons could, with relative ease, rise in the ranks and reach positions of power and eminence, the difference in religion always kept the Jews apart. Only converts seem to have found relatively easy entry into society for themselves and their children; some of the latter even succeeded in penetrating patrician groups, as is attested by the widespread family name or appellative "the Jew" in various lands. However, in practice the ensuing disabilities, even for professing Jews, as we shall see below, need not have been fundamental.[14]

No less instructive is the evidence for Jewish citizens' rights in other parts of Europe. We recall the Jewish *cives* of Marseilles and Arles. Equally sweeping was the declaration of April 2, 1451, in which King Alphonso V stated that "the Jewish communities of the said kingdom [Sicily] are members and citizens of the towns and territories of the said kingdom." Among the numerous provisions adopted by "the Roman people assembled in the public parliament of the city" on February 8, 1310 (at least in their expanded version confirmed by Pope Martin V in 1418), one stated unequivocally that "all Jews and Jewesses, living in the city or residing therein, collectively and severally, together with their families, shall be treated in the city and regarded as Roman citizens in all matters." Similar declarations were also included in many con-

dottas concluded by various central and northern Italian cities with Jewish bankers. For example, in the agreement signed by Reggio Emilia with one Muso (Moses) of Leuccio and his companions on July 30, 1413, the city provided "that the aforementioned shall enjoy all the statutes and ordinances of the municipality of Rezzo [Reggio] and benefit from them like the other citizens and that no one should deprive them of that [right]." Similarly, the first *capitoli* signed in 1437 by the city of Florence with a group of Jewish bankers stated tersely that the latter "shall be treated and considered on a par with the burghers of the city of Florence in their civil and criminal laws." [15]

Such egalitarian provisions were obviously inserted on Jewish initiative. In addressing the count of Montefeltro in 1433 concerning their opening a loan bank in the city of Urbino, two Jewish moneylenders stipulated that "they would be held, treated and considered as burghers and like other burghers of your aforementioned city of Urbino." Quite incisive also was the duke of Mantua in admitting two Jews to the city in 1434.

With certain knowledge and full deliberation [he wrote] we admit Benjamin and Angelo, as well as their children and descendants, both present and future, and make and create them burghers of Our aforementioned city of Mantua. . . . In such a fashion that the said Benjamin and Angelo and their children and descendants shall be burghers and be held, considered, and reputed as citizens of Our aforementioned city. They shall partake of, and enjoy all [general] and special exemptions, dignities and prerogatives partaken of, and enjoyed by the other citizens older and native of Our aforementioned city. They shall have the authority, unrestricted license, and full right of acquiring, having and holding any kind of properties, movable or immovable, and other rights under whatever title in Our aforementioned city, its district and March.

If at times the term "burghers" was not spelled out, the same effect was attained when, for instance, the community of Trapani secured from the Sicilian government in 1470 an approval of its statute and an order to all royal authorities that "the Jews ought to be treated . . . as are treated the Christians of that city." In the following year the viceroy extended a similar privilege to the Jews of Palermo. Certainly, in none of these cases did the royal or ducal government give up its overlordship over Jews. But it rightly saw no contradiction between such postulates of equal treatment of Jewish and Christian burghers and the theory of Jewish "serfdom." Nor did this situation escape the eagle eyes of contemporary jurists. Baldus de Ubaldis simply taught that "the immunity extended to the inhabitants of a certain locality embraces also the Jews." More broadly, Giovanni de Anagni coined a sentence which was often repeated by subsequent jurists down to the seventeenth century. "Jews are considered," he declared, "to be of the same people and of the [political] body of the same city, although they may not be considered members of the same spiritual body." [16]

Actually, burghers' rights did not imply the total incorporation of Jews in the body politic of the respective cities. In general they remained excluded from municipal offices and subject to special Jewish taxation, but they were amply compensated by their vast communal autonomy. Modern scholars have often emphasized the Jewish disabilities far above the positive elements of near-equality. For one example, discussing Jewish burghers' rights in Swiss cities, Fritz Wyler commented: "Although the expression occurs frequently and in all places, it is really but a circumlocution for the Jewish protected status [*Schutzgenössigkeit*]. As a matter of principle Jews were deprived of all rights and duties of burghers (for instance, of standing guard, performing military duties, etc.). Moreover, such burghers' rights were limited in duration; they could be terminated at any time, as well as renounced by the Jews themselves." Our further detailed analysis will show that these reservations are only partially true. Nevertheless, it may readily be conceded that Jews occupied in most European cities a somewhat intermediate position, well defined by Herbert Fischer: "The Jews are not full-fledged burghers [*Vollbürger*], not completely equal members of the corporate group. But neither are they placed in the status of serfs of the chamber, that of special protected subjects. Rather they belong to the city's people and live as members of the burghers' protective association [*Schutzgenossen*]." This ambiguity allowed for many detailed variations from locality to locality and from period to period. It left considerable leeway to legislators, judges, and administrative officials to make necessary adjustments.[17]

RABBINIC INTERPRETATIONS

At considerable variance with these assumptions were the views held by the Jews themselves. True, their intellectual leaders often equated their exilic life with *shi'abud malkhiot* (subjection to [foreign] kingdoms), a concept which in its original talmudic formulation may have been, directly or indirectly, coresponsible for the entire doctrine of Jewish serfdom. Medieval Jews were also well conditioned to receiving violent or contemptuous treatment from their lords and neighbors. However, in no case did they concede more than outward inferiority. In their heart of hearts they still believed themselves to be the chosen people who, temporarily chastised by wrath divine, were nevertheless the Lord's select, destined to return to the land of their forefathers and to see their faith accepted by all the nations of the world. The unsophisticated majority never doubted that in the messianic age there would be a complete reversal of the political conditions and that the Jewish people would also enjoy universal preeminence.

It was to this popular wish-thinking that Geronimo de Santa Fé referred at the disputation of Tortosa when he fulminated against the Jewish expectation that at the end of days the emperor and all Christendom would pay homage to the resurrected Jewish regime in Jerusalem. To which the Jewish delegates replied, without detailed documentation, that all nations were to retain their complete independence and that they would only recognize the messiah's spiritual supremacy. Repudiating any suggestion that the long period of exile and factual subjection to foreign domination had lowered the Jews' human dignity, they also insisted that "nowadays when the Jews live in exile and serve the Lord with much difficulty they merit the greater reward, as a small service performed in subjection and exile is more important and deserving of greater recompense than elaborate services rendered in an era of happiness and prosperity." [18]

From the legal point of view, moreover, their rabbis often reiterated the aforementioned doctrine formulated in the twelfth century by the Tosafist, Isaac b. Samuel of Dampierre, that "in the countries around us Jews have had the right to reside wherever

they wished, like the nobles." Not only the outstanding contro-
versialist, Naḥmanides of Gerona, but also the later Spanish leaders Ḥisdai Crescas the Elder (d. *ca.* 1348), Bonsenior Graciam, and
others insisted upon the Jews' unrestricted freedom of movement.
"In the courts of kings and their palaces," Crescas replied to a
pertinent inquiry (after 1346), "it has been an accepted principle
deeply ingrained in their hearts and in those of their counselors
that the Jews, wherever they may reside, are free to move from
place to place, according to their own choice, with no one having
the right to object or to force them." To which Nehemiah b. Isaac
added, "The law of the Jews is, like that of the knights, that they
are free to journey from place to place." Meir of Rothenburg further claimed that "the [absentee] Jews are not dependent and
obliged to pay taxes [to their lord] wherever they happen to be, as
the Gentiles [villeins] are dependent, but they are like free men
who had lost their possessions, but had not been sold into bondage; this is the customary relation between the government and
the Jews." Of course Meir, most of whose active life was spent during the turbulent years of the German *Interregnum,* would have
been the last to deny the Jews' lack of political power and their
frequent submission to arbitrary decisions of their political su-
periors. Like other Jewish leaders he realized that mighty personages could commit unlawful acts against Jews with perfect impunity, especially if they appealed to the deep-rooted prejudices of
the masses. In more unsettled periods, particularly, it became
doubly important for Jews to secure clear restatements of their ancient privileges safeguarding their freedom of movement. That is
why an assembly of Aragonese communities meeting in Barcelona
in 1354 resolved that the leaders

make every effort to obtain a privilege from our lord, the King, may his
Majesty be elevated, to permit all the Jews living under his domination
to transfer their residence from places in the realm to localities belonging to the nobles or any other place they might choose—which right
they have enjoyed from ancient times—and to revoke every [contrary]
law hitherto promulgated.[19]

To enable their people to live in the dispersion, the rabbis had
long adopted the maxim, first proclaimed by their third-century
Babylonian leader, Mar Samuel, that "the law of the kingdom is

law." They thus recognized all lawfully enacted governmental ordinances, provided these did not infringe upon fundamentals of their faith. But even behind that major concession lurked the unspoken conviction that, in the ultimate sense, Jewish law, derived from the revealed word of God, was superior to all human enactments. Therefore, it was up to the rabbis to decide whether a particular royal decree violated any of their religious fundamentals and should be disregarded. More, even with respect to civil law and such clearly royal prerogatives as taxation, some medieval rabbis drew the distinction between lawful and unlawful enactments. Quoting the difference, stressed by Abraham b. David of Posquières, between the laws of the "kingdom" and those of the "king," Joseph ibn Ḥabib taught that only the former, representing permanent state laws relating to taxation and other legitimate administrative functions, must be respected, but arbitrary expropriations by an individual monarch might well be repudiated. Similarly, an unnamed rabbi of London, cited by Mordecai b. Hillel ha-Kohen, differentiated between the imposition of taxes, a proper exercise of royal power, and illegal confiscatory fines. Adhering to the medieval predilection for custom, he and other rabbis even repudiated taxation going beyond the customary imposts. In such cases, they taught, the ruler was not a true king whose will ought to be respected, but rather acted like a highway robber whose decrees might well be defied. In other words—to use modern terminology—there was an inherent, if hidden, clash in the rivaling doctrines of sovereignty: the Church and the state viewed all rights of Jews in the Christian world as derived from the privileges issued in their behalf by their rulers, whereas from the rabbinic standpoint regulations enacted by kings regarding their Jewish subjects also had to meet the criteria of the truly sovereign, because divinely ordained, Jewish law.[20]

In practice, such a conflict of sovereignties was successfully avoided by mutual concessions and particularly by the state's recognition of Jewish self-government. If any further proof were needed to show that the status of Jews was in no way comparable with that of unfree Christian villeins, such evidence would be manifest in the vast range of communal self-determination which the Jewish people had enjoyed since ancient times and which rather grew in intensity as the segregationist policies of Church and state were more rigidly enforced. In all Christian, as well as Muslim, countries the Jewish community was recognized by law as a corporate body apart entitled not only to regulate its purely religious activities, but also to adjust many civil and political affairs to suit its own needs and traditions. As we shall see, the range of these autonomous functions differed from country to country and from period to period. But such variations in detail did not substantially affect the basic principle that, in their relations with one another, Jews were in the main governed by their own authorities acting on the basis of Jewish law.

In many respects the Jewish communal organization pointed the way for the newly developing northern European cities. What Adalbert Erler considers a major step in the fiscal evolution of the German city had long before been achieved by the Jewish communal leadership. "Nothing shows more clearly," Erler writes, "the magnificent change from city domination [by the lords] to city freedom than precisely the transformation of the individual tax [*bede*] owed the lord into a communal contribution. The latter is characterized by the fixing of a total amount of the impost due the lord, while the city attains the *jus subcollectandi*. . . . The city thus secures the right to allocate the total tax among its members." This right had been exercised by the Jewish communities under both Christendom and Islam from time immemorial. So strong, as a rule, were the Jewish communal controls that the rulers of both East and West often tried to utilize them to their own fiscal advantage either through appointive chief rabbis or through elected representatives. Various regional assemblies of Jewish leaders in the so-called Spanish *colectas,* in Sicily and in Germany were convoked, with governmental approval if not on the kings' initiative, to negotiate about the size of the revenue due to the state and to fix the best means of raising it. Powerful emperors like Sigismund and Frederick III, we remember, invited Jewish leaders from all over the Empire to help them increase that revenue. Can one envisage such national or regional convocations of villeins assembled to vote new taxes or new methods for their effective collection almost on the level of regular diets? [21]

No less extensive and permanent was the judicial self-government of the Jewish communities. Characteristically, in the very first privileges, in which German emperors used the phrase of Jews "belonging to the imperial Chamber," they also insisted upon the latter's right to govern their own affairs. In his decree of 1090 for the Jews of Worms Henry IV expressly forbade the bishop, chamberlain, count, or bailiff to interfere in internal Jewish affairs; they were to leave, in particular, the exercise of all judicial authority to Jewish officials freely elected by their own communal membership.

This principle was constantly reinforced by internal Jewish regulations which attempted to prevent coreligionists from repairing to Gentile courts. The fifteenth-century rabbi, Isaac b. Sheshet Perfet, restated the generally held, if oversimplified, Jewish opinion, "We see with our own eyes that all kings of Aragon have given permission [for us to be] judged according to the laws of our Torah and have ordered their judges thus to administer justice among Jews." This was true not only when Jews repaired to Jewish courts but also in cases, such as in mixed litigations between Jews and Christians, when they appeared before Gentile judges. To quote Perfet again, "It is generally known that, whether the trial takes place before the city council or the bailiff, all is decided upon the basis of Jewish law." We shall see that in various European lands this judicial self-determination was often contested; it was sharply curtailed at times in the case of litigations between Jews and Christians. However, such delimitations often had to be wrung by the respective non-Jewish courts from unwilling rulers insistent upon preserving Jewish judicial autonomy in relations among the Jews themselves. It is small wonder, then, that in all major concerns of his daily life the ordinary Jew had far less contact with the outside authorities than with the leaders of his own community within which he lived as an upright and dignified citizen.[22]

PROTECTION FOR PERSONS AND PROPERTY

With the principle of toleration went, in the first place, safeguards for the Jews' lives, limbs, and possessions. Without such protection Jews could not possibly have resisted both the general xenophobia and the specific anti-Jewish animosities. So long as these forces were more or less dormant, as in the pagan Roman Empire, Jews were adequately protected by the general provisions for the maintenance of public order. But under Christian domination popular resentments often reached a sufficiently high pitch to endanger the peaceful coexistence of the two faiths. Hence the later Roman legislators felt induced to spell out certain protective regulations, although for centuries thereafter, including some of the darkest eras of anti-Jewish hostility, such safeguards were often based on custom and precedent, rather than on clearly formulated laws.

Among the first enactments of this kind are those issued by the Christian emperors Arcadius in 397 and Honorius and Theodosius in 412 (418). "No Jew," wrote the latter, "in so far as he is innocent shall be trampled upon nor shall he be exposed to any insult because of his religious conviction." In 423 Theodosius repeated the same provision with a self-evident qualification. "We demand especially," he wrote, "from Christians, who are such and wish to be so called, that they should not, under the abuse of religious authority, dare to place their hands, contrary to law, upon Jews or pagans who live quietly and do not cause any disturbance." This law was in substance repeated also by Justinian. Fully realizing that legal injunctions alone would not stem popular animosities, some Church Fathers added moral suasion. For example, Augustine exhorted his readers: "You who are in the Church ought not to insult those who have not entered it, but you should rather pray so that they too may enter." These basic principles were invariably upheld also by the medieval churchmen. In their frequently renewed *Constitutio pro Judaeis*, we recall, many popes insisted that "without a judgment of the authority of the land no Christian" was to wound, kill, or rob Jews. Apart from receiving his due punishment, the Church taught, the killer of a Jew out of hatred or cupidity should realize that he had "committed not a slight [religious] sin, and atone for it like for the homicide [of a Christian]." The medieval state, too, dependent as it was on Roman and Christian traditions, reiterated these protective regulations. In a privilege for Domatus and his nephew Samuel, Louis the Pious ordered that "no one should presume, under any illicit pretenses whatsoever, to disturb you, the members of your family, or successors, or to cause you insults." More specifically, the emperor provided that, since Jews were living under his protection, any person committing or instigating the murder of any one of them, "so long as they prove faithful to Us," should pay ten gold pounds to the Treasury. This is also the tenor of Louis' privileges in favor of other Jews.[23]

Confronted with this age-old tradition, the medieval states, outspokenly or tacitly, upheld this principle. In his famous Rhenish privileges of 1090, which remained the fountainhead of the subsequent Central European legislation, Henry IV not only repeated the sweeping injunction that no one should dare attack Jews living under royal protection, but in that of Worms he specifically prescribed that "if any one conspires against, or sets a trap for, any of them [the Jews] so that he be killed, both the instigator and the killer shall pay 12 gold pounds to the royal treasury." In the case of inability to pay, the murderer was to lose both his eyes and his right hand. The wounding of a Jew was punishable by a fine of one gold pound; if committed by a slave, the fine was to be paid by his master who had the alternative of delivering the slave for punishment (ad penas tradat). On finding these provisions ineffective in the emergency of 1096, Henry joined forces with other German princes to proclaim the "peace" for a number of defenseless groups including Jews. These "peace" treaties were subsequently repeated in 1224, 1235, 1254, and frequently thereafter. In the light of these conventions Eike von Repgow taught in his famous law book that "if a Christian slays a Jew or commits any wrong on him, he shall be judged because he has broken the king's peace." Moreover, Henry IV's local privileges of 1090 were expanded over the entire Empire by Frederick I and Frederick II in 1157, 1187, and 1236. These imperial safeguards were further supplemented by many regional and local decrees, including the Austrian privilege of 1244 which, as we recall, served as a model for the subsequent legislation of several neighboring countries. Curiously, the articles protecting the Jews' life and limb appear here after a variety of provisions relating to their economic rights. But the legislator's intent was unmistakable. The Austrian Frederick II provided that any Christian wounding a Jew should pay the Treasury

12 gold marks, while the injured party was to receive 12 silver marks and medical expenses. Injuries without bloodletting were to be punished by a fine of 4 gold marks to the Crown and 4 silver marks to the injured party. Undoubtedly in either case an insolvent assailant was to lose his arm, a penalty provided also for any Christian assailant of a Jewess. Finally, murder of a Jew was to be punished by the death of the murderer and the confiscation of all his property.[24]

Such protective privileges usually implied orders to royal officials to prevent wrongdoings against Jews. Needless to say, in the poorly organized medieval states such orders were not always carried out. While the sheriff of Norfolk effectively protected the Jews of Norwich during the Blood Accusation of 1144, the hearings before the king in 1235 on the Norwich townspeople's complaint "that a greater number [of Jews] than usual dwell in their city" brought out the facts that "the houses of the Jews had on two occasions been set on fire" and that the bailiffs of the town, despite the sheriff's urgings, had failed to intervene. In tenser periods, when attacks on Jews became more frequent, as in 1190 and during the minority of Henry III, the English rulers sought the aid of municipal organs. In 1218 the king's council after "common deliberation" instructed the local authorities not to permit any harm to be done to Jews and, on the initiative of the regent, William Marshal, a number of towns selected twenty-four burghers each, charged with the protection of Jews, especially against hostile Crusaders. On occasion a superior official was appointed to administer the necessary protective measures. We do not know what specific role was assigned to the *magister Judaeorum* of the Carolingian age. But it was probably very much akin to that of the *gardien général des Juifs* whom we have encountered in fourteenth-century France.[25]

Special protective enactments were also needed in connection with territorial changes. The transition from Muslim to Christian rule, in particular, often involved considerable adjustments for Jews, too. The surrendering Muslims at times exacted from the new rulers the promise that Jews would not be appointed to positions of authority over them while, on their part, Jews had to be reassured about their own rights. Such treaties, as we recall, had been concluded by Tudela upon its capitulation in 1115 and by Saragossa in 1118. As late as 1489, when the Moorish rulers of Cadiz surrendered Almeria and other cities, Ferdinand and Isabella had to promise not to grant Jews any jurisdiction over Moors, but they added the clause, "We assure all Jews . . . that they will enjoy the same rights as the said Moorish *Mudejares,* since the said Jews are natives of the said Kingdom of Granada." Similar provisions were also inserted two years later into the treaties of surrender of the rest of Granada.[26]

From time to time kings issued special letters of protection, often amounting to personal safe-conducts, for individual Jews. In 1488, for instance, Ferdinand and Isabella rewarded a Jew, Simuel Abolafia, for his war services with a special order to all Spanish authorities not only to protect him and his associates, but also to let him pass from place to place without the payment of the usual customs duties and tolls. A year later the Catholic monarchs took under their special protection twenty Jews of Malaga and their associates who had been entrusted by the Jewish communities of Castile and Aragon with the task of collecting funds throughout the country for the ransom of Jewish captives. Ten Castilian Jews, dispatched to these captives by Chief Rabbi Abraham Seneor, were even permitted to traverse the archbishopric of Seville and the bishopric of Cordova despite a recent inquisitorial outlawry of all Jewish settlements there.[27]

In practice the issue almost invariably narrowed down to the problem of the punishment of assailants. Although the beneficiaries of fines levied on offenders usually were the rulers, rather than the injured parties, the Jewish communities themselves seemed not to mind that the authorities had thus become financially interested in prosecuting the criminals. In the earlier Middle Ages they sometimes considered it a matter of prestige to have their *wergeld* equal to that of free Christians. Where it was lower, they frequently secured some substitutes, as in the Austrian decree's provision for medical expenses. Absent from safeguards for injured Christians, this indemnity was probably inserted at the request of Jews who had taken it over from their own biblical-talmudic law.

In general the amount and value of the *wergeld* varied in different localities and was subject to alteration from time to time. Hence comparisons between amounts paid for the slaying of free Christians and of Jews are often precarious. Nor did the legislators pay sufficient attention to changes in monetary values and purchasing power. The *wergeld,* originally set in most parts of Aragon during the eleventh and twelfth centuries, was repeated in the subsequent renewals of these laws in codes and *fueros,* though its actual value had substantially declined. Nor did the progressive replacement of financial penalties by physical punishment, even execution, necessarily find immediate expression in the contemporary legislation. The Tortosa custumal of 1279, however, specifically stated that the newly introduced capital punishment for murder was not to apply to the slaying of Jews or Saracens, the penalty for which was to remain unchanged. Most Aragonese statutes placed the *wergeld* for Jewish homicide at 500 solidi (in Calatayud, whose *fuero* was compiled in 1134, at 300 solidi). Bodily harm without bloodletting was punishable by a fine of 60 solidi. In the case of free Christians the *fuero* of Calatayud set the same amount of 300 solidi, whereas the *fuero* of Aragon of 1247 raised the fine to 1,000 solidi or double the sum to be paid by the slayer of a Jew. In Germany Otto Stobbe figured out that, according to the *Sachsenspiegel,* the *wergeld* for the murder of a knight and, according to later laws, also that of a burgher amounted to only 18 silver pounds compared with the equivalent of 20 pounds for the killing of a Jew provided for in the privileges of Henry IV. Considering the decline in the purchasing power of silver between 1090 and the thirteenth-century codes of law, this disparity, if adhered to in practice, was even greater. More frequently, however, the judicial practice leveled down these differences and the *Rechtsbuch nach Distinctionen* doubtless reflects the prevailing usage when it asserts that "in other [nonimperial] secular courts the Jew and the Christian pay the same fine." [28]

Some discrimination was also practiced in penalties inflicted on localities where the murderers were not apprehended. Outstanding examples are the aforementioned decrees of Emperor Frederick II and Pope Honorius IV providing for the payment by such communities of 100 or 50 augustals, dependent on whether the victim had been a Christian or a Jew. In 1377 the Castilian Cortes secured from King Henry II the abolition of such collective responsibility altogether, only promising that local officials would vigorously investigate the murders and bring the criminals to justice. In time the *wergeld* was replaced by capital punishment. When King Pedro I of Portugal (1357–67) ordered, as we recall, the execution of two noble youths who had killed a Jew, he argued that "what they had learned on Jews they would practice on Christians." In the case of mass assaults, to be sure, the authorities had to be more lenient. For instance, the city of Nördlingen accepted a financial settlement from one of its burghers in 1393 for his participation in an attack on Jews "and other quarrels." But he not only had to promise good behavior (*Freundschaft*) in the future, but also had to name his three brothers-in-law as guarantors of this pledge. With the increase of intergroup tensions, however, Jews also required some protection against lesser assaults. Characteristically, most outspoken in this respect was Charles VI's order of July 3, 1393, issued almost on the eve of the final expulsion of Jews from royal France. In this order, addressed to the prefect of Paris and all the seneschals, bailiffs, and judges, as well as to the conservator of Jews, the king referred to the Jews' complaints that "many persons who are their debtors or otherwise their enemies try to commit, and actually commit daily against them, insults, injuries, and villainies by word of mouth or deeds. For instance, they lay their hands upon them, stop their movements, pull off their hats and berets, beat and wound them with knives or sticks, or otherwise assail their persons and property in contempt of Our said protection." The king therefore ordered all his officials to make solemn public announcements threatening severe penalties for such attacks. They were also to furnish transcripts of this decree to any Jewish group asking for them.[29]

Jewish property, too, was frequently singled out for protection in imperial and royal decrees. In his aforementioned law of 423, Emperor Theodosius had provided that, if any Jewish possessions were despoiled, the perpetrators should be made to restitute "not only what they had taken but triple or quadruple damages." Justinian upheld this provision, but he reduced the damages to double the amount of the original loss. This seems to have become the prevailing practice also in the medieval Western lands. Probably taking a cue from existing custom rather than the *Corpus* of Justinian, Louis the Pious ordered payment of double damages in addition to a fine of one gold pound for either the royal or the episcopal Treasury. Other Carolingian privileges were less specific. They generally prohibited the removal or diminution "of any objects belonging to them [the Jews] which appeared to be legally held by them at the time," and forbade the extortion "from the aforementioned Hebrews" of any kind of toll on their journeys. Similarly, in his Spires privilege of 1090, Henry IV stated sweepingly that no one be allowed to take away any of the Jewish "possessions which they own by hereditary rights, be they courtyards, houses, gardens, vineyards, fields, slaves, or any other movable or immovable holdings." Protection of Jewish property became a particular issue whenever fairs wished to attract foreign Jews. In his ordinance of 1179 concerning the city of Étampes, Louis VII specifically provided that "neither the elder of the Jews nor any other man shall seize, on account of debts, any man coming to the fair or any possessions present at the fair on the day of business." [30]

In England, too, John Lackland's charter of 1201 read:

Know that We have granted to all Jews of England and Normandy that they reside in freedom and honour in Our land, and hold of Us all that they held of King Henry, Our father's grandfather, and all that they now rightfully hold in lands, fees, gages and purchases, and that they have all their franchises and customs, as they had them in the time of the said King Henry, Our father's grandfather, in better and more peaceful and honourable enjoyment.

As Jewish property came to be considered part of the royal domain, royal self-interest demanded ever more effective safeguards. That is why the Jews were also allowed by King John "to go wheresoever they will with all their chattels, as Our proper goods, and be it unlawful for any to delay or forbid them." For the same reason they were to be free from all customs duties through the length and breadth of England and Normandy. Ultimately, the lesser nobles complained that both the Crown and the magnates used foreclosures by Jewish moneylenders as a means of transferring many baronial estates to their domains. As late as 1286, Archbishop John Peckham of Canterbury spoke of the "justified clamor" through the whole English kingdom against the acquisition by the queen of noble estates via Jewish usury. Freedom from tolls or, at least, an injunction against charging Jews higher tolls than non-Jews, was included also in many other Jewish privileges. Obviously, under the prevailing medieval system of collecting duties and tolls at the crossing of boundaries between feudal estates, however small, it was not always easy to persuade the local authorities to exempt Jews completely. The Austrian privilege of 1244, therefore, after generally prohibiting the placing of any obstacles or molesting Jews moving from one Austrian place to another, merely demanded that they be charged only such tolls as were customarily collected from Christian burghers of their places of residence.[31]

Of particular interest was freedom from tolls charged for Jewish bodies transported to regional cemeteries, a practice which the mourners could the less effectively resist, as their religious law demanded early burial. Frederick II of Austria specifically outlawed such charges and declared that "if any toll-collector should extort from them [the Jews] any sum of money, he should be punished on a par with one committing the depredation of a corpse, called in the local language *reraub*." With but verbal modifications this provision was taken over by Austria's neighbors and served as a moderate deterrent against such abuses in east-central Europe. In other parts of the Holy Roman Empire, however, Jewish funerary tolls became quite common, as did special charges on Jews conveying merchandise. In time the living Jews, too, became dutiable, leading to the establishment of "corporal taxes" on Jews, a discriminatory and, ultimately, quite humiliating form of taxation which was to agitate the minds of legislators and publicists particularly in the early nineteenth century. Tolls of this kind are recorded quite early in Barcelona and in the County of Roussillon. Elsewhere, as in Tortosa, the native Jews were free from such taxes, but foreigners had to pay them. On the other hand, the Jews of Perpignan and the whole kingdom of Valencia secured in 1247 general exemptions from corporal taxes and even from those paid on animals used for transport.[32]

Of greater importance was the freedom to transmit property to children or other heirs. In antiquity such rights were generally taken for granted. The Christian Roman Empire, however, introduced certain restrictions on the free post-mortem disposal of Jewish property. Jews were allowed neither to disinherit baptized children as demanded by Jewish law, nor to transmit Christian slaves to their heirs, even if they themselves were still permitted to hold them. Despite certain complex regulations concerning their testamentary dispositions, however, Jews could still write wills, a right almost invariably upheld during the Middle Ages. In his aforementioned charter of 1201, John Lackland specifically provided that, upon a Jew's death, his corpse should not be detained above ground for the satisfaction of any private claims, "but let his heir have his money and his debts." No such restriction applied to the claims of the Crown which, in exceptional cases like that of Aaron of York, confiscated the entire estate. Otherwise Jewish heirs usually compromised with the Treasury by paying it an inheritance tax equivalent to one-third of the estate. But some such charges were not infrequently imposed also on estates left behind by other classes of the population.[33]

An interesting variant in these protective provisions was the prohibition of illegal entry into Jewish homes, for whose privacy the Jewish people had long evinced a profound respect. The Deuteronomic legislator had already forbidden creditors to enter their debtors' houses in order to seize pledges for the satisfaction of claims; they had to wait outside. The Talmud quoted the pithy adage: "Even a common weaver shall be governor in his house," anticipating the English phrase of one's home being one's castle. In many cases Jews secured privileges freeing them from involuntary hospitality even to rulers. True, under the constantly increasing fiscal pressures billeting of officials, if not soldiers, in Jewish homes became not infrequent. But the communities of Barcelona, Tarragona, Perpignan, Gerona, and Valencia quite early secured from James I exemptions from that duty. Other Aragonese kings granted similar privileges to the Jews of Lérida and Majorca. Not surprisingly, however, such privileges often irked non-Jews, who had to carry the double burden of hospitality; they also often were disregarded by the royal quartermasters. At times Jews compromised by promising to deliver beds and other equipment for the accommodation of courtiers or soldiers. Ultimately the entire obligation was converted into another Jewish tax. Owing to the greater segregation of German Jewry, actual accommodation of royal courtiers and officials was from the outset replaced by payments in kind. For instance, during the emperor's frequent visits Frankfort Jews had to deliver parchment for his Chancery, bedding and kitchen utensils for his higher officials, and some cash for certain dignitaries. Similar payments are recorded in Nuremberg and other communities. Illegal entry, however, was as a rule subject to penalty, the Austrian privilege of 1244 stating: "Whichever Christian removes by force his pawn from the Jew or applies violence in the latter's home, shall be punished severely as a dissipator of Our Chamber." If judicial records rarely refer to such assaults, this is largely owing to the increasing concentration of Jews within their own quarters which made illegal incursions by outsiders quite perilous.[34]

Clearly, all such broad and detailed legislation, as well as the implied protective devices for Jews living in a predominantly hostile world, were not always effective. The wish so eloquently expressed by Archbishop Wicbold von Holte of Cologne in his decree of 1302 could materialize only if it was supported by a strong administration. It was his intention, Wicbold wrote, that "the said Jews, living quietly and peacefully in the security of their body, tranquillity of their souls and preservation of their property, should in Our days increase in a healthy and fruitful fashion." Wherever the self-interest of the Crown or the ruling classes demanded their violation, these principles were unhesitatingly discarded, however. In the case of kings, barons, bishops, and municipal authorities the line between illegal appropriation of Jewish possessions and legitimate taxation could not easily be drawn, medieval fiscal agents being richly inventive in extorting an endless variety of payments from the Jewish "serfs." Nor did officials hesitate to employ physical torture to break down the resistance of prospective taxpayers so that the difference between judicial torture and uncalled-for bodily assault often was completely obliterated. Only rarely was an official called to account for miscarriage of justice. When in 1300 two Jewish brothers daringly sued the bailiff of Béziers for damages because he had illegally tortured their father to obtain confession of an alleged theft, they secured only the clearing of the defendant's name, not the punishment of the overbearing official. Nor could executions of Jews by irate rulers be prevented any more than those of other defenseless opponents. In fact, the great inconsistencies in the legislative enactments were magnified by the diversities of practical application which opened the gates to an endless variety of arbitrary acts.[35]

Nor was legal protection effective in the case of mass assaults. Whenever Jews were murdered not by single individuals, but by a frenzied mob during some great upheaval, even the instigators as a rule went unpunished. This was the case not only with the Crusaders who, after perpetrating their atrocities, proceeded on their missions, but also with pogromists who remained at home. The punishment of some ringleaders of the English massacres in 1190 and that of cities and individuals involved in the Rindfleisch pogroms of 1298 in Germany were but exceptions confirming the rule that most assailants escaped scot free. The most glaring examples of total impunity occurred in the Black Death era when Charles IV, as we recall, wholly oblivious of his reiterated pledges to protect his imperial "serfs," not only forgave the mass murders of Jews but, on occasion, even granted advance immunity to cities for massacres yet to be committed. Even in relatively quiescent Renaissance Italy, the bishop of Cremona, Giovanni Stefano Botticelli, explained certain disorders by the alleged failure of Jews to wear their distinguishing marks. In his letter to Galeazzo Maria Sforza of April 1468, he also insisted that the Jews themselves had caused the disturbance "by their crimes, perfidy, iniquity, abomination and dishonest mode of living." In the long run, indeed, it was not the protection granted by law, but the interplay of many social, economic, and religious forces which accounted for the security of the Jewish population. Yet, by promulgating certain basic principles, the law set the pace for the regulation of Jewish life at least in times of peace or of slow, imperceptible change. Moreover, certain essential correctives helped redress some of these legal and administrative inadequacies. Bribing of officials, including *douceurs* to highly placed personages, sometimes granted immunity even to guilty Jews. More frequently, these "gifts" helped stave off, or secure some retribution for, acts of violence by private enemies or religious fanatics, as well as forestall some unwittingly injurious decisions.[36]

TREATMENT OF JEWISH CULPRITS

Characteristically, the laws are rather silent on the subject of attacks by Jews on Christians or their property. As a minority, more or less permanently on the defensive, few Jews were likely to indulge in wanton assaults on non-Jews. Yet occurrences of this type could not be totally avoided, since temperamental medieval men often resorted to self-help. An occasional fracas between Christians and Jews may also have left the question open as to who had started the fight. On the whole, Jewish assailants were punished in accordance with the general laws of the respective localities, whose penalties were scaled upwards in accordance with the rank of the injured, not the offending, party.

In time, when execution of murderers began replacing the *wergeld,* Jews were as a rule prosecuted as well as protected on an equal basis. In the formulation of the *Sachsenspiegel,* repeated in various other German law books including that of Magdeburg of 1304, one could actually detect a veiled intent to grant the Jew the much-needed protection. If a Jew slays or injures a Christian, the *Sachsenspiegel* states, "one judges him like a Christian man. If a Christian slays a Jew or does him other [physical] harm, he is judged under the king's peace which he had broken." In practice, either slaying would usually lead to execution, but the Magdeburg law made it clear that only a Jew apprehended during the act (*yn handhaftiger tat*) would be subject to the supreme penalty. The Polish and several thirteenth-century Silesian privileges prescribed the high fine of thirty shillings for a Christian who failed to extend assistance to a Jewish neighbor crying for help at night, but they are silent about the reciprocal duty of a Jew toward his Christian neighbor. In England, too, general equality of treatment is evidenced by the relatively few recorded cases of prosecution of Jewish criminals, which included those for rape (1178–79), assaults on knights (1184–85), and association with outlaws (1193). Realizing that Jews required protection, some rulers went beyond the existing rules of evidence. On May 27, 1423, and February 5, 1443, the Provençal Queen Yolande and King René, respectively, decreed that one must not seize and incarcerate Jews for any crime without solid proofs submitted by the accuser, who was also to be held personally responsible for the expenses of the prosecution if it proved unfounded. Anonymous denunciations were to be totally disregarded. René threatened anyone disobeying this order with a fine of 100 marks and with his personal displeasure. Most significantly, some privileges (for instance, those enacted by the archbishops of Cologne in 1252 and 1302) specifically provided that the Jewish community as a whole should not be held responsible for transgressions of individual members, although these provisions were often observed in their breach, particularly in periods of mass frenzy.[37]

In Spain, on the other hand, there seems to have existed an early dichotomy between the local *fueros* which tried to lower the penalty for murder or injury of a Jew, and the royal privileges which demanded equal treatment. The thirteenth-century custumal of Alba de Tormes and the *fuero* of Sepúlveda postulated the execution of a Jewish murderer of a Christian and the confiscation of his property as against the mere payment of a fine of twenty or one hundred maravedis if a Jew was slain by a Christian. For the wounding of a Christian or a Moor in Sepúlveda the Jew had to pay 10 maravedis, as had a Moorish assailant of a Jew. But if a Christian wounded a Jew his fine was limited to 4 maravedis. All such fines, moreover, were to be divided into equal thirds for the benefit of the injured party or his family, the king or the judge, and the local magistrates. Despite the confirmation of the Sepúlveda custumal by King Ferdinand IV in 1309, however, this was not general Castilian practice. True, in 1313 Queen Maria and Infante Pedro, acting in behalf of Alphonso XI, yielded to the entreaties of the Cortes of Palencia and decreed that in future intergroup killings and assaults the penalties should follow local customs, rather than the royal privileges for Jewish or Moorish subjects. But the queen and the infante themselves essentially withdrew this concession two years later at the Cortes of Burgos.[38]

Such royal "favoritism" was connected, of course, with the kings' unwillingness to lose a Jewish taxpayer through murder, if he was the victim, or through execution if he was the guilty party. That is why even in the Aragonese privileges most favorable to Jews, such as those enacted by James I for the community of

Valencia in 1227 and by James II for that of Saragossa in 1299, monarchs reserved for themselves the fines imposed on the homicide of, or by, a Jew. More, when the Huesca community received in 1212 from Pedro II extensive guarantees for its communal self-government, the king threatened any Jew severing his relations with the community with full-fledged slavery and gave its leaders discretion to sentence transgressors to death by public stoning. In such cases, however, the community had to idemnify the king for the loss of his "serf" by the payment of 1,000 solidi "and no more under any circumstances." [39]

At first the execution of Jewish criminals seems to have followed usual methods. Only a Carolingian capitulary of questionable authenticity provided for the drowning in a sack or the burning of a Jew convicted of having committed "some misdeed against the Christian law or any Christian." In time, however, the general penchant for discriminating against, and humiliating, Jews came to the fore also in this area. Some authorities soon began employing against Jewish criminals the ancient method of hanging them by their feet which, originally reflective of pagan Teuton concepts, was considered particularly contemptible. We hear with increasing frequency of such executions in the last two medieval centuries in both Germany and Aragon. In some German localities hangings of Jews took place slightly outside the official gallows as a demonstration of Jewish inferiority. Sometimes the local authorities achieved that purpose by suspending on either side of the hanged Jew a ferocious dog until he, too, expired. But these chicaneries were neither universal nor endowed with the authority of king or pope; they developed from local observances adopted to give vent to anti-Jewish feelings. Moreover, this penalty was not restricted to Jews. Certainly, the dishonorable execution of Benito Mussolini and his associates by the Italian antifascists is a recent example of apparently unrelated, and yet quite similar inventions of an aroused populace. Curiously, during the Middle Ages this method was generally employed in the execution of thieves, rather than of killers. Its folkloristic and extralegal origins are also evidenced by all sorts of tales. According to one story, a Jew hanged by his feet in Sulzmatt, near Colmar, in 1295 remained alive for eight days and marshaled enough strength to get above the gallows but not enough to escape. Another narrative had it that in Halle in 1462 a suspended Jew finally consented to receive baptism administered to him by a priest who had climbed up a ladder. The new convert was removed to a hospital, but he died there after twenty days.[40]

Another humiliating anti-Jewish custom was apparently first developed in Byzantium. By employing Jewish executioners in the hanging of all criminals, the Byzantine authorities seemingly felt that they thus compounded the indignity for both the hangman and the condemned person. But there is no evidence that that usage ever spread westward, even after its adoption by the Venetian administration on the eastern islands of Crete and Corfu, as well as in Negroponte. The Jews here, and probably also in Morocco (where a case of this kind is recorded in a rabbinic work), strenuously fought this practice and ultimately secured its abolition also in Corfu and Negroponte. The Venetian governor in Cretan Candia merely consented to free the Jewish executioners from performing their duty on Sabbaths and Jewish holidays (1465).[41]

More important were the penalties for assaults by Jews on Jews. Here, too, few legislators were fully articulate, undoubtedly because they left the punishment to the Jewish communal authorities. In his decree of 1201, however, John I of England reserved for the royal judiciary the prosecution for such major crimes as "homicide, mayhem, deliberate assault, housebreaking, rape, larceny, arson, and treasure [trove]." According to the Austrian decree of 1244 and its offshoots, a Jew wounding a coreligionist was to be fined two talents (about 1⅓ marks) payable to the non-Jewish judge presiding over mixed Jewish and non-Jewish affairs. The legislator failed to provide here for any indemnity, including costs of medical treatment, for the injured party, doubtless relying on the Jewish courts' undeviating practice to include such damages in their judgments. Even where Jews exceptionally exercised capital jurisdiction, the actual execution of criminals rested with the state authorities, or to use the ecclesiastical nomenclature, with the secular arm. It appears that relatively few Jews were condemned for acts of violence, in contrast to the fairly large number of those sentenced for monetary transgressions. The Jew of Bitonto,

Apulia, condemned for hiring an assassin to maim or murder five coreligionists, must have been a rare exception. Even in fifteenth-century Florence, where the assimilation of Jews to the mores of their environment had progressed very far, we learn of only four sentences (out of 90 criminal prosecutions of Jews in which the alleged transgression is known) for violent acts. Of the two homicides, one was committed by a baptized Jew. Two other men were accused of poisoning their adversaries—a very common occurrence in Renaissance society. All four defendants, moreover, were condemned only to monetary fines, which always leaves a residuum of doubt concerning the disinterestedness of the judges. Probably far more typical was the plea of the Ratisbon elders in 1460 that "no one of either sex, whatever his age, remembers that a Jew had ever been executed here. For this reason people liked to marry into this community." Two Spanish rabbis could even seriously debate the problem as to whether Jewish judges should continue sitting in judgment over cases of robbery, since "they were so infrequent." These rabbis wished to apply, therefore, the talmudic laws concerning robbery to such more common transgressions as embezzlement by a depositary.[42]

An interesting variant of Jewish penal law was debt bondage. Well known in antiquity, this sanction on insolvency had practically disappeared from Jewish life until it was revived in the medieval West, doubtless under the impact of the parallel provisions of Teuton laws. However, because of the oblivion into which the institution had interveningly fallen and the serious doubts entertained as to its continued validity from the standpoint of both Jewish and state laws, many creditors exacted from their Jewish debtors an advance pledge that, if unable to pay, they would voluntarily submit to such loss of freedom. Apparently because of the frequency of such pledges, a regular formula was adopted in Spain. The decisive passage read:

He [John Doe] has abandoned his body to the aforementioned [Richard Roe] and authorized any bearer of this writ, be he a knight, powerful personage, or any other man who will find him from that time on, that he be allowed to seize his body at any time, in any place and in any kingdom where he will find him and to place him in prison at will until he shall have paid up the aforementioned amount together with the agreed upon penalty as written above. The said [John Doe] also took upon himself that he should not benefit from any act of grace extended to him or which may be extended to him in the future by any king, queen, lord, lady or anybody else in the world, even if the latter should order that, in general, no one seize the Jew's body on account of a debt. All this shall continue until he will have paid up the said amount and penalty as written above.

In fact, however, Jews frequently secured from governments generic exemptions from debt bondage which doubtless superseded these "voluntary" commitments. In a decree of unknown date Alphonso X ordained that "just as a Jew cannot seize a Christian for any debt, so should a Christian be unable to seize a Jew." With reference to a debate in contemporary Burgos, Asher b. Yeḥiel of Toledo stated succinctly that "even if [the debtor] had expressly stipulated in his deed that the creditor might seize his body, such a stipulation is null and void. It is clear that if the debtor has no money to pay, the creditor may neither imprison him, nor use him as his serf, nor sell him on account of his debt." This decision was accepted by Asher's son Jacob, Joseph Karo, and others. Yet the strength of local practice was such that Isaac b. Sheshet Perfet, though on principle agreeing that it had been outlawed, yielded to an approving local ordinance which had contended that without such a safeguard one would "shut off the gates" to prospective borrowers. On his own, R. Isaac suggested a compromise that the debtor might obligate himself in his deed, in the case of insolvency, to go to prison and stay there until the repayment of the loan. This eventuality was, indeed, foreseen in the aforementioned formula. Of a different category was, of course, the practice of some northern communities, recorded by Moses Isserles, to imprison, by court order, a recalcitrant though solvent debtor and thus force him to pay up.[43]

RELIGIOUS SAFEGUARDS

If toleration of Jews was to be meaningful, it also had to include provisions for the free exercise of their religion and the protection of their basic religious institutions. Once he gave up his religion, a medieval Jew, except in cases of mass conversion, was immediately treated as a full-fledged Christian and became subject to the laws governing the particular Christian group which he happened to join. True, new converts often suffered from some social and economic discrimination, but legally they had so definitely ceased to be counted as Jews that any relapse to the old faith, even the observance of one or another Jewish ritual, was treated as criminal apostasy or heresy. In these matters, as in its entire attitude to Jewish religious concerns, the medieval state followed the principles laid down by canon law. It deviated from them only when its interest diverged from those of the Church, or when Jews were influential enough to evade some canonical restrictions with the overt or tacit aid of governmental organs.

A major facet of toleration was, of course, the prohibition of forced conversions of Jews to Christianity. The numerous aspects of this prohibition have been analyzed in our earlier volumes from the standpoint of both canon and Roman laws, and they require but little supplementation from late medieval secular sources. On occasion, to be sure, individual churchmen and secular rulers disregarded it and made Jews adopt Christianity against their will. The best-known and fully documented action of this kind occurred in Portugal in 1496, when the so-called decree of expulsion was turned into an order of wholesale conversion. But rarely do we hear of protests by ecclesiastical authorities; in some, the local clergy appeared among the very protagonists of such compulsion. However, all these were but exceptions confirming the rule of law prevailing in almost all medieval countries, as formulated in Castile's *Siete Partidas:* "No force nor pressure must in any manner be applied to any Jew so that he turn Christian. But the Christians ought to convert them [the Jews] to the faith of our Lord Jesus Christ with good examples, sayings from the Holy Scriptures and cajolery. For our Lord neither requires nor likes worship rendered by force." A similar position was taken by such secular jurists as the author of the *Schwabenspiegel.* During the widespread massacres of Spanish Jews in 1391, John I of Aragon not only scolded his brother, Duke Martin, for his weakness in stemming the attacks in Valencia and Murviedro, but also emphasized that Martin must not allow "that any Jew be forced to submit to baptism except by free choice, for an act of compulsion is neither meritorious nor permissible." A similar order was soon thereafter issued by the queen to the bishop of Barcelona with respect to the family of Ḥisdai Crescas, "Our servant and confidant." [44]

Prohibition of forced conversions was so generally taken for granted that it was not spelled out even in the fundamental privileges of European Jewry. The Austrian decree of 1244 but indirectly alluded to it when it sharply condemned the kidnaping of Jewish children—evidently for conversionist purposes. Frederick II declared tersely, "If any man or woman should abduct a Jewish boy, We wish that he or she be condemned like a thief," that is, sentenced to death as postulated by the biblical legislation elaborated by both the Talmud and canon law. Some Central-European municipal laws, such as that of Iglau and Brünn, provided that the kidnaper of any human being be broken on the wheel. The death penalty was also prescribed by the *Rechtsbuch nach Distinctionen* and other statutes. But all this did not deter certain fanatics from forcibly converting Jewish children, the Freiburg jurist, Ulrich (Udalricus) Zasius, trying, as we recall, to supply a strained rationale for it in his monograph, *Questiones de parvulis Iudeorum baptisandis.*[45]

In return the state often demanded strict conformity within the Jewish community. In 1490 the Viceroy of Sicily, instigated by Jewish envoys from Girgenti, ordered the local *judex Judeorum* to institute proceedings against "some Jews, both male and female, of that community who do not live according to the Mosaic law and hence cause many errors and scandals in the said community." Nor did the Jewish leaders contest, on principle, the king's authority to intervene in such matters. They only tried to stave off interventions by inquisitors which could embroil them in serious controversies. A resolution, adopted by the assembly of the Aragonese Jewish communities in Barcelona in 1354, demanded clear-cut legislation that

the Inquisition into heresies should not relate to Jews except in matters common to all religions such as the denial of the existence of God, or of the revealed character of the Torah. But in regard to religious differences, even such as relate to a Jew's alleged support of a Christian heretic, the stamp of heresy should not be placed on the Jew, for it is impossible to regard as heresy what a Jew rightly considers a part of his faith. It is only appropriate, therefore, that he should be condemned by the ruler alone, be it even to death or to exile, but not by the Inquisition.

Some inquisitors paid little heed to such Jewish requests and on October 12, 1414, Alphonso V had to censure severely the Perpignan cleric for stepping beyond his authority "to the substantial damage of the said Jews and to the prejudice and notorious detriment of Our royal jurisdiction." When the Perpignan inquisitor persisted in his course, he was even more sharply called to account five years later by Queen Maria who expressed her "displeasure" over his "failure to blush for having gone beyond the bounds of his office and arbitrarily raised his hands on someone else's harvest." [46]

More frequent are the legislative references to synagogues. We recall that the ancient Roman populace, and even such ecclesiastical leaders as St. Ambrose, could not quite comprehend the fine distinction drawn by imperial law between the condemnation of the Jewish faith and the protection of houses of worship publicly dedicated to the cultivation of that faith. The compromise finally reached in the fifth century provided that Jews were not to build new synagogues but were to be allowed to keep their old ones in repair. This compromise was more or less faithfully adhered to by both the Church and the state during the entire medieval period. To cite the *Siete Partidas* again, it defined, in its usual verbose manner this middle-of-the-road policy.

The synagogue is a place where the Jews perform their services. It is a house which they must not erect anew in any place of Our dominion unless by Our special order. But those which they have from of old they may repair when ruin threatens or rebuild on the same place where they had been before, but not enlarge them, make them taller, or decorate them. A synagogue constructed in a different manner ought to be taken away from the Jews and given to the major church of its locality. Since the synagogue is a place where the Lord's name is praised, We forbid any Christian to dare to break into or to rob it, or to take anything from it by force. . . . We also forbid Christians to keep animals there or to interfere with, and harass Jews trying to worship there according to their law.

Medieval monarchs, particularly in periods of greater tension, never let the Jews forget this limitation upon their freedom of worship. In 1253 Henry III of England, almost paraphrasing the anti-Jewish resolutions of the Council of Oxford of 1222, even tried to make the prohibition of new synagogues sufficiently retro-active to forbid their maintenance on any sites not thus occupied during the reign of John I some forty years earlier. Complaints that Jews had built synagogues were frequently heard from the clergy, which, in almost all Christian countries, had arrogated to itself the right to grant licenses for the erection of such build-ings. We recall Innocent IV's personal intervention against the "new synagogue of unnecessary height" built by the Jews of Cor-dova (1250). In justification of his anti-Jewish propaganda in Seville, Ferrant Martinez pointed to the twenty-three synagogues which had been built in "the *juderia* of that city against God and the law." More remarkably, similar grievances were sounded also by the French kings Philip III and Philip IV in 1283 and 1299.[47]

Although the royal complaints were couched in strong language and were combined with other accusations of Jewish disregard of state regulations, there is no evidence that they had any immediate effect on existing buildings. Of course, we know less about the his-toric realities of Jewish life than about the pertinent royal legisla-tion. Yet we probably would have heard of Jewish complaints of actual destruction, by decree, of synagogues in periods of relative peace. If carried out, these laws doubtless would also have entailed many changes in real estate ownership which would have left be-hind some traces in court records, particularly since the synagogue usually was the most prominent building in the Jewish street and served to identify the location of other houses. Nor do we hear of many penalties inflicted on Jews who had erected forbidden struc-tures, Queen Joan of Castile's confiscation, in 1379, of a synagogue in the diocese of Oviedo belonging to the rare recorded excep-tions. Not even the irate perorations of the two French kings men-tion fines to be exacted from such "transgressors."[48]

Other monarchs and jurists, however, were more concerned with the reverse aspects of effectively protecting Jewish places of worship. To obviate wanton attacks, the Austrian Frederick II provided in 1244 that "if anyone should with temerity throw stones upon Jewish synagogues [*scolas*], We wish that he pay two talents to the judge of the Jews." In substance, this provision was repeated not only in the east-central European offshoots of the 1244 statute but also in such German law books as the *Rechtsbuch nach Distinctionen,* except that in the latter the size of the fine was left to local laws and usages. With the revival of Roman law in German lands, moreover, some scholarly jurists invoked the laws of the Christian Roman Empire as a direct precedent for the outlawry of the destruction of synagogues. Protective legislation was doubly important in periods of rapid change, such as the Spanish *Reconquista* or when Jewish settlements had to be rebuilt after massacres or expulsions. Jewish communities and their synagogues often suffered also from wars and internal upheavals. Describing the rebellion against King Pedro in Valladolid during the Castilian civil war of 1366–68, the Hebrew chronicler, Samuel Zarza (Çarça) reported: "They [the rebels] shouted, Long live King Henry! They attacked the Jews who lived among them and destroyed their houses. The Jews remained only with their naked bodies and their ruins. Among them they destroyed eight synagogues, exclaiming '*Aru, 'aru,* and they took away all the silver crowns and garlands, tore the scrolls of law and threw them on the streets. Even the destruction of the Temple [of Jerusalem] did not equal it." In ordinary times, too, new communities required special privileges. For instance, in order to attract Jews to Alcolea, Infante Alphonso gave them, in 1320, an extended charter which included the right to build a synagogue and establish a cemetery. Similarly, at the request of Aragon's Jewish representatives, Henry IV took in 1455 all synagogues and Jewish cemeteries under his special protection.[49]

Matters became further complicated by the widespread Jewish practice of holding services in private homes. Many a wealthy communal leader or eminent rabbi preferred to assemble the necessary quorum of ten adult males at his home, sometimes even setting aside a special room for such private worship. In time some private chapels acquired a sanctity of their own. According to the fifteenth-century Italian rabbi, Joseph b. Solomon Colon, "if a citizen had a synagogue in his home, the community must not transfer it to another house." The semipublic character of such congregations was also demonstrated by an early German ordinance, attributed to Gershom, "Light of the Exile," which had provided that "if one lends a [house for use as a] synagogue to the community and he has a quarrel with another member, he may not forbid its use to that man unless he forbids it to all the others." At times kings issued special permits for such private prayer services. Such a favor was extended in 1395 (1396) by King Martin to Joseph Abenafia, "a faithful serf of Our Chamber" in Syracuse, Sicily, because Abenafia, being "engaged in his medical practice in his office for most of the day and night, cannot perform his rites and prayers in the Jews' public synagogue" and, hence, must maintain a private chapel.[50]

Such multiplicity of places of worship became a major issue when the Church began agitating against Jews owning more than one synagogue in any locality. The private chapels were specifically included in Archbishop John Peckham's three orders to the bishop of London in 1281–82, to close down, if necessary through the use of bans, all Jewish houses of worship except one. He also demanded that even these single structures "not be particularly sumptuous or decorated with pictures and pomp." Forty years later Strasbourg's municipal council prohibited Jewish private chapels. Generally the erection of any new synagogue had to be cleared with the local bishop, but James II overruled the bishop of Majorca by allowing Jews in 1331 to erect a synagogue there to replace one which they had previously lost. He argued that this was not really a *new* synagogue. On the other hand, in 1384, before permitting the Jews of Cervera to own a second synagogue Infanta Violante first obtained the consent of the bishop of Vich. Similarly, a year earlier the Zurich city council secured such a permit for its Jewry from the bishop of Constance.[51]

All these prohibitions reflected the legislators' static world outlook which assumed stability in the size of the Jewish population and its geographic distribution. Slightly justified in the declining Roman Empire, it was totally unrealistic in the world of rapid changes characteristic of Europe after the Barbarian Migrations. Because of the expulsions of Jews, as well as their fairly constant voluntary migrations, there were frequent fluctuations in the size of Jewish communities, and the formation of ever new centers of

Jewish life. Some ancient synagogues were allowed to decay, but many more were needed to accommodate both new settlements and the enlarged populations of older cities.

Other social and religious factors contributed to the proliferation of synagogues. With the growing diversity of local synagogue rites and customs throughout the Jewish world, newcomers from other regions often preferred to congregate in their own houses of worship in order to pray according to their accustomed rituals. What Leon da Modena was to write in the seventeenth century was, to some extent, also true of the earlier period: "There are of these synagogues or Schools, more or fewer in each city, proportionable to the number and diversity of the Jews which dwell there. For since the *Levantines, Germans* and *Italians* differ in nothing so much as in the Form of their Liturgies, every one of the Nations chose rather to have a Synagogue by themselves." Independent houses of worship were also necessitated by the gradual expansion, within the Jewish communities, of special charitable, educational, and professional societies, whose members, like their Christian counterparts, often formed brotherhoods holding independent divine services. A society for the visiting of the sick in Saragossa secured from Infante John in 1382 the permission to build a synagogue, to equip it with the necessary facilities including Torah scrolls, and to set aside a separate compartment for women. An undated record, probably written before 1391, mentions five synagogues in Barcelona, including houses of the "confrare del Maldar," doubtless educational (Talmud Torah) associations. Moreover, so long as Jews lived in various expanding town areas, they preferred to have places of worship in the vicinity of their dwellings. On the other hand, at the instigation of Pope Calixtus III, Alphonso V ordered in 1455 the transfer of the synagogue and the Jewish cemetery in Taormina from their location near the church to some other place "as it is only just." [52]

It is small wonder, then, that we have records of at least two synagogues in Marseilles, three in Trani and Breslau, thirteen in Toledo, and allegedly twenty-three in Seville. In the very capital of Latin Christianity the synagogues proliferated at the end of the Middle Ages. The thirteen synagogues recorded in the catacombs of ancient Rome doubtless went out of existence during the

"Dark" Ages. But with the gradual demographic recovery Roman Jewry once more possessed eleven congregations in the early sixteenth century. Not surprisingly, when during the Catholic Restoration the authorities relegated it to a ghetto, they also insisted upon reducing the number of synagogues to one. To accommodate at least the major ritualistic groups, the community arranged for five congregations regularly to meet in separate chambers of the same building which thereafter became famous under the name of *cinque scuole*.[53]

Conflicts of this kind between Jewish law and the state or Church were aggravated by the ecclesiastical propaganda against tall and ornate synagogues, especially those which were built near a church and outshone it externally. At the same time talmudic law had demanded that the houses of worship be built on an elevation and be architectonically impressive. Similarly, the Jews were used to pray aloud, often the whole congregation reciting the prayers in unison. The ensuing noises had already annoyed Gregory the Great. In 1230 and 1253 Henry III relocated the synagogue in London because "all the Jews ought to worship in their synagogues according to their ritual in a subdued voice so that they not be heard by Christians." In the district of Savoca, Sicily, the community was likewise forced on these grounds to remove, in 1470, the synagogue from the vicinity of the church. We recall that this "interference" with the solemnity of Christian worship had induced the generally friendly Emperor Frederick III to initiate the transplantation of the Jewish quarter in Frankfort from the city's center to its periphery. At times Jews were even punished for praying too loudly. In 1288 the Jews of Paris were forced to pay as much as three hundred pounds for that "transgression," which both Philip III and Philip IV specifically singled out for censure in their decrees of 1283 and 1299.[54]

Viewed in their totality, the occasional chicaneries accompanying the erection of new synagogues, or the enlargement or embellishment of some older ones, were far outweighed by definite assurances of royal and municipal protection and the recurrent attempts of the authorities to live up to them. Moreover, the sanctity of a synagogue could in no way be compared with that of the ancient Temple or other celebrated shrines. We have seen how far ancient Judaism had already departed from such territorial moorings, and considered the *house* of prayer decidedly secondary to the congregation as such. For the most part the destruction or confiscation of a synagogue entailed little more than a financial loss for the community; a loss which often was less serious than some new heavy tax. The difficulties encountered in securing ecclesiastical or secular permits likewise reduced themselves as a rule to additional expenditures. Probably the most disagreeable part of these proceedings was their unpredictability in the light of conflicting decisions by rulers and courts. But Jews had long learned to live under conditions of great instability and subjection to contradictory interests, even whims, of persons in power.

Such inconsistencies are well illustrated by conflicting orders issued by Frederick III (II) of Sicily. In 1360 he allowed the Jews of Castrogiovanni to build a new synagogue in lieu of one destroyed outside the city. Thirteen years later, however, he ordered all his officials to assist Fra Simone del Pozzo, the papal inquisitor, in leveling down all synagogues recently constructed in defiance of canon law. In Ferrara Jews were first punished by the Inquisition in 1458 for the erection of an illicit synagogue. Soon thereafter, however, they were allowed to maintain two places of worship, one each of the Italian and Spanish rites. The former, endowed in 1481 by a wealthy member, Ser Samuel Melli, was open for Jewish worship for several centuries. In granting the local Jews a permit to rebuild their synagogue, the abbot of Oña, Castile, stipulated in 1405 that the new building must in no way be distinguished from the neighboring houses. In the turbulent years of 1391–96, however, the king often insisted upon the restoration of synagogues destroyed during the anti-Jewish uprising, and the punishment of the assailants. Several years after the events the clergy and the municipal authorities of Ecija expostulated to the king that they had defied Martinez' orders and refrained from demolishing the local synagogue. They blamed the city's proletariat for the destruction. We also recall that several converts tried to make use of the depopulation of Jewish communities for their private benefit. A newly ordained priest, John Salvador Conmel, petitioned the pope in 1414 that, since the synagogue of Monzón in the diocese of Lérida founded by his grandfather had been converted into a church, the houses and other properties of that synagogue, which had belonged to the two associations of *Cabbarim* (burial society) and Talmud Torah, should be turned into a foundation for the maintenance of a chapel at that church. He indicated that such a foundation might well be used for his support. In the following year the pope favorably responded to a similar request from a former rabbi of Maqueda in the diocese of Toledo who had pleaded that since his conversion he had lost an annual income of some 30 florins from the vineyards and fields which had belonged to his synagogue interveningly converted into a church.[55]

CEMETERIES AND HOLIDAYS

Jewish communities found it no less difficult freely to maintain their cemeteries, which, next to synagogues and schools, ranked highest among their religious institutions. They took no cognizance of the fact, pointed out by Thomas Aquinas, that the Bible had not included burial among the acts of mercy, "but those only which are more clearly necessary." From ancient times Jews considered the maintenance of burial places a major communal responsibility, second only to the family's duty to bury its members. Medieval Jewry often organized special associations, best known under the designation of "holy societies," dedicated to the provision of funerary rites for poor and rich alike. Many distinguished communal leaders did not hesitate to join them and to execute the required menial and unpleasant tasks. So convinced were the rabbis of the importance of early burials that, despite the prevailing denominational segregation particularly in religious rites, talmudic law prescribed that, whenever needed, communities perform such charitable deeds also for non-Jews. Conversely, Jews sometimes found their resting places in general cemeteries, preferably in sections specially assigned to them. But they always tried hard to secure the right to own their "houses of eternity." [56]

In some cases the establishment of a cemetery belonged to the earliest concessions secured by Jewish leaders from friendly rulers, as in Spires (1084), Tudela (1170), or Rostock (1279). In many other areas they had to be satisfied with a central burial ground, such as existed in London for all of England up to 1177, when

Henry II allowed them to acquire land outside the walls of any English city for "an appropriate location for the burial of their dead." For a time, it appears, even the old community of Worms, where a Jewish graveyard is first mentioned about 1220, had to bury its dead in Mayence. Such participation naturally helped to forge the close ties uniting these two Rhenish communities. Legally, too, Meir b. Baruch taught, "A city maintaining a cemetery of its own may force all neighborhood settlers who bury their dead there to appear before its courts." This "has become, I believe, the common practice of Jewish courts everywhere," declared the fifteenth-century rabbi, Israel b. Petaḥiah Isserlein. In his decree of 1410 Archbishop Günther of Magdeburg spoke of foreign Jews "who would migrate to the synagogue or cemetery" of Magdeburg. On the other hand, the city of Augsburg forbade in 1433 the burial of outsiders without special permission by the city council. Understandably, many growing communities resented such dependence and also sought to avoid the considerable expense connected with the transportation of their dead to distant locations. From another rabbinic responsum (by Moses Menz) we learn that it cost six florins merely to bring a body from Landau to Worms; there were additional local expenses in Worms. Since in that particular case the estate of the deceased amounted to less than 100 florins, not enough to cover the widow's marriage settlement, a controversy broke out between the family and the community as to who was to defray these burial costs. Nevertheless many communities were forced to rely, on financial as well as legal grounds, on regional cemeteries, such as were recorded in Ratisbon, Basel, Zurich, and even in such smaller localities as Schweidnitz.[57]

Under the then existing conditions, governments often had to share with the Jewish communities their concern for keeping these burial grounds inviolate. In antiquity Jews could, according to Roman law, exact "funerary amends" from offenders and, like other citizens, they often fortified these pecuniary sanctions with inscriptions containing curses against ghouls. In the Middle Ages, however, special legislation for the protection of Jewish cemeteries became necessary. We recall that the papal *Constitutio pro Judaeis* constantly enjoined the population against the then widely prevalent vandalism. Similar prohibitions had to be enacted by many states. In requesting the pope's permission to grant a privilege to "many Hebrews . . . who wished to live securely and without obstacles" in his duchy, Francesco Sforza of Milan made a point of including in his proposed *capitoli* the prohibition of the desecration of graves, alongside those against killing or assailing Jews or despoiling them of their goods. Frederick II of Austria went to extremes in providing that "if a Christian should with temerity desecrate or invade a Jewish cemetery, he shall be condemned to death by formal judgment and all his possessions under whatever name shall fall to the ducal Chamber," a provision repeated in Přemysl Ottakar's privilege of 1254 and in Rudolph I's decree of 1268. On the other hand, the Hungarian privilege of 1251 omitted that clause, while Ottakar's second privilege, as well as those enacted in Silesia, Poland, and Lithuania, upheld the confiscation of property but otherwise merely prescribed that the guilty be "severely punished in accordance with the customs and laws of our country." Elsewhere, too, the penalties varied. But the general wish to safeguard the peace of these Jewish sacred grounds was incontestable.[58]

Some violations of cemeteries were initiated by the rulers themselves, however. At times executions of criminals, Christian as well as Jewish, were staged at Jewish cemeteries—a practice which even an express prohibition like that in the Cologne archepiscopal decree of 1266 could not entirely eliminate. In 1345 Dukes Wenceslaus and Louis granted the Liegnitz burghers "full authority and license" to use Jewish tombstones in building their city wall. King John of Bohemia in 1345 gave a similar permission to the Breslau burghers "regardless of any objections raised by Jews or anyone else." The burghers thereupon hastily employed fifty laborers for nine days to remove even very recent Jewish tombstones. Other cases of violence are reflected in the decision by Israel Isserlein, the rabbi of Wiener Neustadt, that a community unable to prevent its ruler from pasturing his horses in a Jewish cemetery must otherwise fully uphold the latter's sanctity. After forbidding in 1455 any invasions, desecrations, or sacrileges at synagogues or Jewish cemeteries, Henry IV of Castile added the qualifying clause, "without having first obtained a special order from Me." Despite the reiterated papal injunctions, the lower clergy, too, was often guilty of instigating disorders affecting Jewish cemeteries. The situation in Gerona became so alarming in 1278 that Pedro III threatened the clergy with severe sanctions if such violations of the Jewish graveyard did not stop forthwith.[59]

More frequent and hence more irksome were the forced removals of cemeteries from one city area to another. When in 1360 the Jews of Rome were told to discontinue burying their corpses in the city streets under the sanction of exhumation and a fine of five pounds, they had to establish a new cemetery at some distance from their quarter. Similarly, newly introduced "technical" ghettos often involved also the transfer of burial places to their vicinity. This happened, for instance, in Frankfort in 1462; there a corner of the ghetto was assigned to the new cemetery. In other localities, to the contrary, the Jewish "houses of eternity" were located at a great distance from town, exposing the mourners to abuses by villagers. During the Black Death of 1349 the Barcelona community had to bury its dead with dispatch in a new location without awaiting royal approval, the Jewish elders of Barcelona successfully pleading with Pedro IV that "because of the great distance separating their dwellings from their cemeteries" they had to do it lest healthy survivors be endangered by the corpses. They received a blanket amnesty for this "unlawful" act. Curiously, after Maximilian I in 1510 authorized the city of Colmar in Alsace to expel the Jews, and gave away their cemetery, the community not only sent a delegation to the emperor to persuade him to reverse his decision, but also appealed to the pope, citing the old protective bulls against desecration of Jewish burial places.[60]

Like everything else, Jewish funerals could be taxed over and above the high costs of maintaining the burial grounds. Many landowners, including churches and monasteries, not only exacted higher prices for Jewish cemetery plots, but they also often demanded additional annual rentals. City administrations, such as that of Basel in 1394 or Zurich in 1423, collected fees for every corpse. In Basel the fee for a native Jew was half a florin, for a foreigner one florin. Frankfort charged an annual fee to the surrounding Jewish settlements, an entry in the city ledger for 1424 showing that 100 florins were paid in advance for such a four-year permit. Similar entries appear also in the following years. King

Rupert went further and decided to use the regional cemeteries as an instrument of general law enforcement. In his proclamation of August 17, 1402, announcing to all princes the appointment of Elias of Weinheim and Isaac of Oppenheim as commissioners for the collection of the "golden penny" from imperial Jewry, he declared,

> We also wish to state on Our Royal Roman authority that, if it should happen that some Jews or Jewesses, singly or in groups, should fail to pay the golden penny and should put up resistance to it, in such a case all Jews belonging to the same [regional] cemetery should refuse to have any dealings with them in all matters pertaining to Jewish law. He who will not comply with this order shall be subject to Our and the Roman Empire's severe displeasure [*Ungnade*].

Evidently, the ban here imposed was to include refusal to bury the dead of such recalcitrant families.[61]

As a rule, governments tried to prevent molestation of Jewish funerary processions marching through city streets or the countryside. Understandably, the size of such processions increased in ratio to the importance of the deceased, the rabbis having long been quite articulate in demanding deep and widespread mourning for distinguished intellectual leaders. Otherwise Jews had to refrain from any public displays. In the compromise between Henry IV of Castile and the Estates, arranged by arbiters under the leadership of Alphonso de Oropesa in 1465, Jews were expressly forbidden to hold public processions on account of a drought or a pestilence.[62]

Governmental regulations of other aspects of Jewish religious life likewise followed the lead of the Church. True, the Western states were far more restrained than, for instance, Justinian, who allowed himself various incursions into the domain of Jewish synagogue worship. The West was satisfied with occasional prohibitions of the antiheretical prayer in the '*Amidah* and the concluding liturgical piece, '*Alenu*, which, despite Jewish disclaimers, many Christians regarded as direct attacks upon their faith. But generally the medieval state left the defense of Christianity almost entirely in the hands of ecclesiastical organs, particularly the Inquisition; it merely tried to stave off the latter's infringements on its own preserve. Borderline areas such as conversions of Christians to Judaism were jointly administered by Church and state, since all forms of apostasy and heresy were considered subversive of the existing political structures as well. On the other hand, in matters of minor concern to Christianity, the Jewish community was given full freedom to run its affairs in its own way. We shall see that, because of both tradition and self-interest, the medieval state actually tried to bolster Jewish self-determination in internal religious and communal affairs so as to strengthen the authority of the communal leaders over the rank and file of members.

Observance of Jewish Sabbaths and holidays required special safeguards. Diaspora Jewry had long persuaded the outside world to respect its weekly day of rest and other festivals. Despite Roman misunderstandings of the very idea of the Sabbath, Augustus and his successors prescribed that Jews not be summoned to courts on Saturdays and that, in other ways too, the Jewish holidays be left undisturbed. While some questions arose as to the best methods of preventing Christians from keeping the Jewish Sabbath or Passover, such observance by Jews was safeguarded by the decree of 412, reproduced in the Theodosian Code. With all his intolerance and ineffectual attempts at influencing the dates of the Jewish Passover, Justinian repeated the provisions of that code, merely adding that, just as Christians could not summon Jews on Sabbaths, so must Jews, too, refrain from citing Christians on those days. Basically, these provisions were taken over by the medieval legislators, as stated most clearly in several Castilian *fueros,* including that of Ledesma, the *Libro de los Fueros de Castilla,* and the *Fuero Real.* The latter specifically reemphasized the Jews' reciprocal treatment of Christian parties. This respect for the Sabbath extended also to the return of pawns, which could not be exacted on that day, a provision included also in such German law books as *Das Rechtsbuch nach Distinctionen.*[63]

The *capitoli* arranged with Jewish bankers by the Italian municipalities likewise contained many protective provisions for Jewish holidays. For instance, the detailed stipulations of the city of Vigevano with the Jews, dated May 15, 1435, began with the sharp outlawry of various forms of interference with the Jewish days of rest. True, the populace did not always follow the legislators' lead. Caesarius of Heisterbach emphatically retold a story intended to ridicule the strict Jewish Sabbath observance. A Champagne Jew supposedly fell into a cesspool on Saturday but he staunchly refused to be pulled out in violation of the Sabbath rest commandment. Whereupon the count objected to his being rescued on Sunday, so he had to endure the hardship for another day. Provisions also had to be made for the acquisition by Jews of ritually prepared meats, except that here the competitive interests of Christian butchers often complicated the task of tolerant legislators. All these aspects of Christian-Jewish symbiosis will be mentioned in greater detail in later chapters.[64]

COMMUNAL SELF-GOVERNMENT

As a rule the medieval countries evinced little interest in Jewish religious and ritualistic matters, except in such externals as the building of new synagogues, the latter's height, the number of Jewish butcher shops, and other aspects of public administration. The business conducted in the synagogue, the cemetery, the slaughter houses, and other communal buildings was left almost entirely to the Jewish leaders. Usually the states reserved for themselves only the right of approving the election of communal officials who were expected to administer internal Jewish affairs in accordance with Jewish law and custom.

Closely related to religious functions were the communal activities pertaining to Jewish education and social welfare. Even unfriendly observers sometimes spoke admiringly of widespread Jewish literacy. The popular preacher Berthold of Ratisbon cited the Jews' scriptural expertise in advising his listeners against engaging in religious disputations with them. Such debates, he warned, could only lead to heresy (Berthold estimated that there were one hundred and fifty varieties of Christian heterodoxy), particularly since, as he curiously asserted in another sermon, "the Jews of one house do not believe what the Jews of another house believe." Evidently the preacher had heard about the numerous differences of rabbinic opinion concerning details of Jewish law. In any case, Jewish education was left entirely in the hands of Jews, particularly parents and communal leaders who jointly had the responsibility for providing instruction to male schoolchildren from the age of six or earlier. The state had the less occasion to interfere, as the education of Christians was long controlled by the clergy. Only toward the end of the Middle Ages was there a gradual awakening of the secular spirit. But even rulers, who served as patrons of learning and personally subsidized academies of arts and sciences, exercised little direct jurisdiction over such institutions. Jewish schools of higher learning, whether established by communities or individual scholars, were of interest to governmental authorities only in such external matters as the residential rights of pupils and teachers or the community's fiscal obligations. It was quite exceptional, therefore, that in 1466 the united Sicilian communities secured from King John the privilege of founding, under royal protection, a *studium generale* for all of Sicily. Its objective was, to cite the royal approval: "to provide stipends and graduate doctors, law experts, magisters and others; to present in the said *studium* whatever disciplines are agreed upon by jurists assigned to it and others, as well as to do all other things pertaining to the establishment and maintenance of the said *studium generale*." But this institution, resembling a university rather than a Jewish academy, was so exceptional in nature that governmental cooperation and protection were indeed necessary.[65]

Moreover, the very right of Jews to receive doctorates in medicine and other disciplines had been under extended debate for over a century. No one denied the presence of many Jewish physicians who, despite numerous canonical prohibitions, often attended Christian patients. Yet the right to practice medicine could be secured by special licenses, whereas the title of doctor of medicine implied both more advanced training and superior "dignity." It was precisely because of that *dignitas* that Bartolus taught that Jews should be excluded, as they were (along with women and heretics) from other *dignitates;* he mentioned that at his own university of Bologna two Jewish medical students had been allowed to attend classes, but were refused the doctor's degree. Baldus de Ubaldis even equated holders of medical doctorates with a kind of spiritual militia. These arguments by the two illustrious jurists were often repeated by their successors in civil and canon law. Only slowly were the barriers lowered; at first by papal dispensations. Beginning with fifteenth-century Naples, however, one Italian university after another began conferring doctor's degrees on Jews. That of Padua included some 80 Jews in the roster of its medical graduates in the years 1517–1619, and 149 more in the following 102 years; among them students from far-off Poland. Nonetheless the total number of Jews seeking instruction outside the Jewish school system was always extremely limited. Within that system Jewish teachers undisturbedly pursued their traditional curricula, even educational reforms being left entirely to their discretion or to that of the communal authorities.[66]

Little consideration was also given by medieval legislators to the ramified Jewish social welfare system whose effectiveness, as we shall see in the framework of Jewish social life, far exceeded that of comparable non-Jewish institutions, for the most part likewise administered by ecclesiastical agencies. Once again governmental organs evinced some interest in such externals as the building or fiscal administration of Jewish hospitals and orphanages, the actual operation of which, however, was left to Jewish communal organs, such as the philanthropic associations freely organized by charitable members under the general supervision of communal boards. Although the numerous religious, educational, and charitable institutions and foundations thus played a far greater role in the ordinary Jew's daily life than many high-sounding decrees enacted by emperors or popes, both the Church and the state recognized them as exclusively Jewish concerns.

Quite different, of course, was the problem of Jewish settlement rights. Basically it was the state which admitted new Jewish settlers. It also could withdraw its toleration even from long-established Jewish residents by decree of banishment, individual or collective. In practice, however, it often left all details to the Jewish communal authorities who also were in charge of opening or shutting the gates to newcomers. Out of ancient Babylonian-Jewish precedents the medieval communities developed rules and regulations for admitting new members somewhat similar to those governing the admission of burghers to municipalities. Using the characteristic instrumentality of the *herem ha-yishub* (ban of settlement), later *hezqat ha-yishub* (acquired right of settlement), the elders exercised considerable discretion in protecting their local communities against undue competition by outsiders.

Medieval rabbis often invoked an ordinance attributed to

Gershom b. Yehudah, "Light of the Exile," but gave it different interpretations in accordance with their communities' changing sociopolitical needs. With the expansion of the Western Jewish settlements in the twelfth and thirteenth centuries, the interpretation of the "ban of settlement" became increasingly liberal. Jacob b. Meir Tam actually tried to limit rejections to those "who are overweening, denounce their brethren to Gentiles, or refuse to take part in the communities' tax burdens." The pertinent English agreement called the "Canterbury Treaty" of 1266 excluded only a "liar, improper person or slanderer." Of course, the king could overrule the Canterbury community. But the originators bound themselves to spend all the money necessary to propitiate the Crown and also threatened to expel members already settled, if they assisted undesirable arrivals in evading the ban. This is also the tenor of many stipulations between pioneering Jewish settlers and various royal or municipal powers, whether in the Carolingian capitularies or in the later Italian *condottas*. Even when these "treaties" formally granted the right of settlement only to certain named individuals and their descendants, they usually implied that the recipients could bring with them household help, business associates, and ecclesiastical officials to provide for their material and spiritual needs. In such cases entire communities depended on the good standing and favoritism of these privileged members. Needless to say, the governments did not give up their prerogative of admitting Jewish settlers even against the will of the community. When in 1267 James I of Aragon wished to attract the wealthy Astrug b. Vidal of Carcassonne to Montpellier, he even promised him complete immunity from all civil or criminal prosecution for past obligations or crimes. That such immunity was needed and that it did not completely resolve Astrug's difficulties may perhaps be deduced from his suicide seven years later. But the astonishing fact is not the exercise of such sovereign rights by kings, but rather the frequent delegation of these responsibilities to the Jewish communal elders.[67]

On the other hand, in 1221 the English government threatened recalcitrant Jewish taxpayers with expulsion from the country. It also collected ransom from the Jewish communities for one Moses, son of Le Brun, condemned to death for forgery. Conversely, where, as in Spain, Jews were entitled to pronounce death sentences, the governments usually collected substantial indemnities for the losses thus sustained by the Treasury. Expulsion of a member from a community, sometimes from an entire region or country, naturally had the same fiscal effect. Nevertheless, in his privileges for the community of Barcelona of 1241 and 1272, James I allowed the communal elders "by Our authority to eject or expel [recalcitrant members] from the Jewish quarter, or even from the entire city." While this topographical distinction reflected existing Jewish residences outside the Jewish quarter, in many other localities ejection from the quarter was tantamount to withdrawal of residence rights. In 1229 James himself caused the expulsion of two Calatayud Jews of ill repute and gave the elders the right to condemn them to death without paying the Treasury the usual indemnity in case of their illegal reentry. James II in 1294 instructed the bailiff and judge of Valencia to prevent influential local Christians from hiding Jewish criminals condemned to deportation by their community. Even cities jealously guarding their controls over the admission of new settlers often conceded the Jewish community's right in sharing these controls with respect to its members. Following such a sweeping recognition in the archepiscopal charter of 1252, the city of Cologne promised, in its privilege of 1321, to banish from its confines any Jew declared undesirable by the Jewish communal board. Four years later two Jews were threatened with expulsion from Cologne unless they made peace with their community. More broadly, the French privilege of 1360 gave the right to a board of two rabbis and four Jewish laymen to banish any Jew from the entire kingdom, without stating the reasons. Such sentences could not be appealed, but the king was to receive an indemnity of 100 florins and could confiscate all the property of the condemned. For similar reasons Emperor Rudolph I in 1286 instructed the archbishop of Mayence to seize all property of Jews who had fled "over seas" without royal authorization.[68]

Less rigid than permanent exclusion was temporary suspension of membership rights by communal bans. Anathemas of progressive severity helped to enforce the communal will upon unruly members. Generally it was in the state's interest to strengthen the hand of communal elders, but excommunication usually interfered with the economic pursuits of the affected individuals and thus ultimately reduced the revenue of Crown or city. At times the prohibition of any intercourse with the excommunicated person and his family had, under the medieval system of segregation, almost the effect of civil death.

Hence came the numerous inconsistencies in the medieval legislation with respect to the enforcement of Jewish bans. On the one hand, we find sweeping protective regulations, such as that enacted by the Neapolitan regime in 1484. Emperor Charles IV and King Rupert likewise decreed, in 1348 and 1406 respectively, that he who remained for more than thirty days under a Jewish ban without securing its revocation was to be deprived of all his property. Even after Rupert had tried to restrict the right of issuing excommunications to Chief Rabbi Israel whom he had appointed in 1407, the local rabbis unperturbedly continued to exercise this authority. Ferdinand and Isabella ordered in 1483 the execution of a man condemned for assault and battery on a rabbi who had proclaimed a ban against him. On the other hand, Queen Violante consented in 1390 to the revocation of a ban previously enacted by the Gerona community to enforce a communal statute which had proved unworkable because of the *aljama*'s impoverishment under warlike conditions. At times kings made exceptions for certain favorites, as when Infante John of Aragon forbade the Jewish communities to excommunicate one Jacob Xambell for playing dice with Jews, Christians, or Muslims (1379–82), or when Emperor Frederick III protected one Muschmann against a Jewish excommunication in Judenburg (1467). Moreover, the Jewish ban could also be utilized for fiscal purposes. While on the whole Jewish leadership long effectively resisted the imposition of bans in the service of state powers, Rupert and others succeeded in appropriating for the state fines and other payments exacted by Jewish elders at the revocation of bans. Nor must we overlook the abuses arising from some rabbis' excessive zeal in wielding bans, sometimes merely for the satisfaction of personal grudges, a practice which ultimately blunted the edge of this sanction. Such governmental inconsistencies, however, were very similar to the mixed approaches to ecclesiastical bans within the Christian community.[69]

Medieval states also sought to strengthen the hands of communal elders against would-be informers. The phenomenon of betraying coreligionists to the authorities was not rare in any country, but it became a source of particularly serious complications for the Jewish mass settlements on the Iberian Peninsula. Of course, informing converts enjoyed immunity from Jewish prosecution and were protected, even patronized, by churchmen. But their self-evident bias could more readily be discounted, whereas the testimony of a Jew against Jews always found willing listeners. The lengths to which Jewish leaders would go in stamping out informing is illustrated by Isaac b. Sheshet Perfet's statement that an informer

legally pays the extreme penalty because of the potential ultimate effects of his actions. Even if he had not yet denounced anybody, but merely threatened to do so, we put him to death, as we do a pursuer [of a man with the intent to kill], in order to save the person threatened by that delator. And not only shall the court condemn him to death, but any person who slays him first, as in the case of the pursuer, will perform a meritorious deed.

We have no record of actual lynchings and, hence, cannot tell whether there were any governmental reprisals on their perpetrators or the community as a whole. But at least most Mediterranean governments realized that they could not allow this cancerous growth to destroy the Jewish community, and helped the elders to combat it with all means at their disposal. In 1279 Pedro III of Aragon actually forced two rabbis to issue a sentence of death on a hardened informer. In 1390 Queen Violante appointed Ḥisdai Crescas a special *judex malsinorum* with the right to condemn Jewish informers through the length and breadth of the Aragonese realm, in accordance with the customary procedures.[70]

At times the authorities exercised great restraint in interfering with communal appointments. In 1371 Queen Leonore of Aragon placed the Valencia Jewish elders under a ban for having yielded to governmental pressures in the selection of their rabbi. As a rule, however, the governments were keenly interested in the elections, often extremely complicated, of Jewish elders and rabbis, and usually reserved for themselves the right of final approval. But when Bishop Emmerich of Worms sought outright appointment of Jewish leaders by himself or one of his officials, the Jews resisted fiercely with the full support of the Worms burghers. Community and bishop finally agreed in 1312 that Jews should elect twelve elders and the bishop designate one of them as their chief. This agreement was maintained in later decrees (including those of 1439, 1446, and 1488) and underwent but minor modifications in 1505. If in 1366 Charles IV ordered the sheriff to punish the newly constituted Frankfort community for electing its elders and adopting a new statute without his authorization, this censure merely reflected his reluctance to allow the revival of communities destroyed during the Black Death era without his supervision. Even the royal initiative in the appointment of local Jewish bailiffs in thirteenth-century England probably resulted from consultations with Jewish leaders. Acting on complaints from a Jewish faction, the Sicilian authorities in 1456 (1457) ordered the Jewish officials of Catania to elect as tax assessors "the most appropriate and virtuous men" and prescribed that Jewish elders of the current and preceding years should participate in that election. But they left the ultimate choice to the Jews themselves. On the other hand, a Sicilian viceroy in 1473 ordered the Jewish procurators (*ne'emanim*) of Termini to render accounts of their administration for the preceding three years to both his officials and the then newly appointed Jewish procurator, while another viceroy excused in 1490 the aged Xibitellu Ginni, who had previously served twice as *episcopus* of San Marco Jewry, from the obligation to carry on. Not surprisingly, each electoral act could be turned into a source of royal revenue. *Las Siete Partidas* prescribed a fee of 200 maravedis for the election of a chief rabbi, 100 maravedis for that of a provincial elder, and 20-50 maravedis for that of lesser leaders. These sums were not uniform throughout the realm, however. In 1476 the fee was set by the Cortes of Madrigal at 200 maravedis for an elder or rabbi elected for life in a larger community, but remained at 100 maravedis if he was elected for a specific term. In smaller communities these fees were halved.[71]

Fiscal aspects colored, indeed, all relations between governments and Jewish communal organs. The strenuous efforts made by Charles IV, Rupert, and their successors to appoint imperial "chief rabbis" to facilitate tax collections failed because of the support secured by Jewish resisters from princes and municipalities. Rupert's attempt to camouflage his fiscal motives by praising his appointee, Israel, as "an old and recognized authority in the field of Jewish studies and enjoying among Jews a fine reputation of never having wronged any Jew" did not deceive the German rabbinate which, citing the old rabbinic injunction against acceptance of any government appointments to communal office, placed Israel under a ban. Rupert annulled the ban and persisted in recognizing Israel's chief rabbinate. His successors, too, until the latter part of the sixteenth century, continued to appoint new chief rabbis from time to time. Yet the latter's influence was so minimal that Sigismund and Frederick III substituted for them all-German Jewish conferences to vote subsidies to the Crown. Here the Jews chose their representatives whom they could trust to bear the communities' interests in mind while voting for, and subsequently collecting, the contributions for the Treasury. In countries, on the other hand, with concentrated royal power, both methods worked more smoothly. In thirteenth-century England the so-called *episcopus Judaeorum,* appointed by the king in consultation with Jewish leaders, carried the main burden of supplying the Treasury with Jewish revenue. On one occasion, however, the Worcester Parliament of 1241, a freely elected assembly of six delegates each from the larger communities and of two delegates from each of the lesser settlements, voted the major appropriations demanded by Henry III. The French chief rabbinate, too, during the last span of Jewish life in the royal possessions (1360–94), combined elective Jewish with appointive royal features.[72]

In the Spanish kingdoms the major fiscal role was played by regional *colectas,* consisting of representatives of both regional communities and the lesser settlements grouped around them. In Castile the *rab de la corte* was a more or less permanent fixture of the Jewish communal structure. A document of 1465 describes Samaya (Shemayah) Lubel, a court physician, as "rabbi, chief judge, and tax distributor of all the Jewish communities in My kingdoms and dominions." Despite their dependence on the royal power some of these officials enjoyed the full confidence of their constituents. This is particularly true of Abraham Benveniste, who sought to reform Castilian Jewish community life with the aid of elected spokesmen at the Council of Valladolid of 1432. Characteristically, one resolution adopted by the council read:

No person of Israelitic stock shall have the right to avail himself of any decree, letter of grace, privilege or any other mandate, whether written or oral, issued by our lord the King, or our lady, the Queen, or any other lord or lady, so as to have himself commissioned to serve as rabbi, obtain an agreement or emolument from any of the communities, be appointed scribe, slaughterer, cantor, teacher, court messenger, investigator, or secure any other communal office . . . without the permission of the communities, or the community, to which appertains this particular appointment. . . . This rule shall not apply, however, to the said Rabbi Don Abraham, because it was and is the desire of all the communities that he shall serve as their highest judge and tax distributor, and he accepted this position at the instance of the rabbis and the call of the communities.

Of course, a Jewish assembly could not dictate to the Crown, but the Castilian kings doubtless preferred to select court rabbis acceptable to the Jewish communities. Probably the most permanent concentration of power was found in the chief rabbinate of Portugal (first mentioned in a document of 1278) which thus followed the patterns previously established by the "monarchical" regimes of the Muslim lands. This chief rabbi, *arraby moor,* appointed by the king, was entitled, according to the statute of 1402, to appoint in turn seven regional rabbis who, on their part, controlled the selection of local elders and, together with the chief rabbi, served as courts of appeal from local tribunals. In Sicily, on the contrary, single officers like Joseph Abenafia were overshadowed by regional gatherings of freely elected representatives. In all these cases, nevertheless, the royal power recognized, on principle, the autonomy of Jewish communities; it merely wished to have trustworthy persons in charge of these autonomous operations, particularly in so far as these impinged upon the total revenue from the Crown's Jewish subjects.[73]

JUDICIAL CONFLICTS

Most complicated were the jurisdictional competences of various courts concerning Jewish litigants or accused criminals. On the one hand, he who possessed power usually wished to exercise judicial controls, too, particularly in so far as they yielded substantial judicial fees. On the other hand, the medieval corporate divisions not only produced a multiplicity of courts with varying competences, but also generally fostered the idea that each free person should be judged by his own peers. It decidedly was a sign of servility of the peon masses that they were judged by their lords or the latter's officials. In the Jewish case, moreover, the rabbis had from time immemorial, on theoretical as well as practical grounds, demanded that Jewish parties repair only to Jewish courts.

Efforts were frequently made to secure some role for Jewish judges and the Jewish civil law even in mixed litigations, although a Roman law of unknown date had refused to concede that point. Following the law's renewal in 415, the Theodosian and Justinian Codes stated unequivocally (to quote the latter) that "if there is a litigation between Christians and Jews, it is to be decided not by Jewish elders but rather by ordinary judges." Nor was the Roman tradition ever since 398 that Jewish courts be formally considered but courts of arbitration completely forgotten; it remained in force where, as in Rome, ancient laws had retained a measure of unbroken continuity. Yet various factors now operated to strengthen the hand of Jewish judges. In the Mediterranean countries Muslim rule had firmly established the jurisdictional autonomy of religious minorities. After the Christian reconquest the roles were merely reversed, Muslims becoming the minority group and enjoying extensive judicial privileges. Elsewhere, the growth of feudal institutions favoring judicial independence of various groups facilitated the agreements reached with the states by the new Jewish settlers, whether in the Carolingian Empire or in late medieval Italy, which, as a rule, included provisions for a more or less independent Jewish judiciary. Understandably, Jews could no longer serve as judges or advocates in general courts, and medieval legislators had no need to spell out this exclusion, as did the Christian-Roman emperors. If Bartolus, followed by other jurists, taught that "a Jew or any non-Catholic cannot be an advocate, and a judge admitting him shall be punished," he obviously had legal theory, rather than any actual cases, in mind.[74]

Jurisdiction over Jews, with all its fiscal and administrative implications, depended on the interplay of divergent interests and changing power constellations. With the transfer or pawning, in particular, of Jewish "serfs" by emperors or kings, there usually followed also a transfer of judicial authority over them. Many municipalities, moreover, particularly in Italy, France, and the Holy Roman Empire, successfully strove to arrogate to their own courts full controls over all inhabitants, including Jews. The medieval picture thus offers an enormous variety of jurisdictional rights, often based upon conflicting decrees or local usages which defy generalization. Our evidence, moreover, largely derived from normative sources, often has to be supplemented and corrected through the relatively few extant bits of evidence concerning actual practices.

A most sweeping recognition of Jewish judicial autonomy is included in the imperial privileges of German Jewry which, begun with Henry IV's Worms privilege of 1090, were gradually extended to all of Germany by Frederick I and Frederick II. In its 1236 formulation this basic constitution of German Jewry included the following pertinent articles:

Art. 1: Since we wish that in all judicial matters they [the Jews] should have to turn to Us alone, We order, by virtue of Our royal authority, that no bishop, chamberlain, count, sheriff nor anyone else, except the person elected by themselves from their midst, shall presume to treat with them or against them in any matter or in any judicial proceeding. Only the person whom, in view of their belonging to Our treasury, the emperor, following their own election, had placed at their head [shall be entitled to do so].

Art. 11: If a Jew should have a controversy with a Christian, or a Christian with a Jew, each shall, as the subject may require, institute proceedings and prove his contention in accordance with his law. Just as any Christian may prove through his own public oath and that of a Christian and a Jewish witness that the guarantors placed by him in favor of the Jew have fulfilled [their duty], so may also the Jew through a public oath taken by himself, one other Jew and a Christian prove that the guarantors placed by him in favor of the Christian have fulfilled [theirs]. He shall be forced to do no more by either the plaintiff or the judge.

Art. 14: If the Jews should have among themselves a litigation or another matter requiring judicial decision, they shall be judged by their own peers and not by others. If any untrustworthy person among them should desire to conceal the truth of what transpired among them, he shall be forced to confess the truth by the man who is their bishop [*episcopus*]. Should they, however, be incriminated in a major law-suit, they may bring the matter before the emperor, if they so desire.

It may be noted that the law was not specific in regard to judges in mixed litigations. While internal Jewish controversies were clearly to be settled by Jewish courts subject only to the right of appeal to the emperor or the parties' decision to apply to an imperial tribunal, in conflicts between a Christian and a Jew each had to prove his points through witnesses of both faiths. By inference one may assume that, according to the old Roman principle of *actio sequitur forum rei,* the suit had to be filed in the court of the defendant. A statement to this effect was, indeed, included in a later German gloss. We know of actual cases of Christian plaintiffs appearing before a Jewish court sitting at the synagogue of thirteenth-century Mayence, and of a Jewish judge deciding as an arbiter in a mixed case in Talavera, Castile, in 1432–35. This practice seems to have prevailed in Portugal until 1473–75, when the Cortes of Coimbra and Evora demanded the submission of all Judeo-Christian litigations to the ordinary Christian courts.[75]

The extent to which Jewish courts almost exclusively handled litigations among Jews may also be inferred from the records of the Jewish Exchequer in England. According to Cyril M. Picciotto, only one case in the Exchequer's decisions referred to a Jewish couple. But this 1267 case was apparently brought to the Exchequer only after an appeal from a debate which "had ensued among the Masters of the Jewish law." In contrast, nearly one-sixth of all pleas related to exclusively Christian parties; probably because the controversy originated from a previous Jewish transaction or because the king took up the claims of a Jewish creditor. It is also possible that the Jewish Exchequer's expeditious proceedings induced some Christian litigants to appeal to it, rather than to slow-moving ordinary courts. On the other hand, the constable of the Tower of London retained some jurisdiction in both criminal and civil cases, and in more important matters the king himself or his justiciar sat in judgment. Similarly, there were special courts, such as that of the Chancellor of Oxford University for all members of the University, according to a charter of 1244 which had originated from an anti-Jewish student riot and the ensuing intervention by Robert Grosseteste.[76]

Occasionally, governments and Jews agreed that some central Jewish authority could best handle certain judicial matters on a regional basis. One such chief judge (*dayyan kelali*, misspelled in Italian *dienchelele*) was appointed by King Martin of Sicily in 1395. Allegedly at the instance of various Jewish communities and many individuals Martin asked Joseph Abenafia to serve as

judge, assessor, and corrector concerning hearings, correction, punishment, and decisions in questionable and dubious matters, and any other causes, civil, criminal, and mixed, of all individual Jews residing in any cities, lands, and locations of the said kingdom of Sicily; provided that the aforementioned questions, corrections, doubts, and causes arise between a Jew and a Jew, or emerge with respect to Jews and that, by their very nature, they ought to be corrected, punished, and decided in accordance with Jewish laws, observances, and ceremonies.

Abenafia held sway for many years and had several successors who served with an interruption of but two years in 1421–23. But the institution outlived its usefulness and, by 1447, the Jews themselves paid 600 ounces to the government to terminate the office.[77]

Sometimes there were courts of mixed composition. According to John Lackland's decree of 1204, courts of *legales Christiani et Judaei* were to sit in judgment in mixed cases. Similar courts are recorded in Würzburg after 1412 and in Augsburg until 1436. Matters were decided by a majority vote, so that at least one member of the other faith had to join the majority; otherwise the ensuing deadlock along religious lines prevented any verdict from being rendered without appeal to the king. Such a deadlock occurred, for instance, in 1278 over the claim of the Carmelite convent in Oxford that it had deposited as security with a Jewess Margarina books valued at £20; this contention was denied by the lady. For the most part, however, mixed litigations were submitted to royal officials, under the apparent assumption that the latter's Christian biases were balanced by the royal interest in the welfare of Jewish taxpayers. This practice was so often taken for granted that, in his Castilian code, Alphonso X but casually referred to it in the article devoted to the exemption of Jews from appearing at court on Sabbaths and holidays: "Otherwise We declare that all claims raised by Christians against Jews, or by Jews against Christians, should be deliberated and determined by Our judges in the localities in which they [the Jews] live, and not by their elders." In some places a more or less permanent *judex Judeorum*, that is, a Christian judge appointed by the government, passed judgment over mixed cases; sometimes over all litigations involving Jews. Such justices of Jews are recorded in England, in France before 1291 and after 1360, in many German localities, such as Meissen, in Poland, and elsewhere. A French decree of 1364 empowered this "judge of Jews" to name his deputy. By special concession the Ratisbon Jewish community was allowed to nominate several Christian candidates to the king, who appointed one of them. This privilege in part originated from the special situation in that city where royal controls had to be shared with those of the Bavarian duke, the bishop, and the municipal elders, quite apart from the burgraves to whom the royal authority was intermittently transferred for long periods. A special judicial section of the English Exchequer of the Jews was in charge of problems arising from Jewish loan contracts and fines under the latter's jurisdiction.[78]

Attempts by burghers to secure for their city magistrates exclusive jurisdiction over Jews were for the most part successfully resisted by the royal power in Spain, France, and England. Yet in his anti-Jewish decree of 1412, John II of Castile abolished altogether the Jewish civil jurisdiction and empowered the local *alcaldes* to adjudicate all Jewish litigations, while taking cognizance of the old mores. Many Aragonese cities secured the right to adjudicate conflicts arising from transactions in the market but probably not from those in exclusively Jewish markets. Inconsistencies originated, in particular, from differing local customs, changes in governmental policies, or sheer expediency. The Paris Parlement, informed that the mayor and juries of Chaumon-en-Vexin had customarily adjudicated matters pertaining to Jews, decided in 1300 that if, on investigation, this contention proved justified the bailiff of Senlis should allow that practice to continue. In 1388 Beraut Bresson and Jean Truquan were told that they were no longer to serve as Jewish judges for Paris and Languedoil, but that thenceforth the Jews were to be judged by the provost of

Paris. Curiously, on July 15, 1394, but two months before the expulsion, Charles VI absolved the Jews of Languedoil from penalties for any transgressions then under prosecution, but he insisted that in the future they would be subject to the jurisdiction of ordinary judges, bailiffs, seneschals, and the Paris provost. The German cities were more successful in achieving jurisdictional supremacy because of the general diffusion of power among emperor, secular and ecclesiastical princes, and the municipalities. Acting as preservers of public order the city elders of Cologne intervened even in the purely internal Jewish controversy between the community and its member Salman of Basel (1321–26). In Worms, it appears, the municipal authorities had as early as the twelfth century arrogated to themselves authority over Jewish litigations and, in 1233, the local consuls, on assuming office, pledged themselves to "judge justly in matters affecting a cleric, layman, or Jew." In Strasbourg the city council claimed in 1322 that such practice had long prevailed in the city. In Würzburg the bishop complained in 1253 that he was unable to prevent some Christians (doubtless referring to local judges) from "invading" the rights of his Jews. Municipal jurisdiction is also recorded in Frankfort after 1337, Nuremberg after 1331, and Augsburg after 1436. But there were untold local variations. In Salzwedel the council promised in 1349 together with the margrave's bailiff to assist each Jewish defendant summoned by a Christian plaintiff before the Jewish court, while the Perleberg council even vowed in 1350 to help defend the Jews against the encroachments of the margrave or his officials.[79]

Confusing rivalries of this kind among Jewish, state, and municipal jurisdictions were greatly reduced in the area of criminal law. Because preservation of public order was one of the primary tasks of municipal, as well as state, authorities, they also had to have the right to punish violators, Jewish or Christian. Here the cities' attempt to arrogate to themselves jurisdiction was reinforced by such practical considerations as the ready availability of city magistrates and police organs. Yet state officials were unwilling to relinquish their authority in this field, especially since many transgressions were punished by fines, part or all of which accrued to the benefit of judges or treasuries. Jewish resistance, too, was weakened by the observation that rabbinical courts were not always in a position to enforce their will.

It probably was without any Jewish opposition, therefore, that, in his generally favorable charter for the Jews of 1201, John Lackland reserved for the royal courts, as we recall, the prosecution of "homicide, mayhem, deliberate assault, housebreaking, rape, larceny, arson, and treasure [trove]." Even in Spain, where Jewish courts could impose capital punishment, they encountered considerable opposition in Christian circles. Following the example set by Castile's John I in 1380, the Cortes of Madrigal in 1476 persuaded Ferdinand and Isabella completely to abolish Jewish criminal jurisdiction. The otherwise pro-Jewish Cologne privilege of 1252, we recall, nevertheless reserved for the general courts jurisdiction over Jews accused of theft, forgery, assault and battery, failure to obey bans, or adultery with a Christian or Jewish woman. In 1331 Louis the Bavarian specifically reserved the criminal jurisdiction over Jews to Nördlingen's municipal organs who, however, were to follow the judgment of the Jewish community concerning individual defendants. In Salzwedel, Jews were told to hand over to the city council any Christian criminal caught during the act. At the same time the Augsburg city statute of 1276 restricted the bailiff's right to judge litigations among Jews to "cases of homicide or wounding." In contrast, the city of Toulouse time and again vainly tried to appropriate the jurisdiction, both criminal and civil, over its Jewish inhabitants. Philip III insisted that it remain in the hands of royal seneschals, bailiffs, or special judges appointed by them and, in 1279, he gave strict orders to his provost to watch carefully against any infringement of these royal prerogatives.[80]

Jurisdictional disputes arose also from the Church's attempts to enlarge its judicial authority beyond the ranks of the clergy. In their expansive mood during their intensive warfare against the late medieval heresies, many churchmen, particularly inquisitors, tried to summon Jews, too, before their tribunals. But the latter often successfully appealed against such trespasses on the state's domain.

Charles of Anjou, though greatly indebted to the Church, ordered the seneschal to forbid the appearance of Jews before Inquisitor Rocca, citing an earlier agreement which had restricted inquisitorial proceedings against Jews to three specified transgressions against the Christian faith. Even then, all penalties were to be executed by state organs. In 1288 a French decree prohibited the incarceration of a Jew at a cleric's behest without previous consultation with the seneschal or the bailiff. The Paris Parlement prohibited in the same year any undue inquisitorial interference with Jews under severe fines; the Church was merely entitled to threaten them with ecclesiastical censures, or rather with censures of Christians abetting them in any way. In 1319 it ordered the bailiff of Meaux to withdraw accused Jews from the episcopal jurisdiction in all matters "except such as touch the Catholic faith." In his agreement of 1291 with the royal bailiff the archbishop of Béziers conceded that episcopal jurisdiction had not customarily extended to Jews. Even after the Inquisition had assumed much greater power in southern France Philip the Fair in 1302 and, again, John the Good in 1359 told their officials not to cooperate with attempts by inquisitors to pass judgment on any Jew's secular transgressions; Philip included even sorcery as being beyond the competence of the Holy Office. Under Charles V the government actually threatened ecclesiastics citing Jews before their courts with bodily, as well as financial, penalties (1364). Charles V himself went still further and in 1368 ordered all royal officials to protect Jews even against such clearly religious summonses as those relating to enforced attendance at conversionist sermons or participating in other Church ceremonies. Curiously, the very archepiscopal privileges of 1330 and 1372 for Cologne Jewry expressly exempted Jews from appearing before ecclesiastical tribunals. At the same time the state tried to bridle the excesses of some rabbinic judges as when, in his privilege for Strasbourg Jewry of November 25, 1347, Charles IV provided that no local Jews be cited before Jewish courts outside their city. Similar privileges *de non evocando* are recorded also in other communities while the rabbinic jurists, on their part too, tried to prevent willful chicaneries of this sort.[81]

Problems of judicial evidence likewise were quite complicated. Not only did the rules of evidence in Jewish, canon, and state laws greatly differ from one another, but, especially in periods of heightened tensions, the credibility of witnesses of other faiths appeared suspect. We recall that the early Teuton ordeals had long been abandoned in the case of Jewish parties and witnesses. From Carolingian times it became customary, therefore, to insist that in mixed litigations Jewish and Christian plaintiffs produce witnesses of both faiths. This provision, already included in Louis the Pious' privilege in favor of Domatus (the emperor demanded three witnesses each of both faiths), remained the prevailing rule in the Middle Ages, notwithstanding recurrent attempts to disqualify Jewish witnesses altogether from testifying against Christians. Such disqualification, provided for in Justinian's *Corpus,* was renewed, for instance, by Louis IX in 1272. It was also demanded by several Church councils, beginning with the seventh-century Toledan synods, though not by the more authoritative Third Lateran Council of 1179. Discrimination against Jewish witnesses was also widely practiced in Portugal and Sicily, according to the Palermitan custumal and Frederick III's decree of 1296, although as late as 1483 the burghers of Bari failed to secure from the government their total exclusion. In practice, Jewish witnesses in Christian courts must have found themselves at considerable disadvantage, just as reciprocally Christian witnesses were not accorded equal treatment before Jewish judges. Jewish converts to Christianity, in particular, often appeared suspect to both sides. Their credibility was totally repudiated by Jewish law, while a late-fifteenth-century Neapolitan decree barred them from testifying in mixed Judeo-Christian litigations.[82]

Under these circumstances, it became increasingly necessary for Jews to rely on written instruments, despite objections raised by traditionalists against trusting "mere scraps of paper." In his decree of 1244 for the Jews of Austria, Duke Frederick II provided: "If a Jew lends money on the possessions or writs of the magnates of the land and can prove it by their writs and seals, We shall assign the mortgaged possessions to the Jew and shall defend him against any violence with respect to them." In time, this simple provision was further elaborated and, ultimately, Emperor Frederick III demanded the registration of all claims in a special *Judenbuch,* particularly in Styria. A somewhat similar system had long before been introduced in England. According to J. M. Rigg, the Charter of 1201 "gave to a writ in the hands of a Jew an evidential value which it did not accord to a writ in the hands of a Christian. The effect was to place the Jew at a great advantage over the Christian both for attack and for defense." Because of widespread recriminations the system of chirograph offices was established in 1194. Here all documents were registered under the supervision of two Christian and two Jewish lawyers, as well as two legal registrars, and thus were supposed to furnish indisputable proof. However, even here the prevailing medieval suspicions, reinforced by reiterated forgeries of the very state papers, were not completely allayed. It was, indeed, easy for four chirographers jointly to remove certain documents from the chest; an accusation to this effect seemed credible enough for Edward I in 1274 to place all four men on trial. Hence frequent scrutinies of the chests were clearly indicated and Edward himself had to order investigations in quick succession; for instance on August 6, and December 12, 1276.[83]

Elsewhere many courts preferred the testimony of living witnesses. In his letter of 1205 to Philip Augustus of France, Innocent III voiced the still widely held complaint that "more credence is given to a document which an indiscreet debtor had left with them [the Jews] through negligence or carelessness, than are witnesses presented [by Christian parties]." Many a controversy also arose from the fact that, while certain countries recognized deeds prepared by Jewish notaries and court scribes, others insisted upon the exclusive validity of documents prepared by Christian officials. The very notarial office, long entrusted in Sicily to Jews, was now declared by jurists to be a public office from which Jews must be permanently barred. But Jews could make free use of Christian notaries, though the Sicilian viceroy had specifically to forbid the latter in 1490 to refuse their services to Jewish applicants. Of course, internally Jews continued to use their own scribes who prepared writs in conformity with the pertinent highly elaborate provisions of Jewish law. Such Hebrew deeds were widely used as evidence by non-Jewish authorities also, particularly in real estate transactions in England (the so-called *starrs*), Germany (for instance, at the registry of the Laurenzpfarre in Cologne), Spain, and Portugal. In the latter, however, some zealous or interested

Christian parties induced John I to forbid notaries to use Hebrew in deeds relating to sales, exchanges, or gifts, under the sanction of capital punishment. Alphonso V reduced that penalty to flagellation and deposition from office, but otherwise upheld the prohibition. At the other extreme, some fifteenth-century northern Italian communities (for instance, Vigevano in 1435) were so anxious to attract Jews that they promised to grant *plena fides* even to the bankers' business ledgers.[84]

Understandably, the greatest difficulties arose from the suspicions relating to the truthfulness of oaths. That is why, as we shall see in the next chapter, the formula of the Jewish oath was steadily enlarged and invested with ever more awe-inspiring features. But even if incorporated in formal decrees these ceremonies were of folkloristic rather than legal origin and reflected popular demands rather than deliberate governmental policies.

LEGAL AMBIGUITIES

From our review of the legal status of Jews in late medieval Europe it has become apparent that their position had gradually deteriorated in almost all countries, except perhaps in the peripheral lands of Poland and Hungary. Quite apart from sudden expulsions and massacres, Jews suffered permanently from serious disabilities as well as grave uncertainties concerning the content and efficacy of their privileges. Even the most extensive charters, like those of the Austrian Frederick II in 1244 (also of his east-central European successors) or of the French John the Good in 1360, limited themselves to certain specific provisions and ignored many equally vital areas of law. Such matters, it was doubtless felt, could be left to the customary laws of each region or locality or to the discretion of judges and administrative officials. Clearly, the leeway thus given offered endless opportunities for arbitrary interpretation and application which, in part, stemmed from the legislators' conscious desire not to tie their own hands, but, in part, resulted from the general fluidity of medieval legal institutions. These ambiguities left much room for the interplay of socioeconomic, cultural, and political forces which, in the ultimate sense, determined also the execution of even the most clearly defined laws.

On the whole, the lawgivers' intent was that, so long as Jews were tolerated at all, their lives, limbs, and property must be placed under the full protection of the law. Extensive safeguards were also granted for their free cultivation of their religion and for the undisputed control of their inner life by their own strongly organized self-governing communities. There was, of course, a large gray area on the borderline between internal and external relations, which explains the frequently divergent interpretations as to which authority should determine any particular action. This unpredictability was further aggravated by the conflicting jurisdictions of Church, state, and municipality. However, such differences were often adjusted not by legal formulas, but rather by the operation of group pressures, individual preferences or caprices of persons in power, or successful maneuvres by the parties concerned.

In its totality the Jewish community thus appears as one of a number of corporate bodies within the corporate structure of medieval society. Like the other corporate groups, it lived on the basis of specific privileges which regulated its basic rights and duties, leaving amplification and implementation to local customs. As a rule, the Jewish community enjoyed even fuller self-government than most other corporations. At the same time its rights were often less clearly defined, or willfully disregarded, while its duties were abritrarily expanded to suit the wishes of rulers. Both rights and duties, moreover, frequently differed by locality and period and yet they revealed certain basic similarities which transcended political boundaries and national traditions. Behind them all loomed a certain unifying force derived from the common origin of most of these laws in Roman, Carolingian, and canonical precedents. They were also shaped by the Jews' own powerful will to survive, their long-established religious rationales and ramified rabbinic laws, as well as their remarkable pliability and adjustability to differing sociocultural environments. In short, the late medieval Jewish community simultaneously appeared as one of many corporations *within* the European corporate system and as a corporation of its own kind in many ways placed *outside* the framework of general society.

XLVIII

OUTSIDER

BECAUSE of the Jewish group's extraordinary position in medieval society, the adverse laws affecting it often were more numerous and specific than the protective enactments. In general, states and municipalities closely followed the Church's segregationist and discriminatory program, especially since segregation was the natural counterpart to the Jews' corporate distinctiveness while discrimination served to protect a variety of special interests. The Church was most interested in segregation, but the other corporate groups mainly sought to expand their economic privileges at the Jews' expense. In this endeavor they often encountered the strong resistance of the royal power bent on maintaining the earning capacities of its Jewish "serfs." All of these factors were further complicated, as we shall see in the next chapter, by a vast array of folkloristic suspicions which, colored by the Church's religious teachings, often welled up from the depths of the popular psyche. Out of a combination of these complementary or conflicting forces arose that vast complex of anti-Jewish legal provisions which in their totality present the other side of the medieval Jewish legal picture.

MIXED MATING

In their segregationist efforts the medieval Church and state encountered little Jewish opposition. Jewish leaders may have fought one or another specific enactment, particularly if it seriously interfered with their constituents' ability to earn a living. But, on principle, rabbinic law had long independently aimed at keeping Jews away from too close association with their Gentile neighbors, lest they be totally submerged in the majority peoples. Had not the Bible proclaimed abstention from intimate contacts with idolatrous nations a major prerequisite for maintaining the purity of the Israelitic faith? Jews, as well as Christians, in their diverse ways invoked these biblical injunctions to enhance the solidarity of their respective groups and to stave off the ever-menacing inroads of outside "infidelity." Even "assimilationist" Josephus had emphasized the benefits of Alexandria's separate Jewish quarter so "that, through mixing less with aliens, they might be free to observe their rules more strictly." The Graeco-Roman pagans had not unjustly complained of the *amixia* of both Jews and Christians as the major obstacle to the absorption of these minorities by the growingly uniform Graeco-Roman civilization.[1]

Most pronounced on both the Christian and the Jewish sides was aversion to intermarriage and free sex relations with "unbelievers." Following the postulates of Church Fathers, who in this respect did not differ greatly from contemporary rabbis, Emperor Constantius in 339 declared marriage between a Jew and a Christian woman a *turpis consortium* subject to capital punishment. More broadly Theodosius provided in 388 that "no Jew shall take a Christian wife in matrimony nor shall a Christian be bound conjugally with a Jewess. If any one should commit an act of this kind he shall be regarded as having been guilty of the crime of adultery." This prohibition was repeated verbatim in Justinian's *Corpus*. Although the penalty for adultery underwent some modification under Justinian (the woman was not to be executed but merely committed to a convent for life), there is little doubt that, in the case of Judeo-Christian sex relations, the legislator wished to have both mates condemned to death. These Draconian measures may never have been fully carried into effect, but they remained as permanent reminders for later legislators. In practice, it appears, many medieval states merely fined transgressors, but some Spanish *fueros* insisted on the extreme penalty, those of Teruel (1176) and Cuenca (1190–91) specifying death by burning. The death penalty was also prescribed by the *fueros* of Usagre (*ca.* 1250) and Sepúlveda; the latter, confirmed by Ferdinand IV in 1309, demanded, however, that the "crime" be attested by at least one Jewish and two Christian witnesses. In his own privilege of 1300 for the city of Niebla, Ferdinand more vaguely treated cases of "adultery" between Jews or Moors and Christian women under procedures established in Seville. While the sanctions on illicit relations were thus largely left to local custom, Alphonso X's *Siete Partidas* classified them as capital crimes, unless the Jewess married to a Christian had *previously* been converted to the Christian faith. Waxing rhetorical, Alphonso argued that if the law provided for capital punishment of Christian adulterers, how much more should the same penalty be imposed on Jews having carnal intercourse with Christian women "who are spiritually brides of our Lord Jesus Christ by reason of their faith and the baptism they had received in his name." When, after the bloodshed of 1391, the problem of *conversos* began looming large throughout the Peninsula, John I of Aragon restated in 1393 the death penalty for all sex relations between Jews and Christians, including new converts.[2]

Some Italian jurists argued that, since this ancient prohibition was treated as a marriage impediment, it also should nullify all mixed marriages. But they could not cite any ruling to this effect earlier than a papal decision of 1672 for the city of Rome. In any case, the death penalty was rarely invoked on the Apennine Peninsula; it was for the most part replaced by a monetary fine. A Ferrara ordinance of 1464 removed the pertinent jurisdiction from ecclesiastical and municipal courts and reserved it to the *giudice dei savi*. This regulation was renewed in 1489 and again after Ferrara reverted to direct papal sovereignty in 1598. To forestall temptations, especially during the growingly liberal Renaissance era, the laws more and more stringently forbade any kind of social intercourse. In 1577 the duke of Monferrato prohibited Jews and Christians from visiting each other's homes "in order to sing, play music or dance" together. Jews were not to mediate in Christian marriages as marriage brokers or otherwise. Under the pressure of the Cortes, the Portuguese kings prohibited, as we recall, the entry of Jews into the houses of unmarried Christian women or those whose husbands were absent, except when they were called in as doctors, tailors, masons, or carpenters. Jewish peddlers and wandering craftsmen were allowed to visit farmhouses only if several Christian persons were at home. Conversely, Christian women unaccompanied by adult males were not permitted to visit the Jewish quarter.[3]

Extreme sanctions were also provided north of the Alps and Pyrenees. The ecclesiastical compiler of the *Schwabenspiegel* stated bluntly that "if a Christian fornicates with a Jewess, or a Jew with a Christian woman, they are both guilty of superharlotry [*überhure*] and they shall be placed one upon the other and burned to death; for the Christian has denied the Christian faith." This law was taken over verbatim in the Freising law book. Similarly, a municipal decree of Moravian Iglau in 1249 provided that if, on the testimony of two men, a Jew was convicted of adultery with a Christian woman, both transgressors were to be buried alive. Such executions actually took place from time to time, as in the case of one Jean Allard in seventeenth-century Paris. Allard allegedly had "kept a Jewess in his home in Paris and had several children by her; he was convicted of sodomy on account of this relation and burned together with his paramour, since 'coition with a Jewess is precisely the same as if a man should copulate with a dog.' " To bring home the severity of this trangression Marquardus de Susannis contended that sexual relations with a Jewess were worse than those with a nun. Incidentally, to reduce temptations a delegate sent by the archbishop of Toledo echoed in 1436 the resolution of the provincial council of Alcalá that a Jewish or Moorish physician or carpenter should enter a convent only when accompanied by a Christian. But did not Bernardino da Feltre, on his part, warn his celibatarian disciples to avoid contacts with nuns, quoting the adage that "God has withheld wives from us, but the devil has provided us with sisters"? Curiously, the Church itself was often more moderate. The two councils held in 1267 in Vienna and Breslau, both under the chairmanship of the papal legate, Cardinal Guido, sharply outlawed interfaith sex relations, but they demanded merely a fine of ten marks for the Jewish male and public flagellation, as well as permanent banishment from the city, for the Christian woman.[4]

In practice the penalties varied widely. Even in German-speaking areas, such as Zurich and Constance, Christian girls who had affairs with Jews were merely paraded through the streets wearing a Jewish conical hat and banished (1349, 1378). Most frequently the transgressors escaped with monetary fines. In 1256 Henry III of England remitted a fine to a Jew of Wilton, "on condition that he stand his trial if any will proceed against him for the said crime." Henry may indeed have observed that, in view of the clandestine nature of such affairs, third parties might hesitate to denounce the guilty persons. Failure to prove the accusation usually submitted the informer to severe penalties; sometimes, as in the first Cologne Jewish privilege of 1252, to the same punishment which would have been imposed upon the defendant if proved guilty. That is also why despite the unanimity of the Iberian decrees concerning the death penalty we rarely hear of the execution of any Spanish or Portuguese Jew on this score. The few recorded accusations usually ended with the royal quashing of proceedings because of lack of evidence or personal favoritism. Even a serious prosecution such as that against Lupus Abnexeyl for a variety of crimes including illicit amorous affairs with Christian women ended in 1318 with the dismissal of the case by royal decree. Characteristically, in some Spanish ordinances the enforcement of such prohibitions was left to Jewish authorities, especially the *berure averos* (supervisors of sins), as in Pedro IV's decree of 1377. In 1323 Infante Alphonso did not hesitate to confirm the statute of the Jewish burial society in Huesca which merely called for the expulsion from the society of a member having intercourse with a Christian woman.[5]

As a matter of record, so many Mediterranean Jews kept Christian concubines that they furnished fuel for numerous attacks by Jewish moralists. Abraham Zacuto and Solomon ibn Verga were later to attribute the very expulsion of Jews from Spain to such sinful behavior. The situation was somewhat complicated by the equivocal talmudic law concerning concubinage. Because of frequent biblical references to that ancient legal institution the medieval rabbis were unable totally to outlaw it. Louis M. Epstein well summarizes the discussions among the medieval jurists by saying:

The legal objection to her [the concubine] is very indefinite, even according to Maimonides, but there was a moral revulsion to her and it expressed itself in such objections as that the man becomes thereby estranged from his legitimate family, or that he enjoys marital pleasures without the nuptial benediction, or that he might approach her in time of impurity, because she would be ashamed to observe the law of ritual bathing. These objections sounded rather ethical than legal, and people did not mind them.

In Italy the Jewish leaders assembled at Forlì in 1418 complained of the sexual laxity of the Italian Jews, many of whom considered "Gentile women permitted to them." Similarly, Pope Boniface IX ratified, as we recall, in 1399 an acquittal for lack of evidence of a Foligno Jew who had allegedly claimed that "it is not sinful for Christian women to cohabit [*concubere*] with Jews." In the Provence the prevalence of mixed sex relations was advanced in 1306 as an argument for the attempted expulsion of Jews by Duke Robert of Calabria in the absence of his father, Charles II. That Mediterranean, and especially Spanish, Jews had not only Christian concubines but also Christian wives is borne out by the boast of the famous jurist Moses b. Jacob of Coucy that, on his preaching tour through Spain in 1236, he had persuaded many Jews to discharge their Christian mates.[6]

One wonders, however, how any formal marriage between Christians and Jews was ever accepted by either community. True, weddings as such could still be performed in the presence of but two witnesses without the assistance of either priests or rabbis. But newlyweds overtly persisting in their religious disparity could hardly secure the recognition of their marriage by either Jew or Christian. In most cases the wife doubtless adopted the husband's faith whereupon she was considered by Jewish law a full-fledged proselyte and R. Moses of Coucy would hardly have objected to such unions. Yehudah b. Samuel the Pious went further and, in order to combat social prejudices undoubtedly existing in the Jewish community, taught that "if a Jew of good character marries a woman proselyte of good character, modesty and charity who gets along well with people, his children ought to be preferred to the offspring of a born Jewess who does not possess the same virtues, for the issue of [such] a proselyte are [likely to be] righteous and good persons." Yet it seems that diversity of faith did not necessarily prevent the living together of a couple as "common-law" husband and wife without total rejection by their neighbors. Such cases may have given rise to rumors that many Poitou women had married Jews returning to the province after 1315, rumors which doubtless were highly inflated by Jew-baiters before the Pastoureaux massacres. Nor did Jean Allard apparently have any difficulty in keeping his Jewish concubine at home for several years before the courts intervened.[7]

Most remarkably, Christian public opinion, which sharply condemned relations between Jews and Christian women, was far more tolerant of Christian men having affairs with Jewesses, not only because of the generally prevailing double standard of morality between the sexes, but also because Jewish mistresses were likely to adopt their lovers' faith. Conversely, Jews more strenuously objected to their women having liaisons with Christians than to males keeping Christian concubines. True, in the aforementioned Italian-Jewish conference at Forlì of 1418, relations with Christian women were condemned as "a most grievous sin in addition to the possibility that they thus might beget children outside the faith." Lynching of such sinners caught *in flagranti* still was one of the few cases in which rabbinic law condoned violent popular self-help. Yet in practice but relatively few outraged Jewish families considered death of a guilty female relative preferable to her potential apostasy. Meir b. Baruch of Rothenburg was asked in 1272 about a Jewish woman who had committed adultery with a Gentile during her husband's absence from town. She had denied that charge and offered all sorts of excuses for her suspect behavior, but her father had accused her before the local rabbi of having given birth to a daughter by that Gentile and subsequently murdering the child. Since the wayward woman threatened to convert herself to Christianity, the father had asked for permission to kill her. That permission was, of course, refused him. Similarly two Saragossan brothers were accused of having slain their sister after she had become pregnant by a Christian. But this charge was dismissed by James II in 1311 because of lack of evidence.[8]

At the same time, Christian popular literature actually described seductions of Jewish girls by Christian suitors with considerable sympathy. An English legend about the Virgin centers around a young cleric, a relative of the local bishop, who had fallen in love with a Jewess. The girl resisted his advances for fear of her father. Only on Easter night, when the father was preoccupied with a hemorrhage which had miraculously afflicted many Jews, did the cleric smuggle himself into the girl's room, where he was detected by the irate father in the morning. But when the latter appeared before the bishop another miracle prevented him and his associates from uttering a single word of complaint. The story ends with the defrocking of the cleric and his marriage to his paramour who had interveningly undergone conversion. According to another tale, a young priest so completely lost his head because of his infatuation with a Jewess that he stole golden ornaments from a statue of the Virgin and was, of course, severely punished. The general tenor of these stories is not condemnation of the clerics for seducing Jewish women, but rather satisfaction over a clever prank played on the latter's families. Only one popular story more sympathetically describes the inner struggle of a Jewish girl who had fallen in love with a Christian but preferred death to conversion or an illicit relationship. It is small wonder, then, that even the generally anti-Jewish Spanish poet, Juan de Dueñas, dedicated to a beautiful Jewish lady a poem full of genuine passion which contrasted with his rather stilted descriptions of courtly love in most of the other lyrics included in his *Cancionero*. In short, the cosmic urge often prevailed over both law and public opinion.[9]

The famous story of the Oxford deacon and the Jewess is of a different nature, however. A native of Coventry and a student at the University of Oxford, this unnamed cleric had become so engrossed in the study of Hebrew letters that he underwent conversion to Judaism. Subsequently he fell in love with a Jewish woman and married her. Hence the romantic interest was not the compelling motive in his conversion. Even at his trial before the Council of Oxford in 1222 no one stressed the fact that he had a Jewish consort; according to contemporary chroniclers, he was prosecuted only for apostasy, the desecration of the host, defilement of the crucifix, and blasphemies against the Virgin. These anti-Jewish accusations, which later became commonplace in European folklore, appear here for the first time on English soil.[10]

Regrettably, not only illicit relations which, by their very nature, were secretive, but also more overt unions by marriage or concubinage are recorded only in connection with criminal prosecutions. There must have been numerous other offenders who escaped detection or whose prosecution left no traces in the extant documents, particularly wherever social relations between Jews and Gentiles were very close, as in Spain, the Provence, or in Renaissance Italy. The number of Jews prosecuted in Renaissance Venice for carnal intercourse with Christian women, including nuns, and the high percentage of Florentine Jews condemned on

this score during the fifteenth century doubtless are but a reflection of the general moral laxity prevailing in these great republics
at the height of their glory. Even in the Orthodox German community of Ratisbon there were three such public prosecutions of
Jews in the short span of seven years (1460–67). In reply to the
bishop's intervention in behalf of the first defendant, the city
elders claimed that several other Jews and Christian women were
then in jail awaiting trial and should the accused Jew be allowed
to go free, this would give rise to much gossip against the council.
Conversely, no lesser a person than the provost of Paris, Hughes
Aubriot, was denounced in 1381 for alleged sexual relations with
Jewesses as well as for having allowed baptized Jewish children to
be returned to Jews. These and other allegations, to be sure, came
from political opponents, but they may indeed have contained a
kernel of truth.[11]

A special category consisted of Christian prostitutes. In his
aforementioned decree of 1318, Infante Alphonso of Aragon
acquitted Lupus Abnexeyl of a whole array of accusations, including seduction of Christian women, visits to prostitutes at night "in
the manner of a Christian," and procuring many wives, sisters, and
daughters of honorable men for money. These accusations cast reflection on the state of morals in Spanish society much more than
on that among Jews. Widespread as sexual promiscuity may have
been also in the Jewish community, it certainly did not compare
with the general Iberian moral laxity attested by such foreign visitors as the Pole, Nicholas of Popielowo (Popplau). Reporting in
1484 his impressions during a journey through Spain and Portugal, this observer claimed that, according to rumor, in Galicia,
Andalusia, Biscaya, Portugal, and other parts of the Peninsula, "all
women were whores." If, according to this traveler, even a Valencia countess was available to all bidders at two ducats a night,
many Christian women must have been amenable to amorous ad-
ventures with Jewish men as well. However, lower-class prostitutes
were often little thought of as human beings; some local authorities tried to humiliate Jews by placing them on a par with these
members of the oldest profession. The Avignon municipality, for
example, provided that, if a Jew touched fruit on a stand, he, like
a prostitute, had to purchase it because he had defiled it. A similar

regulation was issued by the *mustassaf* (market supervisor) of Gerona in 1351. Not surprisingly, therefore, some localities had graduated scales of punishment. In their decree of 1420, we recall, the Padua elders provided for penalties ranging from flogging to death dependent on whether the Jew had intercourse with an inmate of a bordello, a nonprofessional lady of easy virtue, or a married lady of good standing. The women in question were to be treated in substantially the same manner. But if a Christian had intimacies with a Jewess both were subject only to flagellation (or a fine of 1,000 lire) and a prison term. There also were frequent inconsistencies. For instance, in Milan, the original fine of 100 lire (or four months in prison in case of insolvency) provided for by the decree of 1439 was replaced in 1470 by the death penalty.[12]

Yet in practice houses of ill repute, presumably inhabited by Christian women, were sometimes (for instance, in Geneva) located in the immediate vicinity of the Jewish quarter. In some cases the city elders merely tried to relegate them to the town's periphery where the Jewish street happened to be placed. But in many older cities the Jewish quarters were centrally located. A brothel close to the Jewish street may actually have served the double purpose of lowering the dignity of that quarter and of enabling Jewish customers to visit the house of ill fame at night without conspicuously violating the curfew. Understandably, Jewish elders often resisted such locations on grounds of both public morals and the implied insult to their community. In some towns, such as Schweidnitz in 1335, the city council had to promise the Jews that it would neither permit the establishment of a house of ill repute nor assign residential quarters to a single prostitute in the Jewish street. Jewish moralists, like Isaac 'Arama, likewise protested against the occasional location of such establishments in, or close to, the Jewish quarter.[13]

Connected with the fear of sexual intimacy also were the numerous canonical prohibitions, often followed by state and city ordinances, against the employment of Christian servants by Jews. We recall Innocent III's fulminations against the "abominations" allegedly taking place between Jewish employers and their Christian maidservants. According to Richard of Devizes, a Christian woman wishing to testify against her Jewish employer in a Blood

Accusation in Winchester was disqualified as an "infamous" person because she had done service for Jews (1192). In Spain, even rabbis complained of some coreligionists acquiring Moorish slave-girls as concubines. Yet, the need of Christian help in Jewish households and the search for gainful employment by Christian women frequently overcame these canonical and civil ostracisms. In the Provence, in particular, the old prohibition against Jews employing Christian servants, still reiterated in the decree of 1294, was completely reversed by King René in 1454. Even in Ratisbon a compromise was reached in 1393; it prohibited only the employment of Christian maidservants under the age of fifty. This decree led to the punishment of a transgressor in 1472. We also recall the stringent conditions under which Christian midwives were allowed to assist in the deliveries of Jewish women. To the same complex of fears also belong the numerous prohibitions against Jews and Christians bathing together. Imported from Byzantium, this outlawry was frequently reemphasized by Christian provincial councils and found its way also into civil legislation. If the still older canonical denunciations of Judeo-Christian conviviality (going back to the Spanish Council of Elvira, *ca.* 300 c.e.) found relatively few echoes in late medieval state and municipal regulations, this was mainly owing to Jewish laws governing the consumption of ritual food and wine which made such contacts less frequent. Even in the southern city of Aix a municipal ordinance of 1295 prohibited Christians and Jews from sharing in the innocent game of dice under the penalty of 50 sous, a third of which was to be paid to the informer.[14]

GHETTO

Clearly, the most effective way of segregating Jews from Christians was to shut them up in quarters of their own, particularly if these were surrounded by walls with one or two gates opened only during the day. We recall that the Church took up the cudgels for that institution on principle, leaving the details to state and local authorities. Since this aspect of the formation of the European ghettos has been discussed above with many illustrations and considerable documentation, we need but offer here some supplementary data relating in particular to state and municipal legislations. Nor must we ignore the fundamental fact that Jewish quarters had a long historic tradition antedating the Christian Roman Empire and that they also met deep-rooted segregationist desires of the Jewish community itself or reacted to a variety of local factors. For example, the Jewish settlement in Rome's Trastevere district, the oldest and most persistent Jewish ghetto in Europe, originated, as we recall, from the location there of numerous Jewish freedmen released by their ancient Roman masters. Most coreligionists who joined them later likewise were proletarians living in that undesirable location which accommodated many poverty-stricken immigrants of other ethnic strains as well.

On the Iberian Peninsula, during both the Moorish expansion and the Christian reconquest, Jewish quarters were often but by-products of the new rulers' conscious policy in resettling their deserted lands. Of course, there was a difference between self-imposed or incidental segregation, particularly characteristic of all ethnically and religiously mixed regions in the ancient and medieval Near East, and a Jewish quarter in a Western land within an otherwise more or less homogeneous population. The physiognomy of Baghdad was little altered by its two Jewish quarters. The motley of races and peoples living apart from one another was a natural aspect of the morphology of any oriental metropolis. Twelfth-century Muslim sectarians, after fleeing from Cordova to Fez, settled in a specially assigned borough as a matter of course. Certainly, a Jewish quarter in ancient Alexandria or Sardes, in medieval Cairo or Cordova, carried no connotation of second-class citizenship.

Nor was inferiority attached at first to Jewish quarters in Europe. Even the decree of Infante John in 1369 which demanded that certain Jews of Cervera, enumerated by name, return to either of the two existing Jewish districts within eight days, was issued after consultation with both the municipal elders and the heads of the Jewish community. In this respect the Cervera quarters did not essentially differ from the old *juderías*, already established in most Spanish cities in Muslim times; for instance, in Burgos, whose two main tenth-century sections had, according to Ibn Ḥauqal (who had visited Spain in 948), been predominantly inhabited by Jews. The following, somewhat oversimplified, description of the conditions in mid-fourteenth-century Aragon, included in an inquiry addressed to R. Nissim b. Reuben Gerondi, is written without any trace of bitterness:

There is a Jewish quarter in the city [here unnamed] called *Calle* which has gates opening to the east and west, people entering from one side and leaving from another. These gates have locked doors similar to those in the Jewish quarters of all other cities such as Gerona and Barcelona. This quarter is entirely Jewish, whereas the rest of the city outside the quarter is all Gentile with no Jews living therein.

Interested only in the joint responsibility of all inmates for the expenses connected with the administration of the quarter, Nissim's responsum may have readily ignored a few individuals living outside the ghetto so long as there was no express prohibition against doing so.[15]

Not until the "holy war" of 1391 were there any concerted Iberian efforts to establish technical ghettos, or quarters embracing all Jews and excluding all non-Jews in the community. If as early as 1243 James I ordered the Tarragona Jews to move into a separate quarter, the situation there may have been in so far exceptional as, in the Muslim period, Jews seem to have so greatly outnumbered the Gentiles that Idrisi called Tarragona "a city of Jews." Separate denominational quarters had long characterized Muslim cities in Spain and elsewhere, without the need of any legal compulsion. A similar order in Pamplona likewise had specific local reasons; it doubtless was in part but a reaction to the widespread massacres of Jews eight years before. Realizing how difficult it had been for Jews, who are said to have suffered 6,000–10,000 casualties, either to defend themselves as they had tried to do in Estelle, or to be helped by the authorities so long as they lived dispersed in various sections of the cities, Philip III decided to set up a separate Jewish quarter surrounded by walls. On the other hand, the Castilian Ferdinand IV and his successors overtly catered to the burghers' competitive appetites when, in a series of partially contradictory decrees in 1301–33, they tried sharply to segregate the Jews from Christians in the small town of Belrado and even to prohibit trade between them in the public market except on one day a week.[16]

These preliminary skirmishes were followed by the great on-slaught after 1391. Within seven years all Jewish domicile in Calatayud was sharply restricted "lest these faithless dirty people infect the purity of Christians through the closeness of their habitation and lest these men, putrefied through the sores of error and crime, corrupt the sanity of the pure Christian mind." More generally, John I of Castile's anti-Jewish decree of 1412, which was largely copied for Aragon by Ferdinand I, included the outspoken provision:

In the first place from now on all Jews and Jewesses, Moors and Moorish women of My kingdoms and dominions shall be and live apart from the Christian men and women in a section or part of the city or village or any place where they have resided. It shall be surrounded by a wall and have but one gate through which one could enter it. All Jews and Jewesses, Moors and Moorish women shall live in the said enclosure thus assigned to them and in no other place or house outside it. They shall begin to move thereto within eight days after these places are assigned to them. And if some Jew or Jewess, Moor or Moorish woman should stay outside the said enclosure, he or she shall by that very fact lose all his or her possessions. The body of such a Jew or Jewess, Moor or Moorish woman shall likewise be at My mercy to impose upon him or her any corporal punishment according to My discretion.

Thereupon the city of Huesca attempted in 1414 to relegate its newly created Jewish quarter to an out-of-the-way and unim-proved location. In Spain, however, the royal bark was decidedly worse than the bite. Despite the prevailing anti-Jewish feelings in certain circles and the segregationist preaching by St. Vicente Ferrer, the close Judeo-Christian social relations could not easily be obstructed. In Gerona, whose Jewish community had been called "wholly liquidated and dead" two years before the 1391 massacres, the Jews had so greatly increased in number that many had to be allowed to reside outside their street. The pertinent de-crees of 1445 were abrogated, however, when in 1448 the city de-cided to enlarge the Jewish quarter and to resettle those outsiders in it. If under the stimulus of Pope Eugene IV's extremist demands of 1442 John II of Castile renewed the provision of 1412, his 1443 decree, too, was so little implemented that at the Cortes of Toledo of 1480 Queen Isabella had to vow that within two years all Jews and Moors would, in fact, be removed to their separate habitations. But she, too, encountered a variety of local obstacles and mutual recriminations by Jews and burghers, so that she and Ferdinand almost immediately began issuing specific exemptions for favored individuals, such as the physician Rabbi Jaco. Progress was further bedeviled by legal complications still under consideration in 1484, 1487, and later, only to give way to new sets of legal problems arising from the disposition of properties left behind by the departing exiles of 1492.[17]

Understandably, any attempt to move a large group into a new quarter caused ideological as well as technical complications. Anticipating by two months the difficulties which were to arise in Huesca as a result of his decree of 1413, Ferdinand I of Aragon warned the authorities of Tamarite de Litera to see to it that the removal of Jews to the new location proceed in an orderly fashion and without any undue hardships. Moreover, while forced to delegate these arduous tasks to lower officials, the monarchs did not wish to yield one iota of their royal prerogatives. When in 1481 a Saragossa prior tried by proclamation to accelerate the transfer of the Jews to their quarter—he also demanded that soon thereafter all exits from that quarter toward Christian houses be permanently sealed off—Ferdinand the Catholic sent him a blistering letter. The king was but slightly appeased on learning that the prior had acted in his capacity of papal commissioner and only after consultation with both the royal authorities and the Jews. On the other hand, Ferdinand did not hesitate to force the Jewish community of Borja in 1484 to relocate a recent convert to Christianity by acquiring his house in the Jewish quarter. Even before the Toledo pledge, which they frequently invoked, the Catholic monarchs had ordered the authorities of Soria in 1477 to remove the Jews into a separate quarter. Yet twelve years later certain Jews still lived in houses located outside the *juderia* with windows looking out on the Church of San Gil "in a fashion that one cannot perform the divine service unseen by them to the great disservice of God, Our Lord." Likewise in 1489 the king and queen had to insist that the governor of Galicia force the Christian houseowners in Orense to vacate their houses located in the Jewish street. On the other hand, in the same period of 1488–91, so to say on the eve of the expulsion, they permitted the extension of the Jewish quarter in Leon where Jews had resided for several centuries. They also ordered the authorities of Cabeçuela to change the location of the newly assigned Jewish quarter since its topographical shortcomings had caused its inmates "much fatigue and damage." In 1490 they allowed the Jews of Trujillo to spend nights outside their quarter. All of which bore out the later testimony of a witness at an inquisitorial trial of 1509–11 that, before 1492, it had been quite customary for Christians to live among Jews and vice versa.[18]

Portugal likewise enacted, in 1412, a new general law regulating ghetto life. Although allegedly adopted at the request of a nationwide Jewish deputation, its main provisions were very harsh, though they marked a substantial reduction of penalties provided in the earlier decree of Pedro the Severe. A Jew found outside his quarter at night after the first signal was to be fined, we remember, the enormous sums of 5,000 or 10,000 livres, or whipped through the streets in the cases of a first, second, or third offense. On the other hand, if he was detained for good reasons he was allowed to spend the night in any Christian house except one inhabited by a woman whose husband was away. If summoned by a Christian, he could leave the quarter at night, provided his guide carried a light. This provision was inserted not only for the benefit of doctors and other Jewish help summoned in emergencies, but also in favor of Jewish tax gatherers who often found night visits productive of revenue. This combination of general severity and individual concessions appears to be a clear indication that the legislators themselves were none too sure of compliance with their orders. Although our records are largely silent on this score, it may be assumed that the majority of Portuguese Jews voluntarily resided in their own quarters. In Lisbon there actually existed two and, from 1457 on, three independent Jewish quarters, the wealthiest inhabitants living close to the great synagogue. But quite a few residents doubtless managed to live on other streets if they had any valid reason for so doing.[19]

In other medieval countries regulations varied. There, too, for the most part the Jewish quarters originated from custom and habit, rather than from legal enactments. Palermo had a Jewish quarter as early as 977. Yet when in 1312 Frederick III [II] ordered the local Jews to move out of the city proper "so that they live separated from the faithful Christians" his order was simply disregarded. A century later (1427) Queen Joanna II of Naples tried to enforce segregation in Lanciano, but within three months she had to revoke that order. Nor had the burghers of Bari any success with their 1463 petition that Jews be forced "to make their habitation and residence together in one locality of the city." In neighboring Lecce the burghers complained four years later that, as a result of the alliance between the king and the Jews, the former "had converted a single community into two communities in the same city." In the North-Italian cities the bankers, invited to residence through special *condottas,* were as a rule given complete freedom to settle and conduct their business in any street they chose. Although few in number, their residences in various parts of Florence necessitated the establishment of two separate Jewish butcher shops on each side of the Arno. Only Piedmont-Savoy came close to enforced separation. Beginning with the rather frivolous argument of the Turin city council in 1425 that segregated Jewish families (then only four in number) could be "better supervised so that they would not lend money at illicit usury," a general decree of Amadeus VIII, in 1430, ordered all Jews in his lands to settle within each city "in a secure closed location, to be called *judaysmus.*" They were not to leave it from sunset to sunrise, except in some emergency such as a fire. Six years later Duke Louis ordered the relocation of Jews inhabiting houses in Turin which could be used for dwellings of doctors or students. Yet it was only in the sixteenth century that the movement to establish technical ghettos gained momentum throughout Italy. It was adumbrated by the famous decision of the Venetian Senate of 1516 which, adopted by a vote of 130 to 44 with 8 abstentions, stated that

all Jews who at present are found residing in the various streets of this Our city, as well as those who might come from elsewhere, shall, until it will be differently decided in accordance with the exigencies of the time, be obliged immediately to proceed to dwell together in the kind of houses located in the *geto* [iron foundry] next to the Church of St. Jerome.

This decision not only initiated a new era in the development of the Italian Jewish quarters, but it also seems fortuitously to have bestowed the name on the entire institution in other countries as well.[20]

Curiously, even in Marseilles, where the Jews enjoyed nearly full burghers' rights, a statute, enacted in 1320 on the initiative of the local inquisitor, ordered all Jews to move into their district within ten days. This statute was observed in its breach, however, and down to the expulsion the quarter remained merely a preferred Jewish residential section. Similar attempts in the Provence were quashed by King René's succinct decree of 1424, "We ordain that the Jews shall not suffer from any innovations with respect to changes in quarters in which they have been wont to dwell." Much freedom existed also in papal Avignon, where some Jews had moved in 1236 from their *vielle juiverie to* the vicinity of the Church of St. Peter. In Carpentras the papal legate had to stipulate in 1460 that Jews must admit Christians to their two quarters during the day. Only in Cavaillon, after lengthy negotiations, was a Jewish quarter established in 1453 over Jewish protests. This situation in the Papacy's French possessions changed after 1555 when they began sharing with its Italian provinces in the enforcement of technical ghettos.[21]

In the northern countries Jewish quarters were likewise, for the most part, extralegal institutions, although in London, where a Jewish quarter is recorded as early as 1115, Jews were forbidden shortly before their expulsion to rent their houses to Christians or lease houses from Christians because they were supposed to live only in their own section. In York, on the contrary, there was no Jewish quarter, a decree of 1278 confirming the Jews' right to live dispersed through the town "as they were wont to do in times past." In Germany, where the Spires quarter of 1084 was established as a distinct privilege for Jews, segregation was increasingly reinforced by legal sanctions, particularly after 1348. In Cologne an anti-Jewish tumult of 1330 forced the city elders to surround the Jewish section by a wall for better defense. In the privilege of 1347 the council authorized the Jewish community to keep its gates under repair, the keys being entrusted jointly to the city's constable and the "Jew bishop." The pact between the archbishop

and the city of Treves of 1362 provided that no more than fifty
Jews should be allowed to live in the Jewish quarter and that
three of its gates should be walled in for better supervision. Similarly, the erection of the ghetto of Frankfort in 1462 followed, as
we recall, a suggestion by the generally friendly Emperor Frederick III. In some cases the location or the size of the Jewish quarter led to the formation of a distinct Jewish "village" or suburb,
even of a regular Jewish city. Combined with the extensive Jewish
communal self-government, such larger concentrations produced,
indeed, the effect of two separate municipalities, a condition
against which the Lecce burghers vehemently protested. This was
the case, at least in early modern times, in the Josefstadt outside
Prague and in Kazimierz outside Cracow.[22]

Otherwise the Jewish quarters were usually allowed to remain
in the cities' central sections. After a careful analysis of "the early
history of the Jewish quarters in Paris," Robert Anchel came to
the general conclusion, applicable also to many other Jewish settlements, that "attracted by the great commercial routes, there
have been Jews in Paris since most ancient times, living in various
quarters both of the Cité and the two banks of the Seine. . . .
They have never ceased to live in some of the sections in which we
find them in ancient times. The rue des Juifs exists today [1940] as
it did in the twelfth century and the historian cannot help but be
moved by the fidelity displayed by generations." The Jewish quarter in the very heart of Cologne paradoxically included its City
Hall and a law of 1341 had to provide that the gate to the quarter
not be locked on evenings when the municipal council was in session. At the same time the city insisted that the acquisition of any
new houses by Jews should require the unanimous consent of the
council; a clause to this effect was actually inserted into the oath of
office of all council members. Such central location also had the
additional advantage of proximity to the castle of the lord or
governor, from which an armed force could speedily be dispatched
to ward off an attack. The Jewish quarter's defensive function is
illustrated by Strasbourg, where the municipal elders temporarily
shut the gates to hold off a mob aroused by the panic of the Black
Death. Defensive purposes were also advanced by Duke Albert III
of Austria in 1371 as the main reason for the establishment of a

separate Jewish quarter in Steyer. Understandably, however, after any major interruption, as when the Jewish exiles began returning to royal France in 1315 or 1359 or to many German localities after the catastrophe of the Black Death, the new quarters assigned to them were often located on the periphery of the cities, which had interveningly used the original Jewish area for the erection of public buildings or given it away to local burghers who subsequently resisted relocation. In other cases, as in Würzburg, Augsburg, or Glogau the growing Jewish population or the city's subjection to two masters necessitated the establishment of an additional Jewish quarter.[23]

Whatever may have been the particular general or local reasons behind the creation of Jewish quarters, in the end segregated living accrued to the benefit of Jewish social and communal life. Hence the institution as such elicited few protests from Jewish leaders who did not even resent the Church-imposed restrictions on the Jews' freedom of movement during Good Friday or the entire Easter week. Jews must have realized that, though these regulations were often dictated by an anti-Jewish animus, they helped reduce clashes with Christians aroused during that week by the services and sermons commemorating Christ's Passion. Of course, they resented specific uncalled-for chicaneries, as when in 1493 the imperial officials placed guards at the Jewish gates in Ratisbon for six weeks lest any person depart without paying his share of a newly imposed tax. During the Blood Accusation there in 1475–76 Jews were not allowed to leave their quarter for fully five months. In 1518 an unsubstantiated rumor that articles stolen from two churches had found their way into the Jewish quarter caused it to be placed under strict surveillance for thirty-two days. However, these police measures were rather exceptional; they were part of the city's campaign to make Jewish life unbearable, a campaign which finally resulted in the ousting of all Ratisbon Jews in 1519.[24]

BADGE

Quite different was the Jewish attitude toward distinguishing marks. Here the Church, ever since the resolution of the Fourth

Lateran Council of 1215, was the clear protagonist, state and municipalities following suit, sometimes reluctantly. On their part the Jews, wherever possible, secured formal exemptions. True, badges were largely a Muslim heritage merely "improved" upon by Western legislators. While certain discriminatory laws affecting Islam's "protected subjects" found no imitators in the West (horseback riding was rarely prohibited, and only sporadically, as in Crete close to Muslim lands, do we find houses labeled by such special signs as wooden figures of the devil), the practices taken over were more rigidly applied. Emulation of Muslim patterns in part accounts also for Emperor Frederick II's speed in embracing the Lateran canon. As early as 1221 he demanded that in Sicily and Naples Jews be distinguished not only by clothing but also by beards appropriate to each man's age under the sanction of confiscation of the transgressors' property and the branding of their foreheads. Religious motivations were soon reinforced by economic factors. On the initiative of the Palermo city council (probably instigated thereto by Christian butchers) Infante Pedro in 1435 ordered all Jewish butcher shops to display a red wheel at least a palm in diameter, so that Christian customers be forewarned against acquiring meats discarded by Jews. But sales of ritualistically disqualified Jewish meats to the Christian public had long before aroused the ire of churchmen, and it always remained in the province of Church councils, and of such leading churchmen as Nicolaus Cusanus and John Capistrano, emphatically to raise the issue of visible distinctions between Jews and Christians and to threaten noncompliance with dire consequences. The story of this ecclesiastical drive has briefly been recited in an earlier chapter and need not be repeated here.[25]

At first both Christians and Jews seemingly took the Lateran Council's professed desire to prevent intimacies between the two groups at its face value. Jewish leaders had long preached against imitation of Gentile ways of life, a preachment which may have induced the Lateran Council to buttress its resolution by the rather irrelevant citation from Num. 15:37–41 relating to the law of fringes. That is why the contemporary German rabbis Isaac b. Moses Or Zaru'a and Meir b. Baruch unemotionally reported that on their visits to France "we had to wear wheels on our garments, for such a law had been enacted against the Jews at that time." Concerned only with the legal problem of whether the badge could be worn on the Sabbath, they adopted the decision of Isaac's French teacher Samson of Coucy that, by being sewn on the garment, the badge had become an integral part of each person's permissible attire. Characteristically, none of these scholars cited the governmental enactments and threatening penalties as an excuse. Only the Castilian Jewish grandees, fearful of interference with their close relations with Gentile statesmen and businessmen, openly opposed the badges. We also possess a sensitive, if oblique, denunciation of any distinguishing marks in a Hebrew elegy by Benjamin b. Abraham 'Anav of Rome.[26]

Some Jews probably saw in the whole scheme but another form of fiscal extortion. Although in the throes of severe internal disturbances, England was the first country to follow the lead of the Lateran Council and to order, in 1218, all Jews to wear on their outer garments two white tables made of linen or parchment "wherever they may go about within or outside the city." But no sooner was the law enacted than the administration began issuing individual exemptions for fees ranging from £4 down to a few pence. This practice was in no way checked by the objections raised by the Council of Oxford in 1222. On the basis of the extant evidence, contends H. G. Richardson, "it is safe to conclude that for a good many years, probably until 1253, no Jew, rich or poor, need unwillingly wear the badge." If in his decree of 1253 Henry III included more forceful provisions long demanded by the Church, this was owing just as much to the general fiscal exhaustion of English Jewry as to political considerations. Not surprisingly, the sharpest orders to wear badges, interveningly changed from one or two tables to a wheel, emanated from Edward I in 1275. This obligation was now formally extended to women from the age of seven, as demanded by English churchmen ever since 1222, although Henry III and his henchmen had surprisingly foregone this potential source of revenue from dispensations granted to the fairly numerous Anglo-Jewish businesswomen. Edward's decree doubtless sought to placate some of those powerful factions which were then irresistibly driving toward the complete elimination of Jews from England.[27]

At times Jewish resistance had to be overcome by drastic means. If in 1219 Ferdinand III of Castile had to yield to the threat of Jewish leaders that they would rather leave the country than wear badges (Pope Honorius III, we recall, acknowledged that the ensuing loss of revenue might cause a calamity), his successor, Alphonso X, felt that he could enforce compliance by threatening in his *Siete Partidas* any Jew appearing in public without a badge with a fine of 10 gold maravedis (in the case of inability to pay, with 10 lashes) for each violation. This famous code of Castilian laws did not secure general compliance until the mid-fourteenth century, however, and in 1313 both the provincial Church Council of Zamora and the Cortes of Palencia had to invoke the example of France and other countries where badges were enforced. Both in Castile and Aragon, moreover, the kings frequently granted exemptions to favorites and even to entire communities. Not until the tense period after 1391 was a sustained effort made to enforce Jewish distinguishing marks. In 1397 Queen Maria for the first time defined the derogatory purposes of the badge, namely to "demonstrate to all the misery of the captive people which it incurred because of its infidelity." There also was now an additional incentive rigidly to segregate Jews from the mass of new *conversos* who otherwise might more readily relapse to their former faith, a fear expressed as early as 1393 by John I of Aragon. In 1405 Henry III approved the resolution of the Cortes of Madrid to make Jews display badges even during appearances at the royal court, though not while traveling on country roads. However, no bystander was to be allowed forcibly to remove a Jew's badgeless garment without specific court orders. Most drastic were the penalties provided in the interrelated anti-Jewish decrees of John II of Castile in 1412, Ferdinand I of Aragon in 1413 and 1415, and Antipope Benedict XIII in 1415. The former went to the extreme of forbidding Jews and Moors to cut their beards and hair in any fashion "other than they had been used to of old," under the severe double sanction of 100 lashes and 100 maravedis. There is no evidence that that part of the law was ever enforced, however. In 1476 the Catholic monarchs complained at the Cortes of Madrigal that Jews (and Moors) often appeared in such splendid and costly attire that "one cannot tell whether they are

Jews or priests or counselors of high estate and authority." In 1483 the royal pair issued a special decree revoking all personal exemptions hitherto granted, "no one excepted." [28]

In Portugal, too, the Papacy and the local clergy conducted an apparently ineffective campaign during the thirteenth century to force the badge upon the large Jewish and Muslim populations. Even the 1325 decree of Alphonso IV at the Cortes of Évora ordering the Jews to affix hexagonal yellow stars to their hats and to cut their hair short, though threatening three-time offenders with confiscation of property and personal slavery, seems to have been observed largely in its breach, despite the praise showered upon the king by a contemporary Portuguese poet. Here, too, the year 1391 ushered in a new effort at enforcement, John I encouraging successful informers by allotting to them half the fine imposed upon the guilty. Yet as late as 1468 the Cortes still bitterly complained of Jews freely walking about without wearing any distinguishing marks.[29]

Provençal Jewry, too, at first successfully pleaded with Charles I that Christian neighbors behaved in a less friendly fashion toward Jews wearing badges. It secured in 1273 the aforementioned blanket exemption in return for an annual payment of two augustals for every person aged ten years or over and one augustal for younger children. But the same fiscal aspects prompted Charles II to reintroduce the badge in 1294, since only a general injunction could assure the collection of both fines and fees for exemptions. Probably this was also the main motive behind Philip the Tall's order to the seneschal of Beaucaire in 1317 to force Jews to wear badges, for "it is not right that persons who make overt profession of Judaism should blush because they are made to wear publicly distinctive signs which render them recognizable as Jews." A host of local ordinances, too, regulated details which often greatly varied from one another. The authorities sometimes inflicted penalties without due process, as when a cleric publicly disrobed a Jew found in Tarascon without his badge (1378). Much room was also left for jurisdictional disputes such as raged in 1234 between the archbishop and the municipal council of Arles. It was only King René who, in 1454, not only reduced the penalty to five sous, but reserved all punishments to royal officials.[30]

Curiously, the Holy Roman Empire (including Switzerland) appeared least eager to enforce the Jewish badge; not because of any pro-Jewish feelings, but rather, as suggested by Otto Stobbe, because the Jews were sufficiently distinguished there by the cone-shaped hats which they had worn from time immemorial. In the illustration of "Feifelein, the Jews' king," included in a fourteenth-century Landshut manuscript, his red clothing and yellow cloak with a purple lining would hardly have distinguished him from his non-Jewish contemporaries, but the shape of his hat made his religious profession unmistakable. Gregory IX exaggerated, therefore, when in addressing a circular letter to the archbishops and bishops of Germany on March 4, 1233, he complained of the "confusion" prevailing in parts of the country because one could not distinguish Jews from Christians. This papal complaint is the more remarkable, as distinctive clothing made priests, nobles, and the various classes of burghers easily recognizable. But the color of the Jewish hat varied greatly; even illuminated manuscripts of the same law book sometimes represented Jews wearing hats of different colors. For instance, in the Heidelberg and Wolfenbüttel manuscripts of the *Sachsenspiegel* the Jews appear with yellow and blue hats, while they wore red hats or berets in Nuremberg. Foreign Jews, however, were made to wear in addition broad capes and in 1343 all Jews were ordered to have their beards trimmed every four weeks. The *Schwabenspiegel* merely prescribed the wearing of a conical hat. In general, shapes and colors of hats differed in various regions and periods and may actually have been left to the wearer's individual discretion. It appears that, with their usual conservatism, most Jews themselves preferred to wear that peculiar headgear.[31]

In the fifteenth century, however, especially under the pressure of such outsiders as Cusanus and Capistrano, the badge spread also to all German-speaking areas. As early as 1434 Emperor Sigismund ordered the city of Augsburg to introduce the yellow wheel. Whatever intentions the original legislators may have had, the populace unavoidably saw in the Jews' distinguishing marks something degrading, since most other classes thus singled out by law were also held in low esteem. Special colors were prescribed, for instance, for the attire of lepers and prostitutes; sometimes also for that of concubines of priests, and other declassed persons. Hence it is not surprising to find quite a few German caricatures of Jews exaggeratedly displaying their cone-shaped hats or wheels. But there also exist medieval representations portraying in a dignified posture the person wearing characteristic Jewish clothing. At any rate, Jewish resistance here, too, was gradually crumbling as the governments of the fifteenth and sixteenth centuries demanded increasing compliance. Ferdinand I's aforementioned decree of 1551 for the Austrian areas was typical of large sections of central Europe. Jews were told to wear upon the left front side of their coat or dress a yellow wheel, according to an enclosed diagram, under the sanction of forfeiting everything found upon them. A third offense was punishable by exile from all Austrian hereditary lands.[32]

Even Italy produced a rather substantial body of segregationist enactments. In Sicily, we recall, a special custodian *del segno* or *della rotella* was appointed in 1366 to collect the numerous fines from disobeying Jews. This office, successively held by Nicoló Papalla, Giovanni di Pino, and Giovanni di Planellario (with a deputy), was specifically continued by the viceroy's decree of 1427. In Venice, where the badge was instituted in 1394, the Senate repeated its ordinance nine times in the course of the following century. It subsequently was so determined to enforce this law that it required the combined efforts of a bishop, the French and English envoys, the papal legate and, finally, of a renowned marshal of France to secure a permanent exemption for the physician and author Jacob Mantino. By the end of the Middle Ages few legislators dared overtly to defy a tradition buttressed by constant reiteration in decrees and synodal resolutions and by the fairly unanimous backing of contemporary juridical luminaries. Even the generally friendly Milanese administration prescribed in 1473 a fine of 10 gold ducats in addition to 4 lashes for any Jew publicly appearing without a badge. If in Vigevano the first *capitoli* contracted with a group of Jewish bankers in 1435 forbade the burghers to force the latter to wear any special attire, the city council reversed itself completely and fifteen years later allowed any passer-by to strip the clothing off a Jew found in the street without the required badge.[33]

Legislative inconsistencies of this type were the more frequent in Italy, as legal theory and tradition often ran counter to the living needs of the moment. In Pisa, where the badge was introduced in 1321, it was later withdrawn. Florence, on the contrary, expressly freed one group in 1437 from that obligation, but within a year and a half the authorities reconsidered and pledged themselves not to repeat this exemption at the renewal of the *capitoli*. They also insisted that all other Jewish inhabitants should wear distinguishing marks. Although in 1446 at the renewal of the agreement with the bankers the exception was reiterated, soon thereafter a new decree enjoined all Jews indiscriminately to wear badges under the severe sanction of a fine of 100 gold florins for each violation. To prove the earnestness of their intention, the authorities arrested a Portuguese Jewish visitor, Amans Joseph, found without his badge and sought to collect the fine even after his conversion to Christianity and escape from prison, holding his guarantors responsible for the full amount. Willy nilly submitting to the Milanese decree of 1473, Cremona Jewry was ready to accept a yellow band around the cap. It pointed to similar practices in Savoy, Mantua, and Germany, although the ladies continued to insist that their dresses and head ornaments sufficiently revealed their Jewish identity.[34]

It would take us too far afield to review here, however superficially, the multitude of regulations concerning the shape and color of the required badges, where and by whom they had to be worn, and other details. Since the main driving force behind this legislation was provincial Church bodies, the shapes, penalties, methods of enforcement, and other details were left to local legislation. Not even the location where the badge was to be worn was always clearly stated. A fourteenth-century French manuscript describing the expulsion of the Jews from France in 1182 prominently displays a Jewish exile wearing the wheel on his hip. True, in his letter of 1234 to King Thibaut I of Navarre, Pope Gregory IX made a specific recommendation. "As We desire," he wrote, "that Jews be clearly discernible from Christians and recognized as such, We order that you impose upon all and every Jew of either sex the wearing of a sign, namely of a round patch of yellow cloth or linen placed upon the outside garment and stitched upon the

heart and another on the back so that he may thus be clearly recognizable. The width of this sign shall be of four digits in circum-
ference." Alphonse de Poitiers used precisely the same verbiage in
his order of 1269. Nonetheless, neither the popes nor the provincial hierarchies were really interested in the specific shape and
other particulars of the distinguishing marks. Before long red and,
particularly, yellow emerged as the preferred colors, partly because of their greater visibility (noted by Goethe) and, partly in
emulation of the long-accepted hues among the minorities of Muslim lands, while the size varied between one and six digits in
diameter. On the other hand, the aforementioned resolution of
the Salzburg synod of 1418 that Jewish women wear little bells remained a legislative curiosity and was not carried out even in that
archbishopric itself. Gregory IX's suggestion that the badge be
worn both front and back likewise found relatively little response.[35]

Not even the age at which Jews had to begin wearing badges was
uniformly established. While in England and in Marseilles children aged seven were told to display them, most laws provided
that men should begin wearing badges from the age of thirteen or
fourteen, women from that of twelve. Nor were the categories of
exempt persons universally accepted or even clearly spelled out.
For the most part Jews traveling from one city to another were exempted since badges might expose them to attack. Physicians were
also frequently given the courtesy of visiting the sick outside their
quarter without such outward signs, although the Marseilles Jewish doctors had to resort in 1384 to a strike during an epidemic of
dysentery before they were given a blanket dispensation. Special
exemptions were frequently granted also to Jewish communal
elders and rabbis, in addition to a host of royal or princely
protégés, either in return for a financial consideration, or out of
general favoritism so rampant throughout the Middle Ages. Sometimes, to be sure, the yellow wheels were minimized even by ordinary Jews. More remarkably, we find in a French manuscript, containing a collection of miracles of the Virgin and evidently written
by a pious Christian, a colorful presentation of a Jew clad in green
with a blue headgear. Although wearing a rose-colored cloak with
a wheel, half red and half white, sewn on the upper left side, this

Jew is presented in an impressive posture. Of course, other artists often depicted Jews in a less appealing, even repulsive or ludicrous, garb.[36]

In subsequent rationalizations, too, private biases readily came to the fore. Speculating on the shape of the Jewish wheel, which he equated with the letter O, a Latin writer, quoted by Johann Jacob Schudt, commented:

There is, my dear friend, a well-known question: Why does the Jew carry an O on his clothes? It is to serve as a permanent reminder of the painful O! for he is rightly subject to eternal sufferings in Hell. Also because we thus express naught in ciphers, for he ought to consider himself as nothing among men. Perhaps also because he lives from usury and, through the addition of this cipher, every number is multiplied [by ten].

This homily is no more fanciful than the explanation that the sign was to remind the Jews of criminals being broken on the wheel. Equally implausible is the suggestion that the wheel or ring was to remind Jews of their alleged desecrations of the host, although this hypothesis is somewhat supported by the parallel obligation of some Christian heretics, accused of using the Eucharist for magic incantations, to wear on their chests or shoulders two pieces of yellow felt in the shape of a host. They had to wear it, according to Inquisitor Bernard Gui, even while serving their life-terms in prison. However, the reverse may be true, and this heresy-identifying symbol may have been borrowed from the Jewish badge. In many German localities Jews were forced to wear both yellow wheels on their chests and yellow conical hats. In Swiss Schaffhausen the city council decreed in 1435 that Jewish residents and visitors should wear on their chests a red badge in the shape of a Jew hat. Historically naïve writers and theatrical performers often presented the ancient Jews, even Jesus himself, clad in such medieval Jewish attire. Paintings such as that of "Jesus Dressed in Purple" in Briga Marittima also depict Jesus wearing a high-pointed hat with a little horn. Similarly, in Peillon a painting of Jesus before Pilate, and another of Jesus scoffed at, show an even taller conical hat as well as a Turkish turban.[37]

Apart from its fiscal aspects, well illustrated for instance by the Paris manuscript recording the royal revenues in France during the years 1298–1301, the badge as such had commercial value. The daughter of an Avignonese Jewish physician, Dieulosal de Stella, borrowed money from another physician. As a pledge for that loan "she deposited with the lender two chests filled with clothing and jewels." As it turned out, they included silk badges for Jewesses, as well as a parchment roll containing the Book of Esther, and two prayer books for the use of Jewish women "in the vulgar Hebrew and Romance languages." It is small wonder, then, that ultimately the pertinent police ordinances became quite explicit; that issued in Tyrol in 1573 actually inserted a picture of the prescribed badge into the text of the ordinance itself. Nevertheless the sixteenth-century jurist Johannes Purgoldt, after describing provisions relating to the badge since their first enactment by Innocent III (whom he mistakenly called Innocent I), resignedly concluded: "Yet they [the Jews] walk around differently. This is but a sign that the princes prefer their gold to the honor of God and holy Christianity." The diverse local practices and their conflicting evaluations by contemporaries are also illustrated in the controversy between the Jews and the city of Ratisbon. In 1516 the Jews claimed that none of them aged fifteen years or more had appeared on the street without a badge. Two years later, the city council complained that, on the contrary, among twenty Jews not one displayed the badge openly, the majority concealing it under their cloaks or in the folds of their garments. Otherwise they usually covered it with their hands. In short, when this initial instrument of segregation was converted into a "badge of shame" some Jews resisted, openly or through some form of evasion, but many submitted to threats and, ultimately, also to the force of habit.[38]

OATHS MORE JUDAICO

Less pronounced was the initiative of ecclesiastical organs in elaborating the ceremonies connected with Jewish oaths, which must rather be attributed to the fervid imagination of an untold array of lay judges and litigants. Behind the various formulas loomed the conviction that no Jew could be trusted. This assumption which had led Byzantine lawgivers to disqualify Jews from testifying against Christians altogether, paralleling the rabbinic objections to non-Jews testifying against Jews, proved economically untenable even in Byzantium. In the West such total exclusion found emulators only in some local custumals, like that of twelfth-century Pisa, which provided that "no heretic, pagan, Jew or Saracen shall be heard against a Christian, when the Christian is unwilling." But even if admitted in court, the Jewish testimony was often impugned by the populace. The average Christian's suspicions, nurtured from the denunciations of Jewish "perfidy" by the theologians (at least as he understood this term without its fine theological nuances), were reinforced by the growing segregation during the Late Middle Ages. That one could not trust any Jew who, by both nature and the dictates of his law, was a cheat and a swindler, had become a commonplace in the medieval literary presentations of Jewish types. John Gower, in his *Confessio Amantis* (*ca.* 1392), makes his Jew proclaim:

> I am a Jewe, and by my lawe
> I shal to no man be felawe
> To keep him trouth in word ne dede.

In his Passion play Arnoul Greban heaps synonyms in calling ancient, and by implication also contemporary, Jewry "a false and perverse nation." The Semur Passion speaks of the "false canaille." [39]

From this general distrust gradually developed the awesome oath *more judaico* which, originally started in connection with the abjuration of recent converts, grew to ridiculous lengths and was often administered in ludicrous forms. The insistence of Jews themselves on very solemn oaths in their internal conflicts contributed to these extravagances. Although the formal talmudic oath taken while holding the Scroll of Laws (*bi-neqiṭat ḥefeṣ*) had largely been discontinued in the geonic age, it was revived in England and other Western lands. But these Jewish approaches were far overshadowed by a combination of legislative biases and popular prejudices. One or another cleric may have been responsible for the insertion of the numerous biblical curses which were to afflict the perjurer. Of ecclesiastical origin doubtless also was the very idea of such horrifying self-condemnations. But one can hardly attribute to the clergy the constant extensions of these formulas which sometimes, as in the Spanish kingdoms, reached the size of 1,500 to 2,000 words. Nor can one blame the Church for the use of similar lengthy maledictions in such purely political oaths of fealty as those sworn by the Paduan Jews to the government of Venice. Suffice it to cite the beginning of one such German formula included in the Gengler edition of the *Schwabenspiegel:*

He [the Jew] shall stand on a sow hide and shall hold his right hand up to his wrist in a volume in which are written the five books of Moses. And he who administers the oath to him shall say the following words which the Jew shall repeat after him: With respect to the objects for which this man sues you that you neither have nor know of them, nor have taken possession of them, nor have them buried in the earth, hidden in walls, or kept under lock; so help you God who created heaven and earth, valleys and mountains, forests, leaves and grass, and so help you the Law which God wrote with His own hand and gave it to the lord Moses on Mount Sinai; and so help you the five books of Moses. But that [if you lie] anything you eat will defile you as it did the king of Babylon; and sulphur and pitch shall rain upon your neck as it rained upon Sodom and Gomorrah; and the same pitch shall flow over you as it did over two hundred or more in Babylon; and the earth shall swallow you as it has Dathan and Abiram; and your soil shall never mingle with other soil nor your dust mingle with other dust in the bosom of Abraham. If you are true and right so help you Adonai. . . .

The oath continues with a series of further maledictions threatening the perjurer with Naaman's leprosy, the Egyptian plagues, and God's vengeance for the crucifixion of Jesus. The authors of this mixture evidently forgot that threats taken from the New Testament could hardly impress any non-Christian.[40]

Even these formidable oaths, however, failed to satisfy the suspicious populace and they had to be taken together with two or more compurgators. Perhaps some legislators realized that, while certain Jews may have been overawed by these horrifying threats, others doubtless found their very excesses ridiculous and paid little heed to them. In time recitation of the ever expanding formulas became too cumbersome for the judges, both Jewish and Christian. To call a halt, Pedro III and Alphonso III ordered in 1286 and 1290 that the lengthy declamations be copied in a book: by merely placing his hand on the volume and saying "Amen" the Jew would bring down upon himself the consequences of these curses. On the other hand, in his 1372 renewal of the law of 1360, Charles V of France explicitly stated that Jewish oaths should be credited only when the opposing Christian party had no persuasive proof to the contrary.[41]

On the whole, it appears, the medieval state was driven in this area by obscure religious and folkloristic forces welling up from the masses. Even where the oath itself was relatively moderate, courts (for instance, in Landshut) added preliminary admonitions intended to inspire awe in the parties or witnesses. Nor were these complex formulas limited to oaths taken on contentious subjects; one is recorded in connection with the simple ratification of an earlier sale of houses by a Jew of Ávila in 1464. At times, as in John Lackland's charter of 1201, the state actually tried to favor the Jewish creditor against the Christian debtor. According to J. M. Rigg's summary, "If a Jew were impleaded by a Christian who failed to produce testimony, he might purge himself by his bare oath on the Pentateuch, whereas in a similar case a Christian, as the law then stood, might be required to wage his law twelve-handed—i.e. with eleven compurgators." On the other hand, where royal self-interest was less one-sided, the government increased the number of persons whose oath had to support the Jewish party or witness against Christians.[42]

A medieval Cologne jurist was clearly wrong in asserting that the formula of the Jewish oath "had been ordered by the divinely appointed Roman emperors and from ancient times had been firmly observed in all Teuton territories." Certainly, the method recorded in an eleventh-century French manuscript actually ran counter to establish Carolingian procedures. According to that provision, whose cruelty was not paralleled until several generations later, one "ought to place on his [the Jew's] throat a wreath of thorns. The same is to be used as a girdle around the knees and a sharp thorny branch, five ells in length, shall be drawn between his thighs until he completes his oath. In this fashion he will purify himself of the accusation and come out unscathed." Not only had Jewish parties and witnesses been specifically exempted from all ordeals by Carolingian law, but this harsh performance clearly ran counter to the more closely Carolingian ceremony recorded in the so-called *Collectio judiciorum Dei*. Evidently that eleventh-century manuscript entry must have sprung from a zealot's overheated fantasy rather than from actual practice. But the constant elongation of the formula of the oath, as well as the consciously degrading ceremonies of placing the Jew on a sowhide or three-legged stool, clearly stemmed not from theological preconceptions but from crude popular fancy thus wishing to emphasize Jewish inferiority. Some ecclesiastical leaders actually frowned upon these humiliating accretions. In 1302, we recall, the archbishop of Cologne prohibited the submission of Jews to "unusual oaths." The bishop of Würzburg issued a similar enactment in 1414, although neither popes nor any outstanding Christian scholastics felt it incumbent upon themselves to interfere in this phase of the administration of justice by state or city. Nor were the penalties imposed upon a Jew falling off the stool and the numerous other petty and vengeful sanctions attributable to any deep lucubrations of friars poring over traditional tomes of Christian lore, but rather to the sadistic propensities of one or another uneducated burgher who happened to be in power.[43]

POLITICAL INFERIORITY

Medieval states were also guided, in part, by the Church's discriminatory postulates with respect to the Jews' occupational choices. But their economic policies, as we shall see in the next volume, were far more deeply affected by the demands of Christian competitors often conflicting with the rulers' attempts to protect the Jews' ability to pay taxes and by the changing economic conditions and class struggles in each country and locality.

Most direct was the Church's role in fostering political discrimination, particularly in barring Jews from positions of trust and confidence in the administration and armed forces of the Western states and cities. It could effectively invoke the withdrawal of the *honos militiae et administrationis* from Jews by the ancient Roman emperors. A Roman law of unspecified date had forbidden Jews to carry arms, and another of 404 had bluntly declared, "We consider that Jews and Samaritans . . . ought to be removed from any military service." A few years later St. Jerome, in his commentary on Isaiah, gloated over the fact "that all the dignity of combatants has been lost among Jews, for they have no right to fight with the sword or to carry arms." This discriminatory provision was repeated in subsequent Roman laws and served as a permanent reminder for medieval legislators.[44]

Rome's western successor states, to be sure, did not immediately follow its example. In a warlike age, when spring was known as the season in which kings went to war, no section of the population could entirely escape the brunt of belligerence. Certainly, when a city was besieged by a foreign enemy everyone, including the Jews, had to take up arms in its defense. During the Spanish *Reconquista,* especially, numerous Jewish "castles" and armed camps were established. Even later in Estella, Navarre, the Jews constructed their houses in such fashion as to help make the city's defenses impregnable. In Cologne the Jews were entrusted with the defense of the *Porta Judaeorum* in 1106 and long thereafter one still spoke there of a *propugnaculum Judaeorum,* showing that Jews were manning a part of the city's ramparts. During his war with Frederick the Handsome, Louis the Bavarian withdrew to the "fortified" cemetery of the Jews of Spires (1315). If German Jews did not take part in distant warlike expeditions, neither did the burghers, who as a rule fought only in behalf of their particular cities. It was truly an exception that Emperor Frederick II imposed upon the Vienna burghers in 1237 the obligation to participate in the empire's outside military ventures lasting one day. But all inhabitants, including clerics, knights, and Jews, were drafted for local defense so frequently that the great rabbinic authorities of the early thirteenth century, Eleazar b. Yehudah Roqeah of Worms and Isaac b. Moses Or Zaru'a of Vienna, permitted their coreligionists to take up arms on the Sabbath. In Spain, in particular, where the size of the Jewish population and its relatively elevated status made Jewish participation doubly desirable, many Jewish combatants were found alongside both Moors and Christians before and during the *Reconquista.* In 1342 Alphonso XI of Castile argued with Pope Clement VI for the retention of a newly erected synagogue in Seville because the Jews "contribute to the necessities of the city and not infrequently go out with the Christians against the Saracens, not fearing to expose themselves to death." As late as 1414 the recorder of the disputation of Tortosa spoke glowingly of some new Jewish converts belonging to the "military race called De la Cavalleria." For permanently manning the royal castle, combined as it was "with great costs and damages," the Jewish community of Soria was freed from all taxation by Henry III in 1397, a privilege renewed by Henry IV in 1455 and 1465. As late as 1474 John II of Aragon ordered the Jews of Cervera to take part in guarding the castle and to perform other necessary services, at least in wartime. It was not without justice that, as we recall, Isaac Or Zaru'a repeated Eliezer b. Joel ha-Levi's earlier observation that "it still is a general practice in Spain for the Jews to go out to war together with the king." [45]

Yet even in Spain the growing animosities favored the replacement of active Jewish participation by financial contributions. The development of medieval chivalry created a class of warriors which, with the aid of peons, conducted most foreign and civil wars. It was in the interest of these nobles to reduce the military services of all other estates, including the clergy, the burghers, and the Jews. Attempts were frequently made to withhold weapons from the very peasants, whose armed assistance was indispensable, and equip them only with knives or bows needed for self-defense, hunting, and the like. When toward the end of the Middle Ages hosts of mercenaries, led by skillful and ruthless *condottieri*, took the place of the feudal armies, personal services by all nonprofessional groups became less and less important. The thirteenth-century *fuero* of Ledesma simply exempted Jews from all military duties. The privilege granted by Infante Alphonso in 1320 to attract Jews to Alcolea included their exemption from all obligations and services, other than the payment of an annual rent of five solidi per house, except for the one inhabited by the communal rabbi. Not surprisingly, the Cortes of Monzón argued in 1376 against the royal demand for a general war tax by stating that "in the past [they] the Christians were wont to serve in person in all wars, and only the Jewish and Moorish communities used to give money to the king." It probably was more than sheer Jew-baiting which determined the Portuguese defenders of Lisbon against the Castilian besiegers in 1385 to remove both Jews and prostitutes from the city as useless for defense and a handicap in the task of feeding the famished population. Apart from outright taxes Jews contributed to their sovereigns' war efforts by billeting soldiers, although for various reasons they often preferred to replace this service, too, by cash payments.[46]

Most important were the Jewish fiscal and logistic services. Jewish financiers and suppliers of weapons, clothing, and food, often played major roles in Spanish wars. We need but remember the great share of Yehudah b. Labi de la Cavalleria and Astrug Jacob Xixon in preserving the kingdom of Valencia for the Aragonese Crown in the 1270s. Samuel b. Abraham Alfaquim (or Abinnaxim) not only served as court physician and royal secretary but in 1279 he arranged for the surrender of the Valencia Muslims and the sale of Muslim captives. He also prepared the charters to govern the Muslim subjects and collected their tribute. Like Joseph Ravaya and Yehudah aben Vives, he was taken along by the king to Sicily, both to assist in the campaign and to help administer the country. Other members of the families Ravaya and Portella negotiated with the royal vassals about the number of soldiers each had to levy; they equipped and fed the army and navy and, in general, helped organize the monarchy's contest against both the rebellious nobles and foreign enemies. By collecting in the 1360s the royal revenue and that due to the militant Knights of St. John (Hospitallers) Don Vidal de la Cavalleria was able to acquire the necessary equipment for a substantial cavalry force. Even a relatively obscure Jew, Genton de Narbona (a native of Narbonne?), was extolled by King Pedro IV of Aragon for the signal services he had rendered during the Aragonese campaign in Sardinia in 1354 and in the subsequent war with Castile in 1359. During the latter Genton lost all his possessions in Almunia because he had resisted the blandishments of the Castilian king and rather than enlist in the latter's services had escaped to Saragossa. On this occasion, one of Genton's brothers and a "sort of uncle" lost their lives, while another brother was carried away into Castilian captivity. In recognition, Pedro freed his faithful servant of all taxes and also of the obligation to wear the Jewish badge (1360, 1363).[47]

Local defense or substitute taxation was also a characteristic obligation of most Italian communities. While according to a law of 1408 the Jews of Messina were expected to defend their section of the city, those of neighboring Sciacca were given in 1402 the choice of paying annually twelve silver ounces in lieu of defending the castle. Several years earlier (1396–97) the community of Girgenti was ordered to equip a company of 200 men for a military expedition. Of unknown provenance was Sicilian Jewry's obligation to furnish flags for some royal castles and galleys, and in certain localities also to clean the castles. But as usual there were not only numerous exemptions for favored individuals, but also many local adjustments. The community of Piazza, for instance, had to furnish flags only once in three years (1408), that of Castroreale apparently performed that service for the first and only time in 1481, while that of Syracuse was completely exempted by a 1402 decree. Here, too, sooner or later Jewish personal services were transformed on the Italian mainland into some kind of taxes. In 1449 the Jews of Piedmont were first formally exempted from military service in return for the payment of 200 florins. Thenceforth, at the beginning of hostilities, the Jewish communities arranged with the government for the exact amounts they were to contribute, subject to revision if the war lasted longer than originally expected. A patriotic Jew, like Menaḥem b. Nathan of Rimini, a native of Rome, voluntarily left a legacy for the repair of the walls of the papal city (1392). Neither in Italy nor in Spain, however, were Jews ever prohibited from bearing arms. In Sicily they actually were the leading metal workers and manufacturers of weapons, so that their expulsion in 1492 inspired widespread apprehensions about their replacement. Similarly, at the time of their enforced conversion in 1496, Jews belonged to Portugal's eminent armorers. Evidently, the 1430 prohibition, included in Alphonso V's code, against Jews appearing armed at the welcoming festivities for the king was, for some unknown reason, limited to such occasions. A Provençal episode of 1355 is likewise illuminating. Here the Jewish self-defense was ironically found guilty of an attack on the Christians of Reillance and fined 2,000 gold florins. But this reprisal was not followed by any sweeping prohibition against Jews bearing arms.[48]

In the north the Jews' right to bear arms became an important issue. In England as early as 1181, we are told by Roger Howden,

Henry II ordered that "no Jew shall keep with him mail or hauberk, but let him sell or give them away, or in some other way remove them from him so that they may remain in the service of the king of England." This may have been a temporary measure, but the underlying idea that the Jew need not be armed for self-defense, since he was under special royal protection, although disproved by the acid test of the Third Crusade, must have played havoc with the Jews' military training in England just as similar erroneous assumptions were to help disarm Continental Jewry. True, exceptions are recorded. This was especially the case of certain converts who, almost immediately upon their baptism, joined the armed forces. One of them, Sir Henry of Winchester, became Henry III's special favorite. According to Edward I, his father had caused this soldier "freed from the Jewish error . . . to be decorated with the Belt of Knighthood out of his affection for him." Another, Roger le Convers, became the king's sergeant-at-arms and member of an élite corps of twenty royal bodyguards. He was one of five guards to accompany Henry III on his campaign in Gascony. But professing Jews became increasingly alienated from the use of arms.[49]

In the Holy Roman Empire matters were further complicated by the "peace" treaties in which, beginning in 1103, Jews were specifically included. Since their demonstrated defenselessness during the massacres of 1096 (even if we discount the underplaying of the Jewish self-defense by contemporary chroniclers, both Jewish and Christian), they, like the women, clerics, and merchants, were given special protection by the royal power with the assistance of imperial lords. With the progress of "peace" legislation went also a progressive disarming of the protected groups which were not supposed to enjoy the double protection of special treaties and personal arms. True, the higher clergy often took an active part in wars. According to Caesarius of Heisterbach, "almost all the bishops of Germany and most abbots use both kinds of swords for the defense and welfare of their subjects." But the lower clergy required special protection and was, like the Jews, forbidden to carry arms. Even with respect to the pursuit of criminals, an obligation resting on the whole population, the *Schwabenspiegel* taught that "clerics, women, sextons, shepherds, and Jews shall not participate in the pursuit personally; but they shall help either by sending substitutes or by contributing materials toward it." Clerics were indeed so often linked together with Jews in legal documents and artistic presentations (for instance, in the illuminated manuscripts of the *Sachsenspiegel*) that the fourteenth-century jurist Johann von Buch felt prompted to remark in his gloss on the *Sachsenspiegel*, "Note here the great difference: weapons are forbidden to priests and clerics for their own honor; they are forbidden to Jews for their ignominy." [50]

German Jews had an additional incentive to abstain from the use of arms as their allegiance to the emperor was increasingly diluted and shared by that to princes, bishops, and cities who were often at odds with one another. Jews doubtless thought it the better part of wisdom not to get involved in the ensuing conflicts. Certainly, the defense of Worms in 1201 against King Otto, which induced Eleazar Roqeaḥ to permit the use of arms on the Sabbath, must have served as a warning of future troubles if they were found defending a losing cause. Under these circumstances, we rarely hear of Jewish fighters in the northern lands where Jewish segregation and anti-Jewish discrimination were at their height. A Zurich Jew, Seligmann, was expelled from the city in the fifteenth century allegedly for no other reason than for his standing one night behind the synagogue equipped with a sword. This whole legislation, whether pursuing anti-Jewish or pro-Jewish objectives, necessarily contributed to the strengthening of the traditional pacifist trends in Jewish social theory and practice.[51]

Neither the rulers nor the majority of Jews were keenly interested in retaining or recapturing the latter's *honos militiae*. But the *honos administrationis* became a more direct bone of contention between state and Church. On principle, the ancient Roman Empire had already excluded Jews and Samaritans from "all administrative offices and dignities" in 438. This law, appended to the Theodosian Code, was repeated by Justinian and was reemphasized by such ecclesiastical writings as the fifth-century *Altercatio ecclesiae et synagogae* which linked this prohibition with the Church's general contention that the Jewish people had become its serf. That is why it primarily stressed the exclusion of Jews from higher offices, which gave the officeholders a measure of control over their subordinates and the public at large. But the implication of all such legal and ecclesiastical rhetoric was that public service of any kind was to be denied to Jews.[52]

In the Middle Ages, however, violations of this principle multiplied. Kings and municipalities benefited from employing Jews in various public and semipublic offices. Fiscal administration, in particular, required the assistance of numerous Jewish tax and toll collectors, as well as semipublic tax farmers. The very Carolingian Empire seems to have made sufficient use of Jewish advisers to lend credence to St. Agobard's exaggerated complaints of Jewish "insolence" and domination over Christians. Popes, too, time and again protested against the employment of Jewish officials, invoking in particular the decisions of the Toledan Councils of 589 and 633. Innocent III persuaded the Fourth Lateran Council to include in its resolutions a special canon (lxix) which read:

Since it is perfectly absurd that a blasphemer of Christ should exercise power over Christians, We, because of the audacity of the transgressors, renew in this General Council the decision of the Council of Toledo [of 589]. We forbid the preferment of Jews in public offices for, under such a pretext, they are able greatly to injure Christians. Should, however, anyone entrust them with such an office he shall, after due warning, be censured by the provincial council—which We order to be assembled annually in the district in which it will meet—by measures at its discretion. At the same time all commercial and other intercourse with Christians shall be denied to such a [Jewish] official until he shall turn over to the use of poor Christians, at the discretion of the diocesan bishop, all that he had earned from Christians through the exercise of his office. He shall also be dishonorably discharged from the office which he had so irreverently assumed. This prohibition extends also to pagans [Muslims].

Violations persisted, however. If under pressure of the Vienna burghers Emperor Frederick II promised, in 1237, to exclude Jews from higher offices and, as in other cases, hypocritically contended that this regulation was enacted in "faithful execution of Catholic principles," he added that it had also been done because from ancient times the imperial authority had imposed perpetual serfdom upon Jews. Perhaps influenced by Frederick, Alphonso X likewise waxed rhetorical and, in his code of laws, emphasized the decline of Jews who had once been "the most honored of peoples and had great distinction over all other nations." But they had become dishonored because of their part in the crucifixion of Christ. Hence the ancient emperors had removed them from all dignities and privileges "in a fashion that no Jew should ever find himself honored by a public office with which he might oppress any Christian in whatever manner." But it was left, as we recall, to Castile's intolerant regime of 1408 to threaten the appointees with flogging and a severe fine for accepting office! [53]

Pledges not to employ Jews in high offices were sometimes entered even in international treaties, as in the aforementioned agreement between the Spanish conquerors of Tudela and its Muslim population, or that of the French Crusaders and Count Raymond VI of Toulouse in 1209. Nonetheless they were often disregarded in the face of political and economic imperatives. Even popes and archbishops (for instance, the elector of Treves) made occasional use of Jewish court bankers, while Ratisbon Jewish leaders were able in 1297 effectively to mediate between the archbishop of Salzburg and the Bavarian duke. Since this problem loomed very large in many countries of Jewish settlement, particularly on the Iberian Peninsula, constant reference to it was made in my treatment of the individual lands. Its economic facets, especially relating to Jewish tax collectors, tax farmers, and physicians (these occupations were sometimes combined in the same persons), will be analyzed more fully in the next volume. We may, therefore, merely conclude with the generalization that Jewish services were most frequently utilized during periods of a country's initial upbuilding or reconstruction, while in eras of comparative stability they could more readily be dispensed with, enabling the rulers to salve their own consciences.[54]

UNIQUE CORPORATION

In this fashion the ecclesiastical doctrine of "Jewish serfdom" underwent a secular reinterpretation to fit the needs and ambitions of Holy Roman emperors and other rulers. While the Church stressed above all Jewish inferiority, the monarchs were more interested in the Jews' direct allegiance and tax payments, as well as their own reciprocal obligations to protect their Jewish "treasure." True, emperors and kings, as well as their bureaucratic

and juridical advisers, often fell back on the ecclesiastical terminology. But, on the whole, their Jewish serfs resembled much
more the Muslim "protected subjects" than contemporary Christian villeins. As a result of many political and socioeconomic developments an ever stronger alliance was thus forged between the
Jewish corporate group and the imperial or royal power which,
though exposing the Jews to both individual whims and storms of
social discontent and political disequilibrium, safeguarded some of
their fundamental rights.

In many details, however, the rulers yielded to outside pressures. We shall see how deeply popular beliefs and biases, even
total misconceptions, were to color the status of medieval Jewry.
The state constantly had to take into account these popular prejudices, as well as the canonical teachings (often strongly abetted by
public opinion) and certain rock bottom demands of the Jewish
community itself, particularly its unwavering insistence on full
liberty of conscience and a large measure of communal self-
determination. Out of the welter of the ensuing contradictory regulations and practices emerged many compromises acceptable to
both the state and the Jews; to the latter under the guise of recognition of "the law of the kingdom." Characteristically, the Church
supported Jewish autonomy as an eminent means of reinforcing
the type of segregation which it constantly preached. If, as a result
of these segregationist policies, Jews had to accept also physical
separation in Jewish quarters and even the more heartily resented
badge and oath *more judaico,* the general impact of these things
helped to strengthen the inner bonds of Jewry.

Some individuals, to be sure, found the atmosphere created by
such water-tight separation quite stifling. Certainly, the Jewish
grandees of Castile, Aragon, or Portugal, of Italy, and the Provence, must have resented the contemptuous treatment frequently
meted out to them by the very nobles who depended on their
bounty or needed their support at court. Jewish intellectuals
collaborating on joint scholarly projects with non-Jewish scholars
sooner or later ran up against a wall of misunderstanding and
atavistic prejudice, which neither they nor their colleagues could
rationally explain. Despite it all, Jews and Christians often maintained far closer social relations (even in the obscure realm of sex)

than one might expect in the light of the stringent segregationist laws and preaching on both sides. But at critical moments there was little reliance on purportedly close friends. Many sensitive Jews, unprepared to make the fateful final step toward conversion, must have decided to withdraw into their Jewish shells. They shared the sentiments expressed by that remarkable Jewish troubadour, Süsskind von Trimberg, who after some years of wandering from one princely court to another, felt utterly rejected and lonesome. Returning to his own people, he sang in parting,

> Henceforth I'll grow a beard, long and grey,
> And live in the old Jewish fashion,
> Quietly proceed along my way,
> Wrapped in a cloak fitting my station.
>
> Deep under my hat which I shall sport
> I shall walk humbly and sadly brood,
> No longer singing the songs of court,
> Since the lords turned me away from their good.[55]

Less acceptable appeared the legal discrimination practiced by the state. While nonadmission to military service and, ultimately, the prohibition to bear arms evoked little articulate resistance from the ever more pacifically attuned Jews, exclusion from public office could have serious consequences. Apart from thus being shut out from an important source of livelihood, the Jewish masses had good reasons to fear the disappearance of influential Jewish officials and courtiers from the councils of state. The *shtadlanut*, that medieval form of lobbying before kings and dignitaries, had become the most important facet of Jewish political activity; in fact, a major safeguard against impulsive and irresponsible acts of rulers. The possible elimination of Jewish advisers to kings and dignitaries loomed, therefore, as a major threat to the very survival of Western Jewry, and most Jewish communities preferred to pay the unavoidable price of occasional sharp retributions for the unsuccessful involvement of such leaders in political intrigues and financial manipulations.

In any case, most Jews realized that they had to rely heavily upon their own resources. Certainly, if the generally rigid hierarchy of orders in medieval society and the submission of the masses of peons to the arbitrary will of the ruling classes were partly mitigated by the Christian idea of charity, Jews, as a religious minority, often despised and haunted, could expect relatively little charity from their neighbors. As a rule they could appeal only to the latter's self-interest. This harsh reality became particularly noticeable in the complex domain of economic endeavor with its numerous discriminatory features which were mitigated only by society's obvious need, so long as it lasted, of Jewish services and contributions. But the realization of the Jews' long-range social usefulness presupposed more sophistication than was possessed by the easily swayed Christian masses which were prone to look for more immediate advantages, or to follow their own deep-rooted prejudices.

"DEMONIC" ALIEN

POPULAR tensions magnified the effects of the discriminatory policies of Church and state. Even the Church, which through the centuries maintained its general polarity of permitting Jews to persist while lowering their social standing, was often deeply affected by the spread of popular prejudices. Its central organs may have stressed toleration in intolerant periods and discrimination in times of relative good will, but on local and regional levels many clerics shared the biases of their lay neighbors. Particularly parish priests and wandering monks, whose education in the principles of Catholic theology and familiarity with the basic decisions of Papacy or universal councils was quite limited, often shared with the peasants and urban proletariat the popular views on Jews and Judaism. In time, the official doctrine itself began to embrace folkloristic elements and, through its local priestly spokesmen, reciprocally helped to color the popular preconceptions concerning the nature of the ever puzzling Jewish minority.

Nor could the vagaries of state policies counteract the circulation of uncontrolled rumors and accusations. Certainly, the main reasons advanced for the toleration of the Jewish people, namely the latter's usefulness to the state treasuries and, on the theological level, its function as witness for the Christian tradition, carried little conviction among the masses. On the other hand, the sharply discriminatory legislation, the relegation of Jews to quarters of their own, their different attire and badges, the awe-inspiring ceremonies connected with the Jewish oath, and the numerous other measures designed to emphasize the inferiority of the people "accursed" by Christ could only intensify the existing hatreds and suspicions. If a farmer or artisan felt aggrieved by exactions of a Jewish moneylender, if he fell victim to machinations of an unscrupulous Jewish merchant or agent—even if his injury was more imaginary than real—he was prone to condemn the whole people whose morality was officially impugned by the intellectual leaders of both Church and state. On the other hand, whenever revolutionary movements of one kind or another sought to overthrow the existing order, Jews served as immediate targets because of the services they had willingly, or forcibly, rendered to the powers that were. Under these circumstances the most outrageous accusations against Jews found ever-willing rumormongers helping to spread them and large segments of the public prepared to believe them.

Growing secularization of European letters and the invention of printing toward the end of the Middle Ages merely aggravated the situation. They not only stimulated the output of polemical pamphlets, biased storiettes, folksongs, and ballads, but also greatly facilitated their dissemination among peoples of the same speech and, via translations, also in other lands. The gradual secularization of the European theater may have removed its earlier concentration upon Passion plays, that perennial focus of anti-Jewish contagion. But it also opened the floodgates to the presentation of unsavory Jewish characters from all walks of public and private life, simultaneously reflecting and intensifying the popular aversions. The stage, in both its original presentations and its ever more numerous adaptations and imitations, thus became an instrument of anti-Jewish warfare, both nationally and internationally. Long before the early 1600s, when Marlowe's *Jew of Malta* and Shakespeare's *Merchant of Venice* became an integral part of the Continental repertories, many an anti-Jewish play had been translated or adapted from one language to another and presented in theaters of many lands.

UNBRIDGEABLE CHASM

Popular antagonisms to Jews appeared under many guises. Unlike the official policies, which were reflected in fairly circumspect decrees and canons, they found expression in the uncontrolled, often anonymous and undatable folk literature and art. It made little difference whether the folk writers and artists knew Jews from direct contact or whether they saw in them mere symbols derived from literature or oral tradition. There was an undiminished output of anti-Jewish legends and narratives in countries where no Jews had lived for several generations. Some writers adumbrated the modern antisemitic adage that their own "best friends" were Jews, but that the generality of Jews was bad. The humanist Konrad Mutian (1471–1526) unblushingly confessed, "I hate the circumcised people, although there are many good men among them who have earned my personal gratitude [*de me bene meriti*]." Above all, the idea of the Jew as Christianity's great antagonist became an integral part of the average man's outlook on the world. One writer and artist after another gave free rein to his imagination in depicting the alleged atrocities and crimes committed by Jews. A medieval German poet wrote, "The children of God that we are,/poisonous worms that you are;/if we were by you controlled,/as you in our power are enrolled,/no Christian would survive the year." This sentiment was reechoed by such diverse Christian personalities as Martin Luther and the seventeenth-century Catholic preacher, Abraham a Sancta Clara. In one of his sermons Abraham exclaimed with total abandon: "After Satan Christians have no greater enemies than the Jews. . . . They pray many times daily that God should destroy us Christians through pestilence, famine and war, aye, that all beings and creatures may rise up with them against the Christians. Can greater scoundrels than these Jews be found anywhere in the whole world?" Not surprisingly, Fritz Kynass, a student of German folklore, has observed that "there exist no [medieval German] folksongs revealing a friendly attitude to Jews." [1]

At times metaphors casually used by homilists resulted in unexpected elaborations by popular fancy. Back in the sixth century St. Caesarius of Arles merely restated the old ecclesiastical doctrine of ancient Israel having been displaced by the new dispensation in saying that "when the apostles' doctrine was transferred to the Gentile nations only the leprosy of sin remained with the miserable Jews." He probably did not anticipate that some listeners might literally connect the Jews with lepers—a connection which in later centuries was to have dire consequences for both groups. Nor did the Christian preachers, who forced Jews to attend their missionary sermons, foresee that, for instance, in Marsala the Jews returning from such forced performances would regularly be pelted with stones by the populace (until forbidden to do so by King Martin in 1399), which would obviously nullify any success of these sermons. Other preachers, however, more consciously helped spread the venom by their own imaginative elaborations of both the traditional lore of the Church and the newly alleged horrors of Jewish behavior. From Agobard to Bernardino da Feltre, indeed through the ages, there were many examples of anti-Jewish pulpit demagoguery. In many details, however, these preachers were disciples, rather than teachers, of a mass of nameless lay Jew-baiters.[2]

Hostility was aggravated by the ambiguity of the term "Jew." In the earlier Middle Ages descent from Jews was not considered a blemish and, in many parts of Europe, distinguished Christian families bore, without any embarrassment, the family name of "Jew" or some variant thereof. Under the growing tensions of the Crusades, however, the term assumed an increasingly pejorative connotation. Had not even St. Bernard of Clairvaux, who in the crucial year 1146 had saved many central-European Jewish communities, equated *judaizare* with usury? Certainly, his rejection of "Antipope" Anacletus II as "Jewish offspring" added its share to the deterioration of the Jewish image in intellectual circles. The accusation of "Judaizing," hurled upon one another with increasing frequency by Christian sectarians, must also have reinforced the picture of the Jew as the great enemy of the established religion. On the Iberian Peninsula, finally, the rise of the large class of *conversos* tended to blur the distinction between a professing and a converted Jew. Harping on Mohammed's legendary animal which was neither male nor female, neither horse nor mule, the author of the *Libro del Alborayque* assailed the Jews' similarly equivocal character (*ca.* 1488). By 1496, four years after all professing Jews had left Spain, Juan del Encina contended that "one no longer knows in these domains and kingdoms what the Jews really are."[3]

Medieval legends frequently combined miracle stories with alleged Jewish crimes against Christianity. That Jews "blasphemed" was the more readily believed, as the mere denial of the divinity and messiahship of Jesus, his virgin birth, and other

Christian dogmas, was tantamount to blasphemy in the eyes of many pious Christians. The few Christians even remotely familiar with the distorted descriptions of the lives of Jesus and Mary in the crudely anti-Christian *Toledot Yeshu* (Life of Jesus), unquestioningly believed that Jewish minds were constantly preoccupied with these "execrable" tales. With the late medieval growth of the veneration of the Virgin in the West, Jews were increasingly accused not only of verbal attacks, but also of direct assaults on statues and paintings of Mary. In view of the widespread belief among Christian masses that possession of an image of the Virgin was the most effective means of warding off demons and staving off diseases, its destruction or defacement was considered both an unpardonable religious offense and a deprivation of families or communities of this sort of supernatural insurance against elementary catastrophes and personal misfortunes. Even so enlightened a monarch as Alphonso X of Castile could sing about Mary that "God could not refuse her anything." True, the king's *cantigas*, from which this statement is taken, contain both pro- and anti-Jewish verses. Others, however, generalized a few incidents, real or alleged, to blame the whole Jewish people. In retribution, many a city (for instance, Ratisbon and Rothenburg in 1519–20), after expelling its Jews, gave the name of Mary to the church consecrated in the place of the old synagogue. Even in Sicily, we recall, several hundred Jews lost their lives in 1474 under the battle cry, "Long live the Virgin and death to the Jews!" [4]

Naturally enough such assaults, actual or imagined, gave rise to many miracle tales. In poetry and prose, in graphic presentation or learned discourse we are told how the assailants were betrayed by the miraculous bleeding or loud outcries of the damaged statue or painting. They were speedily apprehended and executed unless they repented and accepted conversion. A combination of legends uniting the elements of Jewish blasphemies with retribution by demons describes how one midnight a Jewess performed an obscene act before an effigy of the Virgin displayed at the gate of Capua. Thereupon she was seized by two devils and tortured to death. Another Jewess, who expectorated upon a painting, was torn to pieces by a wolf, doubtless another agent of supernatural retribution. Many of these legends, originating in the eastern

Mediterranean, migrated from country to country and reappeared in ever new formulations embellished by the fertile imagination of Western writers and storytellers. Nor was their dissemination completely disinterested. From time to time a shrine was erected to commemorate such a miracle; it soon attracted pilgrims and sick people in search of miraculous healing, and became an important source of income for the church or monastery which owned it.[5]

Occasionally, several localities shared in the benefits of such relics. The piercing of a Christ painting by a Jew as early as 468 had purportedly resulted in blood flowing from the wound, which, distributed through many lands, performed miracles for many centuries thereafter; for instance, in Mantua, as asserted by Pope Leo to Charlemagne. Another miracle arose from a religious controversy between a Christian, blind from birth, and a Jew, who finally offered to accept conversion if the Virgin were miraculously to heal his opponent's blindness. After the latter composed a *responsorium,* in which he "confuted the Jew's errors in a lively fashion," the two disputants met on Candlemas day. The Christian recited his *responsorium* and immediately regained his vision, whereupon fully 500 Jews, including the original skeptic, are said to have adopted Christianity. More significantly, at the pope's order, that *responsorium* was regularly recited on Candlemas Day in Rome. Such legends and folk-tales often achieved greater respectability among the educated classes when they were dramatized by poets of distinction. Early in the sixteenth century Pamphilus Gengenbach composed a lyric entitled "Five Jews" on the theme of the so-called sacrilege of Cambron, which had created a sensation in 1326. Here the main instigator of the attack on a painting of the Virgin in the county of Hainaut (Gengenbach does not mention Cambron) was finally convicted when he lost his duel with a smith who had witnessed the atrocity. A remarkable aspect of that long poem, however, is not the customary dramatic sequence of miracles or even the fact that the Jew was allowed to defend his cause by the ordeal of a duel (Jews had been exempted from ordeals since Carolingian times) but that he continued to deny his guilt despite indescribable tortures. Even more interesting is the purported indifference of a monk who, together with the smith, had witnessed the profanation, as well as that of the abbot and the parish priest to whom it had been reported—all of whom, we are told, tried to quash the prosecution. Emphasis on such indifference may have stemmed from the poet's anticlerical bias. But it doubtless also reflected in part the reality that both ecclesiastical and state organs often tried to exert a moderating influence in the face of such folkloristic accusations.[6]

Of course, some stories may have contained a kernel of truth. That, in reaction to the atmosphere of hatred in which they constantly lived, some Jews may have thrown all caution to the winds appears quite likely. Nor was the Jewish community devoid of its share of deranged persons and criminals, some of whom may have used their contacts with powerful individuals to escape punishment. Matthew Paris describes at length the various crimes committed in 1250 by Abraham of Berkhamsted, a friend of Henry III's brother Richard, Earl of Cornwall. Abraham not only desecrated a picture of the Virgin but also slew his wife for cleaning off the dirt from the Virgin's face. We recall that, because of his "other heavy crimes," the Jewish elders themselves offered 1,000 marks to the earl for Abraham's execution but that he got away with paying a fine of 700 marks to the Treasury. Occasional violent Jewish reactions to conversionist efforts intensified popular ill feeling. It was unusual for a German folksong to depict, with some sympathy, the sufferings of a Jewish girl who, unable to marry her Christian suitor without undergoing conversion, had committed suicide by drowning. More typical was the destruction of the entire community of Clermont in the sixth century when, as we recall, a Jewish assailant poured rancid oil on the head of a former coreligionist, evidently wishing to deride the Christian use of oil for unction. Later Christian folklore ascribed to Jews a more disgusting method of undoing baptism. According to Caesarius of Heisterbach the mother of a converted Jewish girl tried to bring her back to Judaism. Upon learning that the sacrament of baptism was permanent (or indelible, as the jurists styled it), the mother suggested that the sacramental water be washed off by a threefold immersion in human excrements. This narrative doubtless is a throwback to another popular legend describing the devil who, having accidentally fallen into holy water, tried to undo the ensuing damage to his demonic powers by this type of immersion, as well as to the attribution to Jews of a peculiar Jewish body odor which was removed by baptism. A relapsing Jew required such an odiferous ablution to get back his stench.[7]

Another highly popular story, which appeared in many languages and with numerous variations, recited the miracle of a Jewish boy whose clandestine conversion so aroused his father's ire that he was thrown into a blazing furnace. This age-old theme, reminiscent of the Jewish legends concerning trials by fire successfully weathered by Patriarch Abraham and other ancient heroes, was now applied to the youthful convert who, owing to the personal intervention of the Virgin, remained unscathed. Most versions conclude with the aroused Christian populace throwing the heartless father into the flames. Other legends depict the saving of young Jewesses, seduced by Christians and subsequently baptized, from their fathers' revenge by the personal intercession of Mary or Jesus. While this intervention, too, is often followed by the severe punishment of the obstreperous father, many versions prefer to climax the narrative by the father's admission of error and his conversion, singly or together with other Jews. A would-be female convert, allegedly saved by the Virgin from being thrown off a cliff by irate Jews of Segovia, was immortalized in one of Alphonso X's *Cantigas* and in a painting displayed at the Segovia Cathedral. Needless to say, if some unexpected turn of events helped the Jews, this was interpreted not as a divinely ordained "miracle," but as the effect of a lawless intervention by Satan, the Jews' ally. When a planned mass conversion of the Jews of Treves was defeated in 1066 by the sudden death of the hostile Archbishop Eberhard while he conducted services at the cathedral, this coincidence was readily attributed by the Christian chronicler to the magic spell cast by the Jews upon the archbishop.[8]

Understandably, Jewish attacks on Jesus and Mary were more frequently verbal than physical. Reports of such Jewish "blasphemies," though not as frequent as one might expect, reach us from various countries and periods. In Huesca a Dominican monk accused in 1305 one of the city's wealthiest Jews, Açac de Çalema (Isaac b. Solomon), of having uttered "such a great blasphemy that one could not repeat it or hear it without tears." It allegedly referred to Jesus' birth from an adulterous mother and his having been a magician, themes often repeated in the anti-Christian folk-loristic literature. The Dominican appealed to King James II for exemplary punishment of the blaspheming Jew who, through bribery, had been released on bail by the governor. Similarly, in 1487 the Catholic monarchs ordered the imprisonment of one Abraham Farache (Harache) of Aguilar de Campóo because of unspecified blasphemies against the Virgin. The authorities were also to sequester his property until after his trial before the royal court. Astonishing as such audacity may be in the face of threat-ened reprisals, quite a few Jews seem to have lost their tempers at least during religious altercations with Christians. The danger of immediate retribution is well illustrated by another homily by Caesarius of Heisterbach relating to a Paris debate during which the Jewish spokesman disrespectfully commented under his breath about Jesus' flight reported in the Gospels. He was hit over the head by a zealous student in the audience who exclaimed, "And you miserable creature would not have been hit by me with this vise had you kept quiet and fled." In a lighter vein Heinrich Bebel, an early sixteenth-century humorist, depicted a disputation during which the Jew slapped the Christian's face and demanded that the latter turn the other cheek to him. The Christian admin-istered him a severe thrashing instead, justifying it by a gloss on the pertinent New Testament verse. The discussion ended amica-bly enough with the Jew exclaiming, "I see that your gloss is much harsher than your text." [9]

Enmity toward individual Christians, as well as toward the Christian faith as such, was supposed to be deep-rooted among Jews. Taking a cue from the official literature, both theological and legal, the writers of numerous Passion plays and other popular poems saw in Jewish "perfidy" a typical Jewish trait. The figure of Judas Iscariot loomed large in many of these betrayal themes, as it did in the general imagination of Christian peoples. Many medie-val pilgrims visited Judas' reputed Palestinian grave, which some believed was especially selected and a chapel built on it in the traitor's honor by the Palestinian Jews. Pious poets gave free rein to their sadistic impulses in depicting in much gory detail Judas' sufferings in hell. His name was also used prominently in incanta-tions and proverbs, as in the very popular French adage, "Fire lose

thy heat, just as Judas lost his color while betraying the Saviour."
It did not require too much imagination to view his personality as
typical of the whole Jewish people, whose heart was supposed to
be filled with rancor and the desire to betray its Christian hosts.
Characteristically, many German playwrights were more implacable in their condemnation of Judas' suicide than of his treachery.
They may thus have given vent to their resentment of Jewish
heroism during the great massacres when entire communities
chose self-destruction for the "sanctification of the name" of the
Lord, rather than apostasy.[10]

Representative of many Passion plays is that by Arnoul Gréban
which includes the exclamation put into the mouth of the Virgin,
"These accursed Pharisees from whom nothing comes but trea-
son!" Gréban also presents the ancient Jewish priests inciting the
Romans against Jesus as a rebel, an advocate of communism and of
tax dodging. At the same time, like other medieval writers, he de-
nounces the Jews themselves as the perennial rebels and traitors.
These religio-political accusations became particularly vehement
whenever Christianity was threatened by Islam, many Spanish
writers, such as Alphonso de Spina, harping on the alleged alliance
of Moors and Jews against their Christian overlords. Some Spanish
authors were more sympathetic to the Moors and paid homage at
least to their chivalry and bravery, but, in general, the two faiths
were linked together as Christendom's chief enemies. No less a figure than Dante Alighieri found little more blameworthy in the
behavior of Pope Boniface VIII, the "leader of the modern
Pharisees," than his waging war on his neighbors, the Colonnas,
rather than on Jews and Saracens, the common enemies of the
Church. Finally, this conception of the ever treacherous Jew began coloring also the late medieval arts. Unlike the dignified, if
defeated, figure of the Synagogue at the Strasbourg cathedral,
many medieval paintings in Italy, France, and Germany displayed
in a more or less conspicuous place that of a scorpion (sometimes
provided with the sign Sigma, the initial of the synagogue) as the
symbolic representation of Jewish perfidy.[11]

Preconceptions of this kind gave stimulus to, and were in turn
nurtured by, the widespread popular belief in the alliance between Jews and Antichrist. Interdenominational folklore, reach-

ing back to ancient times, had long postulated the appearance of an anti-messiah who would establish a tyrannical, if short-lived, empire immediately before the final advent of the redeemer. This sequence was now elaborated in endless folk tales and legends among Jews, Christians, and Muslims alike. The Christians borrowed some features of their Antichrist from the Armilus legends of the Jewish Aggadah, which reciprocally owed a great deal to the lucubrations of Christian mystics and storytellers. In the Christian legend Antichrist was often a Jew, sometimes one born from a union between a Jewess and Satan. Just as the Muslim legend depicted the *dajjal* as arising in the Jewish quarter of Isfahan, so did many Christian legends place the birth of Antichrist in Babylon or another Middle-Eastern country from where, supported by descendants of the tribe of Dan or other survivors of the Lost Ten Tribes, he would spread his reign of terror through the Western lands.

As early as the mid-tenth century Adson of Toul contended that, on his appearance, Antichrist would claim to be the messiah arisen to save the Jews. The latter would then gather in his support, without realizing at first that they had thus become the unwitting allies of the devil. In thirteenth-century Tortosa a Jew taking his characteristic oath was made to swear "by the Messiah who is called Antichrist for whom you yearn." All these elements were well united in Peter de Blois' *Contra perfidiam Judaeorum* which concludes with the following exhortation to Christian readers:

You thus have arms sent you for the defence of the Faith, use them carefully. For the Jew is always inconstant and shifty. At times he affirms, at times he negates, he quibbles about the literal meaning, or he refers all matters to the times of his own messiah, that is of the Antichrist. After the manner of the devil, his father, he often changes into monstrous shapes. If therefore you wish to apprehend him and stop his transformations, place the library of the Spirit between you so that he may not escape or turn tail but must be slain like Goliath with his own sword.

Even an eminent jurist like Richard de Morins, who had taught canon law in Bologna, after becoming the prior of Dunstable unabashedly reported that he had a vision of two Jews announcing the forthcoming birth of Antichrist. The havoc played by such conceptions was intensified by the deep concern of the masses, particularly in any major European crisis, about Antichrist's forthcoming appearance. Throughout the Middle Ages the idea of an impending end of the world was extremely vivid. We have John Calvin's testimony that "in the Catholic world [papatu] nothing is more widely discussed and well-known than the prospective coming of Antichrist." Even Professor Heinrich von Langenstein of the University of Vienna saw in the "rise of Jewry" portents for such an advent and figured out that, with the help of Jewish money, Antichrist would conquer the world in two and a half years. A number of German plays, too, were devoted to Antichrist and the terrors he was to bring upon the world. True, Jews were not the only culprits. Any group opposing one's own dogma could be stamped Antichrist's ally. Calvin himself, frequently equating Antichrist with the papacy, concludes his aforementioned diatribe: "But they themselves [the Catholics] are so stupid as not to feel the tyranny imposed by him on their necks." [12]

Students of the medieval Passion plays and other semiliturgical performances have long noted a progressive sharpening and vulgarization of the anti-Jewish attitudes. Perhaps the very proliferation of the Easter and Passion plays, as against the Nativity plays performed during the more important Christmas season, was owing not only to the greater dramatic appeal of Jesus' sufferings and death, but also to the opportunity it gave to playwrights and actors to vent their anti-Jewish spleens. One recurrent theme in these plays was derived from a pseudo-Augustinian sermon about efforts by ancient Israelitic prophets to persuade the Jews to recognize Jesus' true messiahship. Like the original sermon, the early plays placed the Jewish spokesmen on a level of parity and made them present their arguments with much dignity. As late as the thirteenth century the so-called Munich Nativity depicted Augustine as presiding over an assembly with Isaiah, Daniel, and the other Israelitic prophets seated on his right, while the "archisynagogus" and his Jewish associates were flanking him to his left. But the Passion play performed in Frankfort in 1469, 1498, and 1506 is not only far cruder in its language with its mixture of German and Latin, but the Jews are presented as haughtily rejecting the Christian message. Sometimes the Jews are made to speak a gibberish reminding the listeners of Hebrew sounds but, in fact, devoid of any meaning. Even the influential city elder of Lucerne, Renward

Cysat (1545–1614), included in the Passion play he produced with great éclat in his home city (from which Jews had long disappeared) a number of supposed Jewish chants consisting of a "strange mixture of sense and nonsense." Cysat admitted that he had used odds and ends of eighteen different languages, including an extremely distorted Hebrew, to ridicule the ancient Jews of Jerusalem and, by indirection, also his Jewish contemporaries.[13]

Another recurrent theme stemmed from the ancient *Altercatio ecclesiae et synagogae* which was now dramatized into a progressive disputation on the merits of the Christian faith. Here, too, in both the text and the accompanying directions for producers, the original equality between the Church and the Synagogue was gradually abandoned. At first, both these figures appear as queens conducting themselves with high dignity, although the debate invariably ends with the Synagogue's defeat and the breaking of her scepter. Later texts present her in a clearly inferior posture: her spokesmen are no longer learned rabbis, but usurers and petty traders who argue their case from the standpoint of financial success, rather than religious merit. True, one of the chief works of this kind, a carnival play written before 1494 by Hans Folz (Falz) of Nuremberg, includes the recitation of the authentic Hebrew profession of faith in the liturgical poem *Adon 'olam* (Lord of the Universe); it is given in a considerably corrupted Latin transliteration but with a fairly accurate German rendition. However, the author also cites dubious rabbinic legends which like the prayer he had evidently borrowed from the older polemical literature, possibly with the aid of a convert. With his penchant for pornography—a leading German literary historian called him "a flowery troubadour, smutty author of comedies, and writer of lascivious carnival plays"—Folz used, in particular, the ancient stories concerning intimacies between Adam and the she-devil, Lilith, to excoriate the Jews as brothers of that union's offspring and to exclaim, "From this speech it is clear as day that you are brethren of the devil!" [14]

"SYNAGOGUE OF SATAN"

Cooperation with the devil, in some respects interrelated with the Jewish alliance with Antichrist, thus became another slogan of medieval Jew-baiting. Once again it received Scriptural support from an irate saying attributed to Jesus. According to the Gospel of St. John, in his altercation with Jewish contestants on Mt. Olive, Jesus had exclaimed: "Ye are of your father the devil, and the lusts of your father ye will do." Similarly, the catchy phrase, "Synagogue of Satan," twice used in the book of Revelation, left an indelible imprint on the minds of many pious Christians. The growing obsession of the medieval man with the devil and demons, which in the popular religion played almost the role of the ancient dualism of Good and Evil, often made of Jesus not the pacifist preacher of humble love but rather a militant leader in the warfare against Satan and his cohorts. In this conflict the "unbelieving" Jews were visualized as Jesus' harshest enemies and hence also as Satan's closest allies.[15]

At times Jews were also associated with the "fallen angels" of the Bible, a notion which David Qimḥi in vain tried to controvert. As early as the fourth century St. Hilarius of Poitiers contended that "before they received the Law Jews were possessed by the demon. . . . For a time the fear of the Law drove it out, but it has now returned in revenge for their repudiation of the grace [of Christ]." Such popular beliefs, relating to Christian heretics as well as Jews, were often nurtured by the authorities for political reasons. In order to eliminate the freedom-loving Stedinger community which staunchly resisted the encroachments of the archbishops of Bremen and the counts of Oldenburg, Gregory IX, in two letters of 1233, accused the former of being "seduced by the devil" and serving him by "shedding blood like water." This incredible denunciation was accepted by the generally skeptical Emperor Frederick II and his allied bishops and princes. Similarly, when Benedict, the forcibly converted York Jewish delegate to Richard Lion-Heart's coronation, wished to revert to Judaism, Archbishop Baldwin of Canterbury exclaimed, "He does not wish to be a Christian, let him be the Devil's man." Peter of Cluny knew of no better way of scolding the Jews for their stubborn rejection of Christianity than by exclaiming, "Will you deny God, whom the Christian Gospel, the profaned pagan temples and the very demons, worse than whom you had become, by divine force acknowledge as God?" Before long the Western Christian masses began believing St. Chrysostom's irate assertion that "the souls of the Jews and the places where they congregate are inhabited by demons." Ultimately, the Jew himself began to be called the devil or, to use the well-known Shakespearean phrase, "Certainly, the Jew is the very devil incarnal." [16]

Such mental associations often found curious expressions as in the medieval German folk song parodies of Jewish prayers. A mere similarity of sound sufficed for the term *Hütchen* or *Gütchen*, standing in the older German for gnomes, through *Grietel*, to wind up in the designation of *Jüdel* for household spirits, some of which were benign pranksters and friendly playmates of children, while others preferred to burn children—an echo of the *Judenknabe*. *Jüdels* were also held responsible for red spots on human faces and other symptoms of disease. Similarly, old folklore saw in fire a preventive against witchcraft and led to the kindling of the so-called Judas Fire a few days before St. Walpurgis Night. On this occasion a song of the *Alte Iötunn* (in Teuton: Old Giants) was turned into a song of the *Alte Juden* (Old Jews).[17]

As a result of this alliance with the Master of Evil Jews were supposed to have developed specific physical characteristics, particularly a strong body odor originating from Lucifer's permanent abode in hell. This odor miraculously disappeared after conversion, when the sprinkling of sacramental waters changed it into a pleasing fragrance. Perhaps for this reason Inquisitor Bernard Gui and others emphasized that, during the ceremonial opening of the purported tomb of Mary Magdalen in 1279 (played up as a major national event by Charles I's Provençal regime), the assembled multitude was greeted by a fine scent emanating from the grave. Even some more sophisticated writers believed in the specific Jewish odor and merely tried to explain it by the Jewish diet of garlic and onions. A German folk parody of the biblical story of Moses' exposure on the Nile depicted the little boy as being approached by a crocodile. But Moses' fears were allayed when the voracious animal declared: "I devour Christians only, but do not want any Jew." Another widespread belief that Jews had horns, as well as animal tails which they succeeded in hiding, was reinforced by the biblical reference to Moses' descent from Mt. Sinai when his face "shone." The Hebrew term *qaran* could also be translated by "had developed horns"; hence, for instance, the horns in Michelangelo's famous sculpture of Moses. This superstition secured a realistic background through the Jews' "horned" hats. It was not too difficult for many a medieval artist to depict the devil himself as wearing a tricornered Jewish hat and a yellow badge. Such alleged Jewish physical characteristics multiplied in time until Johann Jacob Schudt reported, in behalf of a learned contemporary, "that among several hundred of their [the Jews'] kind he had not encountered a single person without a blemish or other repulsive feature: for they are either pale and yellow, or swarthy; they have in general big heads and mouths, pouting lips, protruding eyes and eyelashes like bristles, large ears, crooked feet, hands that hang below their knees, and big shapeless warts, or are otherwise asymetrical and malproportioned in their limbs." [18]

Because of their physical inferiority Jews were supposed to have close relationships with the animal world, particularly the goat. Once again the usually bearded Jew, contrasted with his predominantly clean-shaven neighbors, offered a realistic illustration. Remarkably, popular folklore associated Jews even with swine despite their well-known aversion to that meat. We recall the sow hide often used in connection with the Jewish oath. Incredible though it may seem, the medieval populace believed that a Jewess of Binzwangen near Augsburg once gave birth to twin porkers, an event graphically depicted in a pamphlet of 1574. But had not a medieval poet made a Christian woman recite a poetic complaint to the Virgin for having made her give birth to seven pups? It sufficed for an enemy to substitute a dog for a newly born child to bring about the condemnation of its mother to an extremely painful death for allegedly having had intercourse with an animal. None of the travelers and fiction writers had difficulty in persuading their readers that many distant nations had double noses, four arms or legs, lion's fangs, and the like. Animated by deep-rooted suspicions, the popular mind was even more prone to attribute such physical abnormalities to Jews.[19]

Remarkably, these physical characteristics were not played up in the anti-Jewish medieval literature. True, Nathan Official was once challenged by a converted Jew to deny that "you are the ugliest men of earth, whereas our people [the Frenchmen] are good-looking." Nathan replied by drawing a comparison with flowers: "We Jews, being of pure and white origin, have our faces turn dark, whereas you descended from the red offspring of menstruating women have blond hair and a red complexion." Curiously, red hair was not then considered particularly attractive among Christian writers in either France or Germany. In a fourteenth-century Passion mystery a Burgundian renegade is said to have met Malchus, one of the original chief enemies of Jesus, in a Palestinian cave. Malchus is depicted here as a person, "reddish, with a long face, bearded, and aged between thirty-five and forty years." In other words, a redheaded dolichocephalic person was considered repulsive by these Burgundian writers. The poet Hans Wilhelm Kirchhof describes a red-haired Judas Iscariot and considers all red-haired persons suspect. In graphic arts, too, the Jews often appear as redheads; according to some scholars, because the artists thus wished to express the Jews' similarity to foxes. On the other hand, the Cluniac illustrator of an apologetic tract by the Spaniard Ildefonsus, though apparently working in the tense aftermath of the First Crusade (*ca.* 1100), presents not only ancient Israelites, but also Ildefonsus' seventh-century interlocutors as black-haired men, occasionally identifiable as Jews through their attractive conical hats.[20]

Many people were convinced that Jews were able to obtain favors from Satan and his innumerable demonic helpers supposedly filling the air around man. One Martinus Borrhaus actually computed a total of 2,665,866,746,664 demons floating through the universe and ever ready for all sorts of mischief. To the populace this assistance appeared as the main reason for the Jews' financial success. A folk tale which, starting in Byzantium, reappeared in various guises throughout western Europe from the tenth to the sixteenth centuries, described the vicissitudes of an eastern cleric, Theophilus. Originally very pious, humble, and learned, Theophilus resented his poverty and lack of recognition. This pique led him to a Jew "who with magic fraud had deceived many of the faithful." The latter introduced Theophilus to his partner, the devil, to whom by contract Theophilus surrendered his soul and abjured Jesus and Mary. As a result, he suddenly became very successful, achieved a bishop's see, and, following the advice of his Jewish councilor, governed his diocese with an iron hand. Ultimately, however, Theophilus repented and, after imploring the Virgin, secured the cancellation of his compact with the devil and died in peace. Curiously, when in his initial approach to his Jewish adviser Theophilus asked to be converted to Judaism, he was refused, the legend itself admitting the Jewish aversion to proselytism. But it depicted the Jew as ever ready to persuade Christians to switch their allegiance to the devil, or what the kabbalists liked to call "the other side." [21]

SORCERY AND USURY

Alliance with the devil also seemed to offer to the Christian populace the most plausible explanation for the successes of many Jewish doctors. Even some Jews believed in magic healing, as did the chronicler Aḥimaaz who had extolled his ancestor Shefaṭiah b. Amittai for having, on his journey to Constantinople in 873–76, brought Emperor Basil's daughter back to health by exorcising a demon and locking him up in a lead container sealed with the Lord's name. Satan's friendly intervention allegedly accounted also for the aptitude of some Jews to foretell fortunes and to exercise other magic arts. The Council of Worcester of 1240 not only forbade Christians to indulge in sorcery, but also strongly (*maxime*) insisted that Christians consulting Jewish fortunetellers or taking any magically contrived advice from them be punished at their bishop's discretion. Fifteen years later the Council of Béziers succinctly resolved that "Jews should desist from usuries, blasphemies and sorceries." In 1390 a converted Jew was convicted in London for claiming that, with the aid of magic, he could detect thieves. Even in Spain King Pedro III ordered in 1380 an investigation of a Valencia Jew, Salamies Nasci, accused of "having committed various enormous and horrendous crimes, namely that he had administered poisonous potions to a number of persons of the said city and that he is a fortuneteller [*fatillerius*] and invoker of demons." In 1409 Pope Alexander V included Jews among the practitioners of magic arts whom the inquisitors were to prosecute relentlessly. Even Martin V, one of the most pro-Jewish popes, soon after his election ordered repressive measures against those Avignonese Jews who had invoked demons "with magic chants." [22]

Some of these denunciations realistically reflected the age-old profession of itinerant magicians and wonder healers who made a living from administering potions and selling amulets. A great many ancient gemmas and bowls, bearing Hebrew-Aramaic or, more frequently, Greek inscriptions with Hebraic-sounding divine and angelic names, are still extant in many museums. We also recall that during the pre-Islamic and Islamic Middle Ages, the eastern Jewish masses extensively employed magical amulets for the protection of their families and possessions. At times combined with the international trade in drugs, the sale of magical implements early spread to the West, too.

According to a Christian legend, Heliodorus, an eighth-century Sicilian sorcerer and juggler, owed his mastery to a Babylonian Hebrew magician who had allegedly handed him a paper with which he could force his will upon the devil himself. This legend was not far removed from the Jewish tradition that it was the Babylonian Abu Aaron (Ahron) who had brought the mystic lore of the Orient, in both its theoretical teachings and magical applications, to southern Italy. It is small wonder, then, that Hebrew-Aramaic magical amulets were found, for instance, in Italian Lecce and that, according to the leading Renaissance publicist, Pietro Aretino, Roman prostitutes had learned from Jewish women magical methods for attracting lovers. The romantic poet, Lodovico Ariosto, even described a Spanish Jewish necromancer who was allegedly able to darken the day, turn invisible, assume the shape of an animal, and cause an earthquake. True, Hebraic symbols and names do not necessarily indicate an amulet's Jewish provenance. Just as in antiquity Graeco-Roman pagans frequently invoked the assistance of Iao or Abraxas, names whose meaning and origins they did not know but in whose potency, perhaps for that very reason, they doubly believed, so did medieval Christians use Hebrew-sounding phrases, sometimes totally meaningless, to persuade their gullible public of the efficacy of their ministrations. The necromancer whom Benvenuto Cellini observed at the Roman Coliseum uttering "awful invocations, calling by name on multitudes of demons who are captains of their legions . . . in phrases of the Hebrew" actually was a Sicilian priest. But there is no question about the Jewishness of some peddlers of potions or of small scrolls containing magical formulae which superstitious buyers carried on their chests to ward off evil. Even before the Jews were legally admitted to Florence, Franco Sacchetti observed, "It frequently happens that they [the Florentines] trust a Jew much rather than a thousand Christians." Nor was the populace able clearly to distinguish such vendors from legitimate Jewish druggists; for instance, one Magister Dattilus of Rome who, as early as 1324, was selling medicines in Florence in partnership with a Christian apothecary.[23]

Curiously, the theme of Jewish amulet vendors or magic healers rarely occurs in the medieval mystery and Passion plays. Since the authors had to allot much space to miracles performed by Jesus, they could but incidentally refer to obnoxious Jewish magic. It may perhaps not be too venturesome to suggest that some writers may have feared that audiences, rather than repudiating Jews because of their ability to marshal supernatural forces for medicinal aid or the accumulation of wealth, would be attracted to utilizing their services. We know, of course, that many legislators who strictly forbade Christians to employ Jewish doctors did so themselves. Thomas de Cantimpré unabashedly told in 1258 the story of how he himself had seen and heard a demon who temporarily deprived him of his voice. Even a distinguished abbot like Johann Trittheim (1462–1516) seems to have willfully exposed himself to some dangers only in order to instill in the populace the belief in his own occult powers. Authors and producers of the mystery plays, therefore, often preferred to mention only trite generalities concerning the alliance between Jews and the devil.[24]

Belief in Jewish magic prowess was also nurtured from genuine Jewish traditions. The Jews themselves had long extolled the powers of their revered King Solomon over Ashmodai and other demons. According to ancient legends, further elaborated by the medieval fantasy, this wisest of all men, who understood the language of birds and animals, was also able to communicate directly with the spirits and to force them to do his bidding. These legends, together with certain magical books derived from them, found a widespread following in the Western world also.

Many people believed that, by using a so-called key of Solomon with its garbled Latin transliteration from the Hebrew, they, too, could irresistibly impose their will upon demons. Some Christians even attributed to Solomon writings repudiated by the Jewish leaders. By 1170 Peter Comestor, who through Rashi had learned much of the Jewish Aggadah, ascribed almost all magic books current in his time to the ancient Jewish king. At the same time the Talmud and the Jewish mystical literature circulating in the geonic period furnished enough data on Jewish magical practices to lend support to Archbishop Agobard of Lyons' attacks on "Jewish superstitions" and to the denunciations of the Talmud by Nicholas Donin and others. Not only the originators of the burning of the Talmud in Paris in 1242, but also the new committee of experts in Rome in 1553, contended that "the majority of talmudists are necromancers, heretics and vicious persons." Moreover, the medieval rabbis considered exorcisms and incantations perfectly legitimate, even necessary, pursuits. In a purely legal discussion Isaac b. Joseph of Corbeil decided that agreements concerning rewards for the return of found objects and the like could be disregarded in favor of prevailing rates, but that contracts relating to healing or incantations against demons (according to some rabbis also to marriage brokerage) had to be enforced regardless of the market prices for such services. On the other hand, Isaac b. Moses of Vienna advised his coreligionists to suspend the more symbolic than real practice of bediqat ḥameṣ (search for the leavened bread) on the night before Passover if, because of its mysterious character, it might appear as a magic ritual to the household's Christian servants. Of course, there had also existed within the Jewish community ever since biblical times much opposition to any form of magic. In the Middle Ages not only a philosopher like Maimonides strenuously objected to magic arts in both theory and practice, but even the spokesman of the predominantly "superstitious" German Jewish masses, Yehudah b. Samuel the Pious, contended that "if you see a Jew apostasizing not on account of sex or during an [anti-Jewish] upheaval, you may rest assured that he, his mother or his forebears had engaged in incantations to and manipulations of demons." But these were voices crying in the wilderness against the overwhelming desire of a suffering people who sought in occult arts solace against their individual and collective misfortunes.[25]

Because of their genuine trust in the efficacy of magic practices many Jews doubtless shared their "knowledge" with Christian neighbors, on humanitarian as well as mercenary grounds. The non-Jewish populace the more eagerly absorbed such information as the belief in sorcery and witchcraft increased rather than diminished with the progress of science in the Late Middle Ages. The Church and, under its prompting, the state had their hands full with the prosecution of Christian "witches," a prosecution which was speedily assuming the character of mass hysteria. So rational a theologian as John Calvin readily approved the execution of certain witches. Christian leaders had even more compelling reasons to advocate violent suppression of Jewish "sorcery," as its potential successes tended to arouse doubts in many Christian hearts about the efficacy of the Christian religious preachment. Had not the Church long before been forced to conduct a (far from successful) campaign to persuade peasants to desist from having their crops blessed by Jews? Under these circumstances it is doubly remarkable that we hear relatively little about the prosecution of Jewish "witches." When in 1451 a Messinese Jewess, Gemma, was condemned by the archepiscopal vicar for practicing magic arts, the Jewish community vigorously protested.[26]

At the same time the Christian public, including some of its more educated members, often appreciated the ministrations of talented manipulators of spirits. It was futile for the Council of Narbonne, in 589, to forbid Jews (along with the Goths, Romans, Syrians, or Greeks, that is, the majority of the population) to harbor sorcerers or diviners under the severe fine of six gold ounces. When the Jews' success in the practice of medicine was pointed out to Martin Luther, he replied succinctly, "The devil can do much!" He also recited with relish the story of Albert of Saxony, to whom a Jew had offered an amulet to make him immune from any attack. To test it, Albert hung the amulet on the Jew's neck and killed him with his spear. On the other hand, a 1397 satire claimed that the bishop of Würzburg and his associates had well learned the lessons of the Talmud; "their art is called necromancy; Satan was also with them while they pursued their studies." Curiously, although diversity of belief nurtured mutual suspicions and ancient Jews often had ascribed to Egyptians and other peoples unwarranted use of magic arts, the medieval Jewish sources are relatively silent about contemporary Christian witchcraft. While continuing to attribute events in the past, including the miracles wrought by Jesus, to the employment of magic, they rarely expressed fears of being victimized by the Christians' use of magic arts.[27]

Not surprisingly, the Jewish usurer and money trader occupied an even more focal position on the medieval stage. Since the Passion plays often presented Jews from the time of Jesus in the guise of familiar contemporary figures, bearing well-known Jewish names, negotiations between the ancient leaders and Judas Iscariot lent themselves to particularly persuasive dramatization in the form of bargaining among typical medieval Jewish moneylenders. In some plays Judas' wages were whittled down from the original thirty shillings to thirty pence. Even then the money changers tried to palm off on him defective coins, while Judas, an equally shrewd trader, caught them in the act. Some medieval playwrights, such as Jean Michel, preferred to lower the dignity of Judas by ascribing to him various horrendous crimes including the killing of his father and the marrying of his mother before his conversion to the new religion. Needless to say, they did not bother to explain how he had escaped severe punishment by the Jewish authorities of ancient Jerusalem. The very process of his counting the coins could be developed into a lively dialogue. In some late medieval German performances, Jews were depicted as offering money to the Roman soldiers and inciting them to inflict more severe tortures upon Jesus on his way to, and while on, the Cross. Precisely because bribery of officials had become a daily occurrence, such scenes appeared perfectly plausible to audiences which readily accepted the contention of one of Pamphilus Gengenbach's Jewish characters that he only "needed little silver spears [Länzlein]" to corrupt officials. Several sixteenth-century German writers complained of undue Jewish influence on princes and judges. In an imaginary dialogue with a colleague a rabbi was heard to boast: "When anyone dares to write against us/He no longer anywhere lives securely/From being prosecuted unto death." That such plays were produced in localities like Lucerne, Tyrol, or Antwerp where few, if any, Jews lived in the fifteenth and sixteenth centuries is by no means surprising. The less he knew of contemporary Jews, particularly after 1349, the more inclined was the average Antwerp resident to believe his municipality's influential secretary, Jan (de Clerk) Boendale, who succinctly characterized the entire Jewish people as malignant by nature, avaricious, faithless, deeply corrupted, and full of evil designs. Throughout its history antisemitic propaganda frequently proved most virulent in areas of slight Jewish population density. What was attacked was the prevailing image of the Jew rather than any particular Jewish acquaintances whom one could regard as favorable exceptions.[28]

Popular hostility also found an outlet in numerous folk songs and folk tales, crudely deriding the Jewish peddler. Here we encounter for the first time the cry "Hep, Hep" which was to be revived with great éclat in the German attacks upon Jews in 1819. Various hypotheses have been advanced for the origin of this slogan. Its regnant interpretation as an abbreviation of *Hierosolyma est perdita* (Jerusalem is lost) does not quite fit the usual medieval spelling of "Hepp." Others have suggested that it was merely an abridged form of the word, Hebrew. But the brothers Grimm, distinguished students of medieval German dialects, explained it as a derivative of the then widespread connection between Jews and goats, and the consequent adoption of the goat cry as a symbol for the Jewish people.[29]

Nor did the medieval playwrights overlook the rewarding ancient theme of the burning of the Temple as retribution for the Jewish share in the crucifixion. Here, too, the story of Judas could be used to show that, while the Jewish leaders had paid thirty pence for the person of Jesus, Titus sold thirty Jewish prisoners for the price of one penny. Divine vengeance during the fall of Jerusalem was illustrated by Gregory of Tours through the enormous total of 600,000 Jewish victims, a figure raised by the later Belgian chronicler, Jean des Preis, to 1,100,000. However, both writers doubtless went back, directly or indirectly, to the divergent figures cited soon after 70 by Josephus and Tacitus. More legendary was the story of Vespasian who "since childhood had had some sort of vermin in his nose, whence came his surname of Vespasian." He was cured of this illness, we are told, by believing in Jesus as a miraculous healer, as suggested to him by a messenger from the pro-Christian Pilate. In this fashion history intertwined with legend became a major vehicle of anti-Jewish propaganda among poets, as well as among the official controversialists.[30]

BLOOD ACCUSATIONS

Folkloristic preconceptions affected Jewish life particularly in the recurrent allegations of the use of Christian blood by Jews. Such accusations, far from unusual in the mutual recriminations of pagan groups in the Graeco-Roman world, were hurled against Jews and Christians, too, by some Hellenistic writers. But after 416, the latest recorded anti-Christian accusation, this libel went underground to reappear against the Jews of Norwich in 1144. The enthusiasm for self-sacrifice generated by the Crusading movements, combined with lurid descriptions of the sufferings of ancient saints and martyrs and the ensuing glorification of such witnesses for faith, now created a general psychological receptivity for believing in the martyrdom inflicted upon Christian children by the Jew, Christendom's perennial dissenter. Because it opened the floodgates to fantastic descriptions of these children's sufferings paralleling the ever more gory details used in the depiction of the Passion of Christ or the slaying of ancient saints, and because it furnished justification for sadistic acts including the killing and plunder of entire Jewish communities, it greatly stimulated the popular fancy to indulge in unbridled imaginary descriptions of such murders.[31]

All along the leaders of state and Church kept relatively aloof. The twelfth-century English blood libels of Norwich and Glouces-ter apparently resulted in no prosecutions and no Jewish victims are mentioned in contemporary Hebrew sources. If in Blois in 1171, according to Hebrew chroniclers, the entire community suffered from the bloody vengeance of an aroused populace, this retribution had all the earmarks of popular lynching, rather than of an ordinary trial and condemnation. True, some local priests and monks found it to their advantage to attribute miraculous powers to the remains of such child martyrs. But no leading churchman of that or the following century sought to justify either the Blood Accusation as such or its rumored ritualistic implications. In fact, emperor and pope took a sharp stand against it. We recall that, after a careful investigation of the events in Fulda in 1236, Emperor Frederick II had convoked an assembly of delegates, mainly recruited from informed Jewish converts in several countries. The resolutions of that "Congress" were as outspoken in their condemnation of the ritual murder accusation as any Jewish leader might have desired. No less vigorous was its repudiation by Innocent IV and his successors beginning with the affair in Valréas (in the diocese of Vienne) in 1247. True, two local Franciscan monks, permeated with inquisitorial zeal, had set up the prosecution in Valréas, but they were quickly disavowed by the jurist-pope. Starting with Gregory X, pope after pope inserted a special protective provision to this effect in the papal constitution for the Jews, *Sicut Judaeis*. As late as 1540, Pope Paul III addressed a bull *Licet Judaei* to the bishops of Poland, Bohemia, and Hungary, stating:

We have heard with displeasure from the complaints of Jews of those countries how, for some years past, certain magistrates and other officials, their bitter and mortal enemies, blinded by hate and envy, or as is more probable by cupidity, pretend, in order to despoil them of their goods, that the Jews kill little children and drink their blood.

In 1759 an incident in Poland caused the then Cardinal Lorenzo Ganganelli, later Pope Clement XIV, to submit on orders of Pope Benedict XIV an extensive report to the Holy Office of the Inquisition. Apart from discussing the details of the Polish Blood Accusation, Ganganelli quoted extensively from earlier sources to prove its total unreasonableness.[32]

Many secular princes followed suit. One of the first was Přemysl Ottakar II of Bohemia who reissued, under his own seal, Innocent IV's decree against the Blood Accusation. His young nephew, Henry IV of Silesia, who often consulted him on matters of state policy, went even further. To deter false accusations, he ordained that any ritual murder charge would have to be proved by three Christian and three Jewish witnesses; otherwise the Christian accuser should be subject to the same penalty which he wished to inflict upon the Jewish defendant or defendants. Neither the Bohemian nor the Silesian clergy ever objected to these severe measures and it was for unrelated reasons that the temperamental Breslau bishop, Thomas II, complained in 1286 that "the position of the faithful clergy under the scepter of the said duke [Henry IV] is inferior even to that of the Jews. For the Jews are able to live and pursue their business freely in his country, whereas the clergy, in constant fear of death, can hardly dare to think of entering his land." Similarly, James II of Aragon reacted strongly in 1294 to the unlawful behavior of the authorities (*jurados*) of Saragossa who, on learning about the disappearance of a Christian child, employed a Christian "familiar with magic arts" to detect the missing child. This "expert," after consulting a magical instrument, pointed to a house where the Jews had allegedly murdered the boy and extracted his liver and heart for ritual use. The Jewish community, in grave jeopardy, we recall, located the child in the house of his putative father in Calatayud. The king sharply censured these proceedings "which might have brought about the destruction of Our *aljama*, and also because they run counter to Our faith and law, according to which all magic arts and incantations are to be despised and prohibited." He demanded exemplary punishment of all guilty persons. In 1318 Infante Alphonso without much ado freed Lupus Abnexeyl or de la Penya not only of his alleged sexual transgressions but also of his purported consent "to the theft of little boys and their murder so that he partake of their heart on Good Friday." [33]

In time, however, the libel achieved a certain respectability in both ecclesiastical and government circles. Ironically, it was the scientifically minded Alphonso X of Castile who took the accusation more seriously. In his Code he wrote: "We have heard it said that in certain places the Jews had made and are making on Good Friday a memorial for the Passion of Our Lord Jesus Christ in a mocking manner by stealing little boys and placing them on a cross or, when they cannot obtain little boys, they make wax figures [of Jesus] and crucify them." But he did not leave it to the local authorities to adjudicate such matters and ordered that the alleged culprits be brought before him. By 1475 the clergy of Trent, headed by Bishop Johannes Hinderbach, served as protagonists in the much-debated trial of the Jewish community for the alleged assassination of the child-martyr Simeon (Simoncino), a two-year-old son of the cobbler Andreas Unverdosben. Bernardino da Feltre's incendiary sermons, in which the preacher had "prophetically" predicted the ritual murder, set the stage for this tragic denouement. After an appeal to Rome, the papal commissioner, Bishop Giambattista dei Sindici of Ventimiglia, demanded the quashing of the prosecution and the release of the Jewish prisoners who, under prolonged torture, had been made to "confess" the crime. Yet at the end Pope Sixtus IV failed to rebuke the Trent ecclesiastics and limited himself in 1478 to the merely formal declaration that the court procedure had been *rite et recte factum,* creating the impression of his tacit approval of the verdict itself. Similarly, the ultimate beatification of little Simeon one hundred and ten years after the event, though based on the miracles attributed to his corpse and accepted as true by the Church rather than on the alleged cause of his death, was later invoked very frequently by Jew-baiters as evidence for the Jews' murderous activities. However, here, too, the ultimate driving force was the clamor of the populace, which accused the papal commissioner (and even the pope himself) of having accepted Jewish bribes and forced him out of the city.[34]

Here we also find a progressive sharpening of the anti-Jewish bias. In the twelfth century most accusations were aimed at alleged crucifixions of children during the Christian Easter, supposedly intended to reenact the ancient tragedy at Golgotha. Already in its earliest form at Norwich this action was attributed by a Jewish renegade to an international Jewish assembly in Narbonne—a hint at a Jewish world conspiracy. A thirteenth-century East-European writer retold the story of a monk Eustratios who, during an enemy raid on Kiev in 1096, had been carried away from the Petcherskii monastery and sold to the Jews in Kherson. The latter allegedly crucified their prisoner during their Passover celebration. In the West, too, the transition from Easter to Passover was readily made, with a new rationalization that Jews required the blood of Christian children for their unleavened bread. A combination of both crucifixion and the alleged Jewish ritual is recorded in Bray, France, as early as 1191. These Frenchmen probably never heard of the related tale that, during a Purim celebration in Syrian Inmestar about 415 C.E., some Jews had crucified a Christian boy in commemoration of the hanging of Haman. But they may have learned, however obliquely, of the eleventh-century Byzantine legislation which, perhaps in some way going back to the Inmestar rumor, had included in the oath of abjuration of each Jewish convert a ban on "those who celebrate the festival of Mordecai . . . and those who nail Haman to a piece of wood and, joining it to a sign of the cross, burn them together while hurling curses and anathemas against the Christians." Some such fantastic rumors, upon reaching western Europe, may possibly have added nourishment to the belief that Jews crucified living children during the four-week interval between Purim and Passover and ultimately also that they consumed the victims' blood. There is a strange irony in the total obliviousness, by the French, of the defense attributed to one of their own early women martyrs, Byblis, "How could such men eat children when they are not allowed to eat the blood even of irrational animals?" [35]

Even after the switch from Easter to Passover the connection with Passion Week was never completely lost. Whether or not associated with a Blood Accusation, the mere retelling of the original Gospel story of the Passion, embellished in many details by fervent preachers and playwrights, caused governments and Jewish communities to be on their guard. Jews were often ordered to stay indoors during the crucial Easter weekend or, as in Béziers, during the entire preceding week. Some localities legalized specified attacks on Jews on Palm Sunday in memory of their ancestors' stoning of Jesus, according to the Gospel of John (10:31). We also recall the famous Easter slap in Toulouse which, only after it resulted in a fatality in 1018, was converted into a monetary payment. Sporadic attacks are also recorded in Italy and Aragon, where the kings repeatedly had to instruct the local authorities to protect Jews at such junctures. In Avignon Jews actually observed a so-called *Yom ha-hesger* (the Day of Closing [the Ghetto Gates]), some of their poets composing special liturgical pieces for recitation on that occasion.[36]

FARFETCHED EXPLANATIONS AND EVIDENCE

While realizing the incongruity of Jews lightheartedly violating a biblical prohibition, educated medieval men explained it to their own satisfaction—as doubtless had the Roman contemporaries of Byblis with respect to Christian defendants—by the "culprits'" inveterate hatred of their persecutors. In the Künzelsau carnival play a Jew announces with joy the arrival of Antichrist:

> In your bondage we long have cowered
> Although our Lord had us empowered
> To cause men who fail to worship Him
> Be fast destroyed in life and limb,
> And be martyred like your Jesus Christ.

The crude "Play of the Duke of Burgundy," whose earliest manuscript dates from 1494, presents the defeated Antichrist reciting a long confession of the ways in which he and his Jewish partisans had sought to harm Christians including their kidnaping and slaying of many young children to ridicule the yearly commemoration of the birth of Christ. The author seems completely oblivious that he made that recurrent slaughter coincide with Christmas, rather than the long-accepted Easter or Passover season. In practice, too, Blood Accusations occurred at different dates. It sufficed for a Christian child to die under unusual circumstances, or even temporarily to disappear, in order to evoke the ghost of ritual murder among the ever-suspicious populace. The prevailing association with Passover, however, was doubtless facilitated by some Jewish ceremonies connected with that holiday. As some Christians saw it, the mysterious Jewish unleavened bread, often baked under stringent supervision lest it come in contact with non-Passover food or utensils, in many ways resembled the Catholic host. It was easy enough for them to conclude that, just as the host embodied the blood of Christ, so did the *maṣṣah* preferentially include some Christian blood. Similarly, the red wine, used for the prescribed four cups during the ceremonial Passover meal, so frequently evoked mental associations with blood that the seventeenth-century Lwów rabbi, David b. Samuel ha-Levi, stated that "nowadays we avoid the consumption of red wine because of the false accusations [spread against us] on account of our numerous sins." Finally, the very sumptuousness of that meal, arousing both the curiosity and the envy of Christian onlookers, heightened the aura of mystery. A proverb of Italian, Spanish, and English provenance contended that "a Jew will spend all on his Pasches, a Barbarian

[Turk] on his nuptials, and the Christian on his quarrels and law suits." [37]

Another dish used at the Passover meal, the so-called *haroset,* usually prepared in the Askenazic communities with apples, nuts, and wine, likewise aroused suspicions. Upon learning that, in their general penchant for spiritualizing every object connected with divine worship, some Jewish interpreters had imbued each ingredient with mystic connotations, they easily drew the conclusion that an admixture of Christian blood might heighten the efficacy of the ritual. Had not, despite their general aversion to blood, the Jews themselves admitted the major expiatory function once performed by the blood of sacrificial animals at the Temple in Jerusalem? Ancient and medieval Jewish folklore also attributed to the blood of animals medicinal qualities, although to a lesser extent than did their Gentile neighbors who readily assumed, therefore, that Jewish slayers of Christian children also made use of the victims' blood for magic or healing purposes.

Michael Scot (d. 1232) described the practice of contemporary conjurors who mixed blood with ritual waters in order to attract demons. Christian observers may the more readily have believed in the use of blood as an unguent at circumcision ceremonies, as some Jewish communities used, indeed, a red gum derived from a species of palm—which because of its color was called dragon's blood (*calamus draco*)—to heal the child's wound. Jewish doctors supposedly often used human blood for the cure of patients. Some stories are demonstrably untrue. A widely read tale about an English princess, *Hirlanda,* informs us that a Jewish doctor once recommended to King Richard Lion-Heart, then suffering from leprosy, that he bathe in the blood of a newborn child and consume the child's heart while it still was warm. But the king had never suffered from leprosy. (Incidentally, according to Pliny, blood as a remedy for leprosy and similar diseases had been used by the ancient kings of Egypt.) Only a little less improbable is the story of the Jewish physician who in 1492 allegedly tried to save Pope Innocent VIII by a potion of dissolved pearls. When this medicine failed, he is said to have instilled into the papal veins the blood of three boys aged ten who were procured for a ducat each. The result was tragic: the three children died without saving the pope, and the physician had to flee for his life. If at all true, this story might reflect a Jewish doctor's pioneering attempt at blood transfusion, an experiment which he had not derived from any Jewish source, but rather developed from a technique current among contemporary Christian physicians.[38]

From here it was but a step to a combination of the therapeutic and religious implications of the blood ritual, a combination found as early as the thirteenth century in the encyclopedic work by Thomas de Cantimpré. In his *Bonum universale de Apibus* which, going beyond its narrow subject of "bees" offers a conglomeration of popular scientific and folkloristic concepts, Thomas includes a lengthy excursus on Jewish ritual murder. He writes:

It is hence quite evident that, according to custom, Jews shed Christian blood in every province they inhabit. It has most certainly been established that every year they cast lots in each province as to which community or city should produce Christian blood for the other communities. The holy Gospel reports that, when Pilate washed his hands and said: "I am innocent of the blood of this just person," the most godless Jews cried out: "His blood be on us and on our children!" [Matthew 27:24–25]. St. Augustine appears to allude to this in a discourse, which begins *In cruce,* that as a result of this curse upon their fathers, the criminal disposition is even now transmitted to children by some taint in their blood. The godless posterity inexpiably suffers torment through the violent coursing of this taint through their veins till they repentantly admit themselves guilty of the blood of Christ, and are healed.

Thomas concludes with a story he had heard from a learned Jewish convert that some prophet had told the Jews, "You may be firmly convinced, that only by Christian blood can you be cured of this secret affliction," which gave them the mistaken idea of seeking relief by the annual slaying of a Christian in every province. They simply misunderstood their prophet's remedy *nisi solo sanguine Christiano* which, referring to the blood of Christ, merely meant that Jews could be cured only by partaking, through conversion, in the salvation brought to the Christian world by the blood of its founder. Few of Thomas' readers doubted the existence of such a Jewish malady often appearing as a sort of male menstruation, and the Jews' stubborn persistence in securing the wrong cure. Ultimately, a sixteenth-century German writer, Hans Wilhelm Kirchhof, cited an old proverb that "Jews cannot exist or live without Christian blood." While some persons interpreted that adage figuratively that Jews could not exist without sucking Christian blood through usury, others, including Kirchhof himself, took it literally and quoted in its support Jewish "confessions" of ritual murder. Contending that Jews often preserved blood by mixing it with apples, honey, and ginger for future use, Johann Eck insisted that even those who did not require Christian blood for their health murdered Christians out of hate.[39]

One also wonders to what extent the occasional enforced governmental employment of Jewish hangmen stimulated the popular beliefs in Jewish cruelty. This is indeed the title of the chapter (*De crudelitatibus Judaeorum*) which Alphonso de Spina gave to his description of numerous Blood Accusations in his *Fortalitium fidei* (Fortress of Faith). While, as we recall, Jewish executioners are documented chiefly from Byzantium, Crete, and other East-Mediterranean areas, one is also mentioned, for instance, by the *Chronicle of Mailross* as functioning in England in 1216. The popular mind saw no conflict between such allegations of Jewish proneness to violence and the growingly accepted view that Jews were effeminate and cowardly, a view which doubtless gained in currency with the spreading prohibitions for Jews to bear arms. Even in Spain, where Jews often continued to conduct themselves as *hidalgos,* denigration of Jewish courage was even applied to the sixteenth-century *conversos.* Did not Cervantes speak of them as the *gente afeminada?* With many Spanish authors the diminutive, *judihuelo,* stood for both a little Jewish boy and a coward.[40]

All twelfth-century and many subsequent Blood Accusations were widely circulated without any trial. Wherever defendants were prosecuted before inquisitorial or secular courts, the evidence usually consisted in "confessions" of the accused subjected to severe torture. While torture was then considered by courts, both ecclesiastical and secular, a legitimate means of securing evidence, it was supposed to be employed only after the judges had marshaled sufficient circumstantial proof of the defendants' guilt. In many ritual murder trials the circumstantial evidence, if any, consisted in reports of a miraculous bleeding of the slain child several days after its demise and the like, frequently produced by the prosecution at the last moment.

In all the historically famous trials, for which documentation is still extant, the evidence was of such a tenuous kind. Whenever the authorities intervened speedily and energetically, its spuriousness was quickly discovered. When two Savoy Jews were accused in 1329 of having committed ritual murders "with the knowledge and consent of all the Jews of the County of Savoy," a careful investigation resulted in the confession of the accuser that he had been bribed by a gift of clothes to make the denunciation. On the other hand, it sufficed for inmates of the then newly founded *Domus Conversorum* in London supposedly to detect in 1244 some Hebrew words upon the body of a slain Christian child for Henry III to impose upon all English Jewry the enormous fine of 60,000 marks. After the Ratisbon trial of 1476 it was proved before the emperor that one of the chief "culprits," Josel Jud, had been in Landshut on the day of the alleged murder in Ratisbon. And yet, like the others, Josel had admitted his guilt under torture. Some accusations created a chain reaction. In 1401 a male servant of the bailiff of Diessenhofen, Switzerland, who had killed a four-year-old boy, "confessed" that he had promised to deliver the boy's blood to a Jewish visitor, Michel Vinelmann from Schaffhausen, for three florins. This confession did not save the slayer from the wheel, but in the meantime not only the Jewish visitor but all the Jews of Diessenhofen were burned. During his trial Vinelmann had implicated, under torture, another Schaffhausen Jew, whereupon the whole community of that city, too, was indicted. Although it had sought refuge by escaping, it was overtaken and brought back for trial. Torture again enforced confessions, which were withdrawn at the last moment, however. Yet many Schaffhausen Jews were executed, and the city escaped retribution only by an amnesty granted it by the Habsburg Duke Frederick in 1411. The repercussions of the Diessenhofen-Schaffhausen affair seriously endangered even Zurich Jewry, which was saved from popular wrath only by the city council's dilatory tactics. In short, one must agree with Abbé Elphège Vacandard who, after carefully reviewing the records of the various Blood Accusations, declared that "not a single case has ever been historically established." [41]

Even the renowned conviction of the Jews of Trent of 1475 could have been clearly controverted by consultation of the Jewish calendar. In that year Passover started on a Wednesday evening, whereas Simeon was supposedly slain on the following Friday. Similarly, the slayers' alleged motive to celebrate the Jewish Jubilee year made no sense in 5235 A.M. Moreover, Jews had not celebrated a Jubilee year since the first fall of Jerusalem, if ever. The year 1475 was indeed a Jubilee year, but only for the Church, and the Jews had hardly any reason to commemorate it. In Spain where, despite the allusions in the *Siete Partidas,* few accusations had achieved any notoriety the alleged murder for magical purposes of the *niño* (little boy) of La Guardia became a *cause célèbre* in 1490–91. However, there are serious doubts whether any Christian child at all had then been murdered in La Guardia. No body was ever found, an eighteenth-century priest explaining that "it was universally believed that God had completed the parallel between Christ and the *niño* and, on the third day, had carried the body up to heaven." And yet, because Lope de Vega chose this trial as a subject for one of his famous dramas (written some time between 1604 and 1608), the La Guardia martyrdom achieved very wide currency in the Spanish-speaking world, just as the inclusion of the story of the equally spurious murder of Hugh of Lincoln (in 1265) in Chaucer's *Canterbury Tales* left a permanent imprint on the psyche of untold numbers of English readers. Even a critical nineteenth-century essayist like Charles Lamb could not escape the impact of these *Tales.* Though claiming that in the abstract he had no disrespect for Jews who "are a piece of stubborn antiquity," he added, "I should not care to be in habits of familiar intercourse with any of that nation. I confess that I have not the nerves to enter their synagogues. Old prejudices cling about me. I cannot shake off the story of Hugh of Lincoln." [42]

In time the very frequency of that accusation enhanced its credibility in the eyes of the uncritical majority. How unconcerned the popular writers were over the flimsiness of evidence may be noted from a typical anonymous sixteenth-century German poem. Starting with the alleged Jewish defacement of the Cambron Virgin, the author reproduced a whole array of anti-Jewish accusations and provided them with lurid illustrations. Without much ado he declared that, after slaying little Simeon, the Jews of Trent drank his blood in glasses; he invoked "the whole city of Trent" as witness to the truth of this story. He similarly described another ritual murder of 1475 in Friulí, for which three Jews had been torn apart with iron tongs and burned in Venice. Here he remarked: "All denials will be of no avail against the testimony of the whole land of Italy." In other words, the widespread acceptance of a popular prejudice was in itself proof of its veracity.[43]

Curiously, some government authorities, perhaps out of fiscal self-interest, maintained a measure of *sang-froid* in dealing with such accusations. Their moderation understandably gave rise to the usual suspicions of Jewish bribery. However, bureaucratic machinery often moved very slowly. In March 1563 the city of Worms imprisoned and severely tortured a Jewish resident merely because a journeyman from Fribourg claimed to have seen this Jew receive a Christian child from a woman and bring it into the Jewish quarter. The Jewish community lodged an appeal with the Empire's Supreme Court (the *Reichskammergericht*) but it took almost fifteen months and the posting of a high bail of 20,000 florins before the court forced the city to release the prisoner.[44]

In retrospect, it is difficult to find in the annals of history a more persistent aberration of the mass mind than the belief in Jewish ritual murder. No amount of rational argumentation, no fulminations by popes, emperors, and kings, not even reiterated solemn testimonies of Jewish converts to Christianity could eradicate it. Even a zealous convert like Johann Pfefferkorn, who in all other matters implacably attacked his former coreligionists, futilely protested against these never-dying suspicions. Certainly, one did not need a more persuasive declaration than that signed in 1899 by thirty baptized Jews living in Jerusalem. They declared:

As born Jews, who are intimate with all the ritual prescriptions, uses and traditions of the Jews, and all Jewish sects, and as Christians who believe in Him who is the truth and the light, we hereby testify solemnly before the All-knowing Triune God, by the salvation of our souls and by our honour and conscience, that the accusation against the Jews in general or any Jewish sect whatever, that they are either compelled to use or have used at any time Christian blood or human blood for ritual purposes, is an absolutely mistaken, false calumny.

And yet, even the twentieth century witnessed reiterated revivals of this libel which was ultimately supported by alleged "scholarly" evidence in Tsarist Russia and Nazi Germany.[45]

POISONING

Less widespread and persistent but, in periods of crisis, even more destructive were rumors that in their hatred of Christians Jews were ever ready to poison both individuals and entire cities or regions. Poisons often served indeed as murderous weapons, but there is no evidence of their frequent use by Jews; they certainly could not compare with the efficacious poisoners, high and low, in Renaissance Italy. Yet occasional incidents, like that of an Aragonese Jewish woman accused of poisoning her husband, made such suspicions more realistic than the wholly imaginary ritual murder accusations. Moreover, some poisons were indeed prescribed in legitimate doses by physicians and sold by apothecaries of all denominations. Hence one could readily suspect any doctor or druggist of making use of his "know-how" and supplies to destroy his foes. The low esteem in which drug salesmen were held in twelfth-century England may easily be gauged from their inclusion in Richard of Devizes' list of low-caste characters reputedly living in London in 1192: "Actors, buffoons, eunuchs, garamanters, flatterers, pages, cowards, effeminates, dancing-girls, apothecaries, favourites, witches, vultures, owls, magicians, mimes, mendicants, dancers, people of this kind fill every house." Jews were well represented in the drug trade as in most other mercantile occupations; many were doubtless active importers of rare medicinal herbs from the Orient. Precisely because they were invested with a mysterious aura of healing, these strange herbs readily conjured up in superstitious minds mental associations with magic and deviltry. Informed persons may also have heard that an outstanding treatise on poisons (as well as their antidotes) current in medical circles had been written by an eastern Jew, Maimonides, and translated into Latin by Armangaud de Blaise from a Hebrew version. What, then, was to prevent Jews from using their skills and materials for the destruction of their enemies? [46]

Jewish doctors were particularly suspect. In the Late Middle Ages the increase in general Jew-hatred, as well as the rise of an influential class of Jewish physicians, strengthened these suspicions which were doubtless intensified by competing Christian doctors.

A Franciscan monk in 1489 incited the Sienese population against a local Jewish doctor by reporting in behalf of their revered St. Bernardino that "a Jewish physician of Avignon had boasted on his death-bed of having during his lifetime killed many thousands of Christian patients by prescribing them fraudulent drugs." Early in the sixteenth century the convert Johann Pfefferkorn admitted that, though not a trained physician, he had dabbled in medical practice and that, before his conversion, he had endeavored to poison Archbishop Albert of Magdeburg and Elector Joachim I of Brandenburg. Though unsuccessful in these two cases, he was able, together with some Jewish associates, to administer deadly poisons to thirteen other Christians. Evidently he felt that his conversion had washed away his crimes and he feared no retribution. Martin Luther, too, was convinced that for years Jews had conspired to poison him and even hired assassins for this purpose. He wrote: "If they [the Jews] could kill us all, they would gladly do so; aye, and often do it, especially those who profess to be physicians. They know all that is known about medicine in Germany; they can give poison to a man of which he will die in an hour, or in ten or twenty years; they thoroughly understand this art." (Luther hardly knew that he was echoing a nine-centuries-old accusation against Arabian Jews who had allegedly murdered the first caliph Abu Bakr by serving him poisonous food with effects delayed for more than a year.) A contemporary Czech writer likewise spoke of "a Jew who knew how to prepare a poison which would kill a person in four or eight weeks, in a quarter or half a year, according to one's desire." Hans Wilhelm Kirchhof exhorted his readers to patronize "honest Christian practitioners" rather than Jewish physicians who, he insisted, sought to deprive their Christian patients of life and property. Finally, in 1610 the Vienna medical faculty staked its professional reputation on the assertion that their religious law ordered Jewish doctors to eliminate every tenth Christian patient by the prescription of wrong drugs.[47]

From here was but a step to the accusation that Jews used poison for the mass extermination of Christians, particularly by contaminating wells and streams. The German-speaking areas were the most fertile grounds for the spread of such rumors because of their deep-rooted anti-Jewish feelings and the rapidity with which news traveled from one city to another. Apparently the earliest recorded imputation of well poisoning by Jews came from Troppau (Opava), Silesia, in 1163, followed by others from Breslau in 1226 and Vienna in 1267. However, these libels assumed catastrophic dimensions only in the fourteenth century when an extraordinary succession of cataclysmic pestilences resulted in the disruption of the whole economic and social order in many lands. The panic-stricken people, unable rationally to explain this recurrence of plagues, and especially the mysterious Black Death of 1348–49, were ready to grasp at any straw and they suspected devilish machinations by enemies, particularly Jews.[48]

A report submitted in 1321 by the bailiff of Teruel well illustrates the public's gullibility. A Christian, Diego Perez, was accused of having dropped poison into neighboring waters. Under torture, he confessed that he had done it at the behest of one Simuel Famos and another Jew. When Simuel, however, staunchly refused to admit guilt even under severe torture, Diego declared that he had lied only to satisfy his torturers. He was executed but Simuel, too, was murdered with no formality of trial and sentence. According to the bailiff, the entire Jewish community of Teruel was endangered. Simultaneously, a much larger drama was played out north of the Pyrenees, the protagonists being at first not Jews but lepers, whose number was legion but whose total segregation and low standing had made them regular social outcasts. In revenge, these lepers allegedly conspired to poison the wells all over Europe and thus to eliminate the hated majority. Soon, however, Jews became involved as partners, indeed as the purported initiators of this scheme. A fabricated letter, translated by a convert, served as evidence for a plot hatched by the Muslim king of Granada with Spanish Jewish associates employing the services of lepers. The result was a mass slaughter of French lepers, while 160 Jews of Chinon were burned or committed preventive suicide. Yet Charles IV used this opportunity to mulct the Jews through enormous fines and, in 1322, to renege on the royal pledge of toleration for at least twelve years after their readmission to France in 1315 and to expel them after the passage of but seven years.[49]

These events were far overshadowed by the tragedy of 1348–49.

Italy, whereto the germs of the deadly pulmonary plague, known as the Black Death, were first brought in April 1348 by sailors from the Black Sea region, remained relatively quiescent. But Aragonese Barcelona, Tárrega, Cervera, and Perpignan became the scenes of serious anti-Jewish disturbances, and the communities of Huesca, Lérida, and Monzón escaped serious injury only because they staunchly defended themselves behind the walls of their quarters. The authorities, too, reacted sharply against assailants, condemned by Pedro IV as "impelled by a malignant spirit." Even the populace soon realized that the Jewish communities had also suffered severely from the contagion. Certainly, the decline of the large Jewish population of Saragossa to but one-fifth of its former size, emphasized by Pedro IV in October 1348, and the need of the Barcelona and other Jewries to enlarge their cemeteries could not long escape public notice. Yet these first massacres on the Iberian Peninsula made a sufficient impression on Aragonese Jewry for it to seek permanent preventives. In the Barcelona synod of 1354 its representatives placed at the top of their resolutions a request that the king secure from the pope, either in writing or through influential envoys, an ordinance which would

controvert the evil designs of the people of the land who in the day of wrath, when there happens to be a pestilence or a famine, fill the city quarters with a cry, "All this is the result of Jacob's sin, let us eliminate him from among the nations." Instead of feeling obligated, in such distressing times, to engage in deeds of righteousness and charity before the Lord of mercy they pursue, on the contrary, the foolish way of spreading false rumors about the unfortunate Jews.

The Barcelona delegates further requested that the pope also provide that, if ever individual Jews offended the Christian faith, as some Sevillians had allegedly done, only the guilty persons suffer retribution. Aragonese Jewry's concern was doubtless heightened by both the tragic news arriving from across the Pyrenees and the observation that in the neighboring kingdoms of Castile and Portugal public order had been energetically maintained. Even in Navarre, where popular tensions had led to much bloodshed in 1328, the authorities, perhaps forewarned by these disturbances, now prevented any serious outbreaks.[50]

Remarkably, these Aragonese Jewish leaders seemed unaware of the protective decrees issued by Clement VI in Avignon on July 4 and September 26, 1348, and of their general inefficacy outside the Papal States in stemming the popular violence which proved to be as contagious as the plague itself. Locally, however, the papal administration, aided by such an outstanding Avignonese physician as Guy de Chauliac, who not only performed yeoman service in combating the spread of the disease but also left behind a remarkable analysis of the pest, succeeded in staving off any attacks upon Jews notwithstanding the general panic under which, as De Chauliac observed, "a father did not visit his son, nor a son his father. Charity was dead and hope crushed." In neighboring Dauphiny and Savoy, on the contrary, the populace almost immediately pointed an accusing finger at Jews, the small communities of Chillon and Chambery becoming the pace setters for one of the greatest tragedies in Jewish history. After a prosecution lasting from September 15 to October 11, 1348, the authorities extracted by torture "confessions" from several imprisoned Jews regarding a Jewish world conspiracy "to kill and destroy the entire Christian faith." Under prompting, the accused admitted "that for seven years back no Jew could plead innocence for all had known of it [the conspiracy] and are culpable of the said fact." Their leaders had allegedly sent messengers all the way from Toulouse to Calabria in order to place poison in wells and to provide Christian families with poisoned butter, wine, and other foodstuffs. One of the accused, the Jewish surgeon Balavigny, added that Jews had also injected the poison of basilisks into the air, fully realizing that human bodies once infected would spread the disease by contact. To save their coreligionists from the ensuing pestilence circular letters had warned all Jewish communities to stay away from infected waters for nine days after the beginning of the plague. These "confessions" were confirmed by the discovery of packages of poison purportedly placed by Jews inside wells or cisterns. The Chillon authorities speedily communicated these data to various cities, particularly Strasbourg which, under the pressure of its restless public opinion, had started collecting information about the plague even before the latter reached Alsace.[51]

Scientists of the age, to be sure, though deeply puzzled by the nature of the pestilence which in most affected areas destroyed from one-fifth to two-thirds of the population, did not lend much credence to these tales. They offered multifarious explanations, such as the corruption of the air by an evil constellation of stars, the particular influence of Saturn (this star incidentally had already in ancient legends often been associated with Jews and their Sabbath), and other natural causes. At least one scholar, Conrad von Megenberg, expressed doubts about any Jewish conspiracy and pointed out that the largest German Jewish community of the time, that of Vienna, had been forced "considerably to enlarge its cemetery and to acquire two houses for this purpose. It would have been utter folly if they had poisoned themselves." Moreover, according to rumor, three astrologers, two Christians and the Jew Leo Hebraeus (Gersonides), had as early as 1336–45 predicted the approaching cataclysm. All such considerations, however, were swept aside by the panic-stricken mobs who wanted to vent their wrath on some tangible objects. The result was, to quote Solomon ibn Verga, that "there were universal persecutions in all the lands of Germany and the Provence and sufferings the likes of which had never existed. Yet the German Jews adhered to the sanctity of the Great God and his Torah and did not relinquish their faith." [52]

Jews of the Austrian possessions escaped the wrath of the aroused population only because of the strong measures adopted by Duke Albert II. Elsewhere, too, most princes tried, however ineffectually, to maintain public order. Palatin Rupert even admitted Jewish refugees from Worms and Spires to his city of Heidelberg. Only Margrave Frederick of Meissen personally promoted the bloodshed. Changeable Duke Louis the Elder of Brandenburg first effectively shielded his Jews and, as late as 1350, he admitted refugees to the New March and took them under his protection. But in that very year he suddenly condemned all Königsberg Jews to burning and confiscated their property. Nor did the second thoughts shared by many observers of the great tragedy put an end to the accusation of Jewish well poisoning. As late as 1422, Martin V, following Clement VI's example, saw himself obliged to instruct the Catholic preachers of all ranks to controvert this fable from their pulpits. In Silesia, where the Black Death or a variant thereof did not strike until the 1360s, the Jews suffered immediate retribution, here aggravated, particularly in 1361, by rumors that

Jewish arsonists had been responsible for successive ruinous fires in various Silesian cities. In 1382 the Jews of Halle and two years later those of Magdeburg were again accused of poisoning the wells and suffered sharp retaliation. Prussian Schweidnitz was the scene of similar disturbances in 1448, 1453, and 1543. In short, these accusations, though of far briefer duration than those of ritual murder, nearly terminated all organized Jewish life in Germany. They clearly demonstrated the far-reaching dangers to Jewish survival arising from the irruption of irrational forces if they were not counteracted by an enlightened public opinion.[53]

HOST DESECRATION

Like the Blood Accusation and the rumors of well poisoning the recurrent denunciations of Jewish profanations of the host originated from European folklore, although the Church's share in the diffusion of the underlying assumptions was much greater. Nor did the Papacy take as clear a stand against that accusation as it did against the ritual murder libel. One may perhaps explain that restraint through the vicissitudes of the doctrine of Transubstantiation itself. Achieving its final formulation only at the Fourth Lateran Council of 1215, it still had to combat much opposition and misunderstanding even among the Catholic clergy. Before long the Reformation repudiated its very fundamentals.

Moreover, almost every accusation of profaning the host was combined with that wafer's purported miraculous reaction in the form of bleeding, indestructibility, or even outcry. Such "miracles" were, on the whole, welcomed not only by local churches but also by the hierarchy at large, for the more the Church insisted upon its complex doctrine of Transubstantiation, the more did the man on the street look for some visible signs of the presence of Christ's flesh and blood in the wafer. On the whole, probably more Christians than Jews were accused of stealing hosts and abusing them out of curiosity, or for magic and medicinal purposes. But while an accused Christian implicated at the most a few direct collaborators each Jew was viewed as a representative of his people and, in many cases, endangered the communities of an entire region. Remarkably, without inquiring why, devoid of belief in

Christ's presence in the wafer, a Jew should wish to expose himself and his coreligionists to horrible retribution, the Christian masses simply assumed that, because *they* believed in the Eucharist, Jews, too, would try to use, or abuse, it. This logic was no more far-fetched than the apologists' frequent insistence that Jews repudiated Christ in defiance of their own ancient letters. True, one or another deranged Jew may have tried to test his Christian neighbors' attribution of supernatural qualities to the wafer or to put it to his private use. But not a single case of such an aberration has been conclusively proved.

With the decline of the status of that sacrament under concerted Protestant attacks, the accusations against Jews likewise waned and ultimately totally disappeared. But at the height of the Eucharist's veneration relics of allegedly desecrated wafers, or of implements used in their profanation, could be exhibited to generations of pious pilgrims and thus serve as important sources of income for a local sanctuary. In their quest for rational explanations, some modern scientists have pointed to a natural phenomenon, which to medieval men may well have appeared as a clear demonstration of supernatural intervention. It has been found that the so-called prodigious micrococcus (*Monas prodigiosa* or *Serratia marcescens*), a fungus settling on foodstuffs like flour, bread, cooked rice, or potatoes, produces on contact with light a red dye resembling drops of blood. Many an unwary medieval observer may, indeed, have viewed that "blood" as a literal confirmation of his belief in the wafer representing the flesh and blood of Christ. At times an overzealous or mercenary cleric consciously immersed a wafer in blood, thus fabricating the evidence of a "miracle." [54]

Out of the belief in the Jew's demonic powers and well poisoning also came the ready acceptance of rumors that Jews (or lepers) ground up consecrated hosts and mixed them with other ingredients to poison a well. Although trying to protect Jews against the unruly Pastoureaux, Pope John XXII did not deny that the lepers had abused the host. The Church's ambivalent attitude is well illustrated by Alexander of Hales' answer to his own query: "What is it that sometimes appears as flesh or a child at the altar? It is indeed something of the living Christ." The same position was taken by Duns Scotus, although the majority of theologians denied the continued presence of Christ *after* the mutation. But they left the miraculous mutation as such undisputed. An incident in Bolsena in 1263 made a lasting impression. A German or Bohemian priest, beset by doubts about Transubstantiation, went on a pilgrimage to Rome, but found his doubts resolved by the sight of a bleeding host in Bolsena. This miracle induced Pope Urban IV to promulgate in 1264 the feast of Corpus Christi, for which Thomas Aquinas composed the office. In the following century an anonymous Italian poet wrote a sacred play on this *Miracolo di Bolsena*. Even such a relatively enlightened pope as Alexander VI reputedly carried a consecrated host in a gold box around his neck to ward off diseases and other misfortunes.[55]

Jews long remained unaffected by these internal ecclesiastical developments, although a fourth-century hagiographer describes an inquisitive Jew who, upon viewing the miraculous emergence of flesh and blood from a consecrated host, adopted Christianity. A similar story was told two centuries later by an ecclesiastical compiler of Ravenna. Perhaps as an echo of the Iconoclastic controversy which necessarily affected also the doctrine of Transubstantiation, St. Paschasius Radbertus of Corbie (*ca.* 823) depicted a Jew attending the mass of one Bishop Syrus in the third or fourth century and trying to remove the wafer in order to throw it into his outhouse. But when he put it into his mouth, "it burned him like fire and he suffered horrible pains." Relieved only by the bishop's prayer, he immediately accepted conversion. In the tenth century Gezo of Tortosa advised Christians to steer clear of infidels, particularly Jews, for "as the most unjust and pernicious of men, Jews are accustomed together with their prince the devil to profane the sacraments." These cases invariably referred only to individual Jews prompted by personal curiosity, in contrast to the later mass libels which affected entire communities and regions. Products of the overheated sectarian and Jew-baiting Western animosities at the end of the Middle Ages, they had no counterparts in Byzantine or Islamic lands. Innocent III himself raised this issue when, in his effort to prevent the employment of Christian maidservants by Jews, he wrote, on July 15, 1205, to Archbishop Peter de Corbeille of Sens and Bishop Odo de Sully of Paris that "whenever it happens that on the day of the Lord's Resurrection

[Easter] such nurses accept the body and blood of Jesus Christ, [their employers] force them for three days thereafter to spill their milk into a latrine before again breast feeding the children." Under the assumption that a swallowed wafer would affect the milk in the nurse's breast, this intemperate statesman-pope permitted himself a portentous generalization admittedly based upon mere hearsay (*accepimus*).[56]

Little did Innocent foresee that his unsubstantiated accusation, though not necessarily presupposing concerted Jewish action, would subsequently lend support to unbridled attacks on alleged Jewish profanations of the host and result in the wholesale destruction of scores of communities. The thirteenth century witnessed the rapid spread of that libel, which, like that of the poisoning of wells, readily communicated itself from one city to another and before long covered an entire area. Moreover, like the suspicion of Jewish magic arts and witchcraft, it became embroiled in sharp sectarian controversies.

Unlike the Blood Accusation, however, that of the desecration of the host was limited in duration and geographic extension. The Jesuit Peter Browe compiled a list of recorded accusations against Jews, most of which, 47 in number, occurred between *ca.* 1220 and 1514. Of these no less than 22 arose in the Habsburg hereditary possessions (particularly in Austria and Styria) and the adjacent southern German territories; 14 more were recorded in the rest of the Holy Roman Empire. There were relatively few in France and the Netherlands, although, as we shall presently see, the tragic events of 1290 and 1370 left a permanent imprint upon the literatures of these countries. On the other hand, Jews were expelled from England before this mass libel reached its full maturation. On the Iberian Peninsula, to be sure, Alphonso X included host desecrations and ritual murders among the crimes which he "had heard" attributed to Jews. Occasional local rumors contributed their share to the heightening there of the existing tensions, of which however they were a reflection, rather than the cause. In any case, even less than the Blood Accusation did that issue deeply affect the lives of most Spanish or Portuguese communities.[57]

Many of these anti-Jewish slanders became famous in legend and literature; some gave rise to Church festivals celebrated to the present day. A tremendous impression was made, for example, by the alleged desecration of a Paris host in 1290. First described by a professed participant, the convert Johannes de Thilrode, this so-called *miracle des billettes* became a recurrent theme in French letters, theological and popular, well into the modern age. Despite numerous variations in detail, many Frenchmen believed that a Parisian Jew, Jonathan, had acquired for the high price of ten livres a consecrated wafer merely in order to demonstrate the stupidity of Christians in believing in its supernatural character. However, to the chagrin of the assembled Jews the wafer first resisted all efforts to pierce it. When finally a knife penetrated it, it divided itself into three parts—similar to its liturgical division in church—and began bleeding. A part thrown into boiling water turned into flesh and blood. This miraculous mutation so impressed our *rapporteur*, Johannes, that he and his entire family immediately underwent baptism. It also caused Pope Boniface VIII, who incidentally spoke only of the boiling water turning to blood, to allow the bishop of Paris in 1295 to turn the Jewish house in which the desecration had supposedly taken place into a "Chapelle des billettes." Before long the relic was transferred to the more spacious parish church of Saint-Jean-en-Grévé, further enlarged in 1326 to accommodate the growing throngs of pilgrims. The original instruments allegedly used in piercing the host were displayed at the chapel for some two centuries. The miraculous host itself was purportedly preserved for four hundred years, while the whole sequence was dramatically depicted in the church's stained glass windows. An annual procession, starting from the parish church, commemorated this miracle down to our times, the six-hundredth anniversary in 1890 in a period of growing Franco-Jewish tensions having offered a particularly festive occasion.[58]

Not surprisingly, this much-discussed miracle stirred the imagination of a French poet whose "Play and Mystery of the Sacred Host" was performed for many years; it was witnessed by an observer in Metz in 1513. The author viciously derided even the request for a Bible by a Jewish victim on the stake, purportedly in order magically to stave off the flames. This Jew was supposed to have died chanting, "Let my body, my spirit, my soul/Burn and be consumed with great dispatch./O devils, come and fetch me quickly,/And carry me away to my final goal." [59]

The éclat of the Paris affair was overshadowed by a similar event in Brussels in 1370. The recorded facts are simple: a converted Jewess, Catherine, shortly after Good Friday confessed to her priest that in October she had stolen some hosts from a local chapel and hidden them until the Holy Week. At that time some Jews, doubtless including members of her own family, allegedly submitted these wafers to unspeakable indignities, eliciting the usual miraculous flow of blood. Unable to secure peace of mind, she confessed her guilt to the priest whereupon the Jews were imprisoned and, after severe tortures, admitted their crime. The trial ended with the burning of the whole Brussels Jewish community, which had by that time dwindled to but four families. Many Jews living at a distance, such as those residing in Louvain, were likewise burned, although by no stretch of imagination could they be directly implicated. These facts remained sufficiently dubious to call forth, in 1402, a renewed investigation by the ecclesiastical authorities who, however, confirmed the original sentence.

Far beyond its immediate results this *cause célèbre* served to embitter Judeo-Christian relations in the Low Countries. Although no formal decree of expulsion is recorded, no Jew was allowed to live in Brabant for several centuries. The affair also gave free rein to poetic imagination and the author of a poem, *Miracle de Sainte-Gudule,* depicted a fantastic scene of the condemned Jews dancing around the pyre and chanting "Mamet," the name of the founder of Islam. This doubtless was but a willful distortion of the *Shema'* (Hear, O Lord) recited by the Jewish martyrs while being consumed by flames. In 1436 a commemorative chapel for that miracle was erected on the site of the former synagogue; it was rebuilt in 1735 and still stands in Brussels today. Simultaneously, a second chapel was dedicated in the church of Sainte-Gudule where relics of eleven hosts were permanently preserved; it was reconstructed between 1534 and 1539 in an extremely ornate style. Later, it was adorned by stained glass windows depicting, with much fantastic detail, the theft and maltreatment of the wafer, the execution of the Jewish "culprits," and the wafer's return to the church. Annual processions, ever since held for that "holy sacrament of the miracle," still belong to the major Catholic festivals in Belgium. Each jubilee year, as we recall, even in recent centuries, was celebrated with much pomp and attracted pilgrims from a great distance. Only in the democratic atmosphere of 1870 was there a sufficient revulsion of public opinion to eliminate the planned grandiose celebration.[60]

CONTAGIOUS FURY

By involving Jews of many communities the desecration of the host ranked with the poisoning of wells, rather than with the blood libel. It lent itself to large-scale exploitation of the myth of the Jews' implacable hatred of Christianity and, particularly during its climactic half century from 1290 to 1340, it caused endless sufferings to the Central-European Jewries. Both the so-called Rindfleisch massacres of 1298 and those instigated by the Armleder brothers in 1338 were nurtured by this accusation. The hysteria generated in 1298 in the small Franconian town of Röttingen spread to many parts of southern Germany and penetrated Austria to the vicinity of Vienna. Soon thereafter a Korneuburg priest perpetrated a remarkable fraud. Although the contemporary reports are very hazy about the locale and the number of martyred Jews (the dates range from 1298 to 1308), there is no question that at least two Jews were burned. To cite Pope Benedict XII's letter to Duke Albert II of Austria of 1338,

At one time a cleric sprinkled some blood on an unconsecrated host in the Austrian hamlet of Neuburg and displayed it in the local church. But he confessed in the presence of the bishop of Passau, of blessed memory, and of reliable witnesses still alive today, that he had done it, in order to arouse the suspicion that the wafer had been profaned by Jews in a shameful fashion. For a long time it was revered by the faithful as a true host until it was completely destroyed by insects and moths. Thereupon another cleric, in a devilish delusion, did not hesitate to spatter blood upon another unconsecrated host as he himself admitted it later. As you write, to the present day [this second host] is being revered as the true body of the Lord by the faithful unaware of the fraud.

Although copies of Benedict's letters to the duke and the bishop of Passau must have been deposited in the papal archives, they were ignored by Boniface IX when he permitted in 1396 the erection of a chapel named "for the body of our Lord Jesus Christ" on the site of the alleged miracle.[61]

Benedict's correspondence with Albert was occasioned by a similar libel of 1338 in the Austrian town of Pulka which, as usual, resulted in the preservation of the miraculous wafer in a newly consecrated church, named the Church of the Sacred Blood. Here, however, the anti-Jewish excesses were stemmed, though somewhat belatedly, by Duke Albert II, who had from the outset doubted the veracity of the testimony presented to him. Albert turned to the pope for advice. Sharing the duke's doubts Benedict ordered the bishop of Passau, by chance likewise named Albert II as duke of Saxony (1320–42), to institute a careful investigation and, if trustworthy witnesses were to prove the Jews' innocence, to impose severe canonical sanctions upon the accusers as a deterrent to future crimes of this kind. The bishop also was to remove the unconsecrated hosts from the respective churches. Characteristically, the chroniclers fail to mention the final outcome; they doubtless were unwilling to concede the exoneration of Jews by a joint intervention of duke and pope.[62]

In contrast to Albert, Duke Henry of Bavaria more readily yielded to the pressure of public opinion and condoned the anti-Jewish atrocities committed on this score by the inhabitants of Deggendorf. In a decree of October 14, 1338, he reassured the Deggendorf burghers (as he had three days earlier those of Straubing) that they had not forfeited his good will, and allowed them not only to keep what they had taken from the Jewish victims, "clandestinely or openly," but also to refuse payment of any debts owed to Jews. A host of pilgrims has ever since streamed to the small Deggendorf church and, as late as 1870, 100,000 communions were administered in it. The accusation also inspired an anonymous German author to compose a poem on it; provided with music, it was sung in many communities.[63]

Another *cause célèbre* in Berlin in 1510 had even more tragic consequences. Curiously, according to some sixteenth-century reports (whose credibility has rightly been impugned), at their first appearance in the March of Brandenburg the Jews were confronted with this libel in Belitz (before 1247). However, this accusation, if any, remained a strictly local affair. In contrast, the events of 1510 led to the suppression of all Jewish communal life in the country for almost two centuries. A Jewish chronicler of the period calls Elector Joachim I (1499–1535), under whose reign they took place, "the great enemy and oppressor." But rather than being personally responsible for the prosecution Joachim merely yielded to the virulently hostile public opinion which had long clamored for the expulsion of Jews. To achieve this aim it seized upon the theft from the church in the village of Knoblauch of a gilded monstrance and a copper box containing two consecrated hosts. The thief, Paul Fromm from neighboring Bernau, was soon located, but after his confession he was induced to implicate some Jews. Before long the prosecution extended to the Jewish residents of the entire March and included elements of the ritual murder libel as well. (This is the less surprising as, according to some accounts, both accusations had also been combined in the far-reaching trial which had led to the destruction of the Breslau community in 1453.) Under torture, the defendants made the usual confessions and, ultimately, thirty-eight of them suffered death by burning. Sixty others were acquitted but forced to leave the country, "lest they try something like it in the future, or try unjustly in some fashion to avenge the death of those who had rightly been burned because of their transgressions." They also were made to take a solemn oath (the so-called *Urfehde*) not to return to the country, to steer away any coreligionists wishing to enter it, and not to seek any revenge for their mistreatment.[64]

In this case, however, the judicial murder was discovered within a generation. While attending the Catholic-Protestant debate in Frankfort in 1539, Philip Melanchthon revealed that Fromm had confessed to his priest that he had unjustly dragged in the Jewish names, but that the priest had been prevented by his bishop from divulging that confession. Among Melanchthon's informants were several readily accessible witnesses, including Martin Bucer. Neither Bucer nor Melanchthon was generally friendly to Jews and, although they had their Protestant bias against Catholic relics, their testimony appeared so trustworthy to Joachim II (1539–71) that, notwithstanding Luther's complaints, he admitted to residence in Berlin a number of Jews, including his well-known mint-master, Lippold. He did not dare defy public opinion, however, to the extent of formally abrogating his predecessor's decree of expulsion of 1510. The church of the city of Brandenburg, too, refused to give up its center of attraction. Down to the twentieth century it displayed to visitors knives allegedly used by the Jews to pierce the host, as well as a painting graphically depicting the scene of the profanation.[65]

Frenzied reactions of this type were largely limited to the Holy Roman Empire and adjacent lands. After the *miracle des billettes* in France and the *miracle de Sainte-Gudule* in Brussels, Jews were little affected by host libels in these areas. In England and the Scandinavian countries such miracles, connected with profanations by Christians, rarely excited the imagination of the people and had no effect upon Jews at all. Even in Italy, where occasional incidents flared up, they did not result in large-scale persecutions of Jews in the Central-European fashion. Most remarkably, Switzerland, which had such a sad record with respect to Blood Accusations and well poisonings, proved far less gullible in regard to alleged Jewish desecrations of hosts. Nor did the medieval Swiss churches evince much interest in cashing in on the "miracles of the Sacrament," whether caused by Jewish or non-Jewish perpetrators.[66]

In Aragon and Castile, too, the kings pursued a very prudent policy in this matter. Informed in 1367 that thieves had stolen from a Perpignan church a silver chest containing consecrated hosts and that they had perhaps sold it to, or pawned it with, a local Jew, Infante John ordered the Rousillon governor to investigate the charge, but to be "cautious lest the Jewish quarter suffer damage through a riot or in some other way." This investigation may have involved the distinguished rabbi, Vidal de Tolosa (author of a well-known commentary, *Maggid Mishneh,* on the Maimonidean code) and other scholars and possibly led to the execution of three Barcelona Jews. Ten years later a similar rumor endangered the communities of Huesca and Teruel. Since the Huesca burghers were then trying to shut Jewish competitors out of the city proper, they readily supported the inquisitors who had demonstrably tampered with the evidence. But Pedro IV realized that the accusers acted more out of desire "to destroy the said community and its individual members, as well as Our other communities, than out of zeal for justice or the Catholic faith." Astutely handling this explosive situation, the king overruled his son and averted the danger. In 1383 he ordered the Count of Urgel to investigate a similar accusation against two Lérida Jews "discreetly and with full diligence." But all Aragonese communities felt sufficiently threatened on this occasion to send a delegation to the king. The prosecution was quashed and we learn about these proceedings only from Pedro's order of 1386 that the communities pay the expenses incurred by their delegates. Evidently the peril had passed and the communal treasurers were in no hurry to meet their obligations. Even in the overheated atmosphere of 1408, such rumors in Segovia led only to the execution of the Jewish court physician, Don Meir Alguades, and a few associates, probably because, under torture, Don Meir had also confessed to having poisoned King Henry III. The entire affair gives the impression of a cabal to get rid of an influential leader. Characteristically, these suspicions were soon aimed also at the Castilian *conversos*. During the upheaval of 1449, the Toledan petition included the vague allegation "that some priest of that nation had on a certain day consecrated five hosts, of which he took one, and the others he handed to his brethren. It is not known what happened to them." [67]

No more serious consequences resulted from such rumors in Portuguese Coimbra in 1361, where a Jew, Joseph, was accused of having thrown a host into an outhouse. Only the culprit was punished and in 1397 Pope Boniface IX allowed the erection, on the site of the alleged miracle, of a hospital with a chapel dedicated to its commemoration. The street was renamed the *rua de Corpo de Deos* and, even in modern times, guides, both printed and living, have repeated the story to tourists. [68]

At the same time desecrations of hosts often preoccupied the Iberian peoples, many a Christian being accused of trying to penetrate the mystery of the consecrated wafer. Religious authors also took up this theme. The petition pointing an accusing finger at the *conversos* was fully reproduced by the anti-Jewish writer, Alphonso de Spina, who, as we recall, also told with much relish the story of the Jewish boy in Segovia and his enforced restoration of a miraculous host in 1455. A play entitled *Sacramento de la Eucaristia* resembled similar productions in the northern countries, except that the protagonist here was not a Jew but a Christian skeptic and the miracle brought about the skeptic's death, rather than the usual conversion of the Jewish offender. Of course, after 1575, when this play was written, there no longer were any professing Jews in Spain.[69]

Host accusations were but the most important variants of frequent allegations that Jews had been stealing crosses or manufacturing wax effigies of Christ in order to reenact the crucifixion. Even in Spain, where both accusations were relatively rare, Alphonso X mentioned in his Code the rumor that, when unable to secure little boys for ritual murder, Jews crucified wax images of Christ. So convinced were many Western Christians that Jews went to great lengths in securing crucifixes that they readily circulated stories about individuals daringly assailing public processions and snatching crosses or consecrated hosts from them. One such attack reputedly took place in 1268 at a university procession in Oxford, when a Jew seized the cross "and trod it under his feet, in token of his contempt of Christ." Curiously, instead of being lynched on the spot, the culprit escaped and remained unidentified. It is, of course, possible that a foolhardy or deranged Jew may have committed such an atrocity, but in retribution, all of Oxford Jewry had to pay out of its meager resources for a large marble crucifix with the figures of Jesus and Mary and a smaller cross made of silver. Incidents of this kind, magnified by popular imagination, were often cited as reasons for the regulation that, at the approach of a church procession, Jews withdraw into their houses.[70]

In all these allegations of ritual murders, well poisoning, and desecration of hosts, as in the rapidly spreading witch hunts, the aberration of the medieval mass mind reached a climax. Even persons of gentle disposition, who would recoil from any cruelty to man or animal, often rushed headlong into accusing, condemning, and violently executing such "criminals" on the flimsiest of evidence. Surely they must have known that confessions exacted by severe torture produced no reliable testimony. On balance, it appears surprising that so many Jews succeeded in withstanding unspeakable pain and in staunchly asserting their innocence. Many did it not in order to save themselves, for a most painful death must have beckoned to them as a release from worse sufferings. Only their superior sense of responsibility and the knowledge that admission of guilt might endanger entire communities raised their power of resistance to an almost superhuman level.

In order to understand the admissibility of such enforced confessions as prima facie evidence, it suffices to remember that the well-balanced and religiously tolerant Jean Bodin was perfectly prepared to act upon them in witch trials. In his *Demonomania* he approvingly cited the *Determinatio* of 1398 in which the Paris Theological Faculty had laid down twenty-eight principles starting from the premise that "the demon is considered the persistent and implacable adversary of God and man." Another eminent and personally humane jurist, Henri Boguet (d. 1619), presented in *An Examen of Witches* (which in its original French appeared in eleven editions within a short span of time) a fantastic record of unusual trials before the tribunal of St. Claude presided over by him which resulted in some 600 death sentences against witches. If such frenzy could be unleashed against defenseless Christian women, whose "guilt" often consisted only in prescribing certain remedies for sick or psychologically disturbed persons, how much easier was it to cast aspersions on Jews whose very survival and way of life was a permanent source of wonder! [71]

Rather surprisingly, the sixteenth-century author of the notorious *Endingen Judenspiel* which crudely dramatized an accusation against the Jews of Endingen leading up to their expulsion of 1470, tried to persuade his audience that the Rabbi Elias of the play, who appeared before the city council eight years after his alleged murder of a Christian family of four, had admitted the crime "without torture and pain." Certainly, the thousands of viewers from many localities who, according to an eyewitness of 1616, streamed to see the show and to gaze at the remains of the alleged child-victims believed it to be a perfectly legitimate confession. At times such accusations served sectarian purposes. For instance, the fifteenth-century Croxton *Play of the Sacrament* depicted an alleged desecration of the host by Jews, although at that time the latter had been absent from the English scene for some four or five generations. Its author merely intended thereby to defend the Catholic doctrine of the Eucharist against John Wycliffe's strictures. Jews were thus caught between the sharply contending ideologies during the breakdown of the medieval civilization.[72]

AHASVERUS

Increasing hostility toward Jews came to the fore also in the legend of the Wandering Jew or Ahasverus. Originally this legend, imported from the Middle East, had only indirect Jewish connections. At its first appearance in Europe (in Roger of Wendover's *Flores historiarum*) it described how a distinguished Armenian archbishop on his visit to England had told his British hosts the story of Cartaphilus, one of Pilate's guards. Jesus, struck by him and urged on to march faster toward his execution, allegedly cried out, "I shall go, but you will wait until I come." As a result Cartaphilus became immortal and was still awaiting Jesus' return to earth. Having converted himself to Christianity, he received the name Joseph and led an exemplary life of utter self-denial. This story, somewhat elaborated in Matthew Paris' *Chronicle,* attained a great vogue throughout Western Christendom and was included in a French rhymed chronicle by Philippe Mouskes. It also was interpolated into a fourteenth-century Czech manuscript, containing a versified Czech translation of the *Dialogus beatae Mariae et Anselmi de passione Domini.* Related accounts, though probably of independent origin, appeared also in Italy. An astrologer, Guido Bonatti, reported that such a man, here named Johannes Buttadeus, had visited Forlì in 1267. This unusual name may have conveyed to contemporaries the idea of an "assailant of God" but, according to Paulus Cassel's attractive theory, may have been derived from "Buddha." In Spain we find the even more descriptive name of Espera-en-Dios.[73]

Up to this point the legend merely elaborated a theme suggested by the Gospels. Particularly the saying attributed to Jesus, "Verily I say unto you. There be some standing here which shall

not taste of death, till they see the Son of man coming in his kingdom," had led to the conclusion that one of Jesus' assailants would
become immortal, as drawn by St. Chrysostom in his homily on
the Gospel of John; it was repeated by many ecclesiastical authors
in subsequent generations. The culprit was for the most part
equated with Malchus, Peter's assailant at Gethsemane. Although
occasionally depicted in terms relating to Jews, his punishment by
an endless life of travail did not yet carry the sharply anti-Jewish
accents given it in later Passion plays. According to the Franciscan
Peter of Penna (*ca.* 1350), some scholars doubted reports by pilgrims about a place in Jerusalem pointed out to them as the location where John Buttadeus had ridiculed Christ. They questioned
the very existence of such a person and identified him with another legendary character, John Devout-of-God, an equerry of
Charlemagne, who was supposed to have lived 210 years.[74]

Apart from its Jewish and Buddhist connections, some scholars
have also detected in the story of the Eternal Jew certain ingredients taken over from Teutonic legends about the Eternal Hunter,
a figure widely cherished in the German countryside even in modern times. In some areas the farmers arranged the rows in their
fields in such a way that on Sundays the Eternal Jew might find a
resting place. Elsewhere they assumed that he could rest only upon
a plough or that he had to be on the go all year and was allowed a
respite only on Christmas. Some features of that legend were derived from the Wotan mythology, but they had become integrated
into the Christian tradition.[75]

Soon, however, the anti-Jewish features began to predominate.
Although from the outset everyone realized that Jesus' assailant
had been a Jerusalemite Jew, he now began to be identified with
an unconverted eastern Jew still alive in modern times. This new
version appeared in a short story entitled *Kurze Erzählung von
einem Juden aus Jerusalem mit Namen Ahasversus* which, purportedly published in Leiden in 1602, quickly became a best
seller. Other editions of the same year recorded various places of
publication, a trick sometimes indulged by publishers to convince
the public of the popularity of their product. The booklet was
probably first issued in Basel or, as some recent scholars have suggested, in Danzig. At any rate, it described how in 1542 Paulus

von Eitzen, later bishop of Schleswig, had noticed in a Hamburg church a very tall barefoot stranger with hair hanging down to his shoulders, who, seemingly aged about fifty, impressed all onlookers with his unusual behavior and attire. According to his own purported version,

he was a Jew born in Jerusalem by the name of Ahasverus and had been a shoemaker by trade. He had personally participated in the crucifixion of Christ, had since remained alive, and had traveled through many lands. In confirmation, he described many details of what had happened to Christ as a prisoner brought before Pilate and later before Herod, as well as during the crucifixion. None of that was reported by the evangelists or historians. He similarly told manifold stories and reports concerning changes in government which had taken place in the oriental countries during several hundred years after Christ's passion. He could also give a perfectly good account of the apostles, where each had lived, taught and been finally martyred.

His reports were allegedly verified by Von Eitzen and other scholars. They were elaborated with additional details in subsequent editions of the booklet.[76]

We need not dwell here on the much-debated problem of why the writer selected for this wandering Jew the name of Ahasverus, who in the biblical story of Esther appears as a perfectly sedentary Persian king. It is, of course, possible that the name had some connection with the Oriental patron of seafarers, Al-Khadir, known in Europe under the name of Al-Khisir. Ironically, according to most versions of the legend, this "cobbler" never wore shoes but, because of his perennial wanderings, had soles two fingers thick and hard as nails. More significantly, at least in the German version, Ahasverus appears as a full-fledged personification of the Jewish people. Here we, indeed, have the main themes of participation in the crucifixion, the condemnation to eternal suffering and immortality until the second coming of Christ, the perpetual wanderings, particularly from east to west, and the bearing of witness to the truth of the Christian tradition. Some versions also lay stress on Ahasverus' familiarity with many languages. Understandably, the name of Ahasverus was quite early replaced by that of the Wandering (or Eternal) Jew, apparently first employed in an English ballad antedating the Jewish resettlement under Cromwell. Its anti-Jewish animus is well expressed in its exhortatory refrain:

"Repent therefore, O England!/Repent while you have space;/ And do not (like the wicked Jews)/Despise God's proffered grace." Moreover, this Wandering Jew was soon turned into an ardent adherent of Antichrist, whose appearance in the East had supposedly attracted a large Jewish following.[77]

Whether as a pious, dedicated convert to, or as an opponent of, Christianity and partisan of the Antichrist, the Wandering Jew seemed omnipresent. He appeared all over the Continent and, according to some Icelandic legends, had even penetrated that remote region. Many people contended that they had personally seen him. As late as 1756 Maria Regina Krüger, wife of a professor of mathematics, claimed that she herself had met that man in her native village near Eisleben. He "was of very small stature, had ice-grey hair, a snow-white beard falling down to his chest, and with a very serious mien he walked through the village. Everybody recognized him as the Eternal Jew, and I could not doubt it for a moment when I looked into his eyes." The legend also played into the hands of swindlers. In 1623 a man clad in Turkish attire without trousers or socks, bald-headed and with a very large grey beard, appeared in Ypres. Carrying a pilgrim's staff, from which a flask was suspended, he presented himself as the Wandering Jew and was hospitably received by a local family. After a while he told the daughter of the family that his one hundred twenty-third wife had died but three months before, and seduced the girl after promising to marry her. Before long, however, his real wife appeared on the scene and he turned out to have been a deserter from the army, whereupon he was led to the gallows.[78]

Such incidents, however, did not cure the populace of its belief in the constant reappearance of that strange figure. Of course, there also were some skeptics. In an investigation of the *Historische Nachricht von dem ewigen Juden,* published in Frankfort in 1723, an anonymous author listed the following localities where the Wandering Jew "had allegedly been seen, namely in Armenia, Latvia, Poland, Muscovy, Spain, as well as Lübeck, Hamburg, Rostock, Wismar, Danzig, Naumburg, Saxony and other places; in 1694 even in England and its most prominent localities . . . but who in fact never existed." This booklet was adorned by a wood-cut, showing the Wandering Jew passing by the ruins of the Temple. But the masses never wavered in their belief in this stirring tale. Even in the nineteenth century museums in various places, such as Ulm and Berne, displayed large shoes allegedly worn by the Wandering Jew, although most other folk tales described him as always walking barefoot. The Berne shoes were, indeed, enormous and consisted of some one hundred leather pieces which only a master artisan could have put together. Conceivably, the presence of such relics of an earlier age had induced the mythologists to view the Wandering Jew as being originally a cobbler.[79]

The eternal migrant readily brought to mind the tragic personality of the biblical Cain. Ancient mythological concepts were now revived and homiletically amplified to explain the strange phenomenon. Was not Abel the prototype of Jesus, the innocent son of man, whose offering was accepted by God, but who, for this reason, was slain by his older brother? Certainly, to Christian homilists the biblical story of creation and the first men was not a mere tale but an object lesson in the course of history as it was to unfold under its divine guidance. As early as the days of Tertullian, some homilists had equated the Jewish people with a new Cain who would likewise be "a fugitive and a wanderer . . . in the earth." Distinguished by his Cain's sign, circumcision, so ran the homiletical lesson, the Jew must constantly migrate from place to place, finding no permanent abode. This rationale did not appear at all abstruse to the medieval mind. It was indeed the *leitmotif* of one of Peter of Cluny's letters to King Louis VII. "They [the Jews] should be a sign [for the nations]," also observed Matthew Paris, "like Cain the accursed." Even later, when in Shakespeare's *Richard II* Bolingbroke wished to curse the royal assassin Exton, he found no better phrases than: "With Cain go wander through the shade of night,/And never show thy head by day nor light!" [80]

It is small wonder that the tragic image of the immortal wanderer attracted the attention not only of Jew-baiters, but also of such great poets as Shelley and Goethe. The sudden response to the *Kurze Erzählung* and its very speedy reappearance (before 1930) in no less that 188 editions in German, French, English, Italian, Dutch, Danish, Swedish, Polish, Finnish, and Estonian clearly indicate how well prepared the European folk psyche was for this fantastic tale. The impact of Goethe and Shelley upon imitators was likewise enormous. It has been shown that, from 1774 when Goethe wrote his unfinished poem on the Wandering Jew until 1930, no less than 460 works in various languages on this theme had seen the light of day. As summarized by Joseph J. Gielen, "Ahasverus is the eternal witness of Christ: he is a prophet and preacher who exhorts people to repent; he often serves as a representative of the Jewish people; and particularly in England, the Wandering Jew is used to satirize political affairs or to furnish a survey of current history." In this fashion an essentially medieval irrational theme, reflective of the tensions built up between medieval Jews and their neighbors, germinated a vast and, in part, qualitatively high modern literature which, however, in contrast to its medieval models, often treated the tragedy of the Wandering Jew with fine understanding and sympathy.[81]

CROSSCURRENTS

We must not assume, however, that even in the Late Middle Ages Judeo-Christian relations present only a picture of unmitigated gloom and hostility. Unlike law and theology, or even economics, the daily life of the Jewish people found little reflection in the existing documentation. In the legal sphere the extant decrees and judicial proceedings are on the whole sufficiently precise for us to reconstruct the medieval Jewish status with some accuracy. The major question, often impossible to answer, is the extent to which these laws were applied in practice. Even in theological speculation, subject as it was to personal impulses and temporary exigencies, we may venture certain generalizations, although here, too, we may question whether the bark was not worse than the bite and whether the constantly reiterated arguments reflected existing realities or merely reechoed a centuries-old heritage. Also in the economic sphere, where practice was much more important than theory, we frequently have to depend on normative sources rather than on records of actual daily transactions. Yet the available evidence gives us a fairly adequate picture of the Jewish role in the economic life of many countries, as well as of the converse impact of economic transactions upon the continuity of Jewish existence.

In contrast, the daily relations between the two groups can but partially be reconstructed, since the extant documentation is both meager and slanted; it stresses negative far above any positive aspects of mutual rapprochement. Contemporary chroniclers, in particular, recording dramatic events, had more frequent occasions to mention hostile encounters, including massacres and expulsions, than the more prosaic, because friendly, daily contacts. In belles lettres, too, the presentation of the Jew as an object of hatred, scorn, and derision seemed so much more exciting and likely to secure popular approval than any preachment of mutual toleration. On their part, many rabbis likewise viewed with suspicion any excessively friendly intergroup contacts which might, and often did, result in the apostasy of the Jewish party.

Here and there, nevertheless, we do obtain glimpses of closer collaboration between the two groups. Even the Spanish pietist, R. Jonah b. Abraham of Gerona, advised his readers to follow the example of R. Johanan b. Zakkai and always to greet first all acquaintances, Jewish or Gentile. His advice sharply contrasted with the opposite counsel given to his coreligionists by the Spanish priest, Theotonio, several centuries earlier. Understandably, the most frequently recorded instances stem from the intellectual sphere, since we know much more about the lives and behavioral patterns of outstanding scholars and writers than we do about those of average individuals. Certainly, many students of science and letters, especially if they were interested in the Hebrew language and literature, often found it to their advantage to consult Jewish experts. This was, indeed, the climactic period of collaboration between Jewish and Christian scholars in the translation, often through the use of the Hebrew medium, of Graeco-Arabic works in mathematics, astronomy, and medicine. Such professional cooperation unavoidably also led to closer social contacts. Some of the very theologians who harbored anti-Jewish feelings from time to time consulted Jewish advisers for the better understanding of the Bible. Nicholas de Lyra, about whom it was punned, *si Lyra non lyrasset, Luther non saltasset* (Luther danced to Lyra's lyre), needed Jewish help for the better comprehension not only of the biblical text but also of the medieval commentaries on the Bible, especially that of Rashi. Of course, as in St. Jerome's case, such literary contacts did not necessarily tone down the Christian partner's anti-Jewish animus. While Nicholas restricted his anti-Jewish attacks to a few literary excursuses along the accepted line of Christian polemics, Martin Luther, his disciple in Bible exegesis, was far more vicious in both verbiage and practical application.[82]

Other Christian Hebraists, however, communed with their Jewish friends as genuine colleagues. We need but quote the following entry in Elijah Levita's autobiography concerning his relations with Cardinal Egidio di Viterbo:

Now I swear by my Creator that a certain Christian [Egidio] encouraged me and brought me thus far. He was my pupil for ten years uninterruptedly. I resided in his house and instructed him, for which there was a great outcry against me, and it was not considered right of me. And several of the Rabbis would not countenance me, and pronounced woe to my soul because I taught the law to a Christian, owing to the interpretation assigned to the words, "And as for my judgments, they (i.e. the Gentiles) are not to know them". . . .

When the prince (i.e. Egidio) heard my statement, he came to me and kissed me with the kisses of his mouth, saying "Blessed be the God of the Universe who has brought thee hither. Now abide with me and be my teacher, and I shall be to thee as a father, and shall support thee and thy house, and give thee thy corn and thy wine and thy olives, and fill thy purse and bear all thy wants." Thus we took sweet counsel together, iron sharpening iron. I imparted my spirit to him, and learned from him excellent and valuable things, which are in accordance with truth.

Evidently Elijah was more concerned about the reaction of his own coreligionists than he and Egidio were about the hostility of the Christian public. Some Jewish pietists may even have resented the simple homage paid to an ecclesiastical dignitary. If the latter displayed a cross on his outer garment, onlookers might misinterpret such homage as paying obeisance to an "idolatrous" symbol specifically prohibited in the Talmud. Yet even in orthodox Prague the eminent Jewish scientist and historian, David Gans, could entertain close personal relations with the famous astronomers Johannes Keppler and Tycho Brahe, and translate from the Hebrew into German, at Tycho's request, the Alphonsine Tables, themselves coauthored by Jewish astronomers at Alphonso X's Castilian court. Most congenial was the exchange between Christian and Jewish students of Kabbalah, the former actually finding in Jewish mysticism some support for their Trinitarian dogma—a circumstance which was not to be overlooked later by Jewish opponents of that secret lore. For example, the renowned humanist Giovanni Pico della Mirandola often debated kabbalistic issues with like-minded Jewish scholars, especially the somewhat enigmatic Flavius Mitridates.[83]

Hebrew thus served as a frequent bridge between the intellectuals of the two faiths. Roger Bacon, who knew enough Hebrew to use it in his comments on the biblical text and to comtemplate the writing of a Hebrew grammar, emphasized that it was easy to study Hebrew, as well as Greek, in England because "there is no shortage of teachers. There are Hebrews everywhere, whose language is substantially the same as Arabic and Chaldean, though they differ in certain aspects." Nor did Johannes Reuchlin later encounter any difficulty in acquiring a good command of Hebrew, first through the assistance of Frederick III's court-physician, Jacob Loans, and later, during his sojourn in Rome, under the guidance of Obadiah Sforno, a well-known Bible commentator and humanist philosopher. Sforno's career, incidentally, shows that close association with Christian students did not necessarily impinge upon the orthodoxy of either party. Even his philosophic work was largely devoted to the defense of the Jewish tradition against both Christian strictures and Jewish rationalistic trends. Some Jews were allowed to teach Hebrew at universities, especially in Italy, although theirs were for the most part informal lectureships rather than formal appointments. University students, moreover, in many parts of Europe not only associated with Jewish moneylenders and traders who provided them with their material wants, but often lodged in Jewish-owned houses and were otherwise in contact with Jews.[84]

Most of these examples are taken, to be sure, from Renaissance Italy, where the Judeo-Christian relations had generally become quite friendly. A Scandiano churchman had good reasons to complain about Christian women frequently visiting in Jewish houses and vice versa and about Christian and Jewish children playing together. A Jewish wedding in Modena in 1542 attracted many Christian guests of both sexes even from among the neighboring gentry. The famous banker-scholar Yeḥiel da Pisa entertained in his summer home a number of Christian nobles for whom Mrs. Da Pisa performed on the violin. Jewish musicians and dance masters had Christian pupils. What irked the clergy most was that distinguished Jewish preachers, like Leon da Modena, attracted many Christian listeners. The Church also objected strenuously when in 1484 a Sicilian Christian officially served as godfather (*syndic*) at a Jewish circumcision ceremony. Usually such friendly acts were taken for granted, the Sicilian episode being casually mentioned only because of the fine imposed upon that Christian "culprit." Needless to say, some rabbis, too, frowned upon such intimacy, although Joseph of Arli actually boasted of his numerous Christian friends. A Christian official of Terni befriended Jewish refugees from Civitanova and, according to a Hebrew rendition, stated, "I love you all like myself and I wish to bestow favors upon you for the Lord has never abandoned you all the days of the world. Even as a people in exile, you are beloved by the Creator who at every moment performs miracles for you." Another Italian leader stated succinctly, "I have been a lover of Jews from childhood." [85]

Even in the darkest period of medieval English Jewry in 1286 we hear of a wealthy Jew of Hereford who, at his daughter's wedding, allegedly entertained Christian friends with "displays of silk and cloth of gold, horsemanship and minstrelsy." In his bull *Nimis in partibus* addressed to the archbishops of Canterbury and York at the end of that year, Pope Honorius IV complained, with evident exaggeration, that "Christians and Jews continue meeting in one another's houses. They spend their free time in feasting and banqueting together; hence there is much opportunity for mischief." In fifteenth-century Germany, too, friendly exchanges of gifts are frequently recorded in connection with ritualistic problems. Informed that in Wiener Neustadt a Christian had brought cakes to a Jewish wedding, Israel Isserlein overruled some guests' compunctions by generally allowing Jews to eat breads baked by Christian bakers. He merely advised them as a matter of supererogation to abstain from such consumption during the Ten Days of Repentance from the New Year to the Day of Atonement. This liberality contrasted sharply with the frequent attempts of Christian bakers to persuade their coreligionists that bread baked by Jews, to cite the Arles bakers of 1427, was "dangerous for them to consume." Similarly, Isserlein approved of the practice of Jews sending New Year's gifts to Christians, including the clergy, again adding the reservation that, in order to avoid the appearance of the donors' taking part in a Christian religious ritual, such gifts be dispatched a day before or a day after the holiday. Nor did he see anything objectionable in the custom of sending Christians gifts on the *Lag be-'omer* (the thirty-third day after the inception of Passover), frequently celebrated as a youth festival. Reciprocal Christian expressions of sympathy and respect for Jews, too, were not quite so rare as one might imagine. An Oxford Jew produced in 1244 twelve burghers who testified in his behalf that he had been "brought up among them from infancy, and bore himself ever leally in all manner of lealty." In a lawsuit before the Superior Court of Magdeburg a Christian, referring to a Jew not involved in that litigation, stated, "I know nothing but what is likable and good," about him.[86]

Many other illustrations of the constant interrelations between the two groups will be cited in our description of the internal Jewish social developments and the daily life within the ghetto. We need but remember the frequency of business contacts to realize that the separation of the two groups was not even remotely so watertight as some extremists in either camp might have wished. A large number of non-Jews visited the Jewish quarter daily, whether in quest of less expensive merchandise, to secure a loan, or to pay bills. Conversely, Jewish merchants ventured out of their quarters every day in search of customers or sellers. At times they had to travel extensively through the countryside, visit market places, and generally contact Christians of all classes, including the clergy. These peaceful daily exchanges went unsung and unreported. Only some dramatic incidents were likely to draw the attention of the authorities or contemporary writers. The very fact that a badge became increasingly necessary to distinguish Jews from Christians and that so much effort had to be lavished upon shutting the former off in streets of their own indicates the inherent closeness of intergroup relations.

Most significantly, Jews almost everywhere speedily adopted the local languages and used them even at home and in business dealings with one another. True, most European Jews, unlike their coreligionists in Islamic lands, preferred to write Hebrew not only in their intellectual and communal pursuits but often in their business and family correspondence. In an environment which almost exclusively used Latin in its literary and state papers it would have been rather abnormal for Jews to employ the local dialects in their scholarly letters, communal records, or business contracts. The small size of most communities scattered over a vast continent and extending into the Muslim world and beyond, combined with the basic interdependence of their fate, doubly forced them to resort to the use of a common medium, particularly in fields of religious and cultural concern. Only with the progress of West-European nationalism and the increasing application of local languages in literature did their use increase also among Jews. Here, too, vernacular translations and belles lettres appealing to the broader masses, especially to women for the most part unlearned in Hebrew, were steadily gaining ground. Yet, despite occasional Hebraic influences on the daily speech of various Jewish groups, there never developed in Spain, Italy, England, France, or even Germany, a full-fledged Jewish language of the kind of Yiddish or Ladino, as they were later refined by the Jews of Poland and the Balkans. This high degree of linguistic assimilation revealed a certain feeling of at-homeness of these West-European Jewries which, even if originally developed in the calmer pre-Crusade atmosphere, carried through to the end of the Middle Ages and beyond.[87]

REALM OF UNREASON

In trying to ascertain medieval popular attitudes, we must always bear in mind our lack of real knowledge of the innermost feelings of the vast masses of peasantry, the overwhelming majority of each country's population. In many western countries few Jews were allowed, or willing, to settle in rural districts; even itinerant individuals but rarely stopped off in villages for any length of time. It stands to reason, therefore, that most country folk knew Jews only through some sporadic appearances, if any, of a few atypical persons. As a rule the peasants formed their opinions about Jews and Judaism by what they heard from their parish priests, deduced from some mystery plays, or were told by story-tellers. Even the urban proletariat left behind few direct records. We can infer, of course, some underlying hostility from its occasional violent anti-Jewish riots and massacres. But we must not forget that, between these violent outbursts, there were long intervals of peaceful cooperation when mutual suspicions alternated with deeds of actual friendliness. Nor are we ever certain by whom the recorded cases of mob violence were actually perpetrated; in many cases they doubtless resulted from actions of a ruthless minority with the passive acquiescence, rather than active concurrence, of the majority of the respective populations.

Most of the conclusions reached in this chapter had to be based, therefore, on relatively few literary and artistic monuments extant in the form of Passion and Mystery plays, folk songs and folk tales, or graphic representations in paintings and sculptures adorning churches or illuminating manuscripts. By their very essence such graphic attestations are limited in scope and historic value. Preponderantly intended to illustrate the Gospels or to help the reader visually to understand a religiously oriented manuscript, they naturally carry with them the religious biases of these sources. True, by presenting contemporary Jews in their medieval garb with their medieval speech and gestures, sometimes even as bargainers or usurers, the playwrights came close to expressing their own feelings. But even if their plays were intended for broad urban and rural audiences, they themselves were largely recruited from the clergy or, later, from the urban bourgeoisie. They may have reflected the prejudices of their respective classes, rather than those of the masses.

On the other hand, these masses could not long remain unaffected by the influential opinion molders, although there is no way of ascertaining the extent and enduring quality of that influence. As in the case of modern audiences listening to sermons or attending theatrical performances, the impact of preaching from pulpit or stage may have been short-lived; it may speedily have given way to each individual's personal experiences or desires. Yet, at least in the periods of great political and socioeconomic tensions

which characterized the late Middle Ages, the hostile feelings generated by such performances must have resulted in both immediate reactions and the revival of long-forgotten memories of earlier
animosities.

Of great importance was the gradual transfer of literary leadership from ecclesiastical to lay authors and particularly the rise of
an intelligentsia recruited from the generally anti-Jewish petty
bourgeois class. In the long run this laicization of European letters
was to accrue to the benefit of religious toleration. But at first the
increasingly Jew-baiting Passion and Mystery plays reflected the
transition from the relatively controlled fury of most churchmen
to unbridled savagery in the abuse and caricature of Jews, particularly in Germany. Even Judas became not so much the traitor as
the typical medieval Jewish bargainer and usurer. Nor did such
petty bourgeois authors as Pamphilus Gengenbach hesitate to
lump together the mercenary Christian authorities and the Jews.
Utilizing the phrase of *Judenspiess rennen* which, apparently
derived from the spear of Longinus in the Gospel story of the
Passion, had come to connote Jewish usury, he wrote of cases when
"little silver spears were also needed," that is, when Jews resorted
to the bribery of officials. Obviously, Jews thus gained no immediate advantage from the progressive loss of control by the Church
over the composition and staging of religious plays. They also lost
much through the gradual shift in the Church's attitude from
outright condemnation of actors and acting to the Thomistic distinction between honorable and dishonorable performers. Subsequently the Council of Basel authorized the issuance of charters
for special religious brotherhoods of actors. Finally, the religious
theater, too, was handed over to professional groups which shared
with the other artisan classes and guilds their unrestrained animosity toward Jews.[88]

Limited as the value of our documentation may be, it does point
up the progressive sharpening in Judeo-Christian relations during
the last three centuries of the Middle Ages. These conclusions
which became evident from our review of the increasingly restrictive legislation, the narrowing Jewish economic basis, and the
increasingly bitter religious polemics and disputations, are also
borne out, on a more popular level, by the ever more intensely

Jew-baiting folk literature of the fourteenth, fifteenth, and sixteenth centuries. It is small wonder, then, that these gathering feelings of hostility erupted during those three centuries in a sort of chain reaction of anti-Jewish massacres and expulsions.

L

WANDERER

OUR REVIEW of the religious, political, and folkloristic factors has shown a steady deterioration of the Jewish status in the Late Middle Ages. At the same time the ecclesiastical polarity of tolerating Jews in Christian lands and yet maintaining them on a low social level remained fairly constant, although its formulations were hardened into a ramified canonical legislation. Clearly, Charlemagne or Louis the Pious were no less Christian monarchs than Edward I of England, Philip the Fair of France or Ferdinand the Catholic of Spain. And yet, while the former went out of their way to invite Jews and to bestow upon them a number of far-reaching privileges, these latter-day medieval kings expelled them from their countries. In moments of high tension, to be sure, religious fanaticism played a great, at times a decisive, role. But the explanation of the very leeway given to it in such periods and the origin of the tensions themselves must be looked for elsewhere.

Political and economic relationships were more variable. The conditions differed from country to country and from period to period. Sometimes individual proclivities, even whims, of rulers exercised great influence. The ascendancy and fall of the nobility; the gradual strengthening of state power in the West-European countries while it progressively weakened at the top but grew in the middle echelons of principalities, bishoprics, and cities in the Holy Roman Empire; the internal conflicts within the cities and the temporary rise of artisan classes in their struggle for supremacy with the patrician groups; the greater or lesser dependence of the villein masses upon their feudal lords—all greatly contributed to the improvement or deterioration of Jewish status. Similarly, the growing prosperity characteristic of the twelfth and thirteenth centuries, followed by the economic crises of the fourteenth and early fifteenth centuries; the strengths and weaknesses of economic regimentation; the rise of the great urban centers, particularly in

Italy and the Low Countries, to economic and political power, both domestically and on the international scene; the slow growth and subsequent sudden decline of population of many lands— these, too, had their significant share in shaping the fate of medieval Jewry. No less influential was the growing laicization of the European societies and the emergence of many folkloristic attitudes, theretofore concealed in the depths of the inarticulate masses.

Behind these variables loomed still another major factor which helps to explain some of the changing fortunes of medieval Jews. The twelfth to the fifteenth centuries witnessed a progressive strengthening of national feelings among the European peoples which deeply colored the political and folkloristic factors and subtly pervaded also the economic trends. Not even the religious formulations escaped their impact. It was unavoidable that the new, ever more conscious nationalism in various lands should also exercise a deep influence on the position of Jews in the medieval societies.

MEDIEVAL NATIONALISM

Compared with the modern era dominated by nationalist strife and characterized by a nationalism which was almost deified in Fascist and Nazi totalitarianism, the national sentiment seems to have played a lesser role in the medieval civilization. United by the over-all Catholic *Weltanschauung,* long theoretically adhering to the idea of a universal *corpus Christianum* which, according to some thinkers, embraced also the non-Christian world, the medieval West presented a picture of a fairly homogeneous, intrinsically uniform culture. Thomas Aquinas reflected the dominant ecclesiastical ideas when he taught that the human race should be considered as one mystic body *(corpus)*, whose head is Christ with respect to both the souls and the bodies. "We must consider members of the mystical body, not only as they are in act [Christians], but as they are in potentiality [unbelievers]." The notion of a universal empire, as a counterpart to this *corpus Christianum,* persisted to the very end of the Middle Ages. The fifteenth-century humanist Ennea Silvio Piccolomini, even before his accession to

the papal see as Pius II, still insisted on the Empire's feudal overlordship over all princes and peoples. In periods of crisis, particularly during the Crusades and in contact with the Byzantine world,
this Western unity not only appeared in doctrinal form but also
represented deeply felt emotions on the part of the Western
peoples.[1]

Nevertheless national feeling inescapably came to the fore.
Nationalism, in both its political and its cultural manifestations, is
almost as old as organized humanity. A Polish historian may have
gone too far in claiming that

the nationalisms of the ancient Near East were on the whole sharper,
more violent and more irreducible than modern nationalisms. For the
counterweight of international and supranational factors was far weaker
in the ancient Near East than in the modern period. There was absent,
particularly, that unity of civilization which the Western world has
inherited from the Roman Empire. The civilizations of the ancient
Near East were national civilizations in a much higher degree than all
the subsequent civilizations.

When the nationalities dominated by the Eastern Roman Empire
wished to maintain their national identity in the face of the Greek-
Orthodox steamroller they often resorted to sectarian deviation.
Certainly, the strength of Monophysitism in defiance of the Council of Chalcedon was largely owing to its adherents' semiconscious
attempt to preserve their national distinctiveness. Before it was
abolished by Justinian in 529 the famous University of Athens had
a student body divided by its respective national origins. After the
Islamic expansion the West-Asiatic and North-African peoples
were replaced by the Balkan Slavs who grew into regular nationalities while still under Byzantine domination. This nationalist
wave affected even the Church. As observed by Albert Dufourcq,
"the more the Byzantine Church is 'decatholicized,' the more it
becomes 'nationalized.' " [2]

Similar manifestations soon came to the fore in western Europe.
The University of Paris was divided into four *nationes*. That of
Bologna for a time had no less than thirty-five nations, until it was
finally decided to divide the whole student population into two
major divisions of Citra- and Ultramontanes. The University of
Orléans recognized seven nations, allowed to observe "certain

superstitious celebrations, vulgarly known as the feasts of the nations" which often led to nationalist disturbances. By the sixteenth
century the nationalist recriminations at Cambridge made the
master of St. John's College take a prescribed oath that he "will
not sow hatred or discord, nor bear himself contumeliously to any
man by reason of his country, or race, or other matters of that
kind." The very Church universal had to make allowances for national groupings which sometimes, as in the Council of Constance
(1414–18), led to sharp controversies, for instance, between the
English and the French.[3]

In still another area was the Church forced to recognize the national divisions transcending state boundaries. The papal Chancery established special departments for large units like Gallia,
Germania, Italia, and Anglia, for the purpose of both fund raising
and diplomatic negotiations. Curiously, the rabbis, too, often disregarded political frontiers in favor of larger ethnic groups. Discussing the talmudic law which denied husbands the right to force
wives to move from one country to another, Meir b. Baruch observed that France, England, Germany, and Bohemia belonged to
that category because their inhabitants spoke different languages.
But individual German principalities including Bavaria, Saxony,
Franconia, Alsace, or the Rhine province, all of which shared the
same German language, did not qualify as separate countries in
talmudic terms. Both the rabbis and the Papacy could the more
readily recognize such larger ethnic-cultural entities in a feudally
atomized Europe, as they never considered political boundaries
sacrosanct. To the rabbis all non-Jewish regimes merely represented "foreign domination," while the Christian scholastics persisted in seeing in the state as such an artificial organ, even a necessary evil as the effect of human sinfulness. Practically, too, the ever
changing boundaries involved constant shifts in political allegiance, whereas loyalties to one's religion or class, or, more vaguely,
to a large ethnic-cultural community had earmarks of perma-
nence.[4]

At the same time the ecclesiastical tradition itself contained
enough political elements to foster the rise of national states.
Medieval thinkers could never quite forget Augustine's opposition
to vast empires like the Roman, which he characterized as "in the

eyes of the wicked a gift of fortune, but in the eyes of the good it is a necessary evil" (*necessitas*). Before long the ever recurrent struggles between state and Church, soon enlarged to a European conflict between the Papacy and the Empire, led to the clearer formulation of both the universalist and the nationalist theories of government. At first both the Papacy and the Empire claimed universal supremacy. Emperor Frederick II warned the European kings in 1236 against indulging some "vague luxury of freedom." Invoking his "predecessors," the Roman emperors, who had extended their reign over the whole world including Judea and with respect to whom Jesus had taught "Render unto Caesar" (Matt. 22:21), he demanded that all Christian monarchs pay homage to the Empire. He accused his papal opponent of actually stimulating "the abuse of pestiferous liberty." In the same vein an advocate of the imperial theory, Johannes Teutonicus, declared, "World domination was transferred to the Germans. . . . The emperor is placed above all kings . . . all nations are under him. . . . Jews, too, are under him." No lesser authorities than Bartolus de Saxoferrato and Baldus de Ubaldis taught that any denial of the emperor's world supremacy was a religious "heresy" or "sacrilege." [5]

Like their countryman, Dante Alighieri, however, these two distinguished jurists merely voiced idealistic postulates, rather than reflected existing conditions. Certainly, Jacobus de Albenga was far more correct when he had stated that "Frenchmen, Spaniards and some other provinces, though *de jure* they ought to be subject to the Empire, . . . in fact are not so subjected." To counterbalance these imperial claims Innocent III (in his famous bull *Per Venerabilem* of 1202, which was taken over into the *Corpus juris canonici*) acknowledged that the king of France "recognizes to but a very slight extent any superior in temporal matters." Other popes did not hesitate to encourage the Castilian king Alphonso VI to proclaim himself emperor and, in temporal matters, supreme ruler of all Christianity. [6]

National independence received a powerful rationale under Philip the Fair during France's successful struggle against the two supreme organs of Western Christendom. Some of his juridical associates, such as Pierre Dubois, were able thus to develop the

idea of national sovereignty. Going hand in hand with the growing royal absolutism of the period, the doctrine of national sovereignty was soon combined with that of the divine right of kings
which, reinforcing the drive toward national independence, led
domestically to the concentration of royal power over the centrif-
ugal forces of feudalism. Even the king's person was invested with
a sacred character and *lèse majesté* became a capital crime. This
sacred character of the monarchy also found expression in the
liturgy, with its regular benedictions for the king in churches and
synagogues and in the royal oath. In the name of the national
unity of all Frenchmen Francis I refused in 1526 to implement the
right of secession guaranteed in the treaty with Burgundy of 1484.
Similarly, the mutual bickerings between German and French
Crusaders, or between the representatives of the French and English churches at the ecumenical councils, transcended the boundaries of their home countries and related far more to ethnic-cultural
than to political differences. In short, Halvdan Koht is undoubtedly right in stating that "from the beginning of the twelfth century, European nationalism has a continuous history."[7]

New nationalist emphases translated themselves also into greater patriotic fervor. The idea of dying for one's fatherland, so
highly cherished by ancient Roman patriots, had been replaced by
the antimilitarist early Church following Jewish prototypes with
the concept of religious martyrdom. Even during the early Crusades the intellectual leadership was stressing death in behalf of
one's religious ideal. But while among Ashkenazic Jewry religious
martyrdom was reaching its tragic climaxes in the mass suicide of
entire communities to escape the temptation of apostasy, the doctrine that man must sacrifice his life for his fatherland began
looming larger and larger among the European peoples. Suger, the
twelfth-century abbot of St. Denis, unrestrainedly extolled French
victories and, because of his intense patriotism, merited the designation of *pater patriae*. Tolomeo de Lucca, Thomas Aquinas' contemporary, reasoned that "love for one's fatherland is imbedded in
the root of charity" and that hence such love deserves a place of
honor among the virtues.[8]

The rise of European nationalism in the double meaning of national sovereignty and ethnic-cultural identity has been described

here at somewhat greater length because of its decisive impact on the history of European Jewry. This impact made itself felt first in national self-assertion versus Papacy and Empire and, subsequently, in the ethnic-cultural differentiation from the Jewish minority.

National sovereignty led to the gradual arrogation, by the respective kings, of total overlordship over Jews. We have seen how the purely theological doctrine of Jewish serfdom, first formulated by the Church, had gradually been altered by the Holy Roman emperors, particularly Frederick II, into a serfdom of the imperial Chamber. In its exhausting struggle with the Papacy, however, the Empire lost its grip over its Jewish subjects as well. The ecclesiastical and imperial theories of Jewish serfdom thus progressively gave way to the royal theory which found its classical expression in the aforementioned definition of the English jurist Henry de Bracton. By the end of the thirteenth century there was little question as to who was the real master of Jews. Only sporadically, as in the story of the expulsion of the Jews from France in 1306 or in the occasional appeals to the pope by Jews (or by Christian friends acting in their behalf), do we hear outside the Church and Empire echoes of the old ecclesiastical and imperial doctrines. Basically, the Jews had become attached to the local rulers, be they emperors, kings or dukes, barons or bishops, or even city councils. Of course, this new status was not always so clearly defined as it now appears in retrospective legal theory. In the confused feudal relationships which resulted from a multitude of *ad hoc* actions and reactions, Jews, too, were often dependent on more than one authority, a condition which sometimes alleviated, and at other times aggravated, their general position. But nowhere could they resist the incontestable trend toward national supremacy, least of all in states which achieved a measure of national homogeneity.[9]

By itself this situation does not explain the gradual deterioration of Jewish status in the Late Middle Ages. Since their respective princely masters derived ever greater fiscal benefits from that relationship, it is doubly astonishing that they failed to employ their increasing power for more effective protection of their Jewish "serfs."

We must seek the answer not only in the traditional realms of religious controversy, economic competition, and folkloristic animosities, all of which had also existed to a greater or lesser extent in more tolerant periods, but also in the new type of nationalism gradually taking shape in the Late Middle Ages. Nearly four decades ago I ventured to formulate something approaching an historical "law" that, particularly in medieval Europe, the status of the Jew was most favorable in states of multiple nationality and most unfavorable in national states. Between these two extremes were states which formed but part of a larger ethnic-cultural group and which, for lack of a better term, I called the part-of-a-nationality state (*Nationalteilstaat*). I added then:

The National State, feeling strongly the strangeness of the Jew in its otherwise homogeneous body national, has always tried to eliminate it by full assimilation, which often took the shape of enforced conversion, or by full exclusion, which generally meant expulsion. The State of Nationalities, being composed of many different groups, was less concerned about the existence of another distinct element, and could see more clearly the meritorious qualities of a group different from all others. The wide dispersion of the Jews could even serve sometimes as a cohesive, centripetal force in the State.

In the middle was the part-of-a-nationality state, which revealed some of the intolerant traits of the national state, but lacked its decisiveness and simultaneity of action. It also often evoked tribal, rather than national, enmities. In the case of Jews, tribalism, though also generating much hostility toward them, was as a rule directed against many other tribal aliens and was less dangerous than the national unification of the "host people" which in the Middle Ages often spelled ultimate disaster. In historic reality, needless to say, this factor entered into a variety of combinations with the religious, economic, folkloristic, and sociopolitical forces which accelerated, retarded, or otherwise moderated its operation. However, one hardly need labor the fact of the general medieval xenophobia, reinforced as it long was by the slowness of communications and the almost universal suspicion of strangers. Many proverbs in various lands agreed with the French adage, "Do not look for truth in a man who comes from a distance." Hence the rise of increasingly homogeneous national states in parts of Europe served as an evil augury for the future of Jewry.[10]

Nor was the progressive decline of feudalism and the rise of the middle class of immediate benefit to the Jewish people. On the contrary, this class marched in the vanguard of anti-Jewish movements, partly because of its competitive economic interests and partly because it had become the main exponent of the national idea. Some kings fostered these trends for their own imperialistic and centralizing purposes. Philip the Fair of France, in particular, and Spain's Catholic monarchs effectively placed themselves at the helm of their countries' national unification movements. The anti-Jewish stance of the new class was the more implacable, as burghers did not quite share the restraints of kings interested in Jewish taxation nor those of churchmen tied to an age-old tradition of limited toleration. For a long time the new class had to fight for its own recognition since opponents, like the anonymous cleric of 1440, often contended that only "the three classes of the clergy, the warriors and the farmers were created by God, whereas the fourth class of burghers and usurers was the creation of the devil. . . . The burghers expropriate the soldiers and oppress the workers, while they themselves live a life of leisure [*otiosi*]." Frank Barlow is quite correct in saying that "the [Jewish] ghetto was merely a cell within another ghetto—the town itself." It is small wonder, then, that when the town ghetto began coming into its own, it tried the harder to remove the Jewish ghetto from its midst. In one way or another, it succeeded fairly well in attaining this objective within any growingly homogeneous national state.[11]

The downgrading of the feudal aristocracy, caught in a vise between the growingly absolute monarchy and the increasingly powerful burghers' class, was facilitated by its great wartime losses. So long as military campaigns were conducted principally by the knightly class which often had to finance them from its own resources, the nobility of many lands found itself impoverished, as well as decimated. It sustained further losses from the great mortality during the pestilences of the fourteenth century. For the Jews this transition carried ominous implications. While they often found protectors (however high-handed and contemptuous) in the higher aristocracy, the bourgeoisie, particularly of the "petty" variety, was as a rule inimical to them. Similarly, the growing laicization of the medieval societies intensified their ethno-religious intolerance. We have seen how the relatively restrained ecclesiastical authors and producers of Passion plays gave way to rabidly Jew-baiting middle-class playwrights and performers toward the end of the Middle Ages. The growingly lay spirit promoted mutual rapprochement only in the truly advanced humanistic society of the Italian Renaissance, not north of the Alps. The curious upshot was that the very class which, under the later capitalistic system, proved to be most helpful to Jews in entering its open society, was most hostile and exclusive toward them under the medieval system of regimentation.[12]

ENGLAND

A clear illustration of these trends was offered by medieval England. Even setting aside the union with Normandy, which long remained the center of gravity of the conquerors and also served as a mainspring for the early Anglo-Jewish communities, the inhabitants of the English realm were long divided into an Anglo-Saxon majority and a small, but dominant, Norman minority. So long as this division persisted Jews appeared as but another ethnic group, intrinsically no more foreign than the aristocracy. As protégés of the king, they probably were resented by the Anglo-Saxon peasant masses, though somewhat less than the latter's oppressive Norman landlords. Judeo-Christian relations were sufficiently good to arouse the ire of the clergy which was particularly irked, as we recall, by the alleged favoritism shown the Jews by William II Rufus.

Before long, however, the two major ethnic groups began amalgamating and creating a new English nation, distinguished by a language consisting of an organic blend of Norman-French with Teuton ingredients. At the same time the English monarchy began its struggle for independence from both the Papacy and the Empire. In the latter part of the eleventh century an anonymous York cleric (possibly Archbishop Gerard himself) postulated that both the state and the Church submit to the will of the divinely ordained king. Although perhaps supported by Archbishop Lanfranc and St. Anselm of Canterbury, his demand was too radical for that day; his views and manuscript were allowed to sink into oblivion until they were taken up three centuries later by the nationalist John Wycliffe. The self-assertive Church often was in open conflict with the state and even found a martyr in Archbishop Thomas à Becket. Externally, however, English sovereignty was steadily growing, thus paving the way for, and receiving constant support from, the strong national feelings. As early as 1159, John of Salisbury, aroused by Frederick Barbarossa's presumptuous tone, asked, "Who has appointed the Germans as judges over the nations? Who has conferred that authority on these crude and impetuous men?" In the following century Henry III readily supported the papal claims against the Empire and even tried to place his brother and son on the thrones of Germany and Sicily. English sovereignty also gradually asserted itself against the Papacy. In Henry III's declining years the English monarchy emerged as the relatively most independent power outside the orbit of both the Papacy and Empire. With greater justice than in the days of Bede the Venerable some English thinkers now claimed the *auctoritas imperialis* for England, too. In the mid-thirteenth century the distinguished jurist, Henry de Bracton, well grounded in canon, customary, as well as civil, law, strongly insisted that the English king was not subject to any outside secular power; nor, one might add, to the papal power in temporal matters.[13]

For the Jews this drive for national sovereignty meant, in the first place, growing insistence on royal controls. We have seen how the idea of Jewish "serfdom" under England's royal power had steadily gained ground over the corresponding papal and imperial claims. To lend it some historical sanction, a mid-thirteenth century jurist interpolated into the laws of Edward the Confessor a passage asserting such royal overlordship. Bracton, who insisted upon England's national sovereignty, also offered that classical formulation of Jewish serfdom which was to play havoc with many modern students of the legal status of medieval English Jewry. Jewish dependence on the Crown was clinched by the Assize of Arms of 1181 which forbade Jews to wear weapons because they were under the king's protection. Of course, Jewish security was greatly weakened, since arms could be used to prevent attacks or at least to minimize major disasters, whereas royal protection served at best as a psychological deterrent. In periods of high emotional tension fears of later retribution, particularly under unstable governments and mercenary officials and judges, hardly sufficed to offer Jews a powerful shield.

Parallel with this evolution on top went on the gradual amalgamation of the two ethnic groups. The closer the Normans and the Anglo-Saxons intermingled to develop the characteristics of a single nation, the more pronounced did the Jews' "foreignness" become. With their usual conservatism English Jews continued to use French in their daily speech, even after the Norman aristocracy had begun accommodating itself to the new national language. The recorded names of English Jews, though often translated from the Hebrew (Vives for Ḥayyim, Deleucresse for Solomon or Gedaliah and the like), are predominantly of French origin. Only toward the end of the thirteenth century did Anglo-Saxon names like Bateman (for Benjamin) or even Christian names like Thomas or Peter (for Pereṣ) appear in the records. The badge, too, introduced into England with less difficulty than elsewhere, and the voluntarily worn conical hats, underscored the Jews' alien character. Popular antagonism, reinforced by economic resentments toward a class of wealthy usurers and religious hostility toward infidels, found manifold outlets in acts of aggression against the Jewish minority even during the twelfth century. Blood Accusations, beginning with that of Norwich in 1144, grew into a violent crescendo during the following century. These antagonisms led to the widespread massacres of 1189–90 which left a heritage of great bitterness that cast its shadows upon the entire residual period of Jewish sojourn in the country.[14]

No such violence was allowed again in the following decades. In 1203 John I sharply warned the mayor and barons of London, "We shall require their [the Jews'] blood at your hand if by your fault any ill happen to them, which may God forbid." Nevertheless, the populace staged numerous local riots; among them one in Norwich in 1239 under the excuse that, four years earlier, Jews had forcibly circumcised the son of a physician Benedict, very likely a converted Jew. When, with the aid of soldiers, the sheriff restored order, he was accused of excessive severity. In 1244 students attacked the Oxford Jewry and pillaged many houses, while priests and monks were involved in a similar disturbance in Canterbury in 1261. In most cases the authorities reacted strongly; for instance, in Oxford forty-five rioters were arrested. Less successful were the London Jews whose quarter was ransacked in 1239 because a single Jew had been accused of murder. As a result several Jews, rather than the rioters, were executed and the entire community collectively fined one-third of its property.[15]

The thirteenth-century Church rarely exerted the moderating influence which had characterized its earlier leaders. If, in 1255, the Franciscans, led by their outstanding scholar Adam Marsh, tried to pacify the aroused Londoners, rival Dominicans attributed this action to Jewish bribery. In retribution, the Franciscan order received fewer alms from local devotees for a number of years. More typical was the attitude of Archbishop Stephen Langton who, as we recall, had actually sought to starve the Jews out of England, as some heretics had been starved out under Henry II. A similar effort to stop food sales to Jews in the 1230s likewise had to be checked by the government. The polemical literature also became increasingly sharp. Compared with Crispin's moderate dialogue, the writings of Bishop Bartholomew of Exeter or Peter de Blois were filled with anti-Jewish invective. This contrast between the churchmen's behavior now and that of both their predecessors in England and most of their Continental contemporaries cannot be explained by their ever growing indebtedness to Jewish moneylenders alone.

Evidently, consciously or unconsciously, the ecclesiastical spokesmen thus responded to the growing nationalist feeling against Jews. Understandably, they saw the simplest solution in the Jews' speedy assimilation via conversion. Reacting with extraordinary dispatch to Pope Nicholas III's bull *Vineam sorec* of 1278, the English Church introduced conversionist sermons with the aid of secular authorities which, on January 2, 1280, were ordered by Edward I "to induce the Jews, by such means as they, under the inspiration of the spirit of truth, may think most efficient, to assemble and hear without tumult, contention, or blasphemy, the word of God preached by the friars [Franciscans], and to see that the rest do not interfere with those who become converted." Going beyond anything known on the Continent at that time, Archbishop Peckham, who had served as theological lecturer at the papal palace for several years, closed down, as we recall, all London synagogues except one. "Peckham's zeal," rightly observes Elizabeth O'Neill, "was not tempered by discernment, and he had little gift of sympathy or imagination." By a rather reckless generalization he claimed "that a number of persons of both sexes, in the city of London as elsewhere, who had been converted from the Jewish infidelity to the Christian faith, had returned to their vomit, the Jewish superstition," an accusation echoed in Honorius IV's *Turbato corde* of 1286. Finally, in the critical year of 1290, some clerics, doubtless with the archbishop's tacit approval, resorted to forced conversions in direct violation of the established canon law. This time the civil authorities did not interfere, which is the less surprising, since both the Church and the government preferred the absorption of converted Jews by the English national body to their forcible elimination.[16]

Under clerical influence Edward I also decreed in 1280 that converts should retain half their property. Even prospective converts receiving instruction in the new faith were given room and board in the *domus conversorum* established in 1232. Once again it was Edward I who placed the finances of the *domus* on a firm basis by transferring to it the property confiscated from Jews condemned to death, the one-half of the converts' property which still escheated to the Crown, and other revenues. Most irksome to Jews was the special new poll tax of three pence placed upon each Jew and Jewess from the age of twelve; doubly so, since its collection was often entrusted to converts. Some Jews reacted violently and, in Oxford, attacked one such convert-collector, William le Convers.[17]

This spirit of national intolerance communicated itself also to the barons, particularly in the so-called Barons' War in 1264–66, the nationalist motivations of which have long been recognized. Although Jewish moneylending often played into the hands of the great landlords, to whom the lower barons had to come for assistance when their debts to Jews fell due, it was the higher aristocracy which was mainly responsible for that revolt, gravely affecting many Jewish communities (Canterbury, Northampton, Winchester, Cambridge, Bristol, Worcester, Lincoln, the isle of Ely, and particularly London). The number of Jewish victims is indicated only for the city of London, where, according to Gervaise of Canterbury, the first of two riots resulted in 200 Jewish casualties. Other sources double this number and give for the second London riot the exaggerated figure of 1,500 Jewish victims. Evidently, concomitant with the general destruction of life characteristic of most civil wars, the Jewries of these major communities sustained a severe bloodletting. Needless to say, the barons also gave vent to their economic grievances. In Cambridge and Lincoln they seized Jewish bonds which, in Lincoln, they "trod underfoot in the lanes." On his part, Edward, heir apparent and commander of the royal forces, in 1263 negotiated a loan with two Cahorsin brothers "for the affairs of himself and the realm," and pledged as security "the whole of the Jewry of the realm with the Exchequer of the said Jewry, and all issues belonging to the said Jewry" for more than two years. English Jews were thus caught in a vise between their baronial and urban enemies and their Cahorsin competitors. But above and beyond these obvious economic considerations the strong nationalist sentiments permeating the entire baronial uprising indubitably intensified the rebels' hatred of Jews, which quickly abated when the latter accepted baptism and thereby surrendered their Jewish identity.[18]

Most anti-Jewish were, as elsewhere, the burghers. Once more commercial rivalry, as well as religious and folkloristic animosities, played an enormous role. But this class more than any other also felt the new nationalist stimuli and it deeply resented the numerous foreign advisers brought by Henry III into the country. Its discomfiture grew at the sight of the hated foreigner, Peter de Rivaux, being entrusted by the king in 1232 with "the custody of the King's Jewry of England so that all the Jews of England shall be intendant and accountable to him of all things belonging to the King." Soon thereafter Peter's custody was extended to the Jewry of Ireland "for life." The total exemption of Jews from municipal jurisdiction likewise was very irksome to burghers, since it gave the royal officials many opportunities to intervene in the municipalities' internal affairs. These feelings were hardly assuaged by the numerous charters prohibiting the disposal of burgage tenements to Jews, as well as to religious houses. As the closest neighbor of Jews, the urban population always was in the vanguard of their attackers and furnished both the rumormongers about, and the mass of believers in, Jewish ritual murders and other crimes. The writings of the age, particularly by chroniclers who were often recruited from the burghers' class even if they wore monks' cassocks, reflect this deep hatred. For one example, in describing the confiscation of Jewish bonds by Henry III, Matthew Paris observed that the Jews "were not at all pitied because it is proved, and is manifest, that they are continually convicted of forging charters, seals and coins." It was for good reason, therefore, that, following John I's example, the Regency, led by William Marshal, ordered in 1218 the selection of twenty-four burghers in every potential trouble spot to serve, so to say, as hostages insuring peace. Local officials were also told not to allow any unauthorized persons to interfere with existing Jewish rights of settlement. A similar measure was adopted by the repentant Simon de Montfort himself after the Barons' War. He issued proclamations inviting Jews to return to their former habitats, with twenty-four citizens once again serving as guarantors of their peace in Winchester, Lincoln, and other cities. Of course, Simon's new feeling of responsibility came too late to repair the damage already inflicted upon Jews.[19]

The only radical solution appeared to be for a city to secure from the king or its feudal lord a privilege *de non tolerandis Judaeis*. Such moves got under way in the 1230s, perhaps stimulated by the Leicester decree of 1231 enacted by Simon de Montfort for "my burgesses of Leicester and their heirs." Similar privileges were secured, we recall, by many cities in 1234–43 and were confirmed by a sweeping royal decree of 1253. In 1261 the burghers of Derby secured, for a consideration, a privilege "that no Jew or Jewess by the king and his heirs or others shall henceforth remain to dwell in the said town." More moderately, the abbess and nuns of Romsey secured in 1266 a grant that henceforth no Jew should reside in that town without their license, an authority which they doubtless exercised only in cooperation with the townspeople. These restrictions created twofold resentment in cities (for instance, Wallingford and Winchester) which could not secure similar privileges but, on the contrary, had to accommodate refugees from the "successful" localities. In the burghers' constant struggle with the monarchy for more and more liberties the Jewish issue thus began looming increasingly large.[20]

As coworker with his father during the last years of the latter's regime, Prince Edward doubtless approved of the expulsion from Derby in 1261 and the privilege for the nuns of Romsey in 1266. After his accession to the throne, he did not overrule his officials who agreed to the exclusion of Jews from Winchelsea and Bridgnorth in 1273–74, because "no Jew had at any time customarily lived or dwelled there." In 1275 the driving force was the Queen Mother, Eleanor, who thus sweepingly got rid of all her Jews in the towns under her control. In his characteristic order of January 16, 1275, Edward wrote:

Whereas by Our letters patent We have granted our dearest mother, Eleanor, Queen of England, that no Jew dwell or abide in any of the towns which, by assignment of Our father, King Henry, and Ourself, she, Our mother, has for her dower within Our realm, so long as the same towns shall be in her, Our mother's, hand; and for this cause We have provided, that the Jews of Marlborough be deported to Our town of Devizes, the Jews of Gloucester to Our town of Bristol, the Jews of Worcester to Our town of Hereford, and the Jews of Cambridge to Our city of Norwich, with their Chirograph-Chests and all their goods, and that they thenceforth dwell and abide in the said towns and city among Our other Jews in those places; We therefore command you, that, doing them no injury, either to their persons or to their goods, to conduct them to their new localities.

Much as she disliked Jews in her earlier years, though she greatly benefited from their taxes and gifts, Eleanor probably would not have resorted to this drastic action, were it not for the pressure of her townspeople. Without her cooperation, Jews were banished from Windsor in 1283, from Conway and other localities in 1284.[21]

Most decisively Edward is rightly considered the monarch under whose regime the Franco-Norman and Anglo-Saxon ethnic strains were finally fused into the new English nation, creating a fairly cohesive national state. From the standpoint of Oxford University, Hastings Rashdall observed that the term "nations" ceased to be used there in 1274, "a symbol of that complete national unity which England was the first of the European kingdoms to affirm." From a more general angle William Stubbs commented: "The nation, on whom and by whom he [Edward] was working, had now become a consolidated people, aroused by the lessons of his father's

reign to an intelligent appreciation of their own condition, and attached to their own laws and customs with a steady, though not
unreasoning, affection." Unfortunately for the English Jews Edward had the support of all classes in his drastic measures against
them. In general, by the time he ascended the throne he had become a circumspect, if occasionally still very impulsive, person. He
first tried to achieve the amalgamation of the Jews with the rest of
the population by promoting their voluntary conversion to Christianity. In his basic *Statutum de judeismo* of 1275, he also tried, as
we recall, to make them abandon moneylending in favor of commerce and crafts, even agriculture, thus removing the glaring economic disparity between Jew and Gentile. Obviously, the time
limit of fifteen years was too short. Such a major effort at economic
restratification would have failed even if the Jews had not been
impoverished by the constant expropriations under Henry III
(not completely relaxed under Edward I) and if the English public had been in a more cooperative mood. As it was, the greatly
weakened Jewish community was unable to sustain such a tremendous transformation. Apart from numerous evasions of the
prohibition of usury, some Jews resorted to coin clipping, which
merely added to their condemnation by public opinion.[22]

In view of the near-unanimity among the estates and particularly the pressure of the bourgeoisie, then in the throes of its struggle for extended parliamentary rights, Edward I had no choice
but to command his Jewish "serfs" to leave the country. In preparation he issued on June 18, 1290, secret instructions to have all
archae containing Jewish bonds sealed within ten days. The formal decree of expulsion was promulgated about July 18, which
almost coincided with the Ninth of Ab, the traditional day of great
Jewish catastrophes. The king tried to proceed in an orderly fashion, setting the terminal date for Jewish departure as November 1,
and allowing the exiles to take along their movable property. He
even tacitly condoned their disposal of some immovables. Shortly
before their scheduled emigration he specifically enjoined the authorities, particularly in the Cinque Ports, to extend to them a
helping hand. That some officials failed to live up to the royal
order and that many a tragedy befell the departing Jews was not
the fault of Edward, who severely punished some offenders. Clear-

ly, despite the confiscation of the remaining Jewish property, estimated by B. L. Abrahams at over £15,000, the royal Treasury was going to lose considerable revenue. Whether or not by prearrangement, Parliament immediately voted the payment of a tithe on the property of the clergy and of one-fifteenth on that of nobles and burghers, more than compensating the Crown for its loss of some 2,000 marks of the annual revenue from Jews. We need but remember that when a "fifteenth" had been voted in 1225 to finance the war with France the bishops' contribution alone yielded fully 56,899 marks, 11 shillings, and 9 pence. The tithe contributed by the clergy in 1290, must have surpassed that amount by a substantial margin. In all Edward may well have received more than the £107,000 he then owed in overdrafts to his Lombard creditors. Clearly, the contemporary chronicler Pierre de Langtoft did not exaggerate when he claimed that "there is nobody who opposes it,/To expel the Jews." [23]

Apparently the royal decision startled even contemporaries or near-contemporaries, who indulged in all sorts of speculations concerning Edward's motives. As summarized by Sir B. Lionel Abrahams, the decree of banishment is explained in two chronicles as a concession to the pope or to Queen Eleanor.

In a third, as a measure of summary punishment against the blasphemy of the Jews, taken to give satisfaction to the English clergy; in a fourth as an answer to the complaints made by the magnates of the continued prevalence of usury; in a fifth as an act of conformity to public opinion; in a sixth, as a reform suggested by the King's independent general enquiry into the administration of the kingdom during his absence, and his discovery, through the complaints of the Council, of the "deceits" of the Jews.

While all these explanations, which are not mutually exclusive, contain kernels of truth, the contemporaries, understandably, missed the main underlying factor: England's growth into a national state.[24]

Preoccupation with the Jewish problem deeply affected English national thinking. Although the medieval Anglo-Jewish community had a total career of little more than two centuries, of which the first several decades had marked only slight beginnings, the English people retained vivid, if highly colored, memories of its Jewish minority. With their amazing fortitude, the Jewish exiles left behind but few new renegades; not many more, it appears, than might have abandoned their faith under the more ordinary pressures initiated a decade earlier by the king and Archbishop Peckham. According to Michael Adler's careful investigation, only eighty converts lived in the London *domus conversorum* in 1290, as against ninety-six ten years before. By 1308 their number had dwindled to fifty. Nevertheless, the *domus* continued its operations for many generations, on the chance that an occasional Continental Jew would stray across the Channel and require spiritual, as well as financial, assistance. Popular writers continued to spin the traditional yarns about the Jewish part in the crucifixion of Christ and the blood ritual (Croxton Play, Chaucer, and others). The Jewish usurer remained as the symbol of cunning and cruelty to inspire some of the great Elizabethan writers, including Christopher Marlowe and William Shakespeare, who probably had never laid eyes on a living exemplar of that "accursed" faith. Curiously, more artists now became interested in the traditional theme of the victory of the Church over the Synagogue than in the years before 1290. Almost all the extant English sculptures devoted to that branch of Christian art, which had become standardized on the Continent, belong to the fourteenth century or after. We shall see that when, in the mid-seventeenth century, the British public began discussing the readmission of the Jews to England, these four-century-old feuds still revealed an unexpected vitality and freshness. It required the emergence of a new type of nationalism, no longer dependent on absolute religious conformity, before formal readmission and, ultimately, full equality of English Jewry could become an historic reality.[25]

FRENCH CENTRALIZATION

Growth of English national consciousness was but slightly impeded by the continued English domination over French areas across the Channel. Only the possession of Normandy, the conquerors' mother country, slowed down the amalgamation of the two ethnic groups in England. But with the loss of that province to the French in 1204 (recognized by the English themselves in 1259) this obstacle was removed. The other French territories still

under English control were not only sufficiently different in structure and language to develop, so to say, a political "personality" of
their own, but they also formally remained under the suzerainty of
the French kings to whom, at least theoretically, the kings of England had to pay allegiance as vassals of the realm.

In the Jewish question, however, the large area going under the
name of Vasconia (Gascony) was treated as an appendage to the
English Crown. Edward I's decree of 1288, expelling Jews from
these outlying districts, was but a preliminary test of the efficacy of
such a measure in an area where Jews were both fewer in number
and of lesser economic significance. This test was facilitated by the
king's prolonged stay in Gascony before he returned to England.
That here, too, the burghers were the prime movers appears the
more likely as Bordeaux refused to swear fealty until *after* Edward
and the seneschal took an oath to respect its customs. Once
promulgated in England in 1290, the banishment of Jews had to
be carried out even more strictly in these Continental possessions,
lest the English refugees settle there, as some did in other French
provinces. Yet, because Vasconia did not share in the nascent
English nationalism, some Jews managed to remain in the country, and the king had to instruct his seneschal, Johannes de Haver-
ing, in 1305, "totally to expel all Jews" from the duchy. His
son, Edward II, was obliged to repeat this injunction several times
between 1310 and 1317, all without total effect, although here, too,
the English administration tried to provide for an orderly exodus,
only insisting in 1314 that the prospective exiles themselves cover
the expenses connected with their deportation. The English severely punished those accused of robbing and killing several Jews
at sea. Nonetheless, enough Jews remained in the province to furnish some victims during the Pastoureaux onslaught in 1320, and
small Jewish settlements seem to have persisted in Bordeaux and
elsewhere for many years thereafter.[26]

In France proper the growth of French nationalism was even
more dependent on the development of royal sovereignty. Here
the struggle consisted not only in the assertion of French national
independence from both the Empire and the Papacy, but also in
the gradual weakening of the powerful vassals, some of whom had
rivaled, or even exceeded, the Capetian kings in wealth, size of

subject population, and military power. By the alternate use of persistent diplomatic efforts and warfare the kings finally succeeded in uniting under their scepter most French territories and in molding them into something resembling a national state. This process, which even under the pious Louis IX often involved defiance of the papal will, was demonstrated in Philip the Fair's blunt repudiation in 1297 of Boniface VIII's interference with his war against both the Empire and England: "that the temporal government of his realm depends on him alone, as king, and on no one else, and that he . . . does not intend . . . to submit or subject himself in any way to any living man; but he rather intends to do justice to his fiefs, to defend his kingdom continually, and, together with his subjects, his friends, and his warriors, to further the rights of his kingdom in every way." Some Frenchmen began interpreting the name *Francus* as etymologically derived from *free*, that is free especially from imperial or papal overlordship. Very soon Philip proved his point by forcing the popes to move to Avignon within his easy reach. Progressive further concentration of power in the royal house ultimately converted France in the days of Francis I into a regular national state under the domination of a powerful monarch.[27]

All this boded ill for the future of Jews. No sooner did the nationalist trends manifest themselves in the twelfth century than the riots during the Second Crusade, and the sharp intellectual assaults upon Jewish life and learning by Peter of Cluny and others, were followed by the first major expulsion of Jews from the royal possessions in 1182. As we recall, this move was initiated by Philip II Augustus' councilors who thus responded to popular animosities, rather than the Crown's genuine interests. As soon as Philip II grew up and more fully grasped the Jewish role in the country's economy and fiscal structure, he not only recalled the Jews in 1198, but in a series of treaties with his neighbors tried to attach as large a Jewish population as possible to the royal domain.

Popular hostility persisted, however, and in 1236–39 the preachment of a new Crusade stimulated attacks on the Jewries of Anjou, Poitou, and Brittany. According to a later Hebrew chronicler, more than 3,000 Jews were killed and 500 forcibly converted. These disturbances, which caused great concern to the English

Jews as well, aroused even the generally unfriendly Pope Gregory IX to issue his aforementioned letter of September 1236, to several French bishops, sharply condemning this "unheard of and unprecedented outburst of cruelty. In their mad hatred they have slaughtered two thousand and five hundred of them [Jews], old and young, as well as pregnant women." In April 1240, Duke John of Brittany, in the absence of his crusading father, banished all Jews from his territory. "Having in mind the good of all of Brittany," he wrote invoking an anti-Jewish petition by Breton bishops, abbots, barons, and vassals, "neither We nor Our heirs shall have them in Brittany at any time in the future, nor shall We tolerate that any of Our subjects have them in their lands which are in Brittany." He tried to buttress this order by urging his successors to take an oath faithfully to observe it. Not until such oaths were rendered were the vassals to swear fealty to the new rulers. Reciprocally, the bishops and barons, "not considering themselves sufficiently avenged for Jewish usury by the carnage of 1236," swore not to admit Jews to their territories. Nonetheless, lacking the required confirmation by the king of France, this decree was not carried out and the Jews seem to have disappeared from Brittany only after that province joined royal France in 1491. At least, in a funerary oration of 1514, Queen Ann, whose marriage to Charles VIII had brought about that union, was specifically praised for having caused the elimination of Jews from that region.[28]

Louis IX's idealistic regime led to an expulsion of Jews from royal France in 1251–52, according to Guillaume de Nangis and other contemporary French chroniclers. But Louis was away from France from August 1248 to June 1254, and Matthew Paris doubtless more correctly states that, angered by the existing intimate intergroup relations, the king had

ordered that the Jews be irrevocably expelled from his realm and be removed from his boundaries. But when he was told that it does not please our Lord Jesus Christ that they should be altogether eliminated from under the sky, but that they ought to be symbolically preserved in an accursed state like Cain so that they not be committed to oblivion nor exterminated, he ordered that a small number be preserved under their accustomed captivity and that their misery continue to be manifest to the whole world.

Matthew adds that, on hearing this report, Henry III wished to emulate Louis' example, but reconsidered it when he realized that the Cahorsin usurers were far more guilty than the Jews. Upon his return from the Crusade in 1254, Louis adopted a different method of suppressing Judaism. By issuing stringent antiusury laws, he tried to channel the Jewish energies into agriculture and commerce and thus to remove the economic causes of Jewish separatism. He also intensified his missionary efforts which had earlier caused him to stage the extensive debate on the Talmud and its ensuing public auto-da-fé of 1242. He evidently sensed that, by suppressing the Talmud, he might undermine the loyalty of French Jewry to its faith. Demonstratively to encourage conversions, he personally attended the baptismal ceremony of a Jewess with her three sons and a daughter. On occasion he and other members of the royal household served as godparents at such rites. According to a biographer, in 1261 he maintained in Paris alone eighty converts to whom he paid up to fourteen deniers a day. We also recall the numerous converted children whom he fully supported in the provinces. He also continued, or newly awarded, tax exemptions for converts and their descendants. One such exemption granted by Philip II in 1180 was still being renewed by Philip IV in 1301. Louis was convinced that a combination of all these measures would sooner or later bring about the assimilation of Jews into the French national body, undramatically but no less effectively.[29]

Probably even less serious was the threat of expulsion by Louis' brother, Count Alphonse de Poitiers. In 1248, we recall, Alphonse, while collaborating with the king in raising funds for the forthcoming Crusade, informed the major Jewish communities of his appanage that they would have to leave the country. But he expected the burghers to indemnify his Treasury for the ensuing losses by a new tax of four sous per hearth. However, either the burghers refused or, what appears to have been the original purpose, the Jews offered 1,000 livres and were allowed to stay. The main point in this story is the count's assumption that the burghers were so anxious to get rid of Jews that they would accept a heavy new tax. We find here a minor adumbration of what was going to happen in England forty-two years later. Evidently the astute realist Alphonse sensed better than his idealistic brother the growing nationalist intolerance toward Jews, but he was prepared to substitute the sizable revenue from Jews for the acclaim he might have earned from the burghers by banishing his most dependable taxpayers.[30]

Louis IX's moderate assimilatory endeavors proved no more successful than those of his admirer, Edward I of England. Since the large majority of French Jews effectively resisted conversion, the main effect of his long reign was their growing dispersion into areas dominated by royal vassals, large and small, who received them despite the convention of Melun. Louis' successors first reverted to the older methods of squeezing out maximum Jewish taxation which they badly needed to help finance, in particular, their frequent wars. At the same time the French public increasingly filled the air with grievances about the Jews' financial exploitation, attacks on Christianity, building of new synagogues, continued use of the forbidden talmudic literature, chanting prayers too loudly, sheltering Christian heretics, and the like. The aforementioned dramatic incidents relating to such Jewish martyrs as Samson of Metz (1276) or Rabbi Isaac Males of Toulouse (1278) the auto-da-fé of Troyes (1288), and the *miracle des billettes* in Paris (1290)—all served to inflame anti-Jewish passions. Some of these complaints received formal sanction in Philip IV's abortive decree of expulsion of February 1291, and one less extreme of June 6, 1299. His advisers went further. Responding to the growth of the French national sentiment brought to a high pitch during Philip's successful campaigns, they advocated the total ouster of Jews. Nor was the example of the expulsion of the Jews from Gascony and England lost on the anti-Jewish segment of the French people. Ever impecunious Philip the Fair may have wished to admit a few wealthy Anglo-Jewish exiles, but he quickly yielded to public pressure. The Parlement of Chandeleur of 1291 issued an ordinance, "in the presence and at the recommendation of the King, that all Jews who have arrived in the Kingdom of France from England or Gascony should be expelled from the said French Kingdom within forty days." This well-publicized resolution must have sounded quite ominous to the attentive ears of the native French Jews.[31]

In August 1306, finally, Philip expelled the Jews from all royal possessions. Outwardly this action resembled the ordinance issued by Philip II in 1182. But while the latter had been an impulsive act of a young prince surrounded by imprudent councilors, Philip IV's decree was a deliberate governmental decision, prepared several months in advance, but held in secrecy lest the Jewish victims conceal their belongings or transfer them out of the country. Even more important was the difference in area. The decree of 1182 had embraced only a small segment of French territory, whereas one hundred and twenty-four years later the royal domain included most of France.

Externally, both actions pursued primarily the objective of quickly filling the royal coffers, akin to Philip the Fair's equally drastic expropriation of the Templars in 1307. To make sure of the location of most Jewish holdings Philip promised informers a share of one-fifth of all caches recovered with their assistance. This reward was promised for future recoveries as well, whereas failure to reveal Jewish property was to be severely punished. However, the chorus of approval among the contemporary Christian chroniclers, the lack of any serious opposition on the part of barons whose territories were included without their prior consent, and the option left to the Jews to remain and retain their property if they were willing to adopt Christianity (no such choice was, of course, available to the Templars)—all revealed the people's deep-seated drive to eliminate all professing and, hence, unassimilable Jews from the new national state. To that extent the oft-quoted report by the Austrian chronicler, Ottokar von Horneck, that the expulsion of 1306 was owing to Philip's unwillingness to tolerate Jewish serfs of the Holy Roman Empire, although literally inexact, did reflect the nationalist mood behind the royal decree. A sixteenth-century Hebrew historian used a felicitously descriptive phrase. According to Joseph ha-Kohen, the following royal proclamation was read in all French cities: "Let every Jew leave My country without taking anything with him, or else let him choose another God, and we shall become *one people!*" Following in the footsteps of Samuel Usque, Joseph admits that some French Jews, especially in Toulouse, preferred conversion to the uncertainties of exile. Here these chroniclers' relatively good familiarity with general European history misled them into blaming the spread of Christian heresies in the district of Toulouse (also widely felt as a disruptive factor for France's national unity) on the presence there of a large number of such involuntary converts. This was not an anachronistic allusion to the Albigensian heterodoxies, but rather a reference to the later Christian Reform movements (Usque names specifically the Lutherans) in which, as we shall see, some New Christians played an important role indeed. Joseph thus well sensed that behind Philip's greed also loomed a deeper national motivation.[32]

French patriotism and reluctance to leave a beloved home country is reflected even in some contemporary Hebrew letters. Estori b. Moses Farḥi (ha-Parḥi), author of a comprehensive work on Palestine where he ultimately settled, reminisced of how his parents, who had emigrated from Spain to southern France, were suddenly forced to depart in 1306 without any means. "They dragged me out of the schoolhouse; as a youth [he was about twenty-four years old then] I had to leave my father's house naked and bare. I had to wander from land to land and from people to people whose languages were alien to me." Another contemporary, Yedaiah b. Abraham Penini, surnamed Bedaresi (of Béziers) lent expression to his grief in a poem whose artificiality (each of its thousand words began with the first letter of the alphabet) did not reduce the author's eloquence: "The enemy says: 'I shall take from you what your forefathers have accumulated and shall disperse you to all corners of the earth.' O Lord! Where shall I flee? If I went up on high I should still encounter bitter enemies."[33]

As a financial transaction, Philip the Fair's decree of banishment proved to be a boomerang. The tremendous drop in the value of the French currency, occasioned by Philip's multifarious currency manipulations, which earned him the designation of "money forger" among contemporary canonists, was greatly accelerated by the news that no Jewish or Templar moneylenders and traders would any longer serve the French Crown. Immediately after Philip's death, therefore, his successor Louis X called the Jews back to France in 1315, promising them a minimum stay of twelve years. Cognizant, however, of the national pressures behind the expulsion, Louis tried to justify his restoration of Jews by asserting that he was merely yielding to the "clamor of the people" in need of credit. Yet the popular anti-Jewish sentiments quickly reasserted themselves. It is not impossible that the same individuals changed their minds twice, once in favor of Jews when, during their absence, the Christian moneylenders had turned out to be doubly exacting; and the second time against the Jews when a few years later they were demanding repayment of loans interveningly contracted. Despite the royal assertions, however, even in 1315 many Frenchmen probably looked askance at the return of this ever dissenting group.[34]

In 1320 another agitation for a Crusade led to the formation of unruly mobs of so-called Pastoureaux (Shepherds) commanded by two unsavory characters. It intensified the hatred of Jews in both the provinces unaffected by the expulsion of 1306 and those to which some exiles had returned during the preceding five years. This time neither king nor pope tolerated this rebellious army which often plundered clerical along with Jewish possessions and threatened to overturn the existing order. In Paris the king succeeded in maintaining peace, just as John XXII kept the Pastoureaux off the bounds of the papal possessions. Elsewhere, however, especially in the southwestern regions as well as in the dioceses of Cahors and Albi, Jews suffered severely. These outbreaks of popular hostility should have surprised nobody, since in 1317 and 1320 there had been Blood Accusations in Chinon and Puy, and even the ancient community of Lunel had found itself in great peril when the rumor spread in 1319 that the Jews had parodied the Passion in a public procession. Only the strict royal order to the seneschal of Beaucaire to investigate seems to have prevented bloodshed. Nor did the renewed confiscation and public burning of copies of the Talmud by the Toulouse Inquisitor, Bernard Gui, contribute to the pacification of the frenzied mobs. Hence, atrocities committed by the passing Pastoureaux and even the destruction of the Jewish community of Verdun-sur-Garonne which had found refuge in a tower—this siege greatly resembled that of York Jewry in 1190 and likewise ended, according to Ibn Verga, with the self-immolation of the 200 beleaguered Jews— found no compassionate echo among the non-Jewish bourgeoisie. Despite orders from the higher authorities various local officials, including Bishop Béraud of Albi, were implicated. The city of Albi was ultimately fined 500 livres, later reduced to one-quarter of that amount. Elsewhere, too, a number of officials and burghers cooperated with the "crazy Pastoureaux" as Bernard Gui called them. When the seneschal of Carcassonne, a chronicler points out, ordered the local leaders to protect the Jews, they refused; many actually rejoiced in seeing them destroyed. To be sure, this complacency was occasionally reinforced by the expectation of spoils, such as were obtained by the burghers of Albi and Bourges. The Bourges officials still had to render accounts in 1335 of the goods they had received from Jewish fugitives of 1320, some of which they had misappropriated. But the generally hostile attitude of the southern French population sharply contrasted with the aid extended to its Jewish neighbors by that of Tudela, where the Pastoureaux were vigorously repulsed. In some respects one may indeed see here the contrast between the areas seized by the rising tide of French nationalism and the northern Spanish communities where the nationalist feeling still was quite weak.[35]

No sooner was this danger averted than the alleged Jewish conspiracy with the lepers and the Muslim king of Granada was again to threaten the survival of the entire Franco-Jewish community. Belief in this alleged conspiracy was facilitated by the popular superstition viewing the lepers, because of their alleged descent from Elisha's servant, Gehazi, as somehow related to Jews. It has rightly been observed that rather than from a conspiracy of lepers and Jews against the French, these rumors arose from a French conspiracy against both these groups. The pathetic outcry of a German Jewish poet during the Black Death era applied with full force also to the same accusation of well-poisoning twenty-seven years earlier. The poet Baruch (b. Yeḥiel?) ha-Kohen wrote:

> The vessels they themselves had drugged
> With matter poisoning us, not them.
> That venom which was never found
> Did change the draught, no man had drained,
> Into a sea of burning tears
> Which Thy devoted children wept. . . .
> The true in heart were placed on stakes,
> To make them faithless to their God;
> Not Jew, nor Jewess was there found,
> Who would commit a traitor's crime.[36]

Here, too, the number of Jewish martyrs was very large. In Chinon one hundred and sixty men and women were burned in a single day; among them the distinguished rabbi, Eliezer b. Joseph, who had for many years maintained a far-flung correspondence with Spanish and other scholars, including his pupil Estori Farḥi. The fortitude of these victims made a great impression on the onlookers, a Christian chronicler reporting that many of the condemned jumped into the flames, "chanting and as if they were invited to a wedding." Women threw their children onto the pyre, lest they fall into the hands of their enemies and be forcibly baptized. In Vitry-le-François forty Jewish prisoners resorted to the traditional mass suicide. In contrast to his attitude toward the Pastoureaux movement, however, John XXII remained silent as if he wished to lend credence to the accusation. When he first heard the news in Poitiers, Philip V pretended to believe it himself and ran away to Paris, although, according to Auguste Molinier, he merely sought to use this libel as a means for confiscating much Jewish property. In an order issued in 1321 to the seneschals of Carcassonne, Toulouse, Beaucaire, Saintonge, Poitou, and Limoges, as well as to many bailiffs and the provost of Paris, he ordered a careful inquiry into these crimes which were "so notorious that in no manner could they be concealed." Yet he enjoined the investigators from submitting the defendants to torture, unless they were accused by other Jews or lepers, or there was strong circumstantial evidence against them. Ultimately, the Paris Parlement imposed a large fine of 150,000 livres on the entire Franco-Jewish community. The populace had no such compunctions. A chronicler, who claimed to have seen with his own eyes ill-smelling poison being thrown away by a female leper at the time of her capture, was not quite aware of the irony of his own laudatory comment that "the common people had thus sought justice without appealing to a prefect or bailiff." [37]

Not satisfied with this judgment, the French public demanded a more radical solution, and the new king, Philip VI, breaking all pledges, expelled the Jews from France in 1322. This decree affected again only Jews of the royal domain, including Languedoc. But as in 1306 Burgundy, though frequently at odds with the French monarchy (according to a contemporary chronicler, the Burgundians defeated in 1471 claimed "that God was French this year, just as in times past He had been Burgundian"), followed the French example. Only a few local lords in the interior, like the counts of Bar, defied the royal wishes and accommodated a few exiles. On the other hand, because Jews were then absent from royal France, the French could no longer use them as scapegoats during the Black Death, although various southern communities demonstrably lost almost half of their population. Jews suffered from attacks only in the outlying districts of Savoy, where the whole anti-Jewish movement had started, Toulon, Vergne-en-Gapençais (where 93 Jews lost their lives), and a few other communities. In fact, anti-Jewish riots had broken out in Moustiers and Forcalquier as early as 1340, while in Reillanne the Jews seem to have put up an effective resistance. The result was that the attackers were moderately fined, while the Jewish resisters received severe penalties. A Reillanne Jew, accused of "ravishing Christian children," lost all his property. Although, as in neighboring Avignon, Jews of Marseilles, Arles, and Aix seem to have escaped the bloody vengeance of the populace, Queen Joanna ordered the seneschals of Provence and Forcalquier to collect during the following ten years only half the usual annual imposts from Jews who had suffered greatly from both the pest and Christian attacks.[38]

Before long the absence of Jews was felt severely by the royal Treasury and by some segments of the population at large. The devastation of the Black Death was magnified by the ravages of the Hundred Years' War. By 1359, the great difficulties in raising the huge ransom for King John II which made the king marry off his daughter to Giovanni Visconti, son of the upstart duke of Milan, for money "to the shame of the Crown" (Matteo Villani) also forced him and his son Charles (soon Charles V) to readmit the Jews. In three decrees of 1359–61 John and Charles formally reopened France to Jewish settlement. These privileges included, as we recall, extensive safeguards for Jewish self-government and the right to lend money at the unusually high rate of up to 86⅔ percent. But these very favors added to the general nationalist resentments of the population, then in the throes of great patriotic sacrifices for French freedom. Some circles hoped to persuade the king in 1365–66 to expel the Jews, even if it meant repudiating his own 1359 guarantee of a minimal twenty-year Jewish sojourn, raised by another six years as a result of a new Jewish subsidy in 1364. The circumstances leading up to this attempted reversal are not recorded in the sources. But one wonders whether the triumphant journey of the Holy Roman Emperor, Charles IV, through the east and south of France and his coronation as king of Arles on June 4, 1365, did not revive among many Frenchmen the memories of the imperial claim to overlordship over the Jewish "serfs" everywhere which had allegedly contributed to the banishment of Jews from France in 1306. The king seems to have staunchly resisted all such proposals, however. Although on February 6, 1367, he signed a decree (still extant in the archives) ordering the expulsion of Jews and fully registering their property (it is also mentioned in subsequent decrees of 1368 and 1370), it apparently was never promulgated. Rumors about these negotiations must have filled the Jewish public with grave forebodings, the more so as it drew a parallel with the breach of promise by the French Crown in 1322.[39]

Upon Charles V's death in 1380, the populace, suffering from the severe fiscal exploitation which the king himself had tried to abate in his unusual testament, turned upon its Jewish fellow sufferers. With the outcry, "Let the Jews and the usurers be chased out of Paris," it staged bloody riots in the Jewish street for four days, destroying many lives and bonds of indebtedness. Many Jewish children were wrested from their parents and forcibly baptized. The strong-willed Paris prefect, Hughes Aubriot, not only punished some ringleaders but also secured a royal decree, ordering the restitution of baptized children to their parents. This move did not increase his popularity (already undermined by his intervention against the University during Charles VI's coronation) with either the Church or the mobs. Accused of having favored the Jews because of love affairs with Jewesses, he was deposed and imprisoned. Aubriot again suffered together with the Jews in 1382, when the anti-royal uprising of so-called Maillotins led to new anti-Jewish disturbances. The 1380 riots so impressed the Jews that Samuel Usque dated their final expulsion from France from that event. In fact, they were the beginning of the end. Charles VI who had first persisted in keeping the Jews, ultimately had to give way to the mounting opposition of the various classes of the population, and to issue his decree of expulsion on July 15, 1394. To underscore his financial disinterestedness in this move (in contrast to his predecessors, Philip II and Philip IV), he explained,

We have been for a long time and on many occasions informed by persons deserving of faith, and Our procurators and officers have likewise received many grave complaints and remonstrances which reached them every day, about the excesses and crimes which the Jews had committed and still are committing daily with respect to Christians.

The king claimed that he had examined these complaints and found them justified. He had decided, therefore, after mature deliberation with the Great Council, that thenceforth no Jews should be allowed to live in either Languedoil or Languedoc. Revoking all previous decrees, he ordered the Jews to leave the country by November 3, seven years before the expiration of the period mutually agreed upon after several extensions.[40]

In this fashion Jews were eliminated from most of France. Even from Toulouse, where the decree had not been published until December 7, 1394, more than a month after its terminal date, the remaining Jews (twelve families in the city and seven in the province) had to depart. So did the Jews of Pamiers, despite Count de Foix's initial attempt to disobey the royal order. The peripheral areas of the Franche Comté, Lorraine and, in the south, Provence and Navarre continued to maintain their Jews so long as they were outside the orbit of the French national state. The venerable Provençal communities actually had a new period of flowering during the fifteenth century, particularly under the friendly regime of King René. But no sooner did the Provence become part of France in 1481 than the popular clamor for banishing the Jews could not long be denied.

Louis XI, to be sure, apparently in response to a Jewish delegation from Marseilles, Arles, Aix, Tarascon, and Salon, renewed in 1482 the protective laws for Provençal Jewry. But within two years all these cities, except Salon, witnessed violent attacks on Jews. If in Arles the disturbances were started by unemployed harvesters (*moissonneurs*) from Dauphiny and Auvergne, the local mobs wholeheartedly took up the hue and cry. Shortly thereafter, on

August 19, 1484, Charles VIII himself yielded sufficiently to instruct the Arles consuls not to admit any new Jews to residence. Although the royal administration still continued to tolerate Jews and, in fact, tried to prevent them from escaping without special authorization, the agitation for their exclusion grew in volume and vociferousness. In 1486 the city council of Arles ordered its syndics to propose to the next Assembly of the Estates an outright expulsion of that "accursed race." Similar demands were voiced by the city of Marseilles. Anti-Jewish feelings ran higher and higher, especially after the expulsion of the Jews from Spain in 1492. This much-discussed act of the Catholic monarchs not only invited emulation, but it also brought some Spanish refugees to southern France, which added fuel to the anti-Jewish propaganda. Charles finally yielded and, in July 1493, ordered the Jews to leave Arles within three months, unless they were willing to adopt Christianity. Jewish appeals secured temporary postponements. The Marseilles Jews, too, invoking their old privileges, secured some delay. But by 1500–1501 the remaining Jews of both these communities had to depart. Except for a few individuals, only those Jews were thenceforth found on French soil who either dwelled under papal sovereignty in Avignon and the Comtat, or else had settled in France as New Christians no longer considered Jews.[41]

SPAIN

Far more important for world Jewry were the developments in the Spanish kingdoms of Castile, Aragon, and Navarre. Here the Jewish population was much larger, its affluence, economic diversification, and political as well as cultural role far superior, so that its fate was of decisive importance for the whole Jewish people. When, at the end of the medieval period, it likewise suffered total eclipse, that expulsion made a deep and lasting impression not only upon world Jewry but also upon many non-Jewish contemporaries. The offshoots of the Spanish exiles, moreover, together with the Marranos, who during the subsequent generations were leaving the Peninsula, became a major factor in the development of new communities in both east and west. They served as a yeast in the great socioreligious fermentation which ushered in the new era of world history in the sixteenth and seventeenth centuries.

Here, too, nationalism played an important role. Even before the Muslim conquest of the Peninsula the gradual national fusion of the old Ibero-Romans with the conquering Visigoths had made life for Jews extremely difficult. During the century before 712 Spain witnessed two expulsions or forced conversions which, only because of their ineffectiveness, gave way to increasingly drastic laws aiming at the elimination of Jews in more indirect ways. This sentiment did not completely vanish when the Christians became a minority group under Islam. It survived particularly in the independent northern province of Leon, and it was reawakened during the period of the Christian reconquest when its ethnic and patriotic ingredients were greatly reinforced by the religious zeal of an anti-Muslim Crusade. Ultimately, not only Christians but also Jews who, defying the Almohade regime, continued secretly to profess their outlawed religions welcomed the Christian armies as liberators.[42]

Evidently, the expanding Spanish regimes at first became states of multiple nationalities, each combining large masses of Moors, Jews, and Christians of diverse ethnic origins. But in time these elements began fusing into new nationalities, particularly after the conversion of most Muslims to Christianity, a fusion here, too, stimulated by the twin royal drive for national sovereignty and monarchical supremacy. We recall Jacobus de Abenga's statement that the French and the Spaniards, although *de jure* subject to the emperor, were *de facto* free from his tutelage. Even the leading imperial jurist, Johannes Teutonicus, merely claimed that (according to one version) "the world government, with the exception of the Spanish government, has been handed over to Teutons." Vincentius Hispanus was not alone in extolling his native land as a country "wealthy in horses, celebrated for food, and shining with gold; steadfast and wise, the envy of all; skilled in the law, and standing high on sublime pillars." In *Las Siete Partidas* Alphonso X stated succinctly: "The kings are vicars of God, each one in his kingdom, placed above the nations in order to maintain them in justice and truth in all temporal matters, just as the em-

peror [is placed] in his empire." Among his predecessors Alphonso
VII had actually been crowned in Leon in 1135 as "emperor of
Spain and king of the men of the two religions," that is, of Christians and Muslims, which Ferdinand III (1217–52) changed into
"emperor and king of the three religions," including Jews. Alphonso X, finally, on his mother's side an offshoot of the Hohen-
staufen family, reached out for the German imperial crown itself,
the city council of Pisa grandiloquently inviting him, in behalf "of
the city of Pisa, all Italy and almost the whole world," to ascend
the German throne.[43]

Dependence on the Papacy was not quite so easily shaken off,
however. Nor was the concentration of monarchical power really
accomplished until the days of Ferdinand and Isabella, under
whom the political unity of the Spanish kingdoms began to be
combined with effective royal absolutism. Hand in hand with this
national consolidation went the formation of historical legends
tracing the origins of the Castilian and Aragonese kingdoms to
Pelayo and an alleged realm of Sobrarbe, a reconstruction which
found ready acceptance in the Middle Ages and early modern
times despite its conflict with Catalan counter claims based on an
equally fictitious hero, Otger Cataló, of the days of Charlemagne.
In the Jewish case, royal supremacy chiefly involved the strengthening of that mutual relationship of dependence and protection
going under the name of "Jewish serfdom." The *Libro de los
Fueros de Castilla* bluntly asserted: "The Jews are the king's. No
matter whether they live under the authority of dignitaries,
nobles, or others, or under that of monasteries, all of them belong
to the king, live under his tutelage, and for his service." In reality,
Jews were often controlled by a variety of local powers, particularly the officially recognized royal vassals. This partial decentrali-
zation proved useful to Jews in critical periods when the royal authorities were unable or unwilling to protect them and they had to
seek refuge under the more effective shields of local barons. But
despite these inconsistencies the fate of Jews was essentially linked
with that of the monarchy and its upper-class allies, which made
them vulnerable targets during popular disturbances aimed at the
overthrow or modification of the existing order.[44]

Until the days of the Catholic monarchs the Spanish kingdoms clearly were but part-of-nationality states. Often at war with one another, they rarely collaborated in international affairs. At the Council of Constance, the Spanish "nation," consisting of Aragon, Castile, and Portugal, was sharply divided in almost all votes. As elsewhere, these subgroupings of the same nationality generated enough nationalist, even racial, antagonisms toward Jews, but not enough to bring about any concerted action against them. Yet they resulted in the gradual deterioration of Judeo-Christian relations in the course of the fourteenth century.[45]

Here, too, nationalist resentments often found an outlet in anti-Jewish disturbances, particularly after an external or internal crisis had weakened the props under the established public order. They followed, for instance, the death of Alphonso VI of Castile in 1109, and again that of Alphonso IX of Leon in 1230. Curiously, the same burghers of Toledo who, together with Spanish Crusaders, were to save the Jews in 1212 from attacks by the city's French allies, fifteen years earlier had doubted Jewish loyalty at the approach of Moorish armies. They were oblivious of how much Jews had to lose from Almohade intolerance and how vigorously some of them had already participated in the city's defense. Toledan Jew-baiters never let the Jews forget the role of the latter's ancestors during the Saracen conquest of Spain in 712.[46]

Local riots continued even in the thirteenth century, when Jews were needed to help repopulate the regions deserted by the Saracens. The great disputation at Barcelona sufficiently aroused the populace for it to stage assaults on Jews. In 1268 James I had to stop the throwing of stones upon Jativa Jews on Good Friday. Some attacks may have been initiated by converts from Judaism who thus wished to avenge themselves on their former coreligionists. This is at least the tenor of an inquiry addressed to the Barcelona rabbi, Solomon ibn Adret,

about those converts who spread false rumors. . . and cause the priests in the city to propagate the idea that Christians should not eat from Jewishly slaughtered meat nor drink Jewish wine and [reciprocally] that Jews should not consume Christian bread. For this reason they [the Jews] must spend funds to bribe them [the converts] in order to shut their mouths, and do the same to priests and judges. Similarly, they have to incur annually expenditures on the eve of the well-known holiday [Easter] in order to protect themselves [against expected assaults].

Another significant outbreak took place in Gerona during the Easter holiday of 1278, calling forth strong reprisals by the new king, Pedro III the Great. A year later the king ordered his officials in Huesca to investigate who was responsible for "preparing an ornate little baptismal font [*bastimentum*] resembling a scroll of law and conducting it through the city with derisive chants according to Jewish usage, for the ridicule and contumely of the Jews and their law. Further at whose counsel and teaching did they do it and also elect a king of their own." Probably these pranksters received due punishment but, as elsewhere, the kings were powerless in stemming the rising tide of anti-Jewish plays and *autos sacramentales*. Neither could the penetration into Spanish folklore of the northern accusations of ritual murder and host desecration be stopped by royal fiat. Most disturbances, to be sure, were of a purely local nature and in many cases had specific causes. Yet they revealed deep rumblings of popular Jew-baiting, partially nurtured from aroused nationalist feelings. They augured badly for the subsequent period of political consolidation during the fourteenth century.[47]

It is small wonder, then, that the news about the expulsion of Jews from France in 1306 caused Majorcan Jewry to tremble lest their king emulate that example. These fears were quickly allayed when, on the contrary, some French refugees were rather hospitably received in most parts of Aragon. The community of Barcelona was supposed to take in sixty exiled families, while other communities, including Lérida, opened their gates to ten families each. Some Jews may also have hoped that the national and religious antagonisms would be mainly diverted toward the larger Moorish minority, but they soon learned with dismay how all-embracing ethnic prejudice could be. Anti-Muslim attacks, moreover, such as occurred particularly in the kingdom of Valencia in 1275–76, were somewhat restrained by the fear of Saracen retribution toward Christians living across the border. No such fears protected Jews against the rising nationalist prejudice aimed at both these "alien" subgroups in a growingly unitarian society.[48]

For a long time Jews could depend on the kings' protection,

nurtured on self-interest and fuller understanding of the Jewish contributions to the kingdoms' economy and culture. Even the Pastoureaux and the antileper Crusaders of 1320–21, we recall, entered but a few border areas largely taken by surprise, and devastated only the small Jewish communities of Montclus and Jaca. James II and his son Alphonso speedily intervened with an armed force, Alphonso executing forty rioters brought to Huesca. True, some Teruel judges lent a willing ear to a non-Jewish defendant who, accused of spreading poison in local waters, implicated some Jews under torture, and, notwithstanding his subsequent denials, sentenced both him and several Jews to death. But the royal deputy bailiff successfully shielded the rest of the community. James II also completely disregarded a report from the Majorcan King Sancho that some lepers captured in Avignon had confessed to having poisoned wells in cooperation with Jews. In fact, the Aragonese authorities assisted in the reconstruction of the stricken community of Montclus. While, following a more rigid interpretation of canon law, they forbade baptized children (doubtless forcibly baptized by the attackers) to live among Jews, they temporarily exempted the community from all taxes, and they also extended tax relief to Montclus refugees settled in Huesca and Barbastro. They confirmed such tax privileges in 1331–32, 1334–35, and even in 1336, sixteen years after the event. Even in Navarre, then under French rulers, the Jews of Pamplona were able to withdraw into a tower and, with the aid of a neighborhood baron, effectively to withstand the siege. Yet wherever royal authority weakened Jews suffered severely. This was demonstrated a few years later in Navarre, where, upon the death of Charles I in 1328, the nationalist resentment of the French domination led to a general upheaval which included sanguinary attacks on the Jewish communities of Estella, Viana, Tudela, and others and allegedly cost between 6,000 and 10,000 Jewish lives. Peace was restored only after the coronation of Philip III in 1329, although the king imposed but perfunctory penalties on the offenders and ended up with a general amnesty in 1336. At the same time, some Navarrese refugees found asylum in Aragon, where Alphonso III strictly ordered his officials to protect them from all molestation. But even here Gerona became, in 1331, the scene of a mass attack on the Jewish quarter which destroyed many lives.[49]

Compared with its coreligionists in other countries Spanish Jewry, as we recall, suffered relatively less from popular attacks during the Black Death era. According to Ḥayyim Galipapa, our main, if unreliable, source for these events, Barcelona Jewry lost twenty and Cervera eighteen members, but Tarrega, Solsona, and Salcona suffered three hundred casualties each. In Perpignan some Jews yielded to threats and accepted baptism. But in such communities as Huesca, Lérida, and Monzón Jews offered successful resistance. As elsewhere the motivations of the attackers were quite mixed. Some merely reacted to an unreasoned panic; others saw in such riots an opportunity for looting or getting rid of their debts. But in most cases these appetites were reinforced by growing ethnic-religious intolerance.[50]

Jewish sufferings during the civil war between Pedro I and Henry II of Castile in 1366–68 were mainly caused by the English, French, and Moorish troops brought into the country by the rival monarchs. But the local population, too, actively participated in the massacres and looting. Our main informant, Samuel Zarza (Çarça), claims that, at the outset, the small community of Briviesca lost all of its two hundred Jewish households. When the city of Valladolid staged an uprising against Pedro, the mobs attacked the local Jews, destroyed their houses including their eight synagogues, and tore the scrolls of law and threw them into the street, so that the Jews "were left with nothing but their naked bodies." Both contenders also imposed enormous contributions on the communities under their temporary control, Jews unable to pay being sold into slavery and "there were not enough buyers." The speedy depreciation of the currency issued by Henry to pay overdue wages of his mercenaries, and its subsequent official devaluation, severely hit the few remaining Jewish capitalists. Moreover, there was "in the midst of this turmoil a great famine in the whole realm, especially here in Palencia, and all commodities became so expensive that neither bread nor clothing remained in my home." [51]

1391 AND ITS AFTERMATH

These sporadic attacks were followed by the great catastrophe of 1391 which marked a turning point in the destinies of Spanish Jewry. Overtly the agitation pursued principally religious and social objectives; it was a "holy war" proclaimed by archdeacon Ferrant Martinez of Seville who, ever since 1378, had been preaching there against Jews and Judaism. Martinez also vigorously attacked Jewish usury and other social wrongs, easily arousing the "small people" (*pueblo menudo*), then in a generally revolutionary frame of mind. As usual, greed and expectation of rich spoils likewise contributed their share, as was noted by the chronicler, Pedro López de Ayala. But it was nationalism which largely accounted for the great ease with which this pogrom movement spread from area to area, not only transcending the local and regional peculiarities, but also easily crossing the frontiers from Castile to Aragon. The Church as such vigorously opposed Martinez' subversive propaganda; on several occasions he was sharply admonished by his superior, Archbishop Pedro Gomez Baroso of Seville. In 1389 Don Pedro denounced the archdeacon's preachment as "your erroneous and suspect opinion contrary to our Faith. You have thus become contumacious, rebellious and suspect of heresy." But in those ecclesiastically disturbed times of the Papal Schism Martinez, relying upon his popularity with the masses, ventured to defy the archbishop, who soon thereafter passed away. During the following vacancy Martinez assumed the management of the archdiocese, at least in matters which he considered of prime spiritual importance.[52]

An opportunity for large-scale attacks on Jews offered itself during the regime of a weak regency after the death of John I of Castile. Under Martinez' spellbinding the populace attacked, in June 1391, the Jewish quarter of Seville, killed many Jews, and forced a still larger number to accept baptism. The movement spread to Cordova and Toledo, where Yehudah b. Asher, a saintly and learned scion of Asher b. Yeḥiel, slew his wife and mother-in-law, lest they fall into enemy hands, and committed suicide. Many victims, however, preferred conversion to death. A similar fate befell

Madrid, Burgos, and many lesser Castilian communities. By that time the pogrom movement had gained such momentum that it swept away most hindrances placed in its path even by the far stronger Aragonese government. Some recipients of royal commands to protect Jews, including city councils, churchmen, and royal officials, were themselves seized by the mass hysteria and tolerated, if not actively abetted, the massacres. In Valencia the soldiery, awaiting shipment to Sicily, marched in the vanguard of assailants. In the entire province of Valencia, we are told, only Murviedro escaped the brunt of the attack. Barcelona, too, lost nearly its entire Jewish population through death, flight, or forced conversion, and the community never recovered from that blow. In the Balearic Islands the anti-Jewish propaganda, stimulated by the general revolutionary ferment among the peasantry, found the Jews rendered doubly helpless by the governor's earlier prohibition for them to carry arms even within their quarter (November 1390). On August 2, 1391, 300 Palma Jews were killed, while 800 escaped to the tower. Ultimately, with the connivance of a royal bailiff (later executed) most of these survivors accepted baptism. The converts were promised a cash payment of 20,000 pounds, but they never received it. A list of 111 baptized Jewish householders is still extant; among them, the later famous cartographer, Jafuda (Yehudah) Cresques, whose wife refused to follow him into the new religion, and Isaac Nafusi, a distinguished astronomer, who ultimately succeeded in reaching Palestine, where he returned to his ancestral faith. It took some five months before the government restored order, but only at the price of a general amnesty for "the attacks made on the governor, the Jews and the Jewish quarters, it all having been done in honor of the king and for the public welfare." At the other end of the kingdom, the Perpignan city council reacted to the grave disorders by arguing with the king that he let the Jews join the Christian faith. The king could not disagree with this objective, but he insisted that is must not be achieved by forcible means. The outcome was that many Jews accepted baptism, while others found shelter in the tower, where most of them still lived in 1394.[53]

A remarkably succinct summary of these tragic events has come to light on a flyleaf of a scroll of law, written in 1336 by the great jurist Nissim b. Reuben Gerondi. Nissim's son, Reuben, succeeded in 1391 in salvaging that scroll during his flight and entering on the flyleaf under Elul 28, 5151 (August 29, 1391) a statement which included the following description of the massacres:

The fate of Sodom and Gomorrah overtook the holy communities of Castile, Toledo, Seville, Majorca, Cordova, Valencia, Barcelona, Argawan [Algarve?], Granada, and sixty neighboring cities and villages. . . . Many were sold for bondmen to the Moors; about 140,000, unable to sustain the tortures, apostasized from their pure faith. . . . But provincial governors, princes and barons allowed us and many brethren to find refuge in towers, where they provided us with bread and water. My brother, Don Ḥisdai, with the help of our friend and prince, rescued our families, and I saved all scrolls of Law.

As may be noted from its date, this is an outcry of a sufferer almost immediately after his escape. Although he included Granada which, then still under Saracen domination, was unaffected by this Christian movement and misspelled Argawan—incidentally mentioned also by the later chronicler Samuel Usque (Araguam)—, his testimony is quite valuable.[54]

Spanish Jewry also lost many members through emigration. Among its distinguished leaders Isaac b. Sheshet Perfet and Simon b. Ṣemaḥ Duran settled in Algeria. This large exodus gave a new fillip to the North-African communities, but it left behind a great void on the Iberian Peninsula. Before long even the Crown, which had long resisted the pogromist agitators, agreed that conversion, if attained by less forcible means, might indeed remove a source of aggravation from the tense internal situation.

It was particularly St. Vicente Ferrer who converted both the masses and the royal regimes of Castile and Aragon (not Portugal) to this point of view. Convinced that he was merely acting as a devoted son of his Church, Ferrer could not escape the impact of the underlying nationalist feelings, which, in a large measure, accounted for his signal successes. He worked hand in hand with Pedro de Luna who, as Antipope Benedict XIII, could uphold his papal aspirations only by appealing to the Spaniards' national pride. All along both men also influenced the two regimes to enact ever more restrictive laws which by curtailing the Jews' economic opportunities, especially in moneylending, and by sharpening their segregation in undesirable new quarters would make them more amenable to conversionist suasion. Ultimately, the antipope and the king of Aragon staged that famous disputation of Tortosa which indeed proved effective in bringing about the conversion of many Jewish delegates as well as of large masses of Jews all over the land.[55]

Outwardly, all these proceedings carried religious nomenclature. However, in essence they merely repeated Louis IX's and Edward I's efforts to combine economic restratification with sharp discrimination to bring about the conversion of Jews and their ultimate integration into their national bodies politic. Little did the Spanish leaders realize that when converted *en masse*, Jews never were easily absorbed by the majority but long continued to exist as an identifiable group apart. Spain soon witnessed the rise of a large and influential class of *conversos* or, as their enemies began calling them, *Marranos*. Thenceforth until 1492 Spanish nationalism had to cope with the interlocking problems of assimilating both the substantial new group of *conversos* and the remnant of professing Jews.

Friction between the *converso* group and the Old Christians grew from decade to decade, the latter doubly resenting the New Christians putting their novel legal equality to economic and political advantage. In Castile, then facing a generally tense internal situation, Pedro (Pero) Sarmiento and the artisan classes of Toledo in 1449 seized the reins of government, removed many New Christians from their influential posts, and instituted a sort of Inquisition into the orthodoxy of dubious converts or children of converts. After a while, to be sure, John II of Castile suppressed this uprising, put Sarmiento to flight, and revoked all his anti-Marrano ordinances. But unable to close his eyes to the mutual animosity between the two segments of the Christian population, John, with Pope Nicholas V's approval, reconstituted in 1451 the traditional Inquisition under episcopal supervision. Nevertheless the wound continued to fester, particularly under the unstable reign of Henry IV (1454–74), which ended in a civil war and almost a war of all against all. Jews as well as *conversos* now became the targets of all discontented classes and found little aid in the weak royal administration. In Aragon, to be sure, where the Jewish community never recovered from the blows of 1391–1414, the *converso* problem never assumed the same dimensions. In fact, in 1417 Alphonso V had to take professing Jews under his protection against some hostile converts. Since the king also prevented the burghers of Calatayud from expelling them (1418), revoked the anti-Jewish decree of 1412 (1419), and forbade the Dominican Cerda to preach his accustomed anti-Jewish sermons (1422), the Jews were able to devote themselves more calmly to their urgent tasks of reconstruction. In 1457 Alphonso continued to restrict ecclesiastical interference in Jewish affairs. But here, too, the storm clouds were gathering under the much weaker regime of John II (1458–79). In ever-rebellious Majorca, in particular, even Alphonso's officials had been unable to stem a renewed outbreak of hostility against the Jews on the occasion of a Blood Accusation in 1435 which led the few hundred persons still professing Judaism to accept baptism. Thus ended the Jewish settlement on the Balearic Islands, which back in 418 had had the dubious distinction of being the object of the first forced conversion of Jews in western Europe. Today the Palma Cathedral still displays the great candelabrum and the Torah crowns taken over from the synagogue in 1435.[56]

THE GREAT EXPULSION

Matters came to a head when Isabella and Ferdinand took over the reigns of Castile and Aragon in 1474 and 1479, respectively. Under their joint regime Spain grew into a national state, which needed only the rounding out of its frontiers to include Granada and Navarre, a task achieved in Ferdinand's lifetime. Internally, too, these energetic and intelligent rulers pursued the policy of consolidating monarchical rule and integrating the disparate elements in the population. At the end of their regime Spain emerged as a foremost, fairly well-organized, European power which could undertake its ambitious program of colonial expansion and the defense of Catholicism throughout the Western world. As a part of their international and national commitments, the Catholic monarchs sought fully to absorb the *converso* group and to assimilate, or else to eliminate, the Jewish minority. The latter two enterprises were not unrelated, inasmuch as the presence of professing Jews helped to maintain a large segment of the *converso* population in its secret allegiance to Judaism.[57]

Upon her accession to the throne Isabella was greeted by sporadic disturbances including some aimed at Jews or *conversos*, a heritage of the unsettled years before Henry IV's demise, when serious new attacks upon the *conversos* of Toledo in 1467 were followed by large-scale uprisings against those of Cordova and the rest of Andalusia in 1473–74. The royal commander was unable to stop the Cordovan rebels, led by a brotherhood bearing the ironic name of "Charity." According to the chronicler Diego Enriquez del Castillo, "none of those who escaped dared to live any longer in that city or even to enter it." This revolt was but partially quelled by the intervention of Rodrigo Girón, master of the Order of Calatrava, and the hanging of the principal culprits, whereupon some royal councilors conceived the idea of transporting many *conversos* to the fortress of Gibraltar. But this scheme was withdrawn in 1476. Two years later Isabella decided to establish in the turbulent Andalusian province a special Inquisition which, more effectively than the slow-moving episcopal courts, would come to grips with the complex New Christian problem. She and Ferdinand obtained the necessary permission from Pope Sixtus IV who merely urged the inquisitors to proceed humanely. This momentous authorization, which is to be more fully analyzed in a later chapter, extended to all of Castile and, before long, the rulers established the new tribunals in all parts of Spain, notwithstanding many protests, particularly from Aragon which viewed the entire institution as another vehicle of centralization.[58]

It soon became apparent that even the drastic steps taken by the Inquisition could not solve the problem. The Catholic kings decided, therefore, upon the total elimination of Jews from Andalusia in 1483, probably as but a stop-gap measure before their ultimate expulsion from the whole country. In vain did some Jews secure protection from such powerful lords as Don Rodrigo Ponce de León, marquis of Cadiz, and Don Luis de la Cerda, the first duke of Medinaceli. In view of the ever growing concentration of royal power, these were but brief delaying actions. International considerations may also have influenced the Spanish rulers. Anticipating the unavoidable clash with the expanding Ottoman Empire and probably fearing the intervention of the powerful Turkish navy, which in 1481 had succeeded in occupying Italian Otranto, during their planned invasion of Granada, they may well have suspected the fidelity of their Jewish and *converso* subjects, whose pro-Turkish sympathies were an open secret.

Certainly, the Ottoman conquest of Constantinople in 1453 had made a deep impression on the Spanish Jews and greatly reinforced their messianic yearnings. The opening of the gates of the Ottoman Empire to oppressed western Jews, many of whom now fulfilled their ancient dream of settling in the Holy Land, led some Spanish accusers of Jews to compare them with birds of passage who temporarily sojourned in Spain but who, at the first opportunity, were ready to return to their original habitat. The monarchs were doubtless informed about the messianic dreams of their Jewish subjects and their frequent identification of the Turks with the forces of Antichrist out to destroy Christendom and to liberate the Jews from its yoke. Even a *converso* like Juan de Pineda who, from lowly beginnings, had worked his way up to serve as commander in the Order of Santiago and its representative at the Papal See, was supposed to have declared in 1464 (according to the testimony of a hostile witness at an inquisitorial trial against him twenty-four years later), "You do not know who the Turk is. If the Lord will wish to intercede in our favor, he [the Turk] will be here in Castile before the passage of a year and a half." Yet the economic necessities of the country taught the realistic, if devout, kings that they could not yet dispense with the services of such Jews as Abraham Seneor, his son-in-law Meir Melamed of Segovia, or the new arrival from Portugal in 1473, Don Isaac Abravanel. As late as January 1492, therefore, Ferdinand and Isabella were still signing four-year contracts with Jewish tax farmers, including Seneor and Melamed, as if they expected them to stay on indefinitely. Possibly, the monarchs hoped that at the critical moment most agents would accept conversion, as indeed did Seneor and Melamed, though not Abravanel and others.[59]

When all half-measures failed here, as they had failed in Louis IX's France and in Edward I's England, Ferdinand and Isabella signed on March 31, 1492, their very wordy and repetitious decree of expulsion. Probably because of last-ditch attempts by the Jewish

leaders, especially Seneor and Abravanel who in three successive
interviews with the king allegedly offered him 300,000 ducats for
the withdrawal of the decree, it was not promulgated until the end
of April. The main justification adduced was the great damage
arising from the influence exerted by the Jews upon *conversos* and
even professing Christians in a way prejudicial to the Christian
faith. To prevent future injury of this kind the monarchs decreed:

We command all Jews and Jewesses, of whatever age they may be,
who live, reside, and dwell in Our said kingdoms and dominions, both
natives and non-natives who in any manner or for any cause may have
come to dwell therein, that, by the end of the month of July next of
the present year, they depart from all Our said kingdoms and dominions, with their sons, daughters, man-servants, maid-servants, and
Jewish attendants, both great and small, of whatever age they may be.
They shall not presume to return to, nor reside in them or in any part
of them, either as residents, travelers, or in any other manner whatever, under pain that if they do not act and comply with this law,
and are found to reside in Our said kingdoms and dominions, or should
in any manner arrive there, they incur the penalty of death and confiscation of all their property for Our treasury, which penalty they incur
by the act itself, without further trial, declaration, or sentence. . . .

In the meantime, however, Jews were to be free to travel and trade
in the country and to dispose of their property, until the terminal
date of July 31. They could also export their goods abroad "provided they do not take away gold, silver, coined money, or other
articles prohibited by the laws of Our kingdom." These protective
provisions were reinforced by a special decree of May 14, 1492. To
overcome local resistance Infante Henry added on June 15 and
July 18, 1492, strict orders to two high officials to see to it that the
Catalonian Jews be allowed to depart without anyone "inflicting
on them any injury, damage, vexation, or detention with respect
to persons or property." Exceptionally, Ferdinand even evinced
interest in the fate of the exiles abroad; he addressed an inquiry to
the Republic of Florence, on October 5, 1492, asking for an investigation of the purported robberies committed on some of these
new arrivals on Florentine soil.[60]

Such "charitableness" did not prevent the administration from
simultaneously instructing the local commissioners to register
carefully all Jewish possessions. Nor did it interfere when, as early

as April 1492, the Inquisitors forbade the Christian population, "under the threat of excommunication . . . to receive any goods, movable or immovable which, in any way or manner whatsoever, have belonged or are belonging . . . to Jews or Jewesses." Many Jews, especially from among the majority of exiles seeking refuge in neighboring Portugal, were robbed of their property in transit. Abravanel was singularly fortunate in being allowed to take with him, contrary to the specific prohibition of the edict, 1,000 florins in precious metals and many gold and silver objects, in payment for much larger advances he had made to the Crown on taxes as yet uncollected. It required several royal orders to secure the execution of this special license, however. A similar exception was made in favor of a Granada Jew at the request of its last Moorish king. In all, it appears that well over 30,000 Jewish families left the country, while some 10,000 families remained behind and joined the Neo-Christian group; among the latter Seneor and Melamed, supposedly because Isabella had threatened that, if they left, she would wreak vengeance on the entire Jewish community. Most exiles departed on or before the deadline of July 31 which, according to the Jewish calendar, happened to coincide with Ab 7, readily giving rise to the legend that the great exodus occurred on the Ninth of Ab, that most portentous date of many historic Jewish tragedies. But a few émigrés were detained by the authorities beyond that date because of debts they owed to Christians which they could not pay unless they collected some outstanding loans due them.[61]

Unlike the expulsions from England and France, that from Spain left a permanent imprint on Jewish life and thought. According to a persistent legend, the departing exiles took an oath that neither they nor their descendants would ever return to Spain. This legend was of sufficient potency to discourage Jewish resettlement in Spain; it gave way only under the strains and stresses of the twentieth century. More authentic were the speculations of Hebrew authors on the causes of that great catastrophe. With their usual penchant for self-accusation, they attributed that tragedy to Spanish Jews' sins, rather than to any environmental factors. Joseph Ya'abeṣ pointed an accusing finger at their rationalism and neglect of ritual commandments which had so weakened

Jewish allegiance that many of them were ready to abandon their faith. Abraham Zacuto and Solomon ibn Verga attributed their downfall to their excessive rapprochement with their Gentile neighbors and particularly their intergroup sexual promiscuity. Referring primarily to the massacres of 1391, but clearly having in mind also the tragedy of 1492 of which he was a victim, Zacuto wrote, "We have a tradition that they [the Spanish Jews] took Christian women into their houses and they became pregnant. Their children became Gentiles and afterwards were among the murderers of their fathers." Ibn Verga contended that some of his countrymen had presented a halakhic argument that intercourse with a Christian woman, being subject to flagellation only, was prohibited in a lesser degree than an illicit relationship with a Jewess. Some leading individuals, too, became targets of widespread condemnation. The spectacle, in particular, of Chief Rabbi Abraham Seneor accepting conversion rather than exile understandably aggrieved many émigrés. The anonymous chronicler of 1495 echoed that deeply felt resentment when he contended that Seneor's leadership had never gained the approval of the Jewish community and that the distinguished Toledan rabbi, Isaac de Leon, had long before 1492 punned on the "court rabbi's" name by calling him *sone or* (hater of light).[62]

Among Spanish Christian writers, on the other hand, such as Andrés Bernaldez, there was almost unanimous approval of the expulsion. More remarkably, even such enlightened Italian humanists as Pico della Mirandola, Francesco Guicciardini, and Niccolò Machiavelli had no words of censure. While Pico discussed the banishment mainly from the standpoint of some astrological predictions by Jewish scholars which had failed to materialize, Guicciardini, the famed statesman-historian, emphasized that the great work of Spanish unification accomplished by the Catholic monarchs and the ensuing rise of Spain to the position of a great power sufficiently justified the removal of any obstacle to that unity and greatness. The realist Machiavelli held up Ferdinand as a shining example of a prince acting "in order to gain reputation" and saw in the expropriation of the prospective exiles (whom he erroneously called Marranos), "under the pretext of religion," an illustration of what reasonable monarchs ought to do in strengthening the power of their states. Only much later, particularly in independent Holland, did scholars, pondering over the intervening decline of Spanish power and prosperity, attribute it to that country's ill-considered elimination of its talented and industrious Jewish minority. In any case, in 1492 the most magnificent communal structure of medieval Jewry tumbled under the combined assaults of religious intolerance, economic rivalry, folkloristic prejudice, and inner Jewish weakness—all climaxed by the effects of national unification.[63]

Events in Castile and Aragon unavoidably affected the position of Jews in neighboring Navarre as well. Although the state was not incorporated into Spain until 1512, it strongly gravitated toward that country, rather than France, primarily because of its greater ethnic kinship with Spaniards. Long before 1492 Ferdinand the Catholic intervened in its inner affairs, as when he learned that a number of Castilian *conversos* had found refuge in Tudela and that the city had closed its gates to the inquisitors trying to prosecute them. In a strong letter to the "alcaldes, knights, councilors, and all good people of Tudela" (thus appealing to the population over the heads of its leaders) he expressed his astonishment at good Christians aiding heretics and threatened them with the divine wrath. In fact, neither Tudela nor any other Navarrese cities were really friendly to Jews. Their hostility came clearly to the fore, particularly during the influx of Spanish refugees in 1492. On June 8, several weeks before the July deadline for the latter's departure, the city council of Tafalla consulted that of Tudela about the threatening Jewish "invasion." It wrote:

Undoubtedly we consider it best to inform their Majesties, our lords [King John de Labrit and Queen Catalina] that it is contrary to the service of God, the glory of their Majesties and that of the whole country, to receive Jews, as you have expressed it already, and others will confirm. For it is unquestionably a divine miracle and a curse resting upon them [the Jews] that such a misfortune has befallen them. Let us therefore, honorable Sirs, work with united forces as one man so that no admission be granted to the exiles. Our resolve is firm: we shall not admit even one, so long as the negotiations in this matter are not concluded. We have today deported several Jews who had secretly smuggled themselves into our community. But in order to attain a unanimous resolution for the deputation to be sent to the royal couple, we wish to submit the matter to further careful deliberation and let you know the outcome. You, too, please discuss this matter and let us know the results, lest we express divergent opinions.

Nevertheless, king and queen made a more favorable decision and, according to Hebrew chroniclers, some 12,000 exiles found their way into the Navarrese cities. They were particularly well protected in territories under the control of feudal lords, such as the count of Lerin, whose capital, according to some estimates, in 1495 embraced 66 Jews and 137 Christians.[64]

However, Ferdinand, whose great influence had manifested itself clearly at the Cortes of Pamplona in 1496, exerted unrelenting pressures on the Navarrese rulers. With the aid of the anti-Jewish burghers, he succeeded in persuading them in 1498 to issue a general decree of expulsion, affecting not only the new arrivals but also Jews settled in the kingdom for centuries. In the absence of the royal couple, this decree was promulgated by Bishop John de Lasala who, as Ferdinand's agent, had long lorded it over the country. Here, too, quite a few Jews preferred baptism to departure. In Tudela alone, we are told, no less than 180 Jewish families adopted Christianity. Others escaped to neighboring Provençal and other French territories where, however, they could not publicly profess Judaism. But, subject to less rigid inquisitorial surveillance, they were able to adhere to their Jewish rituals with somewhat less fear and trepidation.[65]

PORTUGAL

Equally dramatic were the final denouements in Portugal. Despite manifold efforts, the Portuguese monarchy was long unable fully to overcome its original dependence on the Papacy and, hence, did not quite so effectively control its episcopate as did the Spanish rulers. During the fifteenth century, on the other hand, Portugal became a major maritime power whose fleets roamed the Atlantic and Mediterranean sea lanes. In Vasco da Gama's expedition of 1498 its sailors circumnavigated Africa and reached the East Indies. The Portuguese also tried to colonize some neighboring North-African territories and began developing certain characteristics of a modern colonial power. All these factors somewhat delimited Portuguese nationalism at home. More, the country constantly lived under the shadow of its more powerful Castilian neighbor, some rulers hoping to unify both countries under one regime. We recall Queen-Regent Leonora's attempt to secure in 1383 the Portuguese throne for her son-in-law King John I of Castile, which, if successful, would have achieved such early unification. Owing in part to a Portuguese (as well as Spanish) nationalist revulsion a native son, though but an illegitimate offshoot of the Portuguese dynasty, enlisted popular support and ascended the throne as John I. Since influential Jewish leaders were found in both camps, the aroused nationalist feelings might have led to sanguinary anti-Jewish riots. But John I's firm leadership averted this danger.[66]

Having escaped the ravages of the "holy war" of 1391 and the officially sponsored missionary endeavors under the leadership of Vicente Ferrer, Portugal was not plagued by a serious *converso* problem. True, in response to Cortes resolutions Alphonso V encouraged conversions and in his Code of Laws provided that, because of their expected bias, Jews, except when appearing as defendants, must not testify at court against converts. However, the total number of baptized Jews was very small and they were quickly absorbed by the majority. Nor was the Muslim minority comparable in size and importance to that in the Spanish realm. Quite early during the Reconquest most Muslims had left the country and the rest were, for the most part, gradually converted to Christianity. Yet in 1449 young hoodlums assailed the Jewish quarter in Lisbon during the king's absence from the city. When Alphonso V ordered the speedy punishment of some ringleaders, the aroused populace repeated its assault on Jews. Since that riot had a decidedly anti-royal tinge as well, Alphonso sharply suppressed the commotion and imposed severe penalties on the plunderers of Jewish homes. However, the Portuguese masses were kept in a state of anti-Jewish tension by both popular writers and the liturgical performers of Passion plays, one of which presented a rabbi carrying a scroll of law among the marchers in the public square. All stories ended, of course, with the victory of the Church over the Synagogue. Nevertheless the greater socio-economic diversification of the Portuguese Jews, their generally amicable social relations with most of their neighbors, and the peculiar characteristics of Portuguese nationalism would probably have prevented any drastic anti-Jewish action, had it not been for the impact of events across the Castilian border.[67]

It was perfectly natural for most Spanish exiles of 1492 to turn to neighboring Portugal as their main haven of refuge. Climatically and socially, even linguistically, the Iberian countries were so much akin that the refugees could look forward to a much easier acclimatization there. With the shorter distance and the perils of the journey somewhat minimized, some 20,000 Jewish families (of the more than 30,000 who preferred exile to conversion) moved across the Portuguese border. The figure of 120,000 new Jewish settlers in Portugal independently given by two Jewish contemporaries appears to come close to reality.[68]

Portugal's John II (1481–95) was ready to admit such a mass of immigrants only if they helped fill his coffers. He arranged, therefore, that, apart from 600 wealthy families, each paying 100 ducats, and a few professionals and artisans whom he wanted to keep, all others should be admitted only for eight months after disbursing a relatively large entry fee, variously given by contemporary chroniclers as upwards of eight cruzados. According to a Hebrew contemporary, the fee was a ducat per capita, in addition to a quarter of all possessions brought in by each family. For better control the Jews were told to enter exclusively at five designated frontier points. The king promised to provide, at their expense, shipping for all exiles wishing to leave at or before the expiration date, but he warned them that all those who would fail to pay the initial fee, or would remain behind after that date, would become royal slaves. This type of slavery greatly differed, of course, from the usual Jewish "serfdom" under Portuguese monarchs, although this term was used here much more sparingly. John II took this arrangement quite seriously and, by delaying shipping during the last crucial month, made certain that not too many refugees could depart. Hence many of those who refused to submit to baptism were indeed turned into slaves. Nor did the king from the outset extend effective protection to the immigrants, many of whom were robbed and even killed by farmers or by roving bands of highwaymen. All these conditions were aggravated by a pestilence then intermittently ravaging the country for some two decades which found easy targets in the crowded camps of undernourished refugees. They thus became doubly unwelcome to their Christian hosts, the city of Lamego claiming that until their arrival it had never suffered from a serious contagion. For this reason as well as out of fear that Spanish immigration would undermine its own position—this fear proved well grounded a few years later—even native Portuguese Jewry revealed certain symptoms of xenophobia toward newcomers who outnumbered it and added one-eighth to the country's population. It allegedly was reprimanded by both the king and its leader, Joseph b. David ibn Yaḥya.[69]

Such was the tragic situation of the majority of refugees upon the accession to the throne of Dom Emanuel (1495–1521). Emanuel, whom Damião de Góis describes as "second to no Christian king in humanity, liberality, clemency, and virtue," was in fact a worthy counterpart to Ferdinand as a shrewd, ambitious, persistent, and self-seeking monarch. Evidently convinced that slavery was not the best means of employing the Jews' energies, he began his reign by releasing them from bondage. But before long the Catholic monarchs began exerting great pressure on him, as they did on the Navarrese rulers, to remove this source of embarrassment to themselves and a possible later obstacle to the unification of the whole Peninsula. After Ferdinand and Isabella agreed that Emanuel should marry their daughter Isabella, the widow of another Portuguese prince, the younger Isabella, whether on her own initiative or following her mother's wishes, withheld her consent until the Portuguese king promised to rid his country of all infidels. The bait was too enticing, for Emanuel stood a good chance to see his children by Isabella ultimately inherit the Spanish throne and thus bring about the unification of both kingdoms under the house of Braganza. This plan did not materialize, except in reverse, when in 1580 Philip II of Spain secured for himself the Portuguese Crown also. But the immediate temptation was enormous and Emanuel readily accepted the condition. After mouthing the usual platitudes about having become convinced that the Jews constantly blasphemed against the Christian faith, the king ordered on December 5, 1496, all Jews to leave Portugal before the end of October 1497, under the penalty of death and the loss of all property for the benefit of the accuser. As to any person who, after the passage of the said time, should receive any Jew, We wish that, by this very act, he should lose all his property and goods for the benefit of the accuser. We also beg, recommend and order the kings, Our successors, with Our blessing and under the penalty of a curse, that at no future time should they allow any Jew to dwell or stay in these Our kingdoms and dominions for whatever cause or reason.

By thus directly encouraging informing, Emanuel made it doubly hard for any professing Jew to remain in the country.[70]

Not that Emanuel really wanted to eliminate the Jews who commercially and fiscally played too important a role in that era of Portuguese expansion and exploration. With ruthless calculation he sought, therefore, by whatever means to convert them and keep them in the country. During the nearly eleven months between the signing of the decree and the Jews' scheduled departure, his police and army displayed both ingenuity and brutality in achieving this aim, particularly by forcibly baptizing all children aged four to fourteen and withdrawing them permanently from parental control, unless the parents, too, accepted conversion. Suggested by a convert, Levi b. Shem Ṭob, this measure was enacted on March 19, 1497, over the protests even of such churchmen as Fernando Coutinho, later Bishop of Silves. Many children of recalcitrant parents were sent away to the island of St. Thomas (Tomé), then in the initial stages of Portuguese colonization, where most of them seem to have perished at the hands of natives, from snakebite, or because they could not stand the climate. Among these child converts was the son of Yehudah Abravanel (Leone Ebreo). Before 1492 the little boy had lived, together with his father and grandfather, Don Isaac, in Spain. Informed by highly placed friends of a court intrigue by some of Ferdinand's advisers to kidnap and baptize the child and thus to induce the boy's loving father and grandfather to accept conversion and stay in the country, the family spirited the boy away to Portugal, probably to the home of an aunt. None foresaw that but a few years later the same fate would befall Portuguese Jewry and that the youngster would then be forcibly converted to Christianity.

As the deadline for departure approached, Emanuel sought to break the resistance of the hard core of unflinchingly loyal Jews by assigning them only three harbors from which they were allowed to leave, and later by concentrating them all in Lisbon. Since shipping was extremely sparse, only a few were able to emigrate on time; the majority was forcibly dragged to the baptismal fonts. To sweeten the pill, the king promised that for twenty years he would not allow any Inquisition into the ways of life of the New Christians, clearly intimating that he would be satisfied with their mere lip service to Christianity. He hoped that at least the children converted at a tender age, and certainly those born after 1497, would become genuine Christians. He also doubtless expected to assuage thereby that segment of Portuguese public opinion which had condemned his violent methods. We need but mention Bishop Geronimo de Osorio, the otherwise admiring historian of his reign. Describing some heart-rending scenes at the forced conversions of Jewish children, the bishop commented that "to hear the cries, sighs, groans, lamentations, and female shrieks that filled the air, was dreadful. Some were so distracted, that they destroyed their children by casting them into wells; others, in fits of despair, made away with themselves." The bishop also roundly condemned the forcible conversion of adults which was "in accordance neither with the law nor with the faith." De Osorio added:

Will any one pretend to maintain that it was consistent with the principles of justice or religion, to force perverse and obstinate minds into the belief of things which in reality they despised and rejected? Will any one pretend to take on himself to prevent the freedom of will, or put fetters on the understanding? This is impossible to be done, and is directly opposed to the doctrine of Christ.

This point of view was to be effectively invoked for several decades in the controversy between the Portuguese Marranos and the Crown when the latter sought papal permission to establish an Inquisition along Spanish lines. The Marranos often argued that, according to canon law, their original conversion had no legal validity and that, hence, the individuals accused of apostasy could not be considered guilty. Not until 1534 did Portugal finally prevail upon the Papacy to authorize the establishment of regular inquisitorial courts in the country.[71]

We shall see that otherwise, too, Emanuel's expectation that all converts would be fully absorbed by the majority after two decades did not materialize and that the Marrano problem was to bedevil the Portuguese regimes for many generations. But the main purpose of eliminating professing Jewish communities from the Peninsula was thus achieved. The national states of Spain and Portugal, whether separate or united under certain monarchs, now had no publicly dissenting Jews in their midst.

ITALY

In contrast to western Europe, where in the course of the last three medieval centuries the major countries achieved a fair degree of national unification, the two large Central-European areas of the Holy Roman Empire and Italy became increasingly disorganized; at times, almost anarchical. While all Germany still recognized the emperor's nominal superiority, Italy did not have even such a minimal theoretical cohesion. Whatever rudimentary unity existed stemmed from Germany, France, or Aragon, which from time to time controlled large areas of the Apennine Peninsula and its adjacent islands. To rationalize German domination over Italy, Holy Roman emperors promoted the myth of the Franks' descent from Troy, making the Germans blood relations of Italians. But few Italians appreciated this alleged common descent, many rejecting even such emperors as Otto III, whose pro-Italian orientation had aroused much opposition in Germany herself. Quite early one began hearing voices demanding a national Italian monarchy "undeterred by savage Gaul and stern Germany." But such occasional postulates of a few thoughtful individuals hardly penetrated the masses who paid primary allegiance to their local regimes. The Papacy, too, whose occupants were not always Italian, had European ambitions but exercised direct sovereignty only over the Papal States. Even there its authority was challenged by the Senate, the populace, and foreign powers.[72]

This situation undoubtedly helped the Italian republics and principalities to develop their rich cultural and economic life which, during the Renaissance era, made them the economic and intellectual foci of the Western world. But politically Italy remained a conglomeration of part-of-nationality states which not only lacked coordination and simultaneity of action, but also largely followed their own specific needs, desires, and moods. Because of their involvement in the great power struggles of the day their policies, with respect to Jews also, often were determined much more by their international relations than by their domestic concerns.

International considerations dominated the papal policies which embraced all of Latin Christianity and, at times, extended their tentacles also to the Eastern Churches and beyond. The popes' international position was endangered, however, when Philip the Fair forced them to move to Avignon. Pierre Dubois expressed (in 1305-1307) the hope that thenceforth the French popes would appoint a majority of French cardinals and thus the Holy See "would no longer be withheld from the French, as has long been the custom because of the craft and natural cunning of the Romans." To some extent Avignon and the Comtat caught something of the rising spirit of French nationalism and for a while proved somewhat less tolerant toward Jews than did the Papacy's Italian possessions. Understandably, this dependence on the French aroused strong German resentments and helped to embroil Louis the Bavarian in his memorable conflict with the Papacy. Nor was St. Catherine the only spiritual leader to demand the return of the popes to Rome, which alone, in her opinion, would publicly reestablish their international position and thus save the Church. On the other hand, while campaigning in 1458 for his own election as pope against Cardinal Guillaume of Rouen, Ennea Silvio Piccolomini (later Pope Pius II) argued with fellow cardinals that Italian candidates ought to enjoy preference. "What is our Italy," he exclaimed, "without the bishop of Rome? We still have the Apostleship, though we have lost the Imperium. . . . A French pope will either go to France—and then our dear country will be bereft of its splendor; or he will stay among us—and Italy the queen of nations will serve a foreign master, while we shall be slaves of the French." But whatever national leanings the individual popes may have had, with respect to the Jewish faith they acted as spokesmen of the Catholic Church at large even when they referred only to local conditions in Rome.[73]

The manifold relations between the Jews and the popes have been described in some detail in earlier chapters. It will suffice therefore to restate here that, in contrast to western Europe, the Papal States never witnessed a total exclusion of Jews. Even partial expulsions were not to come until the era of Counter Reformation. During the Middle Ages proper we hear of but one attempted expulsion, namely that by John XXII in 1321–22. The reports thereon by the later Hebrew chroniclers—there is no confirmation whatever from John's own letters or archives—are based upon nondescript contemporary sources and are quite confused. The following summary by Joseph ha-Kohen is typical:

The pope's sister [Sancha] wished to destroy the Jews and was unable to do so. She requested her brother to expel them from his country and he listened to her, causing much suffering to Israel. But God aroused pity for the Jews in the heart of [Robert], King of Naples, who staunchly defended them against their enemies. Thereupon the Jews gave the woman 20,000 florins so that she became silent, and the matter passed without untoward consequences.

The unreliability of this account is evidenced by the confusion in names, such as Sancha, who was not John's sister, but the wife of Robert of Anjou, the king of Naples. That this story, nevertheless, contains a kernel of truth is evidenced by a contemporary entry in Todros b. Isaac's *Novellae* on the tractate Nazir:

I have written my comments on this tractate in the emergency period of the years [50]82 and the end of 81 [1321] at the time of the lepers' suppression when evil men appeared before the pope, the king of nations, and demanded that he destroy the true Law. The sacred books were indeed burned and they spoke openly about Israel's name no longer being mentioned among the earth's wanderers. They prepared a massacre against the martyrs of the land. But the Lord calmed his [the pope's] anger in the month of Ṭebet [December 1321–January 1322] and our enemies could not fulfill their plans.

Possibly connected with these events is the report, given by Ibn Verga in another context without a date, about an uprising in Rome, when the mob placed the Jews before the alternative of conversion or death. Despite a Jewish offer of a considerable ransom, we are told, the riots continued for three days, during which time some 15,000 Jews in the city and its vicinity allegedly adopted Christianity. Only a few succeeded in escaping to Naples, but "in a short time fate overtook them" there, too.[74]

All that emerges from these unclear accounts is that, in connection with the disturbances of 1320–22, Rome's restless population may have staged some anti-Jewish riots. The pope, as we recall, was quite lukewarm during the attacks on Jews and lepers. Even earlier (in 1320) he had arranged for another burning of the Talmud. To avert the new threat, a delegation of Roman Jews proceeded to Avignon while a solemn fast was proclaimed by their community. The delegates included Kalonymos b. Kalonymos from the circle of Hebrew poets patronized by Robert of Anjou in Naples, who happened to be visiting at that time in Avignon. Particularly in his capacity of Roman senator Robert felt free actively to intervene with the pope and possibly also with the Roman populace. That in recognition of his services the Jews gave him, or his wife Sancha, a Majorcan princess, as well as the pope, handsome presents is more than likely. In any case, whatever dangers faced the Jewish communities of Rome and Avignon at this juncture under the regime of a French pope, doubtless affected by the growing ethnoreligous intolerance of the French public, entailed no permanent untoward results.[75]

We have described this questionable episode at somewhat greater length because, if the allegations were true, John XXII's plan would have marked an abrupt departure from the previous moderately tolerant attitude of the Papacy. If another intolerant outburst occurred in Carpentras in 1350, the papal administration at worst only condoned measures taken by hostile local authorities but in no way altered its basic policy toward Jews. On the contrary, it not only facilitated the expansion of Jews into numerous papal towns and hamlets in central Italy, but even after Sixtus IV had authorized the establishment of the Spanish Inquisition, it admitted Jewish refugees from Spain to the Comtat and Rome. In 1449–52 Jewish arrivals from the Dauphiny, after 1483 from the Provence, in 1492 from Spain, and in 1503–1505 from the Orange principality greatly increased the Jewish population throughout the papal possessions. The popes turned a deaf ear to the petition of Avignon Christian merchants and artisans in 1480 that Jews be expelled. Despite the growing influence of the Catholic monarchs, Alexander VI, himself a Spaniard, even disregarded Ferdinand's official complaint in 1493 that many Marranos had been allowed to settle in Rome. When, after several years, the Roman Inquisition had to intervene against what had become a public scandal, it was satisfied, as we remember, with the culprits' formal abjuration and their promise to behave in good Christian fashion in the future. In short, the contrast drawn by the French chronicler, Jean Froissart, between the humane treatment of Jews in the Pontifical States and the frequent intolerant outbursts in other Christian lands (he referred, in particular, to the Black Death era) held true down to the onset of the Counter Reformation.[76]

Southern Italy, which embraced the majority of medieval Italian Jews, did not develop a full-fledged national movement even after its large residua of Greek- and Arabic-speaking inhabitants had been absorbed with the aid of immigrants from the mainland. More, throughout the Middle Ages the whole South was under foreign domination. Its basically tolerant Muslim regime was replaced by an equally latitudinarian Norman dynasty and by Frederick II. The latter pursued imperial interests encompassing the whole Western world, the very antithesis of either German or Italian nationalism. His successors of the Angevin and of the more enduring Aragonese dynasties divided their attention between their Italian possessions and their home countries. Under these circumstances medieval Naples and Sicily hardly displayed even the characteristics of part-of-a-nationality states.

On the whole, Jews fared rather well under these regimes. Only under Charles II of Anjou did Neapolitan Jews face a real danger when the king banished, in 1288, their coreligionists, as well as the Lombards and Cahorsins, from Anjou and Maine. Since this move coincided with the expulsion of the Jews from Gascony and was followed by that from England in 1290 and, before long, also from France in 1306, it could be viewed as an ominous example for the French administration in southern Italy. Local anti-Jewish forces seized, indeed, the opportunity, as we recall, of staging, in the 1290s, widespread anti-Jewish riots, which resulted in a large-scale conversion of Jews in many localities. No fewer than 1,300 *neofiti* families were granted, in 1294, a broad tax exemption. However, as elsewhere, such mass conversion led to the formation of a new minority, maintaining an intermediate place between professing Jews and original Christians and ever subject to denunciations of heterodoxy. In Apulia the inquisitors demanded in 1333–34 that professing Jews be assigned quarters away from Christians, for numerous converts, "relapsing into their previous error, debase the faith." On the other hand, Joanna I decreed that Apulian Jews should not be forced to denounce relapsed converts. As late as 1454 Alphonso V provided that the *neofiti* should be absolved from further inquisitorial prosecution by a mere oath of abjuration, such as has been preserved from the city of Lucera. Remarkably, this group never completely disappeared from the Italian scene and in the twentieth century some *neofiti* publicly reverted to Judaism. Nonetheless, the impact of Angevin intolerance and popular hostility was sufficiently enduring to cause the loss, by southern Italian Jewry, of that primacy in Central-European Jewish learning which its ancestors had enjoyed in the preceding centuries.[77]

Unlike the Iberian Peninsula, however, Italy did not allow the presence of this convert group seriously to undermine the legal status of professing Jews. True, in 1310 Frederick III of Sicily adopted a number of restrictions of Jewish and Saracen rights suggested to him by the apologist Arnaldo de Vilanova. But he paid no heed to the latter's recommendation that Jews be faced with the alternative of baptism within a year or leaving the country. After this storm blew over, Sicilian and Neapolitan Jewries achieved a relatively uninterrupted period of prosperity during the fourteenth and fifteenth centuries. Even the catastrophic Black Death and the Spanish "holy war" had but relatively minor anti-Jewish repercussions in the Two Sicilies. In June 1392, to be sure, according to an official report, "the inhabitants of the district of Monte San Giuliano attacked the Jews with drawn swords and in the riot violently forced them to accept baptism and to become Christian. A number who refused were unjustly killed." But King Martin V, allegedly "moved by cupidity of acquiring the material goods of the said Jews," quickly reacted and, between June 28 and July 1, issued a series of protective decrees. Citing both papal bulls and earlier royal enactments, he not only outlawed violence and forced baptisms but also forbade the local authorities to impose undue taxes upon the Jews. He also renewed Pedro II's decrees of 1339–40, forbidding the archbishop of Palermo to intervene in local Jewish civil affairs and ordering annual public announce-

ments during the Easter season which threatened with severe
penalties anyone inflicting damage upon Jews. It is small wonder
that, according to Selig Cassel's computation, only three of the
sixty known Jewish communities in Sicily had ever suffered from
large-scale riots.[78]

Governmental attitudes were sufficiently favorable for Alphonso
V to look with a jaundiced eye on the departure of some Jews to
the Holy Land. Yet in 1492 the Jews of Sicily, Sardinia, and the
other Aragonese possessions had to share the fate of their Spanish
coreligionists. True, the decree of expulsion was not promulgated
there at the end of April, as it was in the home country; the viceroy and the municipal authorities acted as if nothing were to happen. On May 23 the city of Palermo issued a proclamation "that
no person, whether a foreigner, or a citizen of whatever standing
and condition he may be, shall presume to injure, molest, disturb,
rebuke, or impose any undue novelty by word or deed in whatever
fashion on the Jews, both aliens and citizens." On June 9, 1492,
but seven weeks before the scheduled departure of Spanish Jewry,
Ferdinand the Catholic again forbade Jewish emigration from
Sicily and the export of gold and silver to the Ottoman Empire.
Yet he ordered the Jews to register all their movables and to deliver their bonds to notaries and but nine days later he issued
the official decree of expulsion. Unlike Spain, Sicily was not yet
ripe for life without Jews, and the decree almost immediately
elicited a storm of protests. In an extensive memorandum of June
20 the leading Sicilian officials assembled in Messina emphasized
the great blow to the island's economy and fiscal structure which
would follow the loss of its Jewry. On July 11 the city of Palermo
argued that the departure of Jewish artisans alone would deprive
the country of both weaponry and agricultural implements. Remarkably, even after the decree of June 18, the viceroy, Ferrando
de Acugna, issued at the Jews' request various protective regulations. While forced to backtrack and, within a few days, to cancel
those provisions which ran counter to the royal decree of banishment, he continued to protect the Jews against undue exactions. It
was probably owing to a large extent to his influence, as well as to
the local protests, that the Jews secured two extensions, until January 12, 1493. At the same time both he and the king tried to per-

suade as many Jews as possible to accept conversion by assuring the New Christians that they would retain all their property and be treated on a basis of absolute equality with the Old Christians. But Ferdinand unflinchingly insisted that thereafter no professing Jews should remain on the Aragonese-controlled islands which included the smaller communities on Malta and Gozzo.[79]

No evidence is available as to how many Jews left Sicily and the other islands. Even more than their Spanish counterparts wealthy Sicilians had every incentive to remain behind and pay lip service to the new religion. For the authorities in Sicily and its island dependencies demanded that the Jews not only pay in full their taxes to the end of 1492 but also that they make up future losses to the Treasury. Probably after much wrangling they settled for the modest sum of 100,000 florins to which the Jews had to add another 5,000 florins for the postponement of the date of expulsion. Through conversion a wealthy Jew could both salvage his property and escape payment of his share in this collective contribution. On the other hand, the numerous paupers as well as most petty merchants and artisans had far less to lose from emigration. In any case, before long, Sicilian exiles appeared in considerable numbers in Naples, Rome, and the Ottoman Empire. The very fact that *neofiti* never constituted an important problem in Sicilian history would actually militate against the assumption of any large-scale conversion.[80]

Jews of the Neapolitan mainland, including many Spanish and Sicilian refugees, received a temporary respite because Naples, including Apulia and Calabria, was ruled at that time by another branch of the Aragonese dynasty. King Ferrante, Ferdinand the Catholic's nephew, staunchly defended the Jews until he died in 1494. Some 4,000 Jewish families are said to have settled in Calabria alone. Commenting in the spring of 1495 on the brotherly reception of the Jewish exiles, the anonymous Hebrew chronicler, himself a new arrival, wrote:

The Neapolitan Jews supplied them [the exiles] with food and sent [messengers] to other parts of Italy to collect money for their support. The city's Marranos lent them money on pledges without interest; even the Dominicans acted charitably toward them. Yet because of their multitude all this help was insufficient. Some died of starvation;

others sold their children to Christians in order to sustain themselves. Ultimately, a pestilence ravaged them, spreading through all of Naples. So many died that the living wearied of burying the dead.

Under Ferrante's son, Alphonso II (1494–95), Neapolitan Jewry suffered severely from a major foreign invasion and the breakdown of internal discipline, since both barons and burghers rebelled against the absolutist regime. On Ferrante's death, they staged attacks on various Jewish communities considered allies of the oppressive monarchy. The situation was further aggravated by rumors that emaciated and penniless exiles from Spain and Sicily had brought with them the ravaging pestilence. At the same time Don Isaac Abravanel's speedy rise to a high position at the court of Ferrante and Alphonso, and his signal services in international and fiscal affairs, merely aroused the envy of rivals. Hence Parliament, convened after Alphonso II's abdication on January 22, 1495, passed, on Naples' initiative, a number of resolutions demanding the expulsion of most Jews from that city; the relegation of the remaining minority to a separate quarter; the reestablishment of the badge; the abolition of special Jewish tribunals; and a general right of preemption for Christians against Jewish competitors. Before these decisions could be implemented, however, the French army, headed by Charles VIII, arrived and occupied the whole country. During the ensuing disturbances there were renewed anti-Jewish riots in both the capital and the provinces; many Jews were killed and their property (including Abravanel's rich library) was looted. While generally keeping aloof and neither encouraging the rioters nor protecting the Jews, some French invaders gladly participated in the looting of Jewish homes.[81]

Having suffered severely during both the brief French occupation and under the restored Aragonese domination (aided by an alliance of Spain, the Holy Roman Empire, and Venice), the Jews felt relieved when Spanish armies occupied the country in 1502. In fact, the Spanish victories were facilitated by Jewish loans. To be sure, with Ferdinand's armies came also an intensification of the inquisitorial procedures against both Marranos and local converts. The burghers, dreading the extension of the Spanish Inquisition with its Sicilian headquarters in Palermo, petitioned the king in 1507 to issue in favor of both the Jews and the New Christians "a general amnesty for each and every crime, however major and enormous, even those under the sanction of natural or civil death or of any kind of fine." This request was formally sponsored by the Parliament of January 15–30, 1507, which also demanded that Jews be allowed to live securely in the realm with their families and property, and enter or leave it without any obstacle or offense. Remarkably, while giving an evasive answer concerning the amnesty which he granted to other citizens for offenses committed before November 1, 1506, Ferdinand ordered the population not to persecute Jews "unduly." The provincial members of Parliament, to be sure, sought simultaneously to secure the cancellation of all debts owed to Jews. Yet in another session at the end of 1508 the majority still demanded the renewal of the security measures previously granted to the settlers from Spain. But soon thereafter (in 1509) Ferdinand, breaking his earlier pledges, allowed an Inquisition, modeled after the Spanish institution, to start operations in Naples as well. He also decreed that "in consideration of how much holy baptism is different from the Jews' depravity and how convenient it should be that the Jews who are separated from the Christians in the observance of the true Catholic faith should also be separated from them and be known as Jews," all Jews, male and female, over ten years of age should wear a [strip of] red cloth on their chests under the penalty of one ounce of gold for each time they would be apprehended without it.[82]

These moves were speedily followed by a general decree of banishment promulgated on November 22, 1510. Combining flattery for the city of Naples which had recognized the truth of Christianity even before Rome did and hence was the most ancient center of the faith (*antiquissima en la religión christiana*) with warnings that for that very reason the kingdom required double vigilance against the Jews' corruptive influence, especially upon the *conversos* of their stock (*de su generación descendiente*), Ferdinand ordered all Jews to leave the country before the end of March 1511 and "never to return." As a result of such a measure, Ferdinand declared,

as experience has clearly shown, Our Spanish Kingdoms have through the divine grace been cleansed of all heresies as far as it depended on

Us and they have greatly benefited from the expulsion of Jews through whose contagion many errors had been caused. This is a well-known matter [*es muy notorio*] and requires no further proof. . . . [Therefore, after March 1511] any Jew found residing or visiting in whatever manner in any part of Our said Kingdom shall incur the penalty of death and the confiscation of all his property for the benefit of Our Chamber and Treasury. He shall incur these penalties by this very fact [of his presence] without any further trial, sentence, or declaration.

Confiscation of property was also to be imposed on those Christians who might help Jewish culprits to evade the decree. On the other hand, the law enabled the new converts of Apulia and Calabria (not the old *neofiti*) and those Spanish settlers who had been condemned by the Inquisition *in absentia* to settle their affairs and leave the country within four months. They were also allowed to take along all their movables except gold and silver. In contrast to his implacable determination in both Spain and Sicily, however, the king soon made an exception: he allowed 200 Jewish families to remain if they paid the Treasury 3,000 ducats annually. It seems that practically all other Jews left the country within the designated period; we possess numerous records of the disposal of property left behind by them. In Lecce, for example, the synagogue was converted into a Catholic church and in Castrovillari the Jewish school was turned over to the municipality. Another expulsion, this time of Marranos, was ordered at the turn of 1514 to 1515. If such measures necessarily discouraged Jews contemplating baptism, their number must from the outset have been quite small, since the Inquisition had interveningly made the life of previously converted Jews quite unbearable.[83]

In the meantime public opinion veered sharply. Realizing the economic shortcomings arising from the absence of Jews and particularly from the excessive usuries charged by Christian bankers, the population clamored that more Jews be allowed to spend at least some time in the country. In 1514 the city of Lanciano secured a privilege of accommodating Jews during its fair. In the following year all of Apulia opened its gates to Jewish refugees from Dalmatia. Some time later even a rabbi established himself in Naples. The city's population expostulated with the king in 1520 that it had "the greatest need to keep Jews" for otherwise it would be unable to pay its taxes. Under the pressure of public opinion Emperor Charles V issued on November 23, 1520, a detailed decree, the first four paragraphs of which stated that Jews could live, do business, and open banks with papal license in the kingdom of Naples; that they were to receive a safe-conduct for five years and be allowed, with the consent of the sovereign, to stay on for another year and a half if the decree were to be revoked; and that they were to pay the royal Treasury 1,500 ducats annually in three installments. To facilitate these payments by the local Jews, interveningly greatly impoverished, they were allowed to invite forty to fifty wealthy Jewish families from abroad to settle in their midst and enjoy the same privileges. Other provisions were equally favorable. In justification, the decree pointed out that "most nefarious usuries had been committed by Christians in an enormous and clandestine fashion during the absence of Jews . . . so that a Christian sucked the blood of another Christian." Hence it was a lesser evil to allow Jews to engage in this sinful trade for the benefit of the populace, as well as that of the royal Treasury.[84]

Jews now began gradually rebuilding their shattered fortunes in the entire kingdom where peace had interveningly been restored. However, these very privileges aroused the ire of zealots, particularly among churchmen. The debate continued under the administration of the powerful viceroy, Pedro de Toledo, whose attitude toward Jews was quite ambivalent. In 1529 he reintroduced the badge and in 1533 he threatened again to expel all professing Jews. But when this radical announcement evoked a storm of protests he accepted, in 1535, a compromise whereby the Jews were to stay for another ten years, subject to an annual tax of 2,000 ducats. Half of this total of 20,000 ducats was to be paid in advance. This arrangement, partially secured through the influential Jewish leader Samuel (son of Isaac) Abravanel and his wife Benvenida, was published in November 1535. It must have had Charles V's approval, since the emperor was at that time visiting Calabria and Naples. Curiously, his sojourn in the capital contributed to the population's ill will toward Jews. The expenses of entertaining him and his court in style weighed so heavily upon the nobles and burghers that many had to pledge their property with Jewish moneylenders. It may well be that Viceroy Pedro merely wished to find a way of relieving the nobles of the realm of their indebtedness by getting rid of their Jewish creditors. Hence, notwithstanding the royal pledge to keep the Jews at least till 1545, and the Parliament's request that this term be prolonged for another five years, Charles V in a decree dated November 10, 1539, ordered all Jews to leave the kingdom within four months. They secured various postponements, but by October 1541 all professing Jews departed, and, during the subsequent three centuries, no organized Jewish community existed in the whole kingdom. The effects of the Jewish exodus and of other adverse facets of the Spanish maladministration were even more sharply felt in parts of the Neapolitan kingdom than in Spain. According to Oreste Dito, the population of Calabria, somewhat unreliably estimated at 160,335 families in 1562, declined to 103,444 in 1648, and to 81,642 in 1661.[85]

These Neapolitan developments down to the tragic finale of 1541 are discussed here in somewhat greater detail because they underscore the difference between southern Italy and the Spanish home country, where nationalist intolerance had been rife for the instantaneous, unopposed elimination of Jews. While in Sicily, long under the heel of Aragonese masters, the opposition to the expulsion, though widespread, was not strong enough to obtain any important relaxation of the Catholic monarchs' determination to banish the Jews, the newly incorporated Neapolitan sections, abetted by the international power struggles, forced both Ferdinand and Charles V to accept various compromises and delays. Even the Spanish viceroys felt that they had to proceed gingerly in ramming through the exclusion of Jews, unpalatable to large segments of the Neapolitan public. Though clearly part-of-a-nationality state, the Kingdom of Naples thus illustrated how its anti-Jewish xenophobia could be overshadowed by the larger fear of seeing its own autonomous evolution submerged by the Spanish imperial power and its most effective instrumentality: the Spanish Inquisition.

The alternating fits of tolerance and intolerance in the various North-Italian republics and principalities have been described in an earlier chapter. We need but point out that the most important center of North-Italian Jewish life at the onset of the sixteenth century was located in the Venetian Republic with its growing control over parts of the *terra firma*, including Padua and Verona. The developments here were affected by the Republic's colonial expansion, which helped to dilute greatly its nationalist intolerance. The Duchy of Milan, Piedmont-Savoy, and Tuscany likewise came under strong international influence. Milan was soon occupied by the Spaniards, a fact which sooner or later was bound also to affect the Jewish status. Savoy, more French than Italian, and Piedmont, more Italian than French, long pursued jointly a purely dynastic policy. Tuscany under its Medicean dukes attempted to play a grandiose European role which, though buttressed by its economic and cultural magnificence, exceeded its genuine resources. Each one of these states pursued independent Jewish policies and whatever manifestations of intolerance toward Jews appeared were owing either to specific local causes, as in Florence, or to international developments, as in Milan. On the other hand, Genoa, though economically suffering losses from the Spanish and southern Italian intransigence toward Jews, was not ready to abandon its own intolerance, making only a few individual and temporary exceptions. The story of these divergent sixteenth-century attitudes, together with the impact of the Counter Reformation, will be told more fully in a later chapter.[86]

In any case, the last three medieval centuries were the period of the greatest and most permanent expansion of the Jews in northern Italy. Despite many instances of friction, even occasional sanguinary riots, Italy as a whole had a relatively clean record when compared with the bloody annals of Jewish history in most other European countries. Among the numerous factors explaining this situation was the relative weakness of medieval Italian nationalism, as well as Italy's pioneering in the new secularized forms of modern civilization in which nationalism was gradually divorced from its intimate ties with religion.

HOLY ROMAN EMPIRE

Equally complicated and lacking in uniformity were the developments in Germany. In the Middle Ages and early modern times German nationalism was permanently at odds with the various regional and tribal feelings which long continued to dominate the life and thought of the people. In foreign countries Germans were best known under the names of one or another tribe. Frenchmen still call the Germans by the tribal name of Alemans; Scandinavians and Estonians usually style them Saxons; while many Balkan peoples know them only as Swabians. The Italians alone, whose history had become closely intertwined with that of medieval Germany and to whom all Germans appeared under the guise of a domineering Empire, thought of them in terms of a single people. They adopted for them the designation of Tedeschi, a derivative of the Latin Teutiscus, first mentioned in Trent in 845. This more or less permanent Italo-German relationship helped to nurture some national sentiments in both countries, but it was not strong enough to create an overriding drive toward national unification until the nineteenth century. On the other hand, these very Italian ambitions were part of the universal imperial aspirations and conflicted with the emperors' self-identification with any German national movement. They injected into the German evolution a universalist counterbalance to regionalism and tribalism. Maximilian I and Charles V still ventured to place on their coins grandiloquent Latin inscriptions reading "What the sun is in the sky, the emperor [Caesar] is on earth." As far as the Jews were concerned, medieval Germany, impeded by these supranational and subnational forces at work, never became a full-fledged national state; its various, more or less sovereign, constitutents were at most part-of-a-nationality states, subject to the pulls and stresses of both universalism and tribalism.The result was the enormous, almost anarchical, variety of actions and counteractions, often dictated by purely local or temporary exigencies, which make the story of medieval Jewry in Germany such a hodge-podge of positive and negative attitudes.[87]

Here we need but refer to the more dramatic expressions of intolerance in riots and massacres, local or regional expulsions. There never was a total banishment of Jews from the whole Empire, similar to the expulsions from England, France, or Spain. The emperors as a rule tried to protect their Jewish "serfs" against intolerant onslaughts in any region or city under their control, nominal or real. If they proved less and less effective, this was mainly owing to their inability to impose the imperial will on increasingly independent princes, bishops, and cities. The events during the First and Second Crusades had left behind a heritage of both animosity and violence which could not easily be repressed. Germany thus became the scene of the most extensive slaughter of Jews and the wholesale destruction of communities, far exceeding in both frequency and geographic extension anything that happened in neighboring lands. At the same time the Empire was too diverse and decentralized a structure to allow for any simultaneity of anti-Jewish action extending beyond certain regions. Only in the Black Death era was there a psychological, similar to the physical, contagion which spread from region to region and gave the superficial appearance of almost concerted action. Even that catastrophic chain of events, however, resulted more from the spread of a mass hysteria than from any preconceived plan.

Local riots occurred on slight provocation even during the relatively peaceful Judeo-Christian symbiosis in the thirteenth century. In sufficed, in 1221, for some Frisian merchants to visit Erfurt, for them, jointly with natives, to attack the Jews and cause the death of at least twenty-one persons. Some of these casualties, to be sure, resulted from self-inflicted Jewish martyrdom which had become so prevalent since 1096 that, after a similar disturbance in Coblenz in 1265, R. Meir of Rothenburg was asked what was to be done with a man who had killed his wife and children but at the last moment was saved by outsiders. The question was raised whether, though suicide for the sake of Heaven and concomitant with it the death inflicted upon others for sacred purposes were clearly condoned, such slaying was to be regarded as murder if the slayer survived. Rabbi Meir exonerated the killer, for any other decision would, in his opinion, have cast aspersion on many revered martyrs of the past.[88]

No less flimsy an excuse than in the Erfurt disturbance of 1221 was given in Frankfort in 1241 for a major riot which, according to a contemporary chronicler, cost some 180 Jewish lives, many Jews perishing in the fire they had themselves started. Since the conflagration consumed more than half of the city, the twenty-four surviving Jews, we are told, headed by their rabbi, feared the wrath of their Christian neighbors and speedily adopted Christianity. In 1243 a number of Jews of both sexes were tortured and subsequently executed in Kitzingen, Bavaria. With special cruelty the corpses were kept for fourteen days on the wheels and only then allowed to be buried in the Würzburg cemetery. Another serious incident in 1263–64 (?) was provoked by a convert to Judaism, who, like most others, had adopted the name of the first Jew, Abraham, and is said to have traveled from place to place in Bavaria, preaching against Christianity. In Sinzig (or Weissenburg) he allegedly destroyed some crucifixes, whereupon he was seized, transported to Augsburg, and executed. But not satisfied with wreaking vengeance on that offender, the populace killed many other Jews as well. Most of these events were commemorated in liturgical poems; one was composed by Abraham b. Moses, apparently the aforementioned Coblenz slayer of his family. Other persecutions are briefly mentioned in both Meiningen and Ortenburg (probably in Baden), the memor book failing to indicate their immediate causes. On the other hand, the persecution in Belitz, Brandenburg, which allegedly took place in 1247 as a result of a Jewish desecration of a host which had miraculously betrayed the evildoers, may have been but the figment of a chronicler's imagination.[89]

In Munich Jews were accused in 1285 of a ritual murder of a Christian child. Without awaiting the outcome of the trial the enraged populace forced most Jews to seek safety in the synagogue, which it speedily set on fire. The number of victims mentioned in contemporary chronicles and poems ranges from 90 to 180. But the Mayence-Nuremberg *Memorbuch* furnished only sixty-eight names, including that of "R. Joseph the Frenchman, his wife and son." Clearly, the Munich mobs were completely oblivious of the sharp denials of the Blood Accusation by Pope Innocent IV and Emperor Frederick II. Little did pope and emperor foresee that the real story of ritual murder libels in Germany had only begun to unfold during their lifetime.[90]

Disturbances of this kind, also in Bachrach, in the Moselle district, and other localities, were but a prelude to a large-scale massacre led by an impoverished nobleman called Rindfleisch. The movement began with an alleged host desecration by the Jews of Röttlingen in the spring of 1298 and soon spread through most of Franconia, Bavaria, and parts of Austria during the temporary weakness of the imperial Crown, then being contested by Adolph of Nassau and Albert of Habsburg. In Rothenburg there were two successive assaults on June 25 and July 18, climaxed by a three-day (July 20–22) siege of a tower in which the Jews offered stout resistance. At the end, to cite an entry in the contemporary memor book, "the tower was captured on account of our numerous sins and all [the inmates] were killed and burned." The number of victims was estimated at 450. Even greater losses were sustained by the community of Würzburg, where a fairly exact account mentions fatalities of some 800 Würzburg and 100 foreign Jews. In Nuremberg a similar list reveals 628 slain; among them the distinguished halakhist Mordecai b. Hillel ha-Kohen, as well as a proselyte who had adopted Judaism in the midst of hostilities, apparently swayed by his admiration for the heroic self-sacrifice of Nuremberg Jewry. Even some antagonistic onlookers spoke with incredulity of the Jews proceeding to the pyre "with dance and song." In all, one hundred and forty-six communities suffered severely. The estimate of 100,000 victims by a Christian chronicler, Gottfried von Ensmingen, is decidedly exaggerated, however, since the entire area under attack did not have that many Jews. Closer to the truth is the figure of 20,000 fatalities cited by a Jewish contemporary. In any case, the substantial losses sustained by a large segment of German Jewry made themselves immediately felt in the economic and fiscal life of the Empire. Albert I, as we recall, reacted sharply and imposed severe fines upon several major cities, particularly Würzburg and Nuremberg, because they had passively stood by during the massacres and had appropriated the victims' possessions. How effective the intervention of local burghers might have been was demonstrated by the ability of both Ratisbon and Augsburg to stave off the assailants. In Ratisbon the burghers, led by the energetic burgomaster Balduin von Färbing and "wishing to honor their city," simply informed the Rindfleisch gangs that they needed more persuasive proof that the latter were merely fulfilling God's wish. On their part, the grateful Augsburg Jews constructed a new so-called Jewish bastion to enhance the city's defenses.[91]

Hardly had these communities partially recovered when some of them, together with others located further west, became the objects of large-scale attacks in 1336–37. Led by two nobles wearing leather patches on their arms and hence called Armleder, as well as by an innkeeper, Johann Zimberli, hordes of pogromists traversed the Rhinelands, Alsace, and Swabia before they again reached Bavaria and spilled over into Austria. Referring only to the latter two regions, a contemporary chronicler stated that the Jews "were barbarically and cruelly killed by poverty-stricken people in all cities throughout Bavaria and Austria, except Ratisbon and Vienna." Terrified at the approach of the blood-thirsty gangs, a number of Jewish communities preferred anticipatory mass suicides. This time, to be sure, some authorities reacted more speedily. While Emperor Louis the Bavarian intervened too late, some cities and princes took up arms in the Jews' defense, clearly realizing that, unless stemmed, this revolutionary movement would overwhelm them, too. Würzburg even sent out an armed detachment to meet a mob marching on the city from Kitzingen and captured forty-seven would-be pogromists. In 1337 its city council broadly decreed that anyone causing damage to a Jew should be banished "for ever" together with his family. Rather belatedly (in 1338) a number of Alsatian cities, including Strasbourg, Colmar, and Haguenau, concluded an alliance with the bishop of Strasbourg and several feudal lords to fight off future assailants. (A similar, even larger, confederacy was concluded in 1345 against all rioters, whether aiming at the clergy, other Christians, or Jews.) Once again Ratisbon distinguished itself in 1336 by holding off the pogromists. Going further, the municipal authorities decreed in 1342 that, in the case of a future "run on Jews," each and every burgher should rush to their defense and "follow the Council's instructions for the honor and necessity of us all and of our city." On the other hand, the neighboring town of Deggendorf utilized the unrest created by a local host accusation to appropriate all Jewish possessions. Similarly, after a riot in Straubing, the Bavarian duke claimed exclusive rights of inheritance to the victims' property, including funds held by Ratisbon Jews. This claim was finally settled by arbitration. A similar rumor in Austrian Pulka, however, was stopped by the aforementioned action of Duke Albert II with the active support of Pope Benedict XII.[92]

Regrettably, the Christian chroniclers—often our main source of information—almost invariably report such anti-Jewish commotions with a strong bias. The Franciscan Johann von Winterthur (Johannes Vitoduranus), for instance, narrates at some length the attacks on Jews in Swiss Ueberlingen and Constance in 1332 and 1334. He not only believes in the Jews' ritual murders and host desecrations, but he also describes, with much sympathy, the Ueberlingen burghers' efforts to evade the expected imperial retribution and their debate as to "how they [the Jews] might be conveniently done away with without the city suffering permanent damage." He unperturbedly reports how 300 (according to other chroniclers, 350–400) Jews were, through a ruse, assembled in a single house and subsequently burned, although he cannot quite suppress his admiration for the victims "singing melodies" in the burning structure. He adds that Louis the Bavarian punished the city and destroyed its walls, not because he considered its judgment unjust, but rather because he had not been previously consulted. To Winterthur's sorrow, only twenty-seven Jews were executed in Constance, while the rest were saved by the intervention of the Austrian dukes, the permanent defenders of Jews. For this reason, the chronicler observes, the dukes died prematurely and "otherwise, too, had prospered very little." Only in time did calmer counsels prevail; a number of later reporters expressed regret over these and subsequent massacres. A Constance chronicler, Seutlonius (Mangold), concluded his narrative with the exclamation: "Woe unto the judges!" [93]

Seutlonius' observation referred particularly to the far greater mass slaughter of 1348–49 which was wholly unprecedented in its geographic extension and in the number of its victims. This stark tragedy has been described in earlier chapters and we need but mention that while in Savoy, where the pogrom movement started, the attacks on Jews followed the outbreak of the Black Death, in most German-speaking areas they preceded it. It sufficed for rumors about its ravages elsewhere to reach Switzerland, Alsace, and the Rhenish communities for the panicky populations readily to blame them on Jewish well poisonings. Some city councils, to be sure, such as Strasbourg, tried to protect their Jews, but they were overwhelmed by mobs usually led by artisan guilds which rebelled against their local masters. This entire anti-Jewish onslaught was, indeed, part of a major social revolution which was spreading like wildfire throughout France and Germany and which made even Emperor Charles IV desist from defending his Jewish "serfs."

On the whole, the mass burning of Jews (*Judenbrand*) proceeded from west to east and from south to north, gradually reaching central Germany and Austria, where, however, Ratisbon and Vienna again successfully defended their Jews. This movement encountered a wave of so-called Flagellants which was expanding from east to west and which, too, was but a reflection of the people's panic in the face of that unexplainable, and hence doubly terrifying, disease. To appease the divine wrath many men and women left their homes and marched through Germany, usually nude from their waists up and submitting themselves to frequent flagellations. At the same time they indulged in much sexual promiscuity and agitated for the overthrow of the existing social order, Jews becoming prime targets for their attacks.

The usual explanations that the massacres were owing either to the panic of a half-crazed population or to the quest for pillage and getting rid of debts are undoubtedly true and have been mentioned by contemporary chroniclers (for instance, in the second and third continuation of the *Chronica* S. Petri Erphordensis). But they do not tell the whole story. In many localities it was the proletariat and the neighboring peasants who joined hands in slaughtering Jews, although neither group was deeply indebted to Jewish moneylenders. On the other hand, when, according to rumor, the Augsburg burgomaster Heinrich Porter, rather than protecting Jews, opened the city gates to "Jew killers" from the outside, he may indeed have been prompted by his heavy personal indebtedness. In some other cases, debt-laden city elders or nobles, without actively promoting the massacres, helped the assailants by their passivity. Some may have been swayed by their exchanges of letters with other cities which confirmed their prejudice against alleged Jewish well poisoners, although, for instance, the Cologne elders in January 1349 warned their Strasbourg confreres not to mistreat the Jews on account of such unverified rumors. Yet but a few months passed until in two waves of persecution, before and after the death of Archbishop Walram on August 14, 1349, the Jews of the whole archbishopric of Cologne, too, suffered severely.

The universality of these onslaughts so impressed contemporaries that Heinrich von Diessenhofen commented:

I might have thought that the end of the Hebrews had now come, if the predictions of Elijah and Enoch had been fulfilled. But since they have not been fulfilled, it is necessary that some [Hebrews] should be preserved so that the Scriptural statement concerning the hearts of the sons turning to the fathers and those of the fathers to the sons be realized. But I do not know where they will be preserved, though I assume that it is more likely that the people and the seed of Abraham will be maintained in regions beyond the sea.

Diessenhofen was evidently unaware that there were several regions in the very Empire which had not massacred Jews. Apart from Vienna and other Austrian communities, Jews were little disturbed in neighboring Bohemia and Moravia, or in some northeastern sections. Moreover, the very bloodshed in Germany stimulated Jewish emigration to Poland where the population suffered relatively little from the Black Death and where, as we have seen, Jews lived under the Crown's fairly effective protection.[94]

Approximately three hundred German communities were annihilated, including some of the most venerable seats of Jewish learning. So great was the destruction of Jewish life that relatively few poets survived to compose dirges on the great martyrdom of their people. The few who did as a rule repeated the traditional theme song of Jewish sinfulness being at the root of these sufferings, as it was voiced in Baruch (b. Yehiel?) ha-Kohen's aforementioned *Ani hu ha-qonen qinah* (I Am He Who Keens This Dirge). Yet few Jews availed themselves of the alternative of conversion. Obviously, the intent to convert Jews and thus to absorb them in the body politic frequently overcame the suspicions of well poisoning and, once converted, the alleged poisoners were left alone. Other Hebrew poets turned to the Lord with queries about why their assailants were allowed to escape punishment or vigorously invoked divine vengeance upon their enemies. But whatever psychological outlets these pained souls found in their lyrical outpourings, they could not gloss over the fact that the Black Death era had almost spelled an end to all organized Jewish life in large sections of Germany and, for a time, cut short an historic career which had begun in the second century or earlier.[95]

ERA OF EXPULSIONS

All appearances to the contrary, the Black Death massacres did not write *finis* to Jewish history in Germany. True, most cities, including the most populous and venerable ones in the west and south, now were emptied of Jews. More, a dangerous precedent was set for large-scale burning of Jews not only as a result of rioting by an aroused populace, but also after some deliberation by rulers or city councils. To be sure, a few of the latter tried to give themselves a semblance of legality. While Jews were rarely given the opportunity to defend themselves, some authorities went through motions of collecting evidence, consisting largely of communications from other cities. Obviously, such "proofs" would not have sufficed for the condemnation of a single defendant in an ordinary court. But in the prevailing hysteria few officials were punctilious about evidence; they accepted widespread rumors precisely because they were so widespread. In many other respects, too, the status of the surviving German Jews after 1350 bore but a remote resemblance to their situation before the Black Death. Even where decrees used the same legal verbiage, they were from the outset intended to be subject to more arbitrary interpretation and revocation.

Insecurity was inherent in the very arrangements made by the returning Jews with the respective authorities. For the most part, settlement rights were now limited in time, not exceeding ten to twelve years. These privileges were renewable, and as a rule were renewed, but at the expiration of each term the rulers could alter the conditions of Jewish sojourn to suit their own needs or simply refuse to renew the agreement with little interference from the emperor. Even the few speedily reconstituted communities rarely got back their communal property and usually had to start from scratch. The very Jewish quarters had in the meantime been occupied, and the returnees had to seek shelter in peripheral, often unsanitary, districts.

Even the lingering suspicions of Jewish well poisoning still persisted. In extending the Jews' right of settlement in 1350 the city council of Perleberg, Brandenburg, entered the reservation that "should it become manifest and proved by truthful men that the said Jews had caused the death of Christians or would cause it in the future, they should suffer for it in accordance with the law notwithstanding prior enactments. It is said that elsewhere Jews have slain men by poisoning." In the first flush of burnings many cities had hoped to fall heir to the Jewish wealth. In practice, they learned to their chagrin, even more than had the French kings, that the liquidation of Jewish property was neither so speedy nor so remunerative as they had expected. Jews had liabilities as well as assets. Many claimants, both legitimate and fraudulent, demanded payment of alleged debts owed them by the exiles, the restoration of pawns, or the fulfillment of other contractual obligations. On the other hand, the Jews' debtors employed all sorts of subterfuges to deny or to reduce their indebtedness. The legal situation of most Jewries, too, had become so complex, their subjection to different authorities, such as city councils, feudal lords, bishops, princes, and emperor had developed over generations in so many contradictory and confusing enactments that it would have taken courts many years to unravel each particular claim to inheritance. If Charles IV with unwonted generosity not only granted amnesty for crimes committed, but also assigned much Jewish real estate throughout Germany to his favorites, he often had to backtrack after finding out that he himself, or some of his predecessors, had disposed of certain Jewish rights to another public authority. Much of Jewish movable property had disappeared, having been looted by assailants or bystanders. A month after the tragedy the Cologne city council asked the local clergy to appeal to their congregations from the pulpit to report to the authorities the whereabouts of any Jewish property and to name burglars and "fences." It took another year before the city reached an agreement with the archbishop, who negotiated until 1356 before striking a compromise with Margrave William of Jülich concerning their respective shares. Even more complicated were the negotiations in Thuringia and elsewhere.[96]

Some cities began welcoming back a few Jews in order to help them recover what they considered legitimate municipal inheritances. Other localities soon felt the loss of the regular Jewish revenue, while their needy residents often clamored for the restoration of Jewish loans extended at less usurious rates and collected with less hardships than had become the accepted practice among the illicit Christian usurers. As a result the Jews speedily reestablished themselves in many localities. We recall that as early as 1349 they reappeared in Lucerne and Augsburg; in the latter first the bishop and, in 1355, the city formally admitted them. In the early 1350s Jews are also mentioned in the important communities of Erfurt, Ulm, Nuremberg, as well as in their old Rhenish centers of Worms, Spires, and Treves. Frankfort readmitted them in 1360. Even Basel, where the city council itself had in 1348 built a shack on an island to burn all Jews, called them back in 1362.

Many other cities followed suit. In most cases, it may be assumed, Jews took the initiative. In Strasbourg they bided their time, probably because of the intense popular animosity demonstrated during the pestilence. But by 1369 a few hardy souls ventured to submit the following petition:

To the honorable Burgomaster and Council of Strasbourg we, poor Jews, offer our services. We herewith request you that you may graciously allow us to live with you, as our forefathers had lived with your forefathers, and as the other free cities of Mayence, Worms, and Spires have graciously conceded to us; also many other cities and great lords, the Roman King, Electors, and other lords, in consideration of the great sufferings and tragedy we have sustained without guilt.

The petitioners played it safe and submitted a similar proposal to the city's guilds, originally the main anti-Jewish driving force in the stark tragedy. Thereupon six Jewish families were admitted for five years. Margrave Frederick III of Meissen who, more than any other German prince, had been personally responsible for the killing of Jews in 1349, twelve years later invited the Erfurt Jew, Freudel, to bring some Jews into his possessions. He promised to treat the new settlers in accordance with their status in Erfurt, and to offer them safe-conducts if they were to leave later. The tenacity of both the Jews and their masters was often amazing. In Magdeburg, where a few Jews had survived the onslaught or returned soon thereafter, they were again accused of having caused a local pestilence in 1357; some were slain, others banished from the city. Yet shortly thereafter the community reestablished itself. It included an influential financier, Schmoll (Samuel) of Derenburg who, as early as 1365, could serve, together with a Christian

burgher, as arbiter in a litigation between the archbishop and the
city. His ramified activities as the archbishop's financial agent attracted the attention of Pope Gregory XI who, on June 15, 1372,
complained to the archbishop that, according to rumor, Schmoll
had erected a synagogue on the site of a Christian chapel. On the
same day the pope also censured the bishop of Naumburg for
favoring his Jewish confidant, Marquard, so that the latter "frequently presides over judgments among Christians and in your
name extorts from them immoderate amounts of money." [97]

Not that the populace completely gave up its cruel methods of
settling differences with Jews. The latter found themselves severely threatened wherever pestilences recurred, as in Paderborn
and its environs after 1383. In 1389 it was the turn of Prague,
which had escaped the brunt of persecutions during the Black
Death, to suffer severely. According to biased reports by churchmen, a priest demonstratively carried a host through the Jewish
quarter. Its inmates, aroused by this display which was perhaps
connected with some missionary exhortation, threw stones at the
priest and allegedly blasphemed against Christ represented by that
host. Some Jewish culprits were immediately arrested, but the
clergy fulminated against the entire community. Preachers supposedly threatened listeners from their pulpits, "If you fail to
avenge the wrongs and insults done to our Lord Jesus, you will
sustain shame and ridicule before the end of this year." An excited
mob proceeded to the Jewish quarter, refusing to listen to the city
elders who promised to punish the prisoners, and set fire to many
Jewish houses together with their inmates. Some three thousand
Jews are said to have lost their lives, while many women and children were forcibly baptized. This figure is doubtless exaggerated.
A Jewish eye-witness, R. Abigdor b. Isaac Kara, in his moving
dirge (still recited on the Day of Atonement in various congregations), speaks but vaguely "of a great many fallen, too numerous to be named." In 1499, as a result of another religious
controversy, eighty Jews were executed. Yet the community did
not suffer the total eclipse indicated by the ecclesiastical writers.
In 1410, on the contrary, King Wenceslaus IV confirmed its right
to use its old cemetery and two years later he ordered the Jews of
Eger to submit an internal quarrel to the decision of the Prague

Jewish elders. Nonetheless these assaults underscored the physical insecurity of Jews even in territories previously immune from attack. Those local communities which, as during the Crusades, lulled themselves into believing that "it could not happen" to them, were bitterly disillusioned. Local riots are indeed recorded in many other localities in the following decades.[98]

Nevertheless, a major change did occurr in the fifteenth century. Perhaps regretful of the hasty actions of the Black Death era and realizing that such brutalities did not pay, princes and city councils now adopted the somewhat more civilized form of eliminating Jews *via* expulsion. This method appeared the more legitimate, as it often consisted in a simple failure to renew an existing temporary residence permit. Elsewhere, too, there was the unwritten understanding that in their "exile" Jews lived only on sufferance and that their toleration could be withdrawn at any time at the discretion of their rulers. An incomplete list of local expulsions during the 1400s, compiled by Johannes Janssen, reads as follows:

The Jews were banished from Saxony in 1432, from Spires and Zurich in 1435, from Mayence in 1438, and from Augsburg in 1439; they were imprisoned in Constance and the neighboring towns in 1446. In 1450, Duke Louis the Wealthy expelled them from Bavaria; in 1453, they were driven out of the bishopric of Würzburg, in 1454 they were banished from Brünn and Olmütz, in 1457, from Schweidnitz, in 1458, from Erfurt, in 1468, from Neisse, and in 1470 from the bishopric of Mayence. . . . From Würzburg, to which they had interveningly returned, they were expelled again in 1498, from Geneva in 1490, the Thurgau and Glatz in 1491, and from Mecklenburg and Pomerania, where they had lived "in almost all hamlets and many villages," in 1492. A year later they were eliminated from the archbishopric of Magdeburg. In 1496, expulsions followed from Styria, Carinthia, and Carniolia, in 1498, from Salzburg and Württemberg. In the same year Emperor Maximilian allowed the city council of Nuremberg to remove its Jews. . . . In 1499 the council of Ulm decreed an expulsion, declaring that thenceforth every one would be free to do whatever he pleased to a Jew found in the city. The expulsion from Nördlingen occurred in 1500.[99]

One such incident stands out both because of its special cruelty and its significant locale. The Vienna *Gezerah* of 1421 had ominous connotations, particularly since it was enacted by Duke Albert V of Austria who later became king of Hungary, Bohemia, and all Germany. A concatenation of circumstances produced this obvious miscarriage of justice. Albert began his reign in Austria in 1411 in dire need of money. He was involved in an unending struggle with the Bohemian Hussites and, on one occasion, burned an entire Hussite village. Hostile feelings toward Jews, frequently accused of siding with these heretics, spread through many classes of the population. In 1419 even the Theological Faculty of the University of Vienna sharply restated the old accusations against Jews so that the duke had to issue a special order against student assaults on them. In this overcharged atmosphere the specter of a Jewish host desecration (of which the Hussites, too, were frequently accused) caused much bitterness and persuaded the duke to let "justice" take its course. After a Christian woman of Enns "confessed" to having given particles of a host to the wealthiest Jew in her town for distribution among all Austrian Jews, she and the Enns Jews were transported to Vienna, submitted to torture, and finally condemned. The affair drew ever wider circles and soon involved all Austrian Jewry. It was of little avail that on March 24, 1421, Albert's father-in-law, Emperor Sigismund, promulgated a special protective privilege for the Austrian Jews, and that Pope Martin V issued a direct reminder that children under twelve must not be converted against their parents' will. Anticipating the imperial decree by an accomplished fact, a major *auto-da-fé* was staged in Vienna on March 12, 1421; it consumed 92 male and 122 female victims (the figures variously given in the sources range from a total of 110 to 400). In addition many Jewish children were converted and sent to monasteries or convents for Christian education. The rest of Austrian Jewry was banished "for ever." A Latin inscription, placed in Vienna's medieval ghetto and still legible in the twentieth century, commemorated "the expiation of the terrible crimes committed by the Jewish dogs who paid the penalty upon the stake." [100]

German Jewry's fears of its new ruler were allayed by Albert's death in 1439 after only two years on the German throne. But it had reasons for concern about a possible change in the traditional attitude of the Papacy, at least as it was represented by its two legates, Nicolaus Cusanus and John Capistrano. While the former limited himself largely to influencing German church councils to tighten up the enforcement of the discriminatory and segregation-ist aspects of canon law, Capistrano vigorously attacked Jews, along with Turks and Hussites, as a grave menace to the Christian world. Of course, it was easier to incite the masses against their close Jewish neighbors than against the more distant heretics and Muslims. It is indeed surprising that his sermons delivered in Latin, often without a German translation, so greatly aroused a populace which could hardly have followed them fully even in its own language. Yet antagonism to Jews was sufficiently ingrained, and it had long enough been nurtured by local propagandists in ecclesiastical and lay publications and theatrical performances, for the listeners to guess at the import of Capistrano's harangues and to be carried away by his obvious fervor. Ennea Silvio Piccolomini was not exaggerating when he wrote in 1455 that "the German peoples consider him a prophet" (quasi prophetam eum habent). Shunning any direct confrontation with German Jews—even in Italy where he had had a disputation with one Gamaliel he had evaded Moses da Rieti's challenge to a debate—Capistrano found an opportunity for anti-Jewish action especially on his arrival in Silesia. He was received with great enthusiasm in Breslau in Feb-ruary 1453, whereupon he magnified some alleged offenses against Christianity by a few Jews into major Jewish crimes. Under his in-fluence forty-one Jewish defendants were executed in Breslau, and seventeen in Schweidnitz. In Liegnitz the prison holding the Jew-ish defendants went up in flames, very likely by arson committed by Jew-baiters impatient with the slow court proceedings. This series of slayings was followed by an expulsion of the Jews from most of Silesia, while children under seven were often held back and delivered to the baptismal font.[101]

The Jews' apprehensions that the actions of King Albert and John Capistrano might herald fundamental changes in the atti-tudes of both the Empire and the Papacy were speedily dispelled through the interventions in their behalf of Emperor Frederick III and Pope Nicholas V. Leading German churchmen, too, often pursued more tolerant policies than princes and city elders. Many fifteenth-century expulsions were initiated by the burghers, often against the wishes of their ecclesiastical overlords. Though mouth-ing the stereotype declarations about the Jews' attempts at converting Christians to Judaism, ritual murders, desecrations of hosts, and support of the Hussites, the cities received little encouragement from the German hierarchy. Characteristically, even where the bishops consented to the elimination of Jews from their diocesan capitals, they often allowed them to continue residing, or even to settle anew, in smaller localities under their jurisdiction. Needless to say, this policy was far from consistently pursued, however, even by the same churchmen.

Developments in the archbishopric of Cologne, partially described above, well illustrate this dichotomy. We recall that, since their readmission in 1372, Jews had lived in the city on the basis of temporary renewals. Serious difficulties arose when in 1415–19 the city tried to protect them against Archbishop Dietrich von Moers' excessive fiscal demands. The ensuing litigation ultimately reached the imperial court, although the archbishop-elector invoked the electors' traditional freedom from imperial interference. A decision favorable to the city, issued by the royal court in 1418, was simply disobeyed by Dietrich. Finally, this matter was settled by arbitration: Archbishop Otto of Treves decided in 1419 that the Jews should pay Dietrich the demanded 25,000 florins, but that otherwise he ought to respect the existing rights of both the city and its Jewry. Growing impatient with these complications, the Cologne city council resolved in 1423 not to renew the Jewish privileges expiring in the following year. Once again religious motivations were advanced, the city pretending to be more pious than the archbishop. On appeal Sigismund urged the city council to postpone action. The archbishop's chamberlain warned the city that it would be held responsible for all fiscal deficiencies accruing to the archepiscopal treasury from the expulsion of Jews. Even Pope Martin V appointed Cardinal Antonius of Aquilea to sit in judgment, the city being invited to a hearing. Finally, an arbiter was elected in the person of Duke Adolph of Jülich-Berg. His decision of July 24, 1425, recognizing Cologne's right not to prolong the Jewish privileges proved immaterial inasmuch as, defying Empire, Papacy, and archepiscopate, the city had already proceeded with its banishment of Jews in October, 1424, though many exiles were able to settle in neighboring localities under the archbishop's reign. An even more protracted litigation between the archbishop and the city of Mayence likewise ended, as we re-call, with the banishment of the Jews from the city and ultimately from the entire archbishopric.[102]

No less disturbing were the expulsions by princes. The destruction of the Jewish communities in Austria in 1421 was followed by the equally ominous, if less cruel, banishment of Jews from Styria, Carinthia, and Carniola under the regime of Emperor Maximilian I. In great need of money for his defense against the Turks and his other ambitious imperial ventures, the emperor allowed himself to be bought off by the Estates' offer of 16,000 pounds as an indemnity for the loss of Jewish taxation. The affair began with a trumped-up accusation against two wealthy Jews. After negotiations extending over two years, Maximilian issued, on March 18, 1496, an "Epistle about the Expulsion of the Jews from Styria," the preamble of which sounded particularly threatening. The emperor emphasized that Jews had desecrated sacraments, martyred and murdered Christian children for ritual purposes, cheated and ruined many inhabitants through forged documents, and caused the latter's unjust imprisonment. In this way a Holy Roman emperor, whose sway now extended into the Netherlands as well, gave personal sanction to these folkloristic libels which had, in part, been formally repudiated by both the popes and his own predecessors. Nevertheless, he left open a convenient loophole by providing that the royal authorities could still admit Jewish individuals to Styria on temporary permits. Since the liquidation of debts owed the Jews kept the administration busy for some two decades, a few Jews were allowed to stay on in Graz and elsewhere to assist in that liquidation. The Graz synagogue was not finally disposed of until half a century after the expulsion. To make sure that the Jews would not be allowed to resettle in their midst, the Styrian Estates secured periodic renewals of the decree of 1496 as part of any new monarch's confirmation of their accustomed liberties. The last renewal is dated October 8, 1731.[103]

Notwithstanding the portentous overtones of the Styrian decree, Maximilian never tried to eliminate the much larger Jewish concentrations in his other hereditary estates, particularly in Bohemia and Moravia. He also resisted fiercely, as we recall, all attempts by the Ratisbon burghers to get rid of their Jews. However, upon his death in 1519, the Ratisbon council finally banished its Jews, Rothenburg following suit in 1520. Thus, two of the remaining ancient German-Jewish communities with centuries of significant history behind them were definitely liquidated. Ten years earlier Jews had also been banished from Brandenburg after a trial and burnings fully reminiscent of the Vienna *Gezerah* of 1421. Nor were these the last expulsions. But the later decrees of banishment were partly intertwined with the ongoing struggle between the Reformation and the Catholic Church and the ensuing Wars of Religion.[104]

NATIONALISM AND INTOLERANCE

Reviewing the European situation about 1520, we note that the Jews had been totally eliminated from western Europe by the expulsions from England, France, and the Iberian Peninsula, all of them embracing evolving national states. The Scandinavian countries in the north never had any sizable medieval Jewish population. In central Europe, on the other hand, neither Italy nor Germany attained their national unification until the nineteenth century. As a result Jews remained in some sections while they were eliminated from others, especially from southern Italy, where a small number persisted only in the Neapolitan kingdom until their total eclipse in 1541. On the other hand, the neighboring Papal States had never witnessed an expulsion of Jews during the Middle Ages. Rome, the "eternal city," had been hospitable to the "eternal" Jewish people without any interruptions at least since the first century. Next to the Papal States the largest sixteenth-century Jewish settlements were concentrated in Italy's northeastern section under the domination of the Venetian Republic which, though characteristically Italian, had, through its vast colonial possessions, become as much an East-Mediterranean as an Italian power. Elsewhere on the Apennine Peninsula Jews were subject to the usual inconsistent policies of part-of-nationality states.

Similarly, the Holy Roman Empire never banished the Jews from the entire country. But its Jewish communities suffered greatly from its ever changing power constellations and increasing popular animosities. Here, too, the greatest agglomeration of Jews came to live in the Habsburg hereditary possessions; characteristically, not in the almost purely German provinces of Austria, Styria, and Carinthia from which they were expelled in the fifteenth century, but rather in the nationally heterogeneous provinces of Bohemia and Moravia. In the rest of Germany, too, Jews survived more frequently in the localities under the rule of Catholic archbishops or bishops than in either the larger princely states or the nearly sovereign imperial cities dominated by a bourgeoisie which was the chief bearer of the growingly intolerant combination of nationalism and religion. The Jewish people would, indeed, have been in a very sad state in the sixteenth century, had it not been for the expansion of the two large multinational states of Poland-Lithuania and the Ottoman Empire.

Expulsions were the radical, and yet the relatively milder, form of intolerance affecting Jews. Though imposing untold hardships on prospective exiles, even in England or Spain which provided for their more orderly departure, banishment appeared as the lesser evil compared with the numerous massacres which, in the Late Middle Ages, embittered Jewish life in an unprecedented fashion. Certainly such a succession of mass attacks as those which, starting with the Rindfleisch and Armleder commotions of 1298 and 1336 and the assaults connected with Pastoureaux Crusaders and the "lepers' " conspiracy in France in 1320–21, culminated in Germany's Black Death destruction of some three hundred communities, and the Spanish unholy war of 1391, had never been witnessed before even in the bloody annals of Jewish history. Nor was it to be repeated again until the Nazi onslaught of the 1940s. In this respect, the fifteenth century may be considered a less trying period in the history of European Jewry than its immediate predecessor.

Viewed in retrospect, however, we must not believe that during the last three medieval centuries all Jews constantly lived in fear and trepidation about assailants lurking around the corner. When telescoped into a single list of pogroms and expulsions, the attacks on Jews appear indeed as an uninterrupted succession of catastrophes. But one must realize that during the thirteenth century (until 1290 in England and 1298 in Germany) there were but relatively few local anti-Jewish attacks with little bearing on Jewish conditions elsewhere. Even Rindfleisch and the Armleders had no contemporary counterparts in other German regions. Martinez' attacks upon Jews did not spill over into neighboring Portugal or the Provence. Only the Black Death generated a mass hysteria throughout western and central Europe which had ominous implications for the very survival of European Jewry, in itself seriously decimated by that frightful pestilence. However, the then most populous Jewish settlements in Spain, Sicily, southern France, and the Papal States, as well as in Bohemia, Hungary, and Poland, suffered relatively little.

Nonetheless the psychological impact of these successive tragedies upon both the Jews and their neighbors was enormous. Between pogroms and expulsions few Jewish communities felt wholly safe or could indulge in any long-term planning except, perhaps, in Italy and east-central Europe, or, as long as they lasted, on the Iberian Peninsula and in southern France. Even in northern Italy many communities had been admitted only on the basis of temporary *condottas* whose mere expiration without renewal would spell the end of their legitimate sojourn.

At the end of the Middle Ages the European Jew thus personified, in his own and his neighbors' minds even more than in actual reality, the Wandering Jew of the legend. Not even friendly observers could view the Jewish position in any terms other than those expressed by Bishop Robert Grosseteste with reference to the biblical story of Cain: "That people is vagabond because of the dispersal, and a fugitive from its own home, namely Jerusalem; vagabond because of the uncertainty of a fixed residence, and fugitive because of the fear of death. Yet they have the proclamation of the Lord [forbidding] that they be slain." [105]

This heritage of many generations deepened the "lachrymose conception of Jewish history" which had long viewed Jewish life in the dispersion as the effect of unmitigated divine wrath. It was further complicated at that time by the presence, side by side with professing Jews, of a large class of Spanish and Portuguese *conversos,* some of whom had become dangerous Jew-baiters, while others staunchly, if secretly, adhered to Judaism. Because of the Inquisition, many New Christians likewise had to seize the wanderers' staffs. Ironically, however, these very victims of Spanish-Portuguese hostility turned out to be the chief pioneers in re-establishing Jewish communities in areas from which Jews had previously been banished and, ultimately, in opening up new Jewish settlements where none had existed before. In this fashion the people of history, steadfastly upholding its historico-ethical monotheism, managed in the very depths of its suffering to maintain its unbroken historic continuity and ultimately to reemerge, scathed but not subdued, into the new era of freedom.

NOTES

ABBREVIATIONS

AFH	Archivum franciscanum historicum
AHDE	Anuario de historia del derecho español
AHR	American Historical Review
AKKR	Archiv für katholisches Kirchenrecht
Annales ESC	Annales Economies, Sociétés, Civilisations
AS	Archivio storico (with identifying name, Lombardo, Siciliano, etc.)
ASPN	Archivio storico per le provincie napoletane
Bab.	Babylonian Talmud (identified by the respective tractates)
Baer Jub. Vol.	Sefer Yobel le-Yitzhak Baer (Yitzhak Baer Jubilee volume), ed. by Salo W. Baron *et al.* Jerusalem, 1960.
BAH	Boletín de la Real Academia de la Historia, Madrid
BEC	Bibliothèque de l'École des Chartes
BIHR	Bulletin of the Institute of Historical Research, London
BJRL	Bulletin of the John Rylands Library
CHE	Cuadernos de historia de España
CJ	Corpus Juris Civilis
EHR	English Historical Review
EJ	Encyclopædia Judaica
Ginzberg Jub. Vol.	Louis Ginzberg Jubilee Volume. 2 vols. New York, 1945. A volume each of English and Hebrew essays.
HJ	Historia Judaica
HJB	Historisches Jahrbuch der Görres-Gesellschaft
Homenaje Millás	Homenaje a Millás-Vallicrosa. 2 vols. Barcelona, 1954–56.
HUCA	Hebrew Union College Annual
HZ	Historische Zeitschrift
JE	Jewish Encyclopedia
JJLG	Jahrbuch der Jüdisch-Literarischen Gesellschaft, Frankfurt a.M.
JNOS	Jahrbuch für Nationalökonomie und Statistik
JQR	Jewish Quarterly Review (new series, unless otherwise stated)
JSS	Jewish Social Studies
Koschaker Mem. Vol.	L'Europa e il diritto romano. Studi in memoria di Paolo Koschaker. 2 vols. Milan, 1954.

M.	Mishnah (identified by the respective tractates)
MGH	Monumenta Germaniae Historica
MGWJ	Monatsschrift für Geschichte und Wissenschaft des Judentums
MIOG	Mitteilungen des Instituts für Österreichische Geschichtsforschung
Miscellanies JHSE	Miscellanies of the Jewish Historical Society of England
MWJ	Magazin für die Wissenschaft des Judentums
Neuman Jub. Vol.	Studies and Essays in Honor of Abraham A. Neuman. Leiden, 1962.
PAAJR	Proceedings of the American Academy for Jewish Research
PG	Patrologiae cursus completus, series Graeca, ed. by J. P. Migne
PL	Patrologiae cursus completus, series Latina, ed. by J. P. Migne
RABM	Revista de Archivos, Bibliotecas y Museos
RBPH	Revue belge de philologie et d'histoire
REJ	Revue des études juives
Resp.	Responsa, or *She'elot u-teshubot*
RH	Revue historique
RHDF	Revue historique de droit français et étranger
RHE	Revue d'histoire ecclésiastique
RHR	Revue d'histoire des religions
RI	Rivista israelitica
RMI	Rassegna mensile di Israel
RQH	Revue des questions historiques
RSI	Rivista storica italiana
SB	Sitzungsberichte der Akademie der Wissenschaften (identified by city: e.g., *SB* Berlin, Heidelberg, Vienna)
TJHSE	Transactions of the Jewish Historical Society of England
TRHS	Transactions of the Royal Historical Society
VSW	Vierteljahrsschrift für Sozial- und Wirtschaftsgeschichte
YB	YIVO Bleter
ZGJD	Zeitschrift für die Geschichte der Juden in Deutschland (new series, unless otherwise stated)
ZGJT	Zeitschrift für die Geschichte der Juden in der Tschechoslowakei
ZKG	Zeitschrift für Kirchengeschichte
ZRG	Zeitschrift der Savigny-Stiftung für Rechtsgeschichte

NOTES

CHAPTER XLVII: CITIZEN OR BONDSMAN

1. St. Bernard of Clairvaux, *De consideratione,* i.3 in *PL,* CLXXXII, 732. Some of these aspects are treated in two of my recent essays entitled " 'Plenitude of Apostolic Powers' and Medieval 'Jewish Serfdom' " (Hebrew), *Baer Jub. Vol.,* pp. 102–24; and "Medieval Nationalism and Jewish Serfdom," *Neuman Jub. Vol.,* pp. 17–48. Nationalism played, indeed, a great role both in the break-up of central controls over Jews by Empire and Papacy and in some refinements of the theory of Jewish serfdom. Other facets of this ramified problem will be discussed in connection with the general impact of medieval nationalism on the destinies of Western Jewry, *infra,* Chap. L.

2. Charles IV's act of donation of February 6, 1350, fully published in A. Bierbach's *Urkundenbuch der Stadt Halle,* p. 357 No. 762; Albert Achilles' oft-cited definition, reproduced in P. E. Spiess, *Archivalische Nebenarbeiten und Nachrichten,* I, 127 f.; *supra,* Vol. IX, pp. 166, 185, 212, 320 n. 36, 340 n. 18. See also the agreement of 1360 between Emperor Charles IV and the Austrian dukes cited *ibid.,* pp. 159 f., 318 n. 28. In Brandenburg Albert Achilles vigorously insisted on the exclusive jurisdiction of his officials, rather than of ecclesiastical courts, in litigations with Jews. In his letter of Jan. 2, 1472, to the Ansbach authorities he exclaimed irately that "he had not so zealously served both chiefs [emperor and pope] in order to suffer constant damage; he had no desire to lose annually three to four thousand florins in Jewish fees and interest." See F. Priebatsch's ed. of the *Politische Correspondenz des Kurfürsten Albrecht Achilles,* I, 305 ff. No. 270.

3. H. Mitteis, "Ueber den Rechtsgrund des Satzes, 'Stadtluft macht frei,' " *Festschrift Edmund E. Stengel* [ed. by E. Kunz], p. 358.

4. A. Pons, "Los Judíos del reino de Mallorca," *Hispania* (Madrid), XVI, 185 ff.; B. Lagumina and G. Lagumina, *Codice diplomatico,* I, 494 ff. No. ccclxxxv, esp. pp. 496, 502; the anonymous monk of Sahagún in his *Chronicle,* ed. by J. Puyol y Alonso in "Las Crónicas anónimas de Sahagún," *BAH,* LXXVII, 151–92, esp. pp. 181 f., with Y. F. Baer's comments thereon in *Die Juden im christlichen Spanien,* I, Part 2, p. 56 No. 70. On Perpignan see *ibid.,* Part 1, pp. 487 ff. No. 330 (1380), 565 ff. No. 371 (1384); *supra,* Vols. IX, pp. 233 f., 349 n. 42; X, pp. 55 f., 325 f. n. 3. In Germany this relationship between monarch and Jew became proverbial. While one popular adage asserted that "the Jews are serfs of the Reich," another added, "Jews live under the princes' peace." See E. Graf, M. Dietherr *et al., Deutsche Rechtssprichwörter,* pp. 53 and 488. The more general views held by medieval Jewish leaders about the nature and scope of their serfdom will be discussed *infra,* nn. 18–20.

Remarkably, just like Frederick II in his Vienna privilege of 1237, Queen Maria of Aragon invoked the ecclesiastical, rather than the royal, doctrine of Jewish serfdom and the canonical stress on the Jews' culpability as the reason for their captivity. But she thus sought to justify her restrictive legislation concerning, in particular, the Jews' obligation to wear distinctive attire. This decree, written in the tense year of 1397, actually underscored the usually pro-Jewish context of phrases relating to Jews as the kings' "treasure" in other Aragonese laws. See Baer, *Die Juden,* I, Part 1, p. 733 No. 464; and, more generally, his *Studien zur Geschichte der Juden im Königreich Aragonien,* p. 14 n. 12. Even the doctrine of the Jews' subservience to the Church could be used as an argument for safeguarding their rights. In trying to defend Quendlinburg Jewry against undue exactions by various lords, Prioress Bertradis in 1273 requested the burghers to protect its lives and property on a par with their own and like that of "the other serfs of the Church." See Aronius, *Regesten zur Geschichte der Juden im fränkischen und deutschen Reiche,* p. 322 No. 763; G. Caro, *Sozial-und Wirtschaftsgeschichte der Juden,* II, 143.

5. Albertus Magnus, *II Summa theologica,* iv.16, in his *Opera omnia,* ed. by S. C. A. Borgnet *et al.,* XXXII, 209; O. Stobbe, *Die Juden in Deutschland,* pp. 13 f.; C. Erdmann and N. Fickermann, eds., *Briefsammlungen der Zeit Heinrichs IV.,* pp. 31 f. No. 13. On the burgeoning realization of the distinction between the monarchs' public and private law property, see G. Post's comprehensive *Studies in Medieval Legal Thought, Public Law and the State, 1100–1222.* The vast range of meanings associated with the term *servitus* may readily be gleaned from the quotations assembled in C. de F. Du Cange, *Glossarium mediae et infimae latinitatis,* new ed. by L. Favre, VI, 454–58. Among the various categories of *servi* those called *servi fiscales* were probably most akin to the Jewish *servi camerae.* On the other hand, some popes actually viewed with jaundiced eyes those kings or abbots who used their own humble, yet honorific, self-description of *servi servorum Dei.* This variegated usage went back, indeed, to both ancient Roman and Hebrew antecedents.

The use, in such thirteenth-century French documents as the Treaty of Melun in 1230, of the designation "serf" *(tamquam proprium servum* in contrast to the 1223 formula: *dominis quibus Judaei subsunt;* see E. J. de Laurière *et al.,* eds., *Ordonnances des roys,* I, 47 Art. 2, 53 f. Art. 2), is the more remarkable as this term had been gradually disappearing from other French records. In his study, "Géographie ou chronologie du servage? Note sur les 'servi' en Forez et en Mâconnais du X⁰ au XII⁰ s." in *Hommage à Lucien Febvre,* I, 147–49, G. Duby has shown that, at the end of the twelfth century, this designation was rarely employed in the official documents of those districts. Whatever bearing that observation may have on the status of peasant serfs, in the Jewish case the term, for reasons discussed above, really began its career only in the thirteenth century. See also *supra,* Vols. IX, pp. 143 f.; X, pp. 54 ff.

6. A. Waas, *Die Alte deutsche Freiheit, ihr Wesen und ihre Geschichte,* p. 29; A. Nitschke, "Die Wirksamkeit Gottes in der Welt Gregors VII.," *Studi Gregoriani,* ed. by B. Borino, V, 115–219, especially pp. 169 ff.; E. Otto, *Adel und Freiheit im deutschen Staat des frühen Mittelalters. Studien über Nobiles und Ministerialen,* p. 37. True, some of these writings reflect the antilibertarian Nazi ideology which dominated most German thinking during the 1930s. But they do offer new insights into the medieval concept of freedom which so greatly differed from that of our modern democracies. A more balanced judgment is found in H. Grundmann's "Freiheit als religiöses, politisches und persönliches Postulat im Mittelalter," *HZ,* CLXXXIII,

23–53. Needless to say, these doctrines of liberty had little to do with the so-called liberties of various corporate bodies, including Jews, safeguarding them against undue governmental interference. Even these liberties, however, were intended to operate in favor of groups, rather than individuals. The latter's range of activity was even more closely circumscribed by such corporate privileges and usages than by state-wide laws.

7. Y. F. Baer, *Die Juden*, I, Part 2, pp. 222 No. 227, 270 No. 275 Art. 23; Part 1, pp. 790 f. No. 485; J. Aronius, *Regesten*, p. 249 No. 585; *supra*, Vol. IX, pp. 151, 314 n. 18. (Italics in William's privilege added for emphasis.)

8. Martin Didacus d'Aux, *Observantiae consuetudinesque scriptae regni Aragonum in usum communiter habitae*, fol. xxix r., cited by Baer in his *Studien*, p. 14 n. 12 (where one may find additional illustrations); T. J. Lacomblet, ed., *Urkundenbuch für die Geschichte des Niederrheins*, I, 189; Laurière *et al.*, *Ordonnances des roys*, I, 646 Art. 5.

9. Jacob Tam's ordinance, quoted by Ḥayyim b. Isaac Or Zaru'a in his *Resp.*, ed. by Judah Rosenberg, fol. 60d No. 179; and by Meir b. Baruch of Rothenburg in his *Resp.*, Lwów, 1860 ed., fol. 7b No. 114; *Tosafot* on B.Q. 113a *s.v. Noderin*; Moses b. Jacob of Coucy, *Sefer ha-Miṣvot [ha-gadol]* (Large Book of Commandments; a code of laws), Positive Comm. 73, Venice, 1522 ed., fol. xix.4, 2b. See also I. A. Agus, *Rabbi Meir of Rothenburg*, I, 140 ff.; *infra*, n. 20; and *supra*, Vol. IV, p. 270 n. 82. The version in *Tosafot* reinforces Isaac b. Samuel's advice by stating that this procedure was quite customary in France. On the general inheritance rights of Jews and their occasional genuine bondage, including debt bondage, see *infra*, nn. 33 and 43.

10. U. Robert, "Catalogue d'actes relatifs aux Juifs pendant le moyen âge," *REJ*, III, 212 ff; R. Lennard, "Peasant Tithe-Collectors in Norman England," *EHR*, LXIX, 580–96, esp. pp. 590, 592 f.; Pierre Dupuy (Simon Vigor), *Histoire du différend d'entre le pape Boniface VIII et Philippe le Bel Roy de France . . . depuis l'an 1296 jusques en l'an 1311*, Preuves, pp. 86 f. On the great variations in the position of the villeins in various parts of medieval Europe see now K. Bosl, "Freiheit und Unfreiheit. Zur Entwicklung der Unterschichten in Deutschland und Frankreich während des Mittelalters," *VSW*, XLIV, 193–219. In practice, it appears, medieval Jews had little difficulty in moving from area to area. The secrecy surrounding in 1414 the "flight" to Brunswick of the "entire community" of Goslar (which had so greatly declined, however, that fourteen years earlier it had difficulty in assembling a quorum of ten male Jews aged thirteen or over for purposes of worship), in order to evade the severe tax imposed upon it by Emperor Sigismund, was necessitated not by any outright prohibition of Jewish emigration, but rather by the Jewish moneylenders' promise to the burghers that they would not suddenly depart together with the pawns. See the data in H. Fischer's essay, "Die Judenprivilegien des Goslarer Rates im 14. Jahrhundert," in *ZRG*, Germanistische Abteilung, LVI, 142 ff. We hear but rarely of a Jew being forced to return to his former residence. Not until 1288 did any French Parlement issue regulations for the recapture of such illegal émigrés. See the excerpt quoted by U. Robert in *REJ*, III, 219 No. 63.

11. C. M. Picciotto, "The Legal Position of the Jews in Pre-Expulsion England," *TJHSE*, IX, 67–84, esp. p. 82; A. A. Beugnot, ed., *Les Olim*, I, 364 f. No. vi; II, 195

No. xxiii, 278 Nos. xii–xiii, 714 No. lxiii; III, 180 No. xlii, etc.; L. Ménard, *Histoire civile . . . de la ville de Nismes*, Paris, 1750–58 ed., I, 414 f. No. lii. See also F. L. Cheyette, "Custom, Case Law and Medieval 'Constitutionalism': a Re-examination," *Political Science Quarterly*, LXXVIII, 362–90. There also were frequent jurisdictional disputes over the authority of the respective courts. Opposing the Toulouse consuls' demand that the local Jews repair to the municipal courts, Philip III insisted on the exclusive competence of his own officials or the special judges appointed by them. In 1279 he ordered his provost to uphold the royal authority. See C. Devic and J. Vaissète, *Histoire générale de Languedoc*, X, Preuves, Part 1, col. 157 note xxxv. This decision was part of the royal campaign to establish the royal supremacy over as many Jews as possible. Another interesting decision, rendered about 1284 by the seneschal of Carcassonne, regulated the status of twenty-seven Jewish residents of Béziers, and by indirection also of all other Jews under dispute. Invoking the shade of Louis IX who, as heir to the viscount vanquished in the Albigensian War, had assumed control over the Béziers Jews and had allowed the bishop to collect only imposts long established by custom, the seneschal proclaimed the general principle that any Jew who had from time immemorial lived in the royal domain remained a royal subject even if he settled in an area under the control of another lord. His children born after his departure from the royal lands, too, if stemming *de natione et genere* from a royal city, were to remain royal subjects. On the other hand, any Jewish outsider establishing his principal residence in royal territory (a sojourn of one year was sufficient to establish a presumption of such a permanent domicile) automatically became a royal subject. See the interesting document published by G. Saige in *Les Juifs du Languedoc*, pp. 213 ff. No. xliii, 3, and the analysis thereof, *ibid.*, pp. 30 ff. See also, more broadly, G. Caumes's juridical dissertation, *Les Jurisdictions royales et seigneuriales de la ville de Béziers de 1229 à 1789; supra*, Vol. X, pp. 56 ff., 83 ff.

12. C. Devic and J. Vaissète, *Histoire générale du Languedoc*, IX, 62 No. xlvii (dating Philip III's deciison in 1278); Saige *Les Juifs du Languedoc*, p. 44 n. 2. So anxious was the archbishop of Narbonne to attract Jews to his sector that, in 1241, his own archepiscopal chapter claimed, with evident exaggeration, that Jews had been favored above Christians. See Vaissète, VIII, Preuves, cols. 1077 ff. No. 346. See also B. Gaillard, "Une Charte inédite du XIIIᵉ siècle en faveur des Juifs de Narbonne," *Mémoires* of the Société d'archéologie de Montpellier, 2d ser. VIII, 102–111 (a document of 1269); *supra*, Vols. IV, pp. 45 ff., 258 ff. nn. 58–60; X, pp. 84 f., 339 f. n. 34; and the literature cited there, to which add A. J. Zuckerman's Columbia University dissertation, *A Vassal Jewish Principality in Carolingian Frankland from 768 to the end of the Ninth Century* (typescript).

13. H. Boos, ed., *Urkundenbuch des Stadt Worms*, I, 267 f. No. 408; A. F. Riedel, ed., *Codex diplomaticus brandenburgensis*, 1st ser. XV, 44 f. No. 57; A. Ackermann, *Geschichte der Juden in Brandenburg a. H.*, p. 4; *Pommersches Urkundenbuch,* ed. by the Stettin Staatsarchiv, V, 530 ff. Nos. 3395–97; M. Wiener, *Regesten zur Geschichte der Juden in Deutschland*, p. 23 No. 146; U. Grotefend, *Geschichte und rechtliche Stellung der Juden in Pommern*, pp. 31 ff.; J. F. Böhmer and A. Huber, eds., *Regesta imperii*, VIII, 42 No. 464; H. Fischer, *Die Verfassungsrechtliche Stellung der Juden in den deutschen Städten*, pp. 150, 158 f., 165 f., 171 No. 6. See also *supra*, Vol. IX, pp. 155, 161, 219 f., 224 f., 316 n. 23, 318 n. 30, 343 n. 27, 345 n. 33. In many cases, as

in Mayence in 1244 when the city secured from the archbishop its full autonomy, the burghers were informed of the archbishop's pledge to uphold *inviolabiliter* the privileges previously granted to Jews. Fischer, p. 80; Aronius, *Regesten*, p. 237 No. 548. On the important evolution in Worms, see G. Kisch's interesting analysis of "Die Rechtsstellung der Wormser Juden im Mittelalter," reprinted in his *Forschungen zur Rechts- und Sozialgeschichte der Juden in Deutschland*, pp. 93 ff., principally based upon the sources published from a Heidelberg MS by Joseph Kohler in 1915. The city's agreement of 1283 with Bishop Simon is reproduced in H. Boos's *Urkundenbuch der Stadt Worms*, I, 267 No. 408. In Frankfort, too, Jewish arrivals were admitted to burghers' rights on a par with Christians after paying the usual fee and submitting proof that they had leased a house for at least one mark annually. In Feldkirch the fourteenth-century municipal statute (Art. xxxvi) also speaks without much ado about Jews as "citizens or sons of citizens" and stresses equal punishment for assaults on them and on their Christian counterparts. See the text, cited from the local archival MS by A. Tänzer in *Die Geschichte der Juden in Tirol und Vorarlberg*, pp. 3 f. See also *infra*, n. 17.

14. See the examples cited by H. Planitz in *Die Deutsche Stadt im Mittelalter*, pp. 253 f., 436 f.

15. P. Hildenfinger, "Documents relatifs aux Juifs d'Arles," *REJ*, XLI, 72 n. 5; B. Lagumina and G. Lagumina, *Codice diplomatico dei Giudei di Sicilia*, I, 499 No. ccclxxxv; H. Vogelstein and P. Rieger, *Geschichte der Juden in Rom*, I, 491 f. App. 5; M. Ciardini, *I Banchieri ebrei in Firenze nel secolo XV e il Monte di pietà fondato da Girolamo Savonarola*, App. p. vii; *supra*, Vol. X, pp. 250 f., 410 f. n. 36.

16. G. Luzzatto, *I Banchieri ebrei in Urbino*, p. 30 (giving the designation of Jews as citizens a much too narrow negativistic conception); B. Lagumina and G. Lagumina, *Codice diplomatico*, II, 105 No. dxxxiv, 112 No. dxxxvii; A. Theiner, *Codex diplomaticus dominii temporalis S. Sedis*, III, 99b No. li (Pope Boniface IX's *capitula* for the city of Anagni of May 4, 1399, which included the provision that the Jews were "to enjoy the privileges and dignities of the said city like the other burghers of that locality"); the Mantua privilege of 1434, reproduced by V. Colorni in his *Legge ebraica e leggi locali*, pp. 369 f. App. iii; Giovanni da Anagni, *In librum quintum decretalium*, Milan, 1492 ed., fol. 63; and *supra*, Vol. X, pp. 273 f., 422 n. 66. In Fribourg, too, the banker and surgeon, Simon de Pierre Chastel, is recorded to have been admitted in 1403 to burghers' rights. See A. Favre, "Les Médecins juifs à Fribourg dans les siècles passés," *Archives* of the Société d'histoire du Canton de Fribourg, VII, 30. See also C. Marciani, "Ebrei a Lanciano dal XII al XVIII secolo," *ASPN*, LXXXI, 173. Colorni, whose first chapter is devoted to the reexamination of the medieval Jewish *status civitatis*, has contributed some valuable data on the views expressed by the glossators of the Roman law (pp. 86 ff.). He overestimates, however, the impact of Jewish serfdom on lowering the status of medieval Jewry, although he steers clear of some of the exaggerations of other jurists and historians. See also *infra*, n. 17.

17. F. Wyler, *Die Staatsrechtliche Stellung der israelitischen Religionsgenossenschaften in der Schweiz*, p. 14 n. 47; H. Fischer, *Die Verfassungsrechtliche Stellung der Juden*, p. 150. The equivocal medieval usage of the term "citizen" is also evi-

denced in the case of peasants. See, for instance, K. Schwarz's recent analysis of "Bäuerliche 'cives' in Brandenburg und benachbarten Territorien. Zur Terminologie verfassungs- und siedlungsgeschichtlicher Quellen Nord- und Mitteldeutschlands," *Blätter für deutsche Landesgeschichte*, XLIX, 103–34. Because of the peculiar nature of the medieval Jewish "citizens' rights," K. Bauer has unsuccessfully tried to distinguish between the terms *samenburger* (cocitizen) applied to Jews in Cologne sources and the corresponding Latin term, *concivis*, used in connection with Christian burghers. See his *Judenrecht in Köln*, pp. 59 ff., 99 App. 3 (1384). We need but recall the Frankfort Jewess expressly called *concivis* in a document of 1348, cited *supra*, Vol. IX, pp. 219, 343 n. 27. On earlier views see also the data assembled by A. Kober in his *Studien zur mittelalterlichen Geschichte der Juden in Köln am Rhein*, p. 14 n. 1. The general picture of the rights and duties of the Jewish burghers in the various cities may emerge a little more clearly from our analysis in this and the following chapters which, however, must constantly be modified by the data relating to the various geographic areas in Vols. IX–X. Nor must we lose sight of the frequent changes in the legal status of the Christian burghers, too, in many medieval localities. See, for one example, E. Rüedi's recent survey of "Das Schaffhauser Bürgerrecht im Wandel der Zeiten," *Schaffhauser Beiträge zur vaterländischen Geschichte*, XL, 7–53.

18. See the protocol of the twenty-fourth session of the disputation of Tortosa of May 17, 1413, in A. Pacios Lopez, *La Disputa de Tortosa*, II, 161 ff.; and its summary by A. Posnanski in "Le Colloque de Tortose et de San Mateo," *REJ*, LXXV, 195 f. See also Y. F. Baer's observations in "Die Disputation von Tortosa," *Spanische Forschungen*, 1st ser. III, 313 f.; his *Toledot ha-Yehudim bi-Sefarad ha-noṣrit*, 2d ed., pp. 335, 533 n. 65 (*A History of the Jews in Christian Spain*, Vol. II [trans. by L. Levensohn *et al.*], pp. 189 f., 482 f. n. 13); and *supra*, Vol. IX, pp. 87 ff. These aspects of the Jewish messianic hope will become clearer in our general analysis of the Jewish messianic doctrines and movements of the pre-Emancipation era.

19. Isaac b. Samuel of Dampierre cited in *Tosafot* on B.Q. fol. 58a, *s.v. I nammi;* Naḥmanides, *Resp.* No. 46, ed. by S. Assaf in *Sifran shel rishonim* (Book of Ancients), p. 88; the statements by other Spanish rabbis excerpted from a Bodleian MS by Baer in *Die Juden*, I, Part 1, pp. 311 ff. No. 224a; the resolutions of the assembly of Aragonese communities in Barcelona in 1354, *ibid.*, p. 357 No. 253 Art. 35; Meir b. Baruch, *Resp.*, Prague, 1608 ed., fols. 24d f. No. 134, 89ab No. 1001; *supra*, n. 7; and Vol. IV, pp. 63 f., 270 n. 82. The curious term *mekhudanim* (dependent or owned) was advisedly used by R. Meir in his second responsum, thereby indicating that Jews were in no one's bondage, but rather free citizens. On the use of this term see the literature cited by E. E. Urbach in his *Ba'ale ha-Tosafot* (The Tosaphists: Their History, Writings and Methods), p. 422 n. 82. This emphasis was doubly necessary in the disturbed period of the German *Interregnum* when this responsum was probably written, but it may also have been pointed against Rudolph I's sharp reformulation of Jewish serfdom, cited *supra*, Vol. IX, pp. 153 f. Similarly, the Barcelona assembly met after the upheaval of the Black Death era, when the very idea of tolerating Jews was in grave jeopardy. In his *Toledot*, 2d ed., pp. 169 f. (in the English trans. by L. Schoffman, *A History of the Jews in Christian Spain*, I, 286 f.) Y. F. Baer slightly overstates the distinction between the Ashkenazic and Sephardic rabbis with

respect to the recognition due to the "law of the kingdom" in this area. See *infra*, n. 20.

20. B.Q. 113a; Joseph ibn Ḥabib, *Nimmuqe Yosef* (Joseph's Motivations; commentary on Alfasi's *Halakhot*), on B.Q. X, Vilna ed., p. 60; Mordecai b. Hillel ha-Kohen, *Sefer Mordekhai* on B.Q. No. 152; Solomon ibn Adret, *Resp.*, I, No. 982 (recognizing the validity of deeds issued by state courts and notaries); III, Leghorn, 1788 ed., fols. 7ab Nos. 15–16, 10bc No. 34; his other responsa, attributed to Naḥmanides, Żółkiew, 1798 ed., fols. 18b–19d Nos. 74–78; with I. Epstein's comments thereon in *The "Responsa" of Rabbi Solomon ben Adreth of Barcelona (1235–1310), as a Source of the History of Spain*, pp. 13 ff.; idem, "Pre-Expulsion England in the Responsa," *TJHSE*, XIV, 194 ff. Ironically, some rabbis debated the legislative rights of kings as if they were a purely halakhic problem. Emphasizing the power of custom, Naḥmanides and Meir Abulafia taught that "if a king enacts a new law, even though he issue it for all [subjects], in so far as it is not part of the legislation of the early kings, it is not valid law in the Jewish sense." Maimonides and Asher b. Yeḥiel, on the other hand, although they, too, were influenced by Spanish-Jewish practices (the former after leaving Spain at an early age always cited Spanish precedents, while Asher spent the last years of his life as chief rabbi of Toledo), more readily acknowledged the royal prerogative to issue novel decrees. See the citations of these and other sources by Joseph Karo in his *Bet Yosef* (Joseph's House; a halakhic commentary) on Jacob b. Asher's *Ṭurim* (The Four Pillars; a code of laws), H. M. No. 369 end; and my comments thereon in *The Jewish Community*, I, 215; III, 52 n. 5.

At times Jewish businessmen tried through private agreements to minimize the effects of royal seizures. According to a Hebrew deed of 1254, still extant in the Public Record Office in London, one Samuel b. Isaac, who had sold a writ of indebtedness in the amount of £25 to a Rabbi Moses Crespin, had to promise to indemnify the purchaser for any loss he might sustain including "if, which Heaven forefend, it [the writ] should be seized by the King or Queen under any pretense." See the Hebrew text and English trans. by M. D. Davis in his ed. of *Sheṭarot: Hebrew Deeds of English Jews before 1290*, pp. 214 ff. No. 93. Incidentally, the mention of the queen in this context was not fortuitous, inasmuch as Queen Eleanor was indeed often hostile to her Jewish subjects. See *supra*, Vol. IX, p. 111; and, on the general rabbinic doctrine of the respect due to the "laws of the kingdom," *supra*, Vol. V, pp. 77 f., 324 f. n. 93. This ramified problem will be more fully considered in connection with the social teachings of the rabbis in a later chapter.

21. A. Erler, *Bürgerrecht und Steuerpflicht*, p. 19; *infra*, Chap. L.

22. Aronius, *Regesten*, pp. 74 ff. No. 171; Isaac b. Sheshet Perfet, *Resp.*, Constantinople, 1547 ed., sigs. 19, 3 No. 239, 25, 4b No. 305; other data analyzed by A. M. Hershman in *Rabbi Isaac Ben Sheshet Perfet and His Times*, pp. 99 ff. To be sure, not even imperial Germany always respected the Jewish judicial autonomy. As elsewhere, the cities, in particular, sought to arrogate to themselves complete jurisdiction over the Jewish inhabitants as well. Internally and externally, the problems of safeguarding their judicial self-determination deeply preoccupied the minds of leading Jews throughout the Middle Ages and early modern times. These aspects, analyzed with respect to the earlier periods *supra*, Vols. II, pp. 265 ff., 418 ff.; V, pp. 58 ff., 317 ff., will be discussed below in this chapter (see nn. 74 ff.) and, more fully,

in a later chapter devoted to a review of the late medieval Jewish communal institutions.

23. *Codex Theodosianus*, xvi.8, 21; 10, 24; *CJ* (Codex), iii, 6, ed. by P. Krüger, II, 63; St. Augustine, *Enarrationes in Psalmos*, lxv, 4–7, in *PL*, XXXVI, 791; the papal bull *Sicut Judaeis*, in the formulation given by Innocent III on September 15, 1199, and reproduced by S. Grayzel in *The Church and the Jews*, pp. 92 f. No. 5; K. Zeumer, ed., *Formulae Merovingici et Carolini aevi*, Nos. 30–31, 52 in *MGH*, Leges, Section V, pp. 309 ff.; J. Aronius, *Regesten*, pp. 30 ff. Nos. 81–83; *supra*, Vols. II, pp. 191 ff.; III, pp. 8 ff., 230 f.; IV, pp. 6 ff., 48 f., 235 f. nn. 2–3, 260 f. nn. 62–63. Without elaborating in detail these protective provisions, the Church took it for granted that, wherever Jews were tolerated at all, they would also be protected against injuries. This was also implied, rather than clearly stated, in Thomas Aquinas' assertion that the Jews' subjection to Christian princes in civil bondage did not "exclude their participation in the order of natural or divine law [*non excludit ordinem juris naturalis vel divini*]." See his *Summa theologica*, ii.2, q.10, art. 12, in his *Opera omnia*, ed. under the sponsorship of Leo XIII [and Benedict XV], VIII, 94b; in the English trans. by the Fathers of the English Dominican Province, p. 146, together with additional data and literature cited *supra*, Vol. IX. pp. 242 ff. nn. 3–5 and 7.

Only in periods of great danger did some churchmen perceive the necessity of intervening in the defense of Jewish lives. The measures taken against the Crusaders by St. Bernard of Clairvaux in 1146 and Gregory IX in 1236 were mentioned *supra*, Vols. IV, pp. 121, 300 f. n. 41; IX, pp. 9 f., 244 n. 8. On the other hand, the Church also promoted legislation, both canonical and civil, aimed at establishing certain specific religious transgressions for which a Jew might forfeit his life; for instance, for blasphemies against Jesus and Mary, attempts at converting Christians, or sex relations with them. But these merely were accepted additions to the criminal codes and remained within the general framework of existing legislations.

24. Aronius, *Regesten*, pp. 71 ff. Nos. 170 Arts. 1 and 13; 171 Arts. 1 and 13; Eike von Repgow, *Sachsenspiegel, Landrecht*, iii.7, 3, ed. by C. G. Homeyer, p. 306; J. E. Scherer, *Die Rechtsverhältnisse der Juden in den deutsch-österreichischen Ländern*, pp. 179 ff. Arts. 9–11, 21; and Scherer's interpretation thereof, *ibid.*, pp. 216 ff.; *supra*, Vols. IV, pp. 70 ff., 274 f.; IX, pp. 149 f. n. 18; and X, pp. 43 f., 320 f. nn. 53–54. Apart from offering Jews additional safeguards, the peace treaties signed by many princes enhanced the severity of sanctions for the slaying of a Jew. While the royal protection still had to adhere to the traditional monetary fines (see the next note), the more "modern" *Landfrieden* compacts could inflict the death penalty without offending the sensitivities of the population accustomed to the doctrine of *de vita componere*, that is, redeeming the criminal's life through financial settlements. In time, however, the death penalty became so widely accepted that "mere royal protection" could likewise be abetted by that sanction. See J. Gernhuber, *Die Landfriedensbewegung in Deutschland bis zum Mainzer Reichslandfrieden von 1235*, pp. 203 f., 214 ff. This distinction remains unimpaired by G. Kisch's strictures in his review of this work in *Tijdschrift voor Rechtsgeschiedenis*, XXI, 355–65, in which he also overstresses the nexus between the progressive disarming of the Jews by law and the need for such peace legislation. See also A. Gerlich, *Studien zur Landfriedenspolitik König Rudolfs von Habsburg;* H. Angermeier, "Städtebünde und Land-

friedenspolitik im 14. Jahrhundert," *HJB*, LXXVI, 34–46; D. Kennelly, "Medieval Towns and the Peace of God," *Medievalia et humanistica*, XV, 35–53; and, more generally, Kisch's data in *The Jews in Medieval Germany: a Study of Their Legal and Social Status*, pp. 107 ff.. 139 ff., 412 f., 427.

25. Thomas of Monmouth, *The Life and Miracles of St. William of Norwich*, ed. by A. Jessopp and M. R. James, pp. 29, 95, 111; T. D. Hardy, ed., *Rotuli litterarum clausarum in turri Londoniensi asservati*, I, 354b, 357; Laurière *et al.*, *Ordonnances des roys*, III, 351 f., 471 ff., 487 f.; Baer, *Die Juden*, I, Part 1, p. 876; H. G. Richardson and G. O. Sayles, eds., *Select Cases of Procedure without Writ under Henry III*, pp. 21 ff. No. 18; and other sources cited by Richardson in *The English Jewry under Angevin Kings*, pp. 110, 182. On the French *gardien général* and John II's intervention in behalf of two Tudela Jews kidnaped to France in 1458, see *supra*, Vol. X, pp. 71 f., 192, 333 f. n. 19, 385 n. 31. At times, it appears, such protective arrangements were invented by officials desirous to collect special fees. The Cologne burgrave, for instance, advanced in the 1220s the claim that "for a long time [*ex antiquo*]" his office had been in charge of safely conducting Jews through the archdiocese in return for an annual fee of 10 marks silver and 6 pounds pepper paid him by the Jewish community. This claim may have been based on a forged arbitration award of 1169, but it was evidently accepted without demurrer by the Jews. See the text in L. Ennen and G. Eckertz's ed. of *Quellen zur Geschichte der Stadt Köln*, I, 554 ff. No. 76; and the debate thereon cited by K. Bauer in his *Judenrecht in Köln*, pp. 14 f.

26. See *supra*, Vol. IV, pp. 30, 247 n. 32; M. Garrido Atienza, *Las Capitulaciones para la entrega de Granada*, pp. 187 No. xv, 235 No. xlv, 238 No. xlvi, and 282 No. lx; M. Gaspar Remiro, *Ultimos pactos y correspondencia intima entre los reyes católicos y Boabdil sobre la entrega de Granada*, pp. 56, 80, 100, 103 f., 111; both summarized by Y. F. Baer in *Die Juden*, I, Part 2, pp. 394 f. No. 368. See also, more generally, D. Gonzalo Maeso, *Garnata al-Yahud. Granada en la historia del judaismo español*.

27. Baer, *Die Juden*, I, Part 2, pp. 390 ff. Nos. 364 and 366–67. See *supra*, Vol. X, p. 391 n. 46; and *infra*, n. 73.

28. Baer, *Die Juden*, I Part 1, pp. 1034 f.; idem, *Studien zur Geschichte der Juden im Königreich Aragonien*, pp. 12 n. 3, 70 f.; J. Amador de los Rios, *Historia social*, I, 406 ff.; *supra*, Vol. IV, pp. 39 f., 253 f., n. 49; Stobbe, *Die Juden in Deutschland*, pp. 43 f.; F. Ortloff, ed., *Das Rechtsbuch nach Distinctionen nebst einem Eisenachischen Rechtsbuch*, iii.17, 48, p. 178. Stobbe could have made his argument even more telling if he had cited the Worms decree's penalty of 12 gold pounds for the slaying of a Jew, which, according to his calculation, would have amounted to 120 silver pounds. This enormous fine was but slightly reduced to 12 gold marks (= 8 gold pounds) plus 12 silver marks in the Austrian decree of 1244. See *supra*, n. 23. See also the fines provided by the local courts of Stendal for injuries inflicted by Christian assailants on Jews, male or female respectively, according to *Ein Stendaler Urtheilsbuch aus dem vierzehnten Jahrhundert*, xxvii.1, ed. by J. F. Behrend, pp. 112 f., excerpted, together with the *Rechtsbuch*, in G. Kisch's *Jewry-Law in Medieval Germany: Laws and Court Decisions concerning Jews*, pp. 88, 141. Occasionally

we learn of actual penalties imposed for mere verbal insults. An entry of 1432 records the payment of 20 denarii by one Seraphino di Montecalvo in Monferrato for having uttered *verba iniuriosa* about Jews. See S. Foa, "Appunti d'archivio di storia ebraica monferrina," *RMI*, XV, 113 f.

29. K. Puchner and G. Wulz, eds., *Die Urkunden der Stadt Nördlingen*, 1350–1399, p. 187 No. 789; Laurière *et al.*, *Ordonnances des roys*, XII, 182; Isambert, *Recueil général*, VI, 731 No. 183; Baer, *Die Juden*, I, Part 2, p. 210 No. 220 Art. 10; *supra*, Vol. X, pp. 23, 161, 334 f. n. 21, 373 n. 51. Charles VI may have been influenced by the example set in the Dauphiny by his own decree of 1355 which included the provision that no one should dare secretly or overtly to threaten Jews under the sanction of the loss of his property and other penalties. See A. Prudhomme, "Les Juifs en Dauphiné aux XIVe et XVe siècles," *Bulletin* of the Académie Delphinale, 3d ser. XVII, 129 ff., 164 ff.; *supra*, Vol. X, pp. 80 f., 338 n. 29; X. Gasnos, *Étude historique sur la condition des Juifs dans l'ancien droit français*, p. 210 Art. xvii.

On the other hand, there doubtless existed many local customs, for the most part prejudicial to Jews, which could not be effectively combated by general regulations. From one of Meir b. Baruch's responsa (Prague, 1608 ed., fol. 25bc No. 140) we learn, at least inferentially, that in a German community the populace felt free to attack a Jew whose house happened to be on fire. Apparently suspecting that the house-owner was guilty of self-inflicted arson (although no reason was given why he should have sought such wanton destruction of his property), the mob threw him into the fire. At the same time it obviously allowed other Jews to enter the burning house and to salvage whatever they could from it. A similar incident seems to be alluded to a century later in the *Minhagim* (Custumal) by Jacob b. Moses ha-Levi Mölln, in the laws of Sabbath and the Day of Atonement, [Johannesburg], 1858 ed., pp. 78, 125 f. Perhaps there was some connection between this "custom" and the ever present suspicions of the Jews' involvement in magic arts. See M. Güdemann, *Geschichte des Erziehungswesens und der Kultur der abendländischen Juden während des Mittelalters und der neueren Zeit*, III, 153; H. J. Zimmels, *Beiträge zur Geschichte der Juden in Deutschland im 13. Jahrhundert insbesondere auf Grund der Gutachten des R. Meir Rothenburg*, pp. 10, 82 n. 26; and *infra*, Chap. XLIX.

30. *Codex Theodosianus* and *CJ*, *loc. cit.* (*supra*, n. 23); Aronius, *Regesten*, pp. 30 ff. Nos. 81 Art. 2, 82 Art. 2; 71 ff. Nos. 170 Art. 2, 171 Art. 2; Laurière *et al.*, *Ordonnances des roys*, XI, 211 f. Art. 25; *supra*, Vol. IV, p. 269 n. 80. Understandably, the practical application of these decrees was far from uniform. Occasionally we do hear of strong reprisals against assailants of Jews. For instance, in 1265, Bishop Henry II of Spires banished three powerful burghers, together with their associates, from the city because they had "with temerity and to spite the empire robbed the possessions of Jews without the cooperation of any judge and had checked the performance of the services customarily due Us from the said Jews in the name of the empire." See A. Hilgard, ed., *Urkunden zur Geschichte der Stadt Speyer*, p. 81 No. 110; Aronius, *Regesten*, p. 292 No. 710. On the other hand, when in 1385 some Jewish representatives at the regional council of Weissenfels were returning home from the meeting, they were assailed by knights and robbed of their possessions. Although the robbers were called to account by the various rulers who had issued safe-conducts to these Jewish leaders, they successfully defended themselves through sheer audacity. According to the chronicler Detmar, a Saxon nobleman who had seized jewelry belonging to Jewish women argued that, since the Jews were recognized en-

emies of Christendom, they were also his private enemies and as such a legitimate warlike prize. See Detmar's *Chronik*, ed. by F. H. Grautoff, I, 329; S. Neufeld, "Die Juden im thüringisch-sächsichen Gebiet während des Mittelalters," *Thüringisch-Sächsische Zeitschrift für Geschichte*, XV, 67 f. It probably was to avoid such misinterpretations of the law that Louis the Bavarian provided in 1336 that none but himself should adjudicate the case of misdeeds committed against the Jews of Mergentheim. See M. Wiener's *Regesten*, p. 40 No. 109.

Clearly, such protection of Jewish property did not apply to the rulers themselves. From the standpoint of royal law all Jewish property belonged to the king and there were hardly any restraints on his use thereof for his own benefit. But in pure theory he was entitled to appropriate the possessions of most of his other subjects as well, the only practical limitations consisting in the ability of the respective classes to resist such encroachments or else, as also in the Jewish case, in the public's inveterate respect for custom.

31. Rigg, *Select Pleas*, pp. 1 f.; John Peckham, *Registrum epistolarum*, ed. by C. T. Martin, III, 937 No. dclxxiv; Scherer, *Die Rechtsverhältnisse*, pp. 181 Arts. 12–13, 223 ff.; and *supra*, Vol. X, pp. 105 f., 349 n. 61. So bent were the English kings on exploiting Jewish possessions that, in a characteristic law of 1233, Henry III declared that "no Jew remain in Our kingdom unless he be of the kind who can serve the king and will find good pledges of his fidelity." See the text, republished with comments by H. G. Richardson in *The English Jewry*, pp. 293 f.; and the slightly diverse formulation used twenty years later, cited *supra*, Vol. X, p. 325 n. 2. It was also principally out of self-interest that the German kings and princes protected Jewish property through royal privileges or "peace" agreements. Although, for reasons to be discussed in the next chapter, the Jews' right to bear arms was increasingly limited both in England and on the Continent, they probably were included in the permission for traveling merchants to carry swords on their vehicles, provided they used them only for self-defense. See the text, ed. by L. Wieland in *MGH*, Constitutiones, I, 195 ff. No. 140; and G. Kisch's rather hesitant comments concerning the application of that law to Jews in *The Jews in Medieval Germany*, pp. 115, 125.

32. Scherer, *Die Rechtsverhältnisse*, pp. 181 f. Art. 13, 223 ff.; and the data assembled by F. Baer in his *Studien . . . Aragonien*, pp. 26 f. We must not, however, lose sight of the fact that in matters of this kind affecting many localities and large groups of burghers and peasants, royal and ducal laws often had to yield to local customs. Probably more representative of actual practice in the Austrian provinces was the Toll Ordinance of Wiener Neustadt compiled in 1310, or but sixty-six years after Frederick II's original enactment. It provided: "While conducting a dead Jew across the border they [the mourners] shall bargain with the toll collectors the best way they can but, if they are residents of Austria or Styria, they have to pay nothing." See the text published in G. Winter's *Urkundliche Beiträge zur Rechtsgeschichte ober- und niederösterreichischer Städte, Märkte und Dörfer vom zwölften bis zum fünfzehnten Jahrhunderte*, pp. 47 ff., 66 Art. 45. On the Jewish cemeteries and burial rites, see *infra*, nn. 56 ff.; they will be more fully described in the chapter dealing with the Jewish communal institutions.

33. *Codex Theodosianus*, xvi.8, 28 (426); 9, 4 (417); other sources analyzed by J. Juster in *Les Juifs dans l'empire romain*, II, 89 ff.; H. Cole, *Documents Illustrative of English History in the Thirteenth and Fourteenth Centuries*, pp. 139 f.; *Rotuli de*

oblatis et finibus, ed. by T. D. Hardy, pp. 391 (Northampton, 1207), 420 (Lincoln, 1208). H. G. Richardson rightly observes that payments to the Crown were exacted also from heirs of Christian landowners before their homage was accepted. See *The English Jewry*, p. 115. See also *supra*, n. 2; and *infra*, Chap. LIV.

34. Deut. 24:10–11; M. Baba Meṣia IX, 13; Bab. 113a; Megillah 12b; Scherer, *Die Rechtsverhältnisse*, pp. 183 Art. 28, 327 f.; J. Régné, "Catalogue des actes de Jaime Ier, Pedro III et Alfonso III rois d'Aragon concernant les Juifs (1213–1291)," *REJ*, LX, 186 No. 130 (1260), 193 f. No. 178 (1262–63); LXI, 34 No. 412 (1269); LXII, 38 No. 474 (1271), 52 No. 566 (1271); Baer, *Die Juden*, I, Part 1, pp. 420 ff. No. 292 Art. 4, 535 ff. No. 356 Art. 6, 876 No. 544 note; M. Kayserling, "Zur Geschichte der Juden in Barcelona," *MGWJ*, XV, 81–95, esp. pp. 94 f. No. F; and other sources cited in Baer's *Studien*, pp. 20 f.; and in Stobbe's *Die Juden*, pp. 38, 213 n. 35. We assume also that in his letter of September 25, 1253, to the dean of the episcopal chapter in Würzburg, Innocent IV advisedly used the terms of *ledere, invadere, vel etiam in aliquo molestare* (offend, invade and molest in some other fashion), referring to the invasion of the privacy of the Jewish quarter and homes as one of the forms of undue oppression. See the text in Aronius, *Regesten*, pp. 253 f. No. 593; and S. Grayzel, *The Church*, pp. 292 ff. No. 132.

35. T. C. Lacomblet, ed., *Urkundenbuch für die Geschichte des Niederrheins*, III, 17 ff. No. 24; A. A. Beugnot, ed., *Les Olim*, III, Part I, pp. 185 ff. No. li.

36. Charles IV's decree of February 1349, cited *supra*, Vol. IX, pp. 158, 317 f. n. 27; L. Fumi, "L'Inquisizione romana e lo stato di Milano," *AS Lombardo*, XXXVII (4th ser. XIII), 299. On Richard I's and Albert I's swift retribution for large-scale assaults on Jews in 1190 and 1298, see *supra*, Vols. IV, pp. 127 f., 134; and IX, pp. 154 f. In 1261 a mob, including some priests, attacked the Jewish quarter in Canterbury, "broke the doors and windows of their houses with axes, brought fire to burn the houses and afterwards beat some of the Jews." Although the king immediately ordered the sheriff to punish the offenders, this episode was merely one of a long series of illegal mass assaults upon Jews. See *Calendar of the Patent Rolls Henry III. A.D. 1258-1266*, p. 229; D'B. Tovey, *Anglia Judaica*, p. 156; M. Adler, *Jews of Medieval England*, pp. 78 f. The broader aspects of the anti-Jewish massacres and the role of governmental authorities in them will be more fully discussed *infra*, Chap. L.

37. Eike von Repgow's *Sachsenspiegel, Landrecht*, iii.7, 2–3, ed. by C. G. Homeyer, p. 306; the Magdeburg-Görlitz code of 1304 Art. 118, in G. A. Tzschoppe and G. A. Stenzel, eds., *Urkundensammlung zur Geschichte des Ursprungs der Städte und der Einführung und Verbreitung deutscher Kolonisten und Rechte in Schlesien und der Oberlausitz*, pp. 69, 473 No. cv; E. T. Gaupp, *Das Alte Magdeburgische und Hallische Recht*, p. 310 Art. 118; *supra*, Vol. IX, pp. 190, 330 n. 61; also excerpted by G. Kisch in his *Jewry-Law in Medieval Germany*, p. 139; other sources cited by Stobbe in *Die Juden*, pp. 159 f.; Kisch in *The Jews in Medieval Germany*, pp. 185 f.; K. Bauer in his *Judenrecht in Köln*, pp. 25, 41; and U. Grotefend in his *Geschichte und rechtliche Stellung der Juden in Pommern von den Anfängen bis zum Tode Friedrich des Grossen*, p. 43 (125); *Pipe Rolls 25 Henry II* (Publications of the Pipe Roll Society, XXVIII, 1907), p. 35; *31 Henry II* (ibid., XXXIV, 1913), p. 222; *Richard I* (ibid., XLI, 1927), p. 121; and other sources cited by H. G. Richardson in *The*

English Jewry, pp. 113, 151 ff.; G. Arnaud d'Agnel, "La Politique de René envers les Juifs de Provence," *Bulletin historique et philologique*, 1908, p. 249.

Protection against false accusations was, of course, not limited to denunciations by Christians. When in 1499 a Jew, Gumprecht, informed the authorities that a fellow Jew had fornicated with two Christian women but was unable to substantiate his accusation, he was fined the large sum of 50 florins. See G. Florian and A. A. von Lersner, *Der Welt-berühmten Freyen Reichs-, Wahl-, und Handelsstadt Frankfurt am Mayn Chronica*, I, 441b.

38. The *Fuero* of Alba de Tormes, Art. 12 in *Fueros Leoneses*, ed. by A. Castro and F. de Onís, p. 297; *Los Fueros de Sepúlveda*, ed. by E. Sanchez, Arts. 37–40, pp. 73 ff.; Queen Maria's and Infante Pedro's decrees of 1313 and 1315 in *Cortes de los antiguos reinos de León y de Castilla*, I, 241 f. Art. 27, 275 f. Art. 23—all summarized in Baer, *Die Juden*, I, Part 2, pp. 32 f. No. 59, 114 f. No. 125, 132 ff. Nos. 139 and 142. See also my remarks *supra*, Vol. IV, pp. 39, 253 f. n. 49.

39. Baer, *Die Juden*, I, Part 1, pp. 70 ff. No. 78, 92 f. No. 91 Art. 1, 157 f. No. 142; and *infra*, n. 68. Of interest also are the special exemptions granted by kings to individual favorites. For one example, in providing his court physician Salomon Caravida with a safe-conduct and general permit to travel through all Aragonese possessions, King Pedro IV exempted him in 1378 from prosecution for any crimes except murder, assault and battery, or being "a traitor, betrayer [*bausator*], heretic, Sodomite, a forger of currency, or else of having committed *lèse majesté* or cohabited with Christian women." See the text published by A. Cardoner Planas in "El Médico judío Šĕlomó Caravida y algunos aspectos de la medicina de su época," *Sefarad*, III, 377–92, esp. pp. 384 f.; *infra*, Chap. LII, n. 15.

40. The Carolingian *Capitula de Judaeis*, vi, in A. Boretius, *Capitularia regum francorum* in *MGH*, Leges, Section 2, I, 1, p. 259 (Boretius, followed by Aronius, doubts the authenticity of this capitulary; see the latter's *Regesten*, p. 29 No. 78); *Annales Colmarienses maiores*, ad 1297 [1296], ed. by P. Jaffé in *MGH*, Scriptores, XVII, 222; in the German trans. by H. Pabst, entitled *Annalen und Chronik von Kolmar*, p. 74; the Brünn *Schöffenbuch*, Art. 432, in *Die Stadtrechte von Brünn aus dem XIII. und XIV. Jahrhundert*, ed. by E. F. Rössler, pp. 201 ff.; *Das Rechtsbuch nach Distinctionen*, iii.17, 40, ed. by Ortloff, p. 176 (also excerpted by Kisch in his *Jewry-Law*, pp. 86, 252); and other sources cited by Stobbe in *Die Juden*, pp. 159 ff., 265 ff. nn. 149, 151. On Majorca, where the Jews obtained a special privilege in 1315 that condemned coreligionists be hanged by the neck, they emphasized that they requested it only "to alleviate the pain." See the text published by A. Morel-Fatio in his "Notes et documents pour servir à l'histoire des Juifs des Baléares sous la domination arragonaise," *REJ*, IV, 47; Baer, *Studien*, p. 87.

The ramified problems of the so-called Jewish execution have been discussed by R. Glanz in "The 'Jewish Execution' in Medieval Germany," *JSS*, V, 1–26; with a "Note" thereon by J. J. Rabinowitz, *ibid.*, pp. 305–308, and Glanz's reply, *ibid.*, VI, 288; and by G. Kisch in "The 'Jewish Execution' in Medieval Germany," *HJ*, V, 103–32 (also *Koschaker Mem. Vol.*, II, 63–93). If one is to accept Karl von Amira's explanation of the Teuton origin of this method of execution, one wonders how that custom had come to Majorca as well. Certainly, the recent antifascists who suspended Mussolini and several associates by their feet acted out of their general wish to add to the ignominy of the performance. Despite a few sporadic instances of both the hanging of Jews by their feet and the use of Jewish executioners (see the next note) in Sicily and other Western lands, there is no reason for assuming that either of these practices had been universally employed in the European Dark Ages and only went into oblivion in most areas outside Germany in the later Middle Ages. C. Roth's pertinent suggestion is unsupported by the available evidence. See his "European Jewry in the Dark Ages: a Revised Picture," *HUCA*, XXIII, Part 2, pp. 156 ff.

41. S. Assaf, "Jewish Executioners: a Contribution to the History of the Jews in Candia" (Hebrew), *Tarbiz*, V, 224–26; J. Starr, *The Jews in the Byzantine Empire 641–1204*, p. 202 No. 149 (1079); idem, "Jewish Life in Crete under the Rule of Venice," *PAAJR*, XII, 50–114, esp. pp. 74 f.

42. J. M. Rigg, *Select Pleas*, p. 2; J. E. Scherer, *Die Rechtsverhältnisse*, pp. 182 Art. 18, 230; N. Ferorelli, *Gli Ebrei nell'Italia meridionale dall'età romana al secolo XVIII*, p. 183; M. Ciardini, *I Banchieri ebrei in Firenze*, pp. 11 f.; Joseph ibn Ḥabib, *Nimmuqe Yosef* (Joseph's Motivations; a commentary on Alfasi's *Halakhot*), on B. Q., VIII, beg.; my *The Jewish Community*, II, 220 ff.; III, 175 ff. See also L. Gauthier, "Les Juifs dans les Deux Bourgognes," *REJ*, XLIX, 258. Scherer's assumption that, after paying the two talents to the judge, the Jewish assailant was free from a fine and medical costs is not evident from the law. Notwithstanding the inherent double jeopardy, very likely the Jewish courts of justice condemned the attacker to such payments in accordance with rabbinic law, as will become clearer from my analysis of the internal Jewish administration of justice in a later chapter.

43. A. Gulak, *Oṣar ha-Sheṭarot* (Thesaurus of Deeds Frequently Used by Jews), p. 211 No. 219; Asher b. Yeḥiel, *Resp.*, lxviii, 10–11, Venice, 1586 ed., fols. 97d f.; Jacob b. Asher, *Turim*, Ḥ. M. No. 97, 31, with Karo's and Isserles' comments thereon; Isaac b. Sheshet, *Resp.*, No. 484, Constantinople, 1547 ed., sig. 45, 1b-d. Pointing out the similarity between this text and the one discussed in a responsum by Meir Abulafia of Toledo (d. 1244), as well as the related even longer documents current in Spain, Baer rightly argued for the Spanish provenance of this formula. See Baer's searching investigation in *Die Juden*, I, Part 1, pp. 1057 ff. It was precisely to such voluntary agreements that Didacus d'Aux referred when he spoke of the legal inability of the Jews to sign away their freedom. See *supra*, n. 7. See also *Los Códigos españoles*, VI (1849), 220 f. (Leyes nuevas); and, more generally, F. T. Valiente's comprehensive review of "La Prisión por deudas en los derechos castellano y aragonès," *AHDE*, XXX, 249–489. On the doubts concerning the legal validity of debt bondage expressed by the "sages of Norwich," see I. Epstein's remarks in *TJHSE*, XIV, 195 n. 35. Such self-restraint of Jewish moneylenders seems to have carried over into their relations with Christian debtors. This is probably the best explanation why Léon Bardinet found in the fifteenth-century documentation of the Comtat Venaissin only two cases of Christian debtors imprisoned by their Jewish creditors as against six Jews incarcerated because they could not pay their debts to Christian moneylenders. The general ratio of Christians indebted to Jews must have been much higher. See Bardinet's "Les Juifs du Comtat Venaissin," *RH*, XIV, 32.

44. Alphonso X, *Las Siete Partidas*, vii.24, 6, ed. by G. Lopez, IV, 646 f.; *Schwabenspiegel*, ccxiv.8, ed. by H. G. Gengler, pp. 176 f.; Aronius, *Regesten*, pp. 327 ff. No. 771, 12; and other sources cited by Kisch in *The Jews*, pp. 200 ff.; Baer, *Die Juden*, I,

Part 1, pp. 656 No. 409, 669 No. 418. See M. A. Ortí Belmonte, "Glosas a la legislación sobre los Judíos en las Partidas," *Boletín* of the R. Academia de Córdoba de Ciencias, XXVI, 41–66; and the extended discussions *supra*, Vols. III–IV in the passages listed in the Index Vol., p. 34 *s.v.* Converts; IX, pp. 12 ff. Understandably, conversion often created financial problems as well. One Regina, daughter of Solomon of Tolosa and wife of a Cervera Jew, was renamed Yolans after her conversion and married a Barcelona burgher. She subsequently sued her former husband for the recovery of her dowry (1482). Instead of taking the state's long-held position that, like all Jewish property belonging to the king, that of a convert should not be alienated from the Jewish community, Infante Henry merely ordered an investigation. The change in attitude is also illustrated by Navarre's readiness to support needy converts from royal funds. This burden had previously fallen upon the shoulders of churchmen. The Navarre Treasury records of 1391 mention the supply of clothing to a Jewish doctor, his wife, and three children, all of whom had been baptized in Montreal in the presence of the king, the latter often serving as godfather at such baptismal ceremonies. See Baer, I, Part 1, pp. 906 f. No. 556, 982 No. 600 n. 3.

45. Scherer, *Die Rechtsverhältnisse*, p. 183 Art. 26, 227; Exod. 21:16; Deut. 24:7; M. Sanh., XI, 1; Bab. 85b–86a; Gregory IX's *Decretales*, iii.33, 2, in *Corpus juris canonici*, ed. by E. Friedberg, II, 587 f.; the Iglau municipal statute, Art. 67 in J. A. Tomaschek, ed., *Deutsches Recht in Oesterreich im dreizehnten Jahrhundert*, pp. 201 ff., 255 f.; the Brünn *Schöffenbuch*, Art. 66 (30) in E. F. Rössler, ed., *Die Stadtrechte von Brünn aus dem XIII. und XIV. Jahrhundert*, p. 360; *Das Rechtsbuch nach Distinctionen*, iii.*17*, 42 and 44, ed. by Ortloff, p. 176; Udalricus Zasius, *Questiones de parvulis Iudeorum baptisandis*. See *supra*, Vol. IX, pp. 16 f., 248 n. 16. That such conversionist zeal was not infrequent is attested by many sources. Several Jews of Borja were accused in 1331 of having pelted with stones and attacked with weapons two Franciscan fathers abducting a Jewish boy who allegedly was willing to undergo conversion. The assailants doubtless considered their attack a legitimate method of self-defense. Yet it cost them 2,500 solidi jac. before Alphonso IV of Aragon quashed the criminal proceedings. See Baer, *Die Juden*, I, Part 1, pp. 264 f. No. 195. See also, more generally, P. Browe, "Die Kirchenrechtliche Stellung der getauften Juden und ihrer Nachkommen," *AKKR*, CXXI, 3–22, 165–91.

46. Lagumina and Lagumina, *Codice diplomatico*, II, Part 1, pp. 504 f. No. dcccvi. The resolutions of the important Barcelona assembly have long been known by historians and are available also in the English summary by L. Finkelstein in his *Jewish Self-Government in the Middle Ages*, pp. 336 ff. They were republished from a Bodleian MS and commented on by Baer in *Die Juden*, I, Part 1, pp. 348 ff. No. 253, esp. pp. 352 f. Art. 4. See also his *Studien*, pp. 63 ff. On Perpignan, see the texts cited by P. Vidal in "Les Juifs des anciens comtés de Roussillon et de Cerdagne," *REJ*, XVI, 14 n. 2, 16. Not surprisingly, as in most other state policies, the attitude of kings to the range of permissible inquisitorial jurisdiction over Jews depended on changing political constellations and needs. Philip the Fair easily reversed himself in this matter in accordance with his constantly changing general ecclesiastical policies. See J. Parkes's pertinent illustrations in *The Jew in the Medieval Community*, p. 140; and, more generally, *infra*, Chaps. LV–LVI., esp. LV, n, 20.

47. Alphonso X, *Las Siete Partidas*, vii.24, 4, ed. by Lopez, p. 45, with Ortí Belmonte's comments thereon in the *Boletín* of the R. Academia de Córdoba, XXVI,

41 ff.; Henry III's decree of 1253 in T. Rymer and R. Sanderson's *Foedera*, I, 293 (on its dependence on the Council of Oxford, see Rigg, *Select Pleas*, pp. xxviii f.); Baer, *Die Juden*, I, Part 2, p. 217 No. 221; the orders issued by Philip III and Philip IV in 1283 and 1299, as reproduced by G. Saige in *Les Juifs du Languedoc*, pp. 212 f. No. xliii, 2; 235 f. No. xliii, 20; and *supra*, Vol. IX, pp. 10 f., 244 f. n. 9.

48. Baer, *Die Juden*, I, Part 2, p. 218 No. 222; *supra*, Vol. X, p. 143. On the pre-eminence of the synagogue see the examples reproduced from the Cologne registry by R. Hoeniger and M. Stern, eds., *Das Judenschreinsbuch der Laurenzpfarre zu Köln* and listed in the Index thereto, p. 228, *s.v.* synagoga. The law books, too, are largely silent on sanctions for such unauthorized buildings or alterations. Only a somewhat belated fourteenth- or fifteenth-century manuscript gloss on the *Sachsenspiegel* (iii.8) speaks vaguely of a fine to be paid by an unauthorized Jewish builder. See Aronius, *Regesten*, pp. 200 f. No. 458 note. Nor were any difficulties encountered by the relatively old Hungarian-Jewish community of Sopron (Ödenburg) when it erected, probably in the thirteenth century, its synagogue discovered by archaeologists in 1954–57. See A. Scheiber, "La Découverte d'une synagogue médiévale à Sopron," *REJ*, CXVIII, 79–93; *supra*, Vols. III, p. 332 n. 50; X, p. 312 n. 31.

49. Scherer, *Die Rechtsverhältnisse*, pp. 182 Art. 15, 226 f.; *Das Rechtsbuch nach Distinctionen*, iii.17, 37, ed. by Ortloff, p. 175; Johann von Buch's *Gloss* on the *Sachsenspiegel*, iii.7, both works excerpted in Kisch's *Jewry-Law*, pp. 48 item 3, 85; Samuel Zarza (Çarça). *Meqor ḥayyim* (Fountain of Life); Baer, *Die Juden*, I, Part 1, pp. 216 ff. No. 175 Arts. 1 and 25; Part 2, pp. 200 f. No. 209, 327 f. No. 314. See *supra*, Vol. X, pp. 147, 367 n. 34. In his early privilege of Jan. 31, 1419, for the Jews of Lombardy, Tuscany, and other Italian communities Pope Martin V likewise emphasized that synagogues ought not to be molested. See F. Vernet, "Le Pape Martin V et les Juifs," *RQH*, LI, 377 f., 411 f. No. 9. The French government, too, recognized the importance of the synagogue. When in 1257–58 Louis IX ordered the restoration of Jewish usury collected from Christian debtors, he allowed the commission to sell Jewish houses for the satisfaction of these claims, but specifically forbade the sale of "ancient" synagogues and cemeteries. Similarly, upon the readmission of Jews to France in 1315 the authorities were ordered to give back to the returnees the synagogues left behind by the exiles of 1306 in so far as they were still available or after paying an indemnity to the intervening purchasers. See Laurière *et al., Ordonnances*, I, 85 f. Art. 3, 596 Arts. 7–8.

In his comments Johannes Scherer overstates the distinction between the synagogue as a house of worship and as a place for the holding of trials. Medieval Jews used their synagogues as all-purpose communal buildings which, like their cemeteries, required special protection against vandals. The assignment of the fine to the Christian *judex Judeorum* need no more refer to the legislator's particular concern for the sanctity of court locations than the same penalty inflicted upon the Jewish assailant of a coreligionist. See *supra*, n. 42. In the protection of synagogues, too, Jews may have sought to involve the self-interest of public officials in the prosecution of offenders. While we do not have many records of such prosecutions, the culprits who in 1318 had stolen scrolls of law from a synagogue in Château-Thierry (hardly for purposes of resale) were indeed condemned by the Paris Parlement. See *Actes du Parlement de Paris*, ed. by E. Boutaric, 1st. ser. II, 223 No. 5230. On the other hand, even friendly Emperor Frederick III granted in 1442 a pardon to one Hanns Breitenbach who, together with several associates, had broken into the synagogue of Friedberg and stolen some objects from it. See Wiener, *Regesten*, p. 80 No. 14.

50. Joseph b. Solomon Colon, *Resp.*, Root 113, Lwów, 1798 ed., fol. [51cd]; Finkelstein, *Self-Government*, pp. 120 Art. 3 (Hebrew), 130 (English); my *The Jewish Community*, II, 125 f.; III, 142 n. 2; Lagumina and Lagumina, *Codice diplomatico*, I, 168 No. 124. The status of such private chapels was not altogether clear. They are mentioned in governmental records mainly in connection with permits for their owners to have them, rather than as objects of special protection. Very likely their attackers were punished only for assault on Jewish property, not for violation of sacred precincts.

51. John Peckham, *Registrum epistolarum*, ed. by C. T. Martin, I, 212 f. No. clxxix; II, 407 ff. Nos. cccxii, cccxvi; *Urkunden und Akten der Stadt Strassburg*, 1st. ser., IV, 2: *Stadtrechte*, ed. by A. Schulte and G. Wolfram, pp. 168 f. Arts. 510–15; F. Fita and G. Llabrés, "Privilegios de los Hebreos mallorquines en el Códice Pueyo," *BAH*, XXXVI, 200 ff. No. 47; Baer, *Die Juden*, I, Part 1, pp. 560 f. No. 368; J. C. Ulrich, *Sammlung jüdischer Geschichten*, pp. 434 ff. App. M (Latin and German); *supra*, Vol. IX, pp. 10 f., 244 n. 9; and, more generally, P. Browe, "Die Religiöse Duldung der Juden im Mittelalter," *AKKR*, CXVIII, 9 ff.

52. Leon da Modena, *Historia dei riti ebraici*, i.10, 8, in the old English trans. by Simon Ockley, entitled *The History of the Present Jews throughout the World*, p. 36; Baer, *Die Juden*, I, Part 1, pp. 531 f. No. 351, 642 No. 399; Lagumina and Lagumina, *Codice diplomatico*, I, 578 f. No. 433. For the most part the ritualistically or regionally diversified congregations started as more or less private assemblies meeting in individual homes. Only after some time were they enabled, financially and politically, to erect synagogues of their own. But the authorities often looked the other way. Only in southern Italy under Aragonese domination were Jews expressly told that they might freely "erect little mosques [synagogues] in any place and do all other things necessary for the observance of their law." See N. Ferorelli, *Gli Ebrei nell'Italia meridionale*, pp. 100 f.

53. A. Crémieux, "Les Juifs de Marseille au moyen âge," *REJ*, XLVI, 31 f.; M. Kayserling, "La Treizième Synagogue de Tolède," *ibid.*, XXXVIII, 142–43; D. Kaufmann, "Les Synagogues de Tolède," *ibid.*, p. 251; P. Riera Vidal, *The Jews of Toledo and Their Synagogue; supra*, n. 47; and Vol. IX, pp. 33, 256 n. 35; G. Carano-Donvito, "Gli Ebrei," *Rivista di politica economica*, XXIII, 838; M. Brann, *Geschichte der Juden in Schlesien*, p. 31; P. Browe, "Die Religiöse Duldung," *AKKR*, CXVIII, 14. See also, more generally, F. Cantera Burgos's comprehensive review of the *Sinagogas españoles* which, besides the synagogues of Cordova (pp. 1–32) and of Toledo (pp. 33–150), discusses 116 other known Jewish houses of worship in medieval Spain. On the situation in Rome before 1500 see A. Milano, "Le Sinagoghe del vecchio ghetto di Roma," *Studi Romani*, VI, 138–59, esp. pp. 143 f. (claiming that at that time there were nine or ten such buildings in the papal capital). See also P. Rieger *et al.*, eds., *Jüdische Gotteshäuser und Friedhöfe Württembergs*.

54. T. Rymer and R. Sanderson, *Foedera*, I, 293; D'B. Tovey, *Anglia Judaica*, p. 192; Lagumina and Lagumina, *Codice diplomatico*, II, Part 1, pp. 102 f. No. 533; M. Bouquet, *Recueil des historiens*, ed. by Delisle, XXII, 761; N. Brussel, *Nouvel examen de l'usage*, I, 603 (*pro eo quod nimis alta cantaverunt*); G. Saige, *Les Juifs du Languedoc*, pp. 213, 236; P. Browe, "Die Religiöse Duldung," *AKKR*, CXVIII, 29 f.; and *supra*, Vol. IX, pp. 35 f., 222, 256 n. 38, 344 f. n. 30. On the obviously forced rabbinic explanations why the talmudic laws concerning synagogue externals might be disregarded, see my *The Jewish Community*, II, 139; III, 147 n. 16.

It stands to reason that when the synagogue was transferred to another locale some adjacent communal buildings were moved also. While the so-called houses of assembly and of the council were usually placed within the synagogue structure, schools, baths, or prisons—the latter occasionally recorded near the synagogue; for instance, in Saragossa, where it was adjacent to the synagogue of the society *bicorolim* (*Biqqur Holim* or for Visiting the Sick)—had to be removed together with it. See M. Serrano y Sanz, *Orígenes de la dominación española en América: Estudios históricos*, I, pp. ix ff., xxiii ff.

55. Lagumina and Lagumina, *Codice diplomatico*, I, 66 f. No. xlix, 87 f. No. lix; R. Starrabba, "Processo di fellonia contro frate Simone del Pozzo, vescovo di Catania (1392)," *AS Siciliano*, I, 429; A. Pesaro, *Memorie storiche sulla Comunità israelitica ferrarese*, pp. 15 ff.; C. Roth, *The History of the Jews of Italy*, p. 188; K. Eubel, "Zu dem Verhalten der Päpste gegen die Juden," *Römische Quartalschrift*, XIII, 36 ff.; Baer, *Die Juden*, I, Part 1, pp. 824 f. No. 508; Part 2, pp. 218 No. 222, 231 f. No. 247, 241 ff. Nos. 256–57 and 259, 253 ff. No. 267, 279 Nos. 283–85; *supra*, Vol. X, pp. 170 f., 375 f. n. 5. The developments leading up to the destruction of the synagogue of Gerona because it was located in a place once occupied by a church are described with full documentation by M. de los Angeles Masiá in his "Aportaciones al estudio del Call gerundense," *Sefarad*, XIII, 287–308. On other crucial changes which took place during the years 1391–1415, including the sharp anti-Jewish decree of Benedict XIII of 1412 and the subsequent disputation of Tortosa, see *supra*, Vol. IX, pp. 87 ff. Of course, kings felt free to seize synagogues like any other Jewish property. In 1336, as we recall, King John of Bohemia did not hesitate to order digging for hidden treasures in the then already widely respected synagogue of Prague and to confiscate outright the 2,000 marks in gold and silver thus recovered. See Wiener, *Regesten*, p. 49 No. 171; and *supra*, Vol. IX, pp. 200 f., 334 f. n. 7.

56. Thomas Aquinas, *Summa theologica*, ii.2, q. 32, art. 2, in his *Opera omnia*, ed. under the sponsorship of Leo XIII, VIII, 251b; in the English trans. by the English Dominican Province, p. 412; Tosefta Gittin, v.5, ed. by M. S. Zuckermandel, p. 328. with the decisions based on these talmudic teachings in Jacob b. Asher's *Turim*, Y. D., Nos. 344 and 367, and in Joseph Karo's and Joel Sirkes's commentaries thereon; and the comparative data offered by J. Schweizer's Basel dissertation, *Kirchhof und Friedhof. Eine Darstellung der beiden Haupttypen europäischer Begräbnisstätten*. A certain measure of interdenominational liberality is evidenced also by an untoward event in Ferrara in 1452. The Order of St. Jerome decided to enlarge its quarters by taking over the local Jewish graveyard which had apparently been in operation for but a short time. To accommodate the monks, the municipality assigned to the Jewish community another location for a burial ground. We hear neither of Jewish objections nor of any compunctions on the monks' part against including Jewish graves

in their monastery's precincts. See A. Pesaro, *Memorie storiche,* p. 12. An interesting example of burial of Jewish corpses in a general cemetery is offered by E. Levy's ed. of "Un Document sur les Juifs du Barrois en 1321–23," *REJ,* XIX, 246–58. Needless to say, tombstone inscriptions, too, could serve apologetic purposes. In their repeated attempts to prove to their Christian compatriots that their local settlements had antedated the Christian era and that, hence, their particular ancestors had not participated in the crucifixion of Jesus, some Jewries pointed to allegedly ancient inscriptions in their cemeteries. The Jewish community of Cividale even erected in 1464 a stone commemorating the existence of a local inscription (since vanished) which supposedly proved the Jews' presence in the city in 604 B.C.E. (!). See the text republished, together with about a dozen other "Hebrew Inscriptions at Cividale," by Z. Avneri in his Hebrew essay in *Tarbiz,* XXXI, 291–96.

57. Aronius, *Regesten,* pp. 69 ff. No. 168 (*locum sepulturae sub hereditaria condicione*), 183 No. 412; Baer, *Die Juden,* I, Part 1, pp. 933 ff. No. 578 Art. 6; L. Donath, *Geschichte der Juden in Mecklenburg von den ältesten Zeiten (1266) bis auf die Gegenwart (1874),* p. 23; Roger Howden (Hoveden), *Chronica,* ed. by W. Stubbs, II, 137; Meir b. Baruch of Rothenburg, *Resp.,* Prague, 1608 ed., end (fol. 114cd); Israel b. Petaḥiah Isserlein, *Pesaqim u-ketabim* (Decisions and Writings on Law), Venice, 1519 ed., No. 65; *supra,* Vol. IX, pp. 189 f., 330 n. 61; P. von Stetten, *Geschichte der Heil. Röm. Reichs-Freyen Stadt Augspurg,* I, 159; Moses b. Isaac Menz (Minz or Mainz), *Resp.,* No. 51, Lwów, 1850 ed., fol. 43bc; and other data cited by Stobbe in *Die Juden,* pp. 269 f. n. 158. See also M. Roblin, "Les Cimetières juifs de Paris au moyen âge," *Mémoires* of the Fédération des sociétés historiques et archéologiques de Paris, IV, 7–19.

Sometimes, in order to attract Jews, the local authorities gave them land for a cemetery. For example, in 1171 the abbot of Sahagún confirmed such a gift by formal contract "for so long as they will be with us; if, however, they should withdraw, it [the plot] should remain with us as our free hereditary property." See Baer, *Die Juden,* I, Part 2, p. 18 No. 36; and for a description of that Jewish community which is well documented from 933 to 1466, see J. Rodriguez, "Judería de Sahagún," *Archivos Leoneses,* VII, 5–77.

58. J. Juster, *Les Juifs,* I, 481 ff.; C. Canetta, "Gli Ebrei del ducato milanese," *AS Lombardo,* VIII, 632–35; Scherer, *Die Rechtsverhältnisse,* pp. 142 Art. 14, 225 f.; *supra,* Vols. II, pp. 286 ff., 336 n. 23; IV, pp. 8 f., 236 n. 4; IX, pp. 11, 245 f. n. 10. In issuing in 1392 a similar protective privilege for the Jewish cemetery of Palermo, King Martin specifically invoked Pope Nicholas III's bull of 1278 and emphasized that he thus tried "to obviate the depravity and avarice of evil men" who were mutilating cemeteries or digging up human bodies in order to collect ransom. Lagumina and Lagumina, *Codice diplomatico,* I, 120 No. lxxxii. Frequent acts of lawlessness of this kind caused even adjustments of rabbinic laws. See my *The Jewish Community,* II, 150 f.; III, 154 n. 28. On the other hand, under peaceful conditions Jews were able, as a rule, to secure some redress by simple lawsuits. An interesting case was recorded in Norwich, where in 1200 Jews sued the burghers for breaking into their cemetery. See F. Palgrave, ed., *Rotuli Curiae Regis,* II, 155; Richardson, *The English Jewry,* p. 114.

59. L. Ennen and G. Eckertz, eds., *Quellen zur Geschichte der Stadt Köln,* II, 543 No. 495; Aronius, *Regesten,* p. 125 No. 289; A. Kober, *Grundbuch des Kölner Juden-*

viertels, 1135–1425, p. 57; G. A. Tzschoppe and G. A. Stenzel, *Urkundensammlung zur Geschichte des Ursprungs der Städte . . . in Schlesien,* p. 557 No. clvi; L. Oelsner, "Schlesische Urkunden zur Geschichte der Juden im Mittelalter," *Archiv für Kunde österreichischer Geschichts-Quellen,* XXXI, 106 No. 6; Israel b. Petaḥiah Isserlein, *Terumat ha-deshen* (Responsa), No. 284, Venice, 1519 ed., sig. 22, lc; cited with approval by Joseph Karo and Moses Isserles on Jacob b. Asher's *Ṭurim,* Y. D. No. 368; Régné, "Catalogue," *REJ,* LXIII, 252 No. 696.

60. C. Rè, ed., *Statuti della città di Roma,* p. 191; Baer, *Die Juden,* I, Part 1, p. 337 No. 243; Part 2, pp. 327 f. No. 314; X. Mossmann, "Étude sur l'histoire des Juifs de Colmar," *Revue de l'Est,* n.s. III, 123. Apart from violations and forcible removals, Jewish cemeteries were also threatened occasionally by governmental seizures. In the tragic year of 1391 the Jews of Jerez de la Frontera were allowed to sell their cemetery to the local Dominicans, but in 1412, responding to the then growing anti-Jewish hostility, Queen Beatrice without much ado gave away the former Jewish graveyard in Villareal to one of her courtiers. In their decree of expulsion of 1492, Ferdinand and Isabella strictly prohibited Jews from selling their synagogues, cemeteries, and other communal possessions, just as Christians were forbidden to buy them. Baer, Part 2, pp. 236 No. 250, 259 No. 270 n.; L. Delgado Merchán, "El Fonsario ó cementerio de los judiós de Ciudad-Real," *BAH,* XL, 169 f.; J. Jacobs, *An Inquiry into the Sources of the History of the Jews in Spain,* p. 148 No. xvi.

61. *Urkundenbuch der Stadt Basel,* ed. by R. Wackernagel and R. Thommen, V, 213 f. No. 204; *Die Züricher Stadtbücher des 14. und 15. Jahrhunderts, II,* 354; Stobbe, *Die Juden,* pp. 217 f. n. 46; G. L. Kriegk, *Frankfurter Bürgerzwiste,* pp. 554 f. n. 245; M. Stern, *König Ruprecht von der Pfalz in seinen Beziehungen zu den Juden,* pp. 7 ff. No. 9. Sometimes, as in Northampton, the community had a special fund set aside for the cemetery's maintenance. See Richardson, *The English Jewry,* p. 134 n. 3. An interesting case arose in Barcelona in 1396. After the disturbances of 1391 Ḥisdai Crescas spent much money and time on the restoration of the Montjuich, the old burial place of the community, which, in the words of King John I, accrued "to the benefit and honor of the whole community in Our dominion." But although Ḥisdai had done it "under personal danger" and with the consent of both the king and the Jewish leaders, he had difficulty in securing reimbursement of his expenses. The small community of Montalban, for instance, requested him to accept a down-payment of 10 gold florins and to wait for the balance until after the Jewish New Year, "for the people are away to harvest the fields." Baer, *Die Juden,* I, Part 1, pp. 726 f. No. 482.

62. Baer, *Die Juden,* I, Part 2, pp. 329 ff. No. 318 Art. 109. On the mourning for intellectual leaders, see my *The Jewish Community,* II, 147 f. It appears that the Christian population resented far less prayers loudly recited by mourners than the sonorous singing in synagogues. Only exceptionally did a Christian council, like that of Narbonne in 589, resolve that "it shall not be permitted for Jews to accompany the body of a deceased person while reciting psalms." See Mansi, *Sacrorum conciliorum . . . collectio,* IX, 1016 canon 9; *supra,* Vol. II, p. 423 n. 56. It must be borne in mind, however, that the recitation of psalms and prayers during Jewish funerals took place in the home, synagogue, or cemetery, rather than on the street. Possibly the clergy assembled at Narbonne was ignorant of Jewish funerary customs and sim-

ply equated them with their own. Even when a whole community mourned the passing of a great leader, most ceremonies took place in the synagogue building, as may be noted from Elijah Capsali's description of such a public mourning for Yehudah Menz of Padua. In this case, we are told, all Jewish shopkeepers had closed their stores and the craftsmen left their workshops to join the services at the synagogue. See the excerpts from the latter's chronicle published by N. Porges in his "Élie Capsali et sa chronique de Venise," *REJ*, LXXIX, 39 ff. No. v; and the French summary thereof, *ibid.*, LXXVII, 34 ff.

Many other Jewish funerary customs may be gleaned from such specialized monographs as L. de Grandmaison, "Le Cimetière des Juifs de Tours," *REJ*, XVIII, 262–75 (discusses other medieval French cemeteries as well); J. M. Castellarnau, "La Cuesta de los Hoyos, ó el cementerio hebreo de Segovia," *BAH*, IX, 265–69; A. Durán Sanpere and M. J. Millás Vallicrosa, "Una Necrópolis judaica en el Montjuich de Barcelona," *Sefarad*, VII, 231–59; other data included in F. Cantera Burgos's brief survey of the "Cementerios hebreos de España," *ibid.*, XIII, 362–67 (with special reference to those of Cordova, Calatayud, and Teruel); S. Simonsohn, "Gli Ebrei a Siracusa ed il loro cimitero," *AS Siracusano*, IX, 8–20; J. Lukaš and J. Lion, *Der Alte jüdische Friedhof in Prag* (Starý židowský Libitow v Praze); A. Grotte, *Alte schlesische Judenfriedhöfe (Breslau und Dyhrenfurth)*; K. H. Bernhardt and F. Treichel, "Der Jüdische Begräbnisplatz in Niederhof (hr. Stralsund)," *Baltische Studien*, n.s. XLVII, 111–36 (although dealing with more recent data, this essay sheds light on earlier Jewish cemeteries as well); *supra*, nn. 46 and 57; Vol. IV, pp. 33, 249 n. 37.

In addition to the studies of cemeteries as such, the various publications relating to funerary inscriptions shed considerable light on the history of the Jewish "houses of eternity." Many of these have been mentioned in the preceding volumes. See also B. Wachstein's outstanding compilation and analysis of *Die Inschriften des alten Judenfriedhofes in Wien*, in Quellen und Forschungen zur Geschichte der Juden in Deutsch-Oesterreich, Vol. IV, Parts I–II; with additional "Randbemerkungen," *ibid.*, Vol. XI; M. Horovitz, *Die Inschriften des alten Friedhofs der israelitischen Gemeinde zu Frankfurt a. M.* (includes materials for the history of those tombstones); such recent monographs as L. Armand-Calliat, "Inscriptions funéraires juives du moyen âge trouvées à Chalon," *Mémoires* of the Société archéologique of Chalon sur Saône, XXXIV, 68–80; Z. Avnéri, "Nouvelles inscriptions tumulaires du premier cimetière de Bâle," *REJ*, CXXI, 181–93 (includes twenty inscriptions uncovered at recent excavations at the University of Basel; supplements the data cited *supra*, Vol. X, pp. 302 f. n. 4); idem, "Hebrew Inscriptions at Cividale" (Hebrew), *Tarbiz*, XXXI, 291–96 (includes 12 inscriptions dating from 1342 to 1733); F. Fita, "El Montjuí de la ciudad de Gerona y la sinagoga y concejo hebreo de Castellón de Ampurias. Escrituras de los siglos XIII, XIV y XV," *BAH*, XLVIII, 169–74; *supra*, n. 56; and other literature, largely relating to somewhat later burial grounds, listed in my *The Jewish Community*, III, 156 f. n. 33. Other aspects of both cemetery and synagogue administration will be discussed in later chapters.

63. *Codex Theodosianus*, ii.8, 26; xvi.8, 20 (412); *CJ* (*Codex*), i.9, 13, ed. by Krüger, II, 61 f., and the observations thereon in Juster's *Les Juifs*, I, 280 ff., 354 ff.; II, 121 ff.; *Fuero* of Ledasma, Art. 393, in *Fueros Leoneses*, ed. by A. Castro and F. de Onís, pp. 271, 284 f.; *Libro de los Fueros de Castilla*, ed. by G. Sanchez, Arts. 219–20; *Fuero real*, iv.2, 7 in *Los Códigos españoles concordados y anotados*, I, 403; all cited by Baer in *Die Juden*, I, Part 2, pp. 31 f. No. 58, 36 f. No. 60, 40 f. No. 61; *Das*

Rechtsbuch nach Distinctionen, iii.17, 28, ed. by F. Ortloff, p. 174; also cited by G. Kisch in his *Jewry-Law,* p. 84.

64. F. Fossati, "Gli Ebrei a Vigevano nel secolo XV," *AS Lombardo,* XXX, 202 f.; P. Browe, "Die Religiöse Duldung," *AKKR,* CXVIII, 29 ff.; Caesarius of Heisterbach, *Dialogus miraculorum,* ed. by J. Strange; in the German trans. by A. Hilka, entitled *Die Wundergeschichten,* I, 157 f. No. 230, with the editor's note thereon, pointing out that a similar story was told about a Magdeburg Jew (*ca.* 1270). Hilka's suggestion, however, that the count who played the trick on the Jew was Thibaut IV does not square with what we know about that ruler's generally favorable attitude toward Champagne Jewry. Curiously, the Castilian *fueros* seemed to have been more concerned with the Jews' breaking the Sabbath laws than with their protection in observing them. On the other hand, even in the Middle Ages the Church often had to struggle against Christians wishing to observe their day of rest together with Jews or in the Jewish manner. On these trends, particularly manifest among Christian sectarians, see *supra,* Vols. IX, pp. 59 f., 268 n. 6; X, pp. 39, 318 f. n. 47; and *infra,* Chap. LV. Protection of Jewish festivals also involved some governments in extending special treatment to individual Jews. In 1389, for example, Albert III of Austria gave three Jewish messengers safe-conducts (including freedom from tolls and duties) to proceed to Trieste for the purpose of acquiring Italian citrons which the Austrian communities needed for the observance of their Feast of Tabernacles. See Scherer, *Die Rechtsverhältnisse,* pp. 534 f.

65. Berthold of Ratisbon, *Vollständige Ausgabe seiner Predigten,* xxv, xxxiii, ed. by F. Pfeiffer and J. Strobl, I, 401, 530; Lagumina and Lagumina, *Codice diplomatico,* II, 28 f. No. cdxci; *supra,* Vol. IX, pp. 56, 266 n. 1. See also M. Scheinert, *Der Franziskaner Berthold von Regensburg als Lehrer und Erzieher des Volkes,* pp. 5 ff. We shall see that the range of interests of Italian Jewry in the Renaissance era was very wide, indeed. A century later (1654) David Provençali and his son Abraham of Mantua appealed to various communities to establish a Jewish college for general studies, including medicine. See M. Güdemann, "Ein Projekt zur Gründung einer jüdischen Universität aus dem 16. Jahrhundert," *Festschrift . . . A. Berliner,* pp. 164–75 (trans. of a circular printed in Mantua, 1564); and text, ed. from a Hebrew MS by S. Z. H. Halberstam and reed. by S. Assaf in his *Meqorot le-toledot ha-ḥinnukh be-Yisrael* (Sources for the History of Jewish Education), II, 115 ff. On the use of the term *studium generale,* even after the adoption of the designation "University" by Paris in 1219 and Oxford in 1245, see A. F. Leach, ed., *Educational Charters and Documents 598 to 1909,* p. xxiii.

66. Bartolus de Saxoferrato, Baldus de Ubaldis, and other jurists, cited by V. Colorni in his broad analysis of *Gli Ebrei nel sistema del diritto comune fino alla prima emancipazione,* pp. 28 ff.; and by A. T. Sheedy in her dissertation, *Bartolus on Social Conditions in the Fourteenth Century,* pp. 154, 234; N. Ferorelli, *Gli Ebrei nell'Italia meridionale,* pp. 117 ff.; A. Ciscato, *Gli Ebrei in Padova (1300–1800),* pp. 217 ff. Among the early medical graduates of the University of Perpignan (1390) was one David Bonet Bonjorn of Gerona, despite the reenactment by the University in the 1380s of its old statute excluding Jews and Saracens from any kind of instruction. See Baer, *Die Juden,* I, Part 1, p. 259 No. 190 n.; M. Fournier, *Les Statuts et privilèges des universités françaises,* II, 655 ff., 679 f., No. 1485 end. The early Italian-

Jewish recipients of the doctor's degree at the university of Ferrara included the well-known Bible commentator, Obadiah Sforno (Servadio di Jacob Sforni) who in 1507 received the *privilegium doctoratus in artibus et medicina.* See A. Pesaro, *Appendice alle Memorie storiche sulla comunità israelitica ferrarese,* p. 43. See also O. Scalvanti, "Lauree in medicina di studenti israeliti a Perugia nel secolo XVI," *Annali* of the Faculty of Jurisprudence of the University of Perugia, 3d ser. VIII, 91–129; I. Zoller (Zolli), "I Medici ebrei laureati a Siena negli anni 1543–1695," *RI,* X, 60–66, 100–110 (includes 11 names, chiefly of the seventeenth century); J. Warchał, "Polish Jews at the University of Padua" (Polish), *Kwartalnik poświęcony badaniu przeszłości Żydów w Polsce,* I, Part 3, pp. 37–72; other monographs listed by Colorni, *loc. cit.;* and, more generally, C. Roth, "The Qualification of Jewish Physicians in the Middle Ages," *Speculum,* XXVIII, 834–43; idem, "The Medieval University and the Jews" (1930), reprinted in his *Personalities and Events in Jewish History,* pp. 91–110; G. Kisch, *Die Universitäten und die Juden. Eine historische Betrachtung zur Fünfhundertjahrfeier der Universität Basel;* various essays by H. Friedenwald collected in *The Jews and Medicine; supra,* Vol. VIII, esp. p. 389 n. 18. The broader aspects of Jewish education and school administration as well as the Jewish contributions to medicine will be more fully analyzed in later chapters.

67. Bab. B.B. 21b f., with the commentaries thereon by the school of Gershom b. Yehudah, Rashi, and the Tosafists; the "Canterbury Treaty" of 1266 in J. M. Rigg's *Select Pleas,* pp. 35 f.; *supra,* Vol. X, pp. 107 f.; M. Adler, *Jews of Medieval England,* pp. 83 ff., 111 f. App. ix; F. de Bofarull y Sans, *Los Judíos en el territorio de Barcelona (siglos X al XIII),* pp. 72 No. lxiii, 109 No. cxxxii. The rabbis saw no irreconcilable conflict between their recognition of the authorities' right to refuse admission to new Jews and their general demand that governments not impede the freedom of movement of their coreligionists. See *supra,* nn. 8 ff. However, Asher b. Yeḥiel was not alone in stating, doubtless with reference to the fourteenth-century Spanish practice, that any Jew was free to settle wherever he pleased. See his *Halakhot* (Legal Commentary on the Talmud), on B.B. II No. 12, Vilna, 1896 ed., fol. 181d; the comprehensive analyses of the rabbinic views by L. I. Rabinowitz in his complementary four essays, "The Origin of the Canterbury 'Treaty' of 1266," *Miscellanies* of the Jewish Historical Society of England, III, 76–79; "The Medieval Jewish Counter-Part to the Gild Merchant," *Economic History Review,* VIII, 180–85; "The Talmudic Basis of the Ḥerem Hayyishub," *JQR,* XXVIII, 217–23; and *The Ḥerem Hayyishub, passim;* as well as my comments in "Rashi and the Community of Troyes" in *Rashi Anniversary Volume* of the American Academy for Jewish Research, pp. 62 ff. See also *infra,* n. 68; and *supra,* Vol. IV, pp. 185, 274 n. 91, 330 f. n. 45.

68. H. G. Richardson, *The English Jewry under Angevin Kings,* pp. 287, 291 f. (publishing the text of the circular addressed in 1221 to the sheriffs and Jewish bailiffs of Cambridge and ten other towns); Baer, *Die Juden,* I, Part 1, pp. 88 f. No. 88 (1229), 96 f. No. 93 (1241), 118 f. No. 106 (1272), 152 No. 137 (1294); L. Ennen and G. Eckertz, eds., *Quellen . . . Köln,* II, 321 ff. No. 308; IV, 120 No. 134; A. Kober, *Cologne,* pp. 41, 67; Laurière *et al., Ordonnances des roys,* III, 467 ff., 475 Art. 3; *supra,* Vol. IX, pp. 153 f., 315 n. 21. Illicit emigration of Jews was often prohibited elsewhere, too; for instance, by Alphonso IV of Portugal (1325–57), Charles II of Navarre (1343–87), John II of Castile in 1412, and Ferdinand I of Aragon in 1413. In

Navarre, Charles II forbade both Christians and Moors to acquire any real estate from Jews without royal permission, a move clearly designed also to impede Jewish emigration. For the most part, the threat of confiscation was combined with that of enslavement of any would-be illicit emigrant seized by the authorities. See *Ordenaçoens . . . Affonso V*, II, 450, lxxiv Art. 14; M. Kayserling, *Die Juden in Navarra, den Baskenlændern und auf den Balearen*, pp. 94 f.; *supra*, nn. 7–8.

Understandably, Jewish communities were rarely expected to cooperate in such prosecution, but they were often called upon to help repopulate devastated Jewish settlements. We recall the royal order of 1393 to Ḥisdai Crescas and two representatives each from the communities of Saragossa and Calatayud to select sixty Jewish families and forcibly resettle them in ruined Barcelona and Valencia. See *supra*, Vol. X, pp. 177, 378 n. 13. Even in fifteenth-century Avignon, where city council and populace often gave vent to their anti-Jewish feelings, the popes as a rule encouraged Jewish immigration. We must thus understand Martin V's order of 1430 to the local Jewish elders not to introduce any innovations which would adversely affect new Jewish settlers. See F. Vernet, "Le Pape Martin V," *RQH*, LI, 422 No. 78.

69. N. Ferorelli, *Gli Ebrei nell'Italia meridionale*, p. 101; M. Stern, *König Ruprecht von der Pfalz*, pp. xxxvi ff., xlvi ff., lii ff., 35 f.; Baer, *Die Juden*, I, Part 1, pp. 625 ff. No. 395; Part 2, pp. 349 f. No. 338 (1483); Wiener, *Regesten*, pp. 64 f. Nos. 71 and 80, 71 ff. App. iv, 90 ff. Nos. 81–82, 106. Recognition of Jewish bans by municipal authorities is also illustrated by the Breslau city council's refusal of a safe-conduct to one Moshe so long as he was not absolved from the Jewish ban "under which he is said to stand" (1431). Cited from a Breslau MS by G. Kisch in *The Jews in Medieval Germany*, pp. 103, 411 f. No. 35. The various stages of the Jewish anathema and its widespread use in enforcing communal controls will be more fully discussed in a later volume.

The Jewish excommunication should not be confused, however, with the imperial ban (*Reichsacht*) which emperors could impose on Jews as on all other subjects. In 1410, at the instance of the Nuremberg municipal council, Rupert placed a Jewish family under such an imperial ban. Five years earlier he had demanded the imprisonment of three Frankfort Jews because they had maintained contacts with persons under an imperial ban and thereby, according to law, had forfeited their own lives and property to the empire. In this case, however, the Frankfort city council succeeded in appeasing the aroused emperor. See Wiener, *Regesten*, pp. 62 No. 62, 68 No. 98. See also M. Stern, *König Ruprecht*, pp. 19 ff. Nos. 23 ff. The aid generally given by governments in the enforcement of Jewish bans is the more noteworthy as even the more Catholic-minded monarchs often hesitated to extend all-out support to parallel bans issued by the Church. See the data analyzed by G. J. Campbell in "The Attitude of the Monarchy toward the Use of Ecclesiastical Censures in the Reign of Saint Louis," *Speculum*, XXXV, 535–55; and *supra*, Vol. IX, p. 258 n. 43.

70. See in particular James I's, Pedro III's, Pedro IV's, and Queen Violante's important decrees of 1241, 1272, 1279, 1377, and 1390, excerpted by Baer in *Die Juden*, I, Part 1, pp. 96 f. No. 93, 117 ff. No. 106, 129 f. No. 116, 459 ff. No. 317, 633 f. No. 396; idem, *Studien*, pp. 42 ff., 88 ff.; A. A. Neuman, *The Jews in Spain*, I, 132 ff., 259 nn. 161–64; Isaac b. Sheshet Perfet, *Resp.*, Nos. 234–39, Constantinople, 1547 ed., sig. 19. The extraordinary deviations of these medieval Spanish jurists from the talmudic laws, both criminal and procedural, are briefly analyzed by A. M. Hershman

in his *Rabbi Isaac Ben Sheshet Perfet and His Times,* pp. 137 ff. No such drastic measures or communal privileges are recorded elsewhere (Jewish capital jurisdiction in Spain was a singular exception), but all Jewish communities tried to stave off informing, with or without the assistance of state authorities. See also D. Kaufmann, "Jewish Informers in the Middle Ages," *JQR,* [o.s.] VIII, 217–38, supplemented by Salomon J. (or S. Z. H.) Halberstam, "A Response of Solomon b. Aderet," *ibid.,* pp. 527–28; and, more generally, *supra,* Vol. V, pp. 17, 45 f., 298 f. n. 15, 312 n. 55; and Vol. X, pp. 130 f., 360 n. 16.

71. Baer, *Die Juden,* I, Part 1, pp. 447 f. No. 307; A. Epstein, "Der Wormser Judenrat," *MGWJ,* XLVI, 157–70, with the comments thereon by M. Frank in his *Qehillot Ashkenaz* (The Jewish Communities and Their Courts in Germany from the Twelfth to the End of the Fifteenth Century), pp. 7 f.; I. Kracauer, *Urkundenbuch zur Geschichte der Juden in Frankfurt a. M.,* I, 84 f. No. 203; idem, *Geschichte der Juden in Frankfurt a. M.,* I, 48 ff.; Lagumina and Lagumina, *Codice diplomatico,* I, 586 f. No. cdxl (1456); II, 124 f. No. dxlv (1473), 487 No. dccxci (1490); Alphonso X, *Las Siete Partidas,* iii.20, 8, ed. by G. Lopez, II, 765, the resolution of the Cortes of Madrigal of 1476 as summarized in *Cortes de los antiguos reinos de León y de Castilla,* published by the R. Academia de Historia, IV, 38; Baer, *Die Juden,* I, Part 2, p. 44 No. 63. While fees varied from country to country, few governments were prepared to extend formal approval without some such tangible consideration. On the Jewish bailiffs in England, see H. G. Richardson in *The English Jewry,* pp. 130 ff., 285 ff.

The Worms situation was not typical, however. To begin with, the elders were elected for life and often replenished their ranks by cooptation—an undemocratic procedure rarely found in Jewish communities. The bishop's participation likewise was more intensive than elsewhere. Even the elders' oath of office was taken in the courtyard of the bishop's palace. Yuspa the Sexton, whose seventeenth-century custumal is our main source of information, makes the point that during that ceremony "all elders cover their heads and they do not appear bareheaded even if the bishop happens to be present." A. Epstein, pp. 162 f. Nor is it surprising that, despite the onerous duties usually resting upon the elders' shoulders (only direct papal intervention absolved in 1430 a Cavaillon elder from personal responsibility for the communal debts), there was no dearth of ambitious candidates. See F. Vernet, "Le Pape Martin V," *RQH,* LI, 421 No. 75. From time to time some overzealous office seekers resorted even to electoral frauds. One such manipulated election in Saragossa in 1480 called forth direct intervention by Ferdinand the Catholic. See L. Serrano y Sanz, *Orígenes de la dominación española,* pp. 490 f. No. xlii. Governments were often more liberal with respect to private foundations, allowing the donors full leeway not only in appointing officers to administer them but also in making statutory provisions about the latter's hereditary succession or other forms of replacement. See, for instance, the statute of a Jewish society in Arles, reproduced by P. Hildenfinger in his "Documents relatifs aux Juifs d'Arles," *REJ,* XLI, 87 ff.

72. Wiener, *Regesten,* pp. 71 ff. App. iv; H. P. Stokes, *Studies in Anglo-Jewish History,* pp. 23 ff., 44 ff., 83 ff., 243 ff.; the detailed analysis of the activities of one such Anglo-Jewish archpresbyter in M. Adler's "Aaron of York and King Henry III," reprinted in his *Jews of Medieval England,* pp. 125–73 (also reproducing Aaron's 1236 patent of appointment as archpresbyter; p. 167); H. G. Richardson, *The English*

Jewry, pp. 124 ff.; *supra*, Vols. IX, pp. 162 f., 319 n. 32; X, pp. 98 f., 346 n. 54. The frequent assumption that, under the pressure of the German rabbinate, Chief Rabbi Israel resigned soon after his appointment in 1407 is controverted by King Conrad's decree eight years later which arranged for a substitute in the case of Israel's death. See W. Altmann, ed., *Die Urkunden Kaiser Siegmunds (1410–1437)*, I, 116 No. 1784; M. Stern, *König Ruprecht*, p. lv n. 1. As late as 1569, Maximilian II nonchalantly referred to the "rabbi whom We have ordained for the common Jewry in Germany." See G. Wolf, "Die Anstellung der Rabbiner und ihr Wirkungskreis," reproduced in his *Kleine historische Schriften*, pp. 139 f. The ramified contributions of the northern Jewish regional chiefs and conferences to Jewish taxation will be more fully analyzed in later chapters. For the time being reference need be made only to the extensive data assembled in my *The Jewish Community*, I, 295 ff.; II, 68 ff.

Only two of these German leaders have been treated in brief biographical studies by M. Stern in "Der Wormser Reichsrabbiner Anselm," *ZGJD*, V, 157–68 (includes the text of Anselm's appointment in 1434; pp. 160 f.) and M. Ginsburger, " 'Le Rabbin de L'Empereur' Jacob de Worms et sa famille," *REJ*, LXXXII, 461–68 (Jacob was appointed by Ferdinand I in 1559). Even the chief rabbis of France after 1360 have remained, both as persons and as incumbents of their high office, rather shadowy figures. See Israel Lévi, "La Lutte entre Isäie, fils d'Abba Mari, et Yohanan, fils de Matatia, pour le rabbinat de France à la fin du XIVe siècle," *REJ*, XXXIX, 85–94; and C. Lauer, "R. Meir Halevy aus Wien und der Streit um das Grossrabbinat in Frankreich," *JJLG*, XVI, 1–42.

73. The resolutions of the Council of Valladolid of 1432, reproduced in an improved version by Baer in *Die Juden*, I, Part 2, pp. 291 No. 287 (iii.7); 321 No. 307, 5; the Portuguese statute regulating the country's chief rabbinate and its subdivisions in the *Ordenaçoens . . . Affonso V*, II, 81, pp. 476 ff., well summarized by M. Kayserling in his *Geschichte der Juden in Portugal*, pp. 9 ff. The latter's renewal in 1440 had become necessary because of the protests of various Jewish communities, led by Lisbon, against the then incumbent Don Juda Cofem. See also *supra*, Vol. X, pp. 160, 372 n. 49; and my *The Jewish Community*, I, 285 ff.; III, 65 ff. The Spanish and Portuguese chief rabbinates, including the personalities of Abraham Benveniste and Abraham Seneor, deserve far fuller treatment than they have hitherto received.

74. *Codex Theodosianus*, ii.i, 10; xvi.8, 22 and 24; *CJ*, i.4, 15; 9, 8 and 15; Bartolus di Saxoferato, *Commentaria* on *Corpus*, 1.8 C. 2, 6, Lyons, 1552 ed.; V. Colorni, *Gli Ebrei nel sistema del diritto comune*, pp. 25 ff. See G. Kisch, "Zur Frage der Aufhebung jüdisch-religiöser Jurisdiktion durch Justinian," *ZRG*, Romanistische Abteilung, LXXVII, 395–401, esp. pp. 397 f. n. 8.; and my debate with him on this score, *ibid.*, LXXIX, 547–49; and, more generally, the detailed illustrations furnished, especially from Italian practices and juridical works, by V. Colorni in his *Legge ebraica e leggi locali, passim*. The persistence of the ancient Roman legal institutions in the Middle Ages is stressed by A. Steinwenter in his "Zum Problem der Kontinuität zwischen antiken und mittelalterlichen Rechtsordnungen," *Jura*, II, 14–43.

The special status of medieval Jewry was well defined in the following statement by the Brünn Law Book: "Jews, however, clerics and nobles, who possess their own judges, must be summoned before those judges, since the plaintiff ought to follow the court of the accused." *Brünner Schöffenbuch*, xiv, ed. by E. F. Rössler in *Die Stadtrechte von Brünn (Deutsche Rechtsdenkmäler, II)*, p. 10; also reproduced by G.

Kisch in his *Jewry-Law in Medieval Germany*, p. 244. Very frequently this judicial autonomy found clear expression in comprehensive communal statutes adopted by Jewish communities and confirmed by rulers. To be sure, in Aragon the royal bailiff often took part in the adoption of such statutes and had the authority to overrule them. Nevertheless, once they were confirmed by the king, the lesser officials had to respect them. This practice was upheld despite occasional protests by the Castilian *Cortes;* for instance, those of Valladolid of 1351 which demanded that Jewish communities not be allowed to issue regulations forbidding members to outbid one another in renting houses from Christians. See Régné, "Catalogue," *REJ*, LXI, 8 No. 253, 41 No. 458; LXII, 66 No. 650; the 1351 resolutions in *Cortes de los antiguos reinos de León y de Castilla*, II, 90 f.; Baer, *Die Juden*, I, Part 2, p. 174 No. 181. See also Baer's *Studien*, pp. 100 ff.; and my *The Jewish Community*, I, 208 ff.

75. R. Hoeniger, "Zur Geschichte der Juden Deutschlands im früheren Mittelalter," *ZGJD*, [o.s.] I, 136 ff.; A. von Daniels and F. von Gruben, eds., *Das Sächsische Weichbildrecht*, I, 174 f. Arts. cxxxv ff., 436; U. Grotefend, *Geschichte*, pp. 32 (114); H. Fischer, *Die Verfassungsrechtliche Stellung*, p. 13 n. 2; Baer, *Die Juden*, I, Part 2, pp. 298 ff. No. 288; *Ordinaçoens . . . Affonso V*, II, 92; M. F. Santarém, *Memórias e alguns documentos para a história e teoria das Côrtes geraes*, II, 32 ff., 44 f., 48, 51; Scherer, *Die Rechtsverhältnisse*, pp. 275 ff.; Kayserling, *Geschichte der Juden in Portugal*, pp. 65 f.; *supra*, n. 74. See also M. Roberti, "Privilegi forensi degli Ebrei di Ferrara," *Atti e Memorie* of the Accademia di scienze of Padua, n.s. XXIII, 155–66. On the somewhat confused situation in fifteenth-century Mayence, see J. S. Menczel, *Beiträge zur Geschichte der Juden von Mainz im XV. Jahrhundert*, pp. 39 ff. In England, too, according to the charter of 1201, "breaches of right among Jews, except for some major crimes, were to be examined and amended among themselves according to their Law." Rigg, *Select Pleas*, p. 2. It may be noted that German proverbs recognize the specific need for Jewish testimony. While one popular saying contended that "No Jew's oath shall prevail over a Christian man," another agreed that "A Jew shall only be convinced [convicted] by another Jew." See E. Graf and M. Dietherr *et al.*, *Deutsche Rechtssprichwörter*, pp. 457 and 512. On the nature of Jewish testimony and other evidence see the complementary essays by B. Cohen, "Evidence in Jewish Law," *Recueils* of the Société Jean Bodin, XVI, 103–115; and H. Jaeger, "La Preuve judiciaire d'après la tradition rabbinique et patristique," *ibid.*, pp. 415–594. So universally was Jewish judicial self-determination on the basis of Jewish law accepted that Gedaliah ibn Yaḥya's report about its repudiation by a pope appears quite suspect. According to him, when Eugenius IV extended the anti-Jewish provisions of his Spanish bull of 1442 to Italy, he forbade Jews to study Jewish law except in so far as it was incorporated in the five books of Moses. See Ibn Yaḥya's *Shalshelet ha-qabbalah*, Venice, 1587 ed., fol. 115a. In general, the very popes who most severely proscribed the use of the Talmud did not deny the right of Jews to live in accordance with talmudic law, even in Rome, where Jewish judicial autonomy was relatively more circumscribed than elsewhere.

76. C. M. Picciotto, "The Legal Position of the Jews in Pre-Expulsion England," *TJHSE*, IX, 73 f.; H. G. Richardson, *The English Jewry*, pp. 148 ff.; C. Roth, *The Jews of Medieval Oxford*, pp. 127 f.; and S. Cohen, "The Oxford Jewry in the Thirteenth Century," *TJHSE*, XIII, 302. See also L. M. Friedman, *Robert Grosseteste and the Jews;* and *supra*, Vols. IX, pp. 248 n. 15; X, p. 349 n. 62. It must be borne in

mind, however, that as in most other relations between Jews and the thirteenth-century English kings even the justices of the Jews were used for the Crown's fiscal interests. In 1250 Henry III dispatched the justices on a special tour through the Jewish communities (*per totam Angliam*), in order to assess their taxable wealth. See Matthew Paris, *Chronica majora*, ed. by Luard, V, 115 f.; in J. A. Giles's English trans., II, 341. It may also be noted that the Provençal Queen Yolande prohibited, in 1424, all prelates and barons from interfering in litigations among Jews. See E. Camau, "Les Juifs en Provence" in *La Provence à travers les siècles*, p. 329. The purpose of this decree evidently was to strengthen the hand of the special *conservator Judaeorum* in civil matters, just as the queen's decree of 1423 had sought to safeguard the rights of Jewish defendants in criminal prosecutions. *Ibid.*, pp. 328 f.; and *supra*, Vol. X, pp. 88 ff., 342 f. nn. 41–42. That Jews often needed special protection may be gauged from such especially biased resolutions as were adopted by the synod of Liège in 1287, forbidding Christian lawyers, unless specifically ordered by courts, to assist Jewish clients in any litigation. See Mansi, *Collectio*, XXIV, 934 (canon xxviii.7).

77. Lagumina and Lagumina, *Codice diplomatico*, I, 166 f. No. cxxiii, 481 ff. Nos. ccclxxviii–lxxx; and other sources reviewed by F. Lionti in "Le Magistrature presso gli Ebrei di Sicilia," *AS Siciliano*, n.s. IX, 332 f.; and by V. Colorni in his *Legge ebraica e leggi locali*, pp. 313 ff. The dissatisfaction of the Sicilian Jewish communities with their *dienchelele* had already become noticeable in 1429. The government had to appoint special commissioners to collect the funds needed to cover the expenses Chief Judge Mose di Bonavoglia incurred while trying to secure from Alphonso V certain privileges for the Sicilian Jews, including the revocation of an earlier decree obliging them to attend missionary sermons by Fra Matteo di Agrigento. This collection dragged on for more than three years. See Lagumina and Lagumina, I, 397 f. No. cccxxv, 403 f. No. cccxxxii, 414 f. No. cccxxxvi.

78. Scherer, *Die Rechtsverhältnisse*, pp. 254 ff., 261 ff., 277 f.; H. Fischer, *Die Verfassungsrechtliche Stellung der Juden*, pp. 123 ff., 167 ff.; J. Jacobs, *The Jews of Angevin England*, pp. 135 Art. 2 (1190), 212 Art. 2 (1201), 331; Rigg, *Select Pleas*, p. 103; Alphonso X, *Las Siete Partidas*, vii.24, 5, ed. by Lopez, IV, 646; Isambert, *Recueil général*, VI, 222; J. M. Rigg and H. Jenkinson, eds., *Calendar of the Plea Rolls of the Exchequer of the Jews*, passim. See also R. Geyer's comments on the Vienna privileges in "Die Mittelalterlichen Stadtrechte Wiens," *MIOG*, LVIII, 591 ff.

79. Baer, *Die Juden*, I, Part 2, pp. 266 f. No. 275 Art. 7; idem, *Studien*, pp. 53 ff.; Boutaric, *Actes du Parlement*, 1st ser. II, 1 No. 2984; Laurière *et al.*, *Ordonnances des roys*, VII, 226 f., 643 f.; L. Ennen and G. Eckertz, eds., *Quellen . . . Köln*, IV, 90 ff. No. 105, 113 f. No. 129; K. Bauer, *Judenrecht in Köln*, pp. 54 f.; A. F. Riedel, *Codex diplomaticus brandenburgensis*, 1st ser. XIV, 94 No. cxxxiii; W. Heise, *Die Juden in der Mark Brandenburg*, pp. 96 f. Despite their obvious bias in favor of their fellow burghers, however, some municipal judges tried to accord fair treatment to Jewish parties, as illustrated by the fourteenth-century Stendal *Urtheilsbuch*. See *supra*, Vol. IX, p. 340 n. 17. On the evolution in Germany, see also the data assembled by H. Fischer in *Die Verfassungsrechtliche Stellung*, pp. 126 ff. An interesting case was decided by the Parlement of Paris in 1323. The municipal elders of Saverdun had caused the hanging of a Jew caught in an adulterous act with a Christian

woman, but they were fined 1,000 livres for infringing on the jurisdiction of royal officials. This severe fine was confirmed by the Parlement. See Boutaric, 1st ser. II, 491 No. 7026. On the other hand, Tortosa, because of the peculiar circumstances of her annexation, seems to have secured from the outset full jurisdiction over her Jews and maintained it despite Pedro IV's objections. If Sancho IV temporarily yielded to the demands of the Cortes of Valladolid of 1293 that Jews be made to repair exclusively to municipal judges, this storm quickly blew over and Alphonso XI even rejected the more moderate postulates of the Cortes of Madrid of 1329 that at least in criminal cases Jews be sentenced by Christian judges in accordance with the *fueros*. See *Cortes de . . . Castilla*, I, 115 Art. 26, 418 f. Art. 44; Baer's *Studien*, pp. 53 ff.; and J. Amador de los Rios, *Historia social*, II, 62, 129.

80. Rigg, *Select Pleas*, p. 2; Baer, *Die Juden*, I, Part 2, pp. 221 f. No. 227, 340 f. No. 330 Art. 11; Wiener, *Regesten*, p. 36 No. 86; *supra*, Vol. IX, pp. 173 f., 323 n. 44; K. Puchner and G. Wulz, eds., *Die Urkunden der Stadt Nördlingen, 1233–1349;* A. F. Riedel, *Codex diplomaticus brandenburgensis*, 1st ser. III, 381 f. No. lxxv; W. Heise, *Die Juden in der Mark Brandenburg*, pp. 96 f.; the Augsburg City Statute of 1276, Art. xix.1 and 10–12; and the supplement to Art. xxvii.8, cited by Fischer in *Die Verfassungsrechtliche Stellung*, p. 129 n. 4; C. Devic and J. Vaissète, *Histoire générale du Languedoc*, X, Part 1, p. 157 n. xxxv. In 1302 Philip the Fair ordered the seneschal of Saintonge to investigate the case of a Jew accused of having "violently kidnaped some Jewess and raped her." On another occasion he instructed the bailiff of Rouen to prosecute local Jews who had illegally practiced medicine among both Jews and Christians. See C. V. Langlois, "Formulaires et lettres du XIIᵉ, du XIIIᵉ et du XIVᵉ siècle," *Notices et extraits des manuscrits de la Bibliothèque Nationale et autres bibliothèques*, XXXIV, Part 1, pp. 18 No. 10, 19 n. 12.

At times such rivalries were settled by the relative strength of the contestants or the mere unwillingness of one or another to get involved in controversy. When in 1336 a Jew, Schmolke, was imprisoned by the city of Berlin because he had insistently demanded from it the payment of 80 marks, Duke Rudolph of Saxony frankly declared that he did not wish to engage in hostilities with the city on account of Jews; he pronounced Berlin free from any obligation toward Schmolke. See F. Voigt and E. Fidicin, eds., *Urkundenbuch zur Berlinischen Chronik*, p. 70; Heise, pp. 79 f. Occasionally, such jurisdictional disputes could be used as weapons in power struggles. In its protracted controversy with the archbishop the city of Cologne in 1258 made the accusation that, on his order, some Jews "were violently and without judicial authority dragged out of their dwellings and incarcerated in the house of Peter de Cranin." See the mutual recriminations reproduced by F. Keutgen, *Urkunden zur städtischen Verfassungsgeschichte*, pp. 158 ff. No. 147, esp. p. 165 item 20.

81. A. de Boüard, *Actes et lettres de Charles I, roi de Sicile concernant la France (1257–1284)*, pp. 293 f. No. 946; Willy Cohn, "Die Judenpolitik König Karls I. von Sizilien in Anjou und in der Provence," *MGWJ*, LXXIV, 435; A. A. Beugnot, ed., *Les Olim*, II, 322 f. No. i Art. 2; Laurière *et al.*, *Ordonnances des roys*, I, 346; IV, 440 f.; V, 167 f.; Isambert, *Recueil*, II, 681, 747; Boutaric, *Actes du Parlement*, 1st ser. II, 291 No. 5848; T. J. Lacomblet, *Urkundenbuch . . . des Niederrheins*, III, 209 ff. No. 259; K. Bauer, *Judenrecht in Köln*, pp. 93 ff. App. 1; Scherer, *Die Rechtsverhältnisse*, pp. 264 ff.; A. Glaser, *Geschichte der Juden in Strassburg*, p. 12. See also the

document excerpted by C. V. Langlois in *Notices et extraits . . . de la Bibliothèque Nationale*, XXXIV, Part 1, pp. 19 f. No. 14.

The stiffened royal attitude in France is well illustrated by the developments in Orléans. In 1245 Louis IX dismissed his bailiff's complaints against the bishop for having summoned a Jew and forced him to answer certain questions, when the bishop proved that he had merely followed a long-accepted usage. However, a second complaint that an episcopal official had arrested an Orléans Jew, beaten him severely, and brought him to the bishop's palace was overruled only after the bishop had under solemn oath denied the allegation. In 1260 Louis himself rejected any ecclesiastical jurisdiction over converts, who were to be treated like Christian burghers. Matters were more definitely settled by the Parlement's ruling of 1288 which was respected also after the return of the Jews to France in 1359. Curiously, in a civil suit of 1385 it was a Jew, David Levy, who secured a favorable judgment from an episcopal official, but this sentence was annulled by the royal bailiff. See T. Cochard, *La Juiverie d'Orléans du VI*e *au XV*e *siècle; son histoire et son organisation*, pp. 146 ff., 195 App. C, 215 App. R. Similarly outspoken was Emperor Frederick III when, in 1478, he addressed the archbishop of Salzburg in behalf of one Yudel of Radkersburg who had been summoned before the archepiscopal court in connection with a loan due him by a Christian borrower. "We and Our Jewry," the emperor declared, "have been given freedom by the Roman See not to have to render account about either capital or interest except before their regular judges in Our lands." *Monumenta Habsburgica*, published by the Vienna Academy, I, Part 2, pp. 354 f. No. xlviii; Scherer, p. 240.

82. K. Zeumer, ed., *Formulae Merovingici et Carolini aevi*, pp. 309 f.; Aronius, *Regesten*, pp. 30 f. No. 81; *CJ*, i.5, 21; *Les Establissements de St. Louis*, i.133, ed. by P. Viollet, pp. 250 ff.; *Ordenaçoens . . . Affonso V*, II, 502 ff., lxxxviii, Arts. 7–9; III, 41 f., xiii Kayserling, *Geschichte . . . Portugal*, p. 15; excerpts from *Foros* of Santarém and Beja, *ibid.*, pp. 339, 341; *Consuetudines Panormitanae*, xv, in W. von Brünneck, ed., *Siciliens mittelalterliche Stadtrechte*, I, 15; II, 267; N. Ferorelli, *Gli Ebrei*, p. 182; and other sources carefully reviewed by Scherer in *Die Rechtsverhältnisse*, pp. 163 ff. On the relative leniency of the Third Lateran Council see W. Herold's observations in his dissertation, *Die Canones des 3. Lateran-Konzils (1179)* (typescript). Jews were not the only ones whose veracity was doubted by Christians. In fact, Church efforts to the contrary, the villeins were also frequently disqualified from testifying at court. See P. Petot, "Serfs d'Eglise habilités à temoigner en justice," *Cahiers de civilisation médiévale*, III, 191–94.

An interesting illustration of the length to which the rabbis went in disqualifying the testimony of converts is offered by a responsum of the fourteenth-century Barcelona sage, Nissim b. Reuben Gerondi. A Jewish woman was abandoned by her husband who, after adopting Christianity, moved to another town and married a Christian girl. Some time later she learned from another convert that her husband had died. Although the rabbis always strained their ingenuity to enable such a stranded woman (a so-called 'agunah) to remarry, they had to dismiss that testimony, for "we must not believe a Jewish apostate even if he speaks unwittingly because he is less trustworthy than a Gentile." Subsequently the putative widow sent a Christian to the locality of her departed husband promising to pay him for the delivery of a letter to the spouse. As expected, the messenger could not hand the letter to the addressee and was informed by the latter's second wife, who had interveningly remarried, of the death of her first husband. Her story was confirmed by local officials who collected testimony to that effect. Nevertheless, R. Nissim, to whom this complicated case was submitted for final decision, was still hesitant to accept either the original testimony of the convert or the new evidence brought back by the messenger. See his *Resp.*, Metz, 1776 ed., fols. 4b ff. No. 3.

83. Scherer, *Die Rechtsverhältnisse*, pp. 183 Art. xxv, 184 f., 275; Rigg, *Select Pleas*, Intro., p. xii; *Calendar of Patent Rolls, 1272–1281*, pp. 158, 184; M. Adler, *Jews of Medieval England*, pp. 93 f. The disappearance of ordeals, however, the role of which in judicial testimony had rapidly declined since the Carolingian age, greatly reduced this procedural differentiation between Jews and Christians. After many futile efforts, the thirteenth-century Church synods (especially the Fourth Lateran Council of 1215) prohibited any liturgical services in connection with ordeals, and the provincial council of Valencia of 1255 denounced some of them as "superstitious and against God." Mansi, *Collectio*, XXII, 1006 f.; XXIII, 893; *supra*, Vol. IV, pp. 40, 49, 69, 77, 254 f. n. 50. See also Baer, *Die Juden*, I, Part 1, pp. 1025 f., 1042 Art. 10; Part 2, pp. 6 f.; and, by way of comparison, C. Leitmeier, *Die Kirche und die Gottesurteile. Eine rechtshistorische Studie;* and H. Nottarp, *Gottesurteilstudien.*

84. Innocent III, *Epistolae*, vii.186 in *PL*, CCXV, 502 ff.; Grayzel, *The Church*, pp. 58 n. 78, 106; Lagumina and Lagumina, *Codice diplomatico*, II, 494 ff. No. 799; *Ordenaçoens . . . Affonso V*, II, 498 f., lxxxv; 513 f., lxxxxiii, Arts. 1–2; F. Fossati, "Gli Ebrei a Vigevano," *AS Lombardo*, XXX, 203. The medieval debates about the eligibility of Jews for the notarial office are briefly summarized by V. Colorni in *Gli Ebrei nel sistema*, pp. 27 f. Not surprisingly, some German rulers, invoking their overlordship over Jews, claimed the right to annul the latter's deeds. From the mid-fourteenth century on so-called *Tötbriefe* (letters of annulment) were arbitrarily issued to various royal favorites and were used, particularly, as a means of penalizing Jews who had emigrated without special authorization. Scherer, *Die Rechtsverhältnisse*, pp. 300 ff.

Because of the complexities of intergroup litigations and the ensuing impediments to satisfactory commercial relations, Spanish Jews tried to secure special protection for their writs and other rules of evidence. It was to obviate many difficulties that Alphonso X prescribed that, in all interdenominational loan contracts between Jews, Christians, and Moors, the deeds must separately record the debtor and his guarantor. If a debt was repaid, the notary was to delete the respective entry in his registry. Nevertheless, the king decided in 1269 that in litigations between Jews and Christians in Burgos the testimony of two "good" Christian witnesses should suffice. See *Los Códigos españoles*, VI, 225 f.; Baer, *Die Juden*, I, Part 2, pp. 48 f. No. 64, 61 No. 79. On the earlier period see also F. Cantera's observations in "La Judería de Burgos," *Sefarad*, XII, 63; the broader discussion *infra*, Chap. LII, nn. 11–12; and such comparative data as may be derived, for instance from R. Trifone, "I Notai nell'antico diritto napoletano," *Studi in onore di Riccardo Filangieri*, I, 243–58.

CHAPTER XLVIII: OUTSIDER

1. Josephus, *War*, ii.18, 7, 488, ed. and trans. by H. St. J. Thackeray, II, 513; and *supra*, Vols. I, pp. 188, 380 f. n. 29; II, pp. 173, 396 n. 2.

2. *Codex Theodosianus*, iii.7, 2; *CJ* (Codex), i.9, 6, ed. by P. Krüger, II, 61; *Forum Turolii*, ed. by F. Aznar Navarro in the *Colección de documentos para el estudio de la historia de Aragón*, Art. 385; *El Fuero de Teruel*, ed. by M. Gorosch, p. 301 Art. 497; *Forum Conche*, xi.53, ed. by G. H. Allen, I, 72; *Fuero de Usagre*, Art. 395, ed. by R. de Ureña y Smenjaud and A. Bonilla y San Martín, p. 138; F. Baer, *Die Juden*, I, Part 1, pp. 716 f. No. 456, 1037 f.; Part 2, pp. 28 ff. No. 56, 41 No. 61 n. (citing the *fuero* of Soria, Art. 543), 44 No. 63, 99 f. No. 109, 115 No. 125 Art. 72 (citing the *Fuero de Sepúlveda*, Art. 72); Alphonso X's *Las Siete Partidas*, iv.2, 15; vii.2, 9, ed. by Lopez, III, 30 f.; IV, 648 f. As pointed out by Baer (I, Part 2, p. 29), the *fuero* of Usagre had taken over almost verbatim the text of a twelfth-century Portuguese *fuero*. Since Majorca and Navarre had likewise provided for the burning of such culprits (A. Pons, "Los Judíos del reino de Mallorca," *Hispania* [Madrid], XVI, 511 f., 514; Kayserling, *Die Juden in Navarra*, p. 71), this penalty enjoyed fairly universal acceptance in all Iberian kingdoms. See also *supra*, Vol. X, pp. 125, 175, 356 n. 7. Apart from the literature listed there see also E. Martínez Marcos, "Fuentes de la doctrina canónica de la IV Partida del Código del rey Alfonso el Sabio," *Revista española de derecho canónico*, XVIII, 897–926. On the progressive sharpening of the ancient Roman legislation, see the literature cited *supra*, Vol. II, pp. 231 ff., 401 f. n. 24, 411 f. nn. 17–18, to which add S. Solazzi, "Le Unioni di cristiani ed ebrei nelle leggi del Basso Impero," *Atti* of the R. Accademia Pontaniana di scienze morali e politiche . . . di Napoli, LIX, 164–70. See also, more generally, the Nazi-oriented study by E. Rumberg, "Der Aussereheliche geschlechtliche Umgang mit Juden in rechtsgeschichtlicher Darstellung," *Rasse und Recht*, I, 397–407.

3. The decisions of the Roman Rota of 1672, cited by H. Vogelstein and P. Rieger in their *Geschichte der Juden in Rom*, II, 306; S. Foa, *Gli Ebrei nel Monferrato nei secoli XVI e XVII*, pp. 108 f.; M. Roberti, "Privilegi forensi degli Ebrei di Ferrara," *Atti e Memorie* of the Accademia di scienze in Padua, n.s. XXIII, 158, 164 f. No. ii; other Italian data analyzed by V. Colorni, in *Gli Ebrei nel sistema del diritto comune*, pp. 40 f.; *Ordenaçoens Affonso V*, ii.67, pp. 435 ff., v.25; and *supra*, Vol. X, p. 394 nn. 51–52. The *capitoli* submitted in 1456 by the Duke of Milan for papal confirmation included a number of these canonical prohibitions and accusations. See C. Canetta, "Gli Ebrei del ducato milanese," *AS Lombardo*, VIII, 632–35. The kings of Portugal, it may be noted, had the less reason to resist public opinion on this score, since they often refused to listen to the Cortes' anti-Jewish resolutions in matters of fiscal interest to themselves. See E. Prestage's brief analysis of *The Royal Power and the Cortes in Portugal*.

4. *Des Schwabenspiegels Landrechtsbuch*, ed. by H. G. Gengler, p. 211 Art. cclxxii; *Das Stadt- und das Landrechtsbuch Ruprechts von Freysing*, ed. by G. L. von Maurer,

I, 204; G. Kisch, *The Jews in Medieval Germany*, pp. 205 ff., 466 f. n. 106; J. A. Tomaschek, *Deutsches Recht in Oesterreich im 13. Jahrhundert auf Grundlage des Stadtrechtes von Iglau*, pp. 296 f. Art. 58; Aronius, *Regesten*, pp. 244 No. 573, 301 ff. Nos. 724–25, 330 f. No. 771; E. P. Evans, *The Criminal Prosecution and Capital Punishment of Animals*, p. 153; Baer, *Die Juden*, I, Part 2, p. 302 No. 289; G. D. Mansi, ed., *Sacrorum conciliorum . . . collectio*, XXIII, 1174 f. Art. xvii; H. Bärwald, "Die Beschlüsse des Wiener Concil's über die Juden aus dem Jahre 1267," *Jahrbuch für Israeliten*, ed. by J. Wertheim, 5620 (1859–60), pp. 181–208; Bernardino da Feltre's advice to his pupils, cited in "De B. Bernardino Feltriensi," *Acta Sanctorum*, September, VII, 827. Jean Allard's case was cited as a precedent by the seventeenth-century Italian jurist Prospero Farinacci in his *Praxis et Theoricae criminalis pars quarta*, Lyons, 1613 ed., quest. 139 No. 24. See Colorni, *Gli Ebrei nel sistema*, p. 43. The penalties differed, however, from locality to locality; for instance, in Augsburg, Iglau, Mayence, and Prague. See R. His, *Das Strafrecht des deutschen Mittelalters*, II, 149.

The hardening of the canonical attitude was demonstrated by the Dominican Bartolomeo Fumi who, in his *Summa aurea armilla* (enlarged ed. Venice, 1587, Art. 17) written under the impact of the Council of Trent, unequivocally demanded the death penalty. See H. Élie's "Contribution" in *RHR*, CXLII, 94. The related theory of Marquardus de Susannis, formulated in his *Tractatus de Judaeis et usuris* (Frankfort, 1604), was wholly in line with his previously published comprehensive *Tractatus de Judaeis et aliis infidelibus* (Venice, 1558), in which he had contended that the slaying of a Jew was less obnoxious than that of a Christian. See *supra*, Vol. IX, pp. 8, 243 n. 6; and G. Landauer, "Zur Geschichte der Judenrechtswissenschaft," *ZGJD*, II, 258. It may also be noted that burning at the stake was a frequent penalty for other sexual transgressions. See J. R. Reinhard, "Burning at the Stake in Mediaeval Penal Law and Literature," *Speculum*, XVI, 186–209.

The concluding clause in the *Schwabenspiegel*, "for the Christian has denied the Christian faith," is not quite so vital for the understanding of the law as Kisch assumes (p. 467 n. 107). Even when legislator or jurist failed to spell out this motivation everybody realized that the Christian was to be so severely punished because of his offense against the Church's religious demands. Yet, as Kisch himself admits, the Fourth Lateran Council had merely demanded the payment of a fine. Later jurists in quest of legal precedents for the extreme sanction found only such secular sources as the ancient Roman codes of law, rather than canonical legislation. See the data quoted by Kisch himself, *ibid.*, pp. 465 f. n. 105.

5. J. C. Ulrich, *Sammlung jüdischer Geschichten*, pp. 109 ff.; L. Löwenstein, *Geschichte der Juden am Bodensee*, pp. 31, 115 n. 23; F. Singermann, *Die Kennzeichnung der Juden im Mittelalter*, p. 39; *Patent Rolls, 1247–1258*, p. 532; L. Ennen and G. Eckertz, eds., *Quellen . . . Köln*, II, 321 ff. No. 308; K. Bauer, *Judenrecht in Köln*, pp. 25 f.; Baer, *Die Juden*, I, Part 1, pp. 209 ff. No. 171 (1318), 229 ff. No. 179 (1323), 459 ff. No. 317 (1377); Solomon ibn Adret, *Resp.*, IV, No. 311, Piotrkow, 1883 ed., p. 87. A Majorcan Jew was burned in 1381 for having cohabited with a nun. See A. Morel-Fatio, "Notes et documents pour servir à l'histoire des Juifs des Baléares sous la domination aragonaise," *REJ*, IV, 37 No. 22 (from J. Villanueva's *Viage literario a las iglesias de España*, XXI, 219); A. Pons, "Los Judíos del reino de Mallorca durante los siglos XIII y XIV," *Hispania* (Madrid), XVI, 511 f., 514. See also *supra*,

Vol. X, pp. 12 f., 332 n. 15; and, on the risks connected with false accusations, see R. His, *Das Strafrecht des deutschen Mittelalters*, II, 136 ff.

6. L. M. Epstein, "The Institution of Concubinage among the Jews," *PAAJR*, VI, 153–88, esp. p. 185; S. Z. H. Halberstam, ed., "The Ancient Ordinances Adopted in Bologna and Forlì in the Years 1416 and 1418 in Behalf of All of Italy" (Hebrew), *Jubelschrift . . . Graetz*, Hebrew section, p. 60; L. Finkelstein, *Jewish Self-Government in the Middle Ages*, pp. 286 (Hebrew), 294 (English summary); K. Eubel, "Weitere Urkunden zu dem Verhalten der Päpste gegen die Juden," *Römische Quartalschrift*, XVII, 186; *supra*, Vol. IX, pp. 33 ff., 255 f. nn. 34 ff.; Camau, *Les Juifs en Provence*, pp. 310 f.; Moses b. Jacob of Coucy, *Sefer ha-Miṣvot* [*ha-Gadol*] (The Large Book of Commandments), Prohibition No. 112 end, Venice, 1522 ed., sign. iv.5, 4d. (It is not surprising that, when the copy of that edition, now in my possession, was submitted in the early seventeenth century to the well-known papal censor Domenico Irosolimitano, or Hierosolymitano, he deleted this passage. However, as in many other cases, his ink proved less durable than that of the printer and the passage is perfectly legible today.)

As in other interfaith relations the Church tried to arrogate to itself jurisdiction over sexual transgressions by Jews. Such a provision had been inserted in William II's privilege for Palermo of 1171 and repeated in another royal decree for that city in 1333. However, it was specifically denied in the decree for Mazzara of 1327. Similarly, a Ferrara ordinance of 1464 expressly reserved the jurisdiction over a Jew's cohabitation with a Christian woman to the *giudice dei savi*. See J. L. A. Huillard-Bréholles, *Historia diplomatica Friderici Secundi*, IV, 171; B. Lagumina and G. Lagumina, *Codice diplomatico*, I, 47 ff. Nos. xlii–xliii; J. E. Scherer, *Die Rechtsverhältnisse*, pp. 282 f.; M. Roberti, "Privilegi forensi," *Atti e Memorie* of the Accademia di scienze in Padua, n.s. XXIII, 163 f. No. 1. For this reason the Paris Parlement actually fined municipal authorities taking independent action. The state also wished to share in the ensuing judicial fees and fines, a Castilian custumal providing for a fine to be collected even from a Jew cohabiting with an unwed Jewess. See Baer, *Die Juden*, I, Part 2, p. 35 No. 60; *supra*, Vol. X, pp. 128, 332 n. 15, 358 n. 11. Jewish sexual ethics, particularly as they affected the internal relations within the Jewish community, will be discussed in a later chapter.

7. Yehudah b. Samuel, *Sefer Ḥasidim* (Book of the Pious), ed. by J. Wistinetzki, p. 279 No. 1097; [J. B.] Vincent, *Les Juifs en Poitou*, pp. 35 f.; *supra*, n. 4. Needless to say, wherever segregation was fairly complete, it was very difficult long to conceal continuing religious disparity after marriage.

8. S. Z. H. Halberstam and L. Finkelstein, *loc. cit.* (*supra*, n. 6); Meir b. Baruch's *Resp.*, ed. Lwów, fols. 22d ff. No. 310, summarized by I. A. Agus in his *Rabbi Meir of Rothenburg*, pp. 283 ff. No. 246; Baer, *Die Juden*, I, Part 1, pp. 201 f. No. 164.

9. A. Mussafia, "Studien zu den mittelalterlichen Marienlegenden, I–V," *SB*, Vienna, CXV, 87 No. 61; Caesarius of Heisterbach, *Dialogus miraculorum*, ii.23, ed. by J. Strange, I, 92 ff.; F. Vendrell, "La Posición del poeta Juan de Dueñas respecto a los Judíos españoles de su época," *Sefarad*, XVIII, 108–13. Similarly, the Veronese writer Leonardo Montagna urged a beautiful Jewish lady to leave the ghetto and "its accursed and strange people unworthy of keeping you company" and to turn

Christian. See G. Biadego, *Leonardo di Agostino Montagna letterato veronese del secolo XV*. See also, more generally, J. de Mata Carriazo, "Amor y moralidad bajo los Reyes Católicos," *RABM*, IX, 57–76. On the literary theme of Christians seducing Jewish girls see also the data cited by F. Aronstein in "Eine Jüdische Novelle von Grimmelshausen," *ZGJD*, V, 237–41. A well-known case in point is Jessica of *The Merchant of Venice* which, because of the figure of Shylock, was to play such a great role in modern discussions on the Jewish question. At the same time, it ought to be noted that, while scolding his Christian listeners for the *turpitudines* committed by both sexes in cellars, Caesarius of Heisterbach emphasized that these excesses were shocking even to Jewish ears. See Caesarius' homilies cited by A. Hilka in his edition of *Die Wundergeschichten des Caesarius von Heisterbach*, I, 27.

10. Thomas Wykes's *Chronicle, ad 1222*, in *Annales monastici*, ed. by H. R. Luard, IV, 62 f.; and the analysis of these data by F. W. Maitland in his "Deacon and the Jewess," reproduced in *The Collected Papers*, I, 385–406; supplemented from Hebrew sources by I. Abrahams in his " 'The Deacon and the Jewess,' Prefatory Notes," *TJHSE*, VI, 254–76; and C. Roth, *The Jews of Medieval Oxford*, pp. 19 ff. It has rightly been observed that the execution of the Oxford deacon established a precedent for the capital punishment of heretics long before the statute *De heretico comburendo* of 1401. The conversion of another cleric, Robert of Reading, in 1275, was likewise prompted by the study of Hebrew letters and but subsequently led to his marriage to a Jewish woman. See the continuation of Florence of Worcester's *Chronicon ex chronicis*, ed. by B. Thorpe, II, 214; in T. Forrester's English trans., p. 354; and the Jewish sources cited by Abrahams, pp. 256 ff. Not surprisingly, some later chroniclers connected Robert's conversion with the expulsion of Jews from England. This is merely one more instance of the biographical-anecdotal type of historiography which reigned supreme in the older literature. See also C. Roth, *A History of the Jews in England*, pp. 83, 273 f. On other proselytes and proselytism in England and elsewhere, see *supra*, Vol. IX, pp. 24, 251 n. 24.

11. E. Camau, *Les Juifs en Provence*, pp. 310 f.; B. Cecchetti, *La Repubblica di Venezia e la Corte di Roma*, II, 12 ff. doc. iv, 100 ff. doc. ii; *Chronique de quatre premiers Valois (1327–1393)*, ed. by S. Luce, pp. 294 f. See also the latter's "Les Juifs sous Charles V et le fonds hébraïque du Trésor de Chartes, en 1372," *RH*, VII, 365 f.; and *infra*, Chap. L, n. 40. On the Ratisbon conditions, see R. Straus, *Urkunden und Aktenstücke zur Geschichte der Juden in Regensburg 1453–1738*, pp. 11 ff. Nos. 44–47, 14 No. 58, 46 No. 168 (24); W. Grau, *Antisemitismus im späten Mittelalter*, pp. 204 f., 304 f.; M. Stern, "Aus Regensburg," *JJLG*, XXII, 25 f. It stands to reason that even in Ratisbon many more cases remained undetected than prosecuted. See also *supra*, Vol. IX, pp. 127 ff., 306 n. 35.

12. Baer, *Die Juden*, I, Part 1, p. 211 No. 171; Nikolaus von Popplau (Nicholas of Popielowo) in J. Liske's Spanish version, *Viajes de estrangeros por España y Portugal*, p. 47; *supra*, Vol. X, pp. 283, 286, 291 f., 391 n. 46; M. de Maulde, *Les Juifs dans les états français du Saint-Siège*, pp. 17 f., L. Batlle y Prats, "Ordenaciones relativos a los Judíos gerundenses," *Homenaje Millás*, I, 84 f.; A. Ciscato, *Gli Ebrei in Padova (1300–1800)*, pp. 162 f., 282 f. No. xxiv; C. Invernizzi, "Gli Ebrei a Pavia. Contributo alla storia dell'Ebraismo nel ducato di Milano," *Bollettino* of the Società Pavese di storia patria, V, 194. See also, more generally, P. Browe, *Beiträge zur Sexu-*

alethik des Mittelalters, which deals, however, mainly with the attitudes to marriage of both canonists and the public.

13. A. Steinberg, *Studien zur Geschichte der Juden in der Schweiz während des Mittelalters,* p. 106; G. A. Tzschoppe and G. A. Stenzel, eds., *Urkundensammlung . . . Schlesien,* p. 251 n. 1; Isaac b. Moses 'Arama, *'Aqedat Yiṣḥaq* (Sacrifice of Isaac; an ethical treatise), 1.20, Lwów, 1868 ed., fol. 162a; I. Abrahams, *Jewish Life in the Middle Ages,* 2d ed., pp. 87 ff., 193 ff. The location of a brothel near the Jewish quarter was discussed in 1567 by the Jews and the city council of Alessandria. See S. Foa, "Gli Ebrei in Alessandria," *RMI,* XXIII, 550 n. 2. Abrahams supplies but meager data on Jewish prostitution in the Middle Ages and the early modern period, for both the Jewish and the non-Jewish sources are rather inarticulate about this aspect of life. Yet occasionally we even hear of a rabbi who considered relations with prostitutes, if indulged in by bachelors, a lesser evil than adultery with Jewish women, or any intercourse with Gentiles. Only in the sixteenth and seventeenth centuries did this problem become sufficiently urgent, however, for several communities to take specific action. See my *The Jewish Community,* II, 313 f.; III, 205 f. nn. 26–27.

14. Innocent III's epistle to Philip Augustus of France, dated January 16, 1205, in his *Epistolae* in *PL,* CCXV, 502 No. 186; Grayzel, *The Church,* pp. 106 f. No. 14; Richard of Devizes, *De rebus gestis Ricardi Primi,* ed. by R. Howlett, p. 435 (J. Jacobs, *The Jews of Angevin England,* p. 152); C. Arnaud, *Essai sur la condition des Juifs en Provence, au moyen âge,* pp. 38 f.; M. Stern, "Aus Regensburg," *JJLG,* XXII, 1 f. These aspects of segregation have often been treated in connection with the legislation of various countries *supra,* Vols. III–IV and IX–X, and they need not be repeated here.

15. See *supra,* Vols. II, pp. 148 f.; IV, pp. 219 f., 265, 392 n. 12, 411 n. 66; IX, pp. 32 ff.; Baer, *Die Juden,* I, Part 1, pp. 321 ff. No. 229, 426 ff. No. 293; T. López Mata, "Morería y judería," *BAH,* CXXIX, 335–84; Abu'l Qasim an-Naṣib ibn Hauqal, *Kitab al-Masalik w'al-mamalik* (Viae et regnae), ed. by M. J. de Goeje; F. Cantera, "La Judería de Burgos," *Sefarad,* XII, 59–104; Nissim b Reuben Gerondi, *Resp.,* Metz, 1776 ed., fol. 32b f. No. 50. The location of the Roman ghetto may have shifted somewhat from ancient to medieval times, but its proximity to the temperamental river Tiber remained unaltered despite the difficulties connected with that habitation.

The medieval Church did not formally demand territorial segregation as a sign of Jewish inferiority, but rather out of fear of Jewish influence leading to Christian infidelity or heresy. It was doubly prompted, therefore, to leave the implementation of its canons to both Jewish isolationism and the popular desire to keep aloof from Jews, which ultimately influenced the states to issue increasingly stringent rules. Apart from the sweeping demands, temporarily included in Eugenius IV's bull of 1442, canon law did not embrace much specific legislation concerning Jewish quarters until the Counter Reformation decrees of 1555 and after.

16. F. Carreras y Candi, "Evolució histórica dels Juheus y juheisants barcelonins," *Estudis universitaris catalans,* III, 404; J. Sanchez Real, "La Judería de Tarragona," *Sefarad,* XI, 340; M. Kayserling, *Die Juden in Navarra, den Baskenlaendern und auf*

den Balearen, pp. 38 ff.; L. Torres Balbás, "Mozarabías y juderías de las ciudades his-
panomusulmanas," *Al-Andalus,* XIX, 172–97; Baer, *Die Juden,* I, Part 2, pp. 101 f.
No. 112; and *supra,* Vol. X, pp. 153 f., 369 f. n. 42.

There also were various transitional stages. Even generally friendly James I of
Aragon in 1273 prohibited Jews and Christians from living together in the same
house. See F. de Bofarull y Sans, *Los Judíos en el territorio de Barcelona,* p. 104 No.
cxxii. On the other hand, when he first assigned a quarter to the Jews of newly
conquered Valencia, James doubtless pursued primarily the aim of pacifying this
rebellious city. See I. Burns, "Social Riots on the Christian-Moslem Frontier (Thirteenth-Century Valencia)," *AHR,* LXVI, 378–400. The king certainly did not foresee
that, after the severe disturbances started by some sailors in Valencia in 1391, this
quarter would turn into a regular technical ghetto. See Baer, *Die Juden,* I, Part 1,
pp. 605 ff. Nos. 415–16; F. Danvila,, "El Robo de la judería de Valencia en 1391,"
BAH, VIII, 358–79; I. Loeb, "Le Sac des juiveries de Valence et de Madrid en 1391,"
REJ, XIII, 239–47 (analyzing the documentary materials supplied by the latter). On
Jewish quarters in Murcia, Seville, and others see J. Villanueva, ed., "Documentos de
la época de D. Alfonso el Sabio," *Memorial histórico español,* published by the Academia de la Historia, I, 13 ff. No. viii, 278 ff. No. cxxviii, esp. p. 285.

17. Baer, *Die Juden,* I, Part 1, pp. 734 f. No. 465 (1398), 802 ff. No. 495 (1414),
964 ff. No. 590 (1336); Part 2, pp. 264 f. No. 275 Art. 1 (1412), 312 No. 296 (1443),
346 f. No. 335 (1480), 359 f. No. 345 (1484), 422 f. No. 387 (1484, 1487); the texts of
the four Gerona decrees of 1445–48, reproduced in L. Batlle y Prats's essay in *Homenaje Millás,* I, 88 ff. As pointed out by Baer, the decree of 1443 (also available in
E. H. Lindo's English trans. in *The History of the Jews of Spain and Portugal,* pp.
221 ff.) is essentially but a renewal of the provisions of 1412. But there was a new
emphasis upon the Jews and Moors being assigned new quarters "in populous and
suitable districts, where they can live and reside commodiously." See the text in J.
Amador de los Rios, *Historia social,* III, 588 f.

18. Baer, *Die Juden,* I, Part 1, pp. 795 f. No. 491, 896 ff. No. 554, 910 f. No. 560;
Part 2, p. 542 No. 425; L. Suárez Fernández, ed., *Documentos acerca de la expulsión
de los Judíos,* pp. 133 f. No. 25 (1477), 212 f. No. 63 (1483), 299 f. No. 110 (1488), 321 f.
No. 126 (1489), 331 f. No. 133 (1489), 347 f. No. 144 (1490), 367 f. No. 161 (1491). Further difficulties arose in connection with the removal of Moorish houses from the
Jewish quarter, as well as from rent gouging by house owners in the growingly
crowded ghettos. In 1487 Ferdinand and Isabella forbade the general of the Hieron-
ymite order to compel the Guadalajara Jews to acquire the Moorish houses, while in
1491 they ordered the Christian house owners of Cáceres to lower the rents in the
Jewish quarter established by royal order but thirteen years before. *Ibid.,* pp. 140 f.
No. 29, 286 f. No. 102, 351 f. No. 148. On the location of the Saragossan ghetto, see L.
Torres Balbás, "La Judería de Zaragoza y su baño," *Al-Andalus,* XXI, 172–90. Other
protective decrees included provisions that newly constructed Christian houses must
not infringe on the walls of Jewish quarters. Such a regulation was issued, for instance, in Fraga. See J. Salarrullana de Dios, "Estudios históricos acerca de la ciudad
de Fraga," *RABM,* XL, 78.

19. *Ordenaçoens Affonso V,* ii.80, 1–11, pp. 471 ff.; M. Kayserling, *Geschichte der
Juden in Portugal,* pp. 49 ff. Here we find a fairly complete enumeration of the fif-

teenth-century *juderías* in the whole realm. See also *supra*, Vol. X, pp. 211 f., 394 n. 52. Unfortunately, the extant nonnormative sources but rarely refer to the Jewish quarters, and there is no way of telling to what extent the severe ordinance of 1412 was obeyed, and what kind of penalties were actually inflicted on transgressors during the remaining eighty-four years of legalized Jewish settlement in the country.

20. N. Ferorelli, *Gli Ebrei nell'Italia meridionale*, pp. 68 f., 100, 104 n. 2; Lagumina and Lagumina, *Codice diplomatico*, I, 35 f. No. xxxv; U. Cassuto, *Gli Ebrei a Firenze nell'età del Rinascimento*, pp. 208 ff.; idem, "I Più antichi capitoli del ghetto di Firenze," *RI*, IX, 203–211; X, 33–40, 71–79; F. Gabotto, "Per una storia degli Israeliti in Piemonte nel medio evo, I: Israeliti a Torino fra il 1425 e il 1430," *Vessillo israelitico*, LXV, 433–37; *Historiae patriae monumenta*, ed. under the sponsorship of King Charles Albert, I (Leges municipales), cols. 222b, 466 ff., 474a; M. D. Anfossi, *Gli Ebrei in Piemonte*, pp. 3 ff.; G. Volino, *Condizione giuridica degli Ebrei in Piemonte*, pp. 19 f.; and, more generally, V. Colorni, *Gli Ebrei nel sistema*, pp. 54 ff.; and G. Volli's brief sketch, "I Ghetti d'Italia,' *RMI*, XV, 22–30, mainly dealing with the modern period. In Padua, too, Jews dwelt in various parts of town, giving rise in 1541 to the complaint of the city council that some of them, "not satisfied to live in their accustomed place together with the other Hebrews, had displayed the audacity of renting houses among Christians in the most beautiful sections of town to the offense of our Lord and to little honor for this city." See Ciscato, *Gli Ebrei in Padova*, pp. 74 ff. Even in Sicily, where both the size of the Jewish settlements and traditions of the Muslim domination induced most Jews to reside in their own quarters, these streets so little resembled technical ghettos that, as the brothers Lagumina have observed (p. x), it was not infrequent to find in them Christian dwellings and even buildings consecrated to Catholic worship. On the situation in Venice and the impetus it gave to the new attitude toward technical ghettos, see L. A. Schiavi, "Gli Ebrei a Venezia e nelle sue colonie," *Nuova Antologia*, CXXXI, 322 f.

The origin of the term "ghetto" from that Venetian location has long been both asserted and rejected. It will suffice to quote here the more recent studies by R. Giacomelli, "Ghetto," *Archivum romanicum*, XVI, 556–63; supplemented by him in "Ancora di 'ghetto,' " *ibid.*, XVII, 415–20; and "L'Origine di 'ghetto,' " *ibid.*, XIX, 443–50, the latter in reply to C. Roth, "The Origin of 'Ghetto': a Final Word," *Romania*, LX, 67–76, 144; and the debate between J. A. Joffe and L. Spitzer on "The Origin of the Word Ghetto," *Yivo Annual of Jewish Social Science*, I, 260–73 (originally published in Yiddish in the *YIVO Filologishe Shriftn*, I–II). Joffe suggested the origin of the term from the Yiddish *gehegter*, i.e., hedged-in plot, similar to the Italian *seraglio* used for the Jewish quarter in Rome, while Spitzer rejects this etymology because "one should strive to explain the word on the basis of the language in question," i.e., Italian. Spitzer's objection also holds substantially true with respect to the more recent suggestion by G. (J.) B. Sermoneta, "Regarding the Origin of the Word 'Ghetto' " (Hebrew), *Tarbiz*, XXXII, 195–206. Pointing out that the term had already appeared in a responsum written by David ha-Kohen of Corfu before 1516 (see his *Resp.*, Constantinople, 1538 ed., No. viii), Sermoneta argues that this designation must have originated from the crowding of Spanish Jewish refugees in the Genoa *quay*, through a subsequent mutation in the Spanish pronunciation before it returned to Italy. Even in Venice this *ghetto nuovo* did not embrace all Jews, however; many lived also in the *ghetto vecchio*. Such multiplicity of Jewish quarters often became necessary both because of sudden increases in the Jewish population and because of certain historic factors, such as the city's division between two masters. This certainly was the case in the ancient community of Narbonne, whose two Jewish quarters, popularly called *Jusaigas*, paid allegiance and taxes to the archbishop and viscount, respectively. See J. Régné, "Étude sur la condition des Juifs de Narbonne du Ve au XIVe siècle," *REJ*, LVIII, 76 ff., 81 ff., 92 ff., 101 ff., 213 ff.; A. Dupont, *Les Cités de la Narbonnaise première depuis les invasions germaniques*, pp. 432, 527 f. (offers a good description of the two Jewish quarters); and, more generally, P. Carbonnel's *Histoire de Narbonne*.

21. A. Crémieux, "Les Juifs de Marseille au moyen âge," *REJ*, XLVI, 29 n. 2; C. Arnaud, *Essai sur la condition des Juifs en Provence*, pp. 41 f.; De Maulde, *Les Juifs dans les états français*, pp. 36 ff.; L. Bardinet, "La Condition civile des Juifs du Comtat Venaissin pendant le séjour des papes à Avignon (1309–1376)," *RH*, XII, 1–47; idem, "Condition civile des Juifs du Comtat Venaissin pendant le XVe siècle (1409–1513)," *REJ*, VI, 1–40; idem, "Antiquité et organisation des juiveries du Comtat Venaissin," *ibid.*, I, 262–92.

22. J. Jacobs, *The Jews of Angevin England*, p. 13; M. Weinbaum, *London unter Eduard I. und II.*, I, 185; M. Adler, *Jews of Medieval England*, pp. 131, 178 f; J. W. F. Hill, *Medieval Lincoln*, pp. 233 f.; I. Herrmann *et al.*, *Das Prager Ghetto*, illustrated by A. Kašpar (also in Czech). See also *supra*, Vol. IX, pp. 35 f., 222, 256 n. 38, 344 f. n. 30; and, on the situation in Cologne, A. Kober's *Cologne*, pp. 82 ff.; and the document reproduced by E. Weyden in his *Geschichte der Juden in Köln am Rhein*, pp. 372 f. No. 23a.

23. R. Anchel, "The Early History of the Jewish Quarters in Paris," *JSS*, II, 60 (also in French in his *Les Juifs de France*, p. 77); A. Glaser, *Geschichte der Juden in Strassburg*, p. 13; P. Lefèvre, "À propos du trafic de l'argent exercé par les Juifs de Bruxelles au XIVe siècle," *RBPH*, IX, 904 f.; V. Preuenhueber, ed., *Annales Styrenses*, p. 58; J. E. Scherer, *Die Rechtsverhältnisse*, pp. 115 f.; *supra*, Vol. X, p. 229; Ellen Littmann, *Studien zur Wiederaufnahme der Juden durch die deutschen Städte nach dem Schwarzen Tode, passim;* Aronius, *Regesten*, pp. 128 f. No. 301, 133 ff. No. 312, 164 f. No. 371; A. Kober, *Cologne* (Jewish Communities Series), p. 83; O. Stobbe, *Die Juden*, pp. 94, 102, 176 f., 275 f. No. 170. See also M. Szulwas (Shulvass), *Die Juden in Würzburg während des Mittelalters*, pp. 14 ff.; and, on the *vicus judaeorum*, mentioned in Rheims as early as 1103, P. Varin, *Archives administratives et législatives de la ville de Reims*, 1st ser. I, 906 No. cccliii n. 1. Another locality bearing the name of Judendorf is discussed by H. Tykocinski in M. Brann *et al.*, eds., *Germania Judaica*, I, 137 f.

A long list of medieval German cities recorded to have embraced one or more Jewish quarters, together with the sources and monographic literature thereon until 1920, is included in A. Kober's intro. to his ed. of the *Grundbuch des Kölner Judenviertels 1135–1425*, pp. 9–21. Kober seems too readily to discount, however, the continuity of these Jewish quarters from ancient times. While there doubtless were many interruptions in the life of any organized Jewish community, the few underground survivors or subsequent arrivals may well have resumed where their more numerous ancestors had left off. Anchel's observation concerning the Paris quarters probably holds true also for many a Rhenish community, particularly that of Cologne, whose Jewish communal organs had twice been addressed by Emperor Constantine, in 321 and 331, and whose medieval Jewish street (*inter Judeos*), first mentioned under Archbishop Anno II (1056–75; Aronius, pp. 2 f. No. 2, 68 No. 163), was among the oldest German ghettos on record. Its synagogue, destroyed during the massacre of 1096, may actually have dated back to the ninth century. The fact that we do not possess the intervening links may be owing entirely to our general paucity of information concerning Cologne Jewry between the fourth and the eleventh centuries.

To a lesser extent the same holds true also of the Jewish quarters in Vienna and elsewhere, notwithstanding the arguments to the contrary, really aimed at the alleged presence of an *enclosed* Jewish quarter in ancient Vindobona, presented by I. Schwarz in *Das Wiener Ghetto*, p. 29. See also H. Planitz's succinct remarks in *Die Deutsche Stadt*, p. 281; and on Switzerland, A. Steinberg's *Studien*, pp. 98 ff.; as well as, from a different angle, W. Stoffers, *Juden und Ghetto in der deutschen Literatur bis zum Ausgang des Weltkrieges*, which, however, supplies data mainly from more recent centuries.

Of a different order, of course, were the French restrictions limiting Jewish residences to larger cities possessing charters from a king or baron. Upon their readmission to France in 1315, Jews were allowed to return only to those localities which their coreligionists had inhabited before the expulsion of 1306. A sharp English decree of April 23, 1269, restricted Jewish residences to localities "where there exists a Jewish community or a chirographs' *arca*." See N. Brussel, *Nouvel examen de l'usage général des fiefs*, p. 601; G. Saige, "De la condition des Juifs dans le comté de Toulouse avant le XIVᵉ siècle," *BEC*, XXXIX, 269 f.; E. J. Laurière *et al.*, *Ordonnances des roys*, I, 596; Grayzel, *The Church*, p. 60; *Close Rolls, 1268–1272*, p. 116; and *supra*, Vol. X, pp. 68, 106, 331 n. 15, 349 n. 62.

24. C. T. Gemeiner, *Reichsstadt Regensburgische Chronik*, III, 581, 837 f.; IV, 342 f.; M. Stern, *Der Regensburger Judenprozess 1476–1480*, pp. 6 f., 17 ff.; W. Grau, *Antisemitismus im späten Mittelalter*, pp. 224 ff. See also A. Schmetzer's description of "Die Regensburger Judenstadt," *ZGJD*, III, 18–39; and, more generally, A. Pinthus's "Studien über die bauliche Entwicklung der Judengassen in den deutschen Städten," *ibid.*, II, 101–130, 197–217, 284–300. The general problems of the structure of Jewish quarters and their internal administration will be discussed in later chapters.

25. K. N. Sathas, *Hellenika anekdota* (Greek Stories), I, xxvi, cited by I. Abrahams, *Jewish Life in the Middle Ages*, 2d ed., p. 298; Lagumina and Lagumina, *Codice diplomatico*, I, 423 ff. No. cccxliv; and particularly, *supra*, Vol. IX, pp. 27 ff., 253 ff. nn. 28 ff. On Frederick II's ukase see the text reproduced in J. L. A. Huillard-Bréholles, *Historia diplomatica Friderici Secundi*, II, 178; R. Straus, *Die Juden im Königreich Sizilien*, pp. 104 f. Because of the very extremes of the 1221 decree, however, Jews and Moors, together amounting to a large segment of the Sicilian population, were able effectively to sabotage it.

26. Isaac b. Moses Or Zaru'a, *Sefer Or Zaru'a*, ii.84, Zhitomir, 1862 ed., I, fol. 20a; Meir b. Baruch of Rothenburg, *Resp.*, Berlin, 1891 ed., p. 8 No. 28; Benjamin b. Abraham 'Anav, *Ototenu lo ra'inu* (We have Not Seen Our Signs), reprinted in S. Bernfeld's anthology, *Sefer ha-Dema'ot* (Book of Tears: Events, Decrees, Persecutions

and Massacres), I, 262 ff. The dates of these statements, of which the first two are verbatim repetitions, are uncertain. R. Meir doubtless tacitly quoted his teacher, Or Zaru'a, who had come to France not long after the Lateran canon had been reinforced by Innocent III's epistle to the French episcopate and the ensuing order by Philip Augustus that two honorable men be appointed in each city to supervise the Jewish seal and wheel (1215–19). See the texts in Grayzel, *The Church*, pp. 140 f. No. 31; Laurière *et al., Ordonnances,* I, 45 item 8. Later Meir himself also visited France, where he apparently witnessed the disputation between R. Yeḥiel of Paris and Nicholas Donin and the burning of the Talmud (1240–42). This sojourn may have persuaded him to include R. Isaac's decision in one of his own responsa, perhaps written in answer to a similar question. See H. Graetz, *Geschichte*, 4th ed., VII, 405 ff., 409 Note 5; *supra*, Vol. IX, pp. 65 ff., 80 ff., 270 f. nn. 13–14, 278 f. nn. 31–33.

Though not yet using the term, *ot ha-qalon* (badge of shame), which was to come into vogue much later when Jews saw in it primarily a symbol of willful degradation, Benjamin's poem, through its *incipit* and reiterated emphasis on signs and clothing, almost certainly refers to the badge. It may have been a response to Alexander IV's renewed insistence in 1257 on the provisions of the Lateran canon, as suggested by Vogelstein and Rieger in their *Geschichte der Juden in Rom*, I, 240, or to that of 1269, as proposed by A. Berliner in his work under the same title, II, Part 1, p. 34. In neither case, however, can this poem be adduced as conclusive evidence for the introduction of the badge into the papal capital itself (see Berliner; and V. Colorni, *Gli Ebrei nel sistema*, p. 50), for which we possess no other testimony until a later date. It certainly was not unusual for decisions of a universal council not to be implemented in the center of Roman Christianity itself. At any rate no detailed regulations are recorded in Rome until the municipal ordinance of 1360, amplified in the decree of 1402, which enumerated the streets in which the Jews were *not* obliged to wear red cloaks. However, in 1360, a general exemption was granted to licensed physicians. Other individual exemptions were enacted in either senatorial or papal decrees from the fourteenth century on. See Vogelstein and Rieger, I, 335 f.; M. Stern's *Urkundliche Beiträge,* I, *passim;* and F. Singermann's dissertation, *Die Kennzeichnung der Juden im Mittelalter*, pp. 28 ff. The need for distinguishing marks was probably greater in Italy than in the northern countries, since in both their physique and their general attire Italian Renaissance Jews seem to have greatly resembled their non-Jewish neighbors. See M. A. Shulvass, *Ḥayye ha-Yehudim be-Italiah* (Jewish Life in Renaissance Italy), pp. 29 ff., 171 ff.; and *infra*, Chap. LVII.

27. T. Rymer and R. Sanderson, eds., *Foedera*, I, Part 1, p. 151 (1218); J. M. Rigg, *Select Pleas*, pp. xlviii f. (1253); Edward I's *Statutum de judeismo* in A. Luders *et al.,* eds., *Statutes of the Realm*, I, 221 f. (1275); H. G. Richardson, *The English Jewry*, pp. 178 ff., 191 ff. That some English Jews actually wore on their garments miniatures of the Two Tables of the Decalogue is illustrated by a few thirteenth-century English manuscripts depicting contemporary Jews. See C. Roth, "Portraits and Caricatures of Medieval English Jews" (1950), reprinted in his *Essays and Portraits in Anglo-Jewish History*, pp. 22–25 and Fig. 3 facing p. 51. In addition to tables or wheels, English Jews often wore cone-shaped hats of the Continental variety, such as appear in at least one of the extant medieval Jewish caricatures in England. See the frontispiece to M. Adler's *Jews of Medieval England*, with his comments thereon, p. 20; and C. Roth, *A History of the Jews in England*, pp. 95 f., esp. n. 1.

28. Alphonso X, *Las Siete Partidas*, vii.24, 11, ed. by Lopez, IV, 649; Baer, *Die Juden*, I, Part 1, pp. 331 No. 237 (1348), 373 f. No. 265 (1360–63), 717 No. 456 (1393), 733 No. 464 (1397), 828 No. 513 (1415), 848 No. 527 Art. 7 (1419), 907 No. 557 (1483), etc.; Part 2, pp. 24 No. 66 (1219), 48 No. 63 (1256–65), 120 No. 133 Art. 7, 131 No. 138 Art. 26 (both 1313), 257 No. 268 (1405), 268 f. No. 275 Arts. 14 and 18, as well as note (1412–13), 302 f. No. 290 (1437), 330 No. 318 Art. 100 (1465); Régné, "Catalogue," in *REJ*, LXI, 30 f. Nos. 390, 392, and 394–95 (James I's 1268 privileges for the communities of Barcelona, Gerona, Perpignan, and Montpellier); U. Robert, "Étude historique et archéologique sur la roue des Juifs depuis le XII⁰ siècle," *REJ*, VI, 81 ff., esp. p. 93; L. Suárez Fernández, *Documentos acerca de la expulsión*, pp. 141 ff. No. 30. Even in the thirteenth century, however, we hear of isolated cases of Jews severely punished for failure to wear badges. See *supra*, Vol. X, pp. 126, 134.

The problem of the badge was complicated in Spain by the generally futile efforts of the authorities, both Christian and Jewish, to stem the excessive display of costly garments, particularly by wealthy women of both denominations. See Baer, I, Part 2, pp. 56 No. 72 Art. 26 (1258), 60 No. 78 Art. 26 (1268), 340 No. 330 Art. 34 (1476), etc. Jewish leaders were ready to cooperate in anti-luxury drives, but they resented the singling out of Jews through badges and often spent substantial sums to stave it off. An interesting controversy on this score is recorded in a responsum by Solomon ibn Adret (V, 69 No. 183). After the elders of an unnamed locality had succeeded, through proper *douceurs*, to secure the reduction of the required badge to half its original size, two members balked against paying their share in the communal assessment and argued that they should have been consulted in advance. Although the two men had hoped to secure total personal exemptions, they were informed by the rabbi that royal grants of immunity from taxation did not free contributors from their share in communal expenditures accruing to their benefit. See also P. Vidal, "Les Juifs des anciens comtés de Roussillon et de Cerdagne," *REJ*, XV, 48; L. Suárez Fernández, pp. 329 f. No. 132.

29. *Ordenaçoens Affonso V*, ii.86, pp. 499 ff.; B. de Brito *et al.*, eds., *Monarchia lusitana (lusytana)*, I, v.3, p. 244; VIII, 243; J. Mendes dos Remedios, *Os Judeus em Portugal*, pp. 146 f.; Kayserling, *Geschichte der Juden in Portugal*, pp. 4 f., 51 ff.; and other sources cited by Singermann in *Die Kennzeichnung*, pp. 22 ff. See also *supra*, Vol. X, pp. 162, 372 f. n. 50.

30. L. Ménard, *Histoire civile . . . de la ville de Nismes*, II, 21 f. No. xvi, Preuves p. 25 No. xv; A. de Boüard, *Actes*, pp. 173 f. Nos. 643, 645; Willy Cohn in *MGWJ*, LXXIV, 431; C. Arnaud, *Essai sur la condition des Juifs*, pp. 49 ff.; E. Camau, *Les Juifs en Provence*, pp. 290 ff., 301; *supra*, Vol. IX, pp. 29 f., 254 n. 31. Philip the Tall's ordinance stresses primarily the stereotyped argument of sexual promiscuity, "cases of which, it is said, occur frequently," while the *Anciennes coutumes d'Alais*, reproduced in the Appendix to A. A. Beugnot's *Olim*, III, Part 2, pp. 1458 ff., esp. pp. 1480 ff. Art. lv, reminded the Jews that they were tolerated only "because of their humble state." Promulgated by the local lord and his nephew for the people of Alais, this custumal generally mouthed, especially in Jewish matters, the usual ecclesiastical phrases. The Jewish badge, it may be noted, also loomed large to the ever greedy administration of Alphonse de Poitiers. See the letters published by A. Molinier in his ed. of the *Correspondance administrative d'Alphonse de Poitiers*, esp. I,

650 ff. Nos. 1003, 1005, and 1008. See also the decrees of 1229, 1269, and 1362 in F. A. Isambert *et al.*, *Recueil général*, II, 234, 344; Laurière *et al.*, *Ordonnances*, III, 603 f.; and the curious penalty of wine offerings reported by S. Luce in "Les Juifs sous Charles V," *RH*, VII, 365. See also the rather good-looking conical hats depicted in an illuminated Cluny MS of *ca.* 1100 and analyzed by M. Schapiro in *The Parma Ildefonsus*, Figures 6–7 (also listing other graphic representations of Jewish hats in medieval MSS; p. 26 n. 71). In many other representations in that MS, however, Jews are sufficiently distinguished by their pronouncedly black hair. The fullest information on both the French legislation and actual practice is offered by the seventy-year-old volume by U. Robert, *Les Signes d'infamie au moyen âge*. Many further details may be culled from the various monographs pertaining to medieval French communities, including the essays in *REJ*. See the numerous entries in the *index* to its first fifty vols., pp. 312 ff. *s.v.* Roue, rouelle. On the fiscal aspects see also *infra*, Chap. LIV.

31. See the reproduction of the Landshut MS in R. Straus, "Ein Landshuter Judeneid," *ZGJD*, V, 42–49; Gregory IX's *Registres*, ed. by Auvray, I, 658 No. 1159; C. Rodenberg, ed., *Epistolae saeculi XIII*, I, 414 f. No. 515; Grayzel, *The Church*, pp. 198 f. No. 69; *Schwabenspiegel*, ccxiv, Art. 10, ed. by Gengler, p. 177; U. F. Kopp, *Bilder und Schriften der Vorzeit*, I, 94 (with illustration); A. Würfel, *Historische Nachrichten von der Juden-Gemeinde . . . Nürnberg*, pp. 24 f.; Stobbe, *Die Juden*, pp. 173 ff., 273 ff. Nos. 165–69; *supra*, Vol. IX, p. 252 n. 26; and *infra*, n. 32. In Cologne, too, the hostile artist who decorated the cathedral choir about 1340 merely depicted Jews wearing conical hats. Only the decrees of 1384 and 1404 for the newly resettled Jews prescribed their distinguishing attire in full detail. See A. Kober, *Cologne*, p. 25; K. Bauer, *Judenrecht in Köln*, pp. 98 ff. App. 3; C. Brisch, *Geschichte der Juden in Cöln*, II, 26 ff. Evidently, here, too, voluntary practice long antedated the legal enforcement.

32. P. von Stetten, *Geschichte der Heil. Röm. Reichs-Freyen Stadt Augspurg*, I, 159; A. F. Pribram, ed., *Urkunden und Akten zur Geschichte der Juden in Wien*, I, 10 ff. On the equally belated regulations issued by Swiss cities, see A. Steinberg, *Studien zur Geschichte der Juden in der Schweiz*, p. 119. Guido Kisch refers to hundreds of illuminated manuscripts of the Middle Ages where Jews are "pictured in different social settings, appearing even before emperors and high Church dignitaries. In spite of their Jewish attributes, that is, beard and hat only, their apparel, carriage and gestures, completely dignified, show them to have been figures far from debased in the conception of the non-Jewish artists." See his "The Yellow Badge in History," *HJ*, IV, 95–144, esp. p. 107. It is, of course, less surprising to find Rabbi Moses Arragel, collaborator in the Spanish translation of Scripture which came to be known as the Alba Bible, depicted as an upstanding scholar. See *supra*, Vols. IX, pp. 30 f., 254 nn. 32–33; X, pp. 188, 382 f. n. 25. To the literature listed there add J. Koch's recent study, *Der Deutsche Kardinal in deutschen Landen. Die Legationsreise des Nikolaus von Kues, 1451–1452*. See also R. Straus, "The 'Jewish Hat' as an Aspect of Social History," *JSS*, IV, 59–72; the illustrations furnished by E. Fuchs in *Die Juden in der Karrikatur*; and, more generally, L. C. Eisenbart, *Kleiderordnungen der deutschen Städte zwischen 1350 und 1700*.

33. Lagumina and Lagumina, *Codice diplomatico*, I, 17 No. xix (1221), 33 No. xxxiv (1310), 80 ff. No. liii (1366), 163 f. No. cxxi (1395), 392 ff. Nos. cccix–xxi (1427);

G. di Giovanni, *L'Ebraismo della Sicilia*, pp. 29 ff.; A. Ciscato, *Gli Ebrei in Padova*, pp. 165 ff.; D. Kaufmann, "Jacob Mantino, une page de l'histoire de la Renaissance," *REJ*, XXVII, 30–60, 207–38, 317, esp. pp. 44 f.; F. Lionti, "Documenti relativi agli Ebrei di Sicilia," *AS Siciliano*, n.s. VIII, 156 ff.; G. Mollat, "Deux frères mineurs, Marc de Viterbe et Guillaume de' Guasconi au service de la papauté (1363–1375)," *AFH*, XLVIII, 69 f.; C. Morbio, ed., *Codice Visconteo-Sforzesco* (Storie dei municipi italiani, VI), p. 418 No. ccxiii; F. Fossati, "Gli Ebrei a Vigevano nel secolo XV," *AS Lombardo*, XXX, 202 f., 209 f.; L. Fumi, "L'Inquisizione romana e lo stato di Milano," *ibid.*, XXXVII, 298 ff.; *supra*, Vol. X, pp. 229 f., 235, 271 ff., 283 (where the Milanese fine of 1,000 ducats is to be corrected to 10). See also the series of documentary studies pertaining to the Sicilian badges by I. Carini in his "Anèddoti siciliani," *AS Siciliano*, n.s. XIII, 402 ff. No. vii; XVI, 206 No. lxxx, 235 No. ciii; XXII, 484 No. xxiv.

34. See B. Blumenkranz, *Juden und Judentum in der mittelalterlichen Kunst*, pp. 23 f.; P. M. Lonardo, "Gli Ebrei a Pisa," *Studi storici*, ed. by A. Crivellucci, VII, 188 ff.; M. Ciardini, *I Banchieri ebrei in Firenze*, pp. vii f. No. i, xix ff. No. v (with his comments thereon, pp. 46 f.); Cassuto, *Gli Ebrei a Firenze*, pp. 38 ff.; C. Bonetti, *Gli Ebrei a Cremona, 1278–1630*, p. 11; D. Kaufmann, "Contributions à l'histoire des Juifs en Italie," *REJ*, XX, 34–72, esp. pp. 44 ff. ("IV: Les Signes jaunes des Juifs à Ferrare, à Rome et à Milan"); and, more generally, the vast material accumulated by G. Rezasco in his "Del segno degli Ebrei," *Giornale ligustico di archeologia, storia e belle arti*, XV, 241–66, 321–51; XVI, 31–61, 259–84; and the briefer surveys by Q. Senigaglia in "La Condizione giuridica degli Ebrei in Sicilia," *Rivista italiana per le scienze giuridiche*, XLI, 93 ff.; and by Colorni in *Gli Ebrei nel sistema*, pp. 48 ff.

Here, too, the clergy usually took the initiative. In her interesting letter to her husband of 1496, Isabella d'Este of Mantua reported that Domenico da Ponzone, a visiting Genoese preacher, wanted to superimpose a yellow hat upon the existing Jewish badge but that she had refused to take action in the duke's absence. See W. Braghirolli, "Isabella d'Este e gli Israeliti a Mantova," *Rivista storica mantovana*, I, 183 ff.; S. Simonsohn, *Toledot ha-Yehudim be-dukhsut Mantovah*, I, 10 f. Joanna II of Naples, on the other hand, tried to reintroduce the Jewish badge in the shape of a *thau* and, yielding to the entreaties of the determined Jew-baiter, Capistrano, issued a very restrictive decree on May 3, 1427. Yet under the pressure of the Jewish moneylenders, who were doubly indispensable to the country during the then widespread economic crisis, she restored the previously existing conditions three months later (August 20, 1427). The queen was able to stand up to the influential rabblerouser, however, only because she was backed by Pope Martin V who, in sharp contrast to his earlier retreats in the Jewish question, this time overruled Capistrano. See N. F. Faraglia, *Storia della regina Giovanna II d'Angiò*, p. 341; N. Ferorelli, *Gli Ebrei*, pp. 66 ff.; J. Hofer, *Johannes von Capestrano*, pp. 109 f., 134 ff.; J. Starr, "Johanna II and the Jews," *JQR*, XXXI, 67–78, esp. pp. 74 f.; and *supra*, Vol. X, pp. 30 f., 402 n. 11.

35. J. Amador de los Rios, *Historia social*, I, 362; II, 22 n. 1, 197 n. 1; Grayzel, *The Church*, pp. 65 ff., 216 f. No. 78; A. Molinier, ed., *Correspondance administrative d'Alphonse de Poitiers*, I, 650 No. 1003; A. Altmann, *Geschichte der Juden in Stadt und Land Salzburg*, I, 131 ff.; *supra*, Vols. III, pp. 140 f.; IX, pp. 31 f., 255 n. 33. The double badge, suggested by Gregory, seems to have been introduced into the Angevin

possessions in southern France, however, if we may judge from the privilege granted in 1276 to J. Bentifac, the provincial procurator of Jewry, whereby the inquisitors were not to force him to wear badges of diverse colors *retro et ante*. See A. de Boüard, *Actes et lettres de Charles I*, p. 296 No. 958; R. Filangieri *et al.*, eds., *I Registri della cancelleria angioina*, XI, 348 ff. Nos. 363–64.

36. A. Crémieux, "Les Juifs de Marseilles au moyen âge," *REJ*, XLVI, 24 f. Unfortunately, not too many graphic reproductions of the bewildering variety of types and colors, provided by local ordinances during the last three centuries of the Middle Ages, have come down to us. Some interesting illustrations appear in U. Robert, *Les Signes d'infamie au moyen âge* (see esp. the reproduction in App. p. 2 Fig. 1); E. Nübling, *Die Judengemeinden des Mittelalters, insbesondere die Judengemeinde der Reichsstadt Ulm* p. lxiv; M. Gerson, "Deux Miniatures avec la roue des Juifs," *REJ*, XV, 114–16 (most other fourteenth-century manuscripts show no Jewish distinguishing marks; see Israel Lévi, "Miniatures représentant des Juifs," *ibid.*, pp. 116–17); J. Bauer, "Le Chapeau jaune chez les Juifs comtadins," *ibid.*, XXXVI, 53–64 (mainly dealing with the early modern period); *supra*, nn. 27 and 32; and, more generally, P. Weber, *Geistliches Schauspiel und kirchliche Kunst in ihrem Verhältnis erläutert an einer Ikonographie der Kirche und Synagog*, esp. pp. 86 ff.; and M. Bulard, *Le Scorpion*, pp. 31 ff.

Lack of uniformity is well illustrated by the situation in Savoy. While elsewhere a white color of low visibility was considered a symbol of innocence, a Savoy edict of 1390 imposed upon the Jews a white badge. At least one Jew was fined 9 solidi in 1404 because he was found in the company of Christians without it. Its color was somewhat later modified to half red and half white. See M. Bruchet, *Le Château de Ripaille*, pp. 174, 383 No. xxxiii. In Avignon the church council of 1326 suggested that females aged twelve or over be made to wear *cornalia* (probably a coiffure with horns). See L. Bardinet, "La Condition civile,' *RH*, XII, 27. But elsewhere the yellow wheel predominated and badges of that color are recorded in the Provence and the Comtat Venaissin (yellow hat), Florence, Rome, and throughout the Holy Roman Empire. See E. Camau, *Les Juifs en Provence*, p. 350; U. Cassuto, *Gli Ebrei*, pp. 38 ff., 366 ff. Apps. vii–viii, 372 ff. App. xiii; E. Rodocanachi, *Le Saint-Siège*, p. 165; A. Pons in "Los Judíos," *Hispania* (Madrid), XVI, 594 No. 69 (Majorca); and various other localities recorded by Robert and Singermann, *passim*.

37. J. J. Schudt, *Jüdische Merckwürdigkeiten*, IV, 246; F. Singermann, *Die Kennzeichnung*, p. 41; C. Molinier, *Histoire de l'Inquisition dans le midi de France au XIII⁰ et au XIV⁰ siècle*, p. 424; U. Robert, *Les Signes*, p. 144; J. C. Ulrich, *Sammlung*, p. 463 App. Aa; M. Bulard, *Le Scorpion*, pp. 33 f. n. 5. Rather inconsistently, a medieval painter of the Passion emphasized the Jewishness of one participant by a yellow badge, although he must have realized that, apart from the few Roman soldiers, all those present had been Jews. On the other hand, Baldwin of Treves' aforementioned presentation of Roman Jewish leaders as wearing the characteristic Jewish hats may not have been wholly unrealistic. See *supra*, Vol. X, p. 413 n. 41. See also B. Blumenkranz, *Juden and Judentum in der mittelalterlichen Kunst*, pp. 46 ff. (also showing how frequently medieval caricaturists emphasized the allegedly "Jewish" crooked or hooked nose, pp. 22 ff.); and *infra*, Chap. XLIX. On the other hand, there were also deviations from the standard presentation of Jews as usurers. No less a master than Albrecht Dürer depicted a *danse macabre* of many damned characters,

including a Jew *and* a usurer, on a mural of the Basel Cathedral. See I. Loeb's remarks in "Le Juif de l'histoire," *REJ*, XX, p. xlvi.

38. L. Lazard in *REJ*, XV, 236 f. with the sources listed there; A. Neubauer's review of G. Bayle's *Les Médecins d'Avignon au moyen âge* in *REJ*, V, 306 f.; *Tiroler Polizeiordnung* of 1573, fol. 15; Johannes Purgoldt, *Das Rechtsbuch*, viii.102, ed. by F. Ortloff, p. 255, reproduced in G. Kisch's *Jewry-Law*, p. 116; C. T. Gemeiner, *Reichsstadt Regensburgische Chronik*, IV, 289 ff., 293 n. 579, 340; O. Stobbe, *Die Juden*, p. 275 n. 169. Complaints about Jews neglecting to wear badges, often exaggerated, were also heard in other countries. In Spain the Cortes had to repeat their demands from time to time (for instance, those of Toro in 1371). There may, therefore, be merit in the contention of a fifteenth-century writer that neither Jews nor Saracens were forced to adhere to these rules and that "all wear the same type of clothing." See Fernando del Pulgar, *Letras—Glosa a las coplas de Mingo Revulgo*, ed. with notes by J. Dominguez Bordona, pp. 185 f.; K. R. Scholberg, "Minorities in Medieval Castilian Literature," *Hispania* (America), XXXVII, 203–209, esp. p. 203.

These and other matters pertaining to the badge have frequently been discussed in the available literature, particularly by U. Robert and G. Rezasco, and in the briefer studies by F. Singermann and G. Kisch referred to in the preceding notes, as well as the other works listed *supra*, Vol. IX, pp. 253 ff. nn. 28–33. The large variety of local laws and customs has also been recorded in the vast monographic literature on individual medieval communities. Precisely because this subject so often preoccupied local legislators and attracted wide popular attention, it has frequently been referred to in Vols. IX–X. In so far, moreover, as this institution necessarily impressed itself also upon the ways of life and mentality of medieval Jewry, it will be analyzed again from the angle of internal Jewish developments in later chapters.

39. *CJ* (Codex), i.v, 21, ed. by P. Krüger, II, 59 f.; (Novellae), xlv.1, ed. by R. Schoell, III, 278 f.; P. M. Lonardo, "Gli Ebrei a Pisa," *Studi storici*, ed. by A. Crivellucci, VII, 172 f.; John Gower, *Confessio amantis*, vii, vv. 3207 f., cited by W. F. P. Stockley in his "Popes and Jewish 'Ritual Murder'," *Catholic World*, CXXXIX, 452 n. 3; Arnoul Greban, *Le Mystère de la Passion*, vv. 20069, 24780, etc., ed. by G. Paris and G. Raynaud, pp. 262, 325; *Passion de Semur* in E. Roy's collection, *Le Mystère de la Passion en France du XIV⁰ au XVI⁰ siècles*, I, 49 v. 2467. See also the numerous variations on this theme in French Passion plays, cited by M. Bulard in *Le Scorpion*, pp. 42 f. Bulard also points out that, while in some contexts Greban and other writers speak mildly of Jewish "errors," in others they do not hesitate to denounce Jewish "treachery" and to speak of Jewish "felons." The transmutation of the term "perfidy" from mere infidelity to perfidiousness is illustrated also by the convert Victor von Carben, where the curious characterization is given of "meek Christians, wise Greeks, and perfidious Jews." See his *De Vita et moribus Judaeorum*, Paris, 1511 ed., fol. 67v. See also *supra*, Vol. IX, p. 259 n. 45.

40. L. Ginzberg, *Geonica*, II, 147; I. Epstein, "Pre-Expulsion England in the Responsa," *TJHSE*, XIV, 198 n. 45; O. Stobbe, *Die Juden*, pp. 153 f.; *Des Schwabenspiegels Landrechtsbuch*, ed. by H. G. Gengler, pp. 178 f. Art. ccxv (a different translation of a text reconstructed from various manuscripts of the *Schwabenspiegel* is offered by G. Kisch in *The Jews*, pp. 277 f.); R. Cessi, "La Condizione degli Ebrei banchieri in Padova nel secolo XV," *Bollettino* of the Museo Civico in Padua, XI, 9

n. 5, citing a text preserved in a Paduan notarial archive. A survival of the old oath of abjuration by converts is found in the formula reproduced by P. M. Lonardo in "Un'Abiura di Ebrei a Lucera nel 1454," *Studi storici*, ed. by A. Crivellucci, XVI, 581–91. See also other sources cited *supra*, Vols. III, p. 322 n. 28; IV, p. 261 n. 63; IX, 259 f. nn. 45–46; and, more generally, my *The Jewish Community*, III, 180 f. n. 31.

On the ever more cumbersome formulas of the oath *more judaico* and the increasingly weird ceremonies connected with administering it, see also E. Biberfeld, "Der Breslauer Judeneid," *Israelitische Monatsschrift* (supplement to *Jüdische Presse*), XXVI, 45–46; XXVII, 2–3; A. Glaser, *Geschichte der Juden in Strassburg*, pp. 21 f. n. 1; the provision included in Rupert von Freysing's law book, ed. by G. L. von Maurer under the title *Das Stadt- und Landrechtsbuch Ruprechts von Freysing*, pp. 493 f. cap. 174; *Coutumes d'Alais* concerning the Jewish oath being administered according to *el sagramental ancian* (ancient formula) reproduced by A. A. Beugnot in *Les Olim*, III, Part 2, pp. 1498 f. No. xxix; Mouynes, "Serment exigé des Juifs habitant Carcassonne, XIII⁰ siècle," *Mémoires* of the Société des Arts . . . Carcassonne, IV, 410 ff. (Romance text); P. Wentzsche, *Ein Elsässischer Judeneid aus dem Anfang des 14. Jahrhunderts;* A. Friss *et al.*, eds., *Monumenta Hungariae Judaica*, V, Part I, p. 97 No. 212; the fifteenth-century Italian formulas cited by F. Glissenti in *Gli Ebrei nel Bresciano*, pp. 16 f.; and by L. Fumi in "L'Inquisizione romana," *AS Lombardo*, XXXVII, 289 f.; the long and complicated forms developed in Spain and analyzed by J. E. Rivas in his "Notas para el estudio de la influencia de la Iglesia en la compilación aragonesa de 1247," *AHDE*, XX, 770 f.; and by F. Bujanda and F. Cantera in their "De camo han de jurár los Judíos," *Sefarad*, VII, 145–47. See also *supra*, Vol. X, pp. 30, 135, 313 n. 34, 361 n. 20, 430 n. 85; and the fifteenth-century Gera MS listed by G. Homeyer in *Die Deutschen Rechtsbücher des Mittelalters und ihre Handschriften*, new ed. by C. Borchling *et al.*, II, 82 No. 375.

Some general aspects of the medieval oaths and the constant elaborations in the formulas recited also by Christian parties, witnesses, and even by the kings of England, France, and Germany are well illustrated by the texts reproduced and analyzed by H. K. Claussen in "Der Judeneid. Ein Beitrag zur Geschichte des Rechtsschutzes," *Deutsche Rechtswissenschaft*, II, 166–89; and by M. David in "Le Serment du sacre du IX⁰ au XV⁰ siècle," *Revue du moyen âge latin*, VI, 5–272. See also G. Kisch's aforementioned essays reprinted in his *Forschungen zur Rechts- und Sozialgeschichte der Juden in Deutschland*, pp. 137–84.

41. J. Amador de los Rios, *Historia social*, I, 558–86 (App. xi); A. Pons in "Los Judíos," *Hispania* (Madrid), XVI, 365 ff., 517 ff. No. 1; Régné, "Catalogue," *REJ*, LXVII, 220 No. 1685; LXIX, 195 No. 2213; Baer, *Die Juden*, I, Part 1, pp. 1029 ff.; Laurière *et al.*, *Ordonnances*, V, 497 f. On the negative impression made by the ceremonies on Jews, see J. C. Ulrich, *Sammlung*, pp. 71 ff.

42. R. Straus, "Ein Landshuter Judeneid aus dem 14. Jahrhundert," *ZGJD*, V, 43; the Ávila document in the National Archives of Madrid, Sección de Clero, Legajo 263; Rigg, *Select Pleas*, Intro., p. xii. It must be borne in mind, however, that German Christians, too, were often required to supply a varying number of helpers and compurgators. See the numerous references listed in Kisch's Index to *The Jews*, *s.v.* Oath. See also F. A. Lincoln's brief remarks on "The Non-Christian Oath in English Law," *TJHSE*, XVI, 73–76, mainly referring to some seventeenth-century de-

bates. This problem was to preoccupy both European legislators and Jewish leaders deep into the Emancipation era and to give rise to an extended polemical, as well as scholarly, literature, such as the monographs by Z. Frankel and L. Zunz mentioned *supra*, Vol. IX, pp. 259 f. n. 46.

43. *Cölner Geschichtsquellen*, I, 188; G. H. Pertz, "Bemerkungen über einzelne Handschriften und Urkunden," *Archiv für deutsche Geschichtskunde*, VII, 222–1022, esp. p. 789; K. Zeumer, ed., *Formulae Merovingici et Carolini aevi*, p. 640 No. 7; and T. J. Lacomblet, ed., *Urkundenbuch für die Geschichte des Niederrheins*, III, No. 24; L. Heffner, *Die Juden in Franken*, pp. 53 ff. App. P; M. Wiener, *Regesten*, pp. 173 f. No. 475; other sources cited by O. Stobbe in *Die Juden in Deutschland*, pp. 153 ff., 262 ff. Nos. 144–48.

44. *Codex Theodosianus*, xvi.8, 16 (404), 24 (418); St. Jerome, *Commentary* on Isaiah, ii (on verse 3:3) in *PL*, XXIV, 60; J. Juster, *Les Juifs*, II, 277 f. This legislation did not prevent imperial Jewry, however, from participating in the defense of various cities and even from staging a major uprising under Heraclius. Like the equally oppressed Samaritans, the Jews were able to take an active part in the Perso-Byzantine wars of the sixth and seventh centuries. See *supra*, Vols. II, pp. 79, 398 nn. 9–10; III, pp. 17 ff., 236 ff.

45. F. de Mendoza, "Con los Judíos de Estella," *Principe de Viana*, XII, 237 f.; F. Idoate Iragui, "Un Registro de Cancillería del siglo XIV," *ibid.*, XVIII, 582; Aronius, *Regesten*, pp. 163 No. 367 (1205), 239 No. 557 (1246); A. Kober, *Studien zur mittelalterlichen Geschichte der Juden in Köln am Rhein insbesondere ihres Grundbesitzes*, p. 17; idem, *Cologne*, pp. 40, 60 f., 65 f., 121, 143; K. Bauer, *Judenrecht in Köln*, pp. 31 f., 65; Wiener, *Regesten*, pp. 26 No. 10; Baer, *Die Juden*, I, Part 1, pp. 885 f. No. 550; Part 2, pp. 163 f. No. 167; F. Keutgen, *Urkunden zur städtischen Verfassungsgeschichte*, p. 211 Art. 3; Isaac b. Moses Or Zaru'a, *Sefer Or Zaru'a*, I, 194 No. 693; *supra*, Vols. IV, pp. 36, 251 n. 43; IX, pp. 92, 285 n. 44; X, pp. 122 f., 151, 192, 203, 355 n. 4, 368 f. n. 39, 390 n. 43. Cuspinian's report that he had read in "trustworthy" sources that King Adolph of Nassau's army in the 1290s "included 30,000 Jews whom the king contemplated sending to battle first," deserves no credence as a factual record. Yet it reveals the acceptance by the German public of the possibility of such a large Jewish participation in the armed forces. See Cuspinian's *Tagebuch*, ed. with explanatory notes by H. Ankwicz. See also the comprehensive review of the Jews' military duties in the thirteenth-century German cities by H. Fischer in *Die Verfassungsrechtliche Stellung*, pp. 98 ff., 188 ff. Note 9 (also reproducing Menaḥem b. Jacob's poem, *Maṣor ba'atah ha-'ir* [The City Came under Siege] which gives a somewhat vague eye-witness account of the siege of Worms in 1201); the data supplied by H. Planitz in *Die Deutsche Stadt im Mittelalter*, pp. 253, 436; and the literature listed *infra*, n. 51.

46. *Fuero* of Ledesma, Art. 393, in *Fueros Leoneses*, ed. by A. Castro and F. de Onís, p. 285 (apparently harking back to regulations enacted by Ferdinand II of Leon); Baer, *Die Juden*, I, Part 1, p. 221 No. 175 Arts. 23–24; Part 2, pp. 31 f. No. 58 Art. 393; Zurita y Castro, *Anales de Aragón*, x.20, ed. Saragossa, II, 369c; Fernão Lopes, *Chronica de-El Rey D. João I*, Lisbon, 1899 ed., I, 52; and J. Mendes dos Remedios, *Os Judeus*, p. 202.

47. Baer, *Die Juden*, I, Part 1, pp. 373 f. No. 265 (1360, 1363); Part 2, pp. 331 f. No. 319 (1465); D. Kaufmann, *GS*, II, 247. On Samuel Alfaquim and his likely identity with Samuel b. Abraham Abinnaxim, see the numerous references in J. E. Martínez Ferrando, *Catálogo de la documentación relativa al antiguo reino de Valencia;* and J. Régné's "Catalogue," analyzed by Y. F. Baer in his *Toledot ha-Yehudim bi-Sefarad ha-noṣrit*, 2d ed., pp. 98, 491 n. 49, 493 n. 63 (*A History of the Jews in Christian Spain*, I, 165, 410 n. 48, 412 n. 63). See also *ibid.*, pp. 75, 102, 261 f., 367, 493 f. n. 67, 529 n. 50 (Hebrew); I, 127, 163 f., 409 f. n. 48 (English); D. Romano's dissertation, *Estudio histórico de la familia Ravaya, bailes de los reyes de Aragón en el siglo XIII;* idem, "Los Hermanos Abenmenassé al servicio del Pedro el Grande de Aragón," *Homenaje Millás*, II, 241–92; and numerous other sources listed *supra*, Vol. X.

Changes in allegiance by statesmen and soldiers, such as that suggested to Genton, were quite common at that time. On one occasion, in 1476, Isabella confiscated all the property of a Madrid Jewish physician, Rabi Jaco, because, "failing to consider the loyalty and fidelity which he owes the said king [Ferdinand], My lord, and Me, as to his natural kings and masters," he had accepted service with the king of Portugal, "Our adversary, and Our other disloyal nobles." Some royal favorites obtained more or less permanent exemption from military services of any kind. For instance, one Yusef Çulama of Ávila, royal cobbler (*çapatero*), was freed from guard duty by John II, Henry IV, and Isabella. See Baer, I, Part 2, pp. 337 ff. Nos. 326 and 328. Curiously, even Milanese Jews, in their petition of 1569 to Philip II against the order to wear badges, pointed out the personal services they had rendered not only to the poor local borrowers, but also to the Spanish garrison. See N. Ferorelli, ed., "Supplica degli Ebrei e pareri del Senato sulla loro permanenza nel Milanese verso la metà del secolo XVI," *Vessillo israelitico*, LXIII, 237 f.

48. The decrees by the Sicilian kings Louis of 1347, Frederick III of 1367, and Martin of 1392, 1398, and 1403, quoted by G. di Giovanni in *L'Ebraismo della Sicilia*, pp. 53 ff.; Lagumina and Lagumina, *Codice diplomatico*, I, 82 No. cxxxviii (1396–97), 188 ff. Nos. cxliv and cxlvii (1398), 228 ff. Nos. clxxii and clxxix (1402–1403), 297 ff. No. ccxxviii (1408); II, 306 No. dclxi (1481); III, 47 No. dcccxciv (1492); M. D. Anfossi, *Gli Ebrei in Piemonte*, pp. 45 f. (chiefly citing events of the seventeenth century); *Ordenaçoens Affonso V*, ii.75 and 83, pp. 471 ff.; M. Kayserling, *Geschichte der Juden in Portugal*, pp. 57 f., 127 f.; L. Bardinet, "La Condition civile," *RH*, XII, 29. Incidentally, the Portuguese decree of 1430 (on which see also J. P. Oliveira Martins, *Os Filhos de D. João I*, pp. 190 ff.) seems to have resulted from some frivolity (and even occasional bloodshed) which had previously accompanied the appearance of Jewish delegations at welcoming ceremonies for royalty. On Sicily, see also the additional data assembled by Q. Senigaglia in "La Condizione giuridica degli Ebrei in Sicilia," *Rivista italiana per le scienze giuridiche*, XLI, 90 f. Obviously, personal military service had become so rare among Italian Jews that the late medieval jurists seem to have taken it for granted that the ancient Roman prohibition still was part of the existing common law and required no further elaboration.

49. The English "Assize of Arms," v, cited by Roger Howden (Hoveden) in his *Chronica*, ed. by W. Stubbs, II, 261; and from there in J. Jacobs, *The Jews of Angevin England*, p. 75. See *supra*, Vol. IV, p. 303 n. 48. On the convert-soldiers see Rymer and Sanderson, eds., *Foedera*, I, 557; *Patent Rolls, 1247–1258*, p. 548 (1257);

1258–1266, pp. 13 (1259), 134 (1260), 177 (1261), 209–222 (1262), 266, 300 (1263), 310 (1264); *Close Rolls, 1254–1256*, pp. 58, 89 ff., 434; M. Adler, *Jews of Medieval England*, pp. 285 f., 294 f. That Roger at the same time served as contractor for the armies, both in England and abroad, is by no means surprising. In 1256 he was entrusted with a diplomatic mission to Spain. Of course, most of these activities would have been denied to him had he remained true to his ancestral faith.

50. Caesarius of Heisterbach, *Commentary* on the Psalms of Ascent (Ps. 119–33), excerpted by A. E. Schönbach in his "Studien zur Erzählungsliteratur des Mittelalters, VII" in *SB*, Vienna, CLIX, Part 4, p. 36; idem, *Dialogus miraculorum*, ed. by J. Strange, II, 27; *Schwabenspiegel*, ed. by Gengler, p. 169 Art. ccvii, 4; Johann von Buch's gloss on the *Sachsenspiegel*, iii.2, reproduced from the Augsburg, 1516 ed. in G. Kisch, *Jewry-Law in Medieval Germany*, p. 42. U. Grotefend has pointed out that the prohibition of the *Sachsenspiegel*, repeated in the Glogau law book, had doubtless become part of the Magdeburg legal system as well. See his *Geschichte und rechtliche Stellung der Juden in Pommern*, p. 19; and, from another angle, H. Fehr, "Das Waffenrecht der Bauern in Mittelalter," *ZRG*, German. Abteilung, XXXV, 111–211; XXXVIII, 1–114; A. Berliner, ed., "Old Records" (Hebrew), *Ha-Medabber le-Yisrael*, I, 47; and I. Abrahams, *Jewish Life in the Middle Ages*, 2d ed., pp. 377 ff. The gradual abrogation of the Jews' right to bear arms in thirteenth-century Germany is analyzed by G. Kisch in *The Jews in Medieval Germany*, pp. 111 ff., 119 ff., 412 ff., and, with some modifications, in his *Forschungen zur Rechts- und Sozialgeschichte der Juden*, pp. 20 ff. See also *supra*, Chap. XLVII, n. 31.

51. See D. M. Shohet, *The Jewish Court in the Middle Ages*, p. 17 n. 5; J. E. Scherer, *Die Rechtsverhältnisse*, pp. 305 f.; Bär, "Die Juden Zürichs im Mittelalter," *Zürcher Taschenbuch*, 1896, p. 119; A. Steinberg, *Studien*, p. 120; K. Seifart, "Streitbare Juden im Mittelalter," *Jeschurun*, ed. by S. A. Hirsch, IV, 315–19; I. Abrahams, *Jewish Life in the Middle Ages*, 2d ed., pp. 377 ff.; and, particularly, the data assembled by M. Ginsburger in "Les Juifs et l'art militaire au moyen âge," *REJ*, LXXXVIII, 156–66; and I. Fischer in his "'Streitbare' Juden im Mittelalter," *Festschrift Armand Kaminka*, pp. 33–37. According to some authorities cited by Ginsburger, Typsiles, the inventor of cannon powder in Augsburg in 1353, was not a Byzantine but a Jew. This is not proved, however. The growing demilitarization of German Jewry is also illustrated by some flags. While the flag furnished by Strasbourg Jewry to the marching burghers (*ca.* 1200), like those in the Italian cities, had military connotations, that displayed by Prague Jews since 1357 had a purely symbolic character. See *supra*, n. 48; Vol. IX, pp. 187, 201, 329 n. 58, 335 f. n. 8. The growth of pacifist sentiments among medieval Jews will be discussed in a later chapter.

52. *Codex Theodosianus*, iii.2 and 6; *CJ* (Codex), i.5, 12, 6, ed. by P. Krüger, II, 53; *Novellae*, xiv, ed. by R. Schoell, III, 277 ff.; *Altercatio ecclesiae et synagogae* in *PL*, XLII, 1133; Juster, *Les Juifs*, II, 243 ff. The formulation in the *Altercatio* referring only to the exclusion from higher offices harkens back to imperial prohibitions antedating 438. But as an ecclesiastical document it seems to have carried special weight in the canonical legislation, including that of the Third and Fourth Councils of Toledo of 589 and 633. See *supra*, Vol. III, pp. 36 ff., 245 ff. nn. 43 ff.; *infra*, n. 53;

and A. Echánove, "Precisiones acerca la legislación conciliar toledana sobre los Judíos," *Hispana sacra*, XIV, 259–79.

53. Mansi, *Collectio*, XXII, 1058; C. J. Hefele, *Histoire des Conciles*, V, Part 2, p. 1387; Grayzel, *The Church*, pp. 310 f. No. xi; Huillard-Bréholles, *Historia diplomatica Friderici Secundi*, V, Part 1, p. 57; Aronius, *Regesten*, pp. 220 f. No. 509; Alphonso X, *Las Siete Partidas*, vii.24, 3, ed. by Lopez, IV, 645; with M. A. Ortí Belmonte's comments thereon in the *Boletín* of the Cordova Academy, XXVI, 41 ff. See also the bitter phrasing in the Vienna municipal statute enacted by Duke Albert I in 1296 as reproduced in F. Keutgen, *Urkunden zur städtischen Verfassungsgeschichte*, p. 213 Art. 5. Among the local variations one may mention the Milanese petition to the pope asking for the exclusion of Jews from public employment, except in agriculture. See C. Canetta, "Gli Ebrei," *AS Lombardo*, VIII, 634 f. In Portugal the law included in the *Ordenaçoens Affonso V* (ii.85, p. 498) succinctly provided "that Jews shall not serve as officials of the king, the infantes, or any other lords." Frederick II's Vienna decree was repeated by him in 1247 and by Přemysl Ottakar in 1251; it was also restated in Duke Frederick II's similar privilege for Vienna in 1239. See G. Winter, *Urkundliche Beiträge zur Rechtsgeschichte ober- und niederösterreichischer Städte*, pp. 9 ff. No. 1; Aronius, *Regesten*, pp. 224 No. 522, 241 Nos. 565–66, 249 No. 584, 331 ff. No. 772; *supra*, Vol. X, pp. 183, 380 n. 20. Exclusion from public office is also indicated in the *Schwabenspiegel*, at least to the extent that a Jew ought not to be appointed a magistrate or elected to princely office (ed. by Gengler, pp. 62 Art. lxxi, 2; 91 Art. ci, 3) and, quite unequivocally, in Johann von Buch's gloss on the *Sachsenspiegel*, iii.2, cited in G. Kisch's *Jewry-Law*, p. 42; Kisch, *The Jews in Medieval Germany*, pp. 300 f. It may be noted, however, that by his singling out Vienna for that prohibition Emperor Frederick intimated that elsewhere the appointment of Jewish officials could proceed unhampered. Certainly, neither he nor any other emperor inserted any such reservation into the general privileges for imperial Jewry. Not surprisingly, therefore, Duke Henry of Mecklenburg, in his statute of 1266 for the city of Wismar, could mention Jewish alongside other ducal and court officials all of whom were to be judged by ducal, rather than municipal, judges. See Aronius, *Regesten*, p. 296 No. 713.

54. See esp. *supra*, Vols. IV, pp. 15, 240 n. 14; IX, pp. 37 f., 231, 257 n. 40, 348 n. 40; X, Chaps. XLIV–XLV, *passim*.

55. Süsskind von Trimberg's poem, "Ich var uf toren vart," reproduced by M. Spanier in his "Süsskind von Trimberg," *ZGJD*, VII, 152. In this essay Spanier offers detailed interpretations of a dozen extant poems by Süsskind and furnishes a comprehensive bibliography relating to this intriguing medieval personality. See also his "Der Spruchdichter Süsskind von Trimberg," *Jahrbuch für jüdische Geschichte und Literatur*, XXXI, 124–36. Yet despite lengthy debates conducted by scholars over several decades, the very problem of Süsskind's Jewishness is not yet definitely resolved. See the arguments to the contrary, marshaled by R. Straus in his "Was Süsskint von Trimperg a Jew? An Inquiry into 13th Century Cultural History," *JSS*, X, 19–30. However, the weight of evidence still favors the presence of this unusual Jew in the ranks of the medieval German *Minnesänger*, implausible as such a degree of assimilation may appear at first glance.

Less astonishing is the presence of such Jewish poet-singers in southern France, although here, too, they suffered from much discrimination and derision as is well illustrated in the poetic altercation between Guiraut Riquier and the probably imaginary Jewish troubadour, Bonfilh, in Narbonne. See the former's "Cinq tensons," ed. by C. Chabaneau in *Revue des langues romanes*, XXXII, 112 f.; with J. Régné's comments thereon in his "Étude sur la condition des Juifs de Narbonne," *REJ*, LXIII, 75 ff. App. iii. See also J. Schirmann, "Isaac Gorni, poète hébreux de Provence," *Lettres romanes*, III, 175–200 (also in Hebrew in *Orlogin*, III, 91–101); and *supra*, Vol. VII, pp. 151, 204, 292 n. 24, 319 n. 92.

CHAPTER XLIX: "DEMONIC" ALIEN

1. Konrad Mutian (Mutianus Rufus), *Der Briefwechsel*, ed. by C. Krause, p. 260 No. 205; O. Frankl, *Der Jude in den deutschen Dichtungen des 15., 16. und 17. Jahrhunderts*, pp. 18, 131 f.; F. Loidl, *Abraham a Santa Clara und das Judentum*, p. 25 (citing Abraham's *Huy und Pfuy der Welt*, Würzburg, 1707 ed., p. 102); Martin Luther, *Von den Juden und ihren Lügen*, in his *Werke*, Weimar ed., LIII, 412–552; and other passages cited by R. Lewin in his *Luthers Stellung zu den Juden*, pp. 47, 109; J. Trachtenberg, *The Devil and the Jews: the Medieval Conception of the Jew and Its Relation to Modern Antisemitism* (also paperback), p. 42; F. Kynass, *Der Jude im deutschen Volkslied*, p. 7. Luther's inconsistent attitude to the Jews will be more fully discussed *infra*, Chap. LVIII. Some authors dragged the Jewish issue into almost any discussion. In his *Joseph: Biblische Komödie*, written in 1540, Theobald Gart, a little known Schlettstadt poet, dramatized mainly the biblical story of Joseph and Potiphar's wife. But in the prologue he did not let the opportunity escape him to denounce the Jews' "obstinate mouth." See the Strasbourg, 1880 ed., p. 26 vv. 39–40.

2. St. Caesarius of Arles, *Sermones*, ed. by G. Morin, I, 532 No. cxxix; F. Lionti, "Gli Ebrei e la festa di S. Stefano Protomartire," *AS Siciliano*, n.s. VIII, 463–82. Lionti also shows the resistance of both the populace and the local authorities to Pope Martin's decree, which had to be reissued by him in duplicate and repeated in 1405. See also E. Wickersheimer, "Lèpre et Juifs au moyen âge," *Janus*, XXXVI, 43–48; *supra*, Vols. II, p. 398 n. 10; III, pp. 244 n. 38, 250 f. n. 58; IX, pp. 208, 338 n. 14; X, pp. 235, 237; and *infra*, n. 49.

3. *Libro del Alborayque*, cited from a Paris MS and analyzed by I. Loeb in his "Polémistes chrétiens et juifs en France et en Espagne," *REJ*, XVIII, 238 ff.; Juan del Encina, *Bucolicas*, *argumento* to the fourth *écloga*, in *Cancionero de las obras*, facsimile of the Salamanca, 1496 ed., fol. 38r.; J. R. Andrews, *Juan del Encina: Prometheus in Search of Prestige*, pp. 173 f. n. 5. Andrews debates the pros and cons of Juan himself being a *converso*. The statement here quoted rather reinforces the affirmative arguments, whereas all the negative deductions from the father's occupation, business relations with the Church, and the like, are inconclusive, since even a professing Jew could have had these attributes. See also *ibid.*, p. 180 n. 5; and, more generally, I. Loeb, "Le Juif de l'histoire et le Juif de la légende," *REJ*, XX, pp. xxxiii–lxi, esp. pp. lii f.; S. Resnick in "The Jew as Portrayed in Early Spanish Literature." *Hispania* (America), XXXIV, 54–58; *supra*, Vols. IV, pp. 11, 121, 237 n. 8, 300 f. nn. 41–42; V, pp. 125 f., 347 n. 56; IX, p. 324 n. 45; X, p. 428 n. 81. To the uncertain cases of whether *Judaeus* is an ethnic-religious designation or a mere family name, add that of the fourteenth-century commentator of Aristotle Themon Jude (son of a Jew?) or Judaeus, cited by L. Thorndike in *A History of Magic and Experimental Science*, III, 587, n. 13.

In his *Reprobración del amor mundano o Carbacho*, written in 1438, Alphonso Martínez de Toledo, "archpriest" of Talavera, on several occasions uses the term *judío* as a synonym for *coward* or *cowardly*, placing Jews on a par with women and priests. See esp. ii.8, ed. by J. Rogerio Sánchez, p. 250. If this attribution reflected more than the author's personal bias, it would show how the originally proud and upstanding Spanish Jewry had become intimidated by the successive blows since 1391. The spreading prohibition for Jews to bear arms, carried over from the northern countries into the Iberian Peninsula, must have not only weakened the military prowess of the Jews but also contributed to the lowering of their dignity in the eyes of their bellicose neighbors. See Y. Malkiel, "En torno a las voces *'judío'* y *'judía,'* " *Homenaje a J. A. van Praag*, pp. 73–80, esp. pp. 75 f.; *supra*, Chap. XLVIII, n. 46; and *infra*, n. 26. On the various shades of meaning associated with the term Jew through the ages, see also my essay, "Who Is a Jew? Some Historical Reflections," *Midstream*, VI, Part 2, pp. 5–16, reprinted in my *History and Jewish Historians: Essays and Addresses*, compiled with a Foreword by A. Hertzberg and L. A. Feldman, pp. 5–22 (also available in a Hebrew and a French trans.) with reference to a recent controversy in Israel.

4. See the data assembled by R. Schröder in his *Glaube und Aberglaube in den altfranzösischen Dichtungen*, pp. 33 ff.; the seven folk songs included in R. von Liliencron's ed. of *Die Historischen Volkslieder der Deutschen vom 13. bis 16. Jahrhundert*, III, 316 ff. Nos. 336–40, 355 ff. Nos. 346–47; his general observations about *Deutsches Leben im Volkslied um 1530;* Alphonso X, *Cantigas de Santa Maria*, xxx, ed. for the Spanish Academy with an historical and critical intro. and an extensive glossary by the Marquis de Valmar, II, 46 f.; L. Geiger, "Die Juden und die deutsche Literatur," *ZGJD*, [o.s.] II, 314 ff.; *supra*, Vol. X, pp. 243, 369 n. 39, 407 n. 28. See also the next note.

In all these matters Jews were not the only culprits, however. Not only were heretics likewise supposed to be guilty of defacing Catholic religious monuments, like that Hussite who had allegedly twice speared the famous painting of the Virgin in the church of Polish Częstochowa, but also soldiers (always suspected of loose morals), jugglers, and vagrants were frequently accused of similar antisocial acts. Yet in the case of Jews suspicions were magnified by their religious disparity and any suspect act of an individual was readily blamed upon the entire community. See the examples cited by J. P. Kaltenbaeck in *Die Mariensagen in Oesterreich*, pp. 308 ff.; H. Loewe, *Die Juden in der katholischen Legende*, pp. 20 ff. These allegations received some additional support from the sweeping attribution of such hostile acts to Jews included in Pope Eugenius IV's bull, *Dudum ad nostram*, cited *supra*, Vol. IX, pp. 272 f. n. 18. In fact, it sufficed for a Jew to remove the painting of a Virgin from a house newly acquired by him to imperil his entire community, as happened to the Norsi family in Mantua. See *supra*, Vol. X, pp. 289 f., 429 f. n. 83.

5. A. Mussafia's "Studien zu den mittelalterlichen Marienlegenden," *SB* Vienna, CXIX, 18 No. 45. Connected with these iconographic legends were also plays related to the Assumption of Mary in which Jews were presented in a variety of hostile roles. See the French, German, Spanish, and Dutch plays from the thirteenth to the sixteenth century, mentioned by H. Pflaum in "Les Scènes des Juifs dans la littérature dramatique du moyen âge," *REJ*, LXXXIX, 122; and, more generally, the data supplied by D. Strumpf in *Die Juden in den mittelalterlichen Mysterien-, Mirakel- und Moralitätendichtungen Frankreichs.*

6. Johannes Nauclerus, *Chronica . . . succinctim comprehendentia res memorabiles*, II, 42 f.; the "Marienlegenden" assembled by K. Goedeke in his *Deutsche Dich-*

tung im Mittelalter, 2d ed. enlarged by H. Oesterley, pp. 132 ff., 142 ff. Nos. 46, 1, and 29; Pamphilus Gengenbach, "Fünf Juden," in his *Gedichte*, ed. by K. Goedeke, pp. 39 ff., 442 n. 5, 557 f.; and other materials assembled by A. Mussafia in his "Studien," *SB* Vienna, CXIII, 917–94; CXV, 5–92; CXIX, No. ix; CXXIII, No. viii; CXXXIX, No. viii. These data are amplified by such more recent investigations as R. W. Southern, "The English Origin of the 'Miracles of the Virgin,'" *Mediaeval and Renaissance Studies*, IV, 176–216; and B. Boyd, *The Middle English Miracles of the Virgin*. In this Columbia University dissertation Miss Boyd also describes (pp. 124 ff.) eighteen such episodes included in the British Museum MS 39,996; among them the story of the "Jewish boy" (No. 7; see *infra*, n. 8), the inability of some Jews to efface a picture of the Virgin (No. 14), and the sudden death of another Jew who had "insulted Our Lady's Image" (No. 16). A great many data of this kind are analyzed, though in a somewhat disorganized fashion, by H. Loewe in *Die Juden in der katholischen Legende*. Loewe also points out the great similarities between Gengenbach's poem and another attributed to his contemporary Thomas Murner. The first edition of the latter, entitled *Entehrung und Schmach*, was published in Strasbourg in 1515 with a series of telling illustrations and was doubtless inspired by the impression which the legend had made on Emperor Maximilian I during his visit to Cambron (pp. 71 ff.). See A. Klasert, ed., "Entehrung Mariae durch die Juden. Eine antisemitische Dichtung Thomas Murners," *Jahrbuch für Geschichte . . . Elsass-Lothringens*, XXI, 78–155; M. Spanier, "Thomas Murners Beziehungen zum Judentum," *Elsass-Lothringisches Jahrbuch*, XI, 89–108 (also, more generally, A. Erler's *Thomas Murner als Jurist);* F. Hachez's extensive bibliography of "La Littérature du sacrilège de Cambron," *Annales* of the Cercle archéologique de Mons, XXVII, 97–152; and other writings listed by J. Stengers in *Les Juifs dans les Pays-Bas au moyen âge*, pp. 116 ff. See also *supra*, Vol. X, pp. 18 f., 307 n. 18; K. Lendi, *Der Dichter Pamphilus Gengenbach. Beiträge zu seinem Leben und seinen Werken;* G. Seewald's Hamburg dissertation, *Die Marienklage im mittellateinischen Schrifttum und in den germanischen Literaturen des Mittelalters* (typescript); and T. Meier, *Die Gestalt Marias im geistlichen Schauspiel des deutschen Mittelalters,* well illustrating the growing veneration of the Virgin during the last centuries of the Middle Ages and its reflection in the contemporary drama. On the widespread pilgrimages to shrines of the Virgin see, for instance, L. Dorn's study of *Die Marienwallfahrten des Bistums Augsburg.*

The theme of the Virgin's plaint over the blindness of the Jews in repudiating Jesus' message and her call for the Jews' penitence was fully elaborated by the author (probably Godefroy de St. Victor late in the twelfth century) of the *Planctus Beate Virginis,* better known under its *incipit* of *Planctus ante nescia.* An anonymous Catalan author makes Mary ask succinctly: "O thou false Jew! How could you be so cruel toward my Son?" See R. A. Aramon i Serra, "Dos planys de la Verge del seglo XV," *Spanische Forschungen der Görresgesellschaft,* XXI, 275 vv. 27–28. This motif appears in many variations in the numerous Western plays of this genre. See also F. Cremaschi, " 'Planctus Mariae.' Nuovi testi inediti," *Aevum,* XXIX, 293–468; K. Young, *The Drama of the Medieval Church,* I, 496 ff.; and S. Sticca's more recent analysis of "The 'Planctus Mariae' and the Passion Plays," *Symposium,* XV, 41–48 (arguing against the derivation of the latter from the former). On the artistic representations, see M. Vloberg, *La Vierge et l'Enfant dans l'art français;* and, more generally, G. Sanoner, "La Vie de Jésus-Christ racontée par les imagiers du moyen âge sur les portes d'églises," *Revue de l'art chrétien,* LV–LVIII (pointing out the relative infrequency of scenes depicting Jesus' circumcision or his chasing the vendors out of the Temple precincts, while his Passion became an increasingly popular theme in the Late Middle Ages; LV, 368 f.; LVI, 302 ff., 308 ff.); B. Blumenkranz, *Juden und Judentum in der mittelalterlichen Kunst;* and *infra*, n. 11. Needless to say, the somewhat less frequent medieval presentations of Old Testament figures offered the artists fewer opportunities for venting their anti-Jewish sentiments. See, for instance, T. Aktuaryus, "Graphische Darstellungen aus dem Alten Testament im 15. Jahrhundert," *Jüdisches Jahrbuch für die Schweiz*, 5680 (1919–20), 143–61; and, more comprehensively, H. Heimann, *The Bible in Art: Miniatures, Paintings, Drawings and Sculptures Inspired by the Old Testament.*

7. Matthew Paris, *Chronica majora*, ed. by Luard, V, 114 f.; in Giles's English trans. II, 340 f.; Caesarius of Heisterbach, *Dialogus miraculorum*, ii.26, ed. by J. Strange, I, 98 f.; Loewe, *Die Juden*, p. 32. The populace did not know that the Jewish requirement of ablutions for new proselytes did not apply to relapsed converts. The minor ceremonies indicated in such cases by rabbinic teachers are cited by A. Jellinek in the appendix to his *Quntras ha-mefaresh* (Bibliography of Early Commentaries on the Talmud), pp. 14 ff. On Abraham of Berkhamsted's later career, see C. Roth, *A History of the Jews in England*, p. 272; and *supra*, Vol. X, pp. 107, 349 n. 63. Less miraculous and doubtless historically more authentic is Caesarius' story about a Louvain Jewish father's unavailing efforts to secure the return of his baptized minor daughter, an affair which involved several leading churchmen. See *Dialogus*, ii.25, ed. by Strange, I, 95 ff.; and *supra*, Vol. V, pp. 113, 340 n. 39.

8. Alphonso X's *Cantigas de Santa Maria*, cvii, ed. by Marquis de Valmar, with J. E. Keller's comments thereon in his "Folklore in the Cantigas of Alfonso el Sabio," *Southern Folklore Quarterly*, XXXIII, 178, 182; *Gesta Treverorum*, Cont. viii, ed. by G. Waitz in *MGH*, Scriptores, VIII, 182; Aronius, *Regesten*, p. 67 No. 160. As observed by B. Blumenkranz, the original version of the Treves incident was much more moderate, but it was sharpened by the copyists in the growingly hostile atmosphere after the First Crusade. See his *Juifs et Chrétiens dans le monde occidental, 430–1096*, pp. 103 f., 131 f., 137. See also the related story of the Limoges Jewish swindler who claimed that, by heaping maledictions on the effigy of their ruler, the Jews could bring about that ruler's death, *supra*, Vols. III, pp. 52 f., 253 f. n. 67; IV, pp. 92, 283 f. n. 2.

On the miracle of little boy, see the polyglot texts edited by E. Wolter in *Der Judenknabe, 5 griechische, 14 lateinische und 8 französische Texte* (listing also 1 Spanish, 2 German, 2 Arabic, and 1 Ethiopic texts). Additional Latin texts were analyzed by T. Pelizaeus in his Halle dissertation, *Beiträge zur Geschichte der Legende vom Judenknaben*. An earlier Greek text wrongly attributed to Johannes Moschos was published by T. Nissen in his "Unbekannte Erzählungen aus dem Pratum spirituale," *Byzantinische Zeitschrift*, XXXVIII, 351–76, esp. pp. 353, 361 ff., and translated into German in his "Zu den ältesten Fassungen der Legende vom Judenknaben," *Zeitschrift für französische Sprache und Literatur*, LXII, 393–403. See also the story retold by Caesarius of Heisterbach in his *Dialogus*, ed. by Strange, III, 18 (where, apparently for the first time, the wrathful father is no longer described as a glazier); and others reported by Mussafia in *SB* Vienna, CXXIII, No. viii, pp. 8, 14, 87. Other versions attributed to Caesarius (one of them places the miracle in Breslau) are quoted from a Xanten and a Bonn MSS by A. Hilka in *Die Wunderge-*

schichten des Caesarius von Heisterbach, III, 147 f. No. 29, 159 f. Nos. 37a–38, and the notes thereon. See also the English stories discussed by R. W. Southern in *Mediaeval and Renaissance Studies*, IV, 191 f.; and by B. Boyd in *The Middle English Miracles of the Virgin*, pp. 36 ff., and other passages listed in her Index, p. 146, *s.v.* "The Jewish Boy."

As pointed out by Otto Weinreich, some such legends were current already in ancient times and in part belong to the pre-Christian Alexander sagas. See his *Der Trug des Nektanebos. Wandlungen eines Novellenstoffs*, pp. 91–122; and other data in Loewe's *Die Juden*, pp. 28 ff. It may be noted that the story penetrated Spain, where it was retold with much gusto in the *Milagros de Nuestra Señora*, xvi: "El niño judío," by the thirteenth-century poet Gonzalo de Berceo. See the text, ed. with notes by A. G. Solalinde, 4th ed., pp. 88 ff. (or with somewhat different explanations in the selection compiled by G. Menéndez Pidal, 7th ed., pp. 107 ff.); and K. R. Scholberg, "Minorities in Medieval Castilian Literature," *Hispania* (America), XXXVII, 204. See also B. Blumenkranz, "Juden und Jüdisches in christlichen Wundererzählungen," *Theologische Zeitschrift*, X, 417–46.

9. Baer, *Die Juden*, I, Part 1, pp. 184 ff. No. 157; Part 2, pp. 386 f. No. 361; A. Hilka, ed., *Die Wundergeschichten des Caesarius von Heisterbach*, I, 121 n. 146, with reference to Matthew 2:13–15; Heinrich Bebel's *Facetiae* (1508), cited by L. Geiger in *ZGJD*, [o.s.] II, 348. That despite all dangers Jewish debaters quite courageously stood their ground is attested by the numerous disputations held, and the polemical letters written, in the Middle Ages. At least Joseph the Zealot and Nathan Official of thirteenth-century France seem to have suffered no immediate reprisals. See *supra*, Vol. IX, p. 277 n. 28. Nor do we hear of any retribution being inflicted upon Josel of Rosheim after his 1539 debate with Martin Bucer, and possibly (as we suggested elsewhere) with John Calvin, in the presence of Emperor Charles V in Frankfort. On the contrary, he seems to have gained status with the emperor and the imperial councilors because of his calm, but unyielding presentation. See S. Stern, *Josel von Rosheim: Befehlshaber der Judenschaft im Heiligen Römischen Reich Deutscher Nation*, pp. 125 ff.; in the English trans. by G. Hirschler, entitled *Josel of Rosheim Commander of Jewry in the Holy Roman Empire of the German Nation*, pp. 172 ff.; my "John Calvin and the Jews," in the *Harry Austryn Wolfson Jubilee Volume*, I, 141–63, esp. p. 156 n. 24; and *infra*, Chap. LVIII. In general, however, only disputations staged by the authorities presupposed certain guarantees for the safety of the Jewish debaters.

10. F. Michel, ed., *Les Voyages merveilleuses de St. Brandan à la recherche du Paradis terrestres: Légendes et vers du XIIᵉ siècle*, pp. 61 ff. vv. 1266 ff.; C. Hippeau, ed., *La Conquète de Jérusalem . . . par le pélerin Richard et renouvelée par Graindor de Douai au XIIIᵉ siècle*, p. 38 vv. 859 ff.; *Li Covenans vivien*, v. 1626, in W. J. A. Jonckbloet's ed. of *Guillaume d'Orange Chançons de geste des XIᵉ et XIIᵉ siècles*, I, 206; R. Schröder, *Glaube und Aberglaube*, pp. 45, 64 f., 78 f.; Pierre de l'Ancre (Lancre), *L'Incrédulité, et mescréance du sortilège plainement convaincue*, cited by Israel Lévi in "Le Traité sur les Juifs de Pierre de l'Ancre," *REJ*, XIX, 235–45, esp. p. 245; other sources cited by M. Lifschitz-Golden in *Les Juifs dans la littérature française du moyen âge (Mystères, miracles, chroniques)*, pp. 42 ff.; Dante Alighieri, *The Divine Comedy: Inferno*, xxvii.85 ff., in Henry Wadsworth Longfellow's English trans. I, 143, 311 ff.; A. Taylor, "Judas Iscariot in Charms and

Incantations," *Washington University Studies*, Humanistic Series, VIII, 3–17. On Judas see also *infra*, n. 28.

Some medieval plays on Jerusalem, however, had more anti-Muslim than anti-Jewish overtones. They voiced complaints about the Saracen occupation of the Holy Places, the generally miserable conditions in the Latin Kingdom of Jerusalem, and the like. See, for instance, E. Asensio, ed., *"Ay Jerusalem! Planto narrativo del siglo XIII,"* *Nueva Revista de Filología española*, XIV, 251–70; and F. W. Wentzlaff-Eggebert's more general analysis of the *Kreuzzugsdichtung des Mittelalters: Studien zu ihrer geschichtlichen und dichterischen Wirklichkeit.*

11. See Arnoul Greban, *Le Mystère de la Passion*, ed. by G. Paris and G. Raynaud, pp. 204 vv. 15,686 ff. (Caiaphas cites Aristotle's *Ethics!*), 213 vv. 16435 ff.; and numerous other examples cited by H. Pflaum in *REJ*, LXXXIX, 111–34; and in *Die Religiöse Disputation in der europäischen Dichtung des Mittelalters*, Vol. I: *Der allegorische Streit zwischen Synagoge und Kirche*. Not surprisingly we find in this area, too, a close resemblance between poetry and theology. It has been shown that, for example, Greban's very popular mystery play was indebted in many details to both the Arras Passion and Nicholas de Lyra's *Postilla*. See E. Roy, *Le Mystère de la Passion en France du XIVᵉ au XVIᵉ siècles. Étude sur les sources et le classement des mystères de la Passion* (with a documentary appendix), I, 276 ff.; A. Rapp, *Studien über den Zusammenhang des geistlichen Theaters mit der bildenden Kunst im ausgehenden Mittelalter;* W. Stammler, *Wort und Bild. Studien zu den Wechselbeziehungen zwischen Schrifttum und Bildkunst im Mittelalter;* and *infra*, n. 88.

Behind these authors stood an age-old legendary tradition, fashioned by a multitude of anonymous writers who did not hesitate to attribute some of their own thoughts to famous teachers like Augustine. The artistic representation of Jewish "treachery" by a scorpion is analyzed, with extensive documentation, by M. Bulard in *Le Scorpion symbole du peuple juif dans l'art religieux des XIVᵉ, XVᵉ, XVIᵉ siècles.* Bulard also shows that the alleged Jewish collaboration with the Muslim enemies of Christianity caused some artists to introduce Muslim flags and other paraphernalia into the very story of the Passion of Christ (pp. 227 ff.). Like the authors of many Passion plays, they evinced little concern about this palpable anachronism. See also the attribution of the cry, *Mamet* (an obvious corruption from Mahomet-Muḥammad) to Jews invoking their Deity, cited *infra*, n. 60; and, more generally, P. Hildenfinger, "La Figure de la synagogue dans l'art du moyen âge," *REJ*, XLVII, 187–96; and the literature listed *supra*, n. 6; and in B. Blumenkranz's *Juden und Judentum*, p. 81 n. 4.

12. Adson of Toul, *Libellus de Antichristo (ca.* 950) in *PL*, CI, 1289–98, esp. cols. 1295 f. (this work was variously attributed to Raban Maur, Alcuin, even Augustine); the twelfth-century *Ludus de Antichristo*, ed. by W. Meyer in his *Gesammelte Abhandlungen zur mittellateinischen Rythmik*, I, 136–70, esp. pp. 150 ff.; P. Steigleder's analysis of *Das Spiel vom Antichrist. Eine geistesgeschichtliche Untersuchung;* J. Amador de los Rios, *Historia social*, I, 572 App. xi, iiia (from a sixteenth-century copy); Peter de Blois, *Contra perfidiam Judaeorum* in his *Opera omnia* in *PL*, CCVII, 870; J. Jacobs, *The Jews of Angevin England*, p. 182; Richard de Morins, the Dunstable prior and annalist, in *Annales monastici*, ed. by H. R. Luard, III, 33; John Calvin, *Commentary* on I John 2:18 in his *Opera quae supersunt omnia*, ed. by W.

Baum *et al.*, LV, 321; Heinrich von Langenstein (de Hassia), "Tractatus contra quendam eremitam de ultimis temporibus vaticinantem nomine Theolophorum" in B. Pez, *Thesaurus anecdotorum novissimus*, I, Part 2, pp. 505–64; O. Hartwig, *Henricus de Langenstein, dictus de Hassia* [*Hessia*], II, 34 f.; and A. Lhotsky, *Quellenkunde zur mittelalterlichen Geschichte Österreichs*, pp. 322 ff.

The great popularity of Antichrist plays is attested by K. T. Reuschel in *Die Deutschen Weltgerichtsspiele* in *Teutonia*, IV, 35–83: "Die Antichristspiele"; and L. Gros's notes on his ed. of *Mystère de l'Antichrist et du Jugement de Dieu* and his *Étude* thereon (with reference to its public performances in Modane in 1580 and 1606). See also I. Schmale-Ott, "Die Fünfzehn Zeichen vor dem Weltuntergang," *Zeitschrift für deutsches Altertum*, LXXXV, 229–34 (analyzing a twelfth-century poem, ed. by H. Eggers in *Beiträge zur Geschichte der deutschen Sprache*, LXXIV, 355–409). Another version of the "fifteen signs" is offered in W. Stammler's ed. of the *Berner Weltgerichtsspiel*, pp. 48 ff. App. ii, Stammler also analyzing some "Weltgerichts-Predigten"; pp. 51 ff. App. iii. Of course, not all Antichrist poems involved Jews. See, for instance, H. de Boor, "Das Antichristgedicht des Wilden Alexander," *Beiträge zur Geschichte der deutschen Sprache und Literatur*, LXXXII, 346–51. Yet they, as well as the nineteen poems reviewed by J. C. Payen, of which only one refers to Antichrist, shed some important, if tangential, light on our theme. See Payen's analysis of "Les *Dies irae* dans la prédication de la morte et des fins dernières au moyen âge," *Romania*, LXXXV, 48–76. Of some interest also are such poems as *La Dança de la Muerte* which presents, among others, a rabbi and a Muslim alfaquim. See the text, ed. by T. A. Sanchez *et al.* in *Biblioteca de Autores españoles*, LVII, 379–85; and, more fully, by C. Appel in "Die 'Danza general' nach der Handschrift des Escorial neu herausgegeben," *Beiträge zum X. Deutschen Neuphilologentag*, Breslau, 1902, pp. 1–42; and J. M. Solá-Solé's recent comments thereon in "El Rabí y el alfaquí en la Dança general de la Muerte," *Romance Philology*, XVIII, 272–83. See also, more generally, H. Preuss, *Die Vorstellungen vom Antichrist im späteren Mittelalter;* E. Liefmann, "Die Legende vom Antichrist und die Sage vom Ahasver; ihre Bedeutung für den Antisemitismus," *Judaica*, III, 122–56; and J. Trachtenberg, *The Devil and the Jews*, pp. 32 ff.

On the background of this legend reaching into pre-Christian antiquity, see W. Bousset, *The Antichrist Legend, a Chapter in Christian and Jewish Folklore*, trans. by A. H. Keane; B. Blumenkranz, *Juifs et Chrétiens dans le monde occidental*, pp. 243 ff.; *supra*, Vol. V, pp. 142 ff. Incidentally the equation of the Papacy with Antichrist long antedated Calvin; it was tellingly used by some antipapal factions among Franciscans, Wycliffites, and the Bohemian predecessors of John Hus. See Calvin's *Institutes of the Christian Religion*, English trans. by F. L. Battle, ed. by J. T. McNeill, II, 1052 n. 16. See also *supra*, Vol. X, p. 385 n. 32.

The progressive Jew-baiting animus permeating the Antichrist presentations on the medieval stage has been illustrated in three plays by H. Pflaum in *REJ*, LXXXIX, 120 f. While the *Ludus de Antichristo*, though deeply nationalistic and looking forward to the Empire's world domination, sympathetically refers to the Jews and depicts them as staunchly resisting the early expansion of Antichrist's power, the subsequent Antichrist plays of Zurich and Künzelsau strongly stress the alliance between the pseudo-messiah and the Jews. They also emphasize the latter's vindictiveness toward their Christian oppressors. See R. Froning's intro. to his ed. of "Das Tegernseer Drama vom römischen Kaisertum deutscher Nation und vom Antichristen" in *Das Drama des Mittelalters*, I, 199 ff.; *Fastnachtspiele aus dem fünfzehn-*

ten Jahrhundert, ed. by A. von Keller, I, 593 ff. No. 68; *Das Künzelsauer Fronleich-namsspiel vom Jahre 1479*, ed. by A. Schumann. See also the vengeful verses quoted from the latter *infra*, n. 37; and the literature cited in the next note. The equation of Antichrist with the Jewish pseudo-messiah was facilitated by the growing conviction that Antichrist would exercise a particular appeal on the souls of the damned, among whom most theologians, as well as the populace, counted the souls of all infidels. It was easy enough, therefore, for a medieval French poet to call the arrival of Antichrist "the grand day of the Jews." See R. Schröder, *Glaube und Aberglaube*, pp. 74 ff.

13. M. B. Evans, *The Passion Play of Lucerne: an Historical and Critical Introduction*, pp. 68 ff. See the brief biographical sketch by W. Frei, *Der Luzerner Stadtschreiber Renward Cysat, 1545-1614;* and M. J. Rudwin, *A Historical and Bibliographical Survey of the German Religious Drama*, where the list of Christmas plays occupies only 5 pages as against 22 pages devoted to the listing of the interrelated plays devoted to the themes of Easter, the Passion, and Mary's Plaints (pp. 22-26, 27-47). The disproportion was somewhat lessened in the sixteenth and seventeenth centuries (pp. 71-75, 75-84). See also W. Werner's more recent *Studien zu den Passions- und Osterspielen des deutschen Mittelalters in ihrem Übergang vom Latein zur Volkssprache*. The evolution of the pseudo-Augustinian sermon in the medieval plays has been ingeniously reconstructed by M. Sepet in "Les Prophètes du Christ. Étude sur les origines du théâtre au moyen âge," *BEC*, XXVIII, 1-27, 211-64; XXIX, 105-39, 261-93; XXXVIII, 397-443 (also reprint), esp. XXXVIII, 398 ff., 409 n. 1, referring to the Frankfort Passion play published by J. C. von Fichard in his "Ordnung des Passionsspiels der St. Bartholomäistiftschule zu Frankfurt am Main," *Frankfurtisches Archiv für ältere deutsche Literatur und Geschichte*, III, 131-58.

Various Passion plays, even if stemming from the same region, for instance, from Laon, Limoges, or Rouen, greatly differed in the choice of prophets attesting the advent of the redeemer. But they all betrayed a pronounced anti-Jewish animus. They diverged, however, in their contemporary implications; only a few, like the Benediktbeuern Christmas play, present a rather overzealous and stubborn archisynagogus "who in everything imitates the Jewish gestures." See K. Young, *The Drama of the Medieval Church*, II, 151, 190 ff.

In another context Sepet graphically described the tremendous impressions such Passion and Mystery plays made on a town's general population, to which they were often introduced with great fanfare. "This was a day of great excitement and magnificence and the town's children long retained its memory." See his *L'Esquisse d'une représentation dramatique à la fin du quinzième siècle*, pp. 9 ff. The public was so insatiable, indeed, that a performance of Simon Greban's *Actes des Apôtres* in Bourges was attended by a host of spectators viewing it in installments over forty days. See H. Niedner, *Die Deutschen und französischen Osterspiele bis zum fünfzehnten Jahrhundert*, p. 122. It appears, on the other hand, that in countries of lesser Judeo-Christian tensions, such as medieval Portugal and early modern Poland, the religious drama displayed less Jew-baiting venom. This observation seems to be borne out at least by the admittedly selected materials analyzed in L. S. Picchio's *Storia del teatro portoghese;* and the few seventeenth-century religious plays included in J. Lewański's ed. of *Dramaty staropolskie* (Old Polish Dramas: an Anthology), Vol. VI. Nor did the Italian plays, even if dealing with anti-Jewish themes, betray feelings of the intensity of their northern counterparts. See, for instance, M.

Bonfantini's ed. of *Le Sacre rappresentazioni italiane: Raccolta di fonti dal secolo XIII al secolo XVI.* Of special Jewish interest are the plays "L'Anticristo e il giudizio finale" by a thirteenth-century author (pp. 43 ff.); Jacopone da Todi's "Il Pianto della Madonna" (pp. 62 ff.); the fourteenth-century "Il Miracolo di Bolsena" (pp. 98 ff.); the fifteenth-century "Miracolo di Teófilo" (pp. 536 ff.); and the sixteenth-century "Storia di Agnolo Ebreo" (pp. 568 ff.). See also E. Re, "Qualche nota sul tipo dell'Ebreo nel teatro popolare italiano," *Giornale storico della letteratura italiana,* 1912, pp. 383–98. Even the Virgin stories in Italy seem to have been permeated with less anti-Jewish animus, if we may judge from the succinct remarks and brief bibliography of G. Cocchiara in "Il Diavolo e la Vergine nella letteratura popolare italiana," *Bollettino* of the Centro di studi filologici e linguistici siciliani, VI–VIII, 358–69.

14. Hans Folz (Falz), *Ein Vasnachtspiel, die alt und neu Ee, die Sinagog, von Ueberwindung der Juden in ir Talmut,* reproduced in A. von Keller's *Fastnachtspiele aus dem fünfzehnten Jahrhundert,* I, 1–33 No. 1 (also *ibid.,* III, 1076; IV, 301, 309 ff.); K. Goedeke, *Grundriss zur Geschichte der deutschen Dichtung aus dem Quellen,* 2d ed., I, 329 f. Regrettably, like the other Folz editions, this text is quite unsatisfactory. See Hans Fischer's review of I. Spriewald's selection from Folz' writings under the title *Auswahl* in *Germanistik,* II, 373–74. See also Miss Spriewald's study of "Hans Folz—Dichter und Drucker. Beitrag zur Folz-Forschung," *Beiträge zur Geschichte der deutschen Sprache und Literatur,* LXXXIII, 242–77. It may be noted that while the *Adon 'olam* is relatively authentic, many speeches placed in the mouths of actors representing Jews are unadulterated nonsense. See M. Schwab, "Mots hébreux dans les Mystères du moyen âge," *REJ,* XLVI, 148–51; and *infra,* n. 17. See also H. Pflaum, *Die Religiöse Disputation,* pp. 84 f. n. 1 (explaining that, contrary to earlier assumptions, the barber Folz had not assembled any rabbinic materials on his own, but that he borrowed heavily from the *Pharetra fidei catholicae* by the Paris prior Theobaldus who, after participating in the renewed condemnation of the Talmud in 1248, had published this anti-Jewish pamphlet between 1254 and 1258; see *ibid.,* pp. 79 f. n. 22; H. Lomnitzer's analysis of "Das Verhältnis des Fastnachtspiels vom 'Kaiser Constantinus' zum Reimpaarspruch 'Christ und Jude' von Hans Folz," *Zeitschrift für deutsches Altertum und deutsche Literatur,* XCII, 277–91; and the later medieval Passion plays included in R. Froning's collection, *Das Drama des Mittelalters.*

It must be borne in mind, however, that not all mystery plays were anti-Jewish. Some playwrights may have included certain satirical scenes in order to amuse the public, rather than to lower the dignity of Jewish contemporaries, although audience reactions may have been hostile to Jews. See R. Hess's recent Freiburg dissertation, *Komische Elemente im romanischen geistlichen Schauspiel des 15. und 16. Jahrhunderts* (typescript). In the relatively friendly Provençal environment a playwright could actually present Jews as pleading *for* Jesus against Caiaphas and Ananias. See A. Jeanroy and H. Toulié, eds., *Mystères provençaux du quinzième siècle,* pp. 188 ff. Similarly, the Provençal liturgical poets who wrote numerous hymns about Mary Magdalen, made but sparing use of the opportunity to contrast her saintly behavior after she met Jesus with her sinful life before. They certainly could have cast broad aspersions on the morals of all ancient Jewish women and by indirection accused also their female contemporaries. They may have been restrained, however, by both their fear of giving nourishment to the folkloristic accusations of the Virgin's infidelity and their own observations of the relatively high standards of sex morality among their Jewish neighbors. See J. Szövérffy, " 'Peccatrix quondam femina': a Survey of the Mary Magdalen Hymns," *Traditio*, XIX, 79–146 (analyzing 160 such hymns).

On the other hand, the growingly hostile German public opinion induced even such secular poets as Heinrich der Teichner, a typical petty bourgeois, to attack Jews. See *Die Gedichte Heinrichs des Teichners*, ed. by H. Niewöhner, esp. III, 34 ff., 72 ff.; and Hans Fischer's comments in his "Neue Forschungen zur deutschen Dichtung des Spätmittelalters (1230–1500)," *Deutsche Vierteljahrsschrift für Literaturwissenschaft und Geistesgeschichte*, XXXI, 303–45, esp. p. 308 n. 15. See also E. Catholy, *Das Fastnachtspiel des Spätmittelalters. Gestalt und Funktion*, esp. p. 43 n. 1 (stressing Folz' need to introduce funny Jewish figures to lighten the seriousness of the play); and the numerous other sources and investigations listed in W. F. Michaels's careful bibliographical review of "Das Deutsche Drama und Theater vor der Reformation. Ein Forschungsbericht," *Deutsche Vierteljahrschrift für Literaturwissenschaft*, XXXI, 106–53; and in R. Tarot's "Literatur zum deutschen Drama und Theater des 16. und 17. Jahrhunderts. Ein Forschungsbericht (1945–1962)." *Euphorion, LVII*, 411–53.

Nor is the Church to be held responsible for some of the fantastically anti-Jewish presentations. While the New Testament and the Christian tradition furnished the main substrata for the plots the Church itself was of a divided mind about allowing local playwrights, and particularly clerics, to give free rein to their imagination. Some leading churchmen, such as Alexander of Hales, even debated the question whether "an actor or one notorious because of another sin" should be admitted to communion. On this negative attitude and its gradual relaxation see P. Browe, "Die Kirchliche Stellung der Schauspieler im Mittelalter," *Archiv für Kulturgeschichte*, XVIII, 246–57; and M. Henshaw, "The Attitude of the Church toward the Stage to the End of the Middle Ages," *Medievalia et humanistica*, VII, 3–17. See also *infra*, n. 88. In any case, it did not prevent individual clerics from using this means for espousing controversial ideas. For one example, a priest is depicted as having a supernatural vision relating to the "Jewish" pope Anacletus II, followed by Anacletus' death. Cited from a Paris MS by Mussafia in *SB* Vienna, CXXXIX, 4. More generally, too, this entire literature is permeated with a theological spirit. See esp. G. Duriez, *La Théologie dans le drame religieux en Allemagne au moyen âge;* R. B. Donovan, *The Liturgical Drama in Medieval Spain;* and E. Prosser, *Drama and Religion in the English Mystery Plays: a Re-Evaluation.*

15. John 8:44; Rev. 2:9 and 3:9. The figure of the devil on the medieval stage, to be sure, was not always that of a malevolent seducer. At times he was assigned a variety of jocular and satirical roles. See H. Wieck's Hamburg dissertation, *Die Teufel auf der mittelalterlichen Mysterienbühne Frankreichs*, esp. pp. 42 ff. Wieck's findings apply to the mystery plays of other countries as well. But the devil's demonic features were sharply accentuated whenever he was brought into contact with Jews. See also A. Axelsen, *Supernatural Beings in the French Medieval Dramas*, pp. 58 ff.; J. P. W. Crawford, "The Devil as a Dramatic Figure in the Spanish Religious Drama before Lope de Vega," *Romanic Review*, I, 302–12, 374–83 (analyzing 9 mystery plays, 14 morality plays, and 4 dramatizations of lives of saints); M. J. Rudwin, *Der Teufel in den deutschen geistlichen Spielen des Mittelalters und der Reformationszeit;* idem, ed., *Devil Stories: an Anthology;* and, more generally, M. Güdemann,

Geschichte des Erziehungswesens und der Cultur der Juden in Deutschland während des 14. und 15. Jahrhunderts, p. 205; and H. C. Holdschmidt, *Der Jude auf dem Theater des deutschen Mittelalters*. Although Holdschmidt's presentation must be used with caution—its shoddiness is well illustrated by its numerous misprints even in the names of authors and titles—he rightly shows how the medieval German stage had become the vehicle of an ever more rabidly anti-Jewish propaganda.

Next to the plays themselves, the directions for the producers often underscored the writers' anti-Jewish animus; they made even ancient Jews appear in medieval garb and talk with typical medieval Jewish gestures. See the *Alsfeld Dirigierrolle*, cited *infra*, n. 28; and the interesting data presented by G. Cohen in his ed. of *Le Livre de conduite du Régisseur et le Compte de dépenses pour le Mystère de la Passion joué à Mons en 1501*. In the play itself the author introduces a number of Jews under fictitious names and describes Judas as his father's slayer who married his own mother. See the pages listed in Cohen's *Index*, pp. 63 f. *s.v.* "Judas" and "Juifs." See also his "La Mise en scène au XIV siècle. La présentation de Marie au Temple . . . Office dramatique latin de Philippe de Mézières joué en Avignon, en 1372 et 1385," *Revue d'histoire du théâtre*, IX, 155–67 (showing the Synagogue, portrayed by a young beardless actor dressed in a torn black coat; he is ultimately ejected from the platform by Archangels Gabriel and Raphael); and his *Etudes d'histoire du théâtre au moyen âge et à la Renaissance*, pp. 163 ff. (similar directions for another fourteenth-century Avignon play); the various papers submitted to the international colloquium of the Centre national de la recherche scientifique in 1963 and ed. by J. Jacquot *et al.* under the title, *Le Lieu théâtral à la Renaissance*, esp. pp. 85 ff. (Venice), 183 ff. (Nuremberg), 215 ff. (Madrid), 473 ff. On the importance attached to gestures in medieval poetry see, from different angles, F. B. Zons, *Von der Auffassung der Gebärde in der MHD. Epik. Studie über drei Hauptarten malerischer Gebärdedarstellung*; M. F. McKean, *The Interplay of Realistic and Flamboyant Art Elements in the French Mystères* (Diss. Catholic University).

16. St. Hilarius of Poitiers, *Commentary* on Matthew 12:22–23 in his *Opera* in *PL*, IX, 992 f.; B. Bamberger, *The Fallen Angels*; Gregory IX's epistles of Oct. 29, 1232, and June 17, 1233, reproduced in C. Rodenberg's ed. of *Epistulae saeculi XIII*, I, 393 f. No. 489, 436 f. No. 539 (the latter summarized in *Les Registres*, ed. by L. Auvray, I, 786 f. No. 1402); and in C. Mackay's English trans. in his *Memoirs of Extraordinary Popular Delusions and the Madness of Crowds*, 3d ed., pp. 474 f.; Archbishop Baldwin cited *supra*, Vol. IV, pp. 125, 302 n. 47; Peter the Venerable of Cluny, *Tractatus adversus Judaeorum inveteratam duritiem*, ii end, in his *Opera* in *PL*, CLXXXIX, 538; St. John Chrysostom, *Adversus Judaeos orationes*, i.3, ii.3 in *Opera* in *PG*, XLVIII, 859 ff.; *supra*, Vols. II, pp. 43, 85; V, pp. 132, 350 n. 64; William Shakespeare, *The Merchant of Venice*, ii.2 in *The Comedies*, Oxford ed. by J. W. Craig, p. 607; and other data analyzed by J. Trachtenberg in *The Devil and the Jews*, pp. 11 ff.

This popular misconception was not restricted to the illiterate masses. No lesser a leader of men than Martin Luther indulged in such reckless assertions as "Verily a hopeless, wicked, venomous, and devilish thing is the existence of these Jews, who for fourteen hundred years have been, and still are, our pest, torment, and misfortune. In fine, they are just devils and nothing more with no feeling of humanity for us heathens." See *Von den Juden und ihren Lügen*, cited in English by E. M. Lamond in his authorized trans. from the German of H. Grisar's standard biography of

Luther, IV, 286. The sharpness of Luther's peroration was by no means mitigated by his similar outburst against the Zwinglians whom he called "endeviled, devilish, yea, ultra-devilish." *Ibid.,* p. 288. See also *infra,* n. 27.

17. See the lyrics cited by F. Kynass in *Der Jude im deutschen Volkslied,* pp. 60 ff.; K. Simrock, *Handbuch der deutschen Mythologie mit Einschluss der nordischen,* 5th ed., pp. 455, 536, 581; and *supra,* n. 14. The attribution to Jews of demonic characteristics was also facilitated by the medieval penchant for calling anything hostile and obnoxious "devilish." Certainly, such designations, frequently applied in popular letters to the New Testament figures of Herod or Caiaphas, and the condemnation of the whole non-Christian world as *le peuple Belzebu* or *les peuples infernax,* easily rubbed off on the unbelieving Jews as well. See the Spanish mystery on Herod (following French and Provençal prototypes), published by H. Corbató in his "Los Misterios del Corpus de Valencía. Critical ed. with notes and an intro.," *Publications in Modern Philology* of the University of California, XVI, 1–172, esp. pp. 67 ff., 83; the confusion in the medieval plays concerning the ancient Judean king analyzed by S. S. Hussey in "How Many Herods in the Middle English Drama?", *Neophilologus,* XLVIII, 251–59; and other illustrations cited by R. Schröder in his *Glaube und Aberglaube,* pp. 64 f. n. 9. At times the legend was more kindly to non-Jewish infidels. In his encounter with a Jew, even a Magus is depicted as an altruistic and kindly person while the Jew is both selfish and conniving. See the summary from a Paris MS by L. Thorndike in *A History of Magic,* II, 278.

18. J. Szövérffy, "'Peccatrix,'" *Traditio,* XIX, 105; K. Wehrhan, *Frankfurter Kinderleben in Sitte und Brauch,* p. 125 Nos. 1918–19; Kynass, *Der Jude,* p. 45; J. J. Schudt, *Jüdische Merckwürdigkeiten,* II, Part 1, pp. 368 f.; I. Lévi, "Les Juifs de la légende," *REJ,* XX, 249–52; I. Loeb, "Le Juif de l'histoire," *ibid.,* XX, pp. lii f. According to a Portuguese tale, a pilgrim recognized through the characteristic odor the Jewish origin of Pope Pius IX! See J. Mendes dos Remedios, *Os Judeus em Portugal,* I, 401 n. 2. Apparently, contrary to the general belief, even the baptism of Pius' ancestor had not eliminated that smell. Incidentally, the prejudice that some Jews' hands touched their knees existed also in Arab folklore but it was largely limited there to exilarchs. See *supra,* Vol. V, p. 297 n. 9.

Conversely, some German stories described how the clandestine conversion of a Jewish boy was detected by his family only because of his new fragrance. See the fourteenth-century version of the "Jewish boy" legend, summarized from a Paris MS by A. Mussafia in *SB,* Vienna, CXIX, Part ix, p. 25; H. Loewe, *Die Juden in der katholischen Legende,* p. 29. Racist bias alone dictated Holdschmidt's contention that medieval authors invariably explained the reputed conversion of Jews after their disputation before Constantine the Great as due to their desire to eat pork rather than to inner conviction. Nor is Luther's statement cited by Holdschmidt as genuinely racialist as he claims. See *Der Jude auf dem Theater,* p. 58, with reference to the carnival play *Kaiser Constantinus,* ed. by A. von Keller in his *Fastnachtspiele aus dem fünfzehnten Jahrhundert,* pp. 796 ff. No. 106 (cf. H. Lomnitzer's aforementioned essay in *Zeitschrift für deutsches Altertum,* XCII, 277 ff.). Only in Spain, where the problem of *conversos* loomed very large, did the contemporary literature reflect the truly widespread distrust of the genuineness of their conversion. See the illustrations assembled by K. R. Scholberg in *Hispania* (America), XXXVII, 203–209; and by E. Glaser in "Referencias antisemitas en la literatura peninsular de la edad de oro,"

Nueva Revista de Filologia española, VIII, 39–62; R. B. Donovan, The Liturgical Drama in Medieval Spain; and infra, Chaps. LV–LVI.

19. Johann Fischart, Wunderzeitung von einer schwangeren Jüdin zu Binzwangen, Strasbourg, 1575 ed. with a woodcut showing the two pigs delivered by the Jewess (reproduced by J. Trachtenberg in The Devil and the Jews, p. 53); Le Chevalier au Cygne et Godefroid de Bouillon, ed. by F. de Reiffenberg, II, 242 vv. 9749 ff., 466 vv. 16578 ff.; R. Schröder, Glaube, pp. 130 ff. These fantasies also underlay some theological figures of speech. In his reiterated attacks upon Jews, St. Bernard of Clairvaux exclaimed: "O intelligence coarse, dense, and as if it were bovine, which did not recognize God, even in his own works!" Subsequently, the preacher argued, with reference to Isaiah's exclamation (1:3) "The ox knoweth his owner," that his condemnation was milder than that implied by the Israelitic prophet who had thus set the Jews below the rank of brute beasts. From another angle Peter de Blois claimed, "We see the Passion of Christ, not only in their [the Jews'] books but also in their faces." See St. Bernard's Sermones in Cantica, lx, in his Opera omnia, PL, CLXXXIII, 1067 f.; Peter de Blois, Contra perfidiam Judaeorum, ibid., CCVII, 825, both also cited by M. Hay in The Foot of Pride. The Pressure of Christendom on the People of Israel for 1900 Years, p. 54.

20. See Z. Kahn, "Le Livre de Joseph le Zélateur," REJ, III, 26; E. Roy's ed. of Le Mystère de la Passion en France, pp. 59 * f.; Hans Wilhelm Kirchhof, Wendunmuth, i.195, ed. by H. Oesterley, I, 238 f.; W. Creizenach, "Judas Ischarioth in Legende und Sage des Mittelalters," Beiträge zur Geschichte der deutschen Sprache, II, 206 f.; M. Schapiro, The Parma Ildefonsus: a Romanesque Illuminated Manuscript from Cluny and Related Works, esp. Figures 7–11, 14–15, and 16. Of course, no reference is made here to the Jewish ancestry of Julian of Toledo. See Figure 86; and supra, Vol. III, pp. 249 f. n. 55. On Malchus and his connection with the Wandering Jew, see infra, n. 74. Another, rather questionable, derivation of the Jews' red hair from Rufus was offered by F. J. Mone in his ed. of Schauspiele des Mittelalters. Aus Handschriften, I, 57. See also the data reviewed by J. Caro Baroja in Los Judios en la España moderna y contemporanea, I, 87 ff.

21. G. Roskoff, Geschichte des Teufels, II, 380; E. F. Sommer, De Theophili cum diabolo foedere, pp. 4 ff.; Hrotswitha of Gandersheim, Lapsus et coversio Theophili vicedomini in her Opera, in PL, CXXXVII, 1101–10; King Sancho's Castigos y documentos, lxxxii, ed. by P. de Gayangos in "Escritores de prosa al siglo XV," Biblioteca de Autores españoles, LI, 215; other versions of the Theophilus legend, cited by K. Plenzat in Die Theophiluslegende in den Dichtungen des Mittelalters (with good bibliography); H. Loewe in Die Juden, pp. 42 ff.; and H. Pflaum in REJ, LXXXIX, 124; M. Güdemann, Geschichte des Erziehungswesens, III, 207 ff.; L. Geiger in ZGJD, [o.s.] III, 298. It should be noted, however, that a related Byzantine story presents an honorable Jew who, because he was helped by a saint to recover his property from a Christian embezzler, adopted Christianity. See P. Devos, "Le Juif et le chrétien. Un miracle de Saint Ménas," Analecta Bollandiana, LXXVIII, 275–308 (reproducing Greek, Coptic, and Ethiopic versions).

22. The Sefer Yuḥasim (Chronicle) of Ahimaaz, cited supra, Vol. III, pp. 180, 315 n. 7, with the comments thereon by J. Starr in The Jews in the Byzantine Empire

641–1204, pp. 128 ff. No. 64; Mansi, *Collectio*, XXIII, 530 canon 15, 882 canon 23; S. Grayzel, *The Church and the Jews*, pp. 73 f., 330 f., 336 f.; C. Pendrill, *London Life in the 14th Century*, pp. 202 f.; A. Rubió y Lluch, *Documents per l'historia de la cultura catalana mig-eval*, II, 232 No. ccxlvii; J. M. Vidal, ed., *Bullaire de l'Inquisition française au XIV⁰ siècle et jusqu'à la fin du Grand Schisme*, p. 487 No. 338; Raynaldus, *Annales*, VIII, 503; F. Vernet, "Le Pape Martin V et les Juifs," *RQH*, LI, 373–423, esp. p. 387; *supra*, Vol. X, pp. 256, 414 n. 44.

By a curious historic irony the popes themselves did not escape the accusation of sorcery. During the Great Schism the Pisa Commission, which in May 1409, held thirteen hearings and listened to eighty-four witnesses, denounced Gregory XII for entertaining close relations with a Jewish physician, Helia (Elijah), "who made use of magic arts or necromancy." The pope had allegedly asked the Jewish magician to ascertain "in which way he could perpetuate himself" and secure the sole occupancy of the Papal See. Benedict XIII, on the other hand, was supposed to have searched for magic books among Saracens and kept in his library a Jewish book in which Jesus' miracles were interpreted as pure magic. See N. Valois, *La France et le Grand Schisme de l'Occident*, IV, 93 ff., 97. The latter accusation may have referred to Benedict's library which, as we recall, contained many Jewish and anti-Jewish tracts, frequently used by that antipope for bitter attacks on Jews and Judaism. See *supra*, Vol. IX, p. 287 n. 2. Not surprisingly, a medieval poet found nothing objectionable in a nephew's praise of an abbot of St. Denis for knowing "more of the art and the learning of necromancy than any other man ever born." See *Gaydon*, vv. 74 f., ed. by F. Guessard *et al.* in their collection of *Les Anciens poètes de la France*, VII, 3. See also *supra*, Vol. X, p. 141. Moreover, magic and particularly fortunetelling also had intimate connections with the far more respectable profession of astrology in which Jews, too, were fully represented. See *supra*, Vol. VIII, pp. 175 ff.; and *infra*, n. 71.

23. J. Starr, *The Jews in the Byzantine Empire*, pp. 95 f. No. 17 (also pointing out that in later legends Heliodorus himself was a Jew); *supra*, Vols. II, pp. 15 ff.; V, pp. 316 f. n. 69; VIII, pp. 44, 293 n. 48; J. Parkes, *The Conflict of the Church and the Synagogue*, I, 160, 164, 299; G. Gabrieli, "Un Amuleto ebraico-aramaico ritrovato in Lecce," *Rivista storica salentina*, XIII (also reprint); Pietro Aretino, *Regionamento dello Zoppino* (1539) in the excerpt reproduced in M. Bontempelli's selection of *Le Più belle pagine di Pietro Aretino*, p. 140; Lodovico Ariosto, *Il Negromante* in his *Opere minore*, ed. by F. L. Polidori, II, 351–422 (this necromancer is described as "a Jew by origin of those who had been chased out of Castile," p. 370) ; Benvenuto Cellini, *The Life*, English trans. by J. A. Symonds, 5th ed., p. 127; W. Ahrens, *Hebräische Amulette mit magischen Zahlenquadraten;* Franco Sacchetti, *Novelle*, Florence, 1724 ed., II, 194 ff. Nos. ccxviii-xix; R. Davidsohn's comprehensive *Forschungen zur ältren Geschichte von Florenz*, III, 166 f. No. 816; idem, *Geschichte von Florenz*, IV, 159; U. Cassuto, *Gli Ebrei*, p. 9; and, more generally, M. Petrocchi, *Esorcismi e magie nell'Italia del Cinquecento e del Seicento;* the comprehensive data assembled by H. Bächtold-Stäubli *et al.*, eds., in the *Handwörterbuch des deutschen Aberglaubens*, esp. IV, 811 ff. (by W. E. Peuckert); and the literature listed in the next note.

The interdenominational use of Hebrew symbols was found also among "jugglers." The latter frequently employed particularly the Hebrew letter *aleph* not only because in the Kabbalah, both Jewish and Christian, it represented the first, divine principle, but also because the Hebrew character seemed graphically to depict a juggler's contortions. See K. Seligmann, *The History of Magic*, pp. 428 ff. and esp. the

Renaissance design of a juggler, reproduced *ibid.*, Fig. 238. On Jewish professional jugglers, see, for instance, *supra*, Vol. X, pp. 153, 369 n. 41.

24. Thomas de Cantimpré, cited by H. C. Lea in his *Materials toward a History of Witchcraft*, ed. by A. C. Howland, with an intro. by G. L. Burr, I, 90 f.; A. Lehmann, *Aberglaube und Zauberei von den ältesten Zeiten an bis in die Gegenwart*, German trans. from the Danish by Dr. Pedersen, pp. 159 ff. Caesarius of Heisterbach, the popular collector of tales and legends, frequently recites miraculous happenings adversely affecting Jews, but he seems consciously to underplay their association with the devil. See P. Schmidt, *Der Täufels- und Daemonenglaube in den Erzählungen des Caesarius von Heisterbach*, to which add the important material accumulated by A. Hilka in the passages of *Die Wundergeschichten* listed in the Indices, *s.v.* Teufel.

25. L. Thorndike, *A History of Magic and Experimental Science*, esp. II, 279 ff.; the remarkable "magical incantation according to the key of Solomon," reproduced by K. Seligmann in *The History of Magic*, p. 296 Fig. 128; the dissertations by F. M. Goebel, *Jüdische Motive im märchenhaften Erzählungsgut*; G. Salzberger, *Die Salomosage in der semitischen Literatur*; St. Agobard of Lyons, *De judaicis superstitionibus* in *PL*, CIV, 77 ff. (*MGH*, Epistolae, V, 185 ff.); M. Stern, *Urkundliche Beiträge über die Stellung der Päpste*, I, 106 ff. No. 105 end; Isaac b. Joseph of Corbeil, *'Ammude golah* or *Sefer Miṣvot qaṭan* (Small Book of Commandments; a code), No. 251, Ladi ed., fol. 96b; Isaac b. Moses of Vienna, *Sefer Or Zaru'a*, II; L. Nemoy, "Maimonides and His Opposition to Sorcery" (Hebrew), *Harofé Haivri*, 1954, Part 2, pp. 102–109; Yehudah b. Samuel, *Sefer Ḥasidim* (Book of the Pious), ed. by J. Wistinetzki, p. 76 No. 210. It should be noted, however, that in stressing theological, rather than ethical, teachings Yehudah did not hesitate to play up the demonic forces of evil. See J. Dan, "Demonological Stories in the Writings of R. Yehudah Hehasid" (Hebrew), *Tarbiz*, XXX, 273–89 (analyzing thirty-one such stories extant in Oxford and Günzburg MSS). See *supra*, Vols. IV, pp. 51 f., 262 ff. nn. 67–68; V, pp. 132 f. nn. 64–65; and the vast accumulation of data from the medieval Jewish folkloristic, homiletical, and halakhic literatures in J. Trachtenberg's *Jewish Magic and Superstition*, esp. pp. 11 ff. See also some additional illustrations in A. Leschnitzer, *The Magic Background of Modern Antisemitism*; C. Roth's brief review of Trachtenberg's *The Devil and the Jews* in *EHR*, LXI, 115–16; and, by way of both comparison and contrast, C. E. Hopkins's dissertation, *The Share of Thomas Aquinas in the Growth of the Witchcraft Delusion*.

Both the realities of Jewish occult practices and their vast exaggeration in the anti-Jewish polemical literature reached back into antiquity and the Muslim Middle Ages. But in later medieval Europe the slurs received a peculiarly vicious coloring and assumed unprecedented dimensions, which endangered the very continuation of the Judeo-Christian symbiosis, all of which did not prevent Jews from borrowing such Christian demonological terms, as *estries, broxa* (both derivations from night birds, but used to designate "witches"), or *werewolf* and incorporating them into their Hebrew usage. See the examples cited by Trachtenberg in his *Jewish Magic*, pp. 38, 278 n. 34.

26. O. Pfister, *Calvins Eingreifen in die Hexer- und Hexenprozesse von Peney 1545 nach seiner Bedeutung für Geschichte und Gegenwart*, pp. 33 ff., 66 ff.; Lagumina and Lagumina, *Codice diplomatico*, I, 508 f. No. cccxc; such recent monographs from

different areas as G. A. Brucker, "Sorcery in Early Renaissance Florence," *Studies in the Renaissance*, X, 7–24; P. Villette, "La Sorcellerie dans le Nord de la France du milieu du XVᵉ à la fin du XVIIᵉ siècle," *Mélanges de science religieuse*, XIII, 39–56, 129–56; W. Krämer, *Kurtrierische Hexenprozesse im 16. und 17. Jahrhundert, vornehmlich an der unteren Mosel;* F. Merzbacher, *Die Hexenprozesse in Franken*, pointing out that, apart from the extensive Jewish self-government, it was only the definite banishment of Jews from the bishoprics of Würzburg (1575) and Bamberg (1565) that spared the Jews prosecutions for sorcery (pp. 67 f.) ; and, more generally, the aforementioned comprehensive work by L. Thorndike; M. Summers's twin studies of *The History of Witchcraft and Demonology*, 2d ed., and *The Geography of Witchcraft;* R. H. Robbins, *The Encyclopedia of Witchcraft;* J. Hansen, *Quellen und Untersuchungen zur Geschichte des Hexenwahns und der Hexenverfolgung im Mittelalter;* idem, *Zauberwahn, Inquisition und Hexenprozess im Mittelalter;* J. Caro Baroja, *The World of the Witches*, trans. from the Spanish by O. N. V. Glendinnen; the telling graphic illustrations reproduced by K. Seligmann in *The History of Magic;* and, with special reference to Jews, M. Mieses, "Heretics Accused of Witchcraft" (Yiddish), *YB*, XIII, 147–71. See also *infra*, n. 71.

27. Mansi, *Collectio*, IX, 1017 can. xiv; J. Parkes, *Conflict*, I, 354; the German satire, probably written by Bernard von Utzingen, and published by R. von Liliencron in *Die Historischen Volkslieder der Deutschen*, I, 161 ff. No. 40, and esp. p. 173 vv. 632 ff. (this generally anticlerical poem makes a representative of an artisan guild express the wish that the city should be rid of both the priests and the Jews and inherit their property, pp. 171 f. vv. 505 f.); Mieses in *YB*, XIII, 162 ff.; *supra*, n. 22. See also the few early data on "Le Juif sorcier" analyzed by Israel Lévi in "Le Juif de la légende," *REJ*, XXII, 232 f.; and, more generally, I. Loeb, "Le Juif de l'histoire et le Juif de la légende," *ibid.*, XX, pp. xxxiii–lxi.

28. See the texts included by R. Froning in *Das Drama des Mittelalters*, II, 457 ff. (Frankfort Passion play of 1493, vv. 2273–84) , 681 ff. (Alsfeld Passion play, vv. 3150–3227), 813 ff. (*ibid.* vv. 6839 ff. where Jews are ridiculed by their appearance before Pilate *cantantes ebraycum*); Jean Michel, *Le Mystère de la Passion (Angers, 1486)*, ed. by O. Jodogne; the Vienna fifteenth-century Easter play, ed. by A. Hoffmann von Fallersleben in *Fundgruben für Geschichte der deutschen Sprache und Literatur*, II, 297–336 ("the Jews dance before Pilate and sing in Jewish [*judisch*]"); K. Goedeke, ed., *Pamphilus Gengenbach*, p. 673 n. 11; R. Brandsteter, "Die Aufführung eines Luzerner Osterspiels im 16.–17. Jahrhundert," *Der Geschichtsfreund*, XLVIII, 277–336; M. B. Evans, *The Passion Play of Lucerne: an Historical and Critical Introduction;* A. Pichler, *Ueber das Drama des Mittelalters in Tirol. Ein seltzam und Wunderbarliches Gespräch, Von zweyen Jüdischen Rabinen gehalten*, 1563, fol. B2a, cited by L. Geiger in *ZGJD*, [o.s.] II, 336 f.; Jan (de Clerk) Boendale's statement in *Der Leken Spieghel*, ed. by M. de Vries, I, 197, and summarized by J. Stengers in *Les Juifs dans les Pays-Bas*, p. 52. On the few Jews still living in the late fifteenth century in the German-speaking parts of Tyrol and the district of Lucerne, see A. Tänzer, *Geschichte der Juden in Tirol und Vorarlberg*, pp. 2 ff.; and A. Steinberg, *Studien zur Geschichte der Juden in der Schweiz während des Mittelalters*, pp. 3 and 9.

As pointed out by R. Froning, the Alsfeld Passion play, after its first performance in 1501, was sharpened in 1511 and 1517 by the interpolation of twenty additional verses elaborating the purported bargaining between Judas, the high priest Caiaphas, and several Roman soldiers. See his intro. to the Alsfeld play in *Das Drama des Mittelalters*, II, 556 f.; H. Legband's dissertation, *Die Alsfelder Dirigierrolle*, pp. 44 f.; Holdschmidt's comments thereon in *Der Jude auf dem Theater*, pp. 104 ff.; more generally, Froning's *Zur Geschichte und Beurteilung der geistlichen Spiele des Mittelalters, insonderheit der Passionsspiele*. On the role of Judas in medieval legend see also J. R. Breitenbucher's dissertation, *Die Judasgestalt in den Passionsspielen* (typescript); W. Creizenach, "Judas Ischarioth in Legende und Sage des Mittelalters," *Beiträge zur Geschichte der deutschen Sprache*, II, esp. pp. 177, 180 f. 185 f., 192 ff.; P. Lehmann, Judas Ischariot in der lateinischen Legendenüberlieferung des Mittelalters" (1930), reprinted in his *Erforschung des Mittelalters: Ausgewählte Abhandlungen und Aufsätze*, II, 229–85; K. Luethi, *Judas Iskarioth in der Geschichte der Auslegung von der Reformation bis zur Gegenwart;* and *supra*, n. 10. Not surprisingly, the tragic figure of the ancient traitor has fascinated many modern writers as well. See, for instance, D. Bagge, "Le Mythe de Judas dans la littérature française contemporaine," *Critique*, XIV, 423–37, which reviews six books published between 1936 and 1956, including a play by Marcel Pagnol, performed in Paris in 1955.

Even when unfavorably depicting Christian usurers medieval poets often attributed to them manifestly Jewish characteristics. In his *Mammons Sold,* for example, published in Nuremberg in 1613, Wolfhart Spangenberg presented a Christian usurer, Reichhart, boasting to Satan of charging compound interest in the Jewish way (*Jüdisch zu nehmen Zins von Zins*), of clipping coins, selling misrepresented wares, distributing forged notes, and pleading fraudulent bankruptcies. "Without inquiring about his misery, I prefer to give the poor man stone instead of bread." See W. Spangenberg's *Augewählte Dichtungen*, pp. 258 ff., 263 f.; and, on the author, see Hans Müller's biographical sketch, "Wolfhart Spangenberg," *Zeitschrift für Deutsche Philologie*, LXXXI, 129–68, 385–401; LXXXII, 454–71. In his *Storia di Agnolo ebreo,* an anonymous fifteenth-century Italian author shows Jews worried over the implications of the new movement for the *monti di pietà*. See the text in M. Bonfantini's ed. of *Le Sacre rappresentazioni italiane*, pp. 568–93. See also K. Burdach's searching observations, "Der Judenspiess und die Longinus-Sage," *Neue Jahrbücher für das klassische Altertum*, XXXVII, 21–56, esp. pp. 25 ff., 36. Occasionally, to be sure, some French authors, evidently no longer personally acquainted with Jewish moneylenders, could depict a Jewish banker in a favorable light. A playwright around 1500, whose miracle play somewhat anachronistically described a miraculous intervention of St. Nicholas in favor of a Jew, presents the latter as extending a loan to an impoverished Christian without any pledge by relying on the debtor's oath in the name of the saint. However, this Jewish lender seems a priori destined to find his way to the baptismal font. See O. Jodogne's analysis of "Le Miracle de saint Nicolas et d'un juif," *Mélanges de linguistique romane offerts à Maurice Delbouille*, II, 313–28.

29. See the literature listed by F. Kynass in *Der Jude*, p. 34 n. 88, and the examples cited *ibid.*, pp. 68 f. Other data have been analyzed in O. Frankl's Vienna dissertation, *Der Jude in den deutschen Dichtungen des 15., 16. und 17. Jahrhunderts*.

30. The sale of thirty Jews for one penny recurs in the recital of *La Prise de Jérusalem ou la Vengeance du Sauveur* (12th cent.), ed. by C. Chabaneau in the

Provençal version (fully described and cited by P. Meyer in his "Notice du manuscrit de la Bibliothèque Nationale, fonds français 25415," *Bulletin* of the Société des anciens textes français, I, 52 ff., 57); in the Catalan version published by P. Bofarull in his "Documentos literarios en antigua lingua catalana (siglos XIV y XV)," *Colección de documentos inéditos del Archivo general de Aragón*, XIII; another *Vengeance*, included in the fourteenth-century *Le Roman d'Arles*, likewise ed. by Chabaneau in the *Revue des langues romanes*, XXXII, 472–542, esp. pp. 478 f., 493 vv. 572 ff.; still another *Vengeance*, published under the telling German title, *Rache Gottes an den Juden durch Titus, Vespasian und dem Teufel in Gestalt des Moses*, by C. Neuhaus in his collection of *Adgar's Marienlegenden*, pp. 213 ff. vv. 66 ff., in part cited by M. Lifschitz-Golden in *Les Juifs*, pp. 63 f., 142 f. See also O. Geister's dissertation, *Die Teufelsszenen in der Passion von Arras und der Vengeance Jhesucrist* (includes unpublished scenes of the devil, pp. 76 ff.; see, for instance, p. 83 vv. 5 ff.).

One wonders whether these legends originated from Baudri de Bourgueil's report concerning the alleged cheap sale of Jewish prisoners by Tancred in the newly conquered Latin Kingdom of Jerusalem. See *supra*, Vols. IV, pp. 110, 294 n. 23, 296 n. 27; IX, 116 f., 312 nn. 13–14; and, on the origin of the Jewish "dice tax," *ibid.*, pp. 322 f. n. 42. This legend, which indeed occurs also in connection with the First Crusade in *Le Chevalier au Cygne*, ed. by F. de Reiffenberg, III, 55 vv. 20470 f., may long have circulated in oral form, just as did many stories directly related to Judas. See, for instance, C. A. Tyre's observations on the Spanish play, *Del Nacimiento y vida de Judas*, written before 1590, which shows greater differences from Jacobus a (de) Voragine's pertinent account in his *Legenda aurea* than would appear justified in a case of sheer literary indebtedness. See Tyre's ed. of *Religious Plays of 1590*, pp. 15 ff., 71–112.

The story of Vespasian's recovery from his alleged illness is told with much gusto in the *Legenda aurea*, lxvii, ed. by T. Graesse, 3d ed., pp. 299 f.; in the English trans. from the Latin by G. Ryan and H. Ripperger, I, 265 f. Jacobus doubtless picked up from some intermediate Christian source this "reply" to the well-known ancient Jewish legend concerning the deadly insect boring in Titus' cranium. See Bab. Giṭṭin 56b; and my remarks thereon *supra*, Vol. II, pp. 93, 369 n. 6. An early Franconian writer actually drew the unusual parallel that, because the Jews had offended God the Father and the Son, they were punished through the instrumentality of a father and a son (Vespasian and Titus). See S. Stein's informative Heidelberg dissertation, *Die Ungläubigen in der mittelhochdeutschen Literatur von 1050 bis 1250*, p. 25. These few examples of the queer mixture of history and legend often injected into the medieval controversial literature, in both prose and poetry, must suffice here. But a comprehensive scholarly monograph on this subject would doubtless prove highly rewarding.

31. *Supra*, Vols. I, pp. 192 f., 382 n. 33; IV, pp. 132 ff., 306 ff. To the literature mentioned IV, 306 n. 56, add J. Trachtenberg's observations in *The Devil and the Jews*, Chaps. IX–X. See also W. Schultze, "Der Vorwurf des Ritualmordes gegen die Christen im Altertum und in der Neuzeit," *ZKG*, LXV, 304–306, also showing how this libel was resuscitated in the 1840s particularly by Georg Friedrich Daumer of Nuremberg. By 1273 the accusation had been sufficiently established for Nathan Official to debate it publicly with Bishop Hugh of Chouteroux. See Z. Kahn's "Étude sur le livre de Joseph le Zélateur," *REJ*, III, 27.

32. See *supra*, Vol. IV, pp. 135 f., 306 n. 57; M. D. Anderson, *A Saint at Stake: the Strange Death of William of Norwich 1144*. Innocent IV's and other papal condemnations of the Blood Accusation, as well as Frederick II's eloquent decree, have in part been quoted *supra*, Vol. IX, pp. 311 f. nn. 10–11. On the events in Valréas see the interesting document ed. with an informative introduction by A. Molinier in his "Enquête sur un meurtre imputé aux Juifs de Valréas (1247)," *Cabinet historique*, XXIX, 121–34. A fuller collection is readily available in M. Stern's ed. of *Die Päpstlichen Bullen über die Blutbeschuldigung* (published anonymously). See also C. Roth, *The Ritual Murder Libel and the Jews. The Report by Cardinal Lorenzo Ganganelli (Pope Clement XIV)*, reproducing with an English trans. the original of Ganganelli's report, first published in the German trans. by A. Berliner in 1888 and soon thereafter republished in Latin and submitted to a careful analysis by I. Loeb in "Un Mémoire de Laurent Ganganelli sur la calomnie du meurtre rituel," *REJ*, XVIII, 179–211. All these authors also cite a number of additional sources. On the numerous earlier Blood Accusations in Poland and attempts by Polish apologists to explain away these papal bulls, see *supra*, Vol. X, pp. 35 f., 316 f. n. 43.

Not surprisingly, a Nazi scholar, H. Schramm, tried to buttress the old ritual murder libel by a pseudo-scientific historical survey of *Der Jüdische Ritualmord*, offering but little information concerning medieval and early modern developments, but concentrating on the accusations of the last hundred years. See also W. F. P. Stockley's brief survey, "Popes and Jewish 'Ritual Murder,'" *Catholic World*, CXXXIX, 450–60. Some of the vast older literature (to 1905) on this subject is listed in H. Hayn's *Uebersicht der (meist in Deutschland erschienenen) Litteratur über die angeblich von Juden verübten Ritualmorde und Hostienfrevel*. A more up-to-date bibliography would be in order.

33. G. A. Tzschoppe and G. A. Stenzel, eds., *Urkundensammlung . . . Schlesien*, p. 69; F. Baer, *Die Juden*, I, Part 1, pp. 152 ff. No. 138, 209 ff. No. 171; G. A. Stenzel, *Urkunden zur Geschichte des Bisthums Breslau*, p. 195 No. cxciii. As explained by M. Brann, Bishop Thomas referred to dangers facing the Silesian clergy at a time when it was locked in deadly combat with the duke whom it had placed under a ban. See Brann's *Geschichte der Juden in Schlesien*, pp. 17 f. On occasion, however, the Blood Accusation could be used to foster political ambitions. In "Une Accusation de meurtre rituel contre les Juifs d'Uzès en 1297," *BEC*, LXXV, 59–66, R. André-Michel has shown how these proceedings first led to a jurisdictional dispute between the bishop who controlled one-quarter of the city and the lay lords who ruled over the rest. Ultimately Philip IV intervened mainly because he was thus able to promote his centralizing efforts. See also *supra*, Vol. X, pp. 140 f., 364 n. 27.

34. Alphonso X, *Las Siete Partidas*, vii.24, 2, ed. by G. Lopez, IV, 644. It is possible, as suggested by H. C. Lea, that Alphonso had written these lines under the impact of rumors, which had emanated in 1250 from Saragossa though not from any Castilian locality, concerning the Jews' crucifixion of a young chorister. See H. C. Lea's *Materials toward a History of Witchcraft*, I, 231; and J. Amador de los Rios's *Historia social*, III, 317 f. n. 1. The Trent affair of 1475, extensively debated in contemporary pamphlets, stirred the imagination of many writers. See *supra*, Vol. X, pp. 286 f., 428 f. nn. 80–81. It received more authoritative support from the inclusion of Simeon's biography in the *Acta Sanctorum*, under March 24 (March, Vol. IX,

cols. 495–502). It has generated a vast literature ever since 1747, when B. Bonelli published his *Dissertazioni apologetiche sul martirio del beato Simone da Trento nell'anno 1475 degli Ebrei ucciso*. Further documentation with a strongly anti-Jewish bias was provided in 1893 by J. Deckert in *Ein Ritualmord actenmässig nach-gewiesen;* and in his *Vier Tiroler Kinder, Opfer des chassidischen Fanatismus: Urkundlich dargestellt*, pp. 1–72. See also the additional bibliography listed in H. L. Strack, *The Jew and Human Sacrifice [Human Blood and Jewish Ritual]; an Historical and Sociological Inquiry*, English trans. by H. Blanchamp, pp. 193 ff.; J. E. Scherer, *Die Rechtsverhältnisse der Juden*, pp. 598 f. n.*; V. Manzini, *La Superstizione omicida e i sacrifici umani;* G. Volli's review of "I Processi tridentini ed il culto del beato Simone da Trento," *Il Ponte*, XIX, 1396–1408; and P. Eckert's totally negative recent findings accepted as valid by Archbishop Alessandro Gottardi of Trent in his pastoral letter of 1965. See R. C. Doty's report in the *New York Times* of Nov. 1, 1965. See also *infra*, n. 44; and M. A. Shulvass's ed. of "A New Hebrew Source for the History of the Blood Accusation in Trent" (Hebrew), *Minḥah li-Yehudah* (Judah Zlotnick [Avida] Jub. Vol.), pp. 189–96, the data of which, however, help but slightly to round out the picture of that prosecution.

35. J. Starr, *The Jews in the Byzantine Empire*, pp. 209 ff. No. 155; Eusebius Pamphilius of Caesarea, *The Ecclesiastical History*, v.1, 26, in the Greek text with the English trans. by K. Lake *et al.;* and, more generally, W. Schultze, "Der Vorwurf des Ritualmordes," *ZKG*, LXV, 304–306. This proximity of Purim and Passover suggested to Selig Cassel and Cecil Roth the idea that the alleged occasional Eastern hangings of the Haman effigy on Purim had stimulated the Western imagination to postulate a similar reenactment of the crucifixion of Jesus during Easter or Passover. See C. Roth, "The Feast of Purim and the Origins of the Blood Accusation," *Speculum*, VIII, 520–26; together with my reservations thereon, *supra*, Vol. IV, p. 308 n. 61. It should also be noted that the Western-type Blood Accusation spread relatively late to the Greek-Orthodox world and that in the Middle Ages it never assumed there the proportions, or entailed the consequences, of the Western libels.

36. See Israel Lévi, "Les Juifs de France du milieu du IXe siècle aux Croisades," *REJ*, LII, 161 ff.; J. Régné, "Catalogue," *ibid.*, LXI, 28 No. 377 (1268); LXIII, 252 No. 696 (1278) ; LXV, 63 Nos. 1034–35 (1282–83); N. Ferorelli, *Gli Ebrei*, p. 60; B. Lagumina and G. Lagumina, *Codice diplomatico*, II, 421 f. No. dccxlvii; *supra*, Vol. IV, pp. 55 f., 265 n. 72; and other sources, cited by C. Roth in "The Easter-Tide Stoning of the Jews and Its Liturgical Echoes," *JQR*, XXXV, 361–70, where a liturgical poem (by one Solomon not further identified) is published from a fifteenth-century Spanish MS (pp. 367 f.).

37. A. Schumann, ed., *Das Künzelsauer Fronleichnamsspiel vom Jahre 1479*, p. 186; "Ein Spil von dem Herzogen von Burgund" in A. von Keller's ed. of the *Fastnachtspiele aus dem fünfzehnten Jahrhundert*, I, 169 ff. No. 20, esp. pp. 179 f.; David b. Samuel ha-Levi, *Magen David* (David's Shield: a commentary on Joseph Karo's *Shulḥan 'Arukh*), Part 1 (O.H.), No. 472, 8 (David's decision is quoted with approval by later commentators); V. S. Lean, *Lean's Collectanea, a*, I, 295. On other diverse dates of the alleged "crimes," see the examples cited by J. Trachtenberg in *The Devil and the Jews*, pp. 135 ff.

38. Michael Scot's *Introduction to Astrology*, cited from a Bodleian MS by L. Thorndike in *A History of Magic*, II, 320 f.; *Hirlanda* in K. Simrock's ed. of *Die Deutschen Volksbücher*, XII, 31 ff.; Pliny, *Historia naturalis*, xxvi.5, Latin text with an English trans. by H. Rackham *et al.* (W. H. S. Jones) , VII, 270 f.; F. Gregorovius, *History of the City of Rome in the Middle Ages*, English trans. by A. Hamilton, VII, 318, quoting Stefano Infessura's *Diario della città di Roma* in L. Muratori's ed. of *Rerum italicarum scriptores*, III, Part 2, col. 1241; and O. Raynaldus' *Annales*, XI, 196 f. No. xxi; Strack, *The Jew*, pp. 62 ff., 138 ff. It should be noted that the historicity of the incident preceding Innocent VIII's demise has seriously been questioned. Gregorovius himself calls it a "horrible fiction" and points out that the Florentine Valori says nothing on this subject. See also the debate on the "Calumnie contro un papa" between P. Perreau and B. Boncompagni in *Giornale degli eruditi e curiosi*, II, 868–69; III, 39–41; Vogelstein and Rieger, *Geschichte der Juden in Rom*, II, 22; and *infra*, n. 47. The Jewish contributions to medical science will be discussed in later chapters.

39. Thomas de Cantimpré, *Miraculorum et exemplorum memorabilium sui temporis libri duo* (later reissued under the title *Bonum universale de Apibus*) ii.29, 17, ed. by Georgius Colverenius, p. 145, cited in H. Blanchamp's different English trans. in H. L. Strack, *The Jew*, pp. 174 ff. (Strack suggests here that the "learned Jew" from whom Thomas had heard the story of the "prophet" was none other than Nicholas Donin, the champion in the struggle against the Talmud, whom Thomas had very likely met in Paris during the famous disputation); Geiler von Keisersberg, "Schiff der Pönitenz," cited by P. Keppler in his "Zur Passionspredigt des Mittelalters," *HJB*, III, 313 f.; Hans Wilhelm Kirchhof, *Wendunmuth*, ed. by H. Oesterley, III, 366 f. (V, 132) ; Johann Eck, *Ains Judenbüechlins verlegung*, fol. Kla; J. Trachtenberg, *The Devil and the Jews*, p. 246 n. 25.

Thomas de Cantimpré's book, written in 1258 and containing a mixture of scientific and superstitious teachings, enjoyed a great vogue for several generations. Its long discussion of demons, including the author's purported personal experiences with a spirit, had their share of responsibility for the growing popular acceptance of medieval demonology. See H. C. Lea, *Materials toward a History of Witchcraft*, I, 90 f. In contrast, only the first conglomeration of stories, verses, and moral exhortations by Kirchhof (Books i–ii) enjoyed great popularity, being republished six times within forty years; the additional sections (iii–viii) were printed only once before Oesterley's edition. See the latter's remarks, V, 14 f. Pope Nicholas V referred to such pseudo-scientific beliefs when, in his bull of 1447 aimed at forced conversions during the Passion Week, he censured rumor-mongering that Jews required the liver and heart of a Christian for Passover use. See the excerpt in M. Stern's *Urkundliche Beiträge*, I, 46 No. 39; and, more generally, J. Marcus's Paris medical dissertation, *Étude médico-légale du meurtre rituel*.

40. See Miguel de Cervantes Saavedra's comedy, *De los baños de Argel*, ii, in his *Comedias y entremeses*, ed. by R. Schevill and A. Bonilla, I, 285; and other examples cited by E. Glaser in his "Two Anti-Semitic Word Plays in the 'Guzmán de Alfarache' [by Matéo Alemán]," *Modern Language Notes*, LXIX, 343–48. See also *supra*, n. 3; A. Castro, *Hacia Cervantes*, 2d ed., esp. pp. 159 f.; and, more generally, M. N. Pavia, *Drama of the siglo de oro: a Study of Magic, Witchcraft and Other Occult Beliefs*.

41. M. Esposito, "Un Procès contre les Juifs de la Savoie en 1329," *RHE*, XXXIV, 785–801; M. Adler, *Jews of Medieval England*, p. 136; the report of the Nuremberg clergyman, Andreas Osiander, *Schrift über die Blutbeschuldigung*, reed. by M. Stern; E. Vacandard, "La Question du meurtre rituel chez les Juifs" in his *Études de critique et d'histoire religieuse*, 3d ser., 313 ff. On the Ratisbon trial see C. T. Gemeiner, *Reichsstadt Regensburgische Chronik*, III, 567 ff.; and M. Stern, "Der Regensburger Judenprozess 1476–1480," *JJLG*, XVIII, 363–86; XX, 157–79 (also reprint). The Diessenhofen-Schaffhausen affair of 1401 and its repercussions in Fribourg, as well as in Zurich, until Duke Frederick's amnesty ten years later, have frequently been described. Suffice it to say that for several generations thereafter the tomb of the little "victim," Konrad, was the center of pilgrimages and the scene of many "miracles." The victorious Reformation put an end, however, to this pious fraud, and nineteenth-century scholars could no longer ascertain the precise locale of that tomb. See E. Im-Thurn and H. W. Harder eds., *Chronik der Stadt Schaffhausen*, I, 101; the report sent by the city council of Schaffhausen to that of Freiburg, reproduced by [J.] H. Schreiber in his ed. of the *Urkundenbuch der Stadt Freiburg im Breisgau*, II, 167 ff. Nos. ccclxx–lxxiii; and other archival data cited in J. C. Ulrich's *Sammlung jüdischer Geschichten*, pp. 24, 103 ff., 208 ff. See also L. Löwenstein, *Geschichte der Juden am Bodensee und Umgebung*, pp. 64 f., 82 ff., 143 f. nn. 60–61, 146 n. 68; A. Steinberg, *Studien*, pp. 138 ff.; *supra*, Vols. IX, p. 229 (Nuremberg, 1467); X, 13, 305 n. 11 (Diessenhofen-Schaffhausen, 1401); and, more generally, the comprehensive, though incomplete, lists of recorded accusations, compiled by J. Jacobs in his appendix to H. L. Strack's article, "Blood Accusation," *JE*, III, 260–67; and by H. Schramm in *Der Jüdische Ritualmord*, pp. 13 ff.

42. Lope Felix de Vega Carpio, *El Niño inocente de la Guardia* in his *Obras* published by the R. Academia Española, V, 71–107; Charles Lamb, "Imperfect Sympathies" in his *Essays of Elia* in *The Works*, ed. by E. V. Lucas, II, 61. The discontinuation of the Jubilee Year during the Second Commonwealth and the denial by some scholars that it was ever observed in Jewish life are discussed *supra*, Vol. I, pp. 85, 332 f. n. 30. The documentation relating to the Blood Accusation of La Guardia is fully analyzed by F. Fita in "La Verdad sobre el martirio del Santo Niño de la Guardia, ó sea El proceso y quema (16 Noviembre, 1491) de Judío Jucé Franco en Ávila," *BAH*, XI, 7–160, 239–40; and in the discussion thereof by I. Loeb in "Le Saint enfant de la Guardia," *REJ*, XV, 203–32; and by H. C. Lea in "El Santo niño de la Guardia," *EHR*, IV, 229–50. See also *supra*, Vol. X, pp. 107, 349 n. 63. The debate between Fita and Lea was resumed a few years later in Fita's "Nuevos datos para escribir la historia de los Judíos expañoles," *BAH*, XV, 313–46, 442–91, 561–600 (with reference to the early stages of the Spanish Inquisition) ; and Lea's *Chapters from the Religious History of Spain Connected with the Inquisition*, pp. 437–68. See also J. Kohn-Zedek's Hebrew homily, *Sefer Ohole Shem (The Tents of Shem): Being an Account of the Trial of Jacob b. Isaac, of the City of Madrid, in the Year 5250 A.M.* (= 1490 C. E.).

Despite Lea's convincing strictures, Fita's views have largely dominated more recent Spanish historiography. They were adopted, among others, by the influential literary historian, M. Menéndez y Pelayo in his intro. to Lope de Vega's *Obras*, V, pp. xix–xxx; and, with minor modifications, in his *Estudios sobre el teatro de Lope de Vega*, reed. by A. Bonilla y San Martín *et al.*, II, 64–79, although he admits that the poet had no access to the original protocols cited by Fita, but had derived all his information from garbled sixteenth-century accounts. See also the careful reexamination of these issues, including Lope de Vega's sources and poetic dramatizations of that event, by E. Glaser in his "Lope de Vega's El Niño inocente de la Guardia," *Bulletin of Hispanic Studies*, XXXII, 140–53. The impression made by *El Niño*'s cruel descriptions on a liberal nineteenth-century student of the Spanish theater may be noted from J. L. Klein's characterization of its author as "the most learned, the most pious and the greatest poet of his nation." Yet this particular drama had turned the playwright, precisely because "of his genius and seductive magic, into Belial's poet, and his art into the work of a devil and the play of a juggler." See Klein's *Geschichte des Dramas*, X, 505 f. The mid-nineteenth-century Austrian dramatist Franz Grillparzer, otherwise a great admirer of Lope de Vega, likewise dismissed his *Niño* as a "revolting piece."

Nor was the *Niño* Lope de Vega's only anti-Jewish play. In his allegorical *La Siega* (The Harvest), the figure of *El Hebraismo* made but a brief appearance, together with Heresy and Idolatry (*Obras*, II, 309–23). Yet the poet was thus able to give vent to his hostility to the *conversos*. So did the other great Spanish dramatist of that age, Pedro Calderon de la Barca, whose religious plays often had strong anti-Jewish overtones. See the texts in A. Valbuena Prat's ed. of Calderon's *Autos sacramentales* in the latter's *Obras completas*, ed. by A. Valbuena Briones *et al.*, Vol. III, pp. 295 ff. For one example, in *El Sacro Parnaso* (1659) Judaism is represented on the stage by an actor "clad as a Jew" and ineffectually debating with both a Roman pagan and several Church Fathers, *ibid.*, pp. 776 ff. See E. Frutos's dissertation *La Filosofía de Calderon en sus Autos sacramentales;* and on their medieval antecedents see B. W. Wardropper, *Introducción al teatro religioso del siglo de oro*, pp. 141 ff. A few other contemporary anti-Jewish writings are listed by H. Pflaum in *REJ*, LXXXIX, 128 f.

43. Thomas Murner, *Entehrung und Schmach der Bildung Mariae von den Juden bewiesen*, ed. by A. Klasert in his "Entehrung Mariae durch die Juden. Eine antisemitische Dichtung Thomas Murners," *Jahrbuch für Geschichte, Sprache und Literatur Elsass-Lothringens*, XXI, 78–155 (argues for Murner's authorship and the dating of this poem in 1515; and reproduces both the text and the woodcuts of the first edition); H. Loewe, *Die Juden in der katholischen Legende*, pp. 71 ff. On the relationship between this author, if it be Murner indeed, and Pamphilus Gengenbach, see *supra*, n. 5.

44. H. Boos, *Geschichte der rheinischen Städtekultur*, I, 28* n. 871. Unfortunately, in most cases we do not have any contemporary records from the Jewish side. See, e.g., *supra*, n. 34.

45. H. L. Strack, *The Jew and Human Sacrifice*, pp. 249 f. In this context Strack reviews the fairly substantial list of converts from Judaism who, in earlier periods, had combated the ritual murder libel. He cites, among others, Johann Pfefferkorn's *Speculum adhortationis iudaice ad Christum*, Cologne, 1509, in which this ardent Jew-baiter conceded the possibility that some Jew may have murdered a Christian child, but emphatically denied any ritualistic motivations. Pfefferkorn concluded with an exhortation to his Christian readers: "Flee from, and avoid accordingly this ludicrous, mendacious talk which, if you wish to consider it closely, contributes no little to casting contempt on the Christians" (Strack, pp. 242 f.). Yet while the Jew-

baiting assertions by Pfefferkorn were taken at their face value, especially by his Dominican friends who helped to disseminate and defend them against Johannes Reuchlin's strictures, this exhortation fell upon deaf ears. See *infra*, Chap. LVII.

Once again one cannot help admiring the fortitude with which Jewish scholars pursued their studies in the midst of the turmoil usually generated by any Blood Accusation. The scribe of a MS, for instance, now preserved at the Bibliothèque Nationale in Paris, unperturbedly completed his task in Arles in 1453, in the midst of such an accusation which imperiled his entire community. See his colophon, published by A. Neubauer and corrected by C. Sirat, in "Glanes dans les manuscrits hébraïques de la Bibliothèque Nationale de Paris," *REJ*, CXVIII, 131–33.

46. Régné, "Catalogue," *REJ*, LXIX, 145 No. 1902; Richard of Devizes, *De rebus gestis Ricardi Primi*, ed. by R. Howlett in *Chronicles of the Reigns of Stephen, Henry II and Richard I*, III, 437; in Jacobs's English trans. in *The Jews of Angevin England*, p. 148; *supra*, Vol. VIII, pp. 234 f., 388 n. 17, 400 n. 38 item 4. It is the less astonishing that such popes as John XXII gave full credence to the rumors of magic poisonings, as John himself almost fell victim to a conspiracy led by Bishop Hughes Géraud of Cahors. In this plot, in which two Jews of Avignon and Toulouse were indirectly involved, poison and wax effigies of John were to be used. See G. Mollat, *Les Papes d'Avignon (1305–1378)*, 2d ed., pp. 44 ff.; S. Grayzel, "References to the Jews in the Correspondence of John XXII," *HUCA*, XXIII, Part 2, pp. 41 f. No. iv.

Of course, some Jewish individuals were convicted of specific crimes and like other transgressors were punished by either Jewish or general courts. In 1474 one Mosse was burned in Ratisbon after admitting that he had taught a number of persons how to mix poisons effectively. See R. Straus, *Urkunden und Aktenstücke zur Geschichte der Juden in Regensburg*, pp. 37 f. No. 140. Even the thirteenth-century German law books reiterated this principle of equal treatment of Jewish and Christian wrongdoers. See, for instance, *Sachsenspiegel, Landrecht*, ed. by C. G. Homeyer, iii.7, 2; *Das Rechtsbuch nach Distinctionen*, iii.17, 38, ed. by F. Ortloff, p. 176; and other sources reproduced by G. Kisch in his *Jewry-Law in Medieval Germany;* see the Index, p. 266 *s.v.* Crimes, committed by Jews. But such legal equality did not prevent the populace from blaming the entire community for each transgression of a single Jew or from assuming that the criminal had acted not from personal motives but because of his hatred of Christians. In view of the frequency of this suspicion Guillaume Bessin's dating of a passage relating to the discouragement of any Christian "who would take a potion from a Jew" in 1321 is far from cogent. This passage, found in the papers of the Rennes diocese, could have been inserted at almost any time during the Late Middle Ages. See Bessin's ed. of *Concilia Rotomagensis provinciae*, p. 175 item 5.

47. L. Wadding, *Annales Minorum*, VII, 235; Schudt, *Jüdische Merckwürdigkeiten*, I, 245 f.; R. Lewin, *Luthers Stellung zu den Juden*, pp. 39 f.; *supra*, n. 12; Vol. V, p. 294 n. 3; G. Bondy and F. Dworský, *Zur Geschichte der Juden in Böhmen*, II, 569 No. 773; Hans Wilhelm Kirchhof, *Wendunmuth*, ed. by H. Oesterly, III, 256 (iv. 281); Louis Lewin, "Die Jüdischen Studenten an der Universität Frankfurt an der Oder," *JJLG*, XIV, 218 ff.; M. Balaban in B. Jacob *et al.*, "Antisemitismus," *EJ*, II, 1002 ff.; and, more generally, E. Wickersheimer, *Les Accusations d'empoisonnement portées pendant la première moitié du XIVe siècle contre les lépreux et les Juifs;*

leurs relations avec les épidémies de la peste. See also the large accumulation of historical, medical, and legal data in Louis Lewin, *Die Gifte in der Weltgeschichte. Toxikologische allgemeinverständliche Untersuchungen der historischen Quellen;* C. J. S. Thompson, *Poisons and Poisoners, with Historical Accounts of Some Famous Mysteries in Ancient and Modern Times;* and J. Glaister, *The Power of Poison.* See also *supra,* n. 38.

48. Bondy and Dworský, *Zur Geschichte,* II, 886 No. 1110; H. Bächtold-Stäubli *et al.,* eds., *Handwörterbuch des deutschen Aberglaubens,* IV, 825 f. (listing the events before and after 1348); G. G. Coulton, *The Black Death;* A. M. Campbell, *The Black Death and Men of Learning.* On the Jewish aspects, see esp. the older but very useful study by R. Höniger, *Der Schwarze Tod in Deutschland: ein Beitrag zur Geschichte des vierzehnten Jahrhunderts;* and *infra,* n. 52. The impact of the Black Death on Europe's population and the ensuing changes in the socioeconomic structure of most western countries have recently become the subjects of close scrutiny; for instance, in Y. Renouard's "Conséquences et intérêt démographiques de la Peste Noire de 1348," *Population,* III, 459–66; W. Abel's "Wüstungen und Preisfall im spätmittelalterlichen Europa," *JNOS,* CLXV, 380–427; E. Kelter's "Das Deutsche Wirtschaftsleben des 14. und 15. Jahrhunderts im Schatten der Pestepidemien," *ibid.,* pp. 161–208; E. Carpentier, "Autour de la peste noire: Famines et épidemies dans l'histoire du XIVe siècle," *Annales ESC,* XVII, 1062–92; and other studies reviewed by E. Keyser in his "Neue deutsche Forschungen über die Geschichte der Pest," *VSW,* XLIV, 243–53. To be sure, important reservations have been advanced by E. A. Kosminsky and others. Certainly, the countries east and south of the Holy Roman Empire suffered far less severely. See B. Zientara, "The Problems of the Economic Depression in the XIV–XV Centuries in the Light of the Most Recent Literature" (Polish), *Przegląd historyczny,* LI, 262–74; and other literature listed *supra,* Vols. IX, pp. 317 f. n. 27; X, pp. 11, 35, 304 n. 8, 316 n. 42; and *infra,* Chaps. L–LI. Be this as it may, the immediate psychological effects upon contemporaries, particularly in Germany and France, even during the less virulent outbreaks of the contagion were enormous and greatly predisposed the populace to believe the worst rumors about its Jewish neighbors.

49. See Baer, *Die Juden,* I, Part 1, pp. 224 f. No. 177; J. de Meyer, *Commentarii sive Annales rerum flandricarum,* xi, fol. 123a; *supra,* Vol. X, pp. 69 f., 332 f. n. 17; and *infra,* Chap. L, nn. 36–37. Remarkably, the accusation that lepers were poisoning wells actually antedated the spread of the pestilence. See the studies cited by L. Thorndike in *A History of Magic,* III, 234 n. 3.

50. Baer, *Die Juden,* I, Part 1, pp. 324 ff. Nos. 230–32, 331 ff. Nos. 238 and 240–45; the text of the Barcelona resolution *ibid.,* pp. 348 ff. No. 253; idem, *Toledot,* 2d ed, pp. 242 f.; A. López de Meneses, "Una Consecuencia de la peste negra en Cataluña: el pogrom de 1348," *Sefarad,* XIX, 93–131, 321–64 (with an extensive documentary appendix); idem, "Documentos acerca de la peste negra en los dominios de la Corona de Aragón," *Estudios de Edad media de la Corona de Aragón,* VI, 291–435; J. Gautier-Dalché, "La Peste noire dans les États de la Couronne d'Aragon," *Bulletin Hispanique,* LXIVbis, 65–80; Kayserling, *Die Juden in Navarra,* pp. 38 ff., 44. Apart from responding to the general panic, the rioters were also trying to get rid of their debts to Jews. It was for good reason that, in his decree of September 12, 1349, Pedro

IV ordered the reconstruction of the Barcelona bonds destroyed during the disturbances and provided that Jewish lenders, erroneously collecting twice on the same claim, should not be automatically condemned for fraud. See Baer, I, Part 1, p. 337 No. 242. On the losses of the Spanish population, see also L. Lliteras Pebro, "Noticias de Arta, referentes al año de la mortalitat de 1348," *Boletín* of the Sociedad arqueológica Luliana, XXXI, 294–98; and, more generally, *supra*, Vol. X, pp. 146 f., 366 n. 33; and *infra*, Chap. LI.

51. Guy de Chauliac, *La Grande chirurgie*, ed. by E. Nicaise, pp. 66 ff., in A. M. Campbell's abridged English rendition in *The Black Death*, pp. 2 ff.; E. Camau, *Les Juifs en Provence*, pp. 318 f. A summary of the Chillon proceedings, communicated to Strasbourg, was first reproduced by Jacob Twinger von Königshoven in his *Chronicle*, ed. by J. Schiltern under the title of *Elsassiche und Strassburgische Chronicke*, pp. 1029 ff., and then reproduced in the *Urkunden und Akten der Stadt Strassburg*, ed. by W. Wiegand *et al.*, 1st ser., V, 167 ff. No. 185. See the numerous other communications received by Strasbourg, *ibid.*, pp. 162 ff. Nos. 173–90; the remarks thereon by A. Steinberg in her *Studien*, pp. 128 ff.; A. Nordmann in his "Histoire des Juifs à Genève de 1281 à 1780," *REJ*, LXXX, 10 ff.; his "Les Juifs dans le pays de Vaud, 1278–1875," *ibid.*, LXXXI, 153 ff.; and his "Documents relatifs à l'histoire des Juifs à Genève, dans le pays de Vaud et en Savoie," *ibid.*, LXXXIII, 71 No. v; A. Glaser in his *Geschichte der Juden in Strassburg*, pp. 12 ff., 65 ff. Nos. i–v; and, more generally, R. Höniger, *Der Schwarze Tod in Deutschland*.

Although it never again reached the tragic dimensions of the Black Death era, the accusation of well poisoning was a recurrent phenomenon affecting non-Jews as well. For one example, during the increasingly bitter religio-political controversies of the Reformation era, Elector John Frederick of Saxony and Landgrave Philip of Hesse claimed that Pope Paul III, "the Antichrist pontifex of Rome, the organ of Satan, . . . had sent out poisoners to infect the wells and stagnant waters so that those [Protestants] who survived the slaughter by iron and arms should be destroyed by poison." The princes supported their accusation by a confession extorted from an Italian traveler. See Joannes Sleidanus, *Commentarii de statu religionis et reipublicae, Carolo Quinto Caesare*, Strasbourg, 1555 ed., fol. 299v; Louis Lewin, *Die Gifte*, pp. 27 f. Lewin also points out that as late as the middle of the nineteenth century the panic occasioned by a cholera epidemic in the Kingdom of Naples generated widespread suspicions that King Ferdinand II (1830–59) himself had ordered the poisoning of waters.

52. Conrad von Megenberg, *Das Buch der Natur. Die erste Naturgeschichte in deutscher Sprache*, ii.33, ed. by F. Pfeiffer, p. 112; in the modern German rendition by H. Schulz, p. 91; Solomon ibn Verga, *Shebeṭ Yehudah*, xxvi, ed. by Wiener, pp. 46 f.; in Wiener's German trans., pp. 92 f.; ed. by Shohet, pp. 70 f.; Thorndike, *A History of Magic*, III, 312 ff. The nature of this pulmonary plague was extensively but inconclusively debated by contemporary physicians, including De Chauliac and Von Megenberg. Their hypotheses, as well as their casual references to Jews, have been carefully analyzed in the aforementioned studies by Höniger and Campbell (*supra*, n. 51); and, more recently, by S. Guerchberg in "La Controverse sur les prétendus semeurs de la 'Peste Noire' d'après les traités de peste de l'époque," *REJ*, CVIII, 3–40. They show that even the scientists of that and the subsequent generations could not entirely escape the folkloristic misconceptions pertaining to Jews.

Curiously, no one endeavored to establish a connection between some specific Jewish maladies and the great pestilence. In time, to be sure, imaginative writers discovered that special illnesses had affected each of the twelve tribes of ancient Israel and had been transmitted to their descendants. See the list summarized from the "fabulist Dudulaeus" by J. J. Schudt in his *Jüdische Merckwürdigkeiten*, II, Part 1, pp. 344 ff. That this nonsense did not enjoy wider acceptance may have been owing to such obvious objections, as voiced already by Christian Wagenseil that, except for the few priests and levites, all medieval Jews were supposed to be descendants of only the two tribes of Judah and Benjamin.

53. A. Koch and J. Wille, eds., *Regesten der Pfalzgrafen am Rhein*, 1214–1508, published by the Badische Historische Kommission, I, 158 No. 2608; L. Löwenstein, *Beiträge zur Geschichte der Juden in Deutschland*, I, 5 ff.; S. Neufeld, *Die Juden im thüringisch-sächsischen Gebiet während des Mittelalters*, Part II (reprinted from the *Thüringisch-Sächsische Zeitschrift für Geschichte und Kunst*, XII), pp. 6 ff.; Part III (*ibid.*, XV), pp. 66 f.; A. F. Riedel, ed., *Codex diplomaticus brandenburgensis*, 1st ser. XIX, 223 No. lxxxiv; A. Ackermann, *Geschichte der Juden in Brandenburg a. H.*, pp. 18 ff.; M. Brann, *Geschichte der Juden in Schlesien*, pp. 50 ff., 64 ff. See also F. Graus, "Autour de la peste noire au XIVᵉ siècle en Bohème," *Annales ESC*, XVIII, 720–24. The most complete list of central-European Jewish communities wiped out during the Black Death is given by S. Salfeld in *Das Martyrologium des Nürnberger Memorbuches*, *passim*, although, as in other matters, this volume is subject to minor corrections in the identification of certain localities. See A. Nordmann's examples in *REJ*, LXXX, 11 f. n. 4, also with reference to A. Neubauer's earlier essay, "Le Memorbuch de Mayence. Essai sur la littérature des complaintes," *REJ*, IV, 1–30. See also the alphabetical list of affected communities compiled by J. Jacobs in his article, "Black Death," *JE*, III, 233–35, and graphically underscored by the attached map; and *infra*, Chaps. L–LI, where reference will also be made to the extremely complex demographic effects of the Black Death.

54. C. G. Ehrenberg in *Mitteilungen über Monas prodigiosa oder die Purpurmonade*, pp. 110–116; his comprehensive *Mikrogeologie. Das Erden und Felsen schaffende Wirken des unsichtbar kleinen selbständigen Lebens auf der Erde*, in the Inhalt des Atlas *s.v.* Blutregen; M. Hay, *The Foot of Pride*, pp. 145 ff.

55. S. Baluze's biography of John XXII in his *Vitae paparum avinionensium*, new ed. by G. Mollat, I, 133 f.; Alexander of Hales, "De sacramento altaris" in his *Quaestiones disputatae* "antequam esset frater," li, Quarachi ed., II, 891–976; and the anonymous *Miracolo di Bolsena*, reproduced by M. Bonfantini in his ed. of *Le Sacre rappresentazioni italiane*, pp. 98–114. Additional data are supplied by P. Browe in *Die Eucharistischen Wunder des Mittelalters*, pp. 139 ff., 184 ff.; and by J. Heuser in his Bonn dissertation, *Heilig-Blut im Kult und Brauchtum des deutschen Kultraumes*. Incidentally, no less a person than Pope Gregory IX publicly accused such Christian sectarians as the "Luciferians" of regularly desecrating hosts. See *supra*, Vol. IX, pp. 60, 268 f. n. 7. See also *supra*, Vols. II, pp. 71, 358 f. n. 21; VI, p. 303; IX, pp. 195 f., 203, 210, 212 f., 336 f. n. 10, 340 f. n. 19; and *infra*, n. 72; and Chap. L.

56. *Vitae patrum*, ed. by H. Rosweyd, in *PL*, LXXIII, 301; Agnellus, presbyter, *Liber pontificalis ecclesiae Ravennatis*, ed. by O. Holder-Egger, in *MGH*, Scriptores

rerum langobardicarum, p. 365 No. 133; St. Paschasius Radbertus, *De corpore et sanguine Domini*, vi.3, in *PL*, CXX, 1283; generalized by Gezo of Tortosa (*ca.* 954) in *De corpore et sanguine Domini*, xxxix, *ibid.*, CXXXVII, 390; Innocent III, *Epistolae*, viii.121, *ibid.*, CCXV, 694 ff.; Grayzel, *The Church*, pp. 114 f. No. 18; and *supra*, Vol. IX, pp. 26, 252 n. 26. Paschasius also includes (ix.8) an early version of the story of the "Jewish boy" saved from a furnace with the aid of a miracle by a Eucharist, *PL*, CXX, 1298 ff.; *supra*, n. 8. However, the *oblata* which, according to the *Anonymus Valesianus*, some Ravenna Jews were throwing into the river in 519, had nothing to do with the Eucharist as suggested by some scholars. See *supra*, Vol. III, p. 241 n. 31.

57. P. Browe, "Die Hostenschändungen der Juden im Mittelalter," *Römische Quartalschrift*, XXXIV, 167–97, esp. pp. 173 ff., 177 f.; and, more generally, idem, *Die Eucharistischen Wunder*, esp. pp. 128 ff. See also *infra*, n. 67. Pope John XXII, author of many bulls against witchcraft, was nevertheless careful in not extending his condemnation to Jews. But he failed to stem the avalanche of the contemporary host accusations in southern Germany and Austria. Even his successor Benedict XII reacted only upon the initiative of an Austrian duke. See *infra*, nn. 61–62 and 71. Apart from mass accusations, we hear of many individual prosecutions resulting in what evidently were judicial murders. See, for instance, J. Weill, "Un Juif brulé à Metz vers 1385 pour profanation d'hostie," *REJ*, LIII, 270–72.

58. Johannes de Thilrode's *Chronicon*, xxv, ed. by J. Heller, in *MGH*, Scriptores, XXV, 578; L. Zunz, *Die Synagogale Poesie des Mittelalters*, pp. 25 f., 33; other bibliographical data supplied by F. Hachez in his aforementioned essay on Cambron in the *Annales . . . Mons*, XXVII, 135; and by Browe in *Die Eucharistischen Wunder*, pp. 130 ff.; *supra*, n. 5. This "miracle" is also the subject of an artistic presentation on a tapestry displayed in the monastery of Ronceray in Angers since the sixteenth century. See G. de Tervarent, *Les Enigmes de l'art du moyen âge*, Vol. II: *Art flamand*, pp. 19 ff. See also J. Deneev, "Le Miracle de la sainte hostie et l'église évangélique des Billettes," *La Cité*, XXII, 169–91. It may be noted that J. A. Piganiol de la Force who, in his *Description de Paris, de Versailles, de Marly, etc.*, new ed., II, 60 ff., describes at considerable length the *miracle des billettes*, reports a similar sacrilege allegedly committed in Paris in 1418 by a Swiss soldier who was subsequently executed in effigy. *Ibid.*, III, 372. See also J. Corblet, *Histoire dogmatique, liturgique et archéologique du sacrement et l'eucharistie* (with an extensive bibliography); and P. D[émann], "À propos de deux publications récentes sur le 'Miracle de Billettes,'" *Cahiers sioniens*, IX, 73–78 (referring to two minor publications of 1954–55).

59. L. Petit de Julleville, ed., *Les Mystères*, II, 103 f., 193 f., 574 ff.; M. Lifschitz-Golden, *Les Juifs dans la littérature française*, pp. 89 ff. See also the next note.

60. The *Miracle de Sainte Gudule* in C. G. N. de Vooys's collection of *Middelnederlandse Legenden en Exemplen*, pp. 199 ff. ("Jews in the Exempla"), esp. 216 and n. 2; and, on the later period, the somewhat uncritical survey by S. Ullmann, *Histoire des Juifs en Belgique jusqu'au 18ᵉ siècle*. See *supra*, Vol. X, pp. 19, 308 n. 19. The 1870 debate on the jubilee celebration of the "miracle of Ste. Gudule" produced a new outpouring of writings for and against the original trial and yielded

much critical information, superseding the earlier largely pietistic writings. However, the fullest reexamination of the available evidence was not accomplished until the 1930s, when Canon P. Lefèvre published a series of essays on this subject. See especially his "La Valeur historique d'une enquête épiscopale sur le miracle eucharistique de Bruxelles en 1370," *RHE*, XXVIII, 328–46 (includes text of summary of the investigation conducted in 1402); his "Le Thème du miracle des hosties poignardees par les Juifs à Bruxelles en 1370," *Moyen Âge*, LIX, 373–98; and, more generally, his *Un Culte eucharistique célébré dans les anciens Pays Bas.*

The growth of such legends, even without any anti-Jewish animus, is well illustrated by an Amsterdam chapel which was consecrated under the name of a "Holy Place" in 1346–47. The reason given was that, after the vomit of a dying man had been thrown into a fire, the wafer of his last sacrament was found intact. See the detailed analysis of six pertinent records by R. Post in "The Sacrament of the Miracle in Amsterdam" (Dutch), *Studia Catholica*, XXX, 241–61. See also the vast additional literature on the Brussels miracle analyzed by J. Stengers in *Les Juifs dans les Pays-Bas*, pp. 24 ff., 54, 134 ff. n. 169; and, more generally, the older literature (up to 1906) listed in H. Hayn's aforementioned *Uebersicht der . . . Litteratur über . . . Ritualmorde und Hostienfrevel.*

61. Benedict XII's letter to Albert II of 1338 in Raynaldus, *Annales*, XVI, 124 ff. *ad* 1338 Nos. xviii–xx; his similar letter to the bishop of Passau of the same date, *ibid.*, No. xxi; and other sources cited by S. Salfeld in *Das Martyrologium*, p. 236; Scherer in *Die Rechtsverhältnisse*, pp. 351 ff.; and Browe in *Die Eucharistischen Wunder*, pp. 162 ff. On the Rindfleisch massacres see *supra*, Vol. IX, pp. 154 f., 315 f. n. 22; and *infra*, Chap. L.

62. Raynaldus, *Annales, loc. cit. (supra,* n. 61); F. Kurz, *Österreich unter H. Albrecht dem Lahmen*, p. 155; and the full summary of the Austrian events by J. E. Scherer in *Die Rechtsverhältnisse*, pp. 363 ff. According to Duke Albert's report, it turned out that the Pulka affair, too, had from the outset been trumped up after a Christian had placed a blood-stained host outside the house of the accused Jew. All this did not save the community of Passau from suffering from a similar accusation in 1477. The latter proceedings inspired a local artist to depict the events on a dozen stained-glass windows under the title *Ein grawsamlich geschicht Geschehen zu passaw Von den Juden.* This extremely crude series, misdated 1470, is reproduced by G. Liebe in *Das Judentum in der deutschen Vergangenheit*, App. 8 facing p. 20. The events in Passau, leading up to the expulsion, are also narrated in a folk poem attributed to one Fritz Fellhamer. See O. Frankl's brief description in *Der Jude in den deutschen Dichtungen*, pp. 124 ff.

63. J. C. von Aretin, *Geschichte der Juden in Baiern*, pp. 23 f., 29 ff. (also citing the rhymed inscription permanently recording the slaying of the Jews and placed on the doors of the new memorial church in Deggendorf). See the text of the poem published by R. von Liliencron in *Die Historischen Volkslieder*, I, 45 ff. No. 12. The Deggendorf affair also generated a large bibliography, including such commemorative studies as that by J. Schreiner, *Das Fünfhundertjährige Jubiläum der Kirche zum hl. Grab in Deggendorf.* See also the extensive literature cited by H. Hayn in his *Uebersicht*, pp. 8 ff.; and by Browe in *Die Eucharistichen Wunder*, pp. 147 f. n. 5, 152 n. 28; and the recent dramatic description of a visit to, and various interviews

held in Deggendorf by W. Rabi in his "Un Mythe tenace: la profanation des hosties. Le Scandale de Deggendorf," *L'Arche*, No. 58 (Nov. 1961), 28–33, 69 (includes interesting reproductions of two panels and the memorial inscription at the *Grabkirche*). Even today the annual celebration attracts several thousand worshipers and is a considerable source of revenue to both the church and the townspeople.

64. H. Lichtenstein, "Der Vorwurf der Hostienschändung und das erste Auftreten der Juden in der Mark Brandenburg," *ZGJD*, IV, 189–97 (cogently arguing against any involvement of Jews in the Belitz accusation); D. Kaufmann, "Die Märtyrer des Berliner Autodafé's von 1510," *MWJ*, XVIII, 48–53, Hebrew section (*Oṣar Ṭob*), p. 43; *supra*, Vol. IX, pp. 210, 212 f., 339 ff. nn. 17 and 19. The main source for the Knoblauch affair is an anonymous pamphlet, published in 1511 in Frankfort a. O. and provided with many anti-Jewish woodcuts. It bears a long title, the first sentence of which reads: *Dietzs ist der wahrhafftig Sumarius der gerichts hendel unnd process der gehalten ist worden uff manchfaldig Indicia, aussag, und bekentnus eines Pawl From gnant der das hochwirdig Sacrament samt einer monstrantzien etc. aus der kirchen Knobloch gestohlen*. Another somewhat fuller description is offered by Abbot Johannes Trithemius (of Trittenheim) in his *Annales Hirsaugienses*, St. Gallen 1690 ed., II, 660 ff. The *Sumarius* was reprinted and, together with other sources largely dependent on it, subjected to a careful juridical analysis by F. Holtze in *Das Strafverfahren gegen die märkischen Juden im Jahre 1510*, supplemented by many details in G. Sello, "Der Hostienschändungs-Process vom Jahre 1510 vor dem Berliner Schöffengericht," *Forschungen zur brandenburgischen und preussischen Geschichte*, IV, 121–35. See esp. pp. 133 f. The 1510 affair found many echoes in the contemporary German literature. A poem by one Jacob Winter underscored the rumor that the Jews had sent parts of the stolen host to distant communities, many of which also witnessed certain miraculous reactions. See also E. Wolbe, *Geschichte der Juden in Berlin und in der Mark Brandenburg*, esp. p. 61, citing the oath of the Jewish expellees.

The developments in Breslau in 1453 are analyzed by M. Brann in his *Geschichte der Juden in Schlesien*, pp. 124 ff. with the documentary appendix thereto No. v, pp. lxxi ff. See also J. Fischer, "Ein Neues Dokument zur Geschichte der Judenaustreibung aus Schlesien im Jahre 1453," *MGWJ*, LXVI, 299–305 (report of one of three royal commissioners sent to Breslau to investigate). A similar tragedy of the Jewish community of Sternberg, Mecklenburg, in 1492, had likewise become the subject of extensive literary reportage, particularly by the humanist historian, Nicolaus Marschalk. See L. Geiger's data in *ZGJD*, [o.s.] II, 309 ff.; III, 295 f. This "miracle" soon attracted sufficient international attention for Pope Leo X to feel obliged to send a gold chalice to the chapel holding the recovered wafers. See the detailed description by L. Donath in his *Geschichte der Juden in Mecklenburg*, pp. 50 ff., 312 ff. Apps. J and K, reproducing excerpts from the contemporary protocols. Donath also cites extensively from several articles published by G. C. F. Lisch in his *Mecklenburgische Jahrbücher*, esp. IV, 86–90, XII, 207–26, also referring to a special Brotherhood of the Sacred Blood established in Sternberg in 1503 (*ibid.*, p. 226). See also W. Lampen, "The Sacred Blood of Sternberg" (Dutch), *Algemeen Nederlansch Eucharistisch Tijdschrift*, VI, 230; and other literature listed by H. Hayn in his *Uebersicht*, pp. 22 f.; and by Browe in *Die Eucharistischen Wunder*, p. 138 n. 50.

65. Josel of Rosheim, *Diary*, xxii, ed. by J. [I.] Kracauer in his "Rabbi Joselmann de Rosheim," *REJ*, XVI, 92 f., 99 f.; H. Bresslau, "Aus Strassburger Judenakten," *ZGJD*,

[o.s.] V, 316 ff.; Josel's *Trostschrift an seine brüder wider Buceri büchlin*, excerpted in L. Feilchenfeld's *Rabbi Josel von Rosheim*, pp. 126, 181; S. Stern, *Josel von Rosheim*, pp. 136 f. (German), 171 f. (English). See the lucid summary of these events by A. Ackermann in his *Geschichte der Juden in Brandenburg a. H.*, pp. 31 ff. On the generally unfriendly attitudes of Bucer and Melanchthon toward Jews, see *infra*, Chap. LVIII.

66. "In our Zurich archives," writes the well-informed Johann Caspar Ulrich, "as well as in Swiss chronicles, in manuscript or in print, there is no trace of our Swiss Jews ever having been suspected of that evil act [the profanation of hosts]." See his *Sammlung jüdischer Geschichten*, pp. 93 f. This is the more remarkable as, in his general description of medieval Jewish life, Ulrich reveals considerable theological bias and recounts with much relish the records pertaining to crimes committed by Jews which he, curiously, arranges in the sequence of the Ten Commandments. See L. Rothchild's observations in his *Johann Caspar Ulrich von Zürich und seine "Sammlung jüdischer Geschichten in der Schweiz,"* p. 54 (236). See also P. Browe's list in *Die Eucharistischen Wunder*, pp. 139 ff.

67. Baer, *Die Juden*, I, Part 1, pp. 352 No. 253 (1354), 398 ff. Nos. 282 and 284 (1367), 547 f. No. 361 (1383), 577 f. No. 379 (1386); Part 2, p. 319 No. 302 (1449). See also *ibid.*, p. 331 No. 318 par. 123 (1467); idem, *Toledot*, 2d ed., pp. 249 ff., 278 ff., 388, 452 ff.; J. Miret y Sans, "El Procès de les hosties contra els Juheus d'Osca en 1377," *Anuari* of the Institut d'estudis catalans, IV, 59–80, esp. pp. 61 n. 2, 68 n. 2; H. Graetz, *Geschichte der Juden*, 4th ed., VIII, 95 f. (citing Alphonso de Spina and Solomon Usque). On the mistaken date of the Segovia events, given by both Usque and Joseph ha-Kohen, see I. Loeb, "Joseph Haccohen et les chroniqueurs juifs," *REJ*, XVI, 221 f. Generally, the Christian Spaniards themselves lost faith in confessions obtained by torture, and valiantly struggled to secure special exemptions. But the usual qualification that persons of ill fame might continue to be forced to confess what they knew to be true cast a cloud on all such privileges (also extended to some Aragonese Jewish communities) and left much leeway to local judges and administrators. We shall see that this was indeed to become the standard procedure in inquisitorial trials. See Baer's *Studien*, pp. 86 f.; and *infra*, Chap. LV.

68. J. Amador de los Rios, *Historia social*, II, 276 n. 2; K. Eubel, "Weitere Urkunden zu dem Verhalten der Päpste gegen die Juden," *Römische Quartalschrift*, XVII, 185. One wonders whether the Coimbra incident helped persuade the Portuguese Cortes, meeting in Elvas in May, 1361, to adopt their sharply segregationist resolution. See M. F. Santarém de Barros, *Memórias e alguns documentos para a história e teoria das Côrtes geraes. . . . em Portugal*, new ed., II, Part 2, p. 28 Art. 40; M. Kayserling, *Geschichte der Juden in Portugal*, p. 24

69. Alphonso de Spina, *Fortalitium fidei*, II, vi.i; *supra*, Vol. IX, pp. 304 f. n. 30; V. H. Buck, ed., *Four Autos sacramentales of 1590*, pp. 9 ff., 23–43. Equally innocuous from the Jewish standpoint were such Italian plays as Paolo Uccello's *Particolare della storia dell'Ostia profanata*, reproduced by M. Bonfantini in *Le Sacre rappresentazioni italiane*, pp. 521 ff., with the telling illustrations in Figs. lxiii–lxx.

70. *Close Rolls, 1268–1272* pp. 14 f., 22 f.; Tovey, *Anglia judaica*, pp. 168 ff.; C. Roth, *The Jews of Medieval Oxford*, pp. 151 ff. Prince Edward, the later King Ed-

ward I, happened to be in Oxford during the 1268 outrage and it was he who initiated the punitive action against the entire community. This incident doubtless
deepened his antipathy toward the Crown's Jewish "serfs," although, since the iconoclastic assailant was never identified, the act might have been committed by a
Christian *agent provocateur,* perhaps in the hope that the ensuing attack on the
Jewish quarter would enable him to partake of the plunder or to secure release
from debts.

71. Jean Bodin, *De magorum daemonomania seu detestando lamiarum ac mag-
orum cum Satana commercio;* H. Boguet, *An Examen of Witches [Discours des
Sorciers] Drawn from Various Trials . . . of This Sect in the District of . . . Saint
Claude,* English trans. by E. A. Ashwin, ed. by M. Summers. Ironically, Jean Bodin
himself may have been of Jewish descent if Robert Berg is correct in "Le Demi-juif
Jean Bodin," *Revue juive de Lorraine,* XIII, 29–35. See also G. Roellenbleck, *Offen-
barung, Natur und jüdische Ueberlieferung bei Jean Bodin;* Jacob Guttmann,
"Ueber Jean Bodin in seinen Beziehungen zum Judentum," *MGWJ,* XLIX, 315–48,
459–89 (also reprint); and, more generally, J. H. Franklin, *Jean Bodin and the
Sixteenth-Century Revolution in the Methodology of Law and History.* See also K. Seligmann, *The History of Magic,* esp. pp. 238 ff.; C. G. Loomis, *White Magic. An Introduction to the Folklore of Christian Legend;* R. H. Robbins, *The Encyclopedia of
Witchcraft and Demonology.* Here the article on 'Jewish Witchcraft' (pp. 281–82) is
extremely sketchy and includes some unjustifiable generalizations. Of considerable
interest, from another angle, is E. Delcambre's analysis of "La Psychologie des in-
culpés lorrains de sorcellerie," *RHDF,* XXXII.

72. The Croxton Play of the Sacrament in O. Waterhouse's ed. of *The Non-Cycle
Mystery Plays,* pp. 54–87; *Das Endinger Judenspiel,* ed. by K. von Amira, p. 92. This
rather inferior German play was read in German schools as late as 1870. On the
historical background of that trial, the legal inadequacies of which were pointed out
by Von Amira, and the ensuing expulsion of the Jews from that locality in 1470, see
I. Kracauer, "L'Affaire des Juifs d'Endingen de 1470," *REJ,* XVI, 236–45. The interrelations between magic and heresy, as viewed from the standpoint of Inquisitors,
will be discussed *infra,* Chap. LV. In general, however, it is extremely difficult to
assess the respective shares of the Church and the laity in the development of these
persecution complexes. Even a drama like the Croxton Play is essentially a secular
product, notwithstanding its inclusion in the *Non-Cycle Mystery Plays* by the Early
English Text Society. See E. D. Coleman, *The Jew in English Drama: an Annotated
Bibliography,* p. ix; and *infra,* n. 88.

73. Roger of Wendover, *Flores historiarum,* ed. by H. O. Coxe, IV, 176 ff.; in J. A.
Giles's English trans, II, 512 ff.; Matthew Paris' relatively minor elaboration in his
Chronica majora, ed. by H. R. Luard, III, 161 ff.; V, 340 f.; Philippe Mousk's *Chronique rimée,* ed. F. de Reiffenberg in the *Collection de chroniques belges inédites,* II,
491 ff.; the fourteenth-century versified Czech translation of *Dialogus beatae Mariae
et Anselmi de passione Domini* in *Svatovitský rukopis,* ed. by A. Patera, as cited by
A. Yarmolinsky in "The Wandering Jew: a Contribution Toward the Slavonic Bibliography of the Legend," *Studies in Jewish Bibliography . . . in Memory of Abraham Solomon Freidus (1867–1923),* p. 320; Guido Bonatti, *De astrologia tractatus,*
Basel, 1600 ed., p. 209; P. (S.) Cassel, *Ahasverus, die Sage vom ewigen Juden.*

Almost contemporary with the English version is another Italian report, from a Florentine MS dated in 1274, first communicated by T. Cassini in his "Rime inedite dei secoli XIII e XIV," *Il Propugnatore*, XV, Part 2, pp. 335 ff. No. i. Giovanni Buttadeo frequently appeared also in fourteenth and fifteenth-century letters. See esp. the two succinct older, but still valuable, essays by G. Paris, "Le Juif Errant," (1880, 1891), reproduced in his *Légendes du moyen âge*, pp. 147–86, 187–221; and S. Morpurgo, *L'Ebreo errante in Italia;* as well as L. Neubaur's comprehensive studies, especially *Die Sage vom ewigen Juden*, 2d ed.; and *Neue Mitteilungen über die Sage vom ewigen Juden*. See also B. H. van't Hooft, "The Legend of the Wandering Jew in a Rolduc Indulgence" (Dutch), *Historisch Tijdschrift*, XIV, 97–142 (relating the legend to the letter of 1234 and reproducing in his Appendix several early excerpts, pp. 133 ff.); and the older, but still interesting, popular summary by F. Helbig, *Die Sagen vom "Ewigen Juden," ihre poetische Wandlung und Fortbildung.*

74. Matt. 16:28; St. John Chrysostom, *Homiliae*, lxxxiii, on John 18:10, *PG*, LIX, 447 ff.; Ludolphus de Saxonia (Cartusian prior of Strasbourg, *ca.* 1370), *Vita Jhesu Christi descripta juxta seriem quatuor evangeliorum*, Part 2, Chap. lx; *La Passion de Notre Seigneur* in *Mystères inédits du quinzième siècle*, ed. by A. Jubinal, II, 139 ff., 186 ff., 193 ff.; both cited by L. Neubaur in *Die Sage vom ewigen Juden*, 2d ed., pp. 4 f.; C. Kohler's ed. of Peter of Penna's (de Pennis') *Libellus de locis ultramarinis* in *Revue de l'Orient Latin*, IX, 358. On Malchus, see *supra*, n. 20. See also P. B. Bagatti, "The Legend of the Wandering Jew: a Franciscan Headache," *Franciscan Studies*, n.s. IX, 1 ff.; W. Zirus, *Der Ewige Jude in der Dichtung, vornehmlich in der englischen und deutschen*, pp. 5 ff. In another Passion play, referred to as "Ste. Geneviève," the popular figure of Malchus is identified as the valet of the high priest, Jesus' chief accuser. See E. Roy, *Le Mystère de la Passion en France (Revue Bourgignonne*, XIII), p. 59*.

75. K. Simrock, *Handbuch der deutschen Mythologie mit Einschluss der nordischen*, 5th ed., pp. 206 f.; W. E. Puckert, ed., *Deutsche Sagen*, Vol. I: *Niederdeutschland*, p. 53 No. 91. See also the older but still useful study of J. G. Grässe, *Die Sage vom ewigen Juden, historisch entwickelt;* and, on the nexus between the legends of Judas, Antichrist, and the Eternal Jew, E. Liefmann's succinct remarks on "Die Legende vom Antichrist und die Sage vom Ahasver; ihre Bedeutung für den Antisemitismus," *Judaica*, III, 122–56.

76. *Kurze Erzählung von einem Juden aus Jerusalem mit Namen Ahasverus, welcher bei der Kreuzigung Christi selbst persönlich gewesen, auch das Crucifige über Christum hat helfen schreien und um Barnabam bitten*, reproduced with a subsequent German "Memorial to the Christian Reader Concerning that Jew," and an Intro. by K. Simrock in *Die Deutschen Volksbücher*, VI, 417–51. The various theories concerning its original place of publication, including Basel, Schleswig, Strasbourg, and particularly Danzig, are briefly reviewed by Zirus in *Der Ewige Jude*, p. 9. On the crucial encounter between Paulus von Eitzen and the Wandering Jew in Hamburg, see also P. Johansen, "War der Ewige Jude in Hamburg?" *Zeitschrift* of the Verein für Hamburgische Geschichte, XLI, 189–203. Despite the story's great popularity, copies of the original edition were no longer readily available in European libraries before 1893. See L. Neubaur's foreword to *Die Sage vom ewigen Juden*, 2d ed. But such scarcity is not surprising in the case of popular writings

which often were used up soon after their publication, but rarely served as collectors' items to be preserved in private or public libraries. See, in general, J. P. Seguin, *L'Information en France avant le périodique. 517 canards imprimés entre 1529 et 1631;* and C. Nisard, *Histoire des livres populaires ou de la littérature du colportage depuis le XVᵉ siècle,* which also offers the text of a noteworthy French poem and some interesting general observations on the older literature relating to the Wandering Jew, I, 553-78.

77. I. Friedländer, "Zur Geschichte der Chadhirlegende," *Archiv für Religionswissenschaft,* XIII, 92-110, esp. p. 110 (following a suggestion by Mark Lidzbarski) ; W. Chappell and J. W. Ebsworth, eds., *The Roxburghe Ballads,* VI, 693 ff. The indebtedness of that ballad to the *Kurze Erzählung,* at least in the MS preserved in the Bagford Collection, is evidenced by its reproduction of a German woodcut of the Wandering Jew. That the author of the *Kurze Erzählung* and his imitators saw in the Wandering Jew a personification of the Jewish people had already been suggested by Johann Jacob Schudt who commented: "This itinerant Jew is not an individual person, but rather the entire Jewish people which has been dispersed and is wandering all over the world ever since the crucifixion of Christ and which, according to Christ's testimony, is to remain alive until the End of Days." See *Jüdische Merckwürdigkeiten,* v.14: "Vom dem in aller Welt vermeinten umherlaufenden Juden *Ahasverus,*" I, 488-512; IV, 308-311, esp. I, 490 f. On the combination of the Ahasverus and Antichrist legends, see E. Liefmann's observations in *Judaica,* III, 122-58; and *supra,* n. 12.

78. M. R. Krüger, *Schreiben an den Herrn Professor Carl Anton darinnen bewiesen wird, dass es einen ewigen Juden gebe,* cited by L. Neubaur in *Die Sage vom ewigen Juden,* pp. 22 ff.; the Ypres story reported from a MS chronicle by Emil Varenbergh and summarized by Neubaur in his *Neue Mitteilungen,* pp. 20 ff. On the difficulties encountered with gullible pilgrims in the Holy Land by local Franciscans, some of whom were themselves by no means above believing both the legend and the presence in Jerusalem of the Wandering Jew in a secluded locality, see the brief remarks by P. B. Bagatti in "The Legend of the Wandering Jew," *Franciscan Studies,* n.s. IX, 1-9.

79. Neubaur in *Die Sage,* p. 118 n. 52; K. Simrock, *Handbuch der deutschen Mythologie,* p. 151. See also F. Fita, "Judío errante de Illescias 1484-1514," *BAH,* VI, 130-40 (here we deal with a real, not legendary, wandering Jew who had spent the years 1492-1514 migrating through many lands and reappearing in Spain as a New Christian) ; B. d'Agostini, " 'L'Ebreo errante' si era fermato sulla scalineata di Sant'Ignazio," *Giornale di Vicenza* of August 21, 1953 (allegedly the visitor's name was Giovanni Battista Mondin) ; and many other local recollections cited in the various bibliographies, mentioned *infra,* n. 82.

80. Gen. 4:12; Peter the Venerable of Cluny, *Epistolae,* xxxvi in *PL,* CLXXXIX, 366 ff.; Matthew Paris, *Historia Anglorum,* ed. by F. Madden, III, 103 f.; William Shakespeare, *The Tragedy of King Richard the Second,* Act V, Scene 6, vv. 43-44, Oxford ed. by J. W. Craig *et al.,* III, 165; *supra,* Vol. IV, pp. 122 f., 301 n. 43. The connection between the Wandering Jew and Cain was well recognized by the nineteenth-century Polish poet, Jan Karłowicz, although his main theory connecting both

legends with solar mythology seems farfetched. See Karłowicz's "Jew the Perennial Migrant: a Medieval Legend Retold and Critically Analyzed" (Polish), *Biblioteka Warszawska*, III, 1–13, 214–32. Understandably, the tragic figure of Cain had already attracted the attention of ancient theologians, both Orthodox and sectarian. On its enduring role in the Judeo-Christian religious controversies, see *supra*, Vols. II, pp. 136 f., 381 f. nn. 10–11; VI, 480 f. n. 91; and *infra*, Chap. L, n. 105.

81. J. J. Gielen, *De Wandelende Jood in Volkskunde en Letterkunde* (The Wandering Jew in Ethnology and Literature); idem, "L'Evolution de la légende du Juif Errant," *Neophilologus*, XVII, 57–63; A. H. Krappe, "Sur l'origine de la légende du Juif Errant," *ibid.*, XX, 145–48 (explaining the name of Ahasverus and his cobbler's trade through the story, reported by Ṭabari, about the death of the Persian king Khosroe II); A. M. Killen, "L'Evolution de la légende du Juif errant," *Revue de littérature comparée*, V, 5–36; H. Glaesener, "Le Type d'Ahasvérus aux XVIIIᵉ et XIXᵉ siècles," *ibid.*, XI, 373–97; B. H. van't Hooft's aforementioned essay in *Historisch Tijdschrift*, XIV, 97–142; W.-E. Puckert and O. Laufer, *Volkskunde: Quellen und Forschungen seit 1930*, pp. 197 ff. (Ahasverus in the Scandinavian legends). On Goethe's conception see esp. J. Minor's *Goethes Fragmente vom ewigen Juden und vom wiederkehrenden Heiland;* A. Soergel, *Ahasver-Dichtungen seit Goethe;* B. H. van't Hooft's "Der Ewige Jude bei Goethe und August Vermeylen," *Neophilologus*, XVIII, 101–112; J. G. T. Grässe, *Der Tannhäuser und Ewige Jude; zwei deutsche Sagen in ihrer Entstehung und Entwickelung historisch, mythologisch und bibliographisch verfolgt und erklärt*, 2d ed.; G. Vabre Pradal, *La Dimension historique de l'homme ou Le Mythe du Juif Errant dans la pensée d'Edgar Quinet;* see also D. Daube, "Ahasver," *JQR*, XLV, 243–44 (equating the name with the royal "simpleton" of the rabbinic legend); G. K. Anderson's recent study, *The Legend of the Wandering Jew; supra*, n. 73; the older literature listed by L. Neubaur in his "Bibliographie der Sage vom ewigen Juden," *Zentralblatt für Bibliothekswesen*, X, 249–67, 297–316; XXVIII, 495–509; and his "Zur Geschichte und Bibliographie des Volksbuchs von Ahasverus," *Zeitschrift für Bücherfreunde*, n.s. V, Part 2, pp. 211–23. One may also note that a large collection of 1,500 vols. dealing with the *Legend of the Wandering Jews* was assembled by W. Easton Luttit, Jr., and donated to the Brown University Library.

82. Jonah b. Abraham Gerondi, *Sefer ha-Yir'ah* (Book of Fear [of the Lord]; an ethical tract), fol. 3b. On the great popularity of this work, see A. T. Schrock, *Rabbi Jonah b. Abraham of Gerona*, pp. 88 f., 163.

83. Elijah Levita, *Masoreth ha-Masoreth* (The Tradition of the Masorah; a Philological Treatise), ed. by C. D. Ginsburg, Intro., p. 96 with reference to Ps. 147:20; Israel Isserlein, *Terumat ha-deshen*, No. 196, Venice, 1519 ed., sign. 12c; David b. Solomon Gans, *Neḥmad ve-na'im* (Desirable and Pleasant: an astronomical miscellany), fol. 9ab; U. Cassuto, *Gli Ebrei*, pp. 278 ff., 299 ff., 316 ff. See also G. E. Weil, "L'Archétype du Massoret ha-Massoret d'Élie Lévita," *Revue d'histoire et de philosophie religieuses*, XLI, 147–58. Among Levita's distinguished Christian pupils was also Sebastian Münster. See G. E. Weil, "Une Leçon de l'humaniste hébreu Elias Lévita à son élève Sébastien Münster," *Revue d'Alsace*, XCV, 31–40 (from the Basel 1531 ed. of David Qimḥi's Commentary on Amos). Levita's philological tracts enjoyed great popularity among Christian Hebraists for several generations. As late as 1660,

the famous halakhist Shabbetai Kohen, then a refugee in Holleschau, Moravia, sent a copy of one of Levita's tracts to his friend, the philosopher Valentin Vidrich of Leipzig, with a letter overflowing with sentiments of friendship and mutual devotion. Many other Jews, including booksellers, must likewise have been instrumental in supplying Hebrew books to non-Jewish scholars. See Shabbetai b. Meir Kohen's letter of Feb. 3, 1660, to Vidrich, published by J. S. Byk in *Bikkure ha-'ittim*, X, 43-44. On Pico see also I. Abrahams, "Pico della Mirandola," *HUCA* Jub. Vol., pp. 317-31; F. Secret, "Pico della Mirandola e gli inizi della cabala cristiana," *Convivium*, XXV, 31-45. See also idem, *Le Zôhar chez les kabbalistes chrétiens de la Renaissance;* idem, *Les Kabbalistes chrétiens de la Renaissance.* The relations between Christian and Jewish humanists will be more fully discussed *infra*, Chap. LVII. See, more generally, A. Berliner, *Persönliche Beziehungen zwischen Christen und Juden im Mittelalter.*

84. Roger Bacon, *Compendium studii philosophiae*, vi–vii in his *Opera quaedam hactenus inedita*, ed. by J. S. Brewer, pp. 391 ff., 432 ff.; V. Colorni, "Spigolature su Obadià Sforno: la sua laurea a Ferrara e la quasi ignota edizione della sua opera OR 'AMIM nella versione latina," *RMI*, XXVIII, 78–88. Bacon realized that Christian students mastered Hebrew in different degrees. On one occasion he claimed that one could learn Hebrew in three days, but elsewhere he stated that it took thirty years to acquire a good command of it. See S. A. Hirsch, "Early English Hebraists: Roger Bacon and His Predecessors" (1899) in *A Book of Essays*, pp. 1–72. On the situation at the English, Italian, and other universities see B. Smalley, *Hebrew Scholarship Among Christians in XIII Century England;* C. Roth, *The Jews of Medieval Oxford*, pp. 126 ff.; and, more generally, his brief comments on "The Medieval University and the Jew" (1930), reprinted in his *Personalities and Events in Jewish History*, pp. 91–111; and G. Kisch, *Die Universitäten und die Juden.* See also B. Bischoff, "The Study of Foreign Languages in the Middle Ages," *Speculum*, XXXVI, 209–24. We must also bear in mind that the medieval universities were an integral part of the ecclesiastical establishment and that the Church closely supervised the students' conduct. The latter often were also financially dependent on the clergy's support and were not completely free even in their financial dealings with Jews.

85. See A. Z. Schwarz, "Letters on the Confiscation of Hebrew Books in 1554" (Hebrew), *Alim*, II, 50 f.; I. Sonne, ed., *Mi-Pavlo ha-rebi'i 'ad Pius ha-ḥamishi* (From Paul IV to Pius V: a Hebrew Chronicle of the Sixteenth Century), vi–viii, pp. 68 (with the editor's n. 21 thereon), 78, 82 f.; A. Marx, "Rabbi Joseph of Arli as Teacher and Head of an Academy in Siena," *Ginzberg Jub. Vol.*, Hebrew section, pp. 271–304, esp. p. 300; H. Hildesheimer, *Simon von Trident*, p. 3; and, more generally, M. Shulvass, *Ḥayye ha-Yehudim*, pp. 168 ff.; and C. Roth, *The Jews in the Renaissance*, pp. 21 ff.

86. W. W. Capes, ed., *Registrum Ricardi de Swinfield, episcopi Herefordiensis, A.D. MCCLXXXIII–MCCCXVIII*, pp. 120 ff.; Raynaldus, *Annales*, IV, 10 f. *ad* 1286 Nos. xxv–xxvii; *supra*, Vol. X, pp. 112 f., 351 n. 69; Israel b. Petaḥiah Isserlein, *Terumat ha-deshen*, No. 195, Venice, 1519 ed., signature 12b f.; M. Pollak, *Die Juden in Wiener-Neustadt. Ein Beitrag zur Geschichte der Juden in Oesterreich*, German trans. from the Hungarian by M. Mezei, ed. by L. Moses, pp. 82 ff. (these and other ritualistically oriented inquiries to rabbis reflect a wide spectrum of social relations, most of which remained unmentioned because they had no religio-legal implica-

tions); L. Bardinet, "Les Juifs du Comtat Venaissin au moyen âge," *RH*, XIV, 38 n. 1; the Magdeburg testimony cited from a Breslau MS by G. Kisch in *The Jews in Medieval Germany*, p. 326.

Popular proverbs, too, were not always hostile. One might contrast an adage like "If you wish to cheat a Jew you must be a Jew," with one stating that "it takes nine Jews to cheat one Basler and nine Baslers to cheat one Genevan." Another fairly neutral proverb contended that "everything is gauche like with the Jews." Nor is the well-known saying, "If you beat my Jews, I beat yours," reflective of any deep antipathy. See the collection of *Die Deutschen Sprichwörter*, ed. by K. Simrock in *Die Deutschen Volksbücher*, V, esp. p. 279. Of course, these proverbs are not datable; hence some of them may be of more recent vintage. But on the whole popular sayings transmitted from the Middle Ages seem to be somewhat less antagonistic to Jews than the folk songs and folk poetry. Curiously, despite the great interest of Jewish apologists and historians, including Abraham Berliner, Moritz Güdemann, and Israel Abrahams, in all aspects of medieval Judeo-Christian relations, these scattered data about more or less friendly intergroup contacts have never been carefully assembled and analyzed. Notwithstanding its broad title, A. Berliner's *Persönliche Beziehungen zwischen Christen und Juden im Mittelalter*, concentrates almost exclusively on the relatively few intellectual exchanges among scholars. A truly comprehensive monograph dealing with all aspects of Judeo-Christian social relations during the Middle Ages clearly is a scholarly desideratum. Even J. Katz's recent study *Exclusiveness and Tolerance: Jewish-Gentile Relations in Medieval and Modern Times* uses principally rabbinic data of the early modern period.

87. Some dialectal differences which in time emerged under the influence of the Hebrew language and talmudic modes of thinking will be discussed in a later chapter. Along with the adoption by Jews of the languages of their environments, there also was a far-reaching onomatological assimilation, such as had already characterized the Jews living in Hellenistic and Arab lands. Even in northern Europe, names derived from animals (Baer, Wolf, and the like) which were widely employed by local non-Jews came into common use also in many Jewish communities. In some cases these were but translations (or adaptations) from Hebrew, mostly biblical, first names whose use was retained for internal Jewish purposes, particularly in connection with religious ceremonies. But family names, wherever such existed, were of predominantly local origin. See the data assembled since the days of L. Zunz's pioneering *Namen der Juden* (1837, reproduced with corrections in his *GS*, II, 1–82) especially by U. Cassuto in *Gli Ebrei*, pp. 231 ff.; M. Roblin in "Les Noms de famille des Juifs d'origine ibérique," *Revue internationale d'Onomastique*, III, 65–72; and P. Mendel, "La Langue et les noms des Juifs en France au moyen âge," *Almanach-Calendrier* of the Communautés israélites de la Moselle, 1955, pp. 88–92.

88. H. Niedner, *Die Deutschen und französischen Osterspiele bis zum 15. Jahrhundert*, pp. 135 f., 138, 141 f., 147; Hans Fischer, "Neue Forschungen zur deutschen Dichtung," *Deutsche Vierteljahrsschrift für Literaturwissenschaft*, XXXI, 308 n. 15; O. Schlisske, *Die Apostel in der deutschen Dichtung des Mittelalters*, pp. 71 ff., 102 f.; K. Goedeke, ed., *Pamphilus Gengenbach*, p. 673 n. 11; A. Leitzmann and K. Burdach, "Der Judenspiess und die Longinus-Sage," *Neue Jahrbücher für das klassische Altertum*, XXXVII, 21–56; P. Browe, M. Henshaw, and other writers, cited *supra*, n. 14.

Growing lay influence on the Passion plays is incontestable even if we decide the controversial question of their supposed liturgical origins in the affirmative. See R. von Stephasius's observations, with special reference to Pilate, in her dissertation, *Die Gestalt des Pilatus in den mittelalterlichen Passionsspielen*, pp. 37 f. In contrast to the earlier plays, moreover, almost invariably inspired if not altogether written by the clergy, those composed after the twelfth century by predominantly lay authors borrowed ideas and facts even from the New Testament apocrypha directly, rather than through the mediation of the medieval ecclesiastical tradition. See H. Rupp, *Deutsche religiöse Dichtungen des 11. und 12. Jahrhunderts;* and G. Duriez's complementary Lille theses, *Les Apocryphes dans le drame religieux en Allemagne au moyen âge;* and *La Théologie dans le drame religieux en Allemagne au moyen âge.* On the general conversionist overtones in the lay literature, see *supra*, Vol. V, pp. 342 f. n. 44. See also E. Schwenkfeld's Marburg dissertation, *Die Religionsgespräche der deutschen erzählenden Dichtung bis zum Ausgang des 13. Jahrhunderts*, which, however, sheds more light on the religious debates with pagans and Muslims than those with Jews; S. Stein's aforementioned dissertation, *Die Ungläubigen in der mittelhochdeutschen Literatur;* and C. Lehrmann's brief general review of *L'Element juif dans la littérature française*, Vol. I: *Des Origines à la Révolution.*

CHAPTER L: WANDERER

1. Thomas Aquinas, *Summa theologica*, iii.8, 1–3 in the Jubilee ed., XI, 126 ff. (with Cardinal Cajetan's interesting comments thereon, *ibid.*, p. 130); in the English trans. by the English Dominican Fathers, 2d ed., XV, 136 ff.; Ennea Silvio Piccolomini (Pope Pius II), *De ortu et auctoritate imperii Romani*, x, ed. by G. Kallen. See J. B. Toews, "Dream and Reality in the Imperial Ideology of Pope Pius II," *Medievalia et humanistica*, XVI, 77–93; and, more generally, the remarkable material brought together by O. Gierke in his long-recognized standard work, *Political Theories of the Middle Age*, trans. by F. W. Maitland, esp. pp. 103 f. n. 7, 109 ff. nn. 16–17, 125 ff. nn. 53 ff.; and by R. Wallach in *Das Abendländische Gemeinschaftsbewusstsein im Mittelalter*. See also Henri de Lubac's *Corpus mysticum: L'Eucharistie et l'église au moyen âge*, 2d ed., esp. p. 358 App. C, citing and analyzing the declaration by St. Bruno of Würzburg (11th century): *Vel certe terra est Ecclesia, id est corpus Christi mysticum;* and W. Kölmel, "Einheit und Zweiheit der Gewalt im Corpus mysticum. Zur Souveränitätslehre des Augustinus Triumphus," *HJB*, LXXXII, 103–47. Even where the phrases used were "Christianity" or "the Church," they could often embrace the non-Christian world as well. See G. B. Ladner's analysis in "The Concepts of 'Ecclesia' and 'Christianitas' and Their Relation to the Idea of Papal 'Plenitudo Potestatis' from Gregory VII to Boniface VIII," *Miscellanea historiae pontificiae*, XVIII, 49–77.

In this respect the Church outlook did not greatly differ from the Jewish, which likewise conceived humanity as a single body, even though it attributed to Israel the highest rank among the nations. This is true even of extremists like Yehudah Halevi or Aaron b. Joseph ha-Levi who, through this special elevation, tried to explain the reason why the Torah was given to Jews. See Aaron's *Sefer ha-Ḥinnukh* (Book of Training; on the six hundred and thirteen commandments), Intro., Venice, 1601 ed., fols. 10b f.; and *supra*, Vol. VIII, pp. 123 ff., 133, 340 ff.

2. T. Walek-Czernecki, "Le Rôle de la nationalité dans l'histoire de l'antiquité," *Bulletin* of the International Committee of Historical Sciences, II, Part 2, p. 307; A. Dufourcq, *L'Avenir du christianisme*, IV, 339 n.; St. Gregory Nazianzien, *Orationes theologicae*, xliii.15 in *PG*, XXXVI, 513 ff. See E. R. Hardy, Jr., "The Patriarchate of Alexandria: a Study in National Christianity," *Church History*, XV, 81–100; and, more generally, E. L. Woodward, *Christianity and Nationalism in the Later Roman Empire*, esp. pp. 5 n. 1, 16, 43 f., 48, 66 n. 1. Walek-Czernecki's thesis contrasts with that of Eduard Meyer who claimed that in antiquity only the Jews, the Persians, and the Greeks developed into real nationalities. However, this difference of opinion is more semantic than basic. See my *Modern Nationalism and Religion*, pp. 7, 275 n. 6. On the nationalist ingredients in the early Christian sectarian struggles see also E. Peterson, "Das Problem des Nationalismus im alten Christentum," *Theologische Zeitschrift*, VII, 81–91.

Obviously, the national idea took on different forms under different civilizations. The nationalism of the early Christian sects was not quite the same as the national movements underlying sectarianism within Islam, although both types developed in the same geographic area. See F. Taeschner, "Kulturgemeinschaft und nationale Sonderheiten im mittelalterlichen Orient," *Zeitschrift für Missionswissenschaft,* XXXV, 128–41 (with special reference to the three major nationalities of Arabs, Turks, and Persians which, beginning with the eleventh century, undermined Islamic unity). The national idea of the medieval West again had peculiarities of its own. But in all its diverse forms nationalism also had many common features including its profound effects on the life of the Jewish minority.

3. See the "Statute of the German Nation" of October 4, 1382, excerpted by L. Thorndike in his *University Records and Life in the Middle Ages,* pp. 255 f. No. 93 (also *ibid.,* pp. 169 ff. No. 69); L. Rigaud, "La Nation germanique de l'ancienne Université d'Orléans," *Revue d'histoire de l'Eglise de France,* XXVII, 46–71; G. G. Coulton, "Nationalism in the Middle Ages," *Cambridge Historical Journal,* V, 20; G. C. Powers, *Nationalism at the Council of Constance (1414–1418),* pp. 59 ff., 104, 108 f., 119; L. R. Loomis, "Nationality at the Council of Constance," *AHR,* XLIV, 508–27; and, more generally, H. Finke, "Die Nation in den spätmittelalterlichen allgemeinen Konzilien," *HJB,* LVII, esp. pp. 335 ff. See also the recent jubilee volume *Das Konzil von Konstanz. Beiträge zur seiner Geschichte und Theologie,* ed. by A. Franzen and W. Müller.

Taught by the Constance experiences, the ecclesiastical leaders tried to avoid such nationalist divisions at the Council of Basel two decades later. However, they were unable to turn back the wheels of history and the national differences came strongly to the fore at that Council also. A century later Francis I of France tried to prevent the convocation of the Council of Trent altogether and subsequently attempted to sabotage it. See I. Rogger, *Le Nazioni al Concilio di Trento durante la sua época imperiale, 1545–1552,* esp. pp. 85 ff. At that time, of course, the Reform movement was in full swing, a movement which, from the days of Wycliffe on, was strongly interlaced with national aspirations. See *infra,* Chaps. LVIII–LIX.

4. Meir b. Baruch, *Resp.,* Cremona ed., No. 117; Joseph Karo, *Bet Yosef* on *Turim* E. 'E. No. 75; I. A. Agus, *Rabbi Meir of Rothenburg,* I, 319 f. No. 283; R. W. Carlyle and A. J. Carlyle, *A History of Mediaeval Political Theory in the West,* V, 441. R. Meir followed here the German, rather than the French, nationalistic doctrines. In their struggle over the Rhenish frontier, the French invoked the territorial-historical principle of boundaries drawn by rivers like the Roman *limes,* whereas the Germans emphasized the linguistic unity of the population on both sides of the Rhine. See Wallach, *Das Abendländische Gemeinschaftsbewusstsein,* p. 38; and particularly the illustrations furnished by M. Lugge in her *"Gallia" und "Francia" im Mittelalter,* pp. 160 ff., 190 n. 670. True, after the spread of the Aristotelian doctrines in western Europe Thomas Aquinas taught that the state was a "natural" institution. But his view did not prevail until the era of Enlightenment. See T. Gilby, *Principality and Polity: Aquinas and the Rise of State Theory in the West,* esp. pp. 122, 319 f. In Thomas' day another leading Dominican contended that he who loved his native land had not yet overcome Nature in favor of Grace. Also, in contrast to Meir of Rothenburg and the German defenders of their Rhine province, St. Stephen of Hungary (997–1038) had glorified his own kingdom because it embraced various ethnic and linguistic groups, claiming that "a kingdom of a single language and the

same mores is senseless and fragile." See K. Lamprecht, *Deutsche Geschichte*, 6th ed., I, 16 f., 29; St. Stephen's *Monita ad filium* in *PL*, CLI, 1240.

History has proved St. Stephen wrong, however, and shown that national unity based upon linguistic identity has, as a rule, endured much longer than mere political coexistence. Boundaries redrawn in the name of the dynastic principle and for the satisfaction of the rulers' imperialist appetites failed to obliterate the deep-rooted linguistic-cultural divisions. With particular reference to Belgium, T. H. Reed has rightly emphasized the enduring nature of the Franco-Flemish linguistic frontier over many centuries. See *supra*, Vol. X, pp. 16, 306 n. 15. On the earlier differences between the state and nation see the debate in E. Sestan's *Stato e Nazione nell'alto medioevo;* and F. Gaeta's remarks thereon under the same title in *Nuova rivista storica*, XXXVIII, 228–38.

5. St. Augustine, *De civitate Dei*, iv.15, ed. with an English trans. by G. E. Mc-Cracken *et al.*, (Loeb Classical Library), II, 56 ff.; J. L. A. Huillard-Bréholles, *Historia diplomatica Friderici Secundi*, IV, 873; VI, 685 f.; K. Hampe, ed., *Die Aktenstücke zum Frieden von S. Germano 1230*, p. 101; Johannes Teutonicus, cited from MSS by G. Post in "Two Notes on Nationalism in the Middle Ages," *Traditio*, IX, 298 f.; Bartolus de Saxoferrato, *Commentaria* on Justinian's *CJ*, Digest, 49.15, 24; Baldus de Ubaldis, *Concilia*, III, cons. 218; both cited by W. Ullmann in "The Development of the Medieval Idea of Sovereignty," *EHR*, LXIV, 3 ff., 6. See also H. Grundmann, "Freiheit als religiöses, politisches und persönliches Postulat im Mittelalter," *HZ*, CLXXXIII, 40 f.

6. Jacobus de Albenga, cited from a British Museum MS by G. Post in *Traditio*, IX, 302; Gregory IX's Decretal, iv.17, 3 in *Corpus juris canonici*, ed. by E. Friedberg, II, 714 ff.; R. Menéndez Pidal, *El Imperio hispánico y los cincos reinos*, pp. 155 ff.; H. J. Hüffer, "Die Mittelalterliche spanische Kaiseridee und ihre Probleme," *Saeculum*, III, 425–43; *supra*, Vol. IV, pp. 28, 245 f. n. 30. From this angle the very canon law became a source of the modern idea of sovereignty. See F. Calasso, *I Glossatori e la teoria della sovranità; studio di diritto comune pubblico;* S. Mochi Onery, *Fonti canonistiche dell'idee moderne dello stato*. Even in Italy the imperial idea became the less popular as German "arrogance" was ever more deeply resented. See P. Amelung's data in *Das Bild des Deutschen in der Literatur der italienischen Renaissance*. See also, more generally, R. Folz, *L'Idée d'empire en Occident du Ve au XIVe siècle;* M. David, *La Souveraineté et les limites juridiques du pouvoir monarchique du IXe au XVe siècle.*

It may be noted that not only the emperors but also the popes extensively used the Bible in support of their claims. Innocent III argued that in ancient Israel the priesthood had long antedated the kingdom, the latter being condemned as sinful in the Book of Samuel. See his address cited *supra*, Vol. IX, pp. 138 f., 308 f. n. 4; J. Funkenstein, "Samuel und Saul in der Staatslehre des Mittelalters," *Archiv für Rechts- und Sozialphilosophie*, XL, 129–40; and, on that usage as early as the days of Charlemagne, E. Rieber's dissertation, *Die Bedeutung alttestamentlicher Vorstellungen für das Herrscherbild Karls des Grossen und seines Hofkreises*. The figure of King David loomed particularly large in both the literary and the graphic presentations. See H. Steger, *David rex et propheta; König David als vorbildliche Verkörperung des Herrschers und Dichters im Mittelalter*. It would take us too far afield to list the innumerable publications on the struggle between the medieval Papacy and the Empire. But the following, more recent, studies (in addition to those listed *supra,* Vol. IX, pp. 308 f. nn. 2 and 4) may be of some use to readers: W. Goetz, *Translatio imperii: ein Beitrag zur Geschichte des Geschichtsdenkens und der politischen Theorien des Mittelalters und in der frühen Neuzeit;* the essays collected by F. Kempf in his ed. of *Sacerdozio e regno da Gregorio VII a Bonifacio VIII;* and Kempf's debate with W. Ullmann on "Die Päpstliche Gewalt in der mittelalterlichen Welt" in *Saggi storici intorno al papato (Miscellanea historiae pontificiae,* XXI), pp. 117–69.

7. H. Hauser, *Le Traité de Madrid et la cession de la Bourgogne à Charles Quint;* idem, *Le Principe de nationalités: Ses origines historiques,* esp. pp. 12, 15; H. Koht, "The Dawn of Nationalism in Europe," *AHR,* LII, 279. See the pertinent discussion by W. Mohr, "Zur Frage des Nationalismus im Mittelalter," *Annales Universitatis Saraviensis,* Philosophie-Lettres, II, 106–16. Typical of the mutual ethnic animosities are not only the accusations of the French Crusaders that their German fellow-combatants were lazy and unwilling to fight, but also an exclamation like that of the Sicilian Peter of Eboli who, although generally a partisan of the emperor, once irately inquired: "Who can tolerate the Teutonic rabble?" See Wallach, *Das Abendländische Gemeinschaftsbewusstsein,* pp. 33 ff. On the growingly "sacred" character of the monarchy, see E. H. Kantorowicz, *Laudes regiae: a Study in Liturgical Acclamations and Medieval Ruler Worship;* C. Ghisalberti, "Sulla teoria dei delitti di lesa maestà nel diritto comune," *Archivio giuridico Serafini,* CXLIX, 100–179; M. David, "Le Serment de Sacre du IX⁰ au XV⁰ siècle. Contribution à l'étude des limites juridiques de la souveraineté," *Revue du moyen âge latin,* VI, 5–272 (includes an analysis of the biblical precedents, pp. 24 ff.). That this elevation into the realm of the sacred applied to the office, rather than to the person of the king, has been convincingly demonstrated, with the aid of the royal symbolism of the time, by P. E. Schramm *et al.* in their *Herrschaftszeichen und Staatssymbolik,* esp. III, 1083. Nevertheless the doctrine that "The Prince is Not Bound by the Laws," as espoused by the fourteenth-century glossator, Franciscus Accursius (Accorso) was bound to increase the dependence of Jews on the whims of their rulers. See B. Tierney's pertinent essay in *Comparative Studies in Society and History,* V, 378–400. This doctrine, going back to a saying by the jurist, Ulpian, and taken over in Justinian's *CJ,* had been contrasted as early as the first century by a Jewish delegation in Rome with the rabbinic view that even God abides by his own commandments. See D. Daube, "Princeps legibus solutus," *Koschaker Mem. Vol.,* II, 461–65.

8. Suger, *Oeuvres complètes,* ed. by A. Lecoy de la Marche, pp. 116, 398; Tolomeo de Lucca, *De regimine principum,* iii.4, ed. by J. Mathis, pp. 41, 413 ff.; and other data analyzed by E. H. Kantorowicz in his *"Pro patria mori* in Medieval Political Thought," *AHR,* LVI, 472–92. The literature on the growth of national sovereignty is enormous. Suffice it to cite here the following recent publications in addition to those mentioned in the previous notes: F. Bock, *Reichsidee und Nationalstaaten. Vom Untergang des alten Reiches bis zur Kündigung des deutsch-englischen Bündnisses im Jahre 1341;* F. A. von der Heydte, *Die Geburtsstunde des souveränen Staates: Ein Beitrag zur Geschichte des Völkerrechts, der allgemeinen Staatslehre und des politischen Denkens;* and, particularly, the enlightening analysis by E. H. Kantorowicz in *The King's Two Bodies: a Study in Medieval Political Theology,*

despite certain qualifications recently suggested by E. Nineham in "The So-Called Anonymous of York" *Journal of Ecclesiastical History*, XIV, 31–45; and by E. Lewis in his "King above Law? 'Quod principi placuit' in Bracton," *Speculum*, XXXIX, 240–69. See also the vast collection of excerpts from primary sources in an English trans. assembled in E. Lewis's *Medieval Political Ideas;* and G. Post, *Studies in Medieval Legal Thought. Public Law and the State, 1100–1322.*

9. See *supra,* Vols. IX, pp. 137 ff., 308 ff. nn. 1 ff.; X, pp. 53 ff., 325 ff. nn. 1 ff.; and Chap. XLVII, nn. 1 ff.; and my discussions of these aspects in *Baer Jub. Vol.,* pp. 102–24; and *Neuman Jub. Vol.,* pp. 17–48.

10. See my "Nationalism and Intolerance," *Menorah Journal*, XVI, 406; S. Singer's collection of *Sprichwörter des Mittelalters*, I, 119 No. 91. The harshness of the medieval national state toward Jews is the less astonishing as, observing the nationalist disagreements among Crusaders, Bishop Gervais of Prémontré had written to Innocent III that Germans should not be made to march with Frenchmen, for "it is said that they had never agreed in any solemn partnership." In extreme cases even English monks, generally sworn to their Orders' pledges of charity, preached that it was no more sinful to slay an Irishman than to kill a dog or any other brute animal. See J. de Fordun, *Scottichronicon cum supplementis ac continuatione*, xii.26 ff., ed. by W. Bower, II, 259 ff., 264; G. G. Coulton in the *Cambridge Historical Journal*, V, 18 f., 30 f. During the nineteenth-century drive for national unification, to be sure, German and Italian historians were apt to detract from the values of tribalism and regionalism. But these values were deeply cherished in the Middle Ages and even found eloquent modern spokesmen in such romantic rebels against French centralism as Maurice Barrès. A more balanced analysis of the mutual relationships between these groupings is offered by K. S. Bader in his essay, "Volk–Stamm–Territorium," *HZ*, CLXXVI, 449–77.

11. C. G. Crump in his and E. F. Jacob's collection of essays entitled *The Legacy of the Middle Ages*, p. 11; the St. Blazier MS of 1440, cited by F. J. Mone in his ed. of *Schauspiele des Mittelalters*, II, 22 n.; A. Leitzmann and K. Burdach, "Der Judenspiess und die Longinus-Sage," *Neue Jahrbücher für das klassische Altertum*, XXXVII, 51 f.; F. Barlow, *The Feudal Kingdom of England 1042–1216*, p. 122. The rise of the bourgeoisie was facilitated by the growing social mobility which even in the regimented society of the Late Middle Ages allowed enterprising individuals to move from one group to another. A soldier-adventurer like Mercadier, Richard I's commander in France, could achieve great eminence, although no one really knew his ancestry. We recall the speedy rise of two Anglo-Jewish converts in the days of Henry III. See *supra,* Chap. XLVIII, n. 49; and other examples cited by Crump, pp. 18 f.

12. See J. R. Strayer, "The Laicization of French and English Society in the Thirteenth Century," *Speculum*, XV, 76–86; G. de Lagarde, *La Naissance de l'esprit laïque au déclin du Moyen Âge*, new ed. For this reason even in such part-of-nationality states as the Holy Roman Empire the gradual achievement of near-sovereign status by many cities augured badly for the toleration of Jews. See O. Brunner, "Souveränitätsproblem und Sozialstruktur in den deutschen Reichsstädten der früheren Neuzeit," *VSW*, L, 329–60.

13. A. Brackmann, "Die Ursachen der geistigen und politischen Wandlung Europas im 11. und 12. Jahrhundert," *HZ*, CXLIX, 234 f.; John of Salisbury, *Epistolae*, lix, in his *Opera omnia*, in *PL*, CXCIX, 39; Bede the Venerable, *Historia ecclesiastica gentis Anglorum*, v.10, in his *Opera omnia*, VI, *PL*, XCV, 243 f.; R. Folz, *L'Idée d'Empire en Occident du Vᵉ au XIVᵉ siècle*, pp. 50 ff., 64 ff.; C. H. McIlwain, *Growth of Political Thought in the West*, p. 268. See also F. Tautz, *Die Könige von England und das Reich 1272–1377. Mit einem Rückblick auf ihr Verhältnis zu den Staufern*. On Bracton's teachings relating to the authority of the English Crown, see *supra*, Vol. X, pp. 54 f., 92 f., 325 n. 2, 344 n. 46; and, more generally, F. Schulz, "Bracton on Kingship," *EHR*, LX, 136–76; and B. Tierney, "Bracton on Government," *Speculum*, XXXVIII, 295–317 (pointing out the English jurist's relative unfamiliarity with the more advanced Continental discussions on constitutionalism vs. absolutism). See also H. G. Richardson's recent study, *Bracton: the Problem of His Text*. The dynamic changes which took place between the reigns of John I and Edward I are analyzed in the comprehensive presentation by F. M. Powicke, *The Thirteenth Century, 1216–1307* (with a few references to Jews). William Stubbs is not altogether wrong when he speaks of nationalism in the later stages of pre-Conquest England. See his *The Constitutional History of England*, 3d ed., I, 230 ff. If one wished to press the point, this factor may have contributed to the paucity of Jews, and of any records pertaining to them, before William the Conqueror. See *supra*, Vol. IV, pp. 76 f., 276 f. nn. 98 and 100.

14. J. Jacobs, *The Jews of Angevin England*, p. 338; *supra*, Chap. XLVIII, n. 49; H. P. Stokes, *Studies in Anglo-Jewish History*, pp. 63 ff.; I. Loeb's observations on Hebrew transliterations of French names in English *starrs* in his reviews of the *Papers Read at the Anglo-Jewish Historical Exhibition, 1887* in *REJ*, XVI, 296–99, and of M. Davis's *Sheṭarot*, *ibid.*, XVIII, 151–52; M. Adler, *Jews of Medieval England*, pp. 20 f.; C. Roth, *A History of the Jews in England*, pp. 93 f., 277. The general use of French by the English Jews is also illustrated by the English Tosafists' exclusive application of French equivalents to explain talmudic terms. See the comments by Darmesteter, Blondheim, and others cited *supra*, Vol. VI, p. 347 n. 58. If, according to Richard of Devizes, a French Jew advised a young man not to go too far into England, since there he would find few people familiar with the Romance language (*De rebus gestis. . . . Ricardi Primi*, ed. by Howlett, p. 438), this counselor evidently had only English Christians in mind. Giraldus Cambrensis depicts the journey of a Jew toward Shrewsbury accompanied by two local deacons, named Peche (*Peccatum*) and Dayville (*Diabolus*). When Peche described the boundaries of his deaconry between places called Mala platea and Bad-pass, the Jew punned, "It will be a wonder if good luck ever returns me safely from this country, whose archdeacon is sin, whose deacon is the devil, which you enter by a Bad-Place and leave in a Bad-Pass." See Giraldus' *Itinerarium Kambriae*, ii.13, in his *Opera*, ed. by J. S. Brewer and J. F. Dimock, VI, 146. The dialects spoken by the Jews of England and elsewhere will be analyzed in a later chapter.

15. John's decree of July 29, 1203, in *Patent Rolls, 1203*, p. 33; in Jacobs, *The Jews of Angevin England*, pp. 217 f., erroneously quoting the date of July 22, 1204, from Tovey's *Anglia Judaica*, pp. 67 f.; Matthew Paris, *Chronica majora*, ed. by H. R. Luard, III, 543; H. Rashdall, *The Universities of Europe in the Middle Ages*, new ed. by F. M. Powicke and A. B. Emden, III, 85 f.; C. Roth, *The Jews of Medieval*

Oxford, pp. 126 f.; M. Adler, *Jews of Medieval England*, pp. 78 f.; idem, "Jewish Tallies of the Thirteenth Century," *Miscellanies JHSE*, II, 8–23. A full analysis of the Norwich affair is given by W. Rye in "The Alleged Abduction and Circumcision of a Boy at Norwich in 1230," *The Norfolk Antiquarian Miscellany*, I, Part 2, pp. 312–44. See also the document published in J. M. Rigg's *Select Pleas*, pp. xliv ff. App. No. i. Felix Liebermann has pointed out that the accusers of the Norwich Jews had to resort to at least "one gross lie and three self-contradictions." See his review of Rigg's *Select Pleas* in *EHR*, XVII, 554.

The student riot in Oxford had many far-reaching results. It raised the question of the sheriff's right to imprison students without the cooperation of University authorities. Robert Grosseteste, as bishop of Lincoln, insisted that the imprisoned rioters, being chiefly student-clerks, be tried by an ecclesiastical court. This petition was granted and ultimately the prisoners were released, allegedly because of insufficient evidence. See the story briefly told by Thomas Wykes in his *Chronicon* in *Annales monastici*, ed. by H. R. Luard, IV, 91; *Close Rolls, 1242–47*, pp. 181, 241 f.; and summarized by C. Roth in *The Jews of Medieval Oxford*, pp. 127 ff. See also A. Ballard and J. Tait, eds., *British Borough Charters, 1216–1307*, pp. lxiv, lxix, 174 f., 302.

16. *Annales monasterii de Burton, 1004–1263*, in *Annales monastici*, ed. by Luard, I, 346 ff.; Mansi, *Collectio*, XXII, 1172, canons 39–40; S. Grayzel, *The Church and the Jews*, pp. 314 f. No. xvi; Bartholomew of Exeter, *Dialogus contra Judaeos ad corrigendum et perficiendum destinatus (1180–84)*, cited from a Bodleian MS by R. W. Hunt in "The Disputation of Peter of Cornwall against Symon the Jew" in *Studies . . . Frederick Maurice Powicke*, pp. 147 f.; Peter de Blois, *Contra perfidiam Judaeorum* in his *Opera omnia* in *PL*, CCVII, 825–70; E. O'Neill, "John Peckham," *Encyclopaedia Britannica*, 11th ed., XXI, 33; Peckham's letter to Edward I of November 2, 1281, in his *Registrum epistolarum*, ed. by C. T. Martin, I, 239; D. L. Douie, *Archbishop Pecham*, pp. 309 f., 322 ff.; *Patent Rolls, 1272–1281*, p. 356; *Rotuli parliamentorum*, I, 46a; *supra*, Vols. IX, p. 274 n. 21; X, pp. 101 ff., 347 f. nn. 57–58; Chap. XLVII, n. 51. If, in his *Anglia Judaica*, pp. 82 ff., D'Bloissiers Tovey mentions that the prior of Dunstable admitted several Jews to residence in his possessions against an annual payment of two silver spoons, these exceptions merely confirm the rule that religio-national intolerance had sharply increased since the twelfth century when Jews and clerics freely associated with one another. See the examples cited by J. Jacobs in *The Jews of Angevin England*, pp. 337 f. No. vii.

17. *Patent Rolls, 1281–1292*, pp. 397 f.; M. Adler, *Jews of Medieval England*, pp. 279 ff., 301; *supra*, Vol. IX, pp. 18 f., 248 f. n. 17. Because the English Church steadfastly favored the peaceful assimilation of Jews, its spokesmen rarely advocated expulsion. If, as early as 1190, the abbey of St. Bury had initiated the expulsion of the Jews from an entire borough, this move arose from specific local causes. In fact, four decades later it was Bishop Robert Grosseteste whose intervention secured the postponement of the expulsion of Leicester Jewry from 1231 to 1253. See his *Epistolae*, v, ed. by H. R. Luard, pp. 33 ff.; reproduced in an English trans. by L. M. Friedman in his *Robert Grosseteste and the Jews*, pp. 12 ff., 23 f.; and *supra*, Vols. IV, pp. 84, 281 n. 11; IX, pp. 248 n. 15, 288 n. 4; X, pp. 349 n. 62. True, in this letter the distinguished scholar also fulminated against Jewish usury, but neither did he spare his own coreligionists. On his very deathbed he denounced Pope Innocent IV for allowing the Cahorsins to extort from debtors interest and expenses well in excess of the

43⅓ percent permitted to Jews. The pope was but "slightly corrected" by this reprimand and rather rejoiced at Grosseteste's death. See Matthew Paris, *Chronica majora*, ed. by Luard, V, 448, 460. See also the essays ed. by D. A. Callus, *Robert Grosseteste, Scholar and Bishop. Essays in Commemoration of the Seventh Centenary of his Death*, esp. pp. 70 ff., 163 ff., 178 ff.; and F. M. Powicke's general evaluation of "Robert Grosseteste, Bishop of Lincoln," *BJRL*, XXXV, 482–507. Simon de Montfort's final decree of expulsion of the Jews from Leicester in 1253 is published in Latin with an English trans. by S. Levy in his "Notes on Leicester Jewry," *TJHSE*, V, 39, 41.

18. See *supra*, Vol. X, pp. 105 f., 349 n. 61; and O. H. Richardson, *The National Movement in the Reign of Henry III and Its Culmination in the Barons' War*. Although using the term "national" in an almost exclusively political sense, Richardson rightly points out that "in connection with the Barons' War the first political poem in English makes its appearance, for the first time the English language is used in public documents, and knowledge of the English tongue is made in certain sections of the country the test of patriotism" (p. 213). See also, more generally, E. F. Jacob, *Studies in the Period of Baronial Reform and Rebellion, 1258–1267*, esp. pp. 32, 236 f., 340; and P. Walne, "The Barons' Argument at Amiens, January, 1264," *EHR*, LXIX, 418–25; LXXIII, 453–59, which illustrates the bitterness among the barons toward the foreigners introduced into England by Henry III, a bitterness which rubbed off on the Jewish "aliens" as well.

Not surprisingly, the news of the baronial attacks on Jews spread to the Continent. See S. Salfeld, ed., *Das Martyrologium des Nürnberger Memorbuches*, pp. 23, 67, 153. These riots, more costly in Jewish lives than any which had taken place in England since 1190, are but sketchily mentioned by W. Rye in "The Persecutions of the Jews in England" in *Papers Read at the Anglo-Jewish Historical Exhibition, 1887*, pp. 164 f. Monetary losses occasioned by the destruction of buildings and pillage must likewise have been very great. Only the bonds of moneylenders, upon which the wrath of the rebels was concentrated with redoubled fury, could be partially recouped by the royal orders of 1266, recorded in *Patent Rolls, 1258–1266*, pp. 585, 603. Certainly, the setback sustained by the entire Jewish population, including the majority of petty traders, artisans, communal officials, and public charges, was in no way compensated by the few opportunities now offered to wealthy Jewish bankers to foreclose estates of the defeated aristocrats, as suggested by Rigg in his *Select Pleas*, pp. xxxvii f.

19. Matthew Paris, *Historia Anglorum*, III, 76; *Patent Rolls, 1216–1225*, p. 157, *1225–1232*, pp. 493 f.; *1258–1266*, pp. 322 f., 421 f.; *Close Rolls, 1264–1268*, pp. 19, 42, 82 f.; *Calendar of the Charter Rolls*, I, 163, 166 ff. (1232). The anti-Jewish English folklore which, though less widespread than on the Continent, revealed the growing popular hostility, was discussed *supra*, Chap. XLIX.

20. S. Levy in *TJHSE*, V, 39, 41; *Close Rolls, 1231–1234*, pp. 466, 515 f.; *1234–1237*, pp. 20, 275, 425; *1237–1242*, p. 393; *1242–1247*, p. 149; *Patent Rolls, 1258–1266*, pp. 153 (1261), 613 (1266); J. M. Rigg, *Select Pleas*, pp. xlviii f. App. ii; and *supra*, Vol. X, pp. 106 ff., 349 f. nn. 62–64. The series of local expulsions of the 1230s and 1240s continued beyond Henry III's regime. See A. Ballard and J. Tait, eds., *British*

Borough Charters, pp. xlix f., lxxviii, 49 (Warton, 1246–71, and Bridgetown Pomeroy, 1268), 86, 93 (Chard, 1235 and 1271–72), 87 (Burton-on-Trent, 1273); and *infra,* n. 21. These charters seem to have been fairly well observed despite the exception inserted into Henry III's decree of 1253, allowing Jewish resettlement "by special licence of the King." We recall that, out of desperation, some hard-pressed Jewish communities themselves resorted to restrictive covenants, like the "Canterbury Treaty" of 1266, whereby they tried to stem the influx of undesirable newcomers.

21. Rymer and Sanderson, *Foedera,* I, 503, 634; *Close Rolls, 1272–79,* p. 130; J. M. Rigg, *Select Pleas,* p. 85; *Patent Rolls, 1272–1281,* p. 76; A. Ballard and J. Tait's ed., *British Borough Charters,* p. 142; *infra,* n. 24. There were some changes after the promulgation of the order of Jan. 12, 1275. On Cambridge, see H. P. Stokes, *Studies,* pp. 188 ff. Sooner or later Jewish expellees were forced to dispose also of their real estate left behind, the burghers of Bridgnorth, for instance, resenting even the occasional brief visits of such houseowners. See *Close Rolls, loc. cit.;* and, more generally, H. G. Richardson, *The English Jewry under Angevin Kings,* pp. 20 ff.

22. E. Jenks, *Edward Plantagenet (Edward I) the English Justinian; or The Making of the Common Law;* H. Rashdall, *The Universities,* III, 58; W. Stubbs, *The Constitutional History of England,* 3d ed., II, 305 ff.; *supra,* Vol. X, pp. 110 ff., 351 f. nn. 67 ff. In *The English Jewry,* pp. 213 f., H. G. Richardson has plausibly argued that the legislation in 1275–90 was not in the main the work of the royal councilors but rather of Edward himself who "was neither English nor heroic." However, he clearly responded to the wishes of the English people by trying to absorb the Jews in the body politic through both religious conversion and economic integration. In the former area he apparently worked hand in hand with Archbishop Peckham. By 1280, indeed, the *domus conversorum* had no less than 97 (or 96, according to Adler) inmates, a sizable number for the relatively small Anglo-Jewish population. See K. Knoll, *London im Mittelalter,* p. 130; M. Adler, *Jews of Medieval England,* pp. 308 f., 350 ff. App. v. Yet, both king and archbishop were disappointed by the slow progress of their conversionist efforts.

23. T. Rymer and R. Sanderson, eds., *Foedera,* ed. by A. Clarke and F. Holbrooke, I, 736; H. G. Richardson, *The English Jewry,* pp. 228 f.; Pierre de Langtoft, *The Chronicle in French Verse, from the Earliest Period to the Death of King Edward I,* ed. by T. Wright, II, 187 ff.; F. A. Cazel, Jr., "The Fifteenth of 1225," *BIHR,* XXXIV, 69 ff.; F. M. Powicke, *King Henry III and the Lord Edward: the Community of the Realm in the Thirteenth Century,* II, 732; B. L. Abrahams, "The Condition of the Jews of England at the Time of Their Expulsion in 1290," *TJHSE,* II, 76–105; C. Roth, *A History of the Jews in England,* pp. 85 f., 275 f. n. e ; and *supra,* Vol. X, pp. 352 f. n. 71. The immediate effects of the banishment on such local communities as Canterbury and Bristol are discussed by M. Adler in his *Jews of Medieval England,* pp. 98 ff., 231 ff.

We cannot tell what role the newly convened Parliament played in the expulsion. But the fact that it had made such a recommendation as early as 1281 would seem to indicate that it continued to exert pressures in this direction in the intervening nine years. It, in turn, may have been prompted by petitions, largely unrecorded, from various classes of the population. These were as a rule shunted to lower officials (in the Jewish case to the Justices of the Jews) where they were largely pigeonholed. See B. Wilkinson, *Constitutional History of Medieval England 1216–1399*, III, 144 No. xvi.

24. B. L. Abrahams, "The Expulsion of the Jews from England in 1290," *JQR*, [o.s.] VII, 75–100, 236–58, 428–58, esp. pp. 449 f., quoting the respective chronicles. The contemporaries realized, of course, the importance of the economic factor, although they were not cognizant of such modern categories of thinking as underlie P. Elman's study of "The Economic Causes of the Expulsion of the Jews in 1290," *Economic History Review*, VII, 145–54. The economic factor is also overemphasized by S. A. Singer in "The Expulsion of the Jews from England in 1290," *JQR*, LV, 117–36 with no new data. See also the earlier observations by G. H. Leonard, "Expulsion of the Jews from England by Edward I: an Essay in Explanation of the Exodus, A. D. 1290," *Transactions* of the Royal Historical Society, V, 103–46; and the more recent interpretations by C. Roth in *A History of the Jews in England*, pp. 68 ff., 85 ff.; and by H. G. Richardson in *The English Jewry*, pp. 213 ff., 228 ff. Roth also discusses the few recorded places in which some of the exiles were to find new abodes, temporary or permanent (p. 87). On the long-debated number of English Jews affected by the Expulsion, see *infra*, Chap. LI.

To the adherents of the "lachrymose conception of Jewish history" the explanation was even simpler: the perennial martyrology of the Jewish people in exile. This school of thought, to which most Hebrew chroniclers of the Late Middle Ages and early modern times belonged, also found eloquent representatives among leading modern Jewish historians, including L. Zunz and H. Graetz. The holocaust under the Nazis necessarily reinforced this point of view. See, for instance, J. Ben-Jacob, *The Motif of Catastrophe in Jewish History*.

25. M. Adler, *Jews of Medieval England*, pp. 305 f., 308, 350; L. Edwards, "Some English Examples of the Medieval Representation of Church and Synagogue," *TJHSE*, XVIII, 63–75; B. Blumenkranz, *Juden und Judentum in der mittelalterlichen Kunst*, esp. pp. 21, 25 f.; *supra*, Vol. IX, pp. 256 f. n. 39. The struggle for the readmission of the Jews to England under Cromwell will be discussed in a later volume.

26. C. Bémont, ed., *Recueil d'actes relatifs à l'administration des rois d'Angleterre en Guyenne au XIIIe siècle* (mainly non-Jewish materials from the years 1254–74); M. Kayserling, *Die Juden in Navarra*, pp. 216 f. App. P; F. Michel, *Rôles gasconnes*, III, 187 ff. Nos. 3048–49, 3063, 3090 and 3092, 461 No. 4786. See *ibid.*, II, 329 No. 1067, 486 f. No. 1571; III, 55 No. 2054; and *supra*, Vol. X, pp. 114 f., 353 n. 72. The Jewish material has been culled by C. T. Martin in "Gascon Rolls," *TJHSE*, II, 170–79, esp. pp. 176 ff. Nos. 12–17. See also Y. Renouard's recent publication of *Gascon Rolls Preserved in the Public Record Office, 1307–1317;* and, more generally, E. C. Lodge, *Gascony under English Rule*, p. 204; and C. Bémont's bibliographical survey, *La Guyenne pendant la domination anglaise, 1152–1453*. These sharply intolerant measures must, from the outset, have affected but a small Jewish minority in the total Gascon population estimated at only 625,000 in 1316 by Y. Renouard in his "Conjectures sur la population du duché d'Aquitaine en 1316," *Moyen Âge*, LXIX (Jubilee Vol.), 471–78. This was, indeed, a reversal of the situation earlier in the century when the English had protected the Jews against Poitou mobs. In 1221 Henry III had strictly ordered the mayor and city council of Niort, "to maintain and

protect Our Jews of Niort, not to tax them nor to let others tax them in any fashion without Our command; nor are you to cause them any damage or to permit anyone else to cause it." See T. D. Hardy, ed., *Rotuli litterarum clausarum*, I, 480. The implications of the continued French sovereignty over *Wasconia* and the frequently confused divisions of authority in the English administrative system itself are well analyzed by P. Chaplais in his "The Chancery of Guyenne 1259–1453," in *Studies Presented to Sir Hilary Jenkinson*, pp. 61–96, esp. pp. 67 f.; and his "La Souveraineté du roi de France et le pouvoir législatif en Guyenne au début du XIVᵉ siècle," *Moyen Âge*, LXIX (Jubilee Volume), 449–69; and other data furnished by [J. B.] Vincent in *Les Juifs en Poitou*, pp. 5 f.; T. Malvezin in his *Histoire des Juifs à Bordeaux*, pp. 41 ff.; and H. G. Richardson in *The English Jewry*, pp. 232 f.

27. Pierre Dupuy, *Histoire du différend d'entre le Pape Boniface VIII. et Philippe le Bel Roy de France*, Actes et preuves, pp. 27 f.; cited here in a variant from the English trans. by E. Lewis in his *Medieval Political Ideas*, II, 529; W. Ullmann, "The Development of the Medieval Idea of Sovereignty," *EHR*, LXIV, 12; H. Wieruszowski, *Vom Imperium zum nationalen Königtum; vergleichende Studien über die publizistischen Kämpfe Kaiser Friedrichs II. und König Philipps des Schönen mit der Kurie;* M. delle Piane, "Saggio sull'ideologia nazionale nella Francia di Filippo il Bello," *Studi senesi*, LXVI–LXVII, 65–96; H. Kämpf, *Pierre Dubois und die geistigen Grundlagen des französichen Nationalbewusstseins um 1300.* See also *supra*, Vol. X, pp. 53 f., 325 f. nn. 1 and 4. On the growth of the royal power in France see also P. E. Schramm, *Der König von Frankreich. Das Wesen der Monarchie vom 9. bis zum 16. Jahrhundert.*

28. Solomon ibn Verga, *Shebeṭ Yehudah*, ed. by Wiener, p. 114; in Wiener's German trans., p. 234; ed. by Shohet, p. 148 (summarizing the lost chronicle by Shem Ṭob Sonzolo); Matthew Paris, *Chronica majora*, ed. by Luard, III, 369; in Giles's English trans., I, 34; idem, *Historia Anglorum*, ed. by F. Madden, II, 391 f.; Gregory IX's bull, *Lachrymabilem judaeorum* in his *Registres*, ed. by L. Auvray, II, 471 f. Nos. 3308 ff.; Grayzel, *The Church and the Jews*, pp. 226 ff. No. 87, 344 f. App. C. Gregory IX sent a similar note to King Louis IX on the same day; Auvray, p. 472 No. 3312; Grayzel, pp. 228 ff. No. 88; and *supra*, Vol. IX, pp. 9 f., 244 n. 8. The usual assumption that Duke John's vigorous decree was the result of the fanaticism generated by the Crusading movement is undoubtedly right. But elsewhere the same Crusading enthusiasm no longer produced such dire results. See G. A. Lobineau, *Histoire de Bretagne*, I, 242; E. Durtelle de Saint-Sauveur, *Histoire de Bretagne des origines à nos jours*, I, 207 ff. (on the duke's relations with both the barons and the Capetian monarchs); L. Brunschwicg, "Les Juifs de Nantes et du pays nantais," *REJ*, XIV, 85 ff.; I. Loeb, "Les Expulsions des Juifs de France au XIVᵉ siècle," *Jubelschrift . . . H. Graetz*, pp. 39 f. n. 2.

29. Matthew Paris, *Historia Anglorum*, ed. by F. Madden, III, 103 f.; S. Le Nain de Tillemont, *Vie de Saint-Louis, roi de France*, V, 295 ff.; *supra*, Vol. X, pp. 60 f., 328 f. nn. 7–8. Louis IX's conversionist efforts found a careful investigator (on the basis of Treasury records) in the seventeenth-century author Vyon d'Hérouval. See L. A. Bruel, ed., "Notes de Vyon d'Hérouval sur les baptisés et des convers et sur les enquêteurs royaux, au temps de saint Louis et de ses successeurs (1234–1334)," *BEC*, XXVIII, 609–21. Some additional data have come to light since. See also, more

generally, J. Levron, *Saint Louis ou l'apogée du moyen âge;* G. Maillet, *La Vie religieuse au temps de S. Louis.*

There is much confusion in the sources concerning Louis' attempt to expel the Jews in the middle of the century. Even the dates, if given at all by the respective chroniclers, range from 1251 to 1254. See Guillaume de Nangis' description of Louis' eastern exploits, only tangentially related to French Jews, in *Gesta sanctae memoriae Ludovici regis Franciae* in M. Bouquet, ed., *Recueil des historiens des Gaules,* XX, 309–465, esp. pp. 370 f.; his *Chronicon, ibid.,* esp. pp. 555 f.; *Vie de Saint Louis* by the Father Confessor of Queen Marguerite, *ibid.,* p. 66 (neither chronicler refers to the expulsion of Jews); the anonymous *Chronicum Normanniae* for the years 1169–1259 (continuation to 1272), *ibid.,* XXIII, 214 f. (Judaei fugati sunt per totum regnum Franciae et regno ejecti); and the collective chronicle of the St. Catherine Monastery of Rouen, *ibid.,* p. 402 (both giving the date of 1252); Shem Ṭob Sonzolo cited by Ibn Verga, *loc. cit. (supra,* n. 28); and other sources mentioned by I. Loeb in "Les Expulsions," *Jubelschrift . . . H. Graetz,* p. 39 n. 1. Most likely the king, after his return from the Middle East to which Sonzolo specifically refers, never really intended to go through with the banishment of Jews whom he had so vigorously sought to attach to his royal Treasury by the Treaty of Melun of 1230. True, the death of his mother and erstwhile regent, Blanche of Castile, removed her moderating influence from his inner circle. See M. Brion's biography of *Blanche de Castille.* But gradual economic and religious absorption, rather than abrupt elimination, appeared to him as the more promising approach.

30. H. Clouzot, *Cens et rentes dus au comte du Poitiers, à Niort, au XIIIᵉ siècle* (based on documents in the Trésor de Chartes of the Archives Nationales); [J. B.] Vincent, *Les Juifs en Poitou,* pp. 13 f.; *supra,* Vol. X, pp. 62 f., 329 n. 9. Our reconstruction of Louis' and Alphonse's original motivations is admittedly hypothetical. But unfortunately the laconic contemporary chroniclers give us no inkling of what went on in the minds of these brothers and what, if any, advice they may have received from their counselors. Not even the numerous references to Jews in Alphonse's ample correspondence give us any unequivocal clues. In any case no order of expulsion is included in the otherwise fairly complete documentary publications by E. J. Laurière *et al.* and F. A. Isambert *et al.* Nor did Philip the Fair invoke this precedent in his decree of expulsion of 1306 which, in view of his and his compatriots' great reverence for the shade of St. Louis, he would hardly have failed to do. In any case, Jews were not banished either from royal France or from Alphonse's appanage at that time. But the fact that such a radical step was seriously considered and that the French public, particularly the bourgeoisie, was expected to favor it wholeheartedly is symptomatic of the rising trend toward French national homogeneity.

31. C. V. Langlois, "Formulaires et lettres du XIIᵉ, du XIIIᵉ et du XIVᵉ siècle," *Notices et extraits des manuscrits* of the Bibliothèque Nationale, XXXIV, Part 1, p. 18 No. 11; Isambert *et al., Recueil,* II, 683; Laurière *et al., Ordonnances,* I, 137; *Ordonnances de Louvre,* I, 317. On the increase in popular libels and accusations from the beginning of Philip IV's regime and the growing hostility toward Jews reflected in contemporary French letters, see U. Robert, "Catalogue d'actes relatifs aux Juifs pendant le moyen âge," *REJ,* III, 223 No. 91; *supra,* Vol. X, pp. 65 f., 330 f. n. 13; and Chap. XLIX, *passim.* Notwithstanding shifts within the court cama-

rilla the royal regime, on the whole, cherished the Jewish revenue, while overtly repeating Louis IX's pious professions concerning the prohibition of usury. In all recorded instances the authorities supported Jewish claimants against Christian debtors and tried to facilitate their financial transactions. Philip III so greatly appreciated that source of income that he forced the bishop of Béziers to return to him some Jews who had moved from the city area under royal to that under episcopal control. This royal contention is doubly remarkable, since, as late as 1230, the bishops of Béziers had claimed supreme authority over the Jews of the entire city. See C. Devic and J. Vaissète, *Histoire générale de Languedoc*, IX, 62 No. xlvii; Louis IX's detailed privilege of 1220 for Bishop Bernard of Béziers, reproduced in J. H. Albanès's ed. of *Gallia christiana*, VI, instrumenta, cols. 151 ff. No. xxiv; J. Petit, *Charles de Valois (1270–1325)*, pp. 319 n. 7, 322 n. 2; T. Reinach's remarks thereon in his "Charles de Valois et les Juifs," *REJ*, XLII, 103–10; L. Lazard, "Les Revenus tirés des Juifs de France dans le domaine royal (XIII⁰ siècle)," *ibid.*, XV, 251 ff. Nos. 10, 11, 15, 17, 20, 41, 53bis, 62, and 63; G. Saige, *Les Juifs du Languedoc*, p. 30; and other sources listed by G. Caro in his *Sozial- und Wirtschaftsgeschichte der Juden*, II, 293 f.; and *supra*, Vol X, pp. 63 f., 329 f. n. 10.

32. The continuation of Guillaume de Nangis' chronicle by a Benedictine monk of St. Denis for the years 1301–1348, in Bouquet, *Recueil*, XX, 594 (giving the date of August, 1306); *Chronique de Saint-Denis depuis 1285 jusqu'en 1328, ibid.*, p. 680 (environ la Magdeleine, that is around July 22); the anonymous chronicler cited *infra*, n. 34; T. Cochard, *La Juiverie d'Orléans*, pp. 74 ff., 202 ff. Apps. H and I; Ottokar von Horneck, *Österreichische Reimchronik*, vv. 91239–777, esp. 91276–78, ed. by J. Saemüller, II, 1186 ff.; Samuel Usque, *Consolaçam ás tribulaçoens de Israel*, iii.20, ed. by J. Mendes dos Remedios, Part 3, pp. xxi ff.; in G. I. Gelbart's English trans. entitled *A Consolation for the Tribulations of Israel*, pp. 301 ff.; in M. A. Cohen's trans., pp. 192 ff.; Joseph ha-Kohen, *'Emeq ha-bakha*, ed. by M. Letteris, p. 57; in M. Wiener's German trans., pp. 46, 180 f. n. 181. See A. H. Benna, "Der Kaiser und der König von Frankreich im Recht des späten Mittelalters," *ZRG*, Germanistische Abteilung, LXVIII, 397–410; I. Loeb, "Les Expulsions des Juifs de France au XIV⁰ siècle," *Jubelschrift . . . H. Graetz*, pp. 39 ff.; S. Luce, "Catalogue des documents du Trésor des Chartes relatifs aux Juifs sous le règne de Philippe le Bel," *REJ*, II, 15 ff., esp. p. 33 No. xxii; L. Lazard, *ibid.*, XV, 241; and P. Girard, "Histoire sociale: Les Juifs de Paris sous Philippe le Bel," *Science historique*, n.s. XXXVIII, No. 17, pp. 8–11; No. 18, pp. 43–46. On the specific background and the precise date of the expulsion, see also *supra*, Vol. X, pp. 66 f., 331 n. 14. That despite his numerous inconsistencies Philip often responded to public pressures has been shown by J. R. Strayer in his "Philip the Fair—a 'Constitutional' King," *AHR*, LXII, 18–32. Nor were his legal advisers immune from public opinion. See F. J. Pegues, *The Lawyers of the Last Capetians*, esp. pp. 42 f., 116 f. See also M. delle Piane, "Saggio sull'ideologia nazionale nella Francia di Filippo il Bello," *Studi senesi*, LXVI–LXVII, 65–96.

It is possible, though we have no documentary evidence for it, that the Toulouse conversions were encouraged by influential local burghers. Like its Jewish community, the city had by 1306 become but a shadow of its former self. Some leaders may have realized that the total loss of a wealthy and intelligent segment of the population would greatly accelerate its decline. See L. Febvre, "Commerce et marchands de Toulouse (1350–1450)," *Annales ESC*, XI, 78–86, with reference to P. Wolff's extensive monograph on this subject, but stressing more strongly the peculiarities of Toulouse. Even after their conversion, many new Christians doubtless continued to live in their old quarter still called the "Jewish street" in documents of 1630 and 1669. See J. Chalande, "La Rue des Juifs à Toulouse aux quinzième, seizième et dix-septième siècles," *Bulletin* of the Société archéologique du Midi de la France, n.s. XXXVII–XXXIX, 367–72. But enough Toulouse Jews must have chosen exile for the sale of their goods to have yielded 40,745 livres for the Treasury within little more than four months. See S. Luce in *REJ*, II, 22, 37 No. xxxiv.

33. Estori b. Moses Farḥi (ha-Parḥi), *Kaftor va-feraḥ* (Knop and Flower: on Palestine and Its Antiquities), Intro., Venice, 1549 ed.; Yedaiah b. Abraham Penini Bedaresi's poem *Alef alefin* (A Thousand Alefs), ed. by S. Vita dalla Volta in his "Letter to the Editor" (Hebrew), *Kerem Chemed*, IV, 57–65 (with notes by M. Mortara); and other sources cited by Graetz in his *Geschichte der Juden*, 4th ed., VI, Part 1, pp. 245 ff. See also J. Chotzner's sketch, "Yedaiah Bedaresi, a Fourteenth-Century Hebrew Poet and Philosopher," *JQR*, [o.s.] VIII, 414–25.

34. *Chronique anonyme finissant en 1356* in Bouquet, *Recueil*, XXI, 139; S. Luce in *REJ*, II, 22 n. 3; A. Grunzweig, "Les Incidences internationales des mutations monétaires de Philippe le Bel," *Moyen Âge*, LIX, 117–72, esp. pp. 129, 142 f. n. 73. That some Jews, especially the banker Héliot of Vésoul, were also active in securing that royal recall is evident from the documentation supplied by G. Saige in *Les Juifs du Languedoc*, pp. 106, 330 f. No. lvii. On the subsequent destinies of Héliot and his associates see L. Gauthier's summary in "Les Juifs dans les Deux Bourgognes," *REJ*, XLIX, 5 f.; and *infra*, Chap. LIII.

35. C. Devic and J. Vaissète, *Histoire générale de Languedoc*, V, 1369 No. ccxxi; IX, 393 f. No. xlviii, 402 n. 44 (by A. Molinier), 403 ff. Nos. lxxiv–lxxv; X, Preuves, col. 603 No. lxxvi; the extremely repetitious reports in the continuation of Guillaume de Nangis' chronicle in Bouquet's *Recueil*, XX, 626; that of Girard de Fracheto's *Chronicon, ibid.*, XXI, 54 f.; John of St. Victor's *Excerpta e memoriali historiarum, ibid.*, pp. 671 f.; Bernard Gui's *E floribus chronicorum, ibid.*, pp. 730 f.; the anonymous *Ex historia satirica regum, regnorum et summorum pontificorum, ibid.*, XXII, 15 (emphasizing the plunder of clerical possessions); the detailed, though topographically rather confused, accounts by the later Hebrew chroniclers, Samuel Usque in his *Consolaçam ás tribulaçoens de Israel*, iii.16, ed. by J. Mendes dos Remedios, Part III, pp. xvi ff.; idem, *A Consolation for the Tribulations of Israel*, trans. by G. I. Gelbart, pp. 256 ff. (with ample documentation); or in M. A. Cohen's trans., pp. 186 ff.; Solomon ibn Verga in his *Shebet Yehudah*, vi, ed. by Wiener, pp. 4 ff.; in Wiener's German trans., pp. 6 ff.; ed. by Shohet, pp. 22 ff.; Joseph ha-Kohen, *'Emeq ha-bakha*, ed. by Letteris, pp. 58 ff.; in Wiener's German trans., pp. 46 ff., 182 f.; and the moving, though as usual not specific, anonymous dirge for one of the communities (Anjou?), reproduced with a German trans. by S. Salfeld in *Das Martyrologium*, pp. 352 ff. See the analysis of the sources in F. Baer's *Untersuchungen über Quellen und Komposition des Schebet Jehuda*, pp. 2 ff.; and the general summaries of these events by Graetz in his *Geschichte*, 4th ed., VII, 254 ff.; and by R. Anchel in *Les Juifs de France*, pp. 79 ff. The siege of the Verdun tower is dramatically described by the continuator of Guillaume de Nangis, *loc. cit.* On its similarities to the siege of York Jewry in 1190, see *supra*, Vol. IV, pp. 126 f., 303 n. 49.

Needless to say, the appetite for loot transcended political boundaries. Aragonese Montclus, too, became the scene of a severe disturbance, with the local alcalde sufficiently involved to be arrested thirteen years later. See J. Miret y Sans, "Le Massacre des Juifs de Montclus en 1320," *REJ*, LIII, 258 ff. See also J. M. Vidal, "L'Emeute des Pastoureaux en 1320; Lettre du pape Jean XXII; Déposition du Juif Baruc devant l'Inquisition de Pamiers," *Annales de St. Louis des Français*, III, 121–74 (in S. Grayzel's annotated partial English trans. in *HJ*, XVII, 89–120); John XXII, *Lettres communes*, III, 175 No. 12277, 232 f. No. 12842; and J. Delalande's recent observations on *Les Extraordinaires croisades d'enfants et de pastoureaux au moyen âge* (on such frenetic movements between 1251 and 1458). See also G. Frotscher, *Die Anschauungen von Papst Johannes XXII., 1316–1334, über Kirche und Staat.*

36. II Kings, 5:27; Baruch (b. Yeḥiel) ha-Kohen's poem, *Ani hu ha-qonen qinah* (I Am He Who Keens the Dirge), reproduced in S. Bernfeld's *Sefer ha-Demaʿot*, II, 111 ff.; in A. Löwy's free English rendition in his trans. of L. Zunz, *The Sufferings of the Jews during the Middle Ages*, rev. and ed. with notes by G. A. Kohut, p. 66; H. Gross, *Gallia Judaica*, pp. 584 ff.; Solomon ibn Verga, *Shebeṭ Yehudah*, xliii, ed. by Wiener, p. 86; in Wiener's German trans., pp. 176 ff.; ed. by Shohet, p. 117; Samuel Usque, *Consolaçam*, iii.18, Part 3, pp. xix ff. (Ibn Verga furnishes the larger total of 15,000 victims); idem, *A Consolation*, trans. by G. I. Gelbart, pp. 287 ff.; trans. by M. A. Cohen, pp. 190 ff.

37. The continuation of Guillaume de Nangis' chronicle in Bouquet's *Recueil*, XX, 628 ff.; Chronicle of St. Denis, *ibid.*, pp. 704 f. (also mentioning the general opposition of the people to the king); continuation of Girard de Fracheto's *Chronicle*, *ibid.*, XXI, 55 ff.; John of St. Victor's *Excerpta, ibid.*, pp. 673 f. (emphasizing that "because many Jews were found guilty of that deed, all without discrimination were burnt in many localities; in Paris only the guilty ones"); Devic and Vaissète, *Histoire générale*, IX, 410 ff. n. 6 (by A. Molinier); H. Gross, *Gallia Judaica*, pp. 577 ff., 584 ff.; Anchel, *Les Juifs de France*, pp. 84 ff. On the folkloristic background of the accusation of well poisoning, see also *supra*, Chap. XLIX, n. 49.

38. E. Lavisse *et al., Histoire de France*, IV, Part 2, p. 364 (C. Petit-Dutailles); G. G. Coulton, "Nationalism in the Middle Ages," *Cambridge Historical Journal*, V, 31 ff.; L. Degouverrain, "De l'état des Juifs de Bourgogne lors de leur expulsion du duché en l'an 1306," *Bulletin* of the Société d'études d'Avallon, III, 60–70; E. Lévy, "Un Document sur les Juifs de Barrois en 1321–23," *REJ*, XIX, 246 ff.; *supra*, Vol. X, pp. 69 f., 77 ff., 332 f. n. 17, 326 ff. nn. 25–27; G. Prati, "Albi et la peste noire," *Annales de Midi*, LXIV, 15–25 (showing that nine years after the plague the city, despite new arrivals from the countryside, still had but one-half the population of 1347); P. Wolff, "Trois études de démographie médiévale en France meridionale," *Studi in onore di Armando Sapori*, I, 493–503; A. Crémieux, "Les Juifs de Toulon au moyen âge et le massacre du 13. avril 1348," *REJ*, LXXXIX, 33–72; XC, 43–64, esp. LXXXIX, 58 ff. On the anti-Jewish riots in the Provence and Queen Joanna's decree, see the brief data assembled by E. Camau in *Les Juifs en Provence* (reprinted from his *La Provence à travers les siècles*, IV, 249–367), pp. 317 ff. On the problem of the purported readmission of Jews to France in 1328 and their renewed expulsion in 1346, see *supra*, Vol. X.

39. Laurière *et al.*, *Ordonnances*, III, 473 ff., 487 f.; VII, 675 ff.; Isambert *et al.*, *Recueil*, V, 61 No. 292 (1359), 114 ff. No. 315 (1360), 124 No. 329 (1361); R. Delachenal, *Histoire de Charles V*, II, 220 ff.; III, 211 ff.; V, 410 ff.; I. Loeb in *Jubelschrift . . . H. Graetz*, pp. 46 ff.

40. L. F. Bellaguet, ed., *Chronique du religieux de Saint-Denys, contenant le règne de Charles VI, de 1380 à 1422*, I, 52 ff.; J. Juvénal de Ursins (archbishop of Rheims), *Histoire de Charles VI, roy de France, et des choses mémorables advenues . . . depuis 1380 . . . à 1422*, reproduced in J. F. Michaud and J. J. F. Poujoulat, eds., *Nouvelle collection des mémoires relatifs à l'histoire de France*, new ed., II, 335–569, esp. 340 ff.; S. Luce, ed., *Chronique des quatre premiers Valois (1327–1393)*, pp. 292, 295 f.; L. Douët-d'Arcq, ed., *Choix de pièces inédites relatives au règne de Charles VI*, published by the Société de l'Histoire de France, I, 43 ff. Nos. xxii–xxiii; L. Kahn, *Les Juifs à Paris depuis le VIe siècle*, pp. 29 ff.; E. Déprez, *Hugo Aubriot praepositus parisiensis et urbanus praetor (1367–1381)*, pp. 97 ff., 111 ff.; *supra*, Chap. XLVIII, n. 11; Samuel Usque, *Consolaçam*, iii.20 (cited *supra*, n. 32). As late as 1391, when the pogrom movement ravaged Spain and threatened to spill over the French frontier (according to an anonymous Hebrew litany, some Provençal communities were seriously menaced), the French administration issued a number of safe-conducts to Languedoc Jews. Charles' uncle, Duke John of Berry actually allowed Spanish refugees to pass through his territory on the way to the Provence. See C. Devic and J. Vaissète, *Histoire générale*, IX, 1023 No. c; the anonymous Hebrew poem, *Shime'u kol 'ammim* (Hear All Peoples My Sad Story), in the App. to Wiener's ed. of Ibn Verga's *Shebeṭ Yehudah*, p. 133. On the duke of Berry, see *supra*, Vol. X, pp. 75, 336 n.23.

In all these developments the initiative clearly rested with a hostile public, whereas the royal power tried, however ineffectively at times, to protect its Jews. In this respect Joseph ha-Kohen was right (despite his confusion in dates) in asserting that, after destroying many Jewish lives, the *populace (rabbim)* had "banished the rest from their country against the king's will." See his *'Emeq ha-bakha*, ed. by Letteris, p. 58; in Wiener's German trans., p. 46. Curiously, this reservation is omitted in the equally confused repetition, *ibid.*, pp. 64 and 72, respectively. See also Wiener's comments, p. 182 n. 184; and those by I. Loeb, in *Jubelschrift . . . H. Graetz*, pp. 46 ff.; and *supra*, Vol. X, pp. 73, 334 f. n. 21.

The absence of the usual quest for self-enrichment in the expulsion of 1394 has frequently puzzled investigators. Isidore Loeb, who more thoroughly than anyone else had explored the documentation for the successive French banishments of Jews, admitted in a private letter of May 27, 1890, to Théophile Cochard that "the expulsion of 1394 has always been incomprehensible to me." Nine years earlier, however, he himself had correctly suggested that behind many intolerant moves lurked elements of modern antisemitism. See his letter, cited in T. Cochard, *La Juiverie d'Orléans*, pp. 97 f.; and his review of E. Renan's *Marc-Aurèle et la fin du monde antique*, in *REJ*, III, 319–21. Writing under the impact of the Franco-German racial anti-Jewish hatred which was rearing its ugly head in those years, Loeb did not quite realize, however, the difference between this brand of antisemitism which repudiated conversion of Jews to Christianity, indeed saw in baptized Jews the greater danger to racial "purity," and the medieval nationalism which sought to eliminate the Jewish disparity through religious conversion and thus hoped painlessly to absorb the Jewish minority.

Remarkably, in the midst of the turmoil which was decisively to influence their future lives, Jewish scholars undeterredly pursued their callings. A Carcassonne Jewish physician, Leo Joseph (Dolal?), completed on Ab 21, 5154 (July 20, 1394) his Hebrew translation of the Latin commentary on Ar-Razi's medical work, *Almanzur*, Book ix, to which he added many learned notes of his own. He expanded these notes in a revised version which he achieved, probably in a more hospitable Provençal community, in 1402. See H. Gross, *Gallia judaica*, pp. 616 f.

41. Devic and Vaissète, *Histoire générale*, IX, 970 f. No. lix; A. Lecoy de la Marche, *Le Roi René: sa vie, son administration, ses travaux artistiques et littéraires d'après* . . . *des archives de France et d'Italie*, I, 576 ff.; G. Arnaud d'Agnel, "La Politique de René envers les Juifs de Provence," *Bulletin historique et philologique* of the Comité des travaux historiques, 1908, pp. 247–76; Camau, *Les Juifs en Provence*, pp. 343 ff.; and *supra*, Vol. X, pp. 82 ff., 91 f., 339 ff. nn. 32 ff., 343 n. 44. On the Spanish refugees in southern France, see, for instance, I. Loeb, "Un Convoi d'exilés d'Espagne à Marseille en 1492," *REJ*, IX, 66–76; Camau, p. 345. See also L. Kukenheim, "L'Originalité des communautés juives en Provence," *Actes et Memoires* of the IIIᵉ Congrès international de langue et littérature du Midi de France, Bordeaux, 1961; and, more generally, G. Santel, "Les Villes du Midi mediterranéen au moyen âge: aspects économiques et sociaux (IXᵉ–XIIIᵉ siècles)," *Recueil de Société Jean Bodin*, VII, 313–56, which largely applies also to the fourteenth and fifteenth centuries.

On the other hand, Camau's suggestion that the circulation of a spurious correspondence between the Jews of Spain and Constantinople, in which the former were advised concerning the most effective methods of betraying their Christian hosts, had greatly contributed to the bitterness of the anti-Jewish feeling has little to commend itself. We do not know when, and by whom, this canard was invented. Certainly the gullible public would have swallowed it, as it did a great many others even in the following somewhat more critical generations. See the list of 517 such inventions printed in the years 1529–1631 and analyzed by J. P. Seguin in *L'Information en France avant le périodique*. But it appears that this forgery did not antedate the sixteenth century, when all professing Jews had disappeared from southern France. See I. Loeb, "La Correspondance des Juifs d'Espagne avec ceux de Constantinople," *REJ*, XV, 262–76; H. Graetz, "But réel de la correspondance échangée vers la fin du XVᵉ siècle entre les Juifs espagnoles et provençaux et les Juifs de Constantinople," *ibid.*, XIX, 106–14; and A. Z. Aescoly's "The Correspondence between the Jews of Spain and the Provence and the Jews of Constantinople" (Hebrew), *Zion*, X, 102–139. See also the twin essays by E[mile] F[assin], "Le Viel Arles. Le Montjuif et le cimetière israélite," *Bulletin* of the Société des Amis du Viel Arles, I, 30–33, 87–90; and "Les Juifs d'Arles au moyen âge," *ibid.*, VI, 89–97; and A. Crémieux's data on Marseilles in *REJ*, XLVI–XLVII (also referring to the attacks on the Jewries of Aix and Arles in 1484; XLVI, 258). The legal difficulties facing Jews wishing to resettle in sixteenth- and seventeenth-century France were discussed in a legal "Opinion of the Sorbonne concerning the Settlement of Jews in France (1633)." See S. Simonsohn's analysis in his pertinent Hebrew essay in *Zion*, XXIII–XXIV, 98–101.

42. See the apt remarks on "La Formación de la nacionalidad hispano-visigoda," by A. García Gallo in his "Nacionalidad y territorialidad del derecho en la época

visigoda," *AHDE*, XIII, 168–264; A. Echánove's rather apologetical "Precisiones acerca la legislación conciliar toledana sobre los Judíos," *Hispania sacra*, XIV, 259–79; and *supra*, Vol. III, pp. 36 ff. Racial pride was transmitted by Visigothic Spain even to the Spanish Muslims; it was reflected in Ibn Garcia's arguments about the superiority of the Spaniards over the eastern Arabs and Ibn Sa'id's racialist explanation of the former's cultural superiority over their northern neighbors, cited *supra*, Vol. III, pp. 98, 275 n. 30. See also H. Pérès, "Les Éléments ethniques de l'Espagne musulmane et la langue arabe, au Vᵉ–XIᵉ siècle," *Études d'orientalisme dédiées . . . à Lévi-Provençal*, II, 717–31, esp. pp. 726 ff.

43. On the early manifestations of Spanish nationalism see G. Davis, "The Incipient Sentiment of Nationality in Mediaeval Castile: The *Patrimonio real*," *Speculum*, XII, 351–58 (esp. the quotations from the fifteenth-century *conversos* Alphonso de Cartagena and Moses Diego de Valera, pp. 357 f.); Johannes Teutonicus, *Apparatus* to Compilation III (the qualification *excepto regimine hyspanie* is missing in the improved version cited from MSS by G. Post in *Traditio*, IX, 299 n. 10, 306 f., while Vincentius, not he, was the author of the praise of Spanish natural resources; correct accordingly my quotation in *Neuman Jub. Vol.*, p. 21); Alphonso X, *Las Siete Partidas*, ii.1, 1 and 5, ed. by Lopez, II, 3 ff., 11. See *supra*, Vol. IV, pp. 28, 245 f. n. 30; W. von Schoen, *Alfons X. von Kastilien, ein ungekrönter deutscher König*, esp. pp. 54 ff.; P. E. Schramm, "Das Kastilische Königtum und Kaisertum während der Reconquista (11. Jahrhundert bis 1252)," *Festschrift für Gerhard Ritter*, pp. 87–139; A. M. Steiger, "Alfons der Weise und die Kaiseridee," *Schweizer Beiträge zur allgemeinen Geschichte*, VII, 87–100; W. Berges, "Kaiserrecht und Kaisertheorie der 'Siete Partidas,' " *Festschrift Percy Ernst Schramm*, pp. 143–56; and the essays by Menéndez Pidal and Hüffer, cited *supra*, Vol. IV, pp. 245 f. n. 30. After the Carolingian age no medieval emperor interfered in inner Spanish affairs. Even ambitious Frederick Barbarossa, who fully asserted his sovereignty over Arles and other southern French regions, did not reach out beyond the Pyrenees. If in his "L'Expérience historique nationale et supranationale de l'Espagne," *Journal of World History*, VI, 919–47, L. Díez de Cabral stresses both "experiences" equally, he indirectly shows how the nationalism of the seventh century was replaced by a modified supranationalism of the eighth to eleventh centuries, and how the flourishing nationalism under the Catholic monarchs alternated with the supranationalism under Charles V. There also existed other complicating factors, such as the persistence of a Basque and Catalan nationalism, continuously nurtured from the physical and dialectal disparities of the respective populations. See esp. J. L. Shneidman and C. L. Shneidman, "Factors in the Emergence of Catalan Nationalism during the Thirteenth Century," *The Historian*, XXVII, 311–33. But at least in periods of great ethno-religious upsurge under the Catholic monarchs or Philip II these disparities did not seriously interfere with the processes of national unification or the great national enthusiasm generated by them.

44. See P. E. Schramm, "Das Kastilische Königtum in der Zeit Alfonsos des Weisen (1252–1284)," *Festschrift Edmund E. Stengel*, pp. 385–413; idem, "Der König von Aragonien. Seine Stellung im Staatsrecht (1276–1410)," *HJB*, LXXIV, 99–123 (esp. pp. 120 f.); J. A. Maravall, "El Pensamiento político en España del año 400 al 1300," *Journal of World History*, IV, 818–32; *supra*, Vol. X, pp. 361 f. n. 22; *Libro de los Fueros de Castilla*, ed. by G. Sanchez, Art. 107; Baer, *Die Juden*, Part 2, p. 36 No. 60;

and other sources cited *supra*, Vol. X, pp. 55 f., 325 f. n. 3. Because of its dependence on the Papacy in the early thirteenth century, Aragon is rightly included by A. Luchaire in his *Innocent III, les royautés vassales du Saint-Siège*, pp. 53 ff. But during his long reign James I succeeded in greatly reducing this dependence. Castile always felt considerably freer from papal tutelage, although Alphonso VIII still sought Innocent III's backing for his occupation of Navarre. See *ibid.*, pp. 41 f.

45. See I. de las Cagigas, *Minorías etnico-religiosas de la Edad Media española* (regrettably, Vols. VIII–XI which were to be devoted to the Jewish minority have not yet appeared). On the national conflicts at the Council of Constance, see the literature cited *supra*, n. 3.

46. See *supra*, Vols. III, 92, 272 n. 25; IV, pp. 38, 252 f. n. 46. The disturbances of 1230 are but briefly mentioned in the chronicle *Zekher ṣaddiq* by Joseph ibn Ṣaddiq, Chap. 1, ed. by A. Neubauer in his *Mediaeval Jewish Chronicles*, I. 95 (the dates are rather confused); and in Abraham Zacuto's *Sefer Yuḥasin ha-snalem* (Complete Book of Genealogies; a World Chronicle), ed. by H. Filipowski, fol. 221a. On the generally stormy conditions in the early 1230s, see A. Ballesteros y Beretta, *Historia de España y su influencia en la historia universal*, III, 3, 145 nn. 21 ff. As pointed out by Baer (in his *Toledot*, p. 482 n. 30; and in the English trans., I, 396 n. 30) Matthew Paris may have referred to these events when he wrote that "in those days a large massacre was instituted against the Jews in lands across the sea, particularly in Spain." See his *Historia Anglorum;* and his *Chronica majora*, both cited *supra*, n. 28. The suspicions aimed at Toledan Jewry are alluded to by Shem Ṭob Sonzolo, cited in Ibn Verga's *Shebeṭ Yehudah*, ed. by Wiener, p. 113; in Wiener's German trans. p. 231; ed. by Shohet, p. 146; *Anales Toledanos*, ed. by E. Flórez in *España sagrada*, XXIII, 394.

47. Régné, "Catalogue," *REJ*, LXI, 21 Nos. 336 f., 30 Nos. 386–400; LXIII, 251 f. Nos. 689 and 695 f., 259 No. 734; Solomon ibn Adret, *Resp.*, I, No. 1091; Baer, *Die Juden*, I, Part 1, p. 130 No. 117; H. Wieruszowski, "Peter der Grosse von Katalonien-Aragon und die Juden, eine Politik des gerechten Ausgleichs," *Homenatge à Antoni Rubió y Lluch*, III, 245, 256. Ibn Adret's reference to converts underscored the difficulties confronting Spanish Jewry by the missionary efforts of even such moderate churchmen as Raymond Lull. To the extensive literature listed *supra*, Vol. IX, pp. 289 f. n. 4 item 2 add S. Garcias Palou's analysis of the "Circunstancias históricas que inspiraron la composición de *Tractatus de modo convertendi infideles* del Bto Ramón Llull," *Estudios lullianos*, VII, 189–202; R. J. Z. Werblowsky's review of "Ramon Lull's Liber Predicationis contra Judeos" (Hebrew), *Tarbiz*, XXXII, 207–11; and E. W. Platzeck's recent biography, *Raimund Lull, sein Leben, seine Werke, die Grundlagen seines Denkens*. Of a different nature were the persecutions of Castilian Jews in 1278–80 which arose from Alphonso X's wrath at various Jewish tax agents, headed by Don Çag de la Maleha. We need not take literally the assertions of both the *Chronicle* of Alphonso and the contemporary poet, Todros b. Yehudah Abulafia (in his *Gan Hammeshalim we-haḥidot: Diwan* [Orchard of Parables and Riddles], ed. by D. Yellin, I, 134 ff. No. 405, esp. vv. 45 ff.; II, No. 595) that entire Jewish communities were then imprisoned. Yet there is no doubt that Jews suffered severely. See Baer, *Die Juden*, I, Part 2, pp. 66 ff. No. 84 and particularly the notes thereon; *supra*, Vol. X, pp. 123 f., 355 f. n. 5.

48. J. Villanueva, *Viage literario a las iglesias de España*, XXII, 333 f.; F. Fita and G. Llabrés, "Privilegios de los Hebreos mallorquines en el Códice Pueyo," *BAH*, XXXVI, 123 No. 17; Baer, *Studien*, p. 11 n. 1; J. Jacobs, *An Inquiry into the Sources of the History of the Jews in Spain*, p. 45 Nos. 752 and 756; K. R. Scholberg, "Minorities in Medieval Castilian Literature," *Hispania* (America), XXXVII, 203–209. In his stimulating twin studies, "Journey from Islam: Incipient Cultural Transition in the Conquered Kingdom of Valencia (1240–1280)," *Speculum*, XXXV, 337–56; and "Social Riots on the Christian-Moslem Frontier (Thirteenth-Century Valencia)," *AHR*, LXVI, 378–400, I. R. Burns has shown that, while religious and economic factors played a certain role in generating the anti-Muslim antagonisms, "a Christian Moor would be no safer in time of rioting than was his Moslem brother." Economic motivations actually operated more strongly against, than for, the conversion of Moors. Burns rightly senses behind the operation of these more overt factors the propelling motif of a powerful group prejudice arising from "the concept of a unitary society, with the concomitant effect of a secondary citizenship for the subgroups" (*AHR*, pp. 381, 399).

49. J. Miret y Sans, "Le Massacre des Juifs de Montclus en 1320," *REJ*, LIII, 255–66; M. de los Ángeles Masiá, "Aportaciones al estudio de los 'Pastorellos' en la Corona de Aragón," *Homenaje Millás*, II, 9–30; the Teruel report reproduced by Baer in *Die Juden*, I, Part 1, pp. 224 ff. No. 177; the immediately preceding excerpts, *ibid.*, pp. 964 f. No. 590; H. Finke, ed., *Acta Aragonensia*, III, 390 f. No. 178 (also publishing excerpts from a letter by Bishop Raymond of Urgel to James II insisting that he had publicized the royal order and refused admission to the Pastoureaux); Menahem b. Aaron ibn Zerah, *Ṣedah la-derekh* (Provision for the Way; a code of laws), Intro., Sabionetta, 1567 ed., fol. 16a; Kayserling, *Die Juden in Navarra*, pp. 38 ff.; N. Brussel, *Nouvel examen*, pp. 608 f. n. 6; Jacobs, *An Inquiry*, pp. 46 ff. Nos. 781, 793, 799, 997, 1075 and 1130; A. Rubió y Lluch, *Documents per l'historia de la cultura catalana mig-eval*, I, 90 f. No. lxxiii; A. Goñi Gaztambide, "La Matanza de Judíos en Navarra en 1328," *Hispania sacra*, XII, 5–33; the report of the Commission of Inquiry on the Gerona events in J. M. Millás-Vallicrosa and L. Batlle y Prats, "Un Alboroto contra el call de Gerona en el año 1331," *Sefarad*, XII, 297–335; and *supra*, Vol. X, pp. 151 ff., 369 nn. 40–41; Chap. XLIX, n. 49.

Most of the information concerning these attacks and their effects on Spanish Jewry are derived from the Jewish chroniclers, particularly Samuel Usque and Solomon ibn Verga. Both authors seem to have derived their information, in an often confused and corrupted form, from a common source, which Graetz, by an ingenious argument, had identified with the lost chronicle *Zikhron ha-shemadot* (The Record of Massacres) by Profiat Duran. See his *Geschichte der Juden*, 4th ed., VIII, 393 ff. Note 1. This hypothesis has been controverted, however, by F. Baer after a detailed examination of the sources. See his *Untersuchungen über Quellen und Komposition des Schebet Jehuda*, pp. 2 ff., and the extensive literature listed *ibid.*, pp. 3 f. n. 2.

50. Baer, *Die Juden*, I, Part 1, pp. 324 ff. Nos. 230 ff., 235 and 238; Ibn Verga, *Shebeṭ Yehudah*, xxvi, ed. by Wiener, pp. 46 f.; in Wiener's German trans., pp. 92 f.; ed. by Shohet, pp. 70 f.; Ḥayyim Galipapa, *'Emeq refa'im* (Vale of Rephaim; a polemical tract) cited in Joseph ha-Kohen's *'Emeq ha-bakha*, ed. by M. Letteris, pp. 65 f.; in Wiener's German trans., pp. 51 f., 185 f. See I. Loeb, "Joseph Haccohen

et les chroniqueurs juifs," *REJ*, XVI, 28–56, 211–35; XVII, 74–95, 247–71, esp. XVII, 82; P. León Tello's Madrid dissertation, briefly summarized in her "Problemas de historiografía hispano-hebraica: el Emeq ha-bakha y las crónicas judías españoles," *Revista de la Universidad de Madrid*, IX, 899–900; and the newer Spanish literature on the Black Death, listed *supra*, Vol. X, pp. 146 f., 366 n. 33; Chap. XLIX, n. 50.

Less helpful are the contemporary dirges because of their lack of precision and the general use of stereotypes. We are not even certain whether a poem beginning *Aqonen be-marah* (I Shall Bitterly Bewail), by one Emanuel b. Joseph, refers to Spain or some other country. See the text published from a Calabria *Maḥzor* (Prayerbook for holidays) by L. Landshuth in his *'Amude ha-'abodah* (Pillars of Worship: on medieval Jewish liturgy), App. p. xxvi; and from there reproduced by S. Bernfeld in his *Sefer ha-Dema'ot* (Book of Tears), II, 108 ff. See also the additional literature listed by I. Davidson in his *Oṣar ha-shirah ve-ha-piyyuṭ* (Thesaurus of Medieval Hebrew Poetry), I, 334 No. 7358; IV, 275.

51. Samuel ibn Seneh Zarza, *Meqor Ḥayyim* (Fountain of Life; a philosophical commentary on the Pentateuch), Intro., an excerpt from which was published from a Munich MS by M. Wiener in the App. to his ed. of Ibn Verga's *Shebeṭ Yehudah*, pp. 131 f.; and, with some improved readings, by Baer in *Die Juden*, I, Part 2, pp. 220 f. No. 209; Menaḥem ibn Zeraḥ, *Ṣedah la-derekh*, Intro. fol. 16b; Isaac b. Sheshet Perfet, *Resp.*, No. 197. In his rather confused account of these events Joseph ha-Kohen unthinkingly paraphrased Samuel that "this was a time of suffering for Jacob the like of which had never been before." He even asserted that, because of the prevailing famine and inability to secure food, the Toledo Jews consumed their own children. See his *'Emeq ha-bakha*, ed. by Letteris, pp. 68 f.; in M. Wiener's German trans., pp. 54 f., 193 f. n. 209. See also Immanuel Aboab's *Nomologia o Discursos legales*, II, xxvi, Amsterdam, 1629 ed., p. 290 (claiming that Henry II actually admired the Jews' staunch loyalty to his opponent, Pedro); *supra*, Vol. X, pp. 147, 367 n. 34; Chap. XLVIII, n. 47. Other bloody riots against Jews and *conversos* on the Iberian Peninsula are listed by Amador de los Rios in his *Historia social*, III, 643 ff. App. xi.

Nor must we overlook in this connection the resentments generated in many Castilian cities by the presence of a Jewish and Muslim middle class which played into the hands of the patrician *caballeros* in their struggle against the masses of so-called *pecheros*. Ultimately, even the patrician *alcaldes* lost ground to the royal *regidores* who likewise derived much strength from the Crown's Jewish protégés. See the analysis of these trends in one city in J. Gautier-Dalché's "Sepúlveda à la fin du moyen-âge: évolution d'une ville castellane de la Meseta," *Moyen Âge*, LXIX, 805–828.

52. Pedro López de Ayala, *Crónicas de los Reyes de Castilla*, Pt. IV (Chronicle of Henry III), xx, ed. by E. de Llajuno Amirola, II, 390 f.; Amador de los Rios, *Historia social*, II, 349 ff., 592 App. xiii. Amador's description of these tragic events, closely followed by Graetz in his *Geschichte*, 4th ed., VIII, 52 ff., still offers the most detailed narrative of the anti-Jewish frenzy which spread like wildfire through both Spanish kingdoms, including the Balearic Islands. Some additional information is offered by Baer in *Die Juden* and *Toledot*, and by other authors, mentioned *supra*, Vol. X, pp. 168 ff.; and *infra*, nn. 53–54.

53. L. Suárez Fernández, "Problemas políticos en la minoridad de Enrique III," *Hispania* (Madrid), XII, 163–231, esp. pp. 190 ff., 222 ff. App. ii; J. M. Quadrato, "La

Judería de la ciudad de Mallorca en 1391," *BAH*, IX, 294–312; other sources cited by Fita and Llabres, "Privilegios de los Hebreos mallorquines," *ibid.*, XXXVI, 491 ff.; G. Llabres, "La Conversión de los Judíos mallorquines en 1391," *ibid.*, XL, 152–54; T. López Mata, "Morería y judería," *ibid.*, CXXIX, 358 ff. (on the events in Burgos); H. Sancho de Sopranis, "Contribución a la historia de la judería de Jerez de la Frontera," *Sefarad*, XI, 349–70; F. Cantera's comprehensive biographies, *La Conversión del célebre talmudista Salomón Levi (Pablo de Burgos)*; and *Alvar García de Santa María*, esp. pp. 21 ff.; and L. Serrano y Pineda's *Los Conversos D. Pablo de Santa María y D. Alfonso de Cartagena*.

Jews, too, left behind some records, particularly in the form of dirges. Among the more recently published are those by H. Schirmann in his *"Qinot* [Dirges] on Persecutions in Palestine, Africa, Spain, Germany and France"* (Hebrew), *Qobeṣ 'al Yad*, XIII, 64 ff. No. xiii (unlike most other poems of this kind, this plaint by one Solomon mentions specific localities; the author was identified with Solomon b. David ibn Yaḥya by A. M. Habermann in the essay cited *infra*, n. 71); S. Bernstein, "An Unknown Dirge by R. Yeḥiel b. Asher on the Toledo Massacre of 1391" (Hebrew), *Sinai*, XIV, Nos. 171–76, pp. 209–14; with corrections by A. Mirski in his "Notes on the Poems by R. Yeḥiel b. Asher" (Hebrew), *ibid.*, pp. 399–401; and C. Roth, "A Hebrew Elegy on the Martyrs of Toledo, 1391," *JQR*, XXXIX, 123–50 (publishing an improved version of the anonymous poem *'Adat Yeshurun kulkhem* [All of You the Congregation of Jeshurun]). Some other poems, including two by Yehudah b. David ibn Yaḥya and Isaac b. Sheshet Perfet, are reprinted in Bernfeld's *Sefer ha-Dema'ot*, II, 218 ff. One also wonders whether the "Two Unknown Hebrew Spanish 'Lamentations' (*Qinot*)," published by S. Bernstein in *Homenaje Millás*, I, 155–63, do not refer to these events rather than to those of 1412, as suggested by the editor. The copyist of the Lisbon MS may have misread a *nun* by an *'ayin,* that is, 1391–92 by 1411–12, when anti-Jewish sermons and legislative enactments had replaced the pogroms. As usual such poems are more helpful in gauging the psychological reaction among the Jewish contemporaries than in ascertaining specific facts. See the summary in Baer's *Toledot*, pp. 284 ff. (*A History*, II, 95 ff.); R. Ramirez de Arellano, "Matanzas judías en Córdoba, 1391," *BAH*, XXXVIII, 294–311; F. Danvila, "El Robo de la judería de Valencia en 1391: Apuntes históricos," *BAH*, VIII, 358–79; idem, "Clausura y delimitación de la judería de Valencia en 1390 a 1391," *ibid.*, XVIII, 142–57; R. Chabás, "Los Judíos valencianos, El robo de la judería en 9 julio de 1391," *El Archivo Revista de ciencias históricas*, V, 37 f., 111 f., 184 f., 201 f., 235 f.; and many other sources listed by Baer in his *Toledot*, pp. 526 ff. (*A History*, II, 467 ff.), nn. 1–11; and *supra*, Vol. X, pp. 375 ff.

Many reliable data are preserved in a letter written almost immediately after the events (Marḥeshvan 20, 5152–October 19, 1391) by the influential leader and thinker, Don Ḥisdai Crescas, who, despite his important position with the government, had lost his only son among the martyrs of Barcelona. According to him, seventy communities were destroyed. Occasionally mentioning the number of victims in particular localities, Crescas also stresses where the majority saved its life by accepting baptism, but he furnishes no over-all figures. This letter is reproduced in Wiener's ed. of Ibn Verga's *Shebeṭ Yehudah*, pp. 128 ff.; its relationship to the reports of the Hebrew chroniclers is analyzed by Baer in his *Untersuchungen*, pp. 26 ff.

54. See the Hebrew text of that excerpt, reproduced with an English trans. by A. M. Hershman in his *Rabbi Isaac Ben Sheshet Perfet*, pp. 194 ff. (here quoted with slight variations); Samuel Usque, *Consolaçam*, iii.21. On the validity of these figures

see *supra*, Vol. X, p. 375 n. 2. The location of Argawan or Araguam has long puzzled historians. Its identification with Aragon, though slightly supported by the clearly oversimplified account in Ibn Verga's *Shebeṭ Yehudah*, xxvii, is controverted by the context in both Reuben Gerondi's autograph and Usque's chronicle. Moreover, the province of Aragon largely escaped the persecution, according to the testimony of Profiat Duran (Isaac b. Moses ha-Levi Efodi) in his *Ma'aseh efod* (Work of the Ephod; on Hebrew grammar), ed. by J. Friedländer and J. Kohn, p. 14. Reuben b. Nissim may have had in mind either the district of Spanish Algarve or the city of Algava, both not far from Seville. That city was to be specifically mentioned, together with Seville, in the petition submitted by Jaco Cachopo in 1484 to the Catholic monarchs, among the localities economically ruined by the expulsion of Jews from Andalusia. See Baer, *Die Juden*, I, Part 2, pp. 357 ff. No. 344; and *infra*, nn. 58–59. Incidentally, this new identification would remove one of Baer's objections to Graetz's theory of the indebtedness of both Usque and Ibn Verga to Duran's lost *Zikhron ha-shemadot*. See Baer's *Untersuchungen*, p. 25; and *supra*, n. 49. That the state of tension continued throughout this period was shown by the renewed disturbances in Cordova in 1405, which gave rise to the extensive debates on the Jewish question at the Cortes of Valladolid of that year. See *supra*, Vol. X, pp. 182 f., 380 n. 20.

55. These developments were more fully described *supra*, Vols. IX, pp. 87 ff., 282 ff. nn. 39 ff.; X, pp. 180 ff., 379 ff. nn. 18 ff., where the extensive pertinent literature is likewise quoted. The following publications are particularly relevant to our theme: F. Vendrell, "La Política proselitista del rey D. Fernando I de Aragón," *Sefarad*, X, 349–66 (with a documentary appendix; shows the king in the active role of a missionary and meddler in family affairs); idem, "La Actividad proselitista de San Vicente Ferrer durante el reinado de Fernando I de Aragón," *ibid.*, XIII, 87–104 (with nine documents of 1412–15); J. M. Millás-Vallicrosa, "En torno a la predicación judaica de San Vicente Ferrer," *BAH*, CXLII, 189–98 (not too plausibly arguing that Ferrer, though an unflinching missionary, was not really anti-Jewish). The gradual hardening of Ferdinand's attitude from the time when, as a member of the regency of Castile, he had tried to uphold the minimal Jewish rights and apparently even opposed the severe law of 1412 enacted without his cooperation by Queen Catalina, to his cosponsorship of the disputation of Tortosa, is well illustrated at the hand of documents largely culled from Murcia archives by J. Torres Fontes in his "Moros, Judíos y conversos en la regencia de Don Fernando de Antequera," *CHE*, XXXI–XXXII, 60–97.

56. Baer, *Die Juden*, I, Part 2, pp. 315 ff. Nos. 302, 304 and 306; Part 1, pp. 842 ff. Nos. 525, 530, 537 and the notes thereon; and other sources cited *supra*, Vol. X, p. 388 n. 40. The full text of the Toledan statute is reproduced in M. Alonso's ed. of Alonso de Cartagena's *Defensorium unitatis christianae* (written in response to Sarmiento's attack), pp. 357 ff. App. iii. See the papal bulls in Raynaldus, *Annales*, IX, 540 f. No. xii *ad* 1449, 569 ff. No. v *ad* 1451; M. Stern, *Urkundliche Beiträge*, I, 50 No. 45; B. Braunstein, *The Chuetas of Majorca: Conversos and the Inquisition of Majorca*, pp. 43 f. n. 16; *supra*, Vols. I, p. 370 n. 6; X, pp. 187 ff. On the growing debates for and against the *conversos* climaxed by the completion in 1460 of the Jew-baiting classic *Fortalitium fidei* by Alphonso de Spina, see *supra*, Vol. X, pp. 199 ff.; and *infra*, Chaps. LV–LVI. On Aragon's social revolution, particularly under John II (1458–79), see J. Vicens Vives, *Juan II de Aragón (1398–1479). Monarquía y revolución*

en la España del siglo XV, pp. 181 ff.; and S. Sobrequés Vidal, "Los Orígenes de la revolución catalana del siglo XV—Las Cortes de Barcelona de 1454-1458," *Estudios de historia moderna,* II, 1–96.

57. To the vast literature on the regime of the Catholic monarchs, selectively listed in Vol. X, esp. pp. 388 f. n. 41, add the noteworthy collection of essays included in the three volumes of *Estudios* of the Fifth Congreso de historia de la Corona de Aragón held in Saragossa, 1952 (e.g., B. Llorca's succinct observations on the "Problemas religiosos y ecclesiasticos de los Reyes Católicos," II, 253–73); F. Gomez de Mercado y de Miguel, *Dogmas nacionales del Rey Católico;* J. M. Igual, "El Elemento geográfico en la formación de la unidad española," *Boletín* of the Sociedad Geográfica, LXXXVIII, 443–68; T. Halperín Donghi, "Un Conflicto nacional: Moriscos y cristianos viejos en Valencia," *CHE,* XXIII–XXIV, 5–115; XXV–XXVI, 83–250 (justifying the terminology of a national, rather than purely religious, conflict, since the *moriscos,* like the *conversos,* were officially Christians); A. de la Torre, *Documentos sobre relaciones internacionales de los Reyes Católicos,* Vols. I–III; L. Fernandez de Retana, *Isabel la Católica, fundidora de la unidad nacional;* and J. H. Mariéjol, *The Spain of Ferdinand and Isabella,* trans. into English and ed. by B. Keen. See also such additional bibliographical data as are listed in F. Magallón Antón's "Bibliografía de artículos, documentos, noticias, etc., relativos al reinado de los Reyes Católicos, que han aparecido en la 'Revista de Archivos, Bibliotecas y Museos,' desde su fundación en 1871 hasta 1951," *RABM,* LVII, 711–15, esp. Nos. 30 and 37.

58. S. Mitrani-Samarian, "Le Sac de Cordoue et le testament d'Anton de Montoro," *REJ,* LIV, 236–40; K. R. Scholberg in *Hispania* (America), XXXVII, 205; Alonso de Palencia's *Crónica de Enrique IV,* ii.7, 4; 8, 1–2; 9, 8; 27, 5, in the Spanish trans. from the Latin by A. Paz y Mélia, III, 107 f., 115, 123 ff., 129 ff.; IV, 267 f.; Diego Enriquez de Castillo, *Crónica de Rey Don Enrique Cuarto,* clx, clxiv, in *Crónicas de los Reyes de Castilla desde Don Alfonso el Sabio hasta los Católicos Don Fernando y Doña Isabel,* ed. by C. Rosell, III, 97–222, esp. pp. 214 ff. See also the anti-Jewish petition submitted by the Castilian bishops and magnates to Henry IV on December 5, 1464 and reproduced by M. Salvá and P. Sainz Baranda in their edition of *Colección de documentos inéditos para la historia de España,* XIV, 369–95, esp. pp. 373 f.; M. Kayserling, "Un Chansonnier marane Antoine de Montoro," *REJ,* XLIII, 259–67; C. Gutiérrez, "La Política religiosa de los Reyes Católicos en España hasta la conquista de Granada," *Miscelanea Comillas,* XVIII, 227–69; B. Llorca, "Problemas religiosos y eclesiasticos de los Reyes Católicos," *Estudios* of the Fifth Congreso de Historia de la Corona de Aragón, II, 253–73, esp. pp. 257 ff., 261 ff.; N. López Martínez, *Los Judaizantes castellanos y la Inquisición en tiempo de Isabel la Católica; supra,* Vol. X, pp. 206 f., 388 f. n. 41, 392 n. 47; and *infra,* Chap. LV.

Curiously, Pope Sixtus IV, who reluctantly had given the permission to establish the Spanish Inquisition, was forced to defend it in 1483 against Ottoman strictures. In his reply to the Porte's complaints about the ensuing maltreatment of the Spanish Muslims, the pope insisted that the latter enjoyed extensive rights and that only the public invocation of the Messenger was prohibited, just as Christians were not allowed to ring church bells in Islamic lands. See his letter of April 8, 1483, in Raynaldus, *Annales,* XI, 52 ff. No. xlv *ad* 1483. On the Marranos, see *ibid.,* Nos. xlvi–l. Nor must one overlook the part played by papal nuncios in the Spanish developments. See J. Fernández Alonso, "Nuncios, colectores y legados pontificios en España de 1474 a 1492," *Hispania sacra,* X.

59. H. Sancho de Sopranis, "Un Documento interesante sobre la expulsión de los Judíos," *Archivo hispalense,* 2d ser., V, 225–28 (on four Jewish vassals of the duke of Medinaceli, probably dating from 1483–84); Baer, *Die Juden,* I, Part 2, p. 471 No. 399; and other data assembled by him in his essay on "The Messianic Movement in Spain during the Period of the Expulsion" (Hebrew), *Zion,* V, 61–77; *infra,* n. 60; R. Carande, "La Economía y la expansión de España bajo el gobierno de los Reyes Católicos," *BAH,* CXXX, 213–55, esp. pp. 230 f. (rather apologetic); and *supra,* Vol. X, pp. 205 f., 391 f. n. 46. Ferdinand's lifelong preoccupation with the Ottoman advances is well described by J. M. Doussinague in *La Política internacional de Fernando el Católico,* pp. 46 ff., 230 ff., 516 ff. App. 1, 548 f. App. 16. Of course, local forces contributed to the Andalusian disturbances. See M. Méndez Bejarano, *Histoire de la juiverie de Seville,* pp. 144 ff.; V. Romero Muñoz, "Andalusia en la obra política de Isabel I de Castilla," *Archivo hispalense,* XIV, 129–70; R. Ramirez de Arellano and Díaz de Morales, *Historia de Córdoba. Desde su fundación hasta la muerte de Isabel la Católica.* In other parts of Castile, too, popular hostility came to the fore in the sharp segregationist and discriminatory ordinances issued by city councils such as that of Burgos from 1476 on. See L. Serrano, *Los Reyes Católicos y la ciudad de Burgos (desde 1451 a 1492),* pp. 187 ff., 238. It is not impossible that the late signing of contracts was a purposeful act on Ferdinand's part; he may have wished thus to spring an even greater surprise on his fiscal agents. Certainly, an act of this kind would not have been out of character with this master of duplicity, praised for that very characteristic by Niccolò Machiavelli, the famous ideologist of the *raison d'état.* See B. Netanyahu, *Don Isaac Abravanel,* pp. 53 ff.; and J. M. Doussinague's admiring sketch, "Fernando el Católico, maestro de diplomacia," *Conferencias* at the Escuela diplomática of Spain's Foreign Ministry, 1943–44, pp. 9–44.

60. Amador de los Rios, *Historia social,* III, 608 f. App. v; Baer, *Die Juden,* I, Part 1, pp. 914 ff. Nos. 565–66; Part 2, p. 429 No. 389. On the edict of expulsion, often reprinted, see *supra,* Vol. X, pp. 392 f. n. 48. The text has also been reproduced, from the original decree itself containing the signatures of the Catholic monarchs and preserved in the municipal archives of Ávila, by M. Romero de Castilla in his colored presentation of *Singular suceso en el reinado de los Reyes Católicos.* It is quoted here, with some variants, from E. H. Lindo's English trans. in *The History of the Jews of Spain and Portugal,* pp. 277 ff.

On the efforts by the Jewish leaders to stave off the edict, see B. Netanyahu, *Don Isaac Abravanel,* pp. 53 ff. While correctly assessing the reasons for the establishment of the new Inquisition as a reaction to the popular drive toward ethnic homogeneity and as part of the design to strengthen royal absolutism, Netanyahu gives a somewhat one-sided interpretation of Ferdinand's fiscal motives in enforcing the expulsion. Clearly, the Catholic monarchs stood to gain substantial revenue from the disposal of property left behind by the exiles. However, they were generally far-sighted enough to realize the long-term losses which they would incur during Spain's greatest economic expansion from the removal of an industrious and commercially gifted population, wholly dependent on the Crown. Nor would they so strongly have promoted the conversion of the wealthier Jewish classes whose property was thus largely removed from the Treasury's reach. Moreover, they could well have followed the French example and forbidden the Jews to take along any possessions, or at least have set the term for the exiles' departure at too close a date for the disposal of any landed property. As a result of their "liberality," they were left, in part, with some communal real estate like synagogues or cemeteries (whose sale was prohibited by a special decree of June 25, 1492; see Jacobs, *An Inquiry*, p. 74 No. 1304), part of which they donated to the Church, while the rest had to be liquidated over a long period of time.

Evidently, the quest for national consolidation, a chief guideline in Ferdinand's domestic policies, was also mainly responsible for his relative moderation which, according to the aforementioned legendary report by Elijah Capsali, was attributed by Isabella to his alleged Jewish ancestry. See *supra*, Vol. X, pp. 201 f., 388 f. n. 41; W. T. Walsh's apologia for *Isabella of Spain: the Last Crusader;* and his debate with C. Roth on the Jewish aspects of her reign in Roth's "Jews, Conversos and the Blood Accusation in Fifteenth-Century Spain," *The Dublin Review*, CXCI, 219–31; and Walsh's "A Reply to Dr. Cecil Roth," *ibid.*, pp. 232–52; and T. de Azcona's more recent *Isabel la Católica. Estudio crítico de su vida y su reinado.*

61. Elijah Capsali, *Liqquṭim shonim mi-sefer De-be Eliyahu* (Various Fragments from the Chronicle De-be Eliyahu), ed. by M. Lattes in his *De vita et scriptis Eliae Kapsali*, p. 73; the anonymous chronicle of 1495 and another eye-witness account by Isaac ibn Faraj, both ed. by A. Marx in "The Expulsion of the Jews from Spain: Two New Accounts," reprinted in his *Studies in Jewish History and Booklore*, pp. 85 f., 101 (Hebrew), 93 f., 103 (English); and other sources cited by Baer in his *Toledot*, pp. 550 f. n. 140 (*A History*, II, 509 f. n. 12); his *Die Juden*, I, Part 2, pp. 409 ff. No. 380, 413 No. 382, 426 No. 387; and the documents assembled by L. Suárez Fernández in his *Documentos acerca de la expulsión de los Judíos*, esp. pp. 391 ff. On the difficulties of travel see E. A. de la Torre, "Viajes y transportes en tiempo de los Reyes Católicos," *Hispania* (Madrid), XIV, 1–48, 365–410 (showing that distances had to be walked at relatively high speed); Baer, *Toledot*, pp. 550 ff. nn. 140–41. See also the description of an exile, Abraham b. Solomon ibn Buqarat, in "A *Qinah* [Dirge] on the Expulsion from Spain" (Hebrew), published from a Günzburg MS by H. H. Ben-Sasson in *Tarbiz*, XXXI, 59–71.

The expulsion itself and its aftermath have frequently been treated. See *supra*, Vol. X, pp. 392 f. n. 48. Among these Duke de Maura's apologetic "Nueva luz sobre la expulsión de los Judíos en 1492," *BAH*, CXXXVII, 187–200, emphasizes especially the element of national unification with reference to N. López Martínez's aforementioned work, *Los Judaizantes castellanos y la Inquisición en tiempo de Isabel la Católica*. Of value also are such local studies as H. Sancho de Sopranis, "La Judería del Puerto de Santa María de 1483 a 1492," *Sefarad*, XIII, 309–24; L. Piles, "La Expulsión de los Judíos en Valencia. Repercusiones económicas," *ibid.*, XV, 89–101; J. Cabezudo Astrain, "La Expulsión de los Judíos zaragozanos," *ibid.*, pp. 103–36 (both describing in detail the liquidation of Jewish property for royal benefit).

No reliable data on the number of the Spanish exiles are available. Andrés Bernaldez, a well-informed, though utterly biased, chronicler, cites a letter by Meir Melamed to his father-in-law Seneor and a statement by another Jewish convert to the effect that the total Jewish population, in 1492, amounted to some 35,000 families in Castile and 6,000 in Aragon. He also furnishes detailed figures for groups of exiles departing from specified ports, but fails to give global numbers of those who chose exile or conversion. Other estimates of the Spanish Jewish population in 1492 range as high as 300,000 souls, as asserted by Abravanel, or from 50,000 to 53,000 families, as cited by the anonymous Hebrew chronicler of 1495. These figures are not quite so far apart as they appear. Since all population estimates were largely derived from unreliable tax computations, a difference of some 25 percent between estimates by various observers represents but a relatively modest margin of error. Even Abravanel's 300,000 figure is not so completely out of line, if we may assume that the average size of a medieval family was in excess of five and a half members. See Andrés Bernaldez' *Historia de los Reyes Católicos D. Fernando y Doña Isabel,* cx ff., Seville, 1870 ed., I, 332 f.; Isaac Abravanel, *Commentary* on the Book of Kings, Intro. in his *Perush 'al nebi'im rishonim* (Commentary on the Former Prophets), Jerusalem, 1955 ed., pp. 602 f.; idem, *Ma'ayene ha-yeshu'ah* (Springs of Salvation: a commentary of Daniel), Intro., fol. 3a–c; Marx in *Studies, loc. cit.;* and *infra,* Chap. LI. Only the figure of 100,000 Jewish families exiled from Spain given to a German traveler, Hieronymus Münzer, who had visited the country in 1494–95 is evidently based on the traveler's, or his informant's, confusion of the number of souls who had reached Portugal with that of families of all exiles. See his *Itinerarium sive peregrinatio per Hispaniam, Franciam et Alemaniam,* partially published by L. Pfandl in his "Itinerarium hispanicum Hieronymi Monetarii, 1494–95," *Revue hispanique,* XLVIII, 1–179, esp. p. 28; and reproduced in a Spanish trans. with notes by J. Puyol in his "Jeronimo Münzer, Viaje por España y Portugal en los años 1494 y 1495," *BAH,* LXXXIV, 32–119, 197–279, esp. p. 67. See L. Pfandl's *Beiträge zur spanischen und provenzalischen Literatur- und Kulturgeschichte des Mittelalters,* pp. 44 ff. The number of immigrants in Portugal is raised to 120,000 by both the anonymous chronicler of 1495 (Marx, *loc. cit.*) and by Abraham Zacuto in his *Sefer Yuḥasin,* ed. by Filipowski, p. 277a. See also Baer, *Toledot,* pp. 551 f. n. 141 (*A History,* II, 510 f. n. 13). Some exiles found the difficulties of travel and adjustment to their new environments more than they could bear. They meekly returned to Spain and submitted to baptism. But their number seems not to have been very large.

62. C. Roth, "Was there a Herem against the Return of the Jews to Spain?" *Judaïsme sephardi,* XV, 675–77; Joseph b. Ḥayyim Ya'abeṣ, *Or ha-Ḥayyim* (The Light of Life: an ethical treatise), Intro., Lwów, 1874 ed., fol. 3a; Zacuto, *Sefer Yuḥasin,* v, ed. by Filipowski, fol. 225a; Ibn Verga, *Shebeṭ Yehudah,* lxiii, ed. by Wiener, p. 95; in Wiener's German trans., pp. 194 f.; ed. by Shohet, pp. 127 f.; the narratives by Abraham b. Solomon Ardutiel in his *Sefer ha-Qabbalah* (Book of Tradition) in Neubauer's *Mediaeval Jewish Chronicles,* I, 111 f.; and the anonymous chronicler of 1495, whose memoir was published by A. Marx in his *Studies in Jewish History and Booklore,* pp. 11, 22 n. 26, 85 ff.

63. Andrés Bernaldez, *Historia de los Reyes Católicos,* Seville, 1870 ed., cx–cxiv, I, 332 ff.; Giovanni Pico della Mirandola, *Adversus astrologos,* v.1. 12 in his *Opera,* Strasbourg, 1504 ed., fols. 158, 164v; Francesco Guicciardini, *Relazione di Spagna* in his *Opere inedite,* ed. by G. Canestrini, VI, 283 f. (calmly discussing the burning of 100 to 200 heretics in Cordova); Niccolò Machiavelli, *Il Principe,* xxi, critical ed. by G. Lisio, p. 101; in the none-too-accurate English trans. by L. Ricci, rev. ed. by E. R. P. Vincent, p. 82. See also E. Shemueli, "European Reaction to the Expulsion from Spain" (Hebrew), *Metsudah,* V–VI, 241–61; idem, *Gerush Sefarad* (The Expulsion from Spain as Reflected by Public Opinion and the Humanists of Europe); and, more generally, G. C. Rossi, "I Re Cattolici in testimoni anze letterarie e storiche italiane del tempo," in *Estudios of the Fifth Congreso de historia de la Corona de Aragón* I, 47–69. See also Y. F. Baer, "The Expulsion of the Jews from Spain" (Hebrew), *Aḥdut ha-'Abodah,* III, 298–307; and his *Toledot,* pp. 401 ff. (*A History,*

II, 300 ff.). Baer's general point of view in the latter standard work, which postulates that sooner or later such a tragic end had to come to any major Jewish community, has been criticized by I. Sonne in his "On Baer and His Philosophy of Jewish History," *JSS*, IX, 61–80. Whether or not one agrees with that philosophy, more fully expounded by Baer in his small volume on *Galut*, one cannot deny that, under the medieval state-and-Church combination, national unification tended to strengthen immeasurably exclusivist tendencies toward Jews. See also V. Marcu's interpretation of *The Expulsion of the Jews from Spain*. On the complex problems of the permanent Jewish heritage of Spain, see particularly the debate centered around Américo Castro's works cited *supra*, Vol. X, pp. 208 f., 393 n. 49. An even more protracted debate has been going on for centuries concerning the long-range effects of the expulsion of the Jews, and of the Moors soon afterwards, on the Spanish economy and society. This subject will be more comprehensively dealt with in later chapters.

64. J. Yanguas y Miranda, *Historia de Navarra*, II, 84 ff., 120, 194, 669; III, 258, 438; Kayserling, *Die Juden in Navarra*, pp. 105 ff., 212 f. App. L; Abravanel's *Commentary* on the Book of Kings, Intro. (*loc. cit. supra*, n. 61); Joseph ha-Kohen, '*Emeq ha-bakha*, ed. by M. Letteris, pp. 85 f.; in Wiener's German trans., pp. 67 f. The figure for Lerin, given by Yanguas, is contrasted by Kayserling (p. 108 n. 2) with the lesser estimates for other communities. On the fate of the new converts in the sixteenth century, see *infra*, Chap. LVI. Tafalla had also been in the forefront of the anti-Jewish agitation in the preceding decades. It was from there that King Francisco Febo (1479–84) issued, in 1482, the so-called *Ordenamiento de Tafalla*, which had stressed particularly the traditional segregationist aspects of ghetto and badge, as well as the prohibition for Jews to hold public office. Together with other representatives of the bourgeoisie, the Talfalla deputies at the Cortes had advocated many further restrictions. See Amador de los Rios, *Historia social*, III, 323 ff. Certainly, from the Jewish point of view the city did not deserve the designation *la buena villa*, on which it prided itself during the fifteenth century!

65. Contemporary chroniclers differ in regard to the effects of the 1498 decree on the Navarrese Jews. While, according to the Hebrew writers, a considerable number of exiles sought refuge in neighboring lands, a Christian author insisted that "not many left the kingdom, for almost all of them converted themselves to the faith." According to this annalist, none of the native Navarrese Jews later rejoined the Jewish community. See J. de Moret, *Anales . . . de Navarra, ad* 1498, cited by Amador de los Rios in his *Historia social*, III, 331 f. We cannot ascertain the exact size of the exodus, since the Jewish chroniclers allude but briefly to the entire Navarrese episode of 1492–98. Nor have local Hebrew poets left behind any of those customary dirges which, despite their general vagueness, sometimes help elucidate both local incidents and psychological reactions.

66. See A. E. Beau, *Die Entwicklung des portugiesischen Nationalbewusstseins;* and his more recent Portuguese essays collected in his *Estudos*, Vol. I (includes interesting essays on "Características da manifestação do sentimento nacional em Fernão Lopes," pp. 63–72; and "A Valização do idioma nacional no pensamento de humanismo português," pp. 349–70). See also, more generally, *supra*, Vol. X, pp. 153 ff.; A. E. Reuter's conclusions regarding the 1289 concordat between King Dinis and Pope Nicholas IV (in her *Königtum und Episkopat in Portugal im 13. Jahrhundert*, pp.

98 ff.) which also apply to conditions in the subsequent two centuries. We shall see that the residual dependence on the Papacy was to affect particularly the protracted negotiations relating to the establishment of the Portuguese Inquisition. See *infra*, Chap. LV. The events leading up to the assumption of power of Dom João de Avis as John I are rightly described by S. Dias Arnaut as *A Crise nacional dos fins do século XIV*, Vol. I. At the same time the Spanish patriots, through the mouthpiece of the Castilian Royal Council, strenuously objected to the Castilian John's proposal to cede Seville and several other areas to Portugal as a price for its submission to him as king. See G. Davis's observations in "The Incipient Sentiment of Nationality in Mediaeval Castile," *Speculum*, XII, 354 f.

67. *Ordenaçãos Affonso V*, lxxii, lxxvii, Vol. II, pp. 434 f., 457 ff.; Ruy de Pina's *Chronica do Senhor Rey D. Affonso V*, cxxx, in the *Collecçaõ de livros inéditos de história portugueza*, ed. by J. Corrêa da Serra, I, 439 f.; A. C. de Sousa, *Historia genealogica de Casa Real Portuguesa*, IV, 40—all cited in Kayserling's *Geschichte der Juden in Portugal*, pp. 63 f.; Amador de los Rios, *Historia social*, III, 340 f. n. 3. In his "Ocorrências da vida judaica," *Archivo histórico portuguez*, II, 185 f., V. Sousa publishes two excerpts from applications of 1451 by persons pleading innocence in the pillage of the Jewish quarter; one accused contended that he had actually tried to defend the Jews. The growing chauvinism of the bourgeoisie found an outlet in the Portuguese Cortes' never-ending complaints (beginning in 1451) about the Jewish display of luxuries. See *supra*, Vol. X, pp. 213 f., 395 f. n. 55. The relations between *The Royal Power and the Cortes in Portugal* are analyzed in E. Prestage's pertinent essay which emphasizes that, although Cortes resolutions "had not the force of law, unless sanctioned by the King" and the very "repetition of their complaints show the small effect they had," they served as a valuable mouthpiece for the Third Estate (pp. 27 f.).

68. The chief Portuguese chronicler of the reign of King Emanuel, Damião de Góis, claims that "more than 20,000 families" some ten to twelve persons strong, were admitted. Abraham Zacuto and the anonymous Hebrew chronicler of 1495, themselves exiles, independently speak of 120,000 Jews having entered Portugal. If, according to Andrés Bernaldez, only 93,000 Castilian Jews had passed through five frontier points, one must add those who entered elsewhere, as well as refugees from Aragon. The two figures of 120,000 persons and 20,000 families thus actually complement each other. See De Góis (Góes), *Crónica do felicissimo rei D. Manuel*, i.10, new ed. by J. Martins Teixeira de Carvalho and D. Lopes, I, 21 f.; Abraham Zacuto, *Sefer Yuḥasin*, ed. by Filipowski, p. 277a; the anonymous chronicler of 1495, ed. by A. Marx in his *Studies in Jewish History*, pp. 85 f. (Hebrew), 93 f. (English); Andrés Bernaldez, *Historia de los Reyes Católicos*, cxi, cxiii, Seville, 1870 ed., I, 339, 343 ff. See also M. Kayserling *Geschichte der Juden in Portugal*, pp. 111 f. n. 3; and H. Graetz, *Geschichte*, 4th ed., VIII, 368 n. 1.

69. See the sources cited in the last note. There also were serious abuses by bureaucrats. As late as 1498 the king ordered the high Portuguese official, Pero Persoa, to render account of the funds he had collected from the Castilian Jews upon their entry into Portugal six years before. See A. Brancamp Freire, "Cartas de quitação del Rei D. Manuel," *Archivo histórico portuguez*, V, 236 No. 538. Our main information concerning the reactions of Portuguese Jewry comes from members of the

Ibn Yaḥya clan, who may, in part, have echoed unreliable family legends. See the letter written by David ibn Yaḥya and reproduced by Graetz in his *Geschichte*, 4th ed., VIII, 482 f. App. 13; and by the generally unreliable chronicler, Gedaliah ibn Yaḥya in his *Shalshelet ha-qabbalah* (Chain of Tradition; a world chronicle), Venice, 1587 ed., fols. 62b f., 115ab f. See also Kayserling, *Geschichte*, pp. 108 ff.

According to another late report, a delegation led by the aged Rabbi Isaac Aboab, and consisting of thirty influential Castilian Jews, appeared before John II and pleaded with him for the admission of refugees. The king allegedly received these men hospitably and assigned them quarters in the city of Oporto, the city charging them but a moderate rental of fifty maravedis each. See the narrative (written some 120 years after the event) by Aboab's descendant, Immanuel Aboab, included in the latter's *Nomologia o Discursos legales*, II, xxvii, Amsterdam, 1629 ed., pp. 299 f. However, this report, although buttressed by the author's recollection of himself having seen the Oporto synagogue erected on that occasion and the house inhabited by his grandfather Abraham Aboab, is unconfirmed by any other source—and quite a few chroniclers, both Jewish and Christian, were keenly aware of the immigration of Spanish exiles to Portugal—and may likewise have been unduly adorned by a family legend. See M. Kayserling's "Immanuel Aboab und seine Nomologia," *Jeschurun*, ed. by S. R. Hirsch, IV, 566–73; idem, *Sephardim. Romanische Poesien der Juden in Spanien*, pp. 118 ff.

70. The 1496 decree is reproduced from a copy in the Lisbon Municipal Archives by Amador de los Rios in his *Historia social*, III, 614 f. App. vii. See also the generally repetitious descriptions of these events by him, Graetz, Kayserling, and others. The date of the decree is somewhat uncertain, however. The copy used by Amador is signed on December 5. See also his remarks, p. 355 n. 1. On the other hand, Zacuto (in his *Sefer Yuḥasin*, p. 227ab) gives the precise date of "December 24th a Sunday, the 29th of Kislev during the Ḥanukkah holiday." This double dating is not only inconsistent in itself (Kislev 29, 5257, happened to fall on Sunday-Monday, Dec. 4–5, 1496), but it also is in part controverted by Zacuto's other statement that the Jews had been allowed eleven months to prepare for their departure. To the end of October 1497 was almost eleven months from early December but not from the Christmas period. Of course, it is quite possible that some time elapsed between the signing of the decree and its promulgation. It was published only after an extended discussion in the Council of State, where opinions were divided about the wisdom of that move. See Damião de Góis' *Crónica de . . . D. Manuel*, i.16–19, ed. by Teixeira de Carvalho and Lopes, I, 33 ff. To underscore Emanuel's purely "political" motives, the edict did not include the Moors. See *supra*, Vol. X, pp. 396 f. n. 60. See also F. Pérez Embid, *El Mudejarismo portugués*, 2d ed.; H. da Gama Barros, "Judeus e Mouros em Portugal em tempos passados (apontamentos histórico-etnográficos)," *Revista Lusitana*, XXXIV, 165–265 (includes 207 documentary excerpts); XXXV.

71. Leone Ebreo expressed his deep grief in a lengthy poem beginning *Zeman hikkah be-ḥeṣ* (Time Has Smitten My Heart with a Sharp Arrow), first published by E. Carmoly in his Hebrew essay "A Biography of Don Isaac Abravanel, His Life, Children, Grandchildren, and Other Relatives" in *Ozar Nechmad*, II, 70 ff.; and republished in C. Gebhardt's *Leone Ebreo*, III, Gedichte, iii.24–25. See Geronimo de Osorio, *De rebus Emmanuelis Lusitaniae regis . . . libri duodecim*, i, Cologne,

1586 ed., fols. 13b f.; in E. H. Lindo's rather free translation in *The History*, pp. 325 ff. De Osorio placed the blame, however, on several royal councilors who had insisted on the legitimacy of this procedure by citing precedents from other Christian lands. This tragedy was also commemorated in "A *Qinah* [Dirge] on the Expulsion from Portugal by R. David ibn Yaḥya" (Hebrew), published from a Montefiore MS by A. M. Habermann in *Oṣar Yehude Sefarad*, V, 11–16, esp. pp. 14 f.

In contrast to many of these precedents, the Portuguese expulsion did not pursue fiscal objectives. It was but coincidental that, after the suppression of the Jewish faith and the dissolution of all Jewish communities, the Crown inherited their communal properties. In the following years John II was able to sell or give away to favorite individuals or the respective cities the synagogues of Silves and Cintra, the Lisbon cemetery, and other holdings. See V. Sousa's data in *Archivo histórico portuguez*, II, 186 ff. On the struggle for the establishment of a Portuguese Inquisition and the persistence of the Marrano problem in the country long after 1534, see *infra*, Chaps. LV–LVI.

72. R. Wallach, *Das Abendländische Gemeinschaftsbewusstsein*, p. 17. Nevertheless some rudiments of Italian nationalism can be detected also in the medieval period. See W. W. Goetz, *Das Werden des italienischen Nationalgefühls* in *SB* Munich, 1939, Part 7; F. Bock, "Nationalstaatliche Regungen in Italien bei den guelfisch-ghibellinischen Auseinandersetzungen von Innocenz III. bis Johann XXII.," *Quellen und Forschungen aus italienischen Archiven*, XXXVIII, 1–48; and A. de Bonis's succinct remarks in "Il Concetto di nazionalità italiana nel medioevo," *Lucania d'oggi*, XVI, 24–26.

73. Pierre Dubois, *De recuperatione Terrae Sanctae*, lxx, in the English trans. by W. I. Brandt, entitled *The Recovery of the Holy Land*, p. 168 No. 111; B. Jarrett, *Social Theories of the Middle Ages, 1200–1500*, pp. 227 f.; G. G. Coulton in *Cambridge Historical Journal*, V, 35 f.; Pius II's *Commentaries* in F. A. Gragg's English trans. in *Smith College Studies in History*, XXII, 99 (excised from the Frankfort, 1614 ed. of the Latin original, p. 30). See also J. B. Toews, "Dream and Reality in the Imperial Ideology of Pope Pius II," *Medievalia et humanistica*, XVI, 77–93. Urban VI (1378–89), the first post-Avignonese pope, was elected by the existing majority of non-Italian cardinals only under the pressure of the Roman population. As a result, within a few months thirteen French members in the College of Cardinals escaped from Rome and elected an antipope, Clement VII. But the election of Italians soon became the rule, subject to but rare exceptions.

74. Joseph ha-Kohen, '*Emeq ha-bakha*, pp. 61 f. (with S. D. Luzzatto's note thereon); in Wiener's German trans., p. 49; Ibn Verga, *Shebeṭ Yehudah*, xiv, xxxix, ed. by Wiener, pp. 37 f., 67; in Wiener's German trans., pp. 74 ff., 133 f.; ed. by Shohet, pp. 60 f., 94; Todros b. Isaac's *Novellae* on Nazir, cited from a Bodleian MS by H. Graetz in his "Burning the Talmud in 1322," *JQR*, [o.s.] II, 104–106. See the most reasonable reconstruction of these events by H. Vogelstein and P. Rieger in their *Geschichte der Juden in Rom*, I, 305 ff. also connecting with them hints in two poems by Immanuel of Rome in his *Maḥbarot* (Maqamae), xiii, xxviii, ed. by A. M. Habermann, pp. 101, 230a (262), 234a (267 f.); the analysis of the Hebrew sources in F. Baer's *Untersuchungen*, pp. 23 ff.; and the discussion of these events *supra*, Vol. X, pp. 253 f., 412 f. n. 40. On John XXII's general attitude toward the Jews see also the literature listed *supra*, nn. 35 and 37.

75. See U. Cassuto, "Quando fù a Roma Calonymos ben Calonymos?" *RI*, I, 181–90. The connection of the Roman riot with John XXII's regime is presented here with extreme diffidence. Reported with no further identification by Ibn Verga alone, it is very doubtful whether such a serious attack really took place. The Spanish apologist may have magnified some recollection of disturbances in Avignon, Carpentras, or Bédarrides. Popular reactions to the Jewish involvement in the later revolutionary movement of Cola de Rienzo may also have given rise to rumors of an anti-Jewish persecution. See *supra*, Vol. X, pp. 254 f., 414 n. 42; A. Frugoni's more recent edition of an anonymous *Vita di Cola di Rienzo;* and A. Frotscher's study cited *supra*, n. 35.

76. Jean Froissart, *Chroniques,* in his *Oeuvres,* ed. by J. M. B. C. Kervyn de Lettenhove, V, 275 (see also the somewhat different version, *ibid.*, p. 277; XVII, 274); *supra*, Vol. X, pp. 260 f., 264 ff.; L. Bardinet in "La Condition civile des Juifs du Comtat Venaissin," *RH*, XII, 2 f., 16 ff., 32; M. de Maulde, *Les Juifs dans les états français*, pp. 6 f. By 1408, Carpentras complained of the increase of Jews beyond the stipulated quota of 90 families. In 1486 its city council again demanded the cessation of the influx of foreign refugees, *ibid.*, p. 7 n. 2. For some reason Carpentras was more hostile to Jews than any other locality in the Comtat. According to an unsubstantiated report, the bishop of Carpentras had expelled the Jews in 1300, a few years before the establishment of the papal regime there. See Fornery's unpublished *Histoire ecclésiastique et civile du Comté Venaissin*, Vol. I, fols. 450 and 459, cited by De Maulde, p. 24 n. 2. Perhaps in connection with the rumored anti-Jewish plan of John XXII, the local bishop appears to have enacted again a decree of banishment in 1322 which seems, at least partially, to have been carried into effect. He formally readmitted the Jews in 1343. As late as 1514 Leo X had to order the bishop of Carpentras not to force Jews to wear badges different in shape from those introduced by Alexander VI. See P. Imbart de la Tour, *Les Origines de la Reforme*, II, 452 n. 1 (2d ed. by Y. Lenhers, II, 454 n. 1).

On the other hand, in 1373 Francesco Bruni, Secretary of the papal Curia, could write about "the great abundance [*magna copia*]" of Jews at the Curia in Avignon. See G. Brucker, "An Unpublished Source on the Avignonese Papacy: the Letters of Francesco Bruni," *Traditio*, XIX, 368 ff.; and, more generally, B. Guillemain, *La Cour pontificale d'Avignon (1300–1376). Étude d'une société*. At any rate, even in the French districts Jewish real estate contracts were identical with those written for Christians. See P. Ourliac, "Notes sur le droit des personnes à Avignon au XVᵉ siècle," *Annales de Midi*, LIV–LV, 508 ff. The same holds true for Roman documents; see, for instance, C. Trasselli, "Un Ufficio notarile per gli Ebrei di Roma (secoli XVI e XVII)," *Archivio* of the R. Deputazione romana di storia patria, LX, 231–44. This tradition was so strong that even the sharply antagonistic Benedict XIII did not permanently alter the status of Comtat Jewry. To the literature listed *supra*, Vol. IX, pp. 282 ff. nn. 39 ff., 287 n. 2, add A. Maier, "Zu einigen Handschriften der päpstlichen Bibliothek von Avignon. Nachtrag zur Edition des Katalogs von 1411," *Archivum historiae pontificiae*, II, 323–28; and F. Stegmüller, "Die *Consolatio theologiae* des Papstes Pedro de Luna (Benedict XIII)," *Spanische Forschungen der Görres-Gesellschaft*, XXI, 209–15 (showing that this tract was but a summary of a fourteenth-century treatise by Johannes von Dambach).

77. C. Minieri-Riccio, *Notizie storiche tratte da 62 registri angioini nell'Archivio di Stato di Napoli*, p. 34; P. Lonardo, *Gli Ebrei a Benevento con documenti inediti,*

p. 12; other sources cited by N. Ferorelli in *Gli Ebrei*, pp. 53 ff.; and particularly the studies by U. Cassuto, V. Vitale, and J. Starr listed *supra*, Vol. X, p. 400 n. 8. In Manfredonia the authorities compiled, in the latter part of the fifteenth century, a complete list of the *neofiti*, "together with their sons and daughters, servants and employees, who are now present in the city." See J. Mazzoleni, "Fonti per la storia dell'epoca aragonese esistenti nell'Archivio di Stato di Napoli," *ASPN*, LXXII, 125–54; LXXIV, 351–73, esp. LXXII, 146. On the persistence of Greek-speaking groups in the area through the thirteenth century and beyond, see A. Gouillou, "Inchiesta sulla popolazione greca della Sicilia e della Calabria nel medio evo," *RSI*, LXXV, 53–68 (in preparation for his comprehensive compilation of *Regestes des actes grecs d'Italie du Sud et de Sicile*).

78. S. (P.) Cassel, "Juden," *Allgemeine Encyclopädie*, ed. by J. G. Ersch and J. H. Gruber, 2d ser., XXVII, 144; the texts of the 1392 decrees in Lagumina and Lagumina, *Codice diplomatico*, I, 109 ff. Nos. lxxvii–xc. At the same time, however, King Martin, on September 1, 1392, permitted the bishop of Mazzara to prosecute some relapsed converts in Monte San Giuliano. *Ibid.*, p. 136 No. xci. On Villanova's intervention see his memorandum reproduced by M. Menéndez y Pelayo in his *Historia de los heterodoxos españoles*, ed. by E. Sanchez Reyes, VII (in his *Obras completas*, XLI), 270 ff. No. xiv, esp. pp. 275 f.; Frederick III's letter of November 25, 1310, to James II of Aragon in H. Finke's ed. of *Acta Aragonensia*, II, 695 ff. No. 438; and *supra*, Vols. IX, p. 290 n. 4 item 6; X, pp. 228 ff. Needless to say, even during the relatively peaceful first half of the fifteenth century, there were occasional anti-Jewish riots as in Taranto in 1414. See N. Vacca, "Per la storia degli Ebrei in Taranto," *Rinascenza salentina*, n.s. IV, 221–29. It appears, however, that unlike other journeys by John Capistrano, that of 1443 to Sicily had no untoward consequences for Jews. See R. Pratesi, "Una Ignorata missione di S. Giovanni da Capestrano in Sicilia (maggio 1443)," *AFH*, LIV, 403–12. There is no evidence that even the employment of Jews in semipublic offices, which in Sicily never assumed the dimensions prevailing in the dynasty's Aragonese homeland, was in any way curtailed by the agitation of that zealous preacher. See F. M. Broglio, "Il Divieto per gli Ebrei di accedere alle cariche pubbliche e il problema della giurisdizione ecclesiastica sugli infedeli nel sistema canonistico e fino alle decretali di Gregorio IX," *Études d'histoire du droit canonique dédiées à Gabriel le Bras*, II, 1071–85; *supra*, Vol. X, pp. 230 f., 235 ff., 402 n. 11, 404 f. nn. 19–21. To the literature listed there add: E. Pontieri's "Alfonso V d'Aragona nel quadro della politica italiana del suo tempo," *Atti* of the Accademia nazionale di scienze morali di Napoli, LXXI, 183–251. See also, more generally, V. d'Alessandria, *Politica e società nella Sicilia aragonese;* Q. Senigaglia's review of "La Condizione giuridica degli Ebrei in Sicilia," *Rivista italiana per le scienze giuridiche*, XLI, 75–102.

79. G. di Giovanni, *L'Ebraismo della Sicilia*, pp. 100 f., 271 f.; C. Roth, *Ancient Aliyot*, pp. 51 f.; M. A. Shulvass, *Roma vi-Yerushalayim* (Rome and Jerusalem), pp. 25 f.; Lagumina and Lagumina, *Codice diplomatico*, III, 45 ff. No. dcccxciv, 86 ff. No. dccccxiii, 152 f. No. dcccclxviii, 154 ff. No. dcccclxx, 167 ff. No. dccccclxxiv, etc.; C. Trasselli, "Sull'espulsione degli Ebrei dalla Sicilia," *Annali* of the University of Palermo, Faculty of Economics and Commerce, VIII, 133 f. See also *infra*, Chap. LI, n. 50.

While many informed citizens objected to the elimination of their Jewish compatriots, others received the news with satisfaction. A Malta notary merely registered the event without comment. But his colleague in Trapani betrayed his anti-Jewish animus when, in September 1494, he started a new volume of his registry "in the third year from the expulsion of the Jews." He followed therein the example of the Catania city elders who after protesting to the viceroy against the expulsion erected, in 1493, a commemorative stone recording this event and started numbering their years from it. See C. Roth, "The Jews of Malta," *TJHSE*, XII, 187–251, esp. pp. 207 ff.; G. di Giovanni, *L'Ebraismo della Sicilia*, pp. 272 f.; G. Policastro, *Catania prima del 1693*, pp. 206 ff., 211; Trasselli in *Annali*, VIII, 146.

80. B. (C.) Roth, "A Contribution to the History of the Exiles from Sicily" (Hebrew), *Eretz-Israel*, III, 230–34; idem, "The Spanish Exiles of 1492 in Italy," *Homenaje Millás*, II, 293–302; *infra*, Chap. LIX. True, according to Carmelo Trasselli, the latest investigator of the Sicilian banishment, the large majority of Jews remained behind and adopted Christianity. He also believes that, from the outset, only some 30,000 persons had been affected by the expulsion, a figure far below that given by other students of Sicilian Jewish demography. However, Trasselli's arguments are in part controverted by his own data concerning the tax revenues from Jews in the district of Palermo alone. Moreover, his reasoning that, because some wealthy Jews preferred conversion to exile, the same held true for the majority is clearly unjustified. According to Trasselli's own example, the wealthy Sala submitting to conversion failed to persuade his own wife to follow him into the new faith, while another prominent Palermo Jew, David the Physician (*lu medicu*), led his entire family and a black slave into exile. See Trasselli's observations in the Palermo *Annali*, VIII, 133 n. 6, 135, 139, 149; Lagumina and Lagumina, *Codice diplomatico*, III, 176 f. No. dcccclxxvii, 264 No. mxxxiv; and, more generally, A. Boscolo, "La Politica di Ferdinando I d'Aragona," *Studi sardi*, XII–XIII, Part 2, 70–254; and F. Giunta's brief critical remarks on "Alcuni recenti studi sulla Sicilia aragonese," *AS Siciliano*, 3d ser. VII, 413–16. See also C. Trasselli's "Sulla diffusione degli Ebrei e sull'importanza della cultura e della lingua ebraica in Sicilia, particolarmente in Trapani e in Palermo, nel secolo XV," *Bollettino* of the Centro di studi filologici e linguistici siciliani, II, 376–82; and, on Sardinia, G. Sorgro, "Note sul tribunale dell'Inquisizione in Sardegna dal 1492–1563," *Studi sardi*, XII–XIII, 313–20; and other literature listed *supra*, Vol. X, pp. 405 f. n. 23.

It should also be noted that, even after 1492, Jews occasionally appeared on these islands, at least for short-term visits. Don Isaac Abravanel had no difficulty in accompanying Alphonso II of Naples (after his abdication) to Mazzara and Messina, although this privilege may have been extended to him only so long as he lived in Alphonso's entourage, as suggested by B. Netanyahu in his *Don Isaac Abravanel*, p. 71. See also S. H. Margulies, "La Famiglia Abravanel in Italia," *RI*, III, 97–107, 147–53.

81. The anonymous chronicler of 1495 in A. Marx's *Studies in Jewish History*, pp. 86 (Hebrew), 95 f. (English, with many variations); F. Lionti, "Le Magistrature presso gli Ebrei di Sicilia," *AS Siciliano*, n.s. IX, 328–71, esp. p. 331; B. Netanyahu, *Don Isaac Abravanel*, pp. 61 ff.; N. Ferorelli, *Gli Ebrei*, pp. 196 ff.; and the sources cited there. See also F. Ruiz Martín's detailed description of "La Expulsión de los Judíos del reino de Nápoles," *Hispania* (Madrid), IX, 28–76, 179–240.

The Neapolitan population, though very changeable, was generally anti-Jewish, as is evidenced by the extant folkloristic records and the popular poetry. Yet, because of the growing economic crisis, aggravated by the barons' revolt, the absenteeism of bishops, and the general political instability, many cities actually requested the government to relieve the incoming Jews from the usual high customs duties, a request heeded, in 1493, in Ferrante's order for Tropea that "the Jews should enjoy the same immunity in customs which are enjoyed by the other inhabitants of the said city." On the developments in Calabria, which soon became the scene of riots and pillage of Jewish communities and of warlike disturbances accompanying the French invasion, see O. Dito, *La Storia calabrese e la dimora degli Ebrei in Calabria dal secolo V alla seconda metà del secolo XVI*, pp. 207 ff., 240 ff., 257 ff., 271 ff., 329 ff. See also F. Elías de Tejada, *Nápoles hispanico* (mainly concerned with political attitudes).

82. N. Ferrorelli, *Gli Ebrei*, pp. 206 ff.; J. C. Lünig, ed., *Codex Italiae diplomaticus.* IV, 793 ff. No. cxx, esp. col. 798 Art. xxiii; A. Marongiu, "Pagine dimenticate della storia parlamentare italiana del cinquecento," *Studi in onore di Riccardo Filangieri*, II, 317–27; *Privilegii et capitoli con altre gratie concessi alla fidelissima città di Napoli et Regno per li Serenissimi Ri di Casa di Aragona*, as confirmed by Charles V and Philip II, Venice, 1588 ed., fols. 61b, 64a, 69ab. See also, more generally, F. Ruiz Martín, "Fernando el Católico y la Inquisición en el reino de Nápoles" in *Estudios* of the Fifth Congreso de historia de la Corona de Aragón, II, 315–36; and the older literature reviewed by E. Pontieri in his "Ferdinando il Cattolico e i regni di Napoli e di Sicilia nella storiografia italiana dell'ultimo cinquantennio," *RSI*, LXIV, 399–422.

As in the broader aspects of national policy, the Neapolitan population's attitude to Jews was extremely changeable. In 1501 the city of Cosenza, Calabria, which had four years before insisted that the few remaining unconverted Jews wear badges, asked the "Great Captain" Hernandez Gonzalo (Gonsalvo) de Cordova to grant freedom of trade and banking also "to Jews and New Christians." Three years later, however, the same municipal council once again demanded the enforcement of a separate Jewish quarter and the badge and a prohibition against Jews maintaining shops in the center of the city in competition with Christian merchants. Again three years passed, and the city requested the reopening of Jewish banks. Similarly, the municipality of Tropea, which had previously been so friendly to Jews, sharply denounced them, in 1506, to Ferdinand the Catholic and demanded their expulsion from both the city and the district. See O. Dito, *La Storia calabrese*, pp. 337 ff.; G. Summo, *Gli Ebrei in Puglia dal XI al XVI secolo;* D. Spanò Bolani, "I Giudei in Reggio di Calabria dal secolo XIII al primo decennio del secolo XVI," *ASPN*, VI, 336–46; S. Pasquale, "Saggio di ricerche archivistiche per la storia degli Ebrei in Calabria nella seconda metà del secolo XV," *Calabria nobilissima*, VIII, 41–48, 109–23 (includes several interesting documents of 1491–97; pp. 119 ff.) and, more generally, A. Rodriguez Villa, *Crónicas del Gran Capitán [Gonzalo Hernández de Córdoba y Aguilar]*; and P. Gasparrini, "Un Ignorato parlamento generale napoletano del 1504 e un altro poco noto del 1507," *ASPN*, LXXV, 203–10 (cites also the text of a Christian oath of fidelity to Ferdinand of 1507, but does not mention the formula, if any, of a similar oath taken by Jews); idem, "Ancora dei parlamenti napoletani del 1504 e del 1507," *ibid.*, LXXVIII, 307–14 (answers Marongiu's strictures in *Studi in onore di Riccardo Filangieri*). On the frequently devious methods employed by Ferdinand in his dealings with the Italian provinces, read between the lines of Baron de Terrateig's comprehensive apologia of the *Política en Italia del Rey Católico, 1507–1516.*

83. L. Amabile, *Il Tumulto napoletano dell'anno 1510,* p. 41; A. L. Antinori, *Raccolta di memorie storiche,* IV, 153; Ferorelli, *Gli Ebrei,* pp. 219 ff.; F. Ruiz Martín in *Hispania* (Madrid), IX, 63 ff.; and particularly *supra,* Vol. X, pp. 245 f., 408 f. n. 32. Ferdinand's decree is quoted here from the original broadside proclamation, a copy of which is available in the Library of the Jewish Theological Seminary. It clearly displays the date of November 22 (21) 1510; correct accordingly that given *supra,* Vol. X. Needless to say, the expulsion did not put an end to the anti-Jewish agitation which now aimed its shafts at the remaining Marranos. The latter were blamed even for the atrocities committed by the Spanish troops during the destruction of Prato in 1512, on which see A. Vannucci, ed., "Tre Narrazioni del sacco di Prato (1512)," *ASI,* I, 227–71; and, more generally, B. Croce, *La Spagna nella vita italiana durante la Rinascenza,* 2d ed. rev., esp. pp. 96 f., 235, 256 f.

84. O. Dito, *La Storia calabrese,* pp. 344 ff.; G. Coniglio, *Il Regno di Napoli al tempo di Carlo V. Amministrazione e vita economico-sociale* (indirectly showing the relative insignificance of Jewish banking at that time; pp. 103 ff.).

85. G. Paladino, "Privilegi concessi agli Ebrei dal Viceré Don Pietro di Toledo (1535–36)," *ASPN,* XXXVIII, 611–36 (includes the text of the decree of Feb. 28, 1535; pp. 623 ff.); G. Coniglio, "Note sulla società napoletana ai tempi di don Pietro di Toledo," *Studi in onore di Riccardo Filangieri,* II, 345–65; G. de Boom, *Les Voyages de Charles V,* pp. 74 f. The agreement of Nov. 10, 1535, and the preceding discussions between Samuel b. Isaac Abravanel and the government are briefly mentioned in D. Kaufmann's "Contributions à l'histoire des Juifs en Italie," *REJ,* XX, 39 ff., 56 ff. No. v. See also such local studies as A. Antonaci, *Otranto. Testi e monumenti (Studi sulla civiltà salentina);* and E. Munkácsi, *Der Jude von Neapel: die historischen und kunstgeschichtlichen Denkmäler des süditalienischen Judentums.* While mainly concentrated on the art-historical aspects, the latter volume sheds some light also on the historical evolution of southern Italian Jewry; for instance, by referring to later inquisitorial trials of Judaizers in 1571 and 1687 (p. 44). On the protracted resistance of the Neapolitan population to the introduction of the Spanish Inquisition, see *infra,* Chap. LV.

86. See esp. *supra,* Vol. X, pp. 277 ff., 285 ff.; and *infra,* Chap. LIX. Suffice it to remember that the very first so-called expulsion of Jews from northern Italy, allegedly promulgated by the Carolingian Emperor Louis II in 855, is of dubious authenticity. It certainly was never carried into effect. See *supra,* Vol. IV, pp. 25 f., 244 f. n. 27. To the literature listed in earlier notes add the following more recent publications: G. Musso, "Per la storia degli Ebrei nella Repubblica di Genova tra il Quattrocento ed il Cinquecento," *Miscellanea storica Ligure,* pp. 203–25 (showing Genoese efforts to induce Yehudah Abravanel to settle in the city), supplemented by V. Slessarev's renewed analysis of "Die Sogenannten Orientalen im mittelalterlichen Genua. Einwanderer aus Südfrankreich in der ligurischen Metropole," *VSW,* LI, 22–65; W. M. Bowsky, "The Impact of the Black Death upon Sienese Government and Society," *Speculum,* XXXIX, 1–34; V. Meneghin, "Due sermoni del B. Bernardino da Feltre," *Studi francescani,* LXI, 212–61. Of special interest are L. C.

Ruggini's searching "Note sugli Ebrei in Italia dal IV al XVI secolo," *RSI*, LXXVI, 926–56, especially with respect to the early Middle Ages. See also the rather lengthy, but avowedly none too far-reaching, list in the Index of C. Roth, *The History of the Jews of Italy*, p. 561, *s.v.* Expulsions; and A. Milano, *Storia degli Ebrei in Italia*, *passim*.

87. D. Schäfer, *Deutsches Nationalbewusstsein im Licht der Geschichte*, p. 17; J. Ficker, *Das Deutsche Kaiserreich in seinen universalen und nationalen Beziehungen*, reprinted in F. Schneider, ed., *Universalstaat und Nationalstaat, Macht und Ende des ersten deutschen Reiches*, pp. 19–158 (in his introductory essay and conclusion the editor shows how Ficker's controversy with Heinrich von Sybel was colored by their respective pro-Austrian and pro-Prussian biases); and the more comprehensive analysis by K. G. Hugelmann in *Stämme, Nation und Nationalstaat im deutschen Mittelalter* (in his *Nationalstaat und Nationalitätenrecht im deutschen Mittelalter*, Vol. I). See also F. G. Schultheiss's concise remarks on *Das Deutsche National-Bewusstsein in der Geschichte;* and some of the literature listed *supra*, nn. 3 ff. While much of that literature reflects the thinking of modern German nationalists, it was able to recapture from the vast and scattered sources some essential ingredients of a burgeoning, if not yet fully conscious, German national feeling. See also O. Redlich, *Rudolf von Habsburg*, pp. 135 ff.; and, from other angles, H. Wieruszowski, *Vom Imperium zum nationalen Königtum; vergleichende Studien über die publizistischen Kämpfe Kaiser Friedrichs II. und König Philipps des Schönen mit der Kurie;* H. Wolfram, *Splendor imperii: Die Epiphanie von Tugend und Heil in Herrschaft und Reich;* G. Barraclough, *The Medieval Empire: Idea and Reality;* and W. Ullmann, "Reflections on the Medieval Empire," *TRHS*, 5th ser. XIV, 89–108 (the latter two showing how the modern conceptions of the medieval empire were molded by later emperors and historians for partisan purposes).

88. Aronius, *Regesten*, pp. 183 ff. No. 413; A. Jaraczewsky, *Die Geschichte der Juden in Erfurt*, pp. 3 ff.; Meir b. Baruch, *Resp.*, Berlin ed., p. 346; S. Salfeld *Das Martyrologium des Nürnberger Memorbuches*, pp. 15 (Hebrew), 130 f. (German). The varying reports concerning the number of casualties in Erfurt are listed by S. Neufeld in *Die Juden im thüringisch-sächsischen Gebiet*, Part 1, p. 50 n. 4. It may be noted that, according to a chronicle cited by Jaraczewsky, *loc. cit.*, the Erfurt burghers tried to protect the Jews and even suffered some casualties. The persecution in Erfurt, which was the more serious as the Jewish settlement there was still very young, had a sufficiently large impact for the community to institute a permanent fast day for Sivan 25. See L. Zunz, *Die Ritus*, p. 127. On the sanctification of self-inflicted martyrdom, see *supra*, Vol. IV, pp. 104, 144 f., 292 n. 18, 309 n. 66.

In time anti-Jewish disturbances became so common and expected that medieval writers and, still more, modern historians were prone to assume anti-Jewish riots even where none occurred. Some complications in Erfurt in 1266 were long construed as a persecution of Jews by the burghers, but on closer examination they turned out to have arisen from an effort by the Erfurt burghers to shield the Jews against undue exactions by their common overlord, Archbishop Werner of Mayence, for which interference they suffered a Church interdict until they capitulated. See Jaraczewsky, pp. 13 f.; H. Fischer, *Die Verfassungsrechtliche Stellung der Juden in den deutschen Städten*, p. 77 n. 1. Correct accordingly the brief summary *supra*, Vol. IX, p. 223.

89. *Annales Erphordenses*, ad 1241, ed. by G. H. Pertz in *MGH*, Scriptores, XVI, 34; Aronius, *Regesten*, pp. 226 f. No. 529, 232 Nos. 539–40 and 542–43, 288 ff. Nos. 697 and 705; I. Kracauer, *Geschichte der Juden in Frankfurt a. M.*, I, 5 ff.; Salfeld, *Das Martyrologium*, pp. 14 ff., 23 (Hebrew), 127 f., 131 ff., 154 (German). Salfeld's account of Abraham the proselyte-preacher is quite confused. Various efforts made to ascertain both the locality and the precise date (probably 1263 or 1264) of "Abraham's" attack on Christianity and its untoward consequences have not proved successful. See Salfeld's note, pp. 132 f. The pertinent liturgical poems assembled by him (pp. 329 ff.) were republished, with additional notes, by S. Bernfeld in his *Sefer ha-Dema'ot*, I, 295 ff. and by A. M. Habermann in *Sefer Gezerot Ashkenaz ve-Ṣarefat* (Records of Anti-Jewish Persecutions in Germany and France), pp. 168 ff., 176 ff., 186 ff. On the Belitz affair see A. F. Riedel ed., *Codex diplomaticus brandenburgensis*, 1st ser. IX, 470 ff. App. xx; and *supra*, Vol. IX, pp. 210, 239 n. 17; and Chap. XLIX, n. 64.

Other early-thirteenth-century persecutions included that in Halle, where the Jewish quarter went up in flames while the survivors were ousted from the city. In retaliation the city's sovereign, Archbishop Albert II of Magdeburg, imposed upon the burghers the large fine of 1,000 marks silver. But the report neither specifies the reason for the attack nor indicates clearly whether it occurred in 1206 or 1207. See *Chronica Reinhardsbrunnensis, a. 530–1338*, ed. by O. Holder-Egger, in *MGH*, Scriptores, XXX, Part 1, p. 571; and the analysis by S. Neufeld in *Die Halleschen Juden im Mittelalter*, pp. 31 f. See also S. von Schultze-Galléra, *Die Juden zu Halle im Mittelalter*.

90. J. C. von Aretin, *Geschichte der Juden in Baiern*, pp. 13, 17 f. Note g; Salfeld, *Das Martyrologium*, pp. 21 (Hebrew), 146 f. (German). The Munich tragedy, too, was commemorated in two litanies reproduced by Habermann in his *Sefer Gezerot*, pp. 198 ff. It is more surprising that in describing the Munich events the sixteenth-century Jesuit M. Rader counted the allegedly slain child among the Bavarian saints. His book on Bavaria, first published in Latin in 1581, appeared in a German translation in Augsburg in 1714 and included an etching with an equally credulous legend. Both are cited by Von Aretin, pp. 19 f.

91. Gottfried von Ensmingen, *Gesta Rudolfi et Alberti regum romanorum, 1273–1299, ad* 1298 in J. F. Böhmer, ed., *Fontes rerum germanicarum*, II, 144; other sources cited by J. E. Scherer in *Die Rechtsverhältnisse*, pp. 349 ff.; Salfeld, *Das Martyrologium*, pp. 29 ff. (Hebrew), 164 ff. (German); Eberhard von Regensburg, *Annales Ratisponenses a. 1273–1305*, ed. by P. Jaffé, *ad* 1298 in *MGH*, Scriptores, XVII, 597 lines 47 ff.; and such local histories as M. Szulwas, *Die Juden in Würzburg*, pp. 37 ff.; and R. Straus, *Regensburg and Augsburg* (Jewish Communities Series), pp. 104 f., 175. Other instances of such defense by burghers were mentioned *supra*, n. 88; Vols. IV, pp. 100 f., 289 f. n. 13; IX, pp. 218 ff., 230 f. See also *infra*, nn. 92–94.

Most figures quoted in the text are derived from the memor books (a designation variously explained, but probably derived from the usual location of such books on the so-called Almemar, the reader's platform, of the various synagogues) which were subsequently used in Jewish divine services for the recitation of memorial prayers for the martyrs. Forty-nine such memor books were closely analyzed by Salfeld in *Das Martyrologium*. These and others still extant were subjected to renewed scrutiny, particularly by M. Weinberg in his "Untersuchungen über das

Wesen des Memorbuches," *JJLG*, XVI, 253–323; and in *Die Memorbücher der jüdischen Gemeinden in Bayern*. On the most distinguished victim of the 1298 massacres see Samuel Kahn, "R. Mordecai b. Hillel ha-Kohen" (Hebrew), *Sinai*, VII, Nos. 76–81, pp. 294–305; Nos. 82–87, pp. 38–47, 314–23; VIII, Nos. 88–93, pp. 44–74, 237–47; Nos. 92–99, pp. 227–47; and S. Schwarzfuchs, "Mordecai ben Hillel et le judaïsme allemand," *REJ*, CXII, 43–52. Mordecai, who had composed a dirge on the martyrdom of the proselyte Abraham in Augsburg in 1265, now became in turn the subject of such a litany by an anonymous author. Both are reproduced by Habermann in his *Sefer Gezerot*, pp. 186 ff. and 230 ff.

92. *Chronica de ducibus Bavariae*, ad 1338, in *Bayerische Chroniken des XIV. Jahrhunderts*, ed. by G. Leidinger, p. 167; Wiener, *Regesten*, p. 50 Nos. 178–79; H. Angermeier, "Städtebünde und Landfriedenspolitik im 14. Jahrhundert," *HJB*, LXXVI, 34–46; "Regensburger Urkundenbuch," in *Monumenta boica*, LIII, 533 No. 982; *ibid.*, XL, 145 f. No. 73; S. Bromberger, *Die Juden in Regensburg bis zur Mitte des 14. Jahrhunderts*, pp. 42 ff., 60 f., 70 ff.; T. Liegel, *Reichsstadt Regensburg und Klerus im Kampf um ihre Rechte* (typescript); H. Fischer, *Die Verfassungsrechtliche Stellung*, pp. 153 ff.; and such general studies of the internal conflicts among the contemporary patrician groups as P. Dollinger, "Le Patriciat des villes du Rhin supérieur et ses dissensions internes dans la première moitié du XIVᵉ siècle," *Schweizer Zeitschrift für Geschichte*, III, 248–58. See also *supra*, Vol. IX, pp. 213 ff., 341 ff. nn. 20 ff. The Armleder massacres, too, elicited a liturgical poem, written by one Isaac b. Solomon and published, with a German trans., by Salfeld in *Das Martyrologium*, pp. 347 ff. See the literature listed *ibid.*, p. 237.

93. Johann von Winterthur (Johannes Vitoduranus), *Chronica*, ed. by F. Baethgen in *MGH*, Scriptores rerum germanicarum, n.s. III, 117 f.; L. Löwenstein, *Geschichte der Juden am Bodensee*, pp. 3 ff., 25 ff., 100 f. n. 3, 115 n. 21. On Winterthur see Baethgen's Intro.; and A. Lhotsky's succinct remarks in his *Quellenkunde zur mittelalterlichen Geschichte Österreichs*, pp. 277 f. Sometimes a writer changed his mind. For instance, Magister Ambrosius of Heiligenkreuz, who, in 1305, had taken up the cudgel for the Korneuburg Jews accused of a host desecration (in his *Tractatus de hostia mirifica*), several years later condemned both some Vienna Jews and their protector, Duke Rudolph III, because of a similar allegation. See his *De actis iudeorum sub duce Rudolfo*, briefly analyzed by Lhotsky, pp. 273 f.

94. See *supra*, Vols. IX, pp. 158 f., 187 f., 196 f., 211 f., 230 f.; X, p. 35; Chap. XLIX, nn. 51 ff.; S. Bromberger, *Die Juden in Regensburg*, pp. 73 f. n. 140 (cogently arguing that, in 1349, as on previous occasions, Ratisbon rather effectively defended her Jews, despite some contrary evidence in the memor books); *Chronica S. Petri Erfordensis moderna*, a. 1072–1335, with Continuations I–III for the years 1334–55, ed. by O. Holder-Egger in *MGH*, Scriptores, XXX, Part 1, pp. 462 f., 470; A. Kober, *Cologne* (Jewish Communities Series), pp. 114 ff.; Heinrich Dapifer von Diessenhofen, *Chronicle* in J. F. Böhmer, *Fontes rerum germanicarum*, IV, 68 ff. How prejudiced even intelligent Germans had become is evidenced by the Erfurt continuator. Though doubting the veracity of rumors about Jewish well poisoning, he nevertheless calmly reported the slaughter of more than 3,000 Jews in Erfurt alone and added the gratuitous remark, "May they rest in hell."

The best analysis of the concurrent anti-Jewish and Flagellant movements in 1348–49 may be found in the aforementioned study by R. Höniger, *Der Schwarze*

Tod in Deutschland. Further insights are gained from some additional interurban correspondence still extant, and particularly the letters received in Würzburg from various other communities, which, although not precisely datable, reveal the state of mind of many other city councils as well. See H. Hoffmann, "Die Würzburger Judenverfolgung von 1349," *Mainfränkisches Jahrbuch für Geschichte und Kunst,* V, 91–114, esp. pp. 98 ff., 103 ff. It nevertheless appears that on the whole cities and princes opposed the massacres. Only Margrave Frederick of Meissen, we recall, stood out as the barbaric exception in actually having stimulated attacks not only by the promise of impunity for the assailants, but also by direct incitation. The greatest individual culprit undoubtedly was Emperor Charles IV, who had cynically shed all responsibility for the protection of his Jews. This rather unusual behavior could hardly be excused even by such admiring biographers as E. Werunsky in his *Geschichte Kaiser Karls IV.,* II, 239 ff. (offering a good chronological survey of the massacres); and J. Pfitzner in his *Kaiser Karl IV.*

Incidentally, Werunsky supplies some interesting illustrations of the extremes to which the popular belief in well poisoning went. Where Jews were not available, mobs attacked converts, as in the lands of the Teutonic Order, or even old Christians, including priests, whose medical ministrations during the pestilence had proved unsuccessful (pp. 254 f.). On the other hand, Pfitzner's attempt to explain Charles' passivity by connecting it with his aversion to both the city leagues and the artisan guilds is unacceptable (pp. 90 f.). The emperor must have known that the guilds were marching in the vanguard of the assailants.

95. Baruch (b. Yeḥiel) ha-Kohen, *Ani hu ha-qonen qinah* (I Am He Who Keens the Dirge), in the English trans. by A. Löwy in his rendition of L. Zunz, *The Sufferings of the Jews During the Middle Ages,* pp. 65 f. Baruch's and other poems are reproduced in S. Bernfeld's *Sefer ha-Demaʻot,* I–II, *passim.* See also *supra,* Vol. IV, pp. 143 ff. The estimate of three hundred Jewish communities destroyed refers largely to organized communal bodies; the number of localities affected was much larger. In the archbishopric of Cologne alone, 29 places have been identified, while in Saxony and Thuringia some 40 localities were stricken. See A. Kober, *Cologne,* pp. 360 f. n. 34; S. Neufeld, *Die Juden im thüringisch-sächsischen Gebiet,* Part 2, pp. 6 f. On the other hand, there were, even within the Empire, localities such as Feldkirch in Vorarlberg which neither suffered from the pestilence nor staged anti-Jewish attacks. See A. Tänzer, *Die Geschichte der Juden in Tirol und Vorarlberg,* p. 7.

The numbers of victims recorded in many sources appear exaggerated. For instance, we are told by a contemporary Christian chronicler that only 100 Jews were slain by pogromists in Erfurt, whereas 3,000 (according to another chronicler, 2,000) died in a self-laid conflagration. (Among the victims here was the distinguished rabbi Alexander Süsslein Kohen.) See the second continuation of the *Chronica S. Petri Erphordensis moderna,* cited *supra,* n. 94; *Sächsische Weltchronik,* ed. by L. Weiland, in *MGH,* Deutsche Chroniken, II, 318 (Thüringische Fortsetzung); Salfeld, *Das Martyrologium,* pp. 78, 83, 361; Neufeld, *loc. cit.* Similarly, the frequently given figure of 600 victims in Basel has been denied by Robert Wackernagel who believes that the total Jewish population there had not exceeded 100 souls. See Mathias von Nuwenburg (Neuenburg), *Chronica,* ed. by A. Hofmeister, in *MGH,* Scriptores rerum germanicarum, n.s. IV, Part 1, pp. 264 ff.; Nicolaus Stulmann von Lauingen, *Chronik vom Jahre 1407,* ed. by J. Würdinger, in the *Jahresbericht* of the Historischer Kreis-Verein im Regierungsbezirk Schwaben und Neuburg, XXXII, 29 f.; R. Wackernagel,

Geschichte der Stadt Basel, II, Part 1, p. 54* (to p. 365). See also M. Ginsburger, "Die Juden in Basel," *Basler Zeitschrift für Geschichte,* VIII, 341 ff. Wackernagel overlooks, however, the fact that the membership of many communities had been swelled before the massacres by refugees from adjacent localities. On the statistical and other uncertainties concerning these tragic developments, see H. Franke's recent discussion in his *Geschichte und Schicksal der Juden in Heilbronn,* pp. 23 ff.

It is equally impossible to ascertain the number of survivors. According to Stulmann's chronicle, 130 Basel children were saved by baptism. Mathias von Nuwenburg (Neuenburg) similarly reports that, notwithstanding the refusal of the majority of Strasbourg Jewry to undergo conversion, "many beautiful women" and "many boys" were involuntarily converted. However, in some cases baptism did not guarantee survival, for in Strasbourg and other localities even some converts were slain, because they had allegedly been personally coresponsible for the spread of the pestilence. See, more generally, the *Urkundenbuch der Stadt Strassburg,* ed. by W. Wiegand *et al.,* V, Part 1, pp. 191 ff., Nos. 204–12.

96. A. F. Riedel, *Codex diplomaticus brandenburgensis,* 1st ser. III, 381 f. No lxxv; Kober, *Cologne,* pp. 116 f.; Neufeld, *Die Juden,* Part 2, pp. 9 ff. Possibly, claims by a few Jewish survivors who could prove their ownership of, or inheritance rights to, some specific property were respected. But we have no evidence to this effect.

97. A. Glaser, *Geschichte der Juden in Strassburg,* pp. 18 f.; *Urkundenbuch der Stadt Strassburg,* ed. by W. Wiegand *et al.,* V, Part 2, pp. 647 f. No. 832; Neufeld, *Die Juden,* Part 2, pp. 14 f., citing the *Magdeburger Schöppenchronik,* p. 223; the *Urkundenbuch der Stadt Magdeburg,* ed. by G. Hertel, I, 302 No. 470, 329 No. 518; the *Geschichtsquellen der Provinz Sachsen,* ed. by P. Kehr, XXII, 281 ff. Nos. 1024 and 1031–32; and other sources commented on by L. Lewinsky in "Drei deutsche Juden betreffende päpstliche Urkunden aus dem Jahre 1372," *MGWJ,* XLVIII, 718–20. See also *supra,* Vol. IX, pp. 188 ff., 329 f. nn. 59–61.

The haste with which some German princes tried to get back their Jews is illustrated by Archbishop Gerlach von Nassau of Mayence. Probably more than any other elector he was instrumental in wresting in 1356 from Charles IV the great concessions of the Golden Bull, including the transfer of the control over Jews in the German electorates to their immediate secular or episcopal rulers. No sooner was this decree promulgated than the archbishop, then still in Nuremberg, took a Jew, Gottlieben of Bischofsheim, under his protection and authorized him to invite other Jews to settle in the archbishopric. Gerlach's liberality soon extended also to such major centers in his domain as Frankfort, Erfurt, and the city of Mayence itself. See the interesting document of 1356 reproduced in F. J. Bodmann's *Rheingauische Alterthümer,* II, 712; other data analyzed by K. A. Schaab in his *Diplomatische Geschichte der Juden zu Mainz und dessen Umgebung,* pp. 97 ff.; *supra,* Vol. IX, pp. 171 f., 322 f. n. 42; and, more generally, Ellen Littmann's *Studien zur Wiederaufnahme der Juden nach dem Schwarzen Tode.*

98. H. Kraft, "Die Rechtliche, wirtschaftliche und soziale Lage der Juden im Hochstift Paderborn," *Westfälische Zeitschrift,* XCIV, Part 2, p. 108; G. Bondy and F. Dworský, *Zur Geschichte der Juden in Böhmen, Mähren und Schlesien,* I, 82 ff. No. 171, 89 f. No. 188; Abigdor b. Isaac Kara, *Et kol ha-tela'ah* (The Whole Catastrophe Which Befell Us), included in the Prague ritual for the afternoon services

of the Day of Atonement and reproduced in S. Bernfeld's *Sefer ha-Dema'ot*, II, 159 ff. See also Joseph ha-Kohen's *'Emeq ha-bakha*, pp. 69 f.; in Wiener's German trans., pp. 55 f., 194 ff. n. 211 (explaining the authorities' failure to protect the Jews by King Wenceslaus' absence from the city); A. Stein, *Die Geschichte der Juden in Böhmen*, pp. 18 f.; *supra*, Vols. IV, p. 120; IX, pp. 202, 336 n. 9. On occasion, however, a city did complain of the mistreatment of Jews in another locality. For instance, Nuremberg raised the question as to why its ally, Nördlingen, had allowed some burghers to slay Jews, although it admitted that this was done "without the local council's will, knowledge or word" (*ca.* 1387). See F. Keutgen, ed., *Urkunden zur städtischen Verfassungsgeschichte*, pp. 517 ff. No. 426, esp. p. 518, Art. 2.

99. J. Janssen, *Geschichte des deutschen Volkes seit dem Ausgang des Mittelalters*, revised and much enlarged by L. Pastor, I, 463 f.; idem, *Erläuterungen und Ergänzungen zu Janssens Geschichte des deutschen Volkes*, ed. by L. Pastor *et al.*; idem, *History of the German People at the Close of the Middle Ages*, trans. from the German by M. A. Mitchell *et al.* The quoted passage is somewhat inaccurately translated in Vol. II, pp. 78 f. See also O. Stobbe, *Die Juden in Deutschland*, pp. 191 ff., 290 ff. nn. 88–89; M. Stern, *Die Israelitische Bevölkerung der deutschen Städte*, I–VII; and *supra*, Vol. IX. Like most other historians, Janssen blamed these expulsions exclusively on Jewish moneylending. He failed to explain, however, why the same cities had shortly before consciously attracted Jewish lenders and why others subsequently reversed their actions and readmitted them. Nor did he pay attention to the rising tide of popular Jew-baiting reflected in the contemporary arts and letters discussed *supra*, Chap. XLIX. Evidently, the particular medieval brand of German national-tribal intolerance, in its intimate tie-up with religion, was then reaching its peak.

100. J. E. Scherer, *Die Rechtsverhältnisse*, pp. 408 ff., 414 n. 4; I. Schwarz, *Das Wiener Ghetto*, p. 7 n. 9; M. Grunwald, *Vienna* (Jewish Communities Series), pp. 32 ff. That the Vienna affair was not a momentary impulsive outburst may be seen from its long duration. Between the first imprisonment of most Austrian Jews in March 1420 and their final execution a year elapsed during which many committed sacrificial suicide. Some chroniclers tell the pathetic tale of the children seized for the purpose of conversion. After starving them for several days, Albert's henchmen tempted their little prisoners by placing ritually forbidden meat before them as a first step toward apostasy. Most of the children are said to have resisted and were either "sold into slavery" or forcibly baptized. The antecedents of that tragedy, briefly described by a near-contemporary Jewish chronicler in his *Wiener Geserah* (it was republished in the Appendix to A. Goldmann, ed., *Das Judenbuch*, pp. 112 ff.), are analyzed by S. Krauss on the basis of numerous extant sources in *Die Wiener Geserah von Jahre 1421*. See, however, O. Stowasser's serious reservations in his review of that volume in "Zur Geschichte der Wiener Geserah," *VSW*, XVI, 104–18, which overstresses, however, the single economic factor in the rising tide of Austrian intolerance. See also Stowasser's intro. to the texts, published thereafter by R. Geyer and L. Sailer, and mentioned *supra*, Vol. IX, p. 333 n. 4, where other pertinent literature is also listed.

101. Israel b. Ḥayyim Bruna (of Brünn), *Resp.*, No. 268, Salonica, 1823 ed., fols. 111b f.; John Capistrano's sermons in Breslau, reproduced by E. Jacob in his *Johannes von Capistrano*, Vol. II; Ennea Silvio Piccolomini's letter of Jan. 10, 1455, to Cardinal

Capranica in L. Wadding's *Annales Minorum, ad* 1455, XII, 308 n. 92; and the remarks by O. Bonmann on "L'Epistolario di S. Giovanni de Capestrano," *Studi francescani,* LIII, 275–98; and other sources analyzed in detail by M. Brann in his *Geschichte der Juden in Schlesien,* pp. 117 ff. (also citing the statement by Moses Rieti from an Oxford MS, pp. 170 f. n. 6); *supra,* Vol. X, pp. 257 f., 415 n. 47. See also O. Bonmann, "Zum Prophetismus des Johannes Kapestran (1386–1456)," *Archiv für Kulturgeschichte,* XLIV, 193–98; and G. Helmrich, *Geschichte der Juden in Liegnitz.* Capistrano was sent to Silesia in order to arouse the public to an anti-Hussite Crusade. But when a few Bohemian subjects (including a Magister Paul of Prague who was of Jewish descent) were imprisoned in Breslau under the suspicion of heterodoxy, George Podiebrad, the regent of Bohemia, forcefully intervened in March 1453 and obtained their release. It was much easier for Capistrano to fulminate against the helpless Jews, on whose "crime" we have divergent reports. While official documents speak of the desecration of one to ten hosts, according to one eye-witness they had been accused of ritual murder. Writing several decades after the event, another contemporary reminisced about having seen the bones of the ritually slain boy in Capistrano's hands. If true, this may have been one of the frequent "miracles" which had become a stock in trade of this papal legate, one reporter asserting that Capistrano had performed forty-seven miracles in the month of March alone. Yet all these obscurities and contradictions did not prevent the final condemnation and execution of the accused Jews. See the data carefully analyzed by Brann, *loc. cit.;* and J. Hofer, *Johannes von Capestrano. Ein Leben im Kampf um die Reform der Kirche,* pp. 481 ff. (Hofer's difficulties with the Nazis, partly on account of this work, are alluded to by O. Bonmann, p. 194 n. 5). On Capistrano's other anti-Jewish activities, see esp. *supra,* Vol. X, pp. 37, 47, 230 f., 323 n. 58, 402 n. 11.

102. See Sigismund's interesting decree of Jan. 5, 1424, reproduced by T. J. Lacomblet in his *Urkundenbuch für die Geschichte der Niederrheins,* IV, 175 f.; and other sources cited by C. Brisch in his *Geschichte der Juden in Cöln und Umgebung,* II, 32 ff.; and by A. Kober in his *Cologne,* pp. 130 ff., 138, 141 ff., 362 ff. n. 42; J. S. Menczel, *Beiträge zur Geschichte der Juden von Mainz im XV. Jahrhundert, passim;* and *supra,* Vol. IX, pp. 172 f., 176 f., 323 n. 43, 325 n. 47. The difficulties the Mayence Jews had under the regime of Adolph II of Nassau in 1462–75 are described, with several interesting quotations from the sources, by K. A. Schaab in his *Diplomatische Geschichte der Juden zu Mainz und dessen Umgebung,* pp. 121 ff. From one such document, dated September 5, 1470, it appears that by that time Jews had already been banished from all the "cities, castles, villages, hamlets, lands, and possessions" of the archbishopric, although Adolph granted some individuals an extension of one year. Cited by Schaab, p. 129. Somewhat different was the situation in Augsburg. By paying the Treasury 900 florins the city had secured permission from Albert II to banish her Jews. But when the king died before signing the pertinent papers, Frederick III's officials imposed upon Augsburg the high tribute of 12,000 (according to other sources, 13,000) florins for having expelled the Jews in 1438 without formal imperial consent. See P. von Stetten, *Geschichte der Heil. Röm. Reichs-Freyen Stadt Augspurg,* pp. 177 f. On the elimination of Jews from Treves, Strasbourg, Würzburg, and other episcopal principalities, see *supra,* Vol. IX, pp. 178 ff.

103. Scherer, *Die Rechtsverhältnisse,* I, 492 ff.; A. Rosenberg, *Beiträge zur Geschichte der Juden in Steiermark;* D. Herzog, *Urkunden und Regesten zur Ge-*

schichte der Juden in der Steiermark (1475–1585), furnishing ample documentation on the events preceding and following the expulsion of 1496; idem, "Kleine Beiträge," *ZGJT*, III–V (marshaling a whole array of arguments, some of them rather forced, against the historicity of the expulsion of the Jews from Gratz in 1439; III, 96 ff., 172 ff.); and other sources cited *supra*, Vol. IX, pp. 200, 334 n. 6.

104. See the data analyzed *supra*, Vol. IX, pp. 234, 350 n. 32. To the literature listed there add P. Schattenmann, "Dr. Johannes Teuschlein und die Rothenburger Judenaustreibung 1519–20 in neuer Schau," *Zeitschrift für bayerische Kirchengeschichte*, XIII, 113–15. See also such detailed descriptions as K. Winkler's "Die 'Judenverfolgung' zu Straubing im Jahre 1435," *Jahresberichte* of the Historischer Verein in Straubing, XL, 16–29. Despite the elimination of Jews from Magdeburg, Brandenburg, and Pomerania (1492–93), some Jews remained in the northeastern parts of Germany. See U. Grotefend, *Geschichte . . . der Juden in Pommern*, pp. 54 ff.

105. Robert Grosseteste's letter of 1231 to Countess Margaret of Winchester in his *Epistolae*, ed. by H. R. Luard, V, 33; in the English trans. by L. M. Friedman in his *Robert Grosseteste and the Jews*, pp. 14 f. The identification of the eternal fugitive Cain with the Jewish people had long become commonplace in the ecclesiastical literature. See, for instance, Augustine's *Civitas Dei*, xv.7, xviii.46, ed. by B. Dombart and A. Kalb, II, 61, 328 f.; in M. Dodd's English trans., II, 61, 277 ff.; Rufinus of Aquileia, *In LXXV Psalmos commentarius* on Ps. 59:12, *PL*, XXI, 879 f.; Martin de León's *Sermones*, iv (*In natale Domini*), ibid., CCVIII, 217; and *supra*, n. 29; Vols. II, pp. 136 f., 381 f. nn. 10–11; VI, 480 f. n. 91; and Chap. XLIX, n. 80.

DATE DUE
